Death and Social Order

in Tokugawa Japan

Harvard East Asian Monographs 282

Death and Social Order
in Tokugawa Japan

Buddhism, Anti-Christianity, and the Danka *System*

Nam-lin Hur

Published by the Harvard University Asia Center
and distributed by Harvard University Press
Cambridge (Massachusetts) and London, 2007

Printed in the United States of America

The Harvard University Asia Center publishes a monograph series and, in coordination with the Fairbank Center for East Asian Research, the Korea Institute, the Reischauer Institute of Japanese Studies, and other faculties and institutes, administers research projects designed to further scholarly understanding of China, Japan, Vietnam, Korea, and other Asian countries. The Center also sponsors projects addressing multidisciplinary and regional issues in Asia.

Library of Congress Cataloging-in-Publication Data

Hur, Nam-lin.
    Death and social order in Tokugawa Japan : Buddhism, anti-Christianity, and the danka system / [Nam-lin Hur].
        p. cm. -- (Harvard East Asian monographs ; 282)
    Includes bibliographical references and index.
    ISBN-13: 978-0-674-02503-5 (hardcover : alk. paper)
    ISBN-10: 0-674-02503-2 (hardcover : alk. paper)
        1. Temples, Buddhist--Japan--Membership--History. 2. Buddhism--Japan--History--1600–1868. 3. Funeral rites and ceremonies, Buddhist--Social aspects--Japan. 4. Religion and state--Japan. I. Title.
    BQ5133.3.J3H87 2007
    294.3'43880952--dc22

2006025369

Index by the author

♾ Printed on acid-free paper

Last figure below indicates year of this printing
17 16 15 14 13 12 11 10 09 08 07

In memory of
Professor Miyata Noboru

ᘓ

Acknowledgments

One day in the late 1980s I came away with a seed of resolution after several inspirational conversations at a luncheon at Princeton's Faculty Club, to which Professor Helen Hardacre had invited me, along with my fellow graduate students. The message that was planted deep in my mind was: "Project your research into the journey of your long-term scholarly life and write a dissertation on a topic that will bring you to a core kernel of Japanese religion and society." This led me to wonder what I might learn about Japanese Buddhism.

Several years later I found myself wrestling with the issues of "death and prayer" in Tokugawa Buddhism, and, by way of the prism of Asakusa Sensōji, this somehow resulted in a thesis. When I set off to turn this thesis into a book, it seemed to be too much to deal with both death and prayer at the same time. At the urging of a silent prayer arising from long walks in a thickly wooded park in Vancouver, I was able to bid farewell to the first half of the task with the publication of *Prayer and Play in Late Tokugawa Japan* (Harvard University Asia Center, 2000). But I still had to tell Professor Hardacre that the other half of the task remained unfulfilled. I thank her for her patience and encouragement, which she kindly extended for a few more years.

When I started the second half of my task, while on sabbatical at the Nihon jōmin bunka kenkyūjo (Jōminken; the Institute for the Study of Japanese Folk Culture) at Kanagawa University in 1999, the issue of "death" loomed large and looked terribly complicated. Over the course of research that required endless pondering and caused much frustration, I was always fortunate enough to find a treasure trove of encouragement and assistance. Professor Miyata Noboru, who advised me at the Jōminken in 1999, remained a perennial source of inspiration and guidance. His humor sometimes returned to me a few days after meeting with him, and it would make me, all alone, burst into laughter. His imagination, flexibility, and serious thought always left me exclaiming "Aha!" and "Naruhodo!" I am deeply indebted to Professor Miyata for this book.

It was truly with much luck and bliss that I started this project at Kanagawa University, which is renowned for its top-notch scholars and researchers, cutting-edge research, excellent library collections, and lively spirit of collaboration. A large chunk of material used for *Death and Social Order in Tokugawa Japan* was collected there, and the basic framework of ideas was incubated there, thanks to the help, kindness, and generosity of, among others, Amino Yoshihiko, Nakajima Michio, Kitsukawa Toshitada, Fukuta Ajio, Tagami Shigeru, Ishii Hideo, Kubota Ryōko, Sekiguchi Hiroo, and Katō Tomoko. In particular, afternoon teatime in the Jōminken office remains a pleasant memory.

Throughout the years devoted to *Death and Social Order in Tokugawa Japan*, Professor Tamamuro Fumio at Meiji University guided me in almost every possible way, from helping me locate some valuable primary sources, to offering suggestions for breaking through obstacles in my research, correcting inaccuracies in my information, answering my many questions, and allowing me access to his personal collections of materials. While writing this book I pored over Professor Tamamuro's numerous works on Tokugawa Buddhism, anti-Christianity, and funerary Buddhism. He was like a walking dictionary that I could consult for advice and wisdom at any time. I often turned to him for long conversations at many an *izakaya* (bar), where I never succeeded in paying. His famed Thursday afternoon graduate seminars, which I attended shamelessly, causing *ojama* (inconvenience) whenever opportunities arose, were invaluable training in reading *komonjo* (old documents). I am very grateful to Professor Tamamuro.

Over the course of the past few years I have been given many opportunities to present my research at various places, conferences, symposia, and *kenkyūkai* (study group) gatherings, including the Association of Asian Studies Annual Meeting, the Center of Japanese Studies at the University of California at Los Angeles, the University of Toronto, Hitotsubashi University, Meiji University, Waseda University, Hallym University, the Korean Institute for Religion and Culture (Hanjongyŏn), and Seoul National University. On many other private occasions, I also had the good fortune to be able to discuss with fellow scholars a wide range of topics related to my project. I thank all of them for their insightful comments, questions, suggestions, and criticisms, all of which enriched the manuscript in one way or another. These scholars include, among others, Yasumaru Yoshio, Wakao Masaki, Nagura Tetsuzō, Shintani Takanori, Ōhashi Yukihiro, Umezawa Fumiko, Shimazono Susumu, Hōzawa Naohide, Sawa Hirokatsu, Kasuya Keisuke, Nakano Satoshi, Kanzaki Noritake, Tairako Tomonaga, Yamamoto Shino, Herman Ooms, Fred G. Notehelfer, Sonja Arntzen, Jacqueline Stone, Alexander Vesey, Duncan Williams, Kim Yongdeok, Keum Jang-Tae, Kim Chong-Suh, Yoon Sungyong, Kang Don-ku, Yun Woncheol, Jang Sukman, Park Kyutae, Lee Chingu, Lee Yongbeom, and Choi Jong-Sung.

My home institution, the University of British Columbia, boasts an excellent library system and has been a great place for me to conduct my research and to teach while writing this book. Japanese librarians Mr. Gonnami Tsuneharu and Ms. Gotō Tomoko and staff members at the interlibrary loan office were most helpful. My colleagues and research assistants at the Asian Studies Department and Centre for Japanese Research, including Michelle Chou, Jiyoon Lee, and Tomoko Kitagawa, always gave me their kind help whenever I needed it. On several occasions I presented parts of my research results at the Centre for Japanese Research, and the feedback from the seminar participants was always appreciated.

A special note of appreciation goes to Professors Yunshik Chang, Chin-hong Chung, and Kang-nam Oh, who always warmed my heart and mind and raised me up whenever the wind blew down the hill. My friends Tong-su, Chin-u, Tŏk-su, Ch'an-il, Nak-bong, Yŏng-sŏng, Yang-hwan, Hŭng-sin, and many others cheered me up whenever I showed up without warning. I thank them for their friendship, which overwhelms me. Special words of thanks go to Seraphina, a legendary poetic figure who forever inspires me when I walk along the beautiful shoreline of Spanish Banks in Vancouver. For my brothers Nam-sŏk and Nam-yong and sister Yŏng-suk, I remain grateful for their understanding and encouragement. Whenever I felt guilty about my lack of filiality toward my father, they were there in my place; and whenever I paid a visit to my mother on the other shore, they stood firmly beside me. I love my son Jin, who has frequently asked me when the book will come out.

Generous financial support from various sources was indispensable for this book. I am grateful to the Japan Foundation, whose fellowship enabled me to embark on this research at the Jōminken in 1999; the Social Sciences and Humanities Research Council of Canada, which provided me with Standard Research Grants in 2002–5; and the University of British Columbia, which, over the past few years, supported me through several UBC-HSS and Kameyama grants.

The critical comments of the anonymous reviewers of the manuscript helped me to revise it and get it into better shape during my sabbatical leave in 2004–5. Of course, any shortcomings or errors are mine alone. The current form of *Death and Social Order in Tokugawa Japan* reflects many of their constructive suggestions and comments. In editing the manuscript Dr. Joanne Richardson kindly exercised her unfailing acumen and guided me through the process of clarifying my prose. I am also deeply grateful to William M. Hammell and the staff of the Harvard University Asia Center for treating this manuscript with impeccable professional care and respect throughout the publication process.

I dedicate this book to Professor Miyata Noboru, whose smile often reminds me of the journey of life that follows and shatters along the contours of clouds that are constantly mutating in the high sky. He was a great scholar and teacher. When I visit his resting place with this book, I shall tell Mrs. Miyata Tomoko that he was indeed a great scholar and friend to all of us.

Contents

Part IV: Funerary Buddhism and Shinto Funerals

Reference Matter

ᘓ

Map and Tables

Map

Tables

Death and Social Order

in Tokugawa Japan

ෆ

INTRODUCTION

The Rise of Funerary Buddhism
in Tokugawa Japan

Buddhism permeated daily life during the Tokugawa period (1600–1868), and Buddhist temples stood in every corner of the country. It is estimated that by the late seventeenth century, there were more than 100,000 Buddhist temples, and this number remained undiminished until the early years of the Meiji period (1868–1912), when an anti-Buddhist movement adopting the motto "abolish the Buddha and discard Śākyamuni" (*haibutsu kishaku*) swept the country.[1] There were more than 100,000 temples (probably between 200,000 and 250,000 if subtemples such as *jiin*, *tatchū*, and *anshitsu* are included) in a country whose population had grown from around 12 million at the turn of the sixteenth century to around 30 million by 1700, and where there were about 73,000 administrative units (about 63,000 village [*mura*] units and 10,000 ward [*machi*] units). This meant that, on average, 300 people (or 60 households, assuming that each family unit has five members) in each village and ward supported at least one or two temples.[2] The Tokugawa Japanese had to shoulder this financial burden in addition to the regular tax obligations and corvée duties owed to the government and to the ruling class.

Almost no village in Tokugawa Japan was without a Buddhist temple and few people were untouched by the activities of Buddhist monks. Nonetheless, Buddhism was not a state religion. Unlike the

Meiji imperial government, for example, which tried to elevate Shinto to the status of a state religion, the Tokugawa regime did not make any attempt to incorporate Buddhist ideas or rituals into its governing principles. It neither forced people to allocate their precious resources to Buddhist temples nor encouraged Buddhist institutions to tap the economic surplus of Tokugawa society. On the contrary, throughout the Tokugawa period, both central (*bakufu*) and local (*han*) governments, which often found themselves vying with Buddhist institutions over the same resources, tried to contain, control, and even in some cases, suppress Buddhism. Given all of this, one might wonder how Buddhist institutions were able to penetrate every corner of the country and how so many Buddhist temples were able to maintain themselves.

As the register of head-branch temples from the Kan'ei era (1624–43) testifies, however, most temples simply could not entrust their sustenance to the mainstay of Tokugawa economic life — agricultural landholdings.[3] Among 2,838 temples listed in the Kan'ei register, 15 percent reported that their income from landholdings was less than one *koku* (= 5.119 bushels) of rice; 52 percent reported income of between one and five *koku*; and 13 percent reported income between six and ten *koku*. According to one estimate, in order to be stable during the 1630s, a temple needed an annual income of at least ten *koku* of rice.[4] As far as the Kan'ei register is concerned, a vast majority of Buddhist temples — 80 percent — had to find extra or supplementary income sources in order to survive.

Where and how were Buddhist temples, which were largely stable and even prosperous throughout the country, able to find financial resources to supplement their mediocre income from agriculture? In an attempt to answer this question, I draw attention to the example of Edo, the shogunal capital that came to embrace a large number of Buddhist temples within a short period of time yet was able to accommodate them without much stress. The mode in which Buddhist temples operated in Edo may be seen as a local issue; however, given that, as far as religious policy was concerned, the shogunal government (i.e., the shogunate, or *bakufu*) set the regulations for all Buddhist temples in the country, it follows that the example of Edo can help us to assess the rise, sustenance and prosperity of Buddhism throughout Tokugawa Japan.

Edo, which served as the de facto capital of Tokugawa Japan, had been a small rural town with no significant religious establishments until Tokugawa Ieyasu (1542–1616) settled there in 1590. Edo's population grew to around 1 million by the late seventeenth century and remained quite stable thereafter. Its dramatic metamorphosis from a rural town into a seventeenth-century megacity was accompanied by a rapid growth in the number of Buddhist temples. According to a *bakufu* survey from the Bunsei era (1818–29) detailing the genesis of religious institutions, Edo was home to more than 1,000 temples—on average, one temple per 1,000 residents. In comparison, all its Shinto shrines numbered only 112.[5] This level of temple density was far less than the national average; however, given that about half of the population were samurai, most of whom were affiliated with temples in their local domains, Edo was—at least, as far as the commoner residents were concerned—clearly a "Buddhist" city.

In order to understand the context of Edo's swift accommodation of a large number of Buddhist temples, it is helpful to look at the findings from the Bunsei-era survey.[6] Data from this survey show that, in the 1820s, Buddhist temples in Edo had the following sectarian distribution outlined in Table 1.

Table 1: Buddhist Temples in Edo

Name of sect	Number of temples	%
Jōdoshū	231	23.6
Nichirenshū	200	20.5
Sōtōshū	156	16.0
Jōdoshinshū	124	12.7
Tendaishū	92	9.4
Rinzaishū	72	7.4
Shingi Shingonshū	65	6.6
Ōbakushū	14	1.4
Kogi Shingonshū	13	1.3
Shugen	7	0.7
Jishū	2	0.2
Shingon Risshū	2	0.2
TOTAL	978	100.0

SOURCE: Asakura Haruhiko ed., *Gofunai jisha bikō bessatsu* (Tokyo: Meicho shuppan, 1987), pp. 7–35.
NOTES: Not included in this survey were: temples related to the shogunal house as prayer halls or funerary temples (such as Kan'eiji, Zōjōji, Gokokuji, Denzūin, Gojiin, and Nishihonganji in Tsukiji); temples located near the city boundary of Edo demarcated by the "vermilion line"; temples serving Shinto shrines as *jingūji*; and many other subtemples (which, in terms of organizational structure, belonged to high-status head temples but were independently run). In other words, Edo temples actually numbered more than what is indicated by Table 1. As I have said, there were more than 1,000 Buddhist temples in Edo.[7]

We notice that Pure Land (Jōdoshū, Jōdoshinshū), Nichiren, and Zen Buddhist (Sōtōshū, Rinzaishū, Ōbakushū) sects were dominant in Edo. The strong presence of the so-called Kamakura Buddhist sects in Edo (which was a newly developed city) stood in contrast to the situations in the more traditional rural villages of the surrounding Musashi area, where such old Buddhist establishments as those associated with the Tendai and Shingon sects were relatively prominent. Before Tokugawa Ieyasu entered the city, Edo's Buddhist temples had been sparse in number and meager in magnitude (notwithstanding a few exceptions, such as Sensōji and Zōjōji). As Edo rapidly developed, Buddhist sects, seeing ample opportunities for growth, vied with each other to expand their footholds. Of these, Jōdoshū, Nichirenshū, Sōtōshū, and Jōdoshinshū (also commonly known as Ikkōshū) turned out to be the most successful.[8]

Table 2 shows the number of temples of each sect established within certain time periods. The year 1600 marks the beginning of the Tokugawa regime, and 1631 and 1663 are the years in which the shogunate reiterated its ban on the construction of new temples. In 1631 (the eighth year of the Kan'ei era) the shogunal government outlawed the building of new temples, ordering the major temples of each sect to survey their branch temples and to enter them in what would later be known as the Kan'ei register of head-branch temples (*honmatsuchō*). The *bakufu* then classified the temples listed in the Kan'ei head-branch register as "old-track temples" (*koseki jiin*) and privileged them over the ones erected after 1631, which were collectively referred to as "new-land temples" (*shinchi jiin*). Officials of the *bakufu* continued to attempt to halt the mushrooming of Buddhist temples throughout Edo.[9] Despite the government's hostility, the number of temples continued to increase. About three decades later, the shogunate once again issued an edict forbidding the opening of "new-land temples" — an edict that was once again promulgated in 1692. The increase in new temples slowed measurably thereafter, and their number eventually stabilized at around 1,000.

Given the status and prestige carried by "old-track temples" throughout the Tokugawa period, it is not surprising that many temples tried to inflate their genealogy when they were surveyed in the early nineteenth century. The older-is-better mindset seemed especially conspicuous among those temples that claimed they had originated before 1600. It is highly unlikely that there were already

Table 2: The Genesis of Buddhist Temples in Edo

Name of sect	Pre-1590	1590–1599	1600–1631	1632–1663	Post-1663	N/A	Total
Jōdoshū	21	21	123	12	6	48	231
Nichirenshū	18	27	96	14	3	42	200
Sōtōshū	25	19	60	9	7	36	156
Jōdoshinshū	20	11	66	9	4	14	124
Tendaishū	21	4	19	2	4	42	92
Shingonshū	3	0	29	5	5	38	80
Rinzaishū	1	2	39	14	9	7	72
Ōbakushū	1	0	1	2	1	9	14
Shugen	2	0	0	0	2	3	7
Jishū	0	0	0	0	0	2	2
TOTAL	112	84	433	67	41	241	978
%	11.5	8.6	44.3	6.8	4.2	24.6	100.0

SOURCES: *Gofunai jisha bikō*, vol. 7, pp. 281–302 and Nittō (1995), pp. 179–81.
NOTE: This table adapts Nittō Kazuhiko's meticulous analysis of the *Gofunai jisha bikō*, to which I added statistics pertaining to the temples managed by *shugen*.

196 temples (see Table 2) in the small town of Edo before the shogunal government was established. Many of these, if they existed at all, must have been obscure religious facilities that hardly qualified to be called "temples."[10] The statistical accuracy of Table 2 should be read with care. Nevertheless, as far as the genesis of Edo's Buddhist temples is concerned, the Bunsei survey reveals some overall historical trends: (1) a vast majority of temples were newly erected within a relatively short period of time, and (2) the vast majority of these were erected during the early decades of the seventeenth century.

Specifically, more than 60 percent of the 231 Jōdoshū temples were founded in the seventeenth century (before 1591, Edo had only 21 Jōdoshū temples). In particular, under the leadership of two major head temples, Chion'in in Kyoto and Zōjōji in Edo (which would, respectively, control 92 and 70 branch temples in Edo), by the 1630s the Jōdoshū saw a dramatic proliferation of its branch temples. In the case of Nichirenshū, the ratio of temples established after 1600 reached 56 percent; and, in the case of Sōtōshū, it exceeded 48 percent. Jōdoshinshū was also quite successful in expanding its branches within the new political center of the nation. More than 60 percent of its temples were established between 1600 and 1662. On the whole, more than half of all Buddhist temples in Edo were erected between 1600 and 1663, whether newly constructed, transformed from obscure prayer halls, or transplanted from other areas. If we take into account those temples whose histories are unknown but whose construction was unlikely to have taken place before 1600, we can see that most of Edo's Buddhist temples came into being in the seventeenth century, particularly in its early to middle decades.

Where in the city were these temples constructed? It is not easy to determine where all of these temples were initially founded because religious institutions in Edo were often subjected to the shogunate's precarious city planning. The transfer of most of the inner-city temples to the outskirts of the city following the Meireki Fire in 1657 was particularly dramatic. Initially, in the early years of the seventeenth century, the shogunate allocated spaces in Hirakawa, Sakurada, and Kanda—all in the vicinity of the shogunal castle—for Buddhist temples. However, due to the rapid growth of city districts and the need to expand and upgrade the shogunal castle, the shogunate began to relocate Buddhist temples to the suburban areas. By 1639 the expansion of the outer moats encircling the castle and the additional appropriation of new tracts of land for the second residences (*naka-yashiki*) and tertiary residences (*shimoyashiki*) of the daimyo families had already forced out many of the inner-city temples. When the Meireki Fire devoured large parts of Edo, the shogunate moved the remaining temples further outwards. Temples located in Kanda and Hirakawa were relocated to Asakusa, Yanaka, or Komagome; those in Kyōbashi to Shiba; those in Inner Ushigome to Outer Ushigome or Kohinata; and those in Inner Azabu to Outer Azabu.[11] It was not until the Genroku era (1688–1703) that Edo temples were relatively stabilized at the surrounding belts of the city along Fukagawa, Honjo, Asakusa, Shitaya, Yanaka, Komagome, Koishikawa, Kohinata, Ushigome, Yotsuya, Azabu, Mita, Takanawa, and Shiba (see Map 1).[12]

Except for the Nishihonganji temple in Tsukiji, all Buddhist temples in the old districts were transferred to the relatively sparsely populated suburban areas that encircled the shogunal castle and the downtown area, as if forming a defensive wall. By the turn of the seventeenth century, some areas were literally transformed into Buddhist districts, showcasing a large number of temples clustered together: Asakusa led the pack with 172 temples, followed by Azabu with 76, Ushigome with 74, Yanaka with 67, Shitaya with 57, and Yotsuya with 53.[13] Many temples were removed from the heavily inhabited inner-city districts that were supposed to constitute their supporting base.

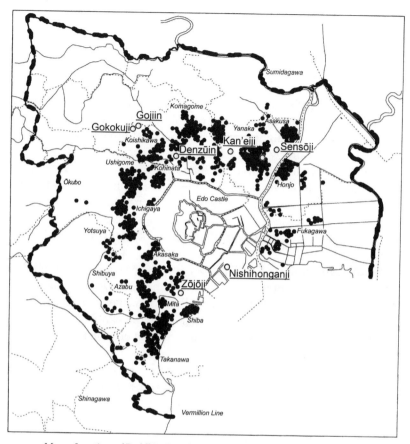

Map 1 Locations of Buddhist Temples in Edo. Adapted from Nittō (1998), p. 11.

Despite a shaky start and mounting density, most of the Buddhist temples in Edo adjusted well to their new environments, as was seen in their ability to embrace tens of thousands of priests, to hold a great number of prosperous religious events, and to erect and maintain innumerable ritual halls, stupas, and other facilities.[14] Given that many of the samurai residents, particularly those belonging to the upper echelon, were affiliated with temples in their local domain or fief, and that Edo was a massive urban hodgepodge containing tens of thousands of transients, it must have been rather difficult for Edo's Buddhist temples to survive. Yet stories of temple poverty were rarely heard, despite the fact that there is no evidence that temples were all richly endowed with land.

The forms of "temple lands" (*keidaichi*) in Edo were various: those granted by the shogun himself (vermilion-seal lands [*goshuinchi*]);

those granted by the government (*hairyōchi*); private land properties subject to government tax (*nenguchi*); new land properties donated by private patrons (*kishinchi*); old lands that had always been exempt from taxation (*jochi*); and front districts (*monzen* or *monzenmachi*) that townspeople could lease for their residence or business. Among these land categories, the vermilion-seal land, exempted from taxation and regarded as an indication to high honor, was granted only to 49 temples of the highest rank. The rice yield, measured in terms of *kokudaka* (amount of *koku*), from this category ranged from 700 *koku* to five *koku*, and its total yield amounted to 5,480 *koku*.[15] On average, the taxable *kokudaka* per temple on vermilion-seal land was a bit more than 112 — an amount that could generate, for instance, an actual income of 34 *koku* of rice at a tax rate of 30 percent. This was certainly not so bad; however, it pertained to only 5 percent of all Edo temples.

As far as income from land properties was concerned, many other temples had to rely upon rent from their *jochi* and/or *monzen*. A bit more than half of all temples held these *jochi* and/or *monzen*, but only a tiny portion of them were able to net a sizable income from renting them out. In terms of the land area over which each temple had a proprietary right, more than 60 percent of the temples commanded less than 1,000 *tsubo* (approximately 303 square meters); and among them, 319 (about one-third) had fewer than 500 *tsubo* — a land area that would not leave much room for rent income after basic temple facilities were accommodated. In particular, many of the Jōdoshinshū and Nichirenshū temples (68 percent and 40 percent, respectively) were built on land that comprised fewer than 400 *tsubo*.[16] In short, for a majority of the Edo temples, land property was simply not a dependable source of income.

So where could the majority of Edo's Buddhist institutions — most of which were newly erected, not associated with old religious traditions, and heavily concentrated in suburban valleys and hills — turn to secure a stable income? Some temples resorted to the business of prayer or votive rites, which generated income in the form of prayer fees, donations, alms-giving, and the sale of such votive items as amulets and talismans. This was clearly the case at Sensōji, which capitalized on the popularity of its renowned Asakusa Kannon as an object of popular worship to garner more than 70 percent of its annual income of 2,000 to 3,000 gold pieces.[17] Buddhist halls, blessed with "miraculous Buddhas and Bodhisattvas," were able to attract crowds of visitors and pilgrims and, in this manner, to rake in a sizable income. But the number of those temples blessed with marketable deities was very few.[18] Furthermore, the fortunes of prayer temples, which owed much to the religious fashion of the time, were often precarious and highly unpredictable. So what, in the final analysis, provided a majority of Buddhist temples — regardless of their sectarian affiliation, prestige, and religious reputation — with financial stability?

The answer is simple: death. During the Tokugawa period, all families were required to be affiliated with a Buddhist temple, and everyone had to die a Buddhist and be given a Buddhist funeral. Not only the funeral but also the postmortem rituals were, to one degree or another, within the religious purview of Buddhist monks who played their priestly role and collected their fees. Naturally, in order to ensure the stable income generated by death-related rituals, almost all Buddhist temples tried to secure funerary patronage from their affiliated households. The enduring relationship between a Buddhist temple and its funerary patron household, cemented from generation to generation through recurring rites and services related to death and ancestral veneration, gave rise to what is commonly known as the *danka* system (*danka seido* or *dankasei*).[19] It was the *danka* system, more than anything else, that sustained Buddhist temples in Tokugawa Japan.

Here, *danka* (also known as *danna*, *dan'otsu*, *danchū*, *dankata*, or *danto*, all of which trace their etymology to the Sanskrit word *dana* [giving]) refers to the funerary patron household or individual who is affiliated with and supports a temple, known as *dankadera* (also called *dannadera* or *bodaiji*, and, in the case of Jōdoshinshū, *tetsugitera*).[20] By binding all Japanese people to the Buddhist care of funerary practices and thereby generating an economy of death, the *danka* system provided Buddhist temples with a stable source of income and, hence, guaranteed sustenance. The *danka* system is commonly, albeit misleadingly, rendered as the "temple parish system" in English. However, as I discuss in Part II, the *danka* system has little to do with the idea of "parish," which connotes a clear geographical setting for the affiliations between patron families and funerary temples. On the contrary, the *danka* system simply indicates the affiliation between patron households (or individuals) and funerary Buddhist temples — an affiliation that is formed when the former, with free will and no restrictions on location, choose the latter. Too often, patterns of affiliation between the household and the temple were so arbitrary, disorderly, and crisscrossed that it was almost impossible to group them into temple-centered parishes that could be adequately demarcated by geographical boundaries.

The *danka* system was a financial foundation not only for Buddhist temples in Edo but also for a vast majority of Buddhist temples throughout the country, regardless of their sectarian affiliation, distribution, and location. In 1879 the Meiji government ordered local governments to conduct a comprehensive survey of Shinto shrines and Buddhist temples and to submit the results. It was a project aimed at gathering new data on the changes that occurred over the past few turbulent years and updating the previous surveys conducted in 1870–71. With regard to Buddhist temples, the government demanded that the survey include information on head-branch relationship and sectarian affiliation, history (year of establishment, founder, and chronicle), administration (current head monk and subtemples), religious facilities and deities enshrined therein, landholding, the number of *danna* (funerary/prayer) households (or patrons), and so on. The survey results in Kōzuke province, for example, provide us with detailed data on how its many temples maintained funerary *danna* patrons.[21]

More than a decade had passed since the Meiji Restoration, and during this period many temples throughout the country, including those in Kōzuke province, had to endure the anti-Buddhist storm of the new era. Nevertheless, the 1880–81 survey reports, entitled *Kōzuke no kuni jiin meisaichō* (Detailed registers of Buddhist temples in Kōzuke province), show that almost all Buddhist temples in the province continued to maintain funerary *danna* patrons.[22] According to the reports, there were a total of 1,361 temples in Kōzuke province. Among them, those that had funerary *danna* patrons numbered 1,283, or a bit over 94 percent. This high ratio of funerary *danna*-holding temples was more or less similar across different sects. In the case of Tendaishū, it was 91 percent, or 322 temples out of 355; in the case of Shingonshū, it was 95 percent, or 414 temples out of 434; and in the case of Zenshū (Sōtō, Rinzai, and Ōbaku), it was 94 percent, or 392 out of 416. Of Jōdoshū's 93 temples only one was without *danna* patrons; and Nichirenshū and Jōdoshinshū, which had 23 and 40 temples, respectively, did not have any that were without funerary *danna* patrons.[23]

Table 3: Ratios of Funerary *Danna*-Holding Temples

Sect	Kakuda	Izu	Shingū	Kurashiki	Ōzu	Hita
Tendaishū	1/1	0/0	0/1	14/17	8/9	4/10
Shingonshū	38/54	11/17	1/3	113/149	28/35	18/30
Zenshū	69/71	234/280	136/140	86/119	84/108	120/176
Jōdoshū	13/13	42/50	7/9	8/8	1/1	48/68
Nichirenshū	3/4	66/73	2/2	44/53	2/2	14/19
Jōdoshinshū	15/15	15/16	8/8	36/42	11/11	190/202
TOTAL	139/158	368/436	154/163	301/388	134/166	394/505
%	88.0	84.4	94.5	77.6	80.7	78.0

SOURCES: The data in each area are based on, respectively, *Kakudaken shoshū honmatsu jigō sonota meisaichō* (1871), *Izu no kuni honmatsu jigō sonota meisaichō* (1871), *Shingūhan shoshū honmatsu jigō sonota meisaichō* (1870), *Kurashikiken honmatsu jigō sonota meisaichō* (1871), *Ōzuhan shoshū honmatsu jigō sonota meisaichō* (1871), and *Hitaken shoshū honmatsu jigō sonota meisaichō* (1871).

NOTES: The numbers before the slash indicate those of *danna*-holding temples; those after it indicate the total numbers of temples in each sect. The category of Zenshū includes Sōtōshū, Rinzaishū, and Ōbakushū; and that of Jōdoshū includes Jishū. In the case of the Shingū, Kurashiki, and Hita areas, subtemples such as *anshitsu* and *tatchū* are all individually counted as they were separately recorded in the reports. These are the only separately counted subtemples. In the case of Ōzu, temples belonging to Zenshū included three Ōbakushū temples, none of which had funerary *danna* households; all others were affiliated with Rinzaishū. Among the Zenshū category in Hita, there were 26 Ōbakushū temples, and, among them, only four had funerary *danna* households.

The number of funerary *danna* patrons held by each temple ranged from just one person (although this was extremely rare) to thousands of persons, indicating that the economic dependence of Buddhist temples upon funerary *danna* holdings was never even. For temples with a small number of *danna* patrons, income generated through the *danka* system must have been supplemented by other sources; however, those blessed with a large number of *danna* patrons could have enjoyed a high level of financial stability with income derived from the provision of death-related services. Despite variations in number, funerary *danna* patrons seemed to be indispensable for the survival and prosperity of the vast majority of temples in Kōzuke province.

Indeed, funerary *danna* patrons were an integral part of temple economy. In some areas the ratio of *danna*-holding temples reached 100 percent, as was seen, for example, in the Shiiya domain (currently parts of Niigata prefecture), where all of its 23 temples had funerary *danna* households.[24] Table 3 clearly shows the high degree to which Buddhist temples were endowed with funerary *danna* patrons.

The data provided here are taken from survey reports conducted in 1870–71, and the samples are chosen from the areas that cover northern Honshū to Kyūshū. Soon after the Restoration the Meiji government, as part of its pro-Shinto policy, surveyed the status of Shinto shrines and scrutinized Buddhist temples. Even though many temples suffered from the prevailing anti-Buddhist sentiment and lost some of their funerary *danna* patrons, a large majority of them still kept their funerary *danna* households—a legacy that bespeaks the firm entrenchment of the *danka* system that had been inherited from the previous period.

As is seen in Table 3, the distribution of temples in terms of sectarian affiliation shows a wide range of variation, with a relatively strong presence of Zen temples in comparison to those belonging to Tendaishū, a discrepancy probably due to the different local characteristics of the areas chosen for study. Nevertheless, without exception, the overall ratios of funerary *danna*-holding temples were very high, ranging from 77.6 percent to 94.5 percent. This suggests that a vast majority of temples throughout the country were involved, to one degree or another, in the business of death-related rituals.

Arimoto Masao, who traces the regional distribution of Buddhist sects during the Tokugawa period, sums up the religious functions of Buddhist temples.[25] According to him, the primary business of Buddhist temples in the Kantō region and its vicinities was to provide funerary rituals and memorial services to their patron households. The preaching of Buddhist doctrine was clearly secondary.[26] The Kinki region and its vicinities, despite the presence of many old and great temples, showed the strong presence in local villages of *miyaza* or "shrine council" organizations, which controlled communal village rituals for Shinto deities. Such organizations often discouraged Buddhists from promoting their teachings on death and afterlife. Nevertheless, Buddhist temples in this region were also, like those in eastern Japan, primarily engaged in the performance of death rituals and postmortem memorial services.[27] Arimoto continues to note that the situation in the areas of Jōdoshinshū was not so different from that in other regions, despite the fact that its sectarian teachings did not officially recognize the ritual efficacy of *nenbutsu*-chanting for the well-being of the deceased.

Based on an analysis of the religious practices of Jōdoshinshū followers in the Okayama area, Nagura Tetsuzō notes that by at least the 1640s, all of them were basically subjugated to the prescription of Buddhist death.[28] To be sure, in some areas, the Jōdoshinshū faithful tried to differentiate their ritual practices pertaining to death and ancestral veneration from those of other sects by emphasizing that their *nenbutsu*-chanting was an expression of gratitude toward the Amida Buddha rather than a devotional offering to their ancestral spirits.[29] But the overall tendency overrode Jōdoshinshū's traditional practices, which, with the complete dissolution of Ikkō *ikki* (a series of revolts by Jōdoshinshū followers who were guided by the Law of the Buddha), were anyway forced to yield to the Law of the King. By the mid-seventeenth century, Jōdoshinshū temples emerged strong in various parts of the country, and these temples, which were not endowed with extensive landholdings, found themselves dependent upon donations and fees paid by lay followers for ritual services related to death and postmortem care. The twelve-article regulations of Higashichōshōji, a Jōdoshinshū temple in the Fukui ward of Echizen, included one straightforward article about what its patrons (*monto*) were expected to do: according to their station in society, they were to strictly conduct all yearly ancestral rites and Buddhist rituals.[30] Indeed, most of the Jōdoshinshū temples imposed a similar set of regulations upon their patrons. The list of regulations was long, including compliance with the shogunal law, contribution to the maintenance of temple buildings, respect for the head monk, hard work, frugality, and so forth. And the key point was always unambiguous: the faithful conduct of death rituals and memorial services within the framework of the *danka* system.[31] More than anything else, it was the economy of death that brought the Tokugawa Japanese to support Buddhist temples.

It should be noted, however, that the *danka* system was not really a legal "system" or "institution" per se; rather, it was a custom, manipulated and entrenched by Buddhist temples, which capitalized on the anti-Christian policy of the Tokugawa *bakufu*. Once established as a custom, it somehow became integrated back into the anti-Christian policy, which was gradually institutionalized into a nationwide system of population surveillance. The *danka* system was never written into law. Despite its lack of legal status, as a public custom, it was applied to the entire populace without exception and exerted enduring influence. In understanding the practice of the *danka* system, therefore, it is essential to comprehend its anti-Christian context—a context that decisively transformed its sphere of practice from private to public.

During the early seventeenth century, in the name of protecting the land of the "divine country," or the "country of the gods" (*shinkoku* — a nativist dictum that would repeatedly be invoked in subsequent anti-Christian pronouncements), the Tokugawa regime decided to eradicate Christianity from Japan and began purging Christian missionaries and their followers, who were collectively referred to as "Kirishitan."[32] Christian missionaries consisted of Roman Catholic fathers (*bateren*) and brothers (*iruman*), both of whom entered Japan between 1549 and the 1630s for the purpose of proselytizing. The term *bateren* is derived from the Portuguese word "padre," and *iruman* from the Portuguese word *irmão*. These terms reflect the fact that the majority of the missionaries — about 300 in total (230 padres and 70 *irmão*) — were Jesuits from Portugal.[33] On the other hand, ever since Francis Xavier's arrival in Japan in 1549, the term "Kirishitan," which comes from the Portuguese word Christão, was used by the Tokugawa Japanese to refer to the Roman Catholic Church, the Christian religion, or its followers. For their part, the Christian missionaries referred to the Japanese who accepted their religion as "qirixitan."[34] Gonoi Takashi estimates that the total number of Kirishitan between 1549 and the 1630s may have reached as high as 760,000.[35] In *Death and Social Order in Tokugawa Japan*, when referring to those Japanese who accepted Christianity during this period, I employ the term "Kirishitan" rather than the terms "Christians" or "Christian converts" in order to minimize possible theological implications as well as to respect the uniqueness of the Kirishitan religion.[36]

In carrying out its anti-Christian policy, the Tokugawa regime relied upon the system of "temple certification," or *terauke*. Under this system, each year all residents were ordered to prove their non-Christian identity by presenting themselves for inspection by the Buddhist temple with which they happened to be affiliated. The temple would then issue them a "certificate" stating that they were affiliated with it and, therefore, had nothing to do with the Kirishitan religion. Those who failed to undergo temple certification were classified as Kirishitan and were put to death.

Here the phrase "Buddhist temple" — a translation of the Japanese words *jiin*, *tera*, or *ji* — refers to the head monk of a temple or the temple itself. In the Japanese cultural tradition, a Buddhist temple is understood to have at least three components: (1) the temple buildings, (2) the Buddhist images and sūtras enshrined within these buildings, and (3) the clergy residing in the temple compound in order to maintain the buildings and to serve the Buddhist deities (represented by iconic images). Conventionally, however, since the head monk (abbot) of a temple represents that institution, the name of the temple often functions as a synonym for its head monk. In some cases, the name of a temple indicates, whether collectively or individually, the members of the clergy belonging to it (without necessarily specifying them).[37] The temple names cited in this book follow this convention.

Notwithstanding the anti-Christian policy in the country of the gods (*kami*), it is curious why the Tokugawa regime chose to adopt a Buddhist rather than a Shinto system of inspection. During the medieval period, Buddhist temples had been a source of political havoc. Furthermore, due to their close affiliation with the imperial court, which the incipient shogunal house had yet to overcome, the strategy of deploying Buddhist temples could have been a risky proposition.[38] As we will see in Part I, however, by the late seventeenth century, the entire population had been subjected to the anti-Christian measure of temple certification, and this anti-Christian system had become fully integrated into the governing apparatus of the Tokugawa regime.

In 1613, Konchiin Sūden (1569–1633), an influential Buddhist adviser who served the first three Tokugawa shoguns, composed an anti-Christian edict entitled "A Statement on Expelling Padres" (*Bateren tsuihō no bun*). Shogun Hidetada presented this to the nation, thereby setting the ground for the anti-Christian policy that would be implemented in the decades that followed. Initially, only those who were identified as Kirishitan were required to obtain written proof from Buddhist temples or village officials with regard to their abandonment of Christianity and affiliation with Buddhism; however, beginning in the 1630s, the shogunate gradually unified the method of religious inspection into a system of temple certification and began to impose this upon the populace. After the Amakusa-Shimabara Rebellion (1637–38), which was condemned as a Christian-inspired revolt, *bakufu* leaders intensified their efforts to root out all Christian elements, ever more vigorously prevailing upon Buddhist temples to carry out the task of religious inspection. By the 1660s, based on the non-Christian certificates of their residents, village officials were ordered to draw up an anti-Christian register, known as a "register of sectarian inspection" (*shūmon aratamechō*), for all residents under their jurisdiction and to submit it to the government.

Within this administrative framework, every year Buddhist temples carried out the role of certifying the non-Christian identity of each resident, and upon this non-Christian certification, village or ward officials annually compiled the "register of sectarian inspection" and submitted it to their higher government office. Here, the inspection by Buddhist monks and the registration by secular officials involved totally separate procedures. Due probably to the obvious link between these two processes, however, scholars often fail to differentiate them, as is seen in the frequency with which the term *terauke* (temple certification) is rendered as "temple registration." *Terauke* applied only to the procedure in which the "*tera*" (i.e., the head monk of a "Buddhist temple") conducted the task of "*uke*" (i.e., "certifying" that persons affiliated with the temple were not Kirishitan). The responsibility for actually registering those who were inspected by Buddhist temples belonged exclusively to village or ward officials, not to Buddhist monks. To be sure, there was no law prohibiting temples from maintaining a private register of their own, and most temples did maintain one; however, this kind of register was known as *kakochō* or *ekōchō*, "register of the past or the dead," consisting of a list of deceased *danna* members and their posthumous names, and it was designed to schedule memorial services for dead patrons, not to conduct anti-Christian inspections for living patrons.

As the annual anti-Christian inspection was put into strict practice, Buddhist monks, who acted like public officials, were quick to transform their religious inspectees into regular funerary patrons and to organize them into the institution of a permanent *danna* relationship or, in other words, the *danka* system. In making Buddhist temples responsible for anti-Christian religious inspection, the shogunate never officially bound the Buddhist inspection to the *danka* system, nor did it authorize Buddhist temples to use the *danka* system to enforce funerary patronage upon the populace. But, over time, the entire populace was, through the assertion of Buddhist temples, locked into the mandate of Buddhist death.

However, as I discuss in Part II, it should also be noted that, despite its political tone of enforcement, the *danka* system was ultimately structured to accommodate, respond to, or resonate with the socio-religious needs of the people. The early modern Japanese, who wanted to deal with the deaths of their family members with dignity, were receptive to the ritual prescriptions of the *danka* system and its links with the anti-Christian policy. Rather than continuing with the medieval approach to death, which had by and large reflected the Buddhist notions of karmic reward and retribution, the early modern Japanese eagerly adopted the hands-on funerary rituals and services of familial Buddhism. Death rituals, not the doctrinal polemics of karma and retribution, were an answer for the socio-religious needs of the new type of family structure that was taking shape in the seventeenth century. Thus, in order to gain a balanced understanding of how the *danka* system came into being and operated, we also need to take into account how changing religious concerns in the changing family structure corresponded to it. The *danka* system was pushed, but at the same time, it was pulled as well.

The process of pulling can be seen through the prism of people's changing concerns with afterlife and hell — concerns that were, for example, reflected into the vicissitudes of the Kumano nuns (*bikuni*). In his discussion of medieval Japanese Buddhism, William R. LaFleur suggests that the idea of "six courses" (*rokudō*) served as "a coherent explanation of the world and of human experience; it was the single most satisfying and comprehensive explanation available to the Japanese people at the time."[39] The *rokudō* refers to the six possible modes of being, which, in hierarchical order, are: gods (*kami*), humans (*ningen*), asuras (*ashura*), animals (*chikushō*), hungry ghosts (*gaki*), and creatures of hell (*jigoku*). After death, in a cycle of ongoing transmigration, one is destined to be reborn into one of these modes of being. This, of course, is in accordance with the law of karmic reward and punishment — a law that was believed to be both inescapable and universal. Within the system of karmic causality, as LaFleur puts it: "Death will result in rebirth, and rebirth always poses the possibility of either progress or slippage to another location in the taxonomy. In strict interpretations, everything depends on the life lived now and the karma engendered in the present. The system thus makes each person individually responsible for his or her own future. Injustice is an impossibility."[40] Progression upward through the *rokudō* taxonomy was, of course, what people hoped for and sought after. Buddhist doctrine even taught that it was not entirely impossible to find a way out of the cycle of birth and death and to enter the realm of Paradise, where transmigration ceases. For the medieval Japanese, however, the desire for a dream-like eternal happiness in Paradise was far outweighed by the looming possibility of slipping into hell. Their anxieties over this led them to undertake all manner of quests for salvation.[41] No matter what they tried to do, they could not escape the agonizing knowledge that the avoidance of hell was their own personal and individual responsibility.

In keeping with the belief that they were personally responsible for their own fate, the medieval Japanese found themselves overwhelmed by the horrible scenes of hell. The "scroll of hell" (*jigoku zōshi*), which depicted a variety of images of unspeakable suffering in the pits of hell, was a regular companion to medieval Buddhist didacticism. During the late medieval period, the *etoki bikuni*, or "painting-recitation nuns"—which included those who were later commonly known as the Kumano nuns—owed much of their religious popularity to their ability to preach about the scroll of hell, which highlighted posthumous sufferings in the hell of *rokudō* cosmology.[42] The terrifying scenes portrayed in the scroll, particularly the "Heart Visualization and the Mandala of the Ten Realms" (*Kanjin jikkai mandara*), which came in various editions, allowed no one to forget the need to safeguard one's future life. In particular, images of ill-fated women writhing in agony in a bloody pond or being punished with childlessness exacerbated women's fear of Buddhist condemnation. The medieval Japanese took very seriously the merciless working of karmic causality, which emphasized the moral responsibility of each individual.

From the early seventeenth century on, however, the painting-recitation nuns began to lose much of their previous appeal as preachers of the *rokudō* cosmology, which had once gripped the medieval Japanese. As time progressed, many of these nuns gradually became street singers, entertainers, prostitutes, wandering mendicants, or the wives of petty Buddhist preachers (*yamabushi*), particularly from the Tenna-Genroku years (1681–1704), which ushered in the boom of a commercial economy.[43] The message of karmic retribution, once a powerful weapon for these street preachers, was being heard less and less. Already in 1661, in his *Tōkaidō meishoki* (Record of famous places along the Tōkaidō Highway), Asai Ryōi (1612–91) commented on what he perceived as Kumano *bikuni*: "While one was not aware of it, [Kumano nuns] stopped chanting. Although still visiting Kumano and Ise, [they] neither practice austerities nor keep precepts. [They] even do not know how to explicate the scrolls, but, instead, only treasure singing. . . . 'One of the five heaviest punishments shall be meted out to those who violate precept-keeping nuns,' says a Buddhist sūtra, but, sadly, it is nuns them-selves who eagerly initiate peddling out [their bodies]."[44]

It is true that the seventeenth-century metamorphosis of *etoki bikuni* was expedited by the Tokugawa government, which tried to do away with itinerant religious entrepreneurs involved in street solicitation. In 1614, Tokugawa Ieyasu determined that public religious solicitations should be subjected to government approval. Thereafter, *bakufu* officials began to tightly regulate solicitation activities in terms of duration, area, and format, while controlling the free movement of wandering religious practitioners. All this was a serious blow to Kumano nuns, whose livelihood depended upon the generosity of public donations.[45] In 1659, for example, the bulletin board at the entrance of Kiji Bridge in Edo warned that the Kumano nuns settled in the residential ward in Inner Kanda should follow government regulations regarding their movements and contact with outsiders.[46] Many of the itinerant nuns, who used to roam the city freely, were gradually segregated into separate settlements as their social functions were transformed. According to the edict on Kumano nuns, which was issued in the 1660s, those who were engaged in religious activities without having "climbed the [Kumano] mountain" and having spent a certain period of time in disciplinary training were defined as illegal mendicants and were subject to control. Many of these mendicant nuns, who could not afford a retreat to Kumano and so failed to obtain a license, were accordingly cut off from the Kumano organization, commonly known as *Hongan jiin* (Temples of the Original Vow), and soon fell into poverty.[47] In 1706, when the shogunate issued edicts banning the solicitations of alms-gathering nuns and warned people to stay away from them in the name of "good moral order," the religious functionality of these women, who had previously captured the religious imagination of the populace with their skillful recitations dealing with the afterlife and hell, was much diminished.[48]

However, it would be naïve to attribute the gradual dissipation of the didactic utility of hell scrolls entirely to the Tokugawa policy of trying to contain the travel of *etoki bikuni*. One must look at the diminishing appeal of the religious message that the fate of one's soul is the consequence of one's own moral behavior and/or religious devotion.[49] By the mid-seventeenth century, the ghastly images of hell were being replaced with the idea of a religious path that promised liberation from the cycle of endless transmigration. And this path featured familial Buddhism, which would be fully institutionalized into the *danka* system, rather than individual Buddhism. The task of saving one's soul through one's own religious actions, which had been a mainstay of medieval Buddhism, gave way to a family-centered ritualism designed to elevate the deceased to the status of an ancestral deity, or *sorei*.[50] One's spirit, which was deified with the help of familial funerary rituals and through ancestral rites of oblation, was known as a *hotoke* (literally, a Buddha) and believed to be a divine being who had wholly transcended the domain of karmic transmigration.[51] Relieved of their anxiety over karmic causality, the Tokugawa Japanese increasingly believed that their spirits could be saved as long as their descendants practiced familial Buddhism, which was now locked into the *danka* system.

Familial death rituals and ancestral rites of oblation were indeed heralded as the solution to what might be dubbed the "problem of death and hell." Yasumaru Yoshio sums up the change: "Dead spirits, which had been an object of worry in the medieval period, were, through the mediation of Buddhism, incorporated into the order of this world; and from the early modern period the practice of venerating ancestral spirits served as the foundation of order in Japanese society."[52] It is ironic that, under the *danka* system, Buddhism ended up neutralizing the notion of Buddhist karma that it had so treasured during the medieval period. The Buddhism related to familial and ancestral death rites, and commonly practiced in Tokugawa Japan, may be referred to as "funerary Buddhism" (*sōshiki Bukkyō*).

To be sure, the term "funerary Buddhism," which correlates with the title of Tamamuro Taijō's book *Sōshiki Bukkyō*, is not free from the burden of ideology. Some scholars and Buddhist critics use this term to underline the negative features of the *danka* system that left Buddhism bereft of its original spiritual value. On the other hand, scholars of Jōdoshinshū practices point out that funerary Buddhism was not as marked in that sect as in others, even though, under the threat of anti-Christian suppression, Jōdoshinshū monks and their followers were all eventually forced to incorporate ancestral rites into their religious practice.[53] The term "funerary Buddhism" is not completely free of controversy; nonetheless, it succinctly cap-

tures the socio-religious nature of Tokugawa Buddhism as it operated within the framework of the *danka* system.[54]

How and when did funerary Buddhism begin to take root in the
family life of ordinary Japanese? In understanding how funerary
Buddhism permeated the populace, we first need to clarify within
what religious context it was practiced. Scholars who regard "ancestor worship" as a quintessential Japanese cultural tradition often
ascribe it to the *danka* system. However, Ōkuwa Hitoshi notes that
the Tokugawa Japanese rarely used the term *sosen sūhai*, which refers
to ancestor worship. What they used, continues Ōkuwa, were such
terms as *senzo matsuri* or *sosen saishi*, which can be rendered as "rites
for ancestors" or "ancestral rites." These concepts stress the ritual
aspect, not the ideational aspect, of ancestral veneration. In a religious context, ancestral rites (*sosen saishi*) and ancestor worship
(*sosen sūhai*) stand in contrast to one another: with regard to the
former, one becomes an ancestor because one's spirit receives ritual
veneration; with regard to the latter, after death one automatically
becomes an ancestor and so becomes an object of ancestral worship.[55] In other words, with "ancestral rites" there can be no ancestors without the offering of rituals, while with "ancestor worship"
there are always ancestors, with or without rituals. Based on this
distinction, Ōkuwa suggests that the concept of "ancestor worship"
fails to capture Tokugawa Japan's notion of ancestral veneration,
which was premised on the religious efficacy of rituals in relation
to creating and maintaining ancestors rather than on the divinity of
ancestors as objects of worship.[56] The universal practice of funerary
Buddhism in Tokugawa Japan, which featured death rituals and
ancestral rites, bespoke the arrival of a new age—an age of ancestral
veneration.

In ancient Japan, the word *hōmuru*, which means "to bury," was
often read as *haburu*, which means "to throw away" or "to discard."
As this indicates, in ancient times funerals often consisted simply
of dumping the dead body.[57] According to the *Shoku Nihon kōki*
(Later chronicles of Japan continued), in 842, Kyoto officials collected
and incinerated as many as 5,500 corpses, all of which had been
abandoned in the inner city and on the riverbeds. The *Nihon sandai
jitsuroku* (Veritable records of three Japanese reigns) states that in 883,
the court ordered local officials to bury the abandoned corpses that
could be seen from the pathways taken by the envoy from Palhae
(Pohai) Kingdom.[58] Similarly, it is said that Kūya (903–72), a well-

known mendicant monk, often gathered dead bodies that had been deserted in the wilderness and cremated them after blessing them by reciting Buddha's name. As the *Konjaku monogatarishū* (Tales of times now and past), the *Shasekishū* (Collection of sand and pebbles) of Mujū Ichien (1226–1312), and other works of narrative literature inform us, the custom of discarding corpses—particularly corpses of the lower classes and of those who had no family—persisted into the medieval period.[59] It is true that courtiers conducted formal funerary services and erected mausoleums for their deceased family members; however, in most cases, as Tanaka Hisao notes, even these aristocrats did not feel obliged to offer regular memorial services for their ancestors, often going so far as to neglect their burial sites.[60]

It was not until the late medieval period that people, both high and low, began to pay serious attention to the well-being of the spirits of their deceased family members. From the early seventeenth century, Buddhist death rituals and memorial services, which were designed to facilitate the process of transforming the deceased's spirit into a benign ancestral deity outside the rule of karma, gained wide currency across all classes.[61] Yanagita Kunio (1875–1962), a founding father of Japanese folklore, characterized the nature of these Buddhist death-related rituals as a process of purifying one's soul so that it could ascend to the status of *kami*. He even determined that this process had nothing to with the notion of improving one's karma.[62] Indeed, the Tokugawa Japanese believed that, once it was posthumously deified, and as long as its descendants venerated it, the spirit of a dead person was assured divine status in a realm not bound to the law of karmic reward and retribution. Attaining the divine status of ancestral *kami* in the Shinto sense required, ironically, not Shinto rituals, but Buddhist rituals of ancestral veneration. The ancestral *kami*, which were created and honored through "Buddhist" rituals, were a major feature of the *danka* system and offered an avenue for the spiritual well-being of early modern families.

The new mode of Buddhist death rituals and ancestral veneration reciprocated a shift in family structure, which was moving from the medieval extended family to a monogamous nuclear family household (*tankon shōkazoku*). In most cases, a stem family, in which there was no more than one couple in each generation made up of father, mother, children, and sometimes grandparents, demanded spiritual support that would foster its independence and solidarity.[63] This support took the form of household-based Buddhist death rituals and ancestral veneration focused upon the stem-lineage of the conjugal family unit. In contrast, in the preceding extended family system, the focus of ritual devotion was the main family lineage, to the detriment of branch family members, who were discouraged from asserting their own independent lineages. For branch family members, the custom of ancestral veneration was a constant reminder of their inferior status and their need to submit to the main family lineage. However, the monogamous nuclear family system in the Tokugawa period had its own means of sanctification, which featured familial Buddhist death rituals, ancestral rites, and notions of filial piety.[64] In Part II, I explore the crisscrossing issues of the *danka* system, death rituals and ancestral rites, and early modern households in Tokugawa society.

I discuss in Part III how, against a backdrop of anti-Christianity, *danna* households, Buddhist monks and institutions, and the state were mutually involved in matters of death and ancestral veneration. Unlike in premodern China and Korea, where Buddhism was commonly understood to be antithetical to family values, early modern Japan championed Buddhism as a way of sustaining harmony between family and society. Empowered with funerary Buddhism, Buddhist monks in Tokugawa Japan took advantage of the inaction and disinterest of other religious traditions. It was always obvious that, given its fundamental makeup, Shinto could not function as a dispenser of death-related rituals. Shinto was extremely sensitive to any source of pollution, and of all sources of pollution, death was considered to be the most defiling. Further, Japanese Confucianism, which had been ascendant among Zen monks and courtiers from the late medieval period, was far removed from the ritual arena of ancestral veneration, standing in stark contrast to Chinese and Korean Confucianism. In Tokugawa Japan, Confucianism was by and large considered to be an intellectual discipline concerned with political economy and social engineering rather than a wellspring of familial ritual life. The religious vacuum created by Shinto and Confucianism thus offered Buddhism a golden opportunity to come to the fore. Although Buddhist monks styled themselves as "renunciants" (*shukkesha*) who had left their families and the secular world, they emerged within the *danka* system as arbiters of family affairs pertaining to death and ancestral veneration.

The role of Buddhist monks as arbiters of family rituals did not pose any problem to the government, even though the *bakufu* was keen to keep the Buddhist clergy in check. Already in the early decades of the seventeenth century, such highly regarded shogunal advisors as Konchiin Sūden and Tenkai (1536–1643), who had experienced the political turmoil caused by the collision between the Law of the Buddha and the Law of the King, made sure that Buddhist institutions served the regime.[65] Family rituals comprised an arena of social control in which Buddhist institutions could offer their service to the Law of the King. When this vision was coupled with the regime's anti-Christian policy, the shogunate could effectively subordinate the Law of the Buddha to its tacit approval of the *danka* system.

Once incorporated into the apparatus of shogunal governance, however, Buddhist temples did not remain passive agents of shogunal policy; rather, they strove to carve out spaces within which they could advance their own ends, often targeting the same pool of resources—whether political, economic, or social—as did the government. The tactics of Buddhist temples usually came down to implementing, through the leverage of annual religious inspection, a variety of schemes designed to secure the patronage of funerary *danna* households. Buddhist death rituals and ancestral rites were promoted as a sort of social "norm" to which the *danna* households were expected to subscribe: people were to die Buddhist and to venerate ancestral deities within the framework of the *danka* system. Every new death reinforced the prescription of Buddhist death, and ancestral rites, which were conducted throughout the year— regularly, on such occasions as the New Year, Higan (celebrations of the vernal and autumnal equinoxes), and Bon (a festival in the seventh month), as well as irregularly—were a constant reminder of the mandate of the *danka* system. Squeezed between the Law of the Buddha and the Law of the King, the Tokugawa Japanese often found themselves struggling to satisfy both.

It should therefore come as no surprise that Buddhist death rituals and ancestral rites, despite their posture as familial affairs, often became a site of competition, resistance, and negotiation between the government, Buddhist temples, and *danna* households. The government tried to keep the growing power of Buddhist temples in check and to tweak various regulatory measures in order to control the Buddhist clergy, while the temples continued to extract income and compliance from the populace. Disenchanted, anti-Buddhist critics charged Buddhist temples and their members of being corrupt and demanded that they start practicing material frugality and clerical honesty. In an extreme case during the 1660s, local lords such as Ikeda Mitsumasa (1609–82) of the Okayama domain, Tokugawa Mitsukuni (1628–1700) of the Mito domain, and Hoshina Masayuki (1611–72) of the Aizu domain, moved to execute a draconian anti-Buddhist measure known as the "retrenchment of Buddhist temples" (*jiin seiri*). Many Buddhist temples in these domains were demolished, and hundreds of Buddhist monks were defrocked and returned to practicing agriculture.[66]

In spite of such pressure and harassment, Buddhist institutions did not back down. Resorting to their right of religious inspection, Buddhist monks stressed the inseparability of anti-Christianity, Buddhist rituals for the dead, and ancestral veneration. These efforts contributed to the integration of family rituals into the governing apparatus of the *danka* system. Over time, rites for a deceased family member were gradually standardized into three stages: a funeral; a series of thirteen postfuneral memorial services, known as the "thirteen Buddhist rites" (*jūsan butsuji*), which were conducted over a period of about three decades; and the annual veneration of the ancestral deity.[67] The Tokugawa Japanese, who followed the multistage ritual practice of Buddhist death, believed that paying homage to ancestral deities was good in itself, indispensable for the well-being of the household, and by extension, good for society in general. Having been brought to funerary Buddhism, *danna* households maintained, or at least tried to maintain, good relations with their funerary temples by fulfilling their obligations to them. In return, funerary temples tended to the religious needs of their patrons. As for the *bakufu*, the social harmony that the *danka* system seemed to foster was something to be protected despite the government's desire to check and control the Buddhist clergy.

That said, however, the *danka* system was not immune from conflict and disruption. Disputes between funerary temples and their patron households were not unusual. In many cases, those disputes took the form of "leaving the *danna* affiliation" (*ridan*) or of "unauthorized egress and ingress" (*fuhō deiri*) to another funerary temple. When a dispute arose, the temple usually tried to avoid losing its funerary patron, while the latter tried to justify switching to another temple. In Tokugawa society, where precedent was taken very seriously, disputes over the issue of "leaving the *danna* affiliation" posed a quandary to the public authorities, who tended to give priority to social stability. When the dispute was aggravated to the point of collective action, it could slip out of control and even develop into a political problem. As far as the government was concerned, a lopsided relationship between a *danna* household and its temple was not desirable. While trying to find the appropriate balance of power between the temple and the household, the public authorities often found themselves facing a delicate issue of social order. Tipping the balance, even slightly, could result in unpredictable chain reactions.

Thus, the manner in which *danna* households, funerary temples, and the state came to terms with the *danka* system reflected the inner dynamics of Tokugawa society—dynamics that were tangled up with socio-ethical arguments for ancestral veneration, with the state apparatus for population surveillance, and with discourses regarding the proper social location of Buddhism. The *danka* system, practiced in terms of claims and counterclaims, rights and obligations, and political control and religious autonomy, was neither static nor monochromatic. Its social topography was complicated by cooperation and competition over money, power, and social influence.

Looking at the larger picture, how did the state utilize the social customs of, and ethical values embedded within, funerary Buddhism for the purposes of social engineering? In a society in which ritual served as a marker of social status, private funeral rituals could not escape the radar of state censure when they become excessively luxurious or pretentious. Public authorities tried to incorporate people who followed various local customs and attitudes into an overarching system of Buddhist death and to make the latter socially accountable. For their part, the people tried to utilize their familial rituals in order to assert a sense of social standing, dignity, autonomy, and/or social resistance.

The *danka* system was never an isolated phenomenon; it was always part of the evolving Tokugawa social system. Thus, the question of why so many temples emerged between the late sixteenth century and the mid-seventeenth century, and of how they were able to maintain themselves, involves analyzing the construction and evolution of Tokugawa society in relation to funerary Buddhism. In Part III, I examine the social practices of the *danka* system, which arose with, was perpetuated by, and adapted to an overabundance of Buddhist temples. In so doing, I shed light on the dynamics of the power relationships among and between religious practice, family, and the state. Through political pressure (anti-Christian religious inspection), ideological persuasion (the imperative of Buddhist death and ancestral veneration), and sentiment (filial piety and social harmony), the agents of the *danka* system (i.e., Buddhism, family, and public authority) demonstrated that the Tokugawa social order remained a site subject to cooperation, competition, and conflict.[68] In illuminating the social matrix of funerary Buddhism, it is therefore important to look at the "perceived norm" of Buddhist death as a socio-religious institution in which the Tokugawa social order was communicated, experienced, and contested. Funerary Buddhism was a corollary of the process of social power that embodied and articulated the basic notions and values of the Tokugawa Japanese.[69]

In order to evaluate the relations of power that characterized the socio-religious practice of the *danka* system, I show in Part IV how Shinto priests strove to circumvent the Buddhist grip on funerary rites. In dealing with this issue, one thing should be clear: no matter how hard Shinto priests petitioned for a "Shinto funeral" (*Shintō sōsai*) for one of their own, public authorities would not countenance them. When their petition (which was often prolonged and disputatious) reached its limit, the government reluctantly allowed the head priest in question and his heir apparent—but only these two—to be granted a Shinto funeral. This kind of exception was rarely granted, and, when it was, it was rarely allowed to extend past one generation. The government's primary concern was to ensure that this did not disrupt the *danka* system, which was now inseparable from the practice of anti-Christian religious inspection. No matter how fed up they were, until long past the twilight of the Tokugawa period, Shinto priests would never be entirely free from the religious dominance of funerary Buddhism.[70]

Indeed, the persistence of the *danka* system speaks to the nature of the social order that, for more than two centuries, underpinned Tokugawa Japan. It was a social order that was institutionalized through anti-Christian religious inspection and cemented through funerary Buddhism. In this way, Buddhism and the Tokugawa state formed a united front for fighting the "wicked enemy" known as Christianity—an alien religion that threatened the peace and order of Japan from without. It was believed that Christian missionaries and their Japanese collaborators were not only corrupting the foundation of the divine country through deceptive religious teachings but also through bribes. It was even argued that each month, the country of Tartar (home to a Mongolian people) sent monies to Japanese Kirishitan![71] The shogunate's perception of Christianity as a threat stood in stark contrast to Christian missionaries' efforts to abide by the law of Japan. Evidence of a Christian threat had not actually been found, but this did not matter.[72] *Bakufu* leaders continued to link the task of rooting out the "national enemy" to that of consolidating an overarching governing order that bound the populace to the *bakuhan* system.

However, the anti-Christian situation could not last forever: with the arrival of a new age, during which the structure of government was massively overhauled in the wake of the Meiji Restoration, radical change began to occur. Amid the increasing pressure of the Western powers, which demanded tolerance of Christianity, Meiji leaders realized that their anti-Christian stance was not sustainable. Charged with implementing a new vision of a Shinto state, they nonetheless tried to replace funerary Buddhism with Shinto funerals, but this did not work out as they had hoped. After a period of trial and error, the Meiji government, which was eventually forced to lift the ban on Christianity, decided to stop manipulating the custom of death rituals that was so deeply rooted in the *danka* system.

In sum, *Death and Social Order in Tokugawa Japan* explores the following major themes: (1) how and why Buddhist institutions came to serve as an administrative vehicle for the anti-Christian policy of the Tokugawa state, thus resulting in the institutionalization of the *danka* system; (2) how Buddhist institutions subjected the entire population to the *danka* system, thereby imbuing death rituals and ancestral rites with a Buddhist character and so incorporating Buddhism into the modus operandi of Tokugawa Japanese households; and (3) how, under the *danka* system, the paradigm of Buddhist death was imposed, contested, and negotiated among the *danna* households, Buddhist temples, and the state—a process that eventually resulted in the backlash of the Shinto funeral movement.

Reflecting the gravity that held sway not only over the religious lives of the Tokugawa Japanese but also over their entire social existence, scholarly works dealing with the issues of the *danka* system and funerary Buddhism are numerous. In recent years, Western scholarship on Tokugawa Japan has moved beyond the level of sketchy or secondary passing citations, with excellent case studies shedding light on a particular Buddhist sect, region, or period (Hardacre 2002; Vesey 2003; Williams 2005).[73] These research achievements, which take seriously the road of social or institutional history, are a great contribution to the study of Tokugawa Buddhism and society. However, many current discussions are still by and large troubled by the most basic errors, as the recurring employment of such key terms as "temple registration" and "temple parish system" attests. These terms are either mistaken, misleading, or simply wrong. The total banishment of such erroneous terms and concepts from future writings is one of the goals of *Death and Social Order in Tokugawa Japan*.

Japanese scholarship on the *danka* system and funerary Buddhism is voluminous, detailed, and informative, and many of its works demonstrate a high level of notoriously meticulous Japanese scholarship. Indeed, when addressing certain specific issues, some of this work is superb. Even though all of these works deal with certain aspects of the *danka* system and funerary Buddhism, it is extremely hard to combine them into a coherent whole because they are heavily compartmentalized, fragmented, narrowly specialized along disciplinary lines, and/or scattered throughout innumerable local case studies. Encountering this scholarship is like coming upon a particularly dense forest.

For example, historical or institutional works on the establishment and practice of the *danka* system (Hōzawa 2004; Morioka 1962; Ōkuwa 1968, 1979; Tamamuro Fumio 1987, 1999; Tsuji Zennosuke 1952–55) do not necessarily shed light on how it was ritually operated and culturally implicated. And works on anti-Christianity (Gonoi 1990; Murai 1987, 2002; Ōhashi Yukihiro 2001; Shimizu Hirokazu 1981) rarely proceed to discuss the issue of how it evolved into the *danka* system and funerary Buddhism. As for the issue of how the *danka* system and funerary Buddhism functioned in terms of death rituals and rites of ancestral veneration, this is for the most part seen as the job of such disciplines as folklore or Buddhist studies. However, scholars in these fields (Akata 1980, 1986; Fujii Masao 1983, 1988; Gorai 1992; Inoguchi 1954; Shintani 1983, 1991), with the exception of a very few (Fukuta 2004; Ōtō 1996; Sasaki 1987), usually take a synchronic approach to their material and do not relate it to the historical specifics of early modern society, economy, and politics. By the same token, historical works that locate the *danka* system and funerary Buddhism within the wider political, social, or cultural context of Tokugawa Japan (Arimoto 1995, 2002; Mori 1993; Toyoda 1982; Yasumaru 1974) usually dissipate into fragmented discussions according to disciplinary or subdisciplinary divisions. Discussions of Shinto funeral movements (Kondo 1990; Okada Shōji 1997; Sakamoto Koremaru 1994) are not an exception: most of them are case studies, with scholars rarely leaving their period specializations to cross the border demarcating Tokugawa and Meiji Japan.

As if reflecting the patchwork nature of the *bakuhan* system that was premised upon the principles of domanial autonomy and self-reliance, extant works on the *danka* system and funerary Buddhism resist interdisciplinary, intersectarian, interperiod, interterritorial, or interregional communication. They are scattered and fragmented. The need to surmount this lack of synthesis and contiguity is paramount. By focusing on death and social order, this book offers a new approach to the far-reaching ramifications of the *danka* system and funerary Buddhism, which were never practiced in isolation from the wider political, cultural, and socioeconomic contexts of early modern Japan.

Cʒ

PART I

The Origin of the Danka System

Oda Nobunaga (1534–82), who endeavored to unify Japan during the Sengoku (or "Warring States") period of the late fifteenth to late sixteenth century, handled two major political problems in a manner that led to his early demise. One of these problems was related to Buddhist forces, particularly those of the obstreperous Ikkō ikki (revolt by Jōdoshinshū followers), which were determined to fight to the death for their autonomy; the other was related to the imperial court, which still retained, if only symbolically, strong political authority. In dealing with these two unrelenting power blocks, which seemed to be incompatible with his "heavenly" ambitions, Nobunaga refused any compromise and pursued two high-handed strategies, which involved: (1) defeating the Buddhist forces through military might and (2) bypassing the imperial court by simply disregarding it. Neither of these strategies proved to be successful.

Nobunaga's battle with Ishiyama Honganji, the Jōdoshinshū temple that was the stronghold of the Ikkō followers, lasted from 1570 until 1580 but did not produce a clear winner. In settling the confrontation, imperial intervention allowed a deal to be struck: Nobunaga, despite the rhetoric of "pardon" upon which he insisted, could do little but watch the Honganji temple move from Osaka to Sagimori in Kii. When they reconciled with Nobunaga, the Honganji adherents were eventually able to preserve what they had fought for: "the Law of the Buddha and the seat of the Saint (Shinran, Founder of Jōdoshinshū)."[1] But Nobunaga was not to be so easily deterred.

In 1567, from his new headquarters at Gifu Castle, Nobunaga resumed campaigns against Buddhist forces under the slogan "blanket the realm with military might" (tenka fubu). *Nobunaga demanded that recalcitrant Buddhists, and by extension, the general population, take that slogan literally: his goal was, simply and solely, to achieve national unification through military subjugation. His ruthless campaigns of destruction against Enryakuji (on Mount Hiei) along with Negoroji and Kokawadera (both in Kii), not to mention the beheading of about 4,000 Kōya* hijiri *(the itinerant practitioners of Mount Kōya), were supposed to show what would happen to those Buddhists who persisted in resisting him. Although the Honganji matter remained a sore spot, Nobunaga determined that the Law of the Buddha would not be free of his authority.*

Nobunaga also snubbed the imperial court. Rather than seeking an imperial anointment, he sought to legitimate his grip on power through applying the principle of the realm under heaven (tenka), *or the heavenly way* (tendō), *which he claimed to possess by virtue of military might. His vision of the heavenly way, under which he strove to promote the welfare of the people through benevolent rule, served as his sole source of justification for eliminating anything that stood in his way. When he ousted Shogun Ashikaga Yoshiaki in 1573, Nobunaga accused him of violating the principle of the heavenly way; and when, in that same year, he forced Emperor Ōgimachi to change the name of the era from Genki to Tenshō ("Heavenly Righteousness"), he did so in order to show that he was in charge of the entire realm under heaven.[2] Having solidified his power base, Nobunaga ensured that he stood above everyone else by declining the emperor's offer of the shogunal title in 1581.*

Ironically, however, Nobunaga's claim to rule by the heavenly way was inevitably destined to collapse: because it was based on military might, his power could be challenged when he faced a stronger military force or a threat from within. By rejecting imperial sanction, which in premodern Japanese tradition shielded the leader from arbitrary political interference, Nobunaga compromised his political position in his complete dependence upon simple military superiority. His demise in 1582 at the hands of one of his own vassals, Akechi Mitsuhide (1528–82), proved that the ideology of military tenka *must eventually succumb to its own logic of control by violence, violence being represented by the dictum "those below overthrow those above"* (gekokujō).[3] *In other words, Nobunaga fell victim to his own karma.*

Unlike Nobunaga, Toyotomi Hideyoshi (1536–98) not only appreciated the legacies of Buddhism and the imperial court, but he also sought to associate himself with both. Initially, Hideyoshi played a game of carrot-and-stick with Buddhist forces. In 1584, he granted those monks of Mount Hiei who survived Nobunaga's carnage permission to rebuild their monastery, along with a donation of land that would yield 1,500 koku of rice; however, Hideyoshi was no more merciful than was Nobunaga toward Buddhist forces that continued to resist. In 1585, he sent an army of 40,000 to Kii to lay waste to Negoro, where "Buddhist bandits" were still insurgent. He then directed his troops to dismantle the last bastion of Honganji adherents in Saika. After the surrender of Saika, which signified an end to the long-standing medieval religious rebellion, Hideyoshi sought reconciliation with the Honganji establishment and awarded it a tract of land in Osaka upon which to build a new temple headquarters.[4]

The next year, Hideyoshi made another move to show his goodwill toward the Buddhist community. He decided to supplant the great statue of Vairocana (the supreme Buddhist protector of the realm), housed at Tōdaiji in Nara, with an imposing Buddhist statue in a grand Tendai temple (named Hōkōji), which was to be built in Kyoto. In constructing this giant statue, Hideyoshi astutely incorporated the Buddhist tradition of "pacifying and protecting the nation" (chingo kokka) into his push for national peace by declaring, in his sword-hunt edict of 1588: "So that the long and short swords collected shall not be wasted, they shall be [melted down and] used as rivets and clamps in the forthcoming construction of the Great Buddha. This will be an act by which the farmers will be saved in this life, needless to say, and in the life to come."[5]

At the same time, Hideyoshi earnestly embraced the legacies of the imperial court. After securing a foothold for national unification, he began to tap imperial authority, which offered him powerful political leverage over rival daimyo. In 1583, he acquired the court title of sangi, *junior fourth rank, and, during the following two years, he took the titles of* gondainagon, *junior third rank;* naidaijin, *senior second rank; and, finally,* kanpaku *(regent of the emperor), junior first rank. All of this happened with unprecedented speed, and for the first time in history, the imperial court helplessly watched as its second most glorious post was taken over by a samurai of obscure origin.*

When it came to chastening enemies, Hideyoshi was swift to make use of the aura of imperial authority. Soon after assuming the title of imperial regent in 1585, he urged the Shimazu family in Kyūshū to surrender to him: "Based on the intention of the emperor, I write. All regions, not to mention Kantō, up to the farthest corner of Ōshū, are all entrusted [to me] by the order of the emperor. The realm is now pacified. But Kyūshū is still in a state of armed conflict. It shall not be tolerated."[6] *Hideyoshi's expedition to Kyūshū, backed by imperial sanction and eased by the compliance of the Ōtomo family of Bungo, brought the resistant Shimazu family to heel. In 1588, after the defeat of the Shimazu family, Hideyoshi invited Emperor Goyōzei and the retired emperor Ōgimachi to his newly built mansion — Jurakutei — and made the country's most powerful warlords, now his vassals, swear before him an oath of three articles, which featured the protection of imperial lands, including those of temples headed by imperial abbots* (monzeki). *This event represented the culmination of Hideyoshi's political career, secured in the tradition of imperial aggrandizement. He demonstrated that his political authority was in the service of, and therefore inseparable from, the emperor's authority. For Hideyoshi, the imperial legacy could not be more useful: it provided his regime with "a framework of tradition, history, and law" and shielded him from questions regarding his humble political origins.*[7]

Furthermore, Hideyoshi merged his pursuit of imperial sanction and Buddhist protection into the national cause of preserving the "divine country" (shinkoku). *In 1587, as grand minister of state* (daijōdaijin, *senior first rank), Hideyoshi proclaimed an edict to expel Christian missionaries: "Japan is the country of the gods, but it has been receiving false teachings from Christian countries. This cannot be tolerated any further."*[8] *In negating Christianity, Hideyoshi accused Christian missionaries of enticing people to become believers, instructing them to destroy shrines and temples, and committing the crime of ruining the teachings of Buddhism, which had been so long cherished in Japan.*[9] *Hideyoshi proceeded to confiscate Nagasaki, which was ceded to the Society of Jesus by Ōmura Sumitada (1533–87), and turned it into his immediate domain; and he destroyed churches and convents in Kinki. After an interval of tolerance during which Christian missionaries functioned as intermediaries in his contacts with Iberian traders, Hideyoshi, triggered by the affair of the Spanish galleon* San Felipe, *yielded to an anti-Christian spasm that entailed the crucifixion of 26 people (including six European Franciscans, seventeen lay Kirishitan affiliated with the Franciscan order, and three Japanese Jesuits) in 1596.*[10] *By keeping his pledge to protect the "country of* kami*" from Christianity, Hideyoshi assumed the role of protector of the imperial institution — the ultimate proprietor of Shinto deities and shrines. At the same time, as the highest imperial liege, Hideyoshi decided that Buddhist teachings were essential to the country of the gods and declared that he was determined to protect them. In this way, the imperial and Buddhist legacies were* directly linked to the well-being of the nation, which was now managed by Hideyoshi's military regime.

However, as was foreshadowed by his ill-fated Hōkōji project, Hideyoshi's vision did not work out well either for him or for his successor. The Hōkōji temple, constructed as a symbol of national peace, was destroyed by earthquake and fire in *1596.* Hideyoshi died in *1598.* Four years later, Hideyoshi's heir, Toyotomi Hideyori *(1593–1615),* began rebuilding the temple only to have it burn down before his task was completed. Finally, in *1612,* Hideyori (who was barely holding on to the diminishing legacies of his father), on the recommendation of the new hegemon Tokugawa Ieyasu, successfully rebuilt the temple — a reminder of past glory that would, as it happened, seal his fate. Ieyasu, who was now looking for an excuse to abolish the remnant of the Toyotomi regime, maneuvered to interpret some Chinese characters, which were inscribed on the bronze bell that hung in the temple, as proof of defiance and eventually destroyed Hideyori and his supporters in the Osaka Campaigns of *1614* and *1615.*[11] Hideyoshi's grand design to incorporate the cherished traditions of the past into his political ambitions could not survive the second generation. In this shattered dream, the Toyotomi regime came to an end without having a chance to fully exploit the political utility of anti-Christianity.

In contrast, Tokugawa Ieyasu, through the leverage of anti-Christianity, was able firmly to incorporate the legacies of the imperial court, Shinto, and Buddhism into the structure of shogunal politics. First, with regard to imperial legacies, Ieyasu (and his successor Hidetada) went so far as to try to establish a bond with the imperial family through marriage. This was an attempt to furbish the shogunal house with blood of the highest nobility.[12] Initially, the imperial court and Emperor Goyōzei resisted Ieyasu's endeavor, which intensified in *1612,* and through the Osaka Campaigns held up the already slow-paced proceedings until shortly before his death in *1617.* However, under the auspices of the "Regulations for the Imperial Court and Courtier Households" (Kinchū narabi ni kuge shohatto), with which the shogunal government overwhelmed the imperial court by confining the emperor to the "pursuit of arts and learning,"[13] Shogun Hidetada carried out his father's wish. Hidetada's ten-year-old daughter Kazuko was married to Emperor Gomizunoo and entered the imperial court in *1620.* She gave birth to a daughter, Meishō, who would be enthroned in *1629.*[14] This familial union provided the finishing touch to the imperial patents sought by the Tokugawa shogunal office.

Unlike his rocky attempt to establish an imperial family bond, Ieyasu's effort to capitalize on Shinto legacies went smoothly. He concentrated on *the idea of promoting the divine country against anti-Christianity. In a 1605 letter informing the Spanish governor of the Philippines about Japan's regulations on foreign trade, Ieyasu warned that Christianity might not be welcome. He explained: "You have many wishes [regarding Christianity], but I cannot allow them. Above all, my country is known as the country of the gods, and the idol worship [to which you are referring] is what our ancestors have treasured generation after generation. Thus I cannot afford to destroy [the tradition] by disregarding [it]. For this reason, you might not be allowed to preach the teachings of your religion in Japan."*[15] *The* shinkoku *banner that was raised against a backdrop of anti-Christianity helped Ieyasu establish himself as the ultimate defender of Japan, a country in which the gods (*kami*) had always been unfailingly revered.*

In embracing Buddhist tradition, Ieyasu demonized Christianity. His strategy was straightforward: by the early 1610s, he had defined Buddhism as the spiritual pillar of the divine country and had equated its defense with the mandate to eliminate Christian elements from Japan — an equation that led to the gradual empowerment of Buddhist temples through the granting of the privilege of carrying out anti-Christian certification. Buddhism, through its full-fledged involvement in the shogunal politics of anti-Christianity, was integrated into the governing apparatus of the Tokugawa regime. In Part 1, we will see how this anti-Christian policy helped to transform imperial, Shinto, and Buddhist legacies into the political basis for the Tokugawa regime and how it gave rise to the danka *system.*

C≈

ONE

Trade, Anti-Christianity, and Buddhism,

1600–1632

It should be noted that Tokugawa Ieyasu was initially, at least in appearance, neither anti-Christian nor pro-Buddhist. As a matter of fact, soon after Hideyoshi died in 1598, Ieyasu tried to invite the Spanish traders in Manila to Kantō under the auspices of the Franciscan missionary Jerónimo de Jesús Castro (in Japan from 1594 to 1599), who had survived Hideyoshi's purge. Ieyasu's plan to develop a trade network connecting Kantō, Manila, and New Spain (Mexico) was not immediately realized, but Castro was granted freedom to promote his religion in Edo and, in 1599, was able to establish a church there.[16] The year after his victory at the Battle of Sekigahara, in an attempt to expand trade, Ieyasu further acknowledged the freedom of Christian missionaries residing in Kyoto, Osaka, and Nagasaki; and, in 1604, he even provided financial assistance to the Jesuit missionaries who, according to João Rodrigues Giram (in Japan from 1586 to 1614), a well-known Jesuit missionary, were having a hard time due to the failure of a Portuguese ship with a cargo of silk (which was captured by the Dutch off Macao) to arrive in Japan in the previous year.[17] Under Ieyasu, the Christian mission seemed destined for smooth sailing.

However, Ieyasu's tolerance of Christianity was not heartfelt; rather, it was a way of maintaining trade with Portugal and Spain.

For the incipient Tokugawa regime, trade with Europeans, who provided reliable access to exotic and precious goods produced in Southeast Asia, was too lucrative to abandon. More important, Ieyasu, as the founder of a new regime, wanted to acquire as much international recognition as possible through the trade network. In more than 150 letters sent to 40 different states (from Korea, to Southeast Asian countries, to Portugal) between 1600 and 1613, Ieyasu informed the world that he was now in control of a newly unified Japan.[18] Following their master's seemingly permissive attitude toward Christianity, such local lords as Nabeshima in Saga, Shimazu in Satsuma, and Date in Sendai also patronized Christian missionaries as a way of promoting trade with the Iberians. An environment conducive to allowing full reign to anti-Christian sentiment had not yet arrived.

This does not mean, however, that Ieyasu's anti-Christian inclination remained completely dormant during this period. In 1606, a year after delivering his anti-Christian message to the governor of the Philippines, Ieyasu warned that the ban on Christianity should be upheld, particularly with regard to the samurai in Osaka, where Hideyori's sympathizers, many of whom were pro-Christian, remained strong. As time went on, Ieyasu's anti-Christian stance gradually came to the surface. In 1609, the Dutch trade factory in Hirado was of particular importance in strengthening Ieyasu's conviction that trade could prosper without Christianity.[19] The Dutch promised that their trade activities had, and would have, nothing to do with Christian missionary work. Within this context, in 1613, upon the suggestion of his foreign advisor William Adams (1564–1620), Ieyasu allowed the English, who had vowed to stay nonreligious, to build a trade base in Hirado.[20]

Interestingly, despite this cautious arrangement, it is not clear how well Ieyasu understood Christianity. For *bakufu* leaders, including Ieyasu, Christianity was still a mysterious, yet somehow disturbing, religion. Konchiin Sūden, a top advisor to Ieyasu, commented: "*Iruman* refer to the Japanese who have become Kirishitan. . . . It is said that they preach a kind of Law of the Buddha."[21] Indeed, Christianity sometimes found a home in the blurred margins of Buddhism, probably owing to the many Buddhist terms that were adopted in order to express Christian concepts.[22] In particular, the varying ranks within Christianity were quite confusing. The Jesuits in Japan could be divided into two groups: the fathers (padres), "with whom the real authority was vested, and who, up to [Alessandro] Valignano's time, were all Europeans," and the brothers (*irmão*), "most of whom were Europeans, but who included about 70 Japanese in 1592."[23] Although the Japanese commonly termed the fathers *bateren* and the brothers *iruman* from a corruption of the corresponding Portuguese words, the distinction was not always well kept. More often, they used the term *bateren* to refer to both fathers and brothers and even to lay Japanese followers. Worse yet, the padres and brothers, who were limited in number, were assisted by the two native officials known as *dōjuku* (catechists) and *kanbō* (lay leaders). Both *dōjuku* and *kanbō*—titles that were modeled on officials affiliated with the Zen monastery—were part of the Japan mission.[24]

While still debating the potential harm of this murkily understood alien religion and the benefits of trade, *bakufu* leaders encountered the Okamoto Daihachi scandal of 1612, which alerted them to the danger that Christianity could pose to the new regime's political order. The root of the scandal goes back to 1608 and an armed clash in Macao between the crew of a vessel belonging to the Christian daimyo Arima Harunobu (1567–1612) and a group of Portuguese sailors—a clash that resulted in more than 60 Japanese deaths. The following year, a Portuguese ship under the command of André Pessoa, who had been involved in the incident, called in at the port of Nagasaki. Harunobu, who was informed of the 1608 clash by Japanese survivors, successfully appealed to Ieyasu for revenge and proceeded to arrest Pessoa, who denied any involvement. After a four-day attack by the joint forces of Harunobu and the Nagasaki magistrate Hasegawa Fujihiro (in office from 1603 to 1617), Pessoa, his crew, and his ship perished at sea.[25] After the attack, Okamoto Daihachi (?–1612), a retainer of State Councilor Honda Masazumi (1565–1637) and a faithful Kirishitan who had fought under the Nagasaki magistrate, came to learn that Harunobu wanted Ieyasu to reward him for his military valor. Okamoto Daihachi suggested to Harunobu that he was willing, on his behalf, to lobby his influential master Honda Masazumi for a shogunal grant of three counties (Fujitsu, Sonogi, and Kishima) in Bizen. These counties had previously belonged to the Arima domain but had been transferred to the Nabeshima domain. Daihachi told Harunobu that Ieyasu was already leaning toward granting him this reward. Swayed by this sweet suggestion, Harunobu offered Daihachi several generous bribes, and the latter cemented the former's hopes with a forged letter from

Ieyasu. In 1612, tired of waiting for the actual transfer of the Bizen land, Harunobu spoke directly to Honda Masazumi, leading to the exposure of Daihachi's fraud.

This was a serious crime flouting the regime's rudimentary law, as it involved not only the forgery of a shogunal letter (even though Ieyasu had already retired at this time), but, more seriously, the shogunate was shocked by the revelation that "a vassal's investiture with land, a matter at the very pith and core of the feudal relationship, could be reduced to a business proposition" between subjects.[26] While investigating Daihachi, who would be condemned to death by fire in the third month of the same year, *bakufu* officials discovered that Harunobu had also offended the shogunal law. During the Portuguese attack, there occurred a dispute between Fujihiro and Harunobu, with the former—the shogunal deputy of Nagasaki— accusing the latter of being too slack. Upset by this reproach, Harunobu plotted, albeit unsuccessfully, to murder Fujihiro. However, plotting to kill a proxy of the shogun is deemed a grave crime, almost as grave as treason. Harunobu was banished to Kai and ordered to commit seppuku, or self-disembowelment, in the fifth month of the same year.[27] Further investigation of Harunobu and his associates revealed that Christianity had infiltrated not only many daimyo and their lieutenants in Kyūshū, but also a circle of Ieyasu's own guards in Sunpu. On top of this, these Kirishitan converts somehow seemed to have formed a network of fellowship and were conspiring to spoil shogunal sovereignty.

Alarmed by the Okamoto Daihachi incident, Ieyasu turned against Christianity and ordered all the vassals of Sunpu Castle to organize themselves into units of ten members each in order to engage in mutual surveillance and to root out Kirishitan converts. This internal scrutiny resulted in the discovery of tens of Kirishitan *hatamoto* (liege vassals to the shogun) and servants upon whom punishment was immediately meted out in the form of transfer and expulsion.[28] The instructions of Andō Shigenobu (1557–1621), a state councilor, to Uesugi Kagekatsu (1555–1623), the daimyo of the Yonezawa domain, tell what happened: "Like this, eight men, who were found to be Kirishitan, were all stripped of their status and immediately expelled from Sunpu. If they try to enter your domain, arrest them, and if they resist, kill them."[29] Within a short period of time, 26 more *hatamoto* vassals were punished, and, to serve as a warning, their punishments were publicized throughout all the domains of the country. In particular, Ieyasu instructed his confidant, Itakura Katsushige (1545–1624), who was the shogunal deputy (*shoshidai*) of Kyoto, to forbid Christianity and to destroy Christian churches in Kyoto—a city that seemed to remain a source of nostalgia for Hideyoshi. Although Katsushige, out of fear of instigating a social uprising, managed to dilute Ieyasu's order, the *bakufu*'s sudden move presaged what was to come.

In line with increasing his anti-Christian stance, Ieyasu sent a state letter to the governor of New Spain in the sixth month of 1612, advising him that Japan would allow trade but not Christianity. This was a final response to a series of requests by Rodrigo de Vivero y Velasco, the former governor of the Philippines, whose ship had been wrecked on the coast of Chiba in 1609 when he was on his way to New Spain to become interim governor. In his audience with Ieyasu during that same year, Velasco expressed three wishes: to protect and free Franciscan missionaries in Japan, to expel Dutch traders, and to treat favorably all Spanish ships from Manila. Although Velasco returned to Mexico almost empty-handed in 1610, his short time in Japan prompted Ieyasu to cultivate his interest in New Spanish trade and in the importation of the technologies pertaining to silver mining.[30] However, in 1611, when Sebastían Vizcaíno, envoy of the governor of New Spain, paid a visit to Ieyasu to thank him for Velasco's rescue, Ieyasu decided to proclaim in a letter delivered to the governor in the following year that trade and Christianity were not compatible. In this letter, Ieyasu first defined Japan as the country of the gods, and then pointed out that: "Since the creation [of Japan], [the Japanese people] have worshipped *kami* and revered the Buddha. The Buddha and *kami* are like . . . traces of each other, identical and not different. The matters of solidifying loyalty and righteousness between the lord and vassals, of ensuring no perfidy, and of building up a strong nation in unity are all pledged to the *kami*. This is the proof of mutual trust."[31]

Unlike his previous assertion of Japan's distinctiveness, which was wrapped in an abstract polemic, in this letter Ieyasu specified precisely why Japan should defend its *shinkoku* ideology against Christianity and how it should do so. Based on the theory that the gods and buddhas were two sides of the same coin, Ieyasu asserted that the lord-vassal relationship, upon which his regime was founded, was premised on an oath of fealty pledged before the gods and buddhas. For Ieyasu, the bonds of fealty and trust between the shogun and the nation's daimyo were divine and inviolable because they were sworn before Japan's traditional deities. The governing structure of his regime—the *bakuhan* system—should be more than an arrangement of political power between the shogunal house and the warlords: it should be a divine covenant that could not allow any interference by alien deities.[32]

As a matter of fact, the unifiers of Sengoku Japan often resorted to an oath of loyalty known as *kishōmon*—a blood oath that could only be broken upon pain of godly punishment—in order to secure allegiance and to prevent defection. For example, Hideyoshi, the quintessential military hegemon, found himself, in his final days, totally dependent upon such oaths. Concerned with the future of his young son Hideyori, who was poised to inherit his not-quite-solidified regime, Hideyoshi pushed senior daimyo to repeat, one after the other, their oaths of loyalty to his son—all of which were sworn in the name of the gods and buddhas.[33] Ieyasu also found vows before the deities helpful for taming unwilling warlords, even though the divine ability of these vows to frighten the signatories into submission seemed to be not quite so strong as before.[34] In 1611, on the same day that Emperor Gomizunoo was enthroned, Ieyasu gathered 22 powerful *tozama* daimyo ("outside" lords who had sided against the Tokugawa at the Battle of Sekigahara) from western Japan at Nijō Castle and had them sign an oath of loyalty to the shogunal house. The three articles that were pledged—all of which were composed by Funahashi Hidekata (1575–1614) and Hayashi Razan (1583–1657) under Ieyasu's direction—were straightforward: to keep the law issued by Shogun Hidetada, not to harbor anyone who violates the law and/or the intention of the shogun, and not to employ any samurai charged with treason or murder.[35] The format of this pledge was similar to that enforced by Hideyoshi on the occasion of Emperor Goyōzei's 1588 visit to Jurakutei. One year after the 1611 pledge, Shogun Hidetada himself imposed a similar pledge upon eleven daimyo in Tōhoku as well as upon 50 daimyo in Kantō and various other regions.[36]

To be sure, Tokugawa sovereignty rested primarily upon the military hegemony that the shogunal house held over the nation's local warlords. But there was no guarantee that the balance of power between the shogun and the daimyo would be perpetuated in favor of the former. In consolidating the *bakuhan* power structure, beginning with his heir Hidetada (who had not yet had the opportunity to prove his military charisma), Ieyasu mobilized the traditional mode of allegiance and fealty, which consisted of a collective vow of commitment to the supernatural beings, against the backdrop of anti-Christianity.[37] The tradition of making a divine pledge toward the shogun and shogunate was exercised whenever a new shogun was installed and high *bakufu* officials assumed their new positions.[38] Given this, Christianity was not presented as simply being a source of heterodox teachings; rather, it was presented as a national enemy against which, under the leadership of the shogun, all the nation's political entities had to unite and fight.

In the eighth month of 1612, the shogunate proclaimed an edict consisting of five articles, one of which contained a clause pertaining to the nationwide ban on Christianity. The second article reads: "The followers of padres (*bateren monto*) are to be prohibited. If there are violators, they shall not be spared punishment."[39] The impact of this decree was immediate, particularly in the Usuki and Oka domains in Kyūshū—a traditional stronghold of Christianity. Kirishitan converts in Usuki were estimated to number more than 15,000 by this time, which is equivalent to about one-fourth to one-third of the domanial population. The lord Inaba Norimichi (in office from 1603 to 1626), who had been lenient toward Christianity, quickly reverted to type, expelling Christian missionaries and arresting and executing their followers.[40] The law of 1612 gradually triggered a nationwide suppression of Christianity. In Edo alone, 22 Kirishitan, mostly group leaders, were executed for "violating the law, becoming the followers of padres, and, on top of that, serving as leaders of [Kirishitan] units" as well as for "returning to Christianity after having sworn a vow to abandon it."[41]

In the twelfth month of 1613, Ieyasu appointed a high-profile state councilor, Ōkubo Tadachika (1553–1628), to a newly created post, Kirishitan magistrate, and then proclaimed, through Shogun Hidetada, the "Statement on Expelling Padres" (*Bateren tsuihō no bun*), which was drafted by Konchiin Sūden.[42] This pedantic edict has long been regarded as a benchmark of the seriousness of the Tokugawa shogunate's endeavor to eradicate Christianity through the concerted religious forces of Shinto and Buddhism.[43]

The edict starts with the claim that "Japan is originally the country of the gods," and it then proceeds to maintain that "Japan is also called the country of Buddha."[44] After arguing that "*kami* and buddhas are different in name but one in their intentions, as tallies are perfectly matched to each other," the edict declares that "[Japan] exceeds any other country in the prosperity of the Law of the Buddha," as is evidenced by the fact that the teachings of the Buddha have advanced eastward.[45] Reiterating that Japan is a country where "*kami* are respected, buddhas are revered, the way of benevolence and righteousness is pursued, and the law of good and evil is rectified," the edict goes on to say that all this is related to the moral foundation of the country: "Those who are accused of crime should prove themselves by pledging before the *kami* and buddhas."[46] The conclusion is straightforward: "That clique of padres contravenes our polity, traduces Shinto, calumniates our righteous teachings, destroys our sense of justice, and corrupts our virtue. . . . They are the enemy of *kami* and buddhas."[47]

Understandably, in identifying the country of the gods with the country of buddhas, the edict relies on the *honji suijaku* theory—the theory of "originals" (*honji*) and "traces" (*suijaku*)—which holds that "buddhas are manifested by myriad deities."[48] Within the context of *honji suijaku* theory, it would make more sense if the "traces" (*kami*) were to assume the role of defending the "originals" (buddhas). But, as it turned out, when dealing with the challenge of Christianity, *bakufu* leaders, not bound by conventional belief, reversed the relationship between Buddhism and Shinto and claimed that buddhas should serve as the protector of the divine country. In justifying why Buddhism came to be recognized as the defender of the divine country, the edict quotes a short verse from the 21st fascicle ("The Supernatural Powers of the Thus Come One") of the *Lotus Sūtra*: "The Buddhas, the Saviors of the world / Dwelling in their great supernatural penetrations / In order to gladden living beings / Display incalculable supernatural powers."[49]

With regard to this reversal in the relationship between buddhas and *kami*, Takagi Shōsaku suggests that one must look at the influence of the thought of Yoshida Kanetomo (1435–1511), who laid the theoretical foundation for what is known as Yoshida (or *Yuiitsu*) Shinto, which maintained the superior stance of Shinto deities over Buddhist deities in terms of *kami* origin and Buddha manifestation.[50] Of particular relevance is his branches-leaves-flowers-fruits theory on the three religions (*sankyō edaha hanami setsu*), which appears in the *Yuiitsu Shintō myōbō yōshū* (Essentials of terminology and doctrine of Yuiitsu Shinto). Based on the argument that Śākyamuni (the Buddha) was born far later than was the country of the gods and that, accordingly, his teachings were transmitted to Japan at a still later date, Kanetomo ranked three teachings—Shinto, Confucianism, and Buddhism—in terms of genesis and derivation.[51]

Our Japan begot the seed, China produced the branches and leaves, and India opened the flowers and fruits. Thus, Buddhism is the flower and fruit of all teachings, Confucianism the branches and leaves of all teachings, and Shinto the roots of all teachings. These two teachings [Buddhism and Confucianism] are derivatives of Shinto, which points to their roots through their branches, leaves, flowers and fruits. When flowers fall down, they return to [their] roots like the teachings of the Buddha advancing eastward [to Japan].[52]

On the surface, *kami* are understood as manifestations of buddhas and bodhisattvas; but, in reality, it is the other way round—buddhas and bodhisattvas are manifestations of *kami*. Kanetomo puts it this way: "What one must understand as the real exoteric teaching is that buddhas and bodhisattvas are the Essence of the *kami*, while the real esoteric teaching reveals that the *kami* are the Essence of the buddhas and bodhisattvas."[53] For Kanetomo, the "fact" that Confucianism and Buddhism "returned" to Japan is proof that Japan, the country of the gods, is, indeed, the source of all three teachings. This is what Sūden meant in the edict by "the eastern transmission of the Law of the Buddha" to Japan and its "prosperity" on its home soil. In short, the country of the gods was established as the birthplace of all teachings, and the gods were established as the original source of all other religions.

Why, though, did buddhas increasingly come to surpass the gods not only in defending the divine country but also in providing religious well-being to the Japanese? With regard to this question, the Yoshida Shintoists offer a convenient answer, as is suggested in the *Jingi seishū* (Orthodox teachings of Shinto deities): "At a certain point in history, Buddhism was transmitted. . . . Prior to its transmission, the gods delivered divine oracles to ensure the well-being of the people. But after its transmission, the gods handed over their role to buddhas and, instead, concentrated on helping the eastward transmission of Buddhism. That is why, among the three countries, Buddhism prospers most in Japan."[54] Given that by the late medieval period, most, if not all, Shinto shrines had fallen under the control of Buddhist monks, who were known as shrine-monks (*shasō*), it appears that this argument is nothing more than an ideological polemic aimed at rescuing the dignity of Shinto. The fact of the matter is that Shinto, unlike Buddhism, was, institutionally, too feeble to defend the divine country. And so Buddhism, which had boasted the tradition of "pacifying and protecting the nation," and was now theorized as an emanation of Shinto, emerged as an effective alternative that could be deployed against the wicked teachings of Christianity.[55]

Nevertheless, the installment of Buddhism as the defender of the divine country in the early seventeenth century was not a sudden twist of fate. It was Kitabatake Chikafusa (1293–1354) who first suggested the *shinkoku*-centered theme of Buddhist service. After proclaiming, in his *Jinnō shōtōki* (Chronicle of the direct descent of gods and sovereigns), that "Great Japan is the divine land; the heavenly progenitor founded it, and the Sun Goddess bequeathed it to her descendants to rule eternally,"[56] Chikafusa argued that the highest purpose of Buddhism is to make people aware of the fact that "[Japanese] sovereigns and ministers alike have received the bright light of divine descent, . . . they are the descendants of deities who received Amaterasu's mandate."[57] The "solemn purpose of Buddhism" for the country of the gods, as put forward by Chikafusa, was further articulated by Yoshida Shintoists and later inherited by national ideologues. One of these ideologues was Zuikei Shūhō (1391–1473), a Zen monk who compiled the monumental *Zenrin kokuhōki* (Chronicle of national treasures for good relations with neighbors)—a collection of Japanese diplomatic documents dating from ancient times. In the preface, Zuikei Shūhō, who repeated the *shinkoku* thesis, went a step farther: he suggested that the divine country was represented by the Law of the Buddha, implying that, whatever happened to Japan, it would be served by Buddhism.[58]

Since this collection had served as a standard text for those involved in diplomatic affairs, there is no doubt that Sūden, who authored the 1613 edict, was most familiar with the *shinkoku* thesis of Buddhist protection suggested in this manual. In fact, it is well known that not only Sūden but also Ieyasu himself was well versed in the assertions of Yoshida Shinto. Ieyasu owed his knowledge to Bonshun (1553–1632), a Shintoist-cum-monk who was a direct descendant (a great-great grandson) of Yoshida Kanetomo. He was once the head administrator of Hōkoku Shrine (established in honor of Hideyoshi), a tutelary shrine of Hōkōji, and, later, he lectured Ieyasu on Shinto thought.[59] Under the strong influence of Bonshun, Ieyasu even specified in 1616 that his funeral was to be conducted according to the procedures of Yoshida Shinto.

By the time of the 1613 edict, Ieyasu seemed to be convinced that Christianity was an evil force that would destroy political stability and social harmony. Within a cultural tradition that held that offenders were judged by the gods, exclusive faith in an alien god that did not recognize other divine beings must have been viewed not only as antithetical to the teachings of Shinto and Buddhism but also as detrimental to social justice in general. Ieyasu linked the sociopolitical order of Tokugawa Japan with the "natural self-working" of the gods and buddhas. Given that "the Christian missionaries were anxious, for the most part, to be seen to conform to the ruling structures of the time" and that "Christian thought, as disseminated by the Iberian missionaries, sought no disruption of the temporal order of things," this was no more than political ideology.[60] As Takagi Shōsaku notes, "Hideyoshi, Ieyasu, and Hidetada were all aware that the country was, in practice, unified and governed by military authority. But at the same time, they were also keenly aware that the ideology of *shinkoku* would help further solidify national unity and strengthen their governance."[61] In fact, when the emperor posthumously elevated Ieyasu (the military hegemon) to the status of a deity (Tōshō Daigongen, or "Great Incarnation Shining over the East"), it was believed that Ieyasu (the god) would help Japan (the country of the gods) prosper in perpetuity.[62] The vision of *shinkoku* was more than a slogan: it was the raison d'être of the Tokugawa political order, which was to be protected at all costs.

Beginning in the first month of 1614, Ōkubo Tadachika, the newly appointed Christian magistrate, began to hunt down Kirishitan and to destroy churches in Kyoto, a stronghold of Christianity.[63] The Kirishitan community in Kyoto, which by that time had eight padres, 27 lay leaders, and tens of thousands of followers, was hard hit. Missionaries and proselytizers were arrested; churches were emptied and destroyed; and lay Kirishitan were forced to abandon their religion on pain of torture, imprisonment, or execution. Although Tadachika was soon fired from his post due to his defeat in an unrelated squabble with the Honda brothers (Masazumi and Masashige), the *bakufu* did not ease up on their anti-Christian activities. In the Echizen, Kansai, and Kyūshū areas, *bakufu* officials rounded up foreign missionaries along with such prominent Kirishitan leaders as Takayama Ukon (1552–1615, a previous Kirishitan daimyo) and Kibe

Pedoro (1587–1639, a Japanese padre ordained by the Society of Jesus in Nagasaki) and expelled them from Japan. In the tenth month of 1614, approximately 400 people, including missionaries (85 Jesuits, four Franciscans, two Dominicans, and two Augustinians) and lay Kirishitan, were rounded up in Nagasaki and permanently exiled to Macao and Manila.[64] With this deportation, known as the "Great Purge of *Bateren*," the shogunate signaled that it would take further measures to eliminate Christian elements from the country of the gods and buddhas.

The expulsion of 1614 was, however, more than a religious purge: it was also, as the case of Takayama Ukon suggests, a strong warning to the nation's defiant warlords. At that time, Ukon was entrusted, along with Naitō Joan (?–1626), another notable Kirishitan, with the supervision of the Kaga lord, Maeda Toshinaga (1562–1614). As a disciple of the great tea master Sen no Rikyū (1522–91), who had been one of Hideyoshi's most trusted associates, Ukon was still sympathetic to the Toyotomi house of Osaka. Ieyasu saw a potential danger lurking in Ukon's covert Kirishitan network, and he feared that it might work against his efforts to annihilate Hideyoshi's legacies.[65] Initially, the *bakufu* decided to banish Ukon and other Kirishitan daimyo to Tsugaru, but Ieyasu overturned that decision and ordered them all out of the country.

This was a decision that had profound implications for trade and diplomacy. In fact, when the news of the Christian expulsion reached Macao, the Society of Jesus attempted, through bribery, appeal, and market maneuvering, to get *bakufu* leaders to reverse Ieyasu's abrupt policy change. A Portuguese trade ship, which had called in at the port of Nagasaki in 1614, refused to unload its cargo of raw silk, which was to be sold at the markets of Kyoto and Osaka. High demand for the suddenly unavailable Chinese raw silk soon led to skyrocketing prices. The shogunate remained unmoved. Frustrated, Portuguese traders began to search for ways to persuade Ieyasu to change his mind; however, their efforts were to no avail. Worse yet, Ieyasu further hardened his anti-Christian stance and ordered the immediate deportation of all Nagasaki Christian prisoners. Christianity, until this point an object of, at most, random suppression, was now treated as a national enemy.[66]

Nagasaki and the Kyoto-Osaka area, which had disproportionately high ratios of Kirishitan, were the primary targets of the anti-Christian crackdown. In Kyoto, in the third month of 1614, 71 Kirishitan were banished to Tsugaru, while ten Kirishitan men were arrested and their wives handed over to a pimp in the red light district. In dealing with Nagasaki, whose 50,000 residents were generally considered to be either Kirishitan or Kirishitan sympathizers, the *bakufu* forced the people to abandon their religion and destroyed churches, vandalizing everything within them, whether Christian images or ritual paraphernalia. The Nagasaki suppression had ripple effects throughout all of the Kyūshū domains. In the Kokura domain, Hosokawa Tadaoki (1563–1645), who had had a famous Kirishitan wife named Hosokawa Garashiya (1563–1600), first conducted a census in order to identify Kirishitan, then forced them to renounce their religion, and then ordered them to submit to temple certification as evidence of having done so. He succeeded in returning 2,047 Kirishitan converts to Buddhism by the fourth month of 1614.[67] This was one of the first examples of Buddhist affiliation being officially recognized as providing proof of one's anti-Christian status.

It is not known to what extent this type of method was followed at the national level, but we do know that it was taken seriously, at least in Kinki and Kyūshū. For example, in 1614, Katagiri Katsumoto (1556–1615) of the Tatsuta domain in Kinki, who had served Hideyori as a house elder but who had defected just before the Osaka Campaigns, acknowledged that he had received a shogunal order stating that "those Kirishitan who have rolled over, converted to a different religion [i.e., Buddhism] and obtained a document from [their] current temple monks should be pardoned."[68] In the Usuki domain of Kyūshū, many Kirishitan were forced to associate themselves with Buddhist temples and then declare themselves to be the latter's funeral patrons. In all cases, the term used to refer to the abandonment of the Kirishitan religion was *korobu* (to roll over), and those who had renounced the Kirishitan religion and switched to Buddhism were called "*korobi* Kirishitan."

In Kansai and Kyūshū, from 1614 on, it gradually became commonplace for Kirishitan, once detected, to prove their *korobi* status by obtaining a non-Christian certificate from their *danna* temple. If a *korobi* Kirishitan failed to remain loyal to his or her *danna* temple, then government officials could remove the label of *korobi* from the designation "*korobi* Kirishitan." In this case, the person in question could be charged not only with being a secret Kirishitan but also with falsely recanting the Kirishitan faith.[69] Thus the enforced association between being non-Kirishitan and being Buddhist began to enter the lives of the early modern Japanese people; however, at this stage, only those who used to be Kirishitan, not the entire population, were required to obtain a Buddhist certificate.[70] Nonetheless, it is significant that the shogunate's measure resulted in the official granting to Buddhist temples limited jurisdiction over the non-Christian identification of residents. For *korobi* Kirishitan, a few lines of script on a temple document made the difference between life and death.

In keeping former Kirishitan under surveillance, why did the Tokugawa shogunate choose to rely upon Buddhist monks rather than upon its own administrators? This is an important question, for this did, indeed, prove to be the first step toward the nationwide implementation of the *shinkoku*-centered theme of Buddhist service—a theme that positioned Buddhism as the polar opposite of Christianity. For Buddhist temples, the *bakufu*'s move to subject "rolled-over" Kirishitan to their supervision meant receiving an unprecedented privilege—one that could be used as leverage for expanding influence and gaining benefits.[71]

It should be noted, however, that there is no evidence that Ieyasu or any other *bakufu* leader really intended to empower Buddhist temples per se. On the contrary, Ieyasu maintained that Buddhist temples and monks did not deserve to accrue power and social influence. As his bitter 1563 experience with the Ikkō *ikki* had reminded him, should they be set free, Buddhist forces, a medieval anathema, could constitute a dangerous power block and spoil his political ambitions.[72] Ieyasu always exercised great caution when taking any action aimed at curbing Buddhism. Only after entrenching his sovereignty in 1612 did he begin to take a series of actions, in the form of "temple laws" (*jiin hatto*), to systematically domesticate major Buddhist sects. Compared to early edicts, which sporadically targeted such great temple complexes as those on Kōyasan (1601), Hieizan (1608), and Ōyama (1609), the edicts of the 1610s, particularly those enacted right after the removal of the Toyotomi faction, were highly coordinated and methodical, as may be seen in the temple laws for Sōtōshū (1612), Shugen (1613), Kantō Tendaishū (1613), Jōdoshū (1615), Shingonshū (1615), Rinzaishū (*Gozan Jissatsu shozan*, 1615), Eiheiji (1615), Sōjiji (1615), and Daitokuji (1615).[73] Through these edicts, Ieyasu sought to enforce a new institutional order and, in so doing, to negate temple extraterritoriality, to remove military elements from Buddhist institutions, to prescribe doctrinal research and disciplinary practice for Buddhist monks, and to impose upon them the duty to pray for the peace and prosperity of the nation and people.[74]

No doubt, Ieyasu's efforts to tame Buddhism were bold and ambitious; however, he did not go so far as to impose a unified set of regulations upon all Buddhists sects. Jōdoshinshū, Nichirenshū, and Jishū, for example, were exempt from Ieyasu's high-handed stipulations, probably either because of their belligerent tendencies (Jōdoshinshū, Nichirenshū) or because of the itinerant preaching of the sect's head monk (Jishū).[75] It would, therefore, be ludicrous to speculate that, when Ieyasu was actively attempting to control Buddhist temples and monks, he was really intending to give them more power. Interestingly, in the temple laws, Ieyasu neither mentioned an anti-Christian policy nor encouraged Buddhism to take an active role in his political cause. In fact, the temple certification system that was applied to the *korobi* Kirishitan in the mid-1610s actually stands in stark contrast to Ieyasu's overall policy toward Buddhism.

In this situation, it was unlikely that the strategy of temple certification, which was applied to *korobi* Kirishitan in Kyūshū and the Kyoto-Osaka area, was going to gain full strength throughout the country any time soon. The idea that Buddhism was the protector of the divine country was put into practice in some areas, but it seemed that many questions would have to be answered before it could be fully implemented at the national level. When Ieyasu died in the fourth month of 1616 in Sunpu, the crisscrossing issues of anti-Christianity, trade, and Buddhism remained a puzzle yet to be solved.

It was Ieyasu's son, Shogun Hidetada, who brought some clarity to these matters. After the Osaka Campaigns that annihilated the Hideyoshi legacy and brought the nation's daimyo under firm control, Hidetada began to pay attention to the signs of a Kirishitan revival activated by Christian missionaries who had now emerged from hiding. Gonoi Takashi estimates that, during the period between 1614 and 1629, Jesuit missionaries were able to gain more than 20,000 new Kirishitan followers while Franciscans garnered more than 26,000 new followers in the Tōhoku region.[76] In the eighth month of 1616, Hidetada issued an edict, signed by five *bakufu* elders and delivered to the nation's daimyo, reiterating the ban on Christianity and restricting foreign trade ships. Hidetada warned that "years ago Shōkoku-sama decreed the ban on the faith of the follow-

ers of the *bateren*. . . . Make sure that there be no adherents of this
religious sect among the peasants and the lower classes."[77] With
regard to "black ships [Iberian ships] and English ships belonging
to this religious sect, if any of them arrive in [your] domains, send
them to Nagasaki or Hirado."[78] Hidetada's message was terse:
Kirishitan must be stamped out across all classes, and trade ships
from Christian countries must be restricted to Nagasaki and Hirado.

In repeating the ban on Christianity, Hidetada mentioned neither
the "pernicious" nature of Christian teachings nor the "destructive"
behavior of Christian missionaries and their followers. He simply
expressed his order in the name of the founder of the Tokugawa
regime, Shōkoku-sama (this title of *daijōdaijin* [senior first rank]
was conferred upon Ieyasu in the third month of 1616, right before
his death). By declaring Ieyasu's anti-Christian initiative an ancestral
law, Hidetada imbued it with an aura of inviolable sanctity and
preempted any attempt to challenge policy made in its name. The
aegis of ancestral law provided Hidetada with the kind of political
latitude that enabled him to impose binding policies upon the entire
nation. Couched in the overarching authority of Ieyasu, Hidetada
effectively subjected European trade to Japan's anti-Christian policy
by limiting commerce to Nagasaki and Hirado.[79] Anti-Christian policy, anointed by the sanctity of ancestral law and privileged over
trade, became an all-purpose weapon in the land of Tōshō Daigongen. The country of the gods, which prospered under the tutelary
protection of Ieyasu the divine, had to be kept from spoilage.[80] And
Christianity had been singled out as the most dangerous source of
that spoilage.

In 1617, the Hidetada government warned Nagasaki residents that
those "lodge masters" (*yadonushi*) who provided accommodation
for Christian missionaries, as well as those ship owners (*funanushi*)
who helped missionaries secretly enter or return to Japan, would
be punished. In the following year, the Nagasaki magistrate offered
cash remuneration to those who provided information on the whereabouts of Kirishitan.[81] This measure was primarily designed to arrest
missionaries who had stayed in or reentered Japan in defiance of the
massive expulsion of 1614.[82] In spite of various anti-Christian measures, however, Christian missionaries never stopped sneaking into
Japan. Although most of them were arrested shortly after reentering
and were summarily executed, their martyrdom (especially that of
Pedro de la Asunción, a Franciscan, and Alonso de Navarrete, a

a Dominican [both of whom perished in the Ōmura domain in 1617]) triggered a zeal for Japanese missionizing among the apostles stationed in Manila and Macao. They began to infiltrate Japan in a more surreptitious manner, starting with seven padres who arrived on a Spanish trade ship in 1618. Smuggled-in missionaries, who numbered around 100 by the early 1640s, remained an ever-present force poised to galvanize the Japanese Kirishitan community.[83]

The shogunate foisted an unforgettably brutal act upon the Kyoto public in 1619 by burning to death 52 Kirishitan. Earlier that year, Kyoto *shoshidai* Itakura Katsushige (1545–1624) "directed his officials to scour for Kirishitan and put all of them into jail without exception. Upon the order, the officials hurriedly sealed the entrances to the ward as was customarily done [when arresting criminals] and deployed guards or watchmen in order to block even a single person from fleeing."[84] The Kirishitan crackdown began in Daiusu Ward (Daiusu refers to "Deus," or "God") in Kamikyō, a well-known Kirishitan ward, and soon spread to the entire city; eventually, it yielded 63 arrests. Among those arrested, as the *Tokugawa jikki* tells in an entry of the 29th day of the eighth month, 52 people, including a pregnant woman and her five children, aged three to thirteen, "were dragged out to the riverbed of Shijō and subjected to death by fire. [Onlookers], old and young, from towns and villages, flocked like clouds and mists to watch [the scene]."[85] This persecution was, in fact, carried out on the order of Shogun Hidetada, who at that time was staying at Fushimi Castle, busying himself with reshuffling daimyo domains in the Kansai area.

Ironically, the tactics that Kirishitan devised to help them evade the penetrating eye of the authorities made them appear yet more "evil" and only contributed to escalating the carnage of suppression. The Hirayama Jōchin affair is a case in point. In the summer of 1620, British and Dutch vessels entered Hirado, dragging a Portuguese junk that they had seized in the Straits of Taiwan. The captors reported to the Japanese authorities that the Portuguese junk, captained by a Japanese, Hirayama Jōchin (?–1622), was hiding two suspicious Europeans who looked like Christian priests. The Portuguese vessel, which possessed a legitimate shogunal document and carried cargo (raw silk, deer hides, sugar, and other goods), was immediately sequestered by the Hirado domain government. Upon instruction from the *bakufu*, the Hirado daimyo (Matsura Takanobu) and the Nagasaki magistrate (Hasegawa Gonroku) arrested and questioned the two Europeans, Pedro de Zúñiga and Luis Flores. The investigation, which was prolonged due to the suspects' denial of their Christian status, became further complicated when Captain Hirayama accused his English and Dutch captors of piracy. However, in 1622, forced questioning, the testimony of witnesses, threats, and torture eventually resulted in Zúñiga confessing that he was an Augustinian missionary (and that he had been to Japan on a previous occasion) and in Flores confessing that he was a Flemish Dominican.[86] A few months later, Zúñiga, Flores, and Captain Hirayama were burned to death, and twelve crew members were beheaded. The three badly burnt corpses and twelve heads were displayed at the execution site for five days—a horrifying spectacle created for the purpose of providing an object lesson.

The Hirayama affair alerted *bakufu* leaders to the potential menace posed by the Spanish and the Portuguese, and immediate misfortune fell upon those Kirishitan imprisoned in the Ōmura domain. In the eighth month of 1622, 21 missionaries (nine Jesuits, seven Dominicans, and five Franciscans) and 34 lay followers (including a Korean couple by the name of Antonio and two three-year-old boys) emerged in chains from their prison cells and were taken to an execution site on the Nishizaka hill in Nagasaki. The death penalty awaiting these unfortunate souls involved a combination of decapitation and immolation at the stake (*hiaburi*). It is said that, in order to prolong their pain while they were being scorched, authorities spread small fagots of wet wood four or so meters away from the stake. The fire was set in the morning, but some of the prisoners struggled, in horrifying torment, until midnight. The slaughter of these unlucky Kirishitan, which came to be known as the "Great Martyrdom of [the] Genna [Era]," offered an unmistakable warning to the Kirishitan community. The victims included not only missionaries and lay Kirishitan but also the landlords who had housed the missionaries, Kirishitan sympathizers, and even some people who simply happened to be the neighbors of the accused.[87]

One year later, 50 Kirishitan, including a Jesuit missionary (Girolamo de Ángelis [in Japan between 1602 and 1623]) and a Franciscan missionary (Francisco Gálvez [in Japan between 1606 and 1614, and 1617 and 1623]), were put to death in the shogunal capital of Edo during a purge known as the "Great Martyrdom of Edo."[88] The execution, carried out in Shiba in the tenth month, demonstrated that anti-Christian suppression would continue under the newly enthroned shogun, Iemitsu (r. 1623–51). Political authority still rested with Hidetada, who would die in the first month of 1632, but executions were conducted in the name of Iemitsu, who had been anointed three months earlier.[89] The *Tokugawa jikki* reads: "Among those [executed] was Hara Mondo, who had previously been expelled for the crime [of being a Kirishitan]. He again committed [that] crime, even though his fingers had been cut off [as punishment]. . . . A shogunal bodyguard named Matsura Sannosuke, who allowed Kirishitan to live in his house, was also punished."[90] Altogether, 24 "criminals" were executed.

The fate of Hara Mondo (1587–1623), nicknamed Joan, bespoke the spiraling intensity of the *bakufu*'s anti-Christian suppression. When Mondo, a captain of the inner guard at Sunpu Castle, was revealed as a Kirishitan in 1612, his punishment was expulsion. Three years later, in 1615, while hiding in the Iwaki domain, he continued to practice his religion and was arrested. Upon being transferred to Sunpu, he was condemned to torture: his fingers and toes were to be mutilated, the sign of the cross was to be branded on his forehead, and he was to be ostracized. Ten years later, he was still a defiant Kirishitan and somehow managed to escape Edo. However, when he was finally captured, the punishment awaiting him was death by fire.[91] To be sure, Mondo had repeated his "crime"; however, by this time, as far as punishment was concerned, there was no distinction being made between proven Kirishitan like Mondo and mere Kirishitan sympathizers. Within less than a month, 37 more people, including 16 children, were put to death in Edo. Among the victims, 13 were non-Kirishitan who had been accused of somehow being on the wrong side of the religious ledger.[92] In Tōhoku during the winter of 1623, around 60 Kirishitan followers, including a missionary, Diogo Carvalho, were arrested, sent to Sendai, and put naked into a prison set up on the river. They all froze to death after undergoing three days of torture and hunger.[93]

The new shogun's fearsome tactics, which were carried out under the guidance of his father, were most strongly expressed in Nagasaki. Mizuno Morinobu, a new magistrate who had been appointed in 1626, had a certain genius when it came to searching out Kirishitan suspects and killing them slowly, with a maximum amount of pain. In 1628 he initiated a unique method for identifying faithful Kirishitan: "trampling on Christian pictures and images," known as *fumie* or *ebumi* in Japanese. This method, which many Kirishitan considered to be akin to treading on the face of their own mother, forced the suspect to stamp either on a wooden or copper plate (initially, paper) that contained the image of the Cross, Christ, or Mary. Ward officials and inquisitors visited residents, forced them to tread on Christian symbols (which were referred to as "Buddhist images") as proof that they were not Kirishitan, and documented the results one by one, trying not to miss the slightest sign of hesitation or embarrassment on the part of the inspectees.[94] During his three-year term, Morinobu brutally executed more than 300 Kirishitan, many of whom were thrown into a boiling hot spring at Unzen. Takenaka Shigeyoshi, who succeeded Morinobu in 1629, was no less ruthless than his predecessor. A Dutch trader in Nagasaki observed: "When Kirishitan imprisoned in the storehouse reached a certain number, the magistrate ordered his retainers to transfer them to Arima to put them into the hell of boiling water."[95] Until his tenure ended in 1632, Shigeyoshi was single-mindedly devoted to the task of hunting down Kirishitan and forcing them to recant. His egregious, unquenchable hatred for Kirishitan drove him to violate their graves and even to torment their infants.[96] The Japanese archipelago had become a hotbed of anti-Christianity.

Nor did European trade remain unscathed amid the ever-increasing anti-Christian suppression. In 1623, the shogunate forbade the Portuguese from settling in Japan and forbade the Japanese from crossing to the Philippines. A year later, *bakufu* leaders decided to sever relations with Spain, "the home country of padres," accusing the Spanish traders of "recklessly spoiling [Japanese] customs with malicious teachings." All the Spanish traders and their Japanese families were expelled from Nagasaki. Along with the departure of the English, who had already closed their Hirado trade factory the previous year due to gloomy prospects, the departure of the Spanish left Japanese trade in the hands of the Dutch and the Portuguese.[97] Nevertheless, in 1626, the *bakufu* proceeded to further restrict Portuguese trade by imposing regulatory procedures designed to ensure the inspection of crew members and cargo. Anyone with any kind of connection to the Society of Jesus was denied entry to Japan. The increasing anti-Christian restrictions eventually led to the suspension of trade with the Portuguese from 1627 to 1630 and with the Dutch from 1627 to 1632, respectively.[98] It appeared to be only a matter of time before European trade was totally subjected to anti-Christian policy.

What happened to Buddhism—which Ieyasu had begun (albeit in a limited fashion) to mobilize as an arbiter of anti-Christianity—during the era of Hidetada (1616–31)? Were Buddhist temples and monks further incorporated into the regime's anti-Christian policy? Not to any significant extent. The method of temple certification for *korobi* Kirishitan continued, but it was not further expanded. Interestingly, *bakufu* leaders did not seem to be concerned with expanding the role of Buddhist temples as the guarantors of non-Christian status. On the contrary, they seemed to want to tame them, as was illustrated in 1627–29 by a Buddhist purge known as the "Purple Robe Incident."

The origin of this incident goes back to Ieyasu's 1613 regulations, which were directed at eight high-status Kyoto temples and which reined in the imperial court's freewheeling practice of conferring ranks and titles upon Buddhist clergy. Ieyasu, who was concerned with the commercial transactions of Buddhist titles, obliged the head monks of these temples to notify the *bakufu* in order to obtain shogunal endorsement before they sought the "purple robe" (*shie*), the highest Buddhist title, from the imperial court.[99] Not satisfied, Ieyasu further tightened the terms of eligibility and the procedure of conferral in the Regulations for the Imperial Court and Courtier Households in 1615.[100] The laws, addressed to major Buddhist sects as well as to the imperial court, set the minimum qualification for the purple robe as follows: all applicants must have practiced Buddhism for at least 30 years, and all applications were to obtain shogunal approval before being forwarded to the emperor.[101] However, the imperial court ignored these regulations and continued to sell titles to status-hungry, often unqualified, monks. Irritated, the *bakufu* decided in 1627 to nullify the "illegal" purple robes acquired after 1615—more than 150 in total. The following year, two major Rinzaishū temples in Kyoto—Daitokuji and Myōshinji—which together faced losing more than 70 purple-robe titles, conveyed a written protest to the shogunate. They questioned the legitimacy of the shogunal regulations, implying that *bakufu* officials, not being familiar with the precedent, might not be suited to assessing an individual monk's capabilities with regard to Buddhist wisdom.[102] *Bakufu* authorities, led by Konchiin Sūden, struck back in 1629 with resolute punishment: Takuan and Gyokushitsu of Daitokuji were expelled to Dewa and to Mutsu, respectively; and Tōgen and Tanden of Myōshinji were expelled to Tsugaru and to Dewa, respectively.[103] Emperor Gomizunoo, who had approved the robes, abdicated in protest, only to have his daughter Meishō (whose mother, Tōfukumon'in, was a daughter of Hidetada) succeed him.

The *bakufu* then proceeded to streamline control by organizing all Buddhist temples hierarchically along sectarian lines. This resulted in a head-and-branch (*honmatsu*) system in which the temples of each sect were to be organized according to head temples and branch temples.[104] The system of the head-branch relationship was soon incorporated into the governing structure of the *bakuhan* system through the *furegashira* ("announcement-head") system, which served as a communication link between Buddhist temples and the government.[105] Under the high-handed supervision of the secular authorities, head temples sought to preserve and promote their diminishing interests by vigorously incorporating lesser temples into their domain. As long as the head temples complied with shogunal rules, the *bakufu* acknowledged their discretionary right to govern branch temples. Nor was the head-branch system necessarily disadvantageous to small temples, which competed among themselves for survival. By being affiliated with big-name temples, branch temples could secure recognition, protection, and, sometimes, prestige.[106]

Aiming to facilitate the head-branch organization, the *bakufu* ordered the nation's head temples in 1631 to submit the registers of their branch temples to the government. In the following year, Zōjōji, in Edo, first submitted its register, entitled "Jōdoshū shoji no chō" (Register of all Jōdoshū temples), and other sects soon followed suit.[107] The collection of head-branch temple registers, known as the Kan'ei head-branch register, helped the shogunate bring Buddhist institutions under its sway.[108] In the long run, the *bakufu*'s grip on Buddhist institutions enabled it to mobilize Buddhist temples as public organs for implementing the regime's anti-Christian policies. Nevertheless, it should be noted that, during the era of Hidetada, the idea of Buddhism serving as protector of the divine country was not particularly popular and did not advance very far.

TWO

From Suppression to Buddhist Inspection, 1633–1651

After the death of his father, Shogun Iemitsu, who quickly strength-ened his own hold on power, dealt with the issues of trade and Christianity.[109] In the second month of 1633, in the name of four state elders, Iemitsu sent an administrative memorandum (consisting of seventeen articles) to the newly appointed Nagasaki magistrates. In this memo, the first of a series of similar administrative orders to be issued annually until 1636, Iemitsu revealed his intention to put foreign trade under tighter shogunal control by banning Japanese foreign travel both out of and back into the country (only those who had been abroad for fewer than five years were to be allowed to return to Japan). He also strictly regulated the import of silk yarn through the "yarn tally" (*ito wappu*) system, which allowed a group of authorized merchants to monopolize the purchase of Chinese raw silk.[110]

At the same time, Iemitsu made clear his desire to eradicate Chris-tian elements, as is evidenced in the anti-Christian clauses spelled out in Articles 4 and 5 of the memo.[111] In Article 4, Iemitsu redefined the jurisdiction of Nagasaki magistrates with regard to collecting and reporting information on Kirishitan: "In case Kirishitan are dis-covered, the two [Nagasaki magistrates] should report [them to the *bakufu*]."[112] The Nagasaki magistrates were authorized to exercise their supervisory power over all the domains of Kyūshū. One year later, in 1634, Iemitsu further empowered the Nagasaki magistrates to conduct "investigations" (*sensaku*) and to put the Kyūshū daimyo under surveillance – an unprecedented move that would subjugate the internal affairs of daimyo domains to shogunal supervision wherever issues related to Christianity were concerned.[113] On the other hand, Article 5 formalized the system of rewarding those who informed on Kirishitan, making this shogunal policy: "The person who informs on an upper Kirishitan shall be rewarded with 100 pieces (*mai*) of silver currency, and the person who informs on a lower Kirishitan will be paid in accordance with the degree of his or her loyalty."[114] As a matter of fact, this system, designed to entice people to spy and inform on each other, was nothing new. It had been tried in Nagasaki in 1618, and it was soon adopted by Itakura Katsushige in Kyoto, as well as by some other local lords, all on their own initiative. The significance of Article 5, however, was that this system of spying was adopted as shogunal policy and was swiftly implemented in shogunal territories. Lured by monetary compensation, people ran around ferreting out Kirishitan; and soon professional hunters, organized into street gangs, began to appear.[115]

Under attack from all sides, the Kirishitan community watched helplessly as Cristovão Ferreira (who was in Japan from 1609 to 1650), a high-ranking Jesuit, became its first apostate padre in 1633. Ferreira, who was captured, collapsed amid the torture of *anatsurushi*, which involves the victim being trussed and placed upside down in a pit filled with excreta. In the face of this torture, Ferreira declared that he "wanted to convert to Zen Buddhism."[116] On top of this apostasy, Ferreira, who, after his conversion, was given the Japanese name Sawano Chūan, began to serve as an inquisitor of Christians, sending shock waves through the Society of Jesus. In a desperate attempt to bring him back to Christianity, in 1642, and again in 1643, groups of Jesuits volunteered to infiltrate Japan. The first group, led by Padre Antonio Rubino (1578–1643), was soon caught and interrogated by the very man whom they had hoped to save; all perished while suspended in the pit, hoping that "the blood of their martyrdom [would] wash away the stain of [their] original sin."[117] Interestingly, the members of the second group, who were also captured and sent to Edo, were all persuaded, under the torture of Inoue Masashige (1585–1661), a *bakufu* official who would leave an indelible mark on the history of anti-Christianity, to abandon their faith. In return they were allowed to live out their lives in jail.[118] Among those jailed was Giuseppe Chiara (who soon assumed the Japanese name Okamoto San'emon), whom Endō Shūsaku used, along with Ferreira, as a model for Rodorigo (the protagonist of his well-known novel *Chinmoku* [Silence]).[119] Christians of rank were in disarray.

From 1634 onward, the Iemitsu government began to devise ever more systematic ways of tracking down Christian elements. One of these involved a comprehensive census conducted in Nagasaki in 1634. The extant 1634 Nagasaki document, known as "Hiradomachi Yokoseuramachi ninzū aratame no chō" (A register of investigation of the Hiradomachi and Yokoseuramachi residents), shows that Buddhist temples conducted religious inspections of all ward residents in order to determine who was affiliated with which Buddhist temple.[120] The inspection results, indicating proof of temple affiliation, can be summed up as follows: among 332 enrollees, 142 (all belonging to either Jōdoshinshū or Zenshū temples) visited their temples; 127 (all belonging to Nichirenshū temples) were in possession of Buddhist scriptures that they had received from their temples; 32 (all belonging to Jōdoshū temples) received the service of *nenbutsu*-chanting; and 31 were unknown.[121] Unlike the previous register, which was applied to *korobi* Kirishitan only, the scope and thoroughness of the 1634 Nagasaki register hinted at the coming trend of temple certification.

Indeed, from the early 1630s, local domains began to apply the method of temple certification to ordinary residents.[122] For example, authorities of the Kumamoto domain, who had initially tried in 1633 to check, through ward officials, the religious affiliation of the residents of Kumamoto and Yatsushiro (who had been under the sway of the well-known former Kirishitan daimyo Konishi Yukinaga), launched domainwide religious inspections through Buddhist temples in 1634. According to the 1634 *shūmon aratame* (sectarian inspection) documents pertaining to Shimōda village in Tamana county, the village elder collected temple certificates (issued by *danna* temples) from 25 household heads and then drew up a roster of family members and submitted it to the domain government. These "sectarian inspection" documents included not only information on the religious affiliation of the villagers listed but also collective anti-Christian pledges to the government.[123] On the surface, the village elder took ultimate responsibility for confirming the non-Christian status of the residents of his village, but it was actually individual *danna* temples that guaranteed and certified each villager's religious innocence. We can find similar examples of "sectarian inspection" by Buddhist temples in the Amakusa islands, Kyoto, and Osaka, even though, at this early stage, it was not conducted on a regular basis.[124]

It was amidst this trend that, in 1635, the shogunate forbade Japanese either to go abroad or, if they were already out of the country, to return home. This decree stemmed from the *bakufu*'s concern that "vermilion ships" (*shuinsen*), which the shogun authorized for trade, were involved in exporting Japanese weapons to Southeast Asia. They were also afraid that these ships, through their extensive networks in Macao and Manila, might be providing financial help to Christian missionaries active in Japan. According to this law, all Japanese were forbidden to travel abroad without special permission.[125] In conjunction with the termination of foreign travel, the shogunate began to rid Japan of anyone related by blood to "southern barbarians." Panicked, those people who were suddenly facing deportation were desperate to hide, be adopted by a "normal family," or, should they be expelled, to sneak back into Japan. But the shogunate blocked all these efforts with the death penalty. By the end of 1636, 287 children born of "barbarian" fathers and Japanese mothers were permanently expelled to Macao.[126] At the same time, the Portuguese traders, who were scattered all over Nagasaki, were collected and confined to a small artificial island, Dejima, which was built off the shore of the city and was connected to it only by a narrow bridge. In the meantime, in the ninth month of 1635, the shogunate urged the nation's daimyo to thoroughly investigate the whereabouts of remaining Kirishitan: "Investigate more strictly all domains and the members of all households. In case these sectarians [Kirishitan] are found, arrest them and then report the matter [to the *bakufu*]."[127]

In line with the shogunal order, Sakai Tadakatsu (1587–1662), an influential state elder, immediately instructed his officials in the Obama domain to organize all residents into five-man groups and to collect temple certificates from them. In stressing that the ban on Christianity was to be enacted through temple certification, Tadakatsu presumed that non-Kirishitan residents would all be affiliated with Buddhist temples. Beginning in 1639, the Obama domain government regularized annual religious inspection by Buddhist temples.[128] Indeed, in many regions, on the pretext of religious inspection, the role of Buddhist temples had already been extended to cover the non-Kirishitan population. In the tenth month of 1635, Nanzenji assured Kyoto officials that the residents in its temple lands and the members of commercial guilds under its control had nothing to do with Christianity. Similarly, one of its subtemples, Jiseiin, reported that the residents of its front district were all non-Kirishitan, and they offered Nanzenji officials a copy of a document signed by six resident representatives: "As far as the matter of Deus was concerned, those associated with the temple [Jiseiin] have all been checked and cleared. From now on, in case those who have signed hereupon hide or do not report [a Kirishitan suspect], even if the Kirishitan suspect is, for example, a relative, punishment shall fall upon all family members."[129]

Apparently, Buddhist temples were making inroads into the general populace, but this does not mean that the practice of temple certification was free of difficulty. There was a two-pronged problem: (1) many households resisted being forced to affiliate with Buddhist temples; and (2) in some areas Buddhist temples were not easily accessible. For example, the Usuki domain in Kyūshū, where anti-Christian policy was vigorously pursued from 1614 on, had to make strenuous efforts to force even *korobi* Kirishitan to affiliate themselves with Buddhism. Not only that, even in the Kanbun era (1661–73) there were still some households that had trouble finding *danna* temples in their vicinity. The situation was not so different in Owari, another domain well known for the persistence of Kirishitan. When, in the 1660s, it was revealed that hundreds of people continued to cling to their Christian faith, domain officials observed that many non-Kirishitan villagers were scrambling to find Buddhist temples to which they could affiliate themselves in order to escape punishment. And they did not mind bribing Buddhist monks.[130] Temple certification was not yet universal, and it seemed as though its full implementation would take far longer than the *bakufu* had hoped.

In addition to temple certification, other tactics for routing Kirishitan were also pursued in the mid-1630s. One of them was the divine pledge, known as the "vow of southern barbarians" (*nanban seishi*). In 1635 the Kyoto shogunal deputy, Itakura Shigemune (1586–1656), imposed upon Kyoto residents (including courtiers, aristocrats, and imperial monks and nuns) an oath of apostasy. In enforcing this oath, Shigemune instructed *korobi* Kirishitan to comply with all three of its articles and to sign at the bottom, while non-Kirishitan only had to deal with those articles relevant to them. Structurally, the preamble of the first article – "Although I had been a Kirishitan from _____ to _____, I truly converted [to Buddhism]" – leads to the second article: "I now regret that I used to be part of a Kirishitan sect; I will never return to Christianity or promote it to my wife, children, or any other dependents." However, the key article is the third: "[If I return to Christianity] in the name of devils, Deus, and Sancta Maria, I shall be subject to all kinds of punishment delivered by God's messengers [Anjo]. Upon death, I shall descend to the hell called Inferno and suffer from the torment of the five coldnesses and the three heats at the hands of all devils."[131] Following this order, the *korobi* Kirishitan in Kyoto started submitting to the government pledges of their conversion, adding yet more items (such as white and black leprosy) to the list of punishments.[132] It is ironic that *korobi* Kirishitan could be exonerated of the crime of having belonged to the Christian faith by pledging to none other than their former icons – God the Father, Jesus, and the Virgin Mary.[133]

Late in the tenth month of 1637, amid multidirectional anti-Christian campaigns, a peasant uprising broke out in the Shimabara domain of Matsukura Katsuie (1597–1638) in Kyūshū. The uprising was, according to the *Tokugawa jikki*, triggered by an incident that involved domain officials imprisoning two villagers in Arima village on the charge of Kirishitan worship.[134] The few villagers who joined together to unleash their long-standing anger at the government soon swelled into thousands. They marched toward Shimabara Castle, destroying Shinto shrines and Buddhist temples and killing monks. Within a few days the rebellion had spread like wildfire into other villages and into the neighboring areas of Amakusa, which were under the control of the Karatsu domain of Terazawa Katataka (1609–47). On the ninth day of the eleventh month, a messenger, dispatched by the shogunal deputies of Kyoto and Osaka, rushed into Edo to transmit the following urgent report: "In the domain of Matsukura Nagato no Kami, Hizen Shimabara, the Kirishitan bandits rose up, mustered their sectarians, and set fire to everything, including the houses of the Matsukura's castle town. They have now shut themselves up in Arie and Arima."[135]

The shogunate wasted no time in condemning the peasant uprisings in Shimabara and Amakusa, better known collectively as the Amakusa-Shimabara Rebellion, a "sectarian revolt" (*shūmon ikki*), and labeled it a Christian-inspired insurrection against the country of the gods. Reminded of the fact that the region did, indeed, encompass the former domains of Kirishitan daimyo Arima Harunobu (Shimabara) and Konishi Yukinaga (Amakusa), *bakufu* leaders did not try to understand what was really at the root of the uprising. Actually, it owed much to the fact that, for too long, peasants had suffered from excessive exploitation in the form of taxes and corvées. Domain officials in Shimabara, for example, set the taxable yield of the domain at more than two times its actual production capacity, which was estimated at 40,000 *koku* of rice.[136] In 1630, Matsukura Katsuie even volunteered to make an excessive contribution (premised on what he could get from a 100,000-*koku* domain) toward the construction of Edo Castle. In order to fulfill the wildly unreasonable goals of tax revenues, the domain government resorted to levying all kinds of new taxes (such as a hearth tax, a window tax, and a shelf tax) on the villagers, severely punishing those who failed to pay their share. Some delinquents were even wrapped in straw bags and thrown into a fire.[137] The situation in Amakusa, where the taxable yield was raised to double its official *kokudaka*, which was originally set at 21,000 *koku*, was no better than that in Shimabara. Not surprisingly, however, all these grueling ills were buried under the overriding perception of the persistence and villainy of this region's Christian legacies.

As if confirming the shogunal perception, the peasant fighters eventually rallied around Amakusa Shirō (Masuda Tokisada, ?–1638), a boy of fifteen or so whom they declared the leader of the revolt and whom they endowed with divine authority. Amakusa Shirō, proclaimed as "an angel from Heaven," seemed to be an ideal leader for peasant rebels engaged in a millenarian struggle for a better world.[138] Indeed, Amakusa Shirō rapidly ignited the until-then dormant messianic quest of Amakusa-Shimabara residents who were still under the heavy influence of *korobi* Kirishitan village leaders. In fact, when Arima Harunobu was transferred to Hyūga in 1614, many of his discontented "masterless samurai" Kirishitan chose, for religious reasons, to become peasants and to stay in their region as village elders or officials. Under the harsh anti-Christian suppression, these village leaders were forced to abandon their religion and to deactivate their secret religious confraternities – a network of Kirishitan fellowship known as *konfurariya*.[139] However, upon the news of the advent of God in the person of Amakusa Shirō, many of them quickly returned to their concealed religion, took up leadership roles, and led the villagers in their quest to renew the world.[140]

By the time the *bakufu* forces, led by Itakura Shigemasa (shogunal envoy, 1588–1638) and Ishigai Sadakiyo (vice shogunal envoy, 1594–1672), arrived at Shimabara on the fifth day of the twelfth month, the Amakusa-Shimabara Rebellion had become a Christian rebellion.

The *bakufu* forces, in a hastily arranged attack launched on the first day of the first month of 1638, experienced a crushing defeat at the hands of rebels who had now firmly fortified themselves at the dilapidated former site of Hara Castle. Shigemasa was killed, and the second in command, Sadakiyo, was injured, barely escaping with his life. Shocked, Shogun Iemitsu mobilized a huge army of 120,000 from western Japan (for a short time he even utilized Dutch cannons and gunpowder), appointed Matsudaira Nobutsuna (1596–1662) as general commander, and then advanced his forces toward the Shimabara peninsula. The peasant rebels at the Hara fortress were soon under siege.[141] At one point the "Christian" rebels successfully waged a surprise night attack on the encircling forces, but they could not sustain their efforts in the face of a shogunal strategy dedicated to exhausting their dwindling stocks of food and weapons. Matsudaira Nobutsuna, judging that the time was right, ordered a general attack on the 28th day of the second month, and the fortress fell within two hours, leaving corpses piled all over the place.[142] The shogunal troops literally exterminated nearly 28,000 human beings, including women and children, who were trying to hold the Hara fortress. In this unutterable "kill everyone" (*minagoroshi*) attack, the shogunal forces themselves suffered some casualties: 1,130 were killed, and 6,966 were injured.[143]

Right after this major rebellion, the shogunate proceeded to restore order to its governing structure. It punished Matsukura Katsuie and Terazawa Katataka (the daimyo responsible for the rebel domains), revised the Laws of Military Households for the nation's local lords, transferred *fudai* daimyo (hereditary vassals to the Tokugawa) into Kyūshū, and transplanted a farming population from neighboring domains to the wasted battlefields. And then, in the ninth month of 1638, Iemitsu issued a decree on the campaign of secret information, delineating the amounts of financial rewards as follows: 200 pieces (*mai*) of silver for those who informed on padres; 100 pieces of silver for those who informed on brothers; and 50 or 30 pieces of silver for those who informed on Kirishitan. The edict ended as follows: "Those who inform on [Kirishitan] will be pardoned, even if they are found to belong to the same sect, and will be given a remuneration [by the shogunal authority]."[144] A critical feature of the edict was that it enticed Kirishitan to inform on their fellow believers by promising to forgive their "previous" crimes as well as to provide them with bountiful rewards. The *bakufu* then ordered details of the rewards to be displayed on public bulletin boards throughout the nation. The reward for informing on padres, set at 200 pieces of silver currency, was worth more than 140 *ryō* of gold *koban*; and even the smallest reward, 30 pieces of silver currency, exceeded 20 gold *koban* in value.[145] Ordinary people could certainly not expect to make this much money in their lifetime.

The significance of this edict was that, for the first time, the shogunal government explicitly adopted the term "Kirishitan" to refer to lay followers of Christianity as distinct from padres, brothers, and Kirishitan leaders of the samurai class, to whom the term *bateren* had been loosely applied.[146] The shogunate now shifted the focus of anti-Christian inquisition to lay followers, and, in order to do this, it tried to expand the reward system (which had initially been tried in Nagasaki and Kyoto) into a national policy.[147] At the same time, the shogunate declared that monies would be paid from the shogunal treasury, thus indicating that, as far as the matter of Kirishitan was concerned, shogunal authority would prevail over domanial autonomy. This was a significant reversal of the cardinal principle of the *bakuhan* system, according to which the *bakufu* had hitherto honored a policy of noninterference in the matters of domanial residents. The shogunate took the occasion of the Amakusa-Shimabara Rebellion as an excuse to execute "national" policies that would bring semi-independent local governments, particularly those of *tozama* daimyo, to their knees.[148]

Along with the reward system, the *bakufu* attempted to impose annual temple certification upon the residents of all shogunal lands. This was modeled after similar but sporadic experiments in Kyūshū and Kyoto.[149] With regard to this, the shogunate introduced a standardized format for the temple certificate:

With regard to the one said here of _____ village, it is true that the person indicated is a patron of the Bodhi of our [Buddhist] sect. In case someone comes out and accuses [the person] of being a Kirishitan, this humble monk will come [to your office] and testify [to the truth].

Year/Month/Date

Temple of _____ sect/Signature[150]

Soon after the shogunate had delivered its instructions, Buddhist temples in the Kantō region began to issue non-Christian certificates.[151] But it would be too much to expect that, on the strength of one shogunal order, the entire population of the region affiliated itself with *danna* temples. There is not even any evidence that, at this time, the system of temple certification was put in place across the Kantō.[152] Nevertheless, what is significant is the fact that the shogunate began to give serious thought to implementing universal temple certification as a means of eradicating Christian elements. In the twelfth month of 1638, the shogunate reiterated to the assembly of daimyo, which had gathered at Edo Castle, the urgency of tracking down Kirishitan in their respective domains.[153]

On another battlefront, *bakufu* leaders moved to address the problem of Portuguese traders, who seemed still to be associated with Christianity. In the seventh month of 1639, Shogun Iemitsu proclaimed an expulsion decree, commonly known as the *Kareutafune tokai kinshirei* ("Ban on the Crossing of the Sea by Galeota [Portuguese Vessels]"). In this decree, which was cosigned by all state councilors, Iemitsu pointed out three misdeeds committed by the Portuguese: providing transportation to missionaries trying to sneak into Japan, attempting to organize a clique of Kirishitan and to promote evil teachings, and sending material assistance to padres and Kirishitan who were in hiding in Japan. For these reasons, Iemitsu declared that Portuguese vessels were to be prohibited from coming to Japan; he warned that those ships that violated his decree would be destroyed and their crews immediately decapitated, thus ending the tenuous working relationship that had developed between the Portuguese traders and the Tokugawa regime.[154] In order to expel the Portuguese, the *bakufu* dispatched Ōta Sukemune (1600–80), a junior councilor, along with about 700 troops, to Nagasaki. With the expulsion of the Portuguese, all relations with the Iberians – relations that had lasted since 1543 – were permanently terminated.

Ōta Sukemune then summoned representatives of Dutch and Chinese traders and informed them of the ban on Portuguese trade and Christianity. The Dutch vowed to continue to stay away from Christianity, as they had done since their arrival in 1606, while the Chinese claimed that they had nothing to do with this religion. Out of fear of Portuguese retaliation, Sukemune delivered the shogunal order of coastal defense and vigilance to the Kyūshū daimyo.[155] The termination of relations with the Iberians was, indeed, a major foreign policy decision – one that would put the doctrine of anti-Christianity over the issues of trade and foreign relations. Devastated, the Portuguese in Macao, whose survival prospects suddenly looked bleak, dispatched a trade ship to Japan in the sixth month of 1640 in search of a repeal of that ruinous decision. But the *bakufu*'s response to the Portuguese, who were called upon to appear before its inspectors in formal dress, was death sentences: "On the charge of arriving ashore in violation of the national prohibition, [shogunal authorities] beheaded on the spot 61 among 74 barbarians who were aboard the ship on the sixteenth day of this month, and they burned the vessel and all its cargo. Only 13 people, doctors and children [in fact, they were blacks who were regarded as non-Christians], were saved and expelled [to Macao] on board another ship."[156]

Shogun Iemitsu then ordered all Kyūshū daimyo to further strengthen the coastal defense, and he dispatched Inoue Masashige to Nagasaki and Hirado. Upon arriving at Hirado, Masashige inspected the Dutch trade factory, demolished their warehouses because one of them bore the graffito "the year of the birth of Jesus," and ordered that the head of the trade factory be replaced annually. In the following year, in the interest of closer surveillance, the *bakufu* decided to relocate the Dutch to the confines of Dejima in Nagasaki, which would remain the only terminus for European trading vessels.[157] The Hirado era of the Dutch, which had lasted more than 30 years, came to an end in the fifth month of 1641. In that same year, Chinese traders were also ordered to relocate to Nagasaki.

While strictly subjecting trade and foreign travel to the national policy (*kokuze*) of anti-Christianity, the Iemitsu government proceeded to establish in 1640 an office that, by the late 1650s, would evolve into the Office of the Inspector of Religious Sects (*shūmon aratameyaku*). Masashige, who had just returned from Kyūshū and had been elevated to the rank of daimyo, was appointed to the post of inspector general.[158] Until being released from this position in 1658, Masashige played a key role in developing ways of eliminating Kirishitan, and he helped, whether intentionally or not, to lay the foundation for the *danka* system, which, by the late seventeenth century, would gain full force. For this reason, Masashige's involvement in anti-Christian policies, which began in 1638 when he was dispatched as a shogunal envoy to Shimabara, deserves special attention.[159]

Shocked by the life-or-death resistance of the "Kirishitan" *ikki*, which he witnessed in Shimabara, Inoue Masashige quickly transformed himself into a champion of anti-Christianity. In the beginning, his approach to Christianity was somewhat erratic – vengeful on one occasion, pacificatory on another. For example, in mid-1639, Masashige had a chance to meet a Dutch captain who was in Edo to pay his annual visit to the shogun. During his conversation with this man, Masashige made a comment about the pro-Christian Portuguese: "I wish I could hang on the cross, without exception, the two Portuguese captains who are in Nagasaki and the Portuguese who are coming [to Nagasaki] this year. If that were to happen, I would be able to match the exact number [of Japanese] who have died for nothing in the past many years because of the Portuguese."[160] However, several months later, Masashige came to deal with three Portuguese padres who had been captured in Sendai and sent to Edo. At first they were unsuccessfully questioned by the *bakufu* court (led by Sakai Tadakatsu, the senior state councilor). When Masashige, then inspector general, took over, he demonstrated his unusual interrogation skills, and, within ten days, succeeded in persuading two of them to recite the *nenbutsu*.[161] Another time, as has been mentioned, Masashige completely demolished Dutch warehouses in Hirado for bearing the date of the birth of Jesus on their walls. At times he seemed unable to forgive even the slightest hint of Christianity.

Over time, however, Inoue Masashige leaned toward placation rather than extirpation and began to be directly involved in the investigation of local Kirishitan across the country. This trend became quite evident after he succeeded in inducing four padres, one brother, and five ardent lay followers – all of whom had been captured in Chikuzen in 1643 – to recite the Buddha's name. Masashige relegated all of these "Buddhist converts" to a prison that had just been built on the ground of his tertiary residence (*shimoyashiki*) in Edo at Koishikawa, far from the previous jail at Tenmachō.[162] Until 1792, when it was demolished, the Inoue Masashige prison, better known as Kirishitan *yashiki* (residence of Kirishitan), was a place where Masashige and other *bakufu* officials sometimes called upon the *bateren* inmates in order to hear their stories about the risks they took entering Japan.[163] One of the padre captives, Ercole Francesco Cassola (in Japan from 1643 to 1644), had even been put into the cell of a female inmate and allowed to live there until he died the following year. When they wanted to officially become a couple, Masashige arranged a ceremony at which the two "shared a bowl of sake" and received the congratulations of their fellow missionary inmates. Giuseppe Chiara, a model for the protagonist of Endō Shūsaku's *Silence*, was also "bestowed a wife."[164] And so Masashige extended his pacificatory treatment to apostate Christian leaders, sometimes even granting them rice and silver (albeit within their miserable prison cells).

It should, however, be noted that Masashige's pacificatory approach had nothing to do with a sudden compassion toward Christians; rather, it stemmed from his own experience, which convinced him that killing alone would not provide an adequate solution to the problem. Masashige commented as follows on the practical merits of his methods: "Killing by hanging upside down, or beheading, or burning at the stake will not prevent padres from crossing [to our country]. I found ways of converting them to the Japanese religious sect. . . . This method has caused the membership of the Christian sect to decrease."[165] Masashige began to emphasize appeasement and conversion. The shogun and his top officials agreed that, after the massive blood-letting of the Amakusa-Shimabara Rebellion, it was time for healing.

In fact, *bakufu* leaders were ill at ease with the deteriorating socio-economic situation, which was becoming increasingly visible in the late 1630s and early 1640s. In particular, the economic hardships of the early 1640s caused by epidemics, natural disasters, and crop failures – collectively known as the Kan'ei famines – seemed to suggest that government by bayonet was not going to cure the ailing social order. Christianity was not the only problem. This time the trouble, which first surfaced in Kyūshū in the middle of the eighth month of 1638, began with the dying of farm animals. Due to mysterious cattle plagues, cows, which were indispensable to agriculture (they were a source of both labor and manure, the latter being mixed with leftover fodder, forage, and rice straw and used as fertilizer), were virtually wiped out in northwestern Kyūshū. And by 1640, the plagues had spread deep into the Chūgoku, Kinki, and Shikoku regions. In the following year, ominous symptoms appeared almost everywhere throughout the country in the form of irregular weather patterns and natural disasters. All of these phenomena combined to produce widespread famines in 1641–43.[166] In a hard-hit village in Shinano, for example, the casualties were staggering: in 1642 alone,

147 villagers starved to death, 92 sold themselves into bondage, 38 families deserted the village, and 82 horses and 83 cows died. The result of this was the loss of about one-third of the village households. The "fatigue of those below" (*shimojimo no kutabire*) began to spread everywhere, including the streets of Nihonbashi in Edo, where hundreds of famished people gathered every day to seek the mercy of those above.[167]

Amid mounting troubles, in the fifth month of 1642, the shogunate instructed the nation's daimyo to conduct anti-Christian inspection in their domains; however, at the same time, it urged them to try to "nurture the people" (*bumin*), saying that the residents of all domains suffered from poverty due to crop failures.[168] The anti-Christian inspection was tied up with the task of nurturing the people. In the eighth month of the same year, the anxious shogunate further moved to counter the nationwide crisis. Sumptuary laws were imposed on diet, drink, clothing, housing, entertainment, and religious rituals and ceremonies; peasants were ordered to increase their efforts to produce grain and to nurture a spirit of communal assistance; the selling or purchasing farm lands was banned; officials were warned against corruption and the harsh treatment of peasants; street vagrants were returned to their home villages; and rice prices were controlled. As was clearly spelled out in the seventeen articles of an edict issued to the shogunal deputies of the Kantō in early 1643, the *bakufu* stepped up its efforts to stabilize society by binding the peasant population to the land and agriculture.[169] The establishment of a self-sustainable peasant class (*hyakushō no naritachi*) was a priority. Within this milieu, which emphasized a spirit of caring and mutual help, repressive social engineering could not prevail as it had before.

Inoue Masashige understood the needs of the time when he was dealing with Kirishitan, who were proving to be quite resilient to terrorism. Instead of threatening them with swords, gallows, and fire, Masashige switched to the strategy of appeasement, aiming to reclaim the "depraved souls" of Christian followers, including padres, by converting them to Buddhism.[170] Similarly, right after the Amakusa-Shimabara Rebellion, Baba Toshishige (?–1657), who was a Nagasaki magistrate from 1636 to 1652, called for prominent Buddhist monks to join him in pacifying the Kirishitan in the region. Suzuki Shigenari (1588–1653), who was appointed shogunal deputy of Amakusa in 1641, invited his brother Suzuki Shōsan (1579–1655), an eminent

Zen monk, to his domain to help him placate the *ikki*-stricken populace. In the post-rebellion era in Kyūshū, *bakufu* officials pushed the Buddhist clergy into joining their spiritual campaigns to reclaim pro-Christian residents.[171] This new approach, which began in Kyūshū, found its way to the central government during the famine crises of the early 1640s. The past tendency of confronting the Kirishitan populace with violence gradually gave way to attempting to persuade and convert it.

On the whole, compared to the previous decades, which were dominated by a violent, monochromatic approach to Kirishitan, the 1640s were gentle, even inclusive. Government authorities seemed to view Christianity as a belief system that deserved a more prudent approach than it had hitherto been granted. If torture had to be used, suggested Masashige, then *mokubazeme* would be a good choice. *Mokubazeme* refers to a form of torture that involves using a wooden horse across which the victim was straddled with heavy weights (usually rocks) tied to his or her legs. This form of torture, Masashige believed, would be neither harsh enough to cause death or sickness nor mild enough to be ignored.[172] Depending on the situation, officials were advised to apply suitable and effective tactics in order to persuade Kirishitan to discard their religion. It was said that Shogun Iemitsu himself once commented: "The law of Jesus is the teaching of the West. For this reason, it would be a loss to our country if we would allow our people, even a single person, to fall into it. What we should do in order to prevent our people from being lost is to try to remedy their religion."[173] From top to bottom, efforts were made to discredit Christianity through edification and counterargument and thereby to bring the religious minds of Kirishitan back to Buddhism.

It is true that since the first decade of the 1600s, Confucian and Buddhist scholars had occasionally disclaimed Christianity. For example, Hayashi Razan wrote a scholastic critique in 1606 entitled *Hai Yaso* (Rejecting Jesus) after having had a dispute with the Japanese brother Fabian Fucan (known as Fukansai Habian, 1565–1621), a one-time Rinzaishū monk who had joined the Society of Jesus in Kyoto in 1586.[174] In 1620, Fabian, who had switched back to Buddhism in 1608, authored *Ha Daiusu* (Deus destroyed) in an attempt to systematically denounce his former religion.[175] Apostate missionaries were not shy about castigating the religion they had deserted. In 1636, Cristovão Ferreira questioned Christianity in the *Kengiroku* (Deceit disclosed), saying that "if [Deus] were the fountainhead of compassion, then why did he create the eight sufferings of human beings and the five decays of heavenly beings in the three worlds [*sangai*] of unforgiving agony?"[176] Beginning in 1630, the *bakufu* banned all books imported through Nagasaki that dealt with, or were in any way related to, Christianity. Within this environment it is unrealistic to imagine that the public would be exposed to any pro-Christian publications.[177] However, even though the publications to which people had access were all severely anti-Christian, it is doubtful that they were terribly effective in swaying Kirishitan to convert to Buddhism.

It was after the Amakusa-Shimabara Rebellion that anti-Christian propaganda began to show some effect. For example, from the early 1640s, the residents of Nagasaki, who had seen a steady increase of new Shinto shrines in the city, joined en masse the vogue of the Ise pilgrimage as part of a movement to denounce the alien religion that had once swept their neighborhoods.[178] The zeal of the Ise pilgrimage, which helped to strengthen phobic sensitivities toward Christianity, spread to various parts of the country. Indeed, the populace in general seemed to have grown more receptive to the binary juxtaposition of good and evil in terms of divine country versus Christianity.[179] The achievement of Suzuki Shōsan, who worked from 1642 to 1645 in the Amakusa islands, is telling. Shōsan, who declared that "Japan is the land of the gods,"[180] preached Buddhism in order to rebut Christian beliefs and, at the same time, to pacify the survivors of Amakusa. All this had the strong flavor of *kami* veneration. Within a period of three years, he was able to found 32 new temples and to register many pro-Christian residents. When he was convinced that the populace had been successfully guided to the safe haven of Buddhism, Shōsan left Amakusa after depositing a copy of his *Ha Kirishitan* (Christians countered) in each of its temples.[181] Suzuki Shōsan's pacificatory campaign was inherited by other Sōtōshū monks, who, with government support, continued to establish new Buddhist temples and to transform former Kirishitan into Buddhists.[182]

On the other hand, at the request of Inoue Masashige, the Kyoto Rinzaishū monk Sessō Sōsai (1589–1649) preached the "orthodox law" to the once Christianity-stricken residents of Nagasaki between 1647 and 1649. Sessō Sōsai's message, based on the argument that Christianity was a Buddhist heresy that was attempting to destroy Japan's cherished religious traditions (Buddhism, Shinto, and Confucianism), was quite direct: "Those who adhere to a religion that attempts to usurp sovereignty betray their own ruler and their obligations to their land. Those who do not venerate their ancestors disregard their own parents' virtue. Those who do not pray at the gods' mausoleum undercut the customs of the country to which they owe their very lives."[183] Under the patronage of the Nagasaki magistrate's office, Sessō Sōsai's preaching, according to one estimate, brought 18,000 residents back to Buddhism – the protector of the country of the gods. Out of respect for Sessō Sōsai's impressive work, the story has it that Shogun Iemitsu wanted to erect a special lecture hall in Nagasaki; however, Sessō Sōsai's sudden death precluded this.[184]

The pacification campaign, which made use of various strategies, was a laboratory within which good Buddhism was pitted against evil Christianity. In popular literature, Christianity was hopelessly demonized, as, for example, in the narratives of *Kirishitan monogatari* (Story of the Kirishitan), a chapbook on the rebellious Kirishitan of Amakusa and Shimabara. The *Kirishitan monogatari*, published in 1639 and widely circulated, helped to popularize a jarred image of how *bateren* and Kirishitan conspired to subjugate the country of the gods. More than 130 variants of this story awakened the populace to the evils of Christianity. As George Elison puts it, "Here the barbarian perfidy was stripped of its cloak, deceit disclosed, and truth revealed triumphant."[185]

Could this kind of propaganda firmly safeguard the Japanese from the intrusion of Christianity? As though testing the effectiveness of the anti-Christian pacification campaigns, the Portuguese again knocked at Japan's door in 1647, sending two vessels – one with 200 crew members and one with 128. The *bakufu*'s reaction to this was swift and resolute: "This barbarian country called Portugal . . . has come again even though trade is forbidden. This is because they worship Christianity." The shogunate immediately ordered the Kyūshū daimyo to deploy 898 ships, put more than 48,000 defense forces on alert, and then dispatched Masashige to Nagasaki.[186] Masashige was ordered to coordinate the forces of the Kyūshū daimyo and the Nagasaki magistrates. Upon arriving at Nagasaki, however, Masashige failed to find any signs that the Portuguese vessels were intent upon "attack and pillage." The Portuguese just wanted to reopen trade with Japan.[187] When they realized that, once again, they were not welcome, the Portuguese retreated without causing any trouble.

Nevertheless, the reappearance of Portuguese vessels was ominous enough to rekindle the nightmarish memory of the Amakusa-

Shimabara Rebellion. Inoue Masashige found himself losing his early confidence in his multilayered approaches to anti-Christianity, including his much-touted interrogatory strategy of pacification. Other *bakufu* officials also seemed to concur with him: "A debate is usually waged [between Kirishitan and officials] on the afterlife – for which neither side possesses proof – and it becomes a hammerheaded debate. Bystanders hear this and think that the officials are on the wrong side; and, worst of all, even retainers often believe that there must be some reason to the Christian sect."[188] It seemed that the method of pacification through doctrinal disputation had fundamental limits and that, indeed, it was even inherently dangerous, for Kirishitan were quick to drag their interrogators into debate and were good at presenting their well-reasoned arguments.

Worse, *bakufu* officials found that Buddhist proselytizers who were mobilized to join the pacification campaign were often more interested in their own religious gain than in the conversion of Kirishitan. For example, for many Buddhist monks who were sent to Kyūshū, Christian pacification provided a golden opportunity to erect new temples and to expand their sectarian bases with the support and protection of the public authorities. Many of them did not seriously tackle the doctrines of Christianity; rather, it appeared that some were more interested in attacking and criticizing rival Buddhist sects.[189]

Inoue Masashige was also troubled to find that the ways in which local daimyo handled the matter of Kirishitan were rarely coordinated: "Kirishitan go into hiding in those domains where the handling of Kirishitan is badly conceived. Because it is easy [for them] to blend into the populace, Kirishitan always manage to survive in those domains."[190] Dismayed at the loopholes of *magireyasuki* ("easy to blend into"), Masashige increasingly doubted that the strategy of "enlightening" (*kyōka*) Kirishitan through anti-Christian exhortation could fulfill the task of eradicating Christian elements. He felt that there should be more systematic and tangible methods of keeping the populace from slipping into Christianity. Where could he find these? He returned to conventional wisdom: "There are domains where the 'southern barbarian' oath and religious inspection are imposed upon the peasants, townsmen, and artisans, preventing Kirishitan from going into hiding."[191] Masashige convinced himself: in enforcing anti-Christianity, after all, the anti-Christian oath, temple certification, the reward system, the enforced trampling of Christian images, and the five-man group could do a far better job than any other method if they were executed more systematically and more thoroughly.[192]

For Inoue Masashige, of all these anti-Christian measures, temple certification, which had been tried out in various domains (Kumamoto, Ōmura, Saga, Hiroshima, Kanazawa, Takada, Mito, Yonezawa) and some shogunal lands such as Osaka, seemed most promising with regard to keeping the whole populace under check. Although he was not yet sure how this should be implemented at the national level across sectarian and domanial differences, Masashige cautioned that, no matter how it was put into practice, Buddhist temples must be wary when dealing with Kirishitan: "*Danna* temples should pay utmost attention when they inspect [their *danna* families], for Buddhist monks are often easily deceived."[193] The Buddhist funeral was regarded as a barometer for determining the non-Christian status of a *danna* family. However, as Masashige saw it, things were not that simple. Even though a Buddhist funeral might be conducted, cunning Kirishitan families could "put the body into a tub at home, place inside the tub a cross made of wooden pieces, tie the tub up tightly, and then bury it in the ground." Masashige warned that if one "exhumes the corpse and checks inside the tub, then one will sometimes discover a Kirishitan."[194] By the late 1640s, the practice of temple certification had yet to be refined as a system capable of solving all these tricky problems. It had a long way to go, but it was nonetheless quite clear to Masashige that the system of temple certification was the best option available.

It was indeed a long detour, but eventually things ended up coming back to where they had been four decades earlier: Buddhism was recognized to be the spiritual guardian of the country of the gods and it would protect it against the intrusion of Christianity. Details of how temple certification should be administered were still to be hammered out, and, as the Buddhist pacification campaign revealed, there were still questions about how to accommodate the "private" interests of Buddhist temples to the "public" cause of anti-Christianity. No less critical was the cooperation of the people who should, in theory, all become Buddhists. But by the end of the Iemitsu era, the direction of anti-Christianity was set.

Soon after Shogun Iemitsu died in 1651, a lampoon appeared on the Nihonbashi bridge in Edo: "Daiyūin-dono [the posthumous Buddhist name for Iemitsu], not in a particularly good mood, arrived at the abode of supreme bliss. . . . Even here [he was] quite bothered by [the matter of] investigating Kirishitan, and he wished that Inoue Chikugo no Kami [Inoue Masashige] could immediately cross the sea with a vow of compassion [for his rescue]."[195] The task that Iemitsu could not fulfill in his lifetime was left to the government of the next shogun, Ietsuna (r. 1651–80).

THREE

Population Surveillance
and Temple Certification, 1651–1709

From the outset, Shogun Ietsuna (r. 1651–80) encountered unwelcome challenges. In the seventh month of 1651, Matsudaira Sadamasa (1610–72), the Tokugawa-descended daimyo of the Kariya domain in Mikawa, tonsured himself and went about asking for alms on the streets of Edo to protest shogunal politics. Deploring the fact that too many *hatamoto* were being impoverished, Sadamasa indicated that he would soon return his fief, residences, and weapons to the *bakufu* in order to provide them with some relief. His eccentric behavior, though castigated as madness and punished with the confiscation of status, was a clear expression of dissatisfaction with the fact that power was too much concentrated in the top echelon of the samurai estate. A few days after the Matsudaira Sadamasa incident, a group of masterless samurai, led by Yui Shōsetsu (1605–51), conspired to stage simultaneous revolts in Edo, Osaka, and Kyoto. Their ill-fated plan, which quickly ended in a rampage of execution and suicide, nonetheless once again revealed the discontent that some samurai felt with regard to the high-handedness of shogunal politics.[196]

Despite a bumpy start, however, thanks to a strong bureaucratic apparatus, the Ietsuna government quickly established stability and led people into an era of peace and prosperity. Enthroned at the age of II, Ietsuna was unlike his strong-willed father and remained almost detached from government decision making in the 1650s; it was his entrusted aides and elders—such as Hoshina Masayuki, Sakai Tadakatsu, Matsudaira Nobutsuna, and Abe Tadaaki (1602–75)—who ran a commanding bureaucracy. With regard to governing style, these top bureaucrats promoted the rule of law, and they preferred to rely upon civil principles rather than upon the military.[197] This transition in the art of governing, from the martial arts (*bu*) to the civil arts (*bun*), set the direction of social engineering.

And so, in the 1650s, anti-Christian policies were increasingly implemented through the civil arts and decreasingly through fear of punishment. This new trend was first signaled by a shogunal directive that reemphasized civilian cooperation and public exhortation. In 1652, prizes awarded to those who informed on Christian missionaries were raised to 200 or 300 pieces (*mai*) of silver; two years later they were raised to 300 pieces for those who informed on padres and to 200 pieces for those who informed on brothers. By the end of the Ietsuna years the prizes were as much as 500 pieces for padres, 300 pieces for brothers, and 50 or 100 pieces for lay followers.[198] By the same token, the shogunate aggressively promoted a public awareness campaign, posting anti-Christian decrees on bulletin boards all over the country: "When one is . . . reported to have hidden a Kirishitan, the punishment shall fall upon all members of his five-man group."[199] This bulletin board campaign was a permanent feature of Ietsuna's anti-Christian policy.

Unfortunately, however, this soft approach to Christianity backfired in 1657, when a large number of Kirishitan were found in Koori village in the Ōmura domain in Kyūshū. Acting on a tip from a villager about an old woman's "suspicious" religious practices—which included the "worship of an image of Saint Mary in the mountain cave and the prophecy of the coming of a new world"—the Nagasaki magistrate and the domain government ransacked the whole village and, within two months, arrested 608 Kirishitan. The large roundups in the Ōmura domain, commonly known as Koori *kuzure* (collapse, or crumbling, in Koori), was the first of its kind and was to be followed by a raid on Bungo in 1660 and on Nōbi in 1661. While conducting an investigation, public authorities found that many residents in the area were quite sympathetic to the prophecy of the coming of a new world. It was a chilling reminder of the Amakusa-Shimabara Rebellion. In 1658 the government swiftly handed down harsh punishments to those found guilty: 411 were beheaded, 20 were sentenced to life in prison, and 78 died during the investigation. Only 99 were released free of charge.[200] In the aftermath, Buddhist funerary rites were imposed on the region and all of the Kirishitan graves were desecrated, with the bones of the deceased being thrown into the sea.

Alarmed that its laid-back anti-Christian policy had led to the fiasco of the Koori *kuzure*, the shogunate quickly moved to reshuffle its administrative organs of religious inspection. By the time those involved in the Koori *kuzure* was brought to punishment, Inoue Masashige, who, over the past decade, had advocated a pacificatory approach, was dismissed as inspector of Roman Catholicism (*Tenshukyō kōsatsu*) for "being senile." This was the post to which he had been appointed in the ninth month of 1657.[201] The architect of anti-Christian policy during the Iemitsu era could not survive the storm of Kirishitan revelation, which deeply disturbed other hard-line *bakufu* leaders. The shogunate then assigned Hōjō Ujinaga (1609–70), a military expert, to the office of shogunal religious inspector. Ujinaga, who was empowered with 6 mounted officials and 30 foot soldiers, quickly switched to a tough, systematic method of routing Kirishitan.[202] Ujinaga was convinced that, in order to put an end to the never-ending problem of Christianity, the government should systematically pursue an age-old strategy that combined surveillance and corporeal punishment. A few months after the departure of Masashige, Ujinaga played a key role in introducing two sets of shogunal decrees: one was issued in the third month of 1659 and ordered the reinvestigation of all Kirishitan, whether pardoned or imprisoned, and their family members and relatives; the other was issued in the sixth month of 1659 and instructed public authorities on how to keep the general populace under surveillance.

The first decree mainly aimed at collecting nationwide data on former Kirishitan and those related to them, whether through blood or marriage, so that, in the years to come, more centralized, comprehensive religious control would be possible. For that, the shogunate instructed the daimyo and shogunal deputies to thoroughly reinvestigate anyone under domestic confinement (*azuke*), whether he or she had been "found guilty of being a Kirishitan but pardoned owing to his or her confession of the crime" or whether he or she had been "found not guilty but still charged due to his or her insufficient disclaimer."[203] In all cases, officials were ordered to determine when and how those sentences had been handed down, how old the person in question had been at the time of sentencing, and his or her name, former employer, social status and current address, and to report the details of their investigation to the office of Hōjō Ujinaga.[204] Along with information on former Kirishitan, the shogunate added that "any information on the relatives and acquaintances of the convicted" should be collected and reported.[205] This was the beginning of a systematic method of collecting data on former Kirishitan and would be further refined throughout the late seventeenth century.

The second shogunal order, which Ujinaga delivered in the presence of State Councilor Matsudaira Nobutsuna to the messengers of the nation's daimyo (who were all summoned to gather at Edo Castle), presaged a long-term *bakufu* goal that would fully materialize in the Kanbun era (1661–72). After reiterating that the ban on Christianity should be strictly applied to everyone, including not only retainers and vassals but also minor servants, the order specified what should be done for those moving around in search of job opportunities—a transient population that, it was feared, might slip through the net of anti-Christian control: "At the time of the replacement of seasonal contract laborers, pay close attention to their guarantors and instruct [employers] to hire [them] only after scrutinizing their religious sect."[206] In the case of peasants and townspeople, it continued, "check their five-man groups and *danna* temples more closely, and when one is found to belong to a suspicious sect, [he or she] must be scrutinized."[207]

Two months after the issuance of the edict, in Hatori village in the Kōza county of Sagami, village officials pledged to the local government that five-man groups would be responsible for detecting Kirishitan, that each villager would acquire a religious certificate from his or her *danna* temple and submit it to the government office, and that anyone who wanted to hire seasonal laborers would do so only after the latter's religious affiliation had been cleared through an investigation of their home villages and *danna* temples.[208] This time, village officials in the Kantō region heeded the shogunal decree and reported that they would make sure that their villages were kept free of Christianity.

Amid all these reinvigorated anti-Christian efforts, however, the shogunate was again hit hard by a series of revelations in Bungo, Owari, and Mino. It seems that a large number of Kirishitan were not only still extant but also strongly united and well disguised. The

Bungo *kuzure* of Kyūshū, which first began in 1659 in Takata (presently Ōita City), a branch domain of the Hosokawa house of Kumamoto, spread into other domains in the province, including some villages under direct shogunal control, the Usuki domain, and the Oka domain. The extensive hunt for hidden Kirishitan—a hunt that, under the direction of the Nagasaki magistrate, lasted more than a decade—produced hundreds of death penalties and terrified the entire region.[209] Along with making arrests and conducting executions, shogunal authorities insisted that the entire population in the region be regularly subject to "trampling on Christian pictures and images"—an order for which domain governments were held accountable.[210]

On the other hand, throughout the 1660s, the Nōbi *kuzure* in Owari and Mino brought harsher punishment and more prolonged agony to those involved than had the Bungo *kuzure*. It was triggered in 1661 by Hayashi Gonzaemon, a *hatamoto* who held a fief in Mino and who reported to the Owari government that Kirishitan had been found in his estate. Upon hearing this report, the Owari government acted swiftly and arrested 24 Kirishitan. Alerted by the revelation of hidden Kirishitan, the shogunate soon dispatched inspectors to Mino and Owari and ordered an intensive manhunt. The Owari domain, which was now in crisis, instituted various anti-Christian measures, including the erection of 38 anti-Christian bulletin boards, the reorganization of the five-man group, and the insistence that Buddhist temples investigate new *danna* families. All these efforts resulted in the arrests of a large number of Kirishitan, most of whom were speedily beheaded—207 in 1664, 756 in 1667, 33 in 1669, and so on. Altogether more than 1,000 people perished.[211] The shogunate must have been shocked to learn that even the Owari domain, which belonged to one of the three Tokugawa collateral houses, was found to harbor so many Kirishitan. Once again, this kind of ongoing revelation of Kirishitan served to convince *bakufu* leaders that the problem of Christianity still existed and that it must be dealt with in a thoroughgoing manner.

The shogunate moved to strengthen its administrative machinery so that it could more effectively handle matters pertaining to Christianity. In early 1662, right after the first revelation of the Nōbi *kuzure*, it added one more senior official to the anti-Christian office: Yasuda Muneyuki, magistrate of construction (*sakuji bugyō*), was appointed to the post of inspector of Roman Catholicism. It is interesting that it was the magistrate of construction, not the magistrate of temples and shrines (*jisha bugyō*), who was assigned, along with the inspector general, to undertake the duties of religious inspection. This indicated that the shogunal administration had decided to deal with Christianity from a political perspective rather than from a religious perspective. The inspector general (Hōjō Ujinaga) was responsible for law enforcement, while the magistrate of construction (Yasuda Muneyuki) was responsible for supervising such public projects as shogunal castles, great temples, and shrines. Both of these offices, to which the responsibility of inspecting muskets and cannons, or *teppō aratame*, was added in 1698, had been directly involved in matters relating to policing and security.[212] As inspectors of Roman Catholicism, each of these men was provided with a shogunal force of 6 mounted officials and 30 foot soldiers. This stood in sharp contrast to the previous "semi-private" way in which the office operated, when Inoue Masashige had to rely upon his own vassals to perform his assigned tasks.[213] Armed with professional military personnel and strong shogunal support, inspectors of Roman Catholicism were fully prepared for the task of uprooting Christianity.

The administrative mechanisms for conducting anti-Christian national policy were being put in good order not only at the *bakufu* level but also at the domain level. As a preemptive measure, the Ietsuna regime first revised the Laws of Military Households in 1663, promulgated by Iemitsu in 1635, adding, for the first time, a strongly worded anti-Christian clause. Article 19 stated: "The Kirishitan sect shall be strictly forbidden in all domains and in all places."[214] In the following year, the *bakufu* proceeded to put this article, now written into the nation's highest law, into practice. The 1664 directive, delivered to all daimyo and shogunal administrators, was truly remarkable in that it provided an overarching framework for the nationwide administration of religious inspection.

After reminding people that, if a Kirishitan were to be discovered, then his or her village elder and five-man group would be subject to punishment, and that there might still be Kirishitan in hiding despite the recent "collapses," the *bakufu* explicitly spelled out how religious inspection should be executed in the daimyo domains (Article 1), in the shogunal estates (Articles 2 and 3), and in the lands of temples and shrines (Article 5), respectively.[215] In the case of daimyo domains (which were defined as a fief of more than 10,000 *koku*), the *bakufu* ordered the "installation [of full-time] officials to inspect the vassals of the [daimyo] house and the entire domain residents every year."[216] In the case of *hatamoto* carrying a fief of no more than 9,000 *koku*, it ordered that "the lords themselves must be responsible for closely examining their vassals, village heads and elders, and villagers, and, in addition, [they must] prepare the registers of five-man groups each year and be ready to submit them whenever the public authority so instructs." This lack of a requirement to install full-time religious inspectors stemmed from the understanding that *hatamoto* would, on their own, have great difficulty maintaining separate religious inspectors. With regard to temples and shrines, whether they had front districts or not, they were under the direction of the magistrate of temples and shrines, who were ordered to "scrutinize all personnel under their jurisdiction." In all cases, by "religious scrutiny" the shogunate meant temple certification. In addition to the task of implementing annual religious inspection, all officials were also instructed to "draw up a list of former Kirishitan who have been converted and submit it to Hōjō Awa no Kami (Ujinaga) and Yasuda Wakasa no Kami (Muneyuki)" (Article 4).[217] With this directive, the shogunate was able to establish a nationwide network of religious inspectors, known as superintendents of religious sects (*shūmon bugyō*), across the public and private fiefs and to put them under the direct supervision of the shogunal inspectors of Roman Catholicism.

As far as the matter of Christianity was concerned, all domains, whether they belonged to daimyo, *hatamoto*, or temples and shrines, were now put under the direct control of the shogunate. This was by no means a small encroachment upon the principle of domain autonomy, which the *bakuhan* system had always honored. As Nagasaki magistrate Kurokawa Masanao (in office between 1650 and 1665) reported in 1664, some domain officials, when appointed, refused to take the office of religious inspection, which had been established by shogunal order.[218] And this was not the only adverse reaction to the unilateral imposition of shogunal will: local domains were, or pretended to be, unsure of how to proceed. Inaba Kagemichi, caretaker of the Usuki domain (in lieu of his father Nobumichi, who was in Edo), wrote Masanao (Nagasaki magistrate) that there were simply not enough Buddhist temples to properly conduct religious inspection. Masanao wrote back: "For the area where there is no temple available nearby, erect one small temple per three, four, or five villages and install a Buddhist monk there. Inspection should be conducted to determine who in which village is certified by which temple of what sect."[219] No excuse was allowed.

The trouble was not that the temples lacked will; rather, it was that they tended to be abusive, and sometimes deceptive, in the manner in which they conducted religious inspection. "Under the pretext of inspecting Kirishitan, [some temples] give a hard time to trustworthy people when they are admitted as *danna*. Those temples that accept *danna* after receiving a gift or bribe shall be subject to punishment," the Owari government warned Buddhist monks in 1661.[220] Amid the panic of the Owari *kuzure*, non-Buddhist villagers rushed to associate themselves with Buddhist temples, and the latter took advantage of this. The government noticed that suspicious people were often made *danna* members upon agreeing to certain financial transactions, and it was not always easy to check the authenticity of such membership.[221] Temple certification in the 1660s remained somewhat fuzzy and troublesome, especially at the fringes.

However, shogunal leaders were not to be deterred. In early 1667, the *bakufu* dispatched special inspectors, commonly known as *shokoku junkenshi* (envoys for tours of inspection throughout the domains), to local domains and shogunal lands in order to check how strictly local governments were observing the shogunal anti-Christian edicts. Among other things, the *bakufu* charged the shogunal inspectors with scrutinizing "whether or not the manner of handling the Kirishitan sect [was] being executed without negligence."[222] Six groups consisting of three inspectors each, and accompanied by a retinue of more than 100 assisting officers, were scattered all over the country (except Kantō), which was divided into six circuits. To the Okayama domain, for example, three shogunal inspectors were dispatched in the first eight months. Upon arriving, they entered villages of their choice without being accompanied by domain officials, had face-to-face meetings with villagers in order to conduct inquiries, and checked first hand how religious inspection was being conducted.[223] For the local daimyo, shogunal inspection was not something that could be ignored; and when it touched the matter of Christianity, it could be deadly. Kirishitan, who had become almost non-existent by the late 1660s, played a key role in helping tip the conventional balance of power between the *bakufu* and the *han* decisively in the favor of the former.[224]

Under the bullish shogunal policy, the entire population became subject to annual religious scrutiny. Without proof of non-Kirishitan status one could not expect to be treated as a legitimate citizen. How seriously was the shogunal policy of anti-Christian inspection taken at the village level? The 1665 inspection roster of Senzushima village in Ashigarakami county of Sagami, for example, shows how village officials dealt with the matter of anti-Christian inspection. The village head and five-man group representatives, who cosigned the roster, pledged in the five-article preface (*maegaki*) that they would take joint responsibility for any error that might occur. Assuring the public authorities that their villagers had strictly obeyed the shogunal law, they declared that there was not a single Kirishitan in their village (this included all servants over the age of 15). As proof, they emphasized that all villagers, both men and women, had acquired non-Christian certificates that were issued and signed by the head monks of their *danna* temples. If the worst should happen (i.e., if a Kirishitan should be discovered), then signatories swore that "the head monk of his or her *danna* temple as well as the village head and elders, and the representative of his or her five-man group [would] come [to the government office] and answer [all questions]. If we are ordered to reinspect religious sects, we will do so. And [we will] recollect all temple certificates, [draw up a new roster], and submit it."[225] The *danna* temples' "crime" of hiding Kirishitan was clearly defined as a collective conspiracy by *danna* temples, village officials, and five-man group representatives. Furthermore, the signatories declared that they would immediately report any and all information concerning former Kirishitan, suspicious individuals, and those who conducted funerals without the approval of their *danna* temples.[226] All in all, deceit was impossible.

Interestingly, however, in a situation where Kirishitan were, in theory, non-existent, the immediate benefactor of this policy was not the government but, rather, the Buddhist temples. As shogunal officials realized, putting the Buddhist clergy in charge of temple certification was like throwing meat to a hungry tiger. There were almost no Buddhist "officials" who would shy away from capitalizing on this potential gold mine. Buddhist monks paid more and more attention to the "business" of religious inspection, which would automatically bring with it the inspectee's life-long commitment to "fee-generating" rituals and ceremonies related to death and ancestral veneration.

Not surprisingly, in the rush to grab customers, Buddhist temples were increasingly at odds over a limited pool of prospective *danna* families. Many temples adopted aggressive, sometimes abusive, tactics in their attempts to carve out new business niches while trying to consolidate their existing ones. On the other hand, temples with slim prospects for gaining new patrons often attempted to extract more financial contributions from the ones they already had. Over time, the unprecedented privileges granted to Buddhist institutions often spawned spoilage, corruption, and even exploitation.[227]

In 1665, the shogunate took steps to make amends for what it regarded as the "disorderly state of . . . all [Buddhist] sects" by issuing two sets of decrees on the same day. One was a nine-article shogunal order (*sadame*), and the other was a five-article injunction (*jōjō*) cosigned by four state councilors.[228] On the whole, these decrees aimed to address problems stemming from Buddhism's misuse of power and prerogatives, including its mistreatment of *danna* families. "One who does not understand the ritual procedures and doctrines of his Buddhist sect should not be appointed head monk of a temple in the first place," warned the shogunate, adding that "performing uncanny rites in the name of a new theory will not be tolerated."[229] In the mid-1660s, it was not unusual to find temples run by monks who were qualified neither by education nor by experience. In order to deal with this problem, the shogunal decree announced that "one who comes from nowhere shall not be allowed to denounce the world without permission, no matter how badly he wants to become a [Buddhist] disciple. In the case of unavoidable circumstances, report the situation to the lord or administrator of your place and follow his instructions."[230] This was an attempt to control the disorderly increase of Buddhist monks by providing regulations pertaining to the acceptance and training of candidates. In fact, as anti-Christian policies continued, an increasing number of people drifted toward Buddhism. Particularly for the uneducated and less fortunate, becoming a Buddhist monk offered both a livelihood and social power. Furthermore, this was a relatively easy career path, for, once accepted by the head monk of a temple, it was just a matter of time before the candidate would be officially ordained.

As Kumazawa Banzan (1619–91), an influential Confucian scholar of the Okayama domain, lamented, the prevalence of low standards inevitably led to there being few genuine monks: "maybe fewer than 100 in 10,000."[231] In most cases, the usual requirements for the official ordination of a monk candidate were apprenticeship and brief attendance at a local sectarian educational center (*inaka danrin*).[232] Some monks who were so ordained could not perform even the most basic rituals without having to refer to a manual.[233] The shogunate did not want to relegate the task of religious inspection to these illiterate, unfit Buddhist monks who were more interested in "decorating temple buildings lavishly and luring merchants and entertainers into temple precincts" than in Buddhist teachings per se. [234]

The shogunate also grew increasingly uneasy at the emerging relationship between Buddhist temples and *danna* families: "[The matter of choosing a *danna* temple], no matter which one it might be, should be left to the will of the *danna* patron. It is not a matter over which monks should compete with each other."[235] In an attempt to reverse the trend in which non-Christian-certificate-issuing temples wielded more and more power over their patron families, the shogunate tried to introduce checks and balances into the Buddhist politics of religious inspection.

Not only the central government but also the local governments heeded the working of temple certification, which seemed to be straying from its original course. In particular, three domain governments close to the shogunal family—Tokugawa Mitsukuni of Mito, Ikeda Mitsumasa of Okayama, and Hoshina Masayuki of Aizu—were determined to set things right. Needless to say, anti-Christianity itself was never a problem: what bothered, even outraged, these increasingly Confucian-minded lords was the fact that anti-Christian religious certification was somehow being carried out only through Buddhist temples. In an attempt to remedy the problematic monopoly of "Buddhist service," these lords launched in the late 1660s extensive reforms that involved "retrenching Buddhist temples" (*jiin seiri*).[236] It is interesting that no sooner had the nation-wide system of temple certification been realized than it was subjected to harsh criticism and revision. The reforms carried out in these domains, particularly the ones in Mito and Okayama, which directly challenged the effectiveness of, and even the rationale behind, Buddhist religious inspection, constituted a tough test for *shinkoku*-centered Buddhist service.[237]

In 1663, Tokugawa Mitsukuni ordered the head of each administrative unit in his domain to investigate, and submit detailed data on, all Buddhist temples and Shinto shrines, including information on landholding, tax exemption, sectarian affiliation, head temple, rank of monks, founder, year of establishment, and the number and social class of *danna* families. The data collected under the title *Mito kaikichō* (A Mito register of [religious] foundations) were arranged according to sectarian subcategories.[238] Two years later, Mitsukuni appointed two religious superintendents, conducted a thorough survey of the religious affiliations of the domain's residents, and inspected the financial status of temples and shrines. Findings from these surveys revealed that a vast majority of Buddhist temples were financially destitute. Among more than 2,000 temples, those with a landholding yielding fewer than five *koku* of rice were close to 90 percent, and those with no *danna* patrons exceeded 20 percent. Many of these petty temples were tended by absentee priests or unqualified monks. Worse yet, domain officials also found that many temples, which had been erected on taxable lands in violation of the shogunal ban on new temples, claimed tax exemption while promoting petty chicanery that passed itself off as Buddhist ritual and prayer.[239] Particularly annoyed with "ignorant monks with no knowledge—no one could be lower than them—who would do preposterous things, delude the people, harm the country, and ruin good customs and manners," Mitsukuni concluded that reforms were urgent.[240] In his view, the willy-nilly growth of Buddhist temples was, in the final analysis, attributable to the growing religious power and social influence of Buddhism that had been unleashed by the system of temple certification.

In the name of protecting legitimate funerary temples carrying out the solemn task of religious inspection, Mitsukuni ordered a crackdown in 1666 on all Buddhist institutions involved in running bogus prayer halls and engaging in spurious exorcisms: 712 temples were summarily demolished, and an additional 170 were closed when their monks were forced to return to the secular world. At the same time, small temples were incorporated into large ones, and temples left with no monks in residence were dismantled. Altogether, 1,098 temples, more than 50 percent of the total, disappeared at a stroke.[241]

The Mito government justified its draconian action by pointing out that a majority of the demolished temples were neither financially nor managerially viable and that, in any case, they were in violation of the shogunal ban on new temples. Temple properties affected by the retrenchment reforms were either transferred to the remaining temples or were disposed of by the government. The families who lost their *danna* temples were ordered to find new ones: "As soon as a temple is decided upon, the family [must] report to domain officials and immediately obtain a new religious certificate."[242] The "temple retrenchment" of Mito, which brought about the massive destruction of Buddhist temples, was an attempt to block the free ride that shogunal policy was providing for Buddhist institutions.

On the other hand, the Okayama domain, resonating with Kumazawa Banzan's staunch anti-Buddhist stance, went further than any other local government in that it even attempted to put an end to the system of temple certification. Disturbed by "too many Buddhist halls and too many world-renouncers," Banzan had urged from the mid-1650s that the number of monks and Buddhist temples be trimmed down.[243] Ikeda Mitsumasa's critical view that current Buddhist teachings had strayed far from what Gongen-sama (Ieyasu) had envisioned as a religion of "public service" intensified and eventually pushed him to take radical measures, which included the introduction of Confucian-style death rituals and the pruning of Buddhist temples.[244] The anti-Buddhist policy peaked in 1666–67, when more than 800 monks were defrocked and 563 temples—close to 60 percent of a total of 1,044 Buddhist temples—were demolished. Compared to the Shingonshū, which lost about 45 percent of its 401 temples, the Nichirenshū, which continued to defy secular authority, lost close to 90 percent of its 397 temples.[245] Although the anti-Buddhist Confucian critics in the domain suggested the idea of removing bogus prayer halls and the illegal structures within which esoteric rituals were being conducted, Mitsumasa paid more attention to subjugating those Buddhist institutions emboldened either by their own political stance or by the system of temple certification.

Mitsumasa's disgust with the "arrogance and luxury" of power-wielding Buddhist temples eventually drove him to initiate a radical change to the system of temple certification. In 1666, he ordered domain residents to submit new non-Christian certificates according to the following format:

I, a Shingon sect [for example] follower for generations, was a *danna* of ____ temple in ____ village in ____ county. But as I have understood Confucianism and learned Shinto, on the ___th day of the ___th month, I came to discard the Law of the Buddha and then to conduct Confucian worship rituals and to have faith in the tutelary deity [*ikidokoro no kami*] of Shinto. Thus, I hereby submit a [non-Christian] certificate I have obtained from ____ Shinto priest.[246]

Immediately after the order to procure Shinto certification (called Shintōuke, or *shinshokuuke*), Okayama residents began to abandon their Buddhist certificates. According to a government survey conducted in 1669, it appeared that more than 95 percent of the domain residents had switched to Shinto certification.[247]

On the surface, the *bakufu* did not seem agitated by this drastic measure on the part of the Okayama domain—a measure that seemed to go against long-standing shogunal policy. When Mitsumasa first reported this new measure to Great State Councilor Sakai Tadakiyo (1624-81), the latter expressed his concern that the Okayama policy, particularly with regard to Buddhist monks, might invite others to follow it, and that, if that happened, then it might cause great confusion and turmoil. But Tadakiyo stopped short of clearly disapproving of it; rather, he advised that, since the Okayama policy was somewhat different from "the great law of the heaven" (i.e., the shogunal position), Mitsumasa further discuss the matter with other state councilors. However, their overall reaction was rather insipid: they were neither negative nor positive. Councilor Abe Tadaaki (1602-75) was the only one who said that he doubted whether there were so many "corrupted" monks in the Okayama domain as was being argued.[248] In the end, Mitsumasa failed to obtain strong endorsement from *bakufu* leaders, but he decided to assume that Tadakiyo had given him tacit approval and, thereupon, proceeded to persuade Hōjō Ujinaga and Yasuda Muneyuki (inspectors of Roman Catholicism) to approve his plan to have Shinto priests conduct religious inspection. The inspectors eventually gave their approval to this new type of religious inspection in Okayama, saying that there would be no other option for those residents who had already discarded Buddhism.[249]

Mitsumasa, relieved by the lack of shogunal interference, pressed his new policy upon the populace more strictly, turning an annual inspection into a monthly one. He boasted that the upgraded inspection, which would ensure that detailed statistics on new deaths and births were available on a monthly basis, would allow officials to trace family changes more thoroughly than had been possible before. In addition, he pointed out that, unlike most of the Buddhist monks who came and went according to the terms of their appointment or contract, sedentary Shinto priests would have a firm knowledge of local residents generation after generation and, thus, would be able to perfect anti-Christian inspection.

What happened to those families who were forced to obtain non-Christian certificates from Shinto priests? Did they all switch from Buddhism to Shinto when dealing with their deceased family members? As a matter of fact, when Mitsumasa imposed Shinto certification, he was kind enough to offer detailed instructions as to how to perform Shinto funerals (*shinsōsai*).[250] Since much of the criticism of Buddhist institutions was related to the manner in which Buddhist death rituals fed off forced religious inspections, one might wonder if the Shinto inspections would prove to be any different.

Interestingly, however, even after most domain residents were put under the anti-Christian jurisdiction of Shinto shrines, Shinto rituals for the deceased were rarely conducted. As Tamamuro Fumio notes in his analysis of documents found in Takehara village in Jōdō county recording the deaths of Kirishitan descendants between 1666 and 1687, the Shinto inspection did not result in a single Shinto ritual being performed, even for these closely watched "pseudo-criminals." Instead, we read this sort of thing: "This woman died of disease at the age of 24 in 1670 and was buried according to a Confucian ritual." Of 69 people who died during this period, 11 were buried according to Confucian rituals while 58 were buried according to Buddhist rituals—84 percent of the total.[251] Swayed by the ideological leadership of Ikeda Mitsumasa and Kumazawa Banzan, some domain residents switched to Confucian rituals; however, the vast majority kept to Buddhist rituals.

Because Shinto funerals were never seriously adopted, Shinto priests, unlike Buddhist monks, had no incentive to enforce religious inspections upon residents. This would only have cost time and administrative resources without much benefit. It must be remembered that for religious practitioners in Tokugawa society, funeral and ancestral rites were a major source of income. From the beginning, Shinto funerals were not a practical alternative to Buddhist funerals for the simple reason that Shinto was extremely sensitive to any source of pollution, and death was the most defiling pollution of all. Not surprisingly, Shinto priests were unenthusiastic about serving the deceased.[252] Nor, in terms of religious service, was Confucianism any more applicable than Shinto: it failed to play any significant role in mortuary rites in Tokugawa Japan (although it did so in China and Korea, where Chu Hsi's *Family Rituals* dominated funerary services). Consequently, Buddhism remained the most effective weapon with which to counter the Christian message of life after death.[253]

Mitsumasa did not push the people to desert Buddhism; rather, he was quite concerned that people might misconstrue his intentions and thoughtlessly abandon all Buddhist ideas and practices, particularly those associated with ancestral veneration. He advised: "One who is a follower of Shinto or Confucianism is fine. One who is not, however, should not discard [his/her] Buddhist temple without reason . . . If a [family] grave is established in a temple, one, even if a practitioner of [Shinto and Confucianism], should send things [to the temple] as before."[254] The Okayama government realized that Shinto inspections could only be enforced at the point of a bayonet. On top of that, state councilor Toda Tadamasa (1632–99) warned Mitsumasa in 1687 that, "although Shinto, Confucianism, and Buddhism all provide service to the shogunal house, religious inspection should be unified with temple certification."[255] In the same year, the Okayama domain eventually declared that, without exception, samurai, peasants, merchants, and artisans would all be subject to temple certification.[256] Thus Okayama's Shinto inspections amounted to nothing more than a short-lived political experiment.

As a matter of fact, institutionally as well as philosophically, Shinto shrines in the late seventeenth century fell far short of being able to handle the task of religious inspection. This is clearly illustrated by a 1663 survey of Shinto shrines in the pro-Shinto Mito domain. This survey—probably the only available source of information on the state of Shinto institutions (e.g., landholdings, deities, priests, buildings, and management) at the village level during this period—explains why Shinto inspection could not be sustained. The Mito data show that many villages in the domain did not have any Shinto shrines. Among more than 500 villages, only 186 had village tutelary shrines (*chinju*, or *chinjusha*). On average, there was slightly more than one Shinto shrine for every three villages, compared with four Buddhist temples (two after the retrenchment policy) for each village.[257] On top of that, many shrines were involved in the worship of Buddhist rather than Shinto deities, and they were being run by Buddhist monks rather than by Shinto priests.

In order to elevate the status of Shinto in village life, Tokugawa Mitsukuni advocated a policy in 1666 that aimed to establish at least one tutelary Shinto shrine in each village, and his successor, Tokugawa Tsunaeda (1656–1718), was seriously engaged in cleansing existing Shinto shrines of Buddhist elements. After a strenuous, long-term effort, the domain government found that its goal had been almost fulfilled by 1696: Shinto shrines had increased from 186 to 593 for 575 villages—at least one shrine for each village.[258] This statistical match, however, did not necessarily mean that all Shinto shrines were prepared to serve as public agents for Shinto inspection. As is shown in the 1696 survey results, compiled under the title of *Chinjuchō* (Register of tutelary shrines), about one-fifth of the shrines still housed Buddhist images as their main deities, and about two-fifths of them were controlled by Buddhist monks rather than by Shinto priests. In addition, more than 30 shrines lacked serving priests and were collectively administered by villagers. The domain government was successful in forcing 72 percent of the shrines to replace their Buddhist images with the "deity bodies" (*shintai*) of Shinto (278 shrines were consecrated with cloth [*hei*] and 35 with mirrors [*kagami*]), but more than one-fourth of the shrines still remained Buddhist.[259] As far as Shinto inspection was concerned, almost half of the shrines were found not to be ready.

Despite challenges and resistance, the system of temple certification had gained a firm foothold at the national level by the end of the 1660s. It is ironic that religious inspection was fully implemented as national policy precisely when its original cause—the problem of Christianity—had virtually ceased to exist. By the end of the 1660s, Kirishitan had been almost entirely wiped out, and Christian missionaries had not tried to infiltrate Japan since 1644 (except for Giovanni Battista Sidotti, an Italian missionary who was caught soon after stepping onto Japanese soil in 1708 and who remained in the Kirishitan *yashiki* prison until his death in 1715).[260] *Bakufu* leaders no longer considered Christianity to be a real threat to the Tokugawa polity; nonetheless, they decided to continue their efforts to eliminate any remaining Kirishitan, no matter how hard they were to find.

In early 1671, the shogunal office of anti-Christianity ordered local government officials to closely watch seasonal servants and laborers. The guarantors of these migrants were to conduct strict annual religious inspections and to report the results to their local officials. At the same time, the *bakufu* repeated that, if a Kirishitan were to be discovered, then the head of the village and the members of his or her five-man group would be subject to joint punishment.[261] Then, in the tenth month of the same year, the shogunate (the office of financial superintendents) further specified to the administrative intendants (*daikan*) of the shogunal lands how the census register of religious inspection should be conducted and reported:

The offices of intendants should pay attention to the matter of the inspection of the Christian sect and direct it without negligence [in their domains]. From now on, record the households of peasants on the population register one by one; tally the number of males and females for each village, county, and province; and, from now on, without negligence, make sure that [you] make and keep a register for your record and forward a one-page report to this office as was done this year. It goes without saying that for men and women under your jurisdiction who move to other places for marriage or employment, inspection records should accompany them. Of course, reductions due to death and to people moving in from elsewhere—[all these changes], except those pertaining to monks, should be recorded, including the sex and age of each person.[262]

After reminding the shogunal deputies that the register was "not just for sectarian inspection only, but also for checking all other matters," the shogunate added: "Make the [upcoming] inspection known [to residents] from the spring or summer, and conduct it in the fall when assistant officials [from the office of intendants] are dispatched for calculating the level of annual taxes or collecting them."[263] This edict, which was signed by three superintendents of finance at the shogunal government and addressed to the administrative deputies of the shogunal lands, soon served for a nationwide guideline for the "register of sectarian inspection."

The register of sectarian inspection, which was commonly referred to as *shūmon aratamechō*, *shūshi aratamechō*, or (rarely) *fumiechō* or even *shūmon aratame goninchō*, was the endpoint of the evolution of temple certification—all residents of Tokugawa Japan were now annually registered and their non-Kirishitan identity individually confirmed by the government. Within this administrative apparatus, which, by the late seventeenth century, was streamlined, village and ward officials throughout the country were all required to record, based on the anti-Kirishitan inspection carried out by *danna* temples, all residents under their jurisdiction and to submit these names to the government. Those who were not registered had no place in Tokugawa Japan—at least, not until the system of temple certification was officially abolished and replaced with a new family registration act in 1871.

The standard format of entries in the "register of sectarian inspection," which was suggested in the *Hōnen zeisho*, a guidebook for local administration compiled in 1685, was as follows.[264] All members belonging to a household unit, regardless of their family or non-family relationship, were recorded on the register in order of household head, spouse, children, and other members (including servants and employees as long as they shared the same residence); and each household unit was then arranged from right to left. Entries for each member of a household unit included, from top to bottom, the names of the Buddhist sect and temple with which he or she was affiliated, the stamp of the temple's head monk, his or her name, and the stamp of the household head. At the end of each household unit, the total number of its members was indicated. At the end of the register, the number of residents, who were categorized by Buddhist sect, was indicated, along with the names of their temples. Finally, the village or ward head put his name and stamp on the document, along with the names and stamps of other village or ward officials.

Since the register of sectarian inspection was compiled for the purpose of identifying the religious status of each resident, the village or ward head was supposed to enter people on the register when they brought a certificate issued by the head of their *danna* temple, who was officially in charge of confirming their non-Kirishitan status. This was the design that the shogunal government had originally intended to implement, but it eventually gave way to a procedure in which the village or ward head first compiled a register and temple heads then endorsed the non-Kirishitan status of their *danna* members by putting their stamp under the latter's names. With regard to a village or ward head, there were three ways to obtain from Buddhist *danna* temples the "temple stamp," which was usually done between the end of the year and the third month of the following year. The first involved village or ward heads summoning all related monks to their residences on a prearranged date, to have them check a newly compiled register, and to conduct a ceremony of seal-stamping that was usually followed by a feast; the second involved village or ward officials traveling to each of the related temples and obtaining their stamps on their registers; and the third involved the ward or village head asking the heads of all related *danna* temples to come to their residences at their convenience and to stamp the registers for their respective *danna* patrons.[265] In the case of the third option, for example, as Nagura Tetsuzō notes in his examination of the Ganshōji diary (1846–66) in Kakudahama village in Echigo, the head monk of the temple usually had to spend a whole month or more on the road just to carry out the job of "temple stamping" for *danna* patrons (who were scattered over a number of villages).[266]

Once he made two copies of the annual register (the original one, which contained all the necessary stamps, and its duplicate), the village or ward head immediately had to submit the original to the government. The duplicate copy, which was kept at his office, was used as a memorandum for writing any changes during the coming year (e.g., deaths, births, marriages, adoptions, and the like) in red ink. All of these changes were to be reflected in a new register, which would be compiled in the new year.[267] The government offices were inundated every year with piles of registers of sectarian inspection from every single village and ward under their jurisdiction. It is said that government officials did not really care about verifying the contents of the registers since it was assumed that the wards and villages were Kirishitan-free. The copies of these collected registers were usually discarded or used as scrap paper after three or four years had elapsed.[268]

The submission and collection of registers of sectarian inspection, however, did not follow the same administrative chain of order, even though local governments were all required to report the results of inspections to the magistrates of temples and shrines at the shogunate.[269] In the case of daimyo domains, village or ward heads submitted the registers to the county intendants, who would summarize the inspection results for the domanial office of temples and shrines, which would collect all inspection results in the domain and report them to the *bakufu*. In the case of shogunal lands under the supervision of intendants, the inspection results were delivered to the shogunal magistrates of temples and shrines through the superintendents of finance, who collected all reports directly from the intendants. On the other hand, the inspection results from the Edo wards were collected by the city magistrates; those from remote urban centers were collected by their respective magistrates; and those from temple or shrine lands were collected by their respective intendants. In all cases, no matter where they originated or where they were collected, each year the inspection results throughout the country ended up with the magistrates of temples and shrines at the shogunate.[270] The administrative paths pertaining to the annual compilation of anti-Christian registers mirrored the patchwork-like form of governance in Tokugawa Japan.

Moreover, because the shogunate delegated much of the register of sectarian inspection to the discretion of local governments, the actual execution of this inspection and its recordkeeping were not standardized.[271] It is known that the registers of sectarian inspection were very scant in the Tōhoku, Shikoku, and Kyūshū regions, and that they are so far missing in Satsuma and Tosa. In the case of Chō-shū, they seem to have been compiled until the mid-eighteenth century, but no traces of them are found thereafter. It is, however, known that the Chōshū government had switched to compiling a census register of its own called *tojaku*.[272] Some domains, probably due to high infant mortality, did not record children until they reached a specific age: in the case of the Kaga domain, this age was 15, while in the Kishū and Hiroshima domains, it was nine. In spite of the principle of annual registration, there were some discrepancies: some domains conducted it twice a year, some every other year, some once every three years, and some were even more sporadic.[273]

What varied was not only the manner in which the register of sectarian inspection was compiled but also its content. Most commonly, the registers contained such information as temple affiliation (temple's sect and name), age, gender, and family relationship. But some registers added more information, such as province of ancestral origin (*hongoku*) and birth (*shōkoku*), landholding (*kokudaka*), occupation, farm animals owned, and so on. Some registers were so detailed that they provided detailed information on servants or seasonal workers who moved in or out of the household, on those who married in or out, and on those who were adopted in or out.[274] It should be emphasized, however, that despite some local variations, the annual compilation and submission of anti-Christian registers was a nationwide phenomenon until the end of the Tokugawa period.

As mentioned before, the shogunal requirement regarding the register of sectarian inspection was fully enforced upon the nation's daimyo and all other governing entities whenthe Kirishitan population was already wiped out. Under these circumstances, most notably between the Genroku (1688–1703) and the Kyōhō eras (1716–35), the register of sectarian inspection was gradually transformed into the census register of sectarian inspection (known as *shūmon nin-betsuchō* or *shūmon ninbetsu aratamechō*) when it incorporated the function of census register, or *ninbetsuchō*.[275] *Ninbetsuchō* (also called *ninbetsu aratamechō*, *nayosechō*, or *ninjuchō*) refers to the census register that, since 1591, had been drawn, along with *kenchichō* (cadastral register), from each village in the country for such administrative purposes as taxation, military recruitment, and social order.[276] Given that no Kirishitan could be found, the function of the register of sectarian inspection was virtually no different from that of the census register. The natural merging of these two constituted an adjustment that indicated that religious registration was now being used for administration purposes rather than for anti-Christian surveillance.

Nevertheless, the insistence on the register of sectarian inspection allowed the shogunate to keep the domain governments under check. The nationwide chains of order that subjugated the populace, Buddhist temples, village and ward officials, and local governments to the anti-Christian policy of annual religious inspection contributed to upholding shogunal authority.[277] By the time of Ietsuna's death in 1680, the system of temple certification, which entailed the annual compilation of sectarian inspection, had been almost perfected, and Tokugawa Japan seemed secure from Christianity.

Ironically, however, the destruction of Christianity diminished significantly the original rationale for religious inspection, and this raised the question of how to justify its perpetuation. This was the task that Shogun Tsunayoshi (r. 1680–1709) inherited from Ietsuna. Tsunayoshi, who knew that he must show his loyalty to ancestral law, approached the problem by making the census registration of sectarian inspection even more thorough than it already was. Three of his measures deserve attention: the scapegoating of Kirishitan descendants who had nothing to do with the Christian faith—a practice that had been tried, if only partially, during the late Kan'ei era, in which all relatives of convicted Kirishitan were closely monitored for the rest of their lives;[278] controlling Buddhist temples through suppressing the defiant Fujufuse sect; and further strengthening the joint responsibility of the five-man group.

With regard to the first measure, the *bakufu* decided in 1687 to draw up a nationwide register of all former Kirishitan and their descendants and relatives and to subject them all to special surveillance. The eight-article edict, issued to the nation's daimyo in the seventh month, spelled out how public authorities should categorize former Kirishitan, and anyone related to them through blood or marriage, as Kirishitan "family groups" (*ruizoku*).[279] Specifically, regarding *korobi* Kirishitan, the shogunate ordered local governments to thoroughly investigate when they had abandoned their Christian faith; whether or not they had informed against their fellow Kirishitan in order to achieve exoneration; how they had been treated; and how they had made a living. Concerning the children of *korobi* Kirishitan, the shogunate stated that those born before their parents converted should be treated in the same manner as were their parents (*honnin dōzen*) and that those born after should be classified as *ruizoku*. Repeating that all former Kirishitan were, after conversion, supposed to be affiliated with Buddhist temples, the shogunate then directed their *danna* temples to check whether or not former Kirishitan had fulfilled their duties as funerary patrons (e.g., by sending fees and gifts, attending a memorial service for their deceased parents, or erecting a Buddhist altar at their homes).[280] If a Kirishitan or a suspicious person were found, the edict continued, then the responsible shogunal deputy or daimyo was to report immediately to the shogunal inspectors of Roman Catholicism (with the informer to be rewarded in cash and protected from retaliation). The shogunate also ordered that, if any Kirishitan *ruizoku* were to move to other domains, then a record should be kept of their movements. Finally, the shogunate specified what should be done when a death occurred: if the person were a former Kirishitan, then the body should be salted first and then handled according to shogunal instructions; if the person were a *ruizoku*, then his/her *danna* temple should take responsibility for inspecting his/her death, updating his/her record, and making a report to the shogunate.[281]

Upon shogunal orders, in 1688, all the nation's daimyo began to submit to the *bakufu* two registers (one for survivors, the other for the dead) pertaining to Kirishitan *ruizoku*.[282] According to Shimizu Hirokazu, who examined the registers of 74 domains collected in the *Kyōto oboegaki* (Memoranda of Kyoto), they numbered 75,988 (52,838 were alive, and 23,150 were dead), and more than 70 percent of them were from Kyūshū.[283] Needless to say, these people were no longer Kirishitan; however, they had to be scrutinized simply because they were descendants of former Kirishitan (often at the remove of two or three generations). Once they had been registered and accused of carrying the blood of Kirishitan, there was virtually no way for these innocent but unfortunate *ruizoku* to avoid heavy social discrimination: they were strictly subjected to surveillance for five generations (if they were a direct descendent of a *korobi* Kirishitan) and for three generations (if they were other *ruizoku*).[284] Public authorities treated them as traitors, and ordinary people shunned them. The detailed regulations pertaining to the Kirishitan *ruizoku*, which the shogunate reintroduced in 1695, were particularly stifling. Twice a year local officials were required to report to the *bakufu* anything that occurred in the lives of Kirishitan *ruizoku*, from being born, marrying, moving, adopting a child, renouncing the world, running away, getting a criminal conviction, getting a divorce, changing a name, changing Buddhist sectarian affiliation, to dying.[285] The Kirishitan *ruizoku* were like social prisoners on permanent probation, as is evidenced by the *bakufu*'s repeated insistence upon receiving reports on them.[286]

The second measure that the Tsunayoshi regime took in order to make religious inspection more thorough was to make sure that the Law of the Buddha faithfully served the Law of the King. All Buddhist sects but one—the Fujufuse subsect of Nichirenshū—showed their willingness, and even eagerness, to follow the shogunal order. However, the Fujufuse, which took a "no-taking, no-giving" stance toward the nonbelievers in the *Lotus Sūtra*, was unyielding: it resisted on the grounds that there should be no communication whatsoever with nonbelievers, including political authorities. Fujufuse leaders maintained that, as far as their faith was concerned, the Law of the Buddha stood above the Law of the King.[287] In 1691 the shogunate struck back resolutely: "The Fujufuse of the Nichiren Sect has been banned, but calling itself Kominato Tanjōji, Himon'ya Hokkeji, Yanaka Kannōji, or Hidenshū [Lands of Compassion subsect], it still spreads the wicked teachings of 'no taking, no giving.' Now the followers of Hidenshū are strictly prohibited."[288] Along with this ban, the shogunate banished some active Fujufuse monks and ordered their followers to change their sectarian affiliation. The Fujufuse subsect was castigated as a "criminal" group—and it had no option but to go underground. Until the end of the Tokugawa period, the *bakufu*'s repeated condemnation and punishment of the covert Fujufuse subsect served as a standing warning to all Buddhist sects: the Law of the King was to prevail over the Law of the Buddha.

As a third measure, Tsunayoshi decided in 1694 to strengthen the five-man group. He decreed that a clause pertaining to annual religious inspection be added to the preface of the five-man group register (*goningumichō*): "The register of sectarian inspection should be submitted by the third month of every year. In case someone is found belonging to a sect banned by law, a report on him or her should immediately be made. Observe what the public bulletin board says and conduct religious inspection with attention. In the case of servants or laborers who are hired after the [regular] religious inspection, the record of their temple certificates should be kept separately."[289] All residents were turned into vigilant agents who were obliged to watch out for each other.

By the time Tsunayoshi died in 1709, the Tokugawa shogunate was secure from Christianity: Christian elements had been rooted out and anti-Christian religious inspection was the law of the land. The only possible Kirishitan remnants consisted of those who went underground and disappeared completely from the public gaze. In the late Tokugawa and early Meiji periods, the existence of these people was confirmed in Nagasaki, the regions of Sotome and the Gotō Archipelago, the islands Hirado and Ikitsuki, the Amakusa islands, Imamura, and (rarely) in Takatsuki of Settsu, and in the Nanbu and Sendai domains. It is estimated that they numbered between 30,000 and 35,000. But these people did not reveal their true religious colors until the end of the Tokugawa period. Furthermore, the strict secrecy, isolation, and self-sufficiency that was crucial to their survival eventually transformed their "Christian" religion into something quite other than was normally understood as constituting Christianity.[290] Deprived of priests and cut off from the sources of their faith, over time these underground Kirishitan ended up merging vestigial Christian elements (i.e., *orashio* prayers in Latin, baptism, certain rites, and the like) into a sort of folk creed built upon "multi-layered beliefs, ancestor worship, orientation towards worldly benefits, and ritualism."[291]

All in all, the entire country was subjugated to the absolute mandate of anti-Christian politics—all in the name of protecting the divine country of the gods through perfecting the administrative apparatus of Buddhism. Buddhist institutions set themselves up as trusted anti-Christian agents, and, in return, they succeeded in turning the entire population into loyal Buddhist patrons who would remain within the *danka* system. Anti-Christianity, in alliance with Buddhism, was an institutional fixture of Tokugawa Japan.

Conclusion

It is ironic that temple certification, which was designed to remove Christian elements from the country of the gods, was fully implemented only after Christianity had already been eliminated. In a situation where the threat of Christianity had ceased to exist, the *bakufu* used temple certification as a mechanism for tightening its control of the nation's daimyo and populace. Similarly, the domain governments, which faithfully followed the shogunal policy of anti-Christianity, used the system of temple certification as leverage for strengthening their own authority and enforcing their domestic reforms.[292] Political calculations were dictated by the shifting needs of different times, but the result was what *bakufu* leaders had been pursuing for more than half a century—the subjection of the entire Japanese population to annual temple certification. During this time, tens of thousands of people were tortured, punished, imprisoned, or executed because of their ill-fated religious affiliation. The Amakusa-Shimabara Rebellion alone claimed the lives of nearly 28,000 people, while another 10,000 to 20,000 perished on the scaffold.[293] The institutionalization of temple certification was slow and extremely brutal.

The social life of the Tokugawa Japanese was absolutely dependent upon temple certification. If one were severed from it, then not only would one be deprived of one's citizenship, but one would also jeopardize the lives of one's family and relatives. Interestingly, however, in imposing this comprehensive shogunal policy upon the nation in the name of "public authority" (*kōgi*), the shogunate compromised its own sovereign authority by granting Buddhist monks the right to inspect people's religious life. Why did the shogunate have to delegate part of its sovereignty to Buddhist monks?

The involvement of Buddhist monks in religious inspection reflected both ideological politics and the reality of the shogunal administrative apparatus. The idea of the country of the gods being protected by Buddhist service, which had originated in the medieval period, was first employed in the form of religious certification for the *korobi* Kirishitan. Once religious certification was found to be effective, public authorities began to apply it to ordinary residents. By the mid-1660s, the entire population of Tokugawa Japan had to declare itself Buddhist. Temple certification started as a tiny seed, and it eventually produced a forest that overwhelmed the entire land.

In theory, the idea of a national policy that would unilaterally affect all daimyo domains was not compatible with the *bakuhan* arrangement of political power, which featured "an intricate web of overlapping authorities." For example, as Mark Ravina notes, "Although bound by ties of vassalage to the shogun, the daimyo of great domains simultaneously saw themselves as sovereign lords."[294] As far as "domestic" affairs were concerned, even the daimyo of small domains, including *fudai* daimyo, were highly protective of their local interests. It is true that, for security and subsistence, many small domains, now freed "from their Sengoku fear" of the stronger, needed the protection of a strong shogunate; nonetheless, they were unwilling to subordinate local autonomy to shogunal authority.[295] In taking measures that might unilaterally encroach upon domain autonomy, the shogunate had to be cautious. A balance of power that favored the *bakufu* over the *han* was not something that was written in stone, as was evidenced by a shift in *bakuhan* politics that was set in motion in the mid-nineteenth century and that eventually led to the collapse of the Tokugawa *bakufu* itself. In this sense, the Tokugawa polity was always subject to the tension and balance between central and local "sovereignties," and this involved an ongoing process of negotiation.[296] Besides, as far as shogunal power over people's religious life was concerned, the shogunate simply did not have the administrative ability to keep an eye on all domain territories.

Its use of Buddhist institutions, which was gradually expanded, helped the *bakufu* bypass the structural constraints of the *bakuhan* system. By the late seventeenth century, Buddhist temples, relatively free from the binding principles of *bakuhan* politics, had already penetrated every corner of the country and had firmly been bound up with the shogunal authority. As an agent for administrating anti-Christian certification on a national level, there was, in fact, no better option than Buddhist monks and their institutions. They were the best option not only because of their comprehensive administrative network (which could be mobilized at no extra cost) but also because of their independent and superior status (which gave them supervisory authority over the general populace).

Indeed, being separated from ordinary residents, Buddhist monks could command special status due partly to their own system of law and organization as well as to their traditional connections with the imperial court. Although bound by a series of regulatory measures issued by the *bakufu*, the final authority concerning Buddhist titles and ranks continued to rest either with the imperial court or with imperial abbacy temples known as *monzeki*. This system gave Buddhism extra clout and prestige over secular politics.[297] Although it is true that the previous authority of the *monzeki* had been significantly depleted during the Tokugawa period, some of them, particularly the newly created Rinnōji *monzeki*, still commanded respect and exerted strong influence.[298] As long as it had to obtain (if only nominally) its shogunal title from the imperial court, the Tokugawa shogunate could not afford to entirely ignore imperial authority. Consequently, it decided to integrate Buddhism into its governing structure through the system of temple certification. Buddhist institutions offered the shogunate a cost-free way of exerting socio-religious control over the populace.

When Kirishitan were discovered in the 1660s having survived in disguise in some pockets of the Kyūshū and Owari-Mino areas, *bakufu* leaders were very much disturbed. In particular, the Koori *kuzure* was ominous enough to bring back the memory of the Ama-kusa-Shimabara Rebellion and to remind people of the danger of renegade Kirishitan. Through temple certification and the surveillance of Kirishitan family groups, the shogunate resolved to keep an eye on the movements of its people. Beyond controlling their religious life, the shogunal government wanted to ensure that people did not have too much freedom of movement.[299] This policy was intended to ensure social order and, at the same time, to foster the stability of the "household" — the institution upon whose taxes the Tokugawa system ultimately depended. Buddhist institutions, which bridged the domains of religion, society, and the state, were an integral part of the Tokugawa system itself.

No matter how they were integrated, however, Buddhist temples did not passively lend their services to the shogunate. On the contrary, once they came to wield the power of religious inspection, Buddhist temples quickly moved to ensure that the recipients of non-Christian certificates became their funerary patrons. For Buddhist institutions, temple certification was, more than anything else, an effective means of securing religious patrons in the name of anti-Christianity. Within this environment, the entire population of Japan was subjected to Buddhist funerary practices. And this, in turn, gave rise to the *danka* system. By the turn of the seventeenth century, the *danka* system had become another social reality with which the Japanese people had to live — a reality that was grounded in the inseparable relationship between those who provided death-related religious services and those who commissioned them.

૭

PART II

The Danka System and Funerary Buddhism

"Having been removed from Christianity, one is expected to have a danna temple." So states the 1687 decree pertaining to the Kirishitan ruizoku (family groups), whereby the shogunate specified the actions expected of former Kirishitan and their descendants and relatives.[1] The list of evidence attesting to one's abandonment of the Christian faith was long: sending gifts (tsuketodoke) to the danna temple on a regular basis, visiting the danna temple on the anniversary of the death of one's parents and on other occasions, keeping a miniature Buddhist image in the household Buddhist altar, and making offerings of flowers. The danna temple was expected to check on these matters without fail. If the person in question had servants, then these people were to be scrutinized as well.[2]

These regulations soon went beyond the bakufu's original intention. Against a backdrop of anti-Christian terror, Buddhist institutions began to apply these danna obligations to the entire populace, as though transforming the whole population into quasi-Kirishitan kin. In a situation where Buddhist monks wielded the "right of religious judgment" (shūhanken), the inspectees, who lacked comparable countermeasures, remained submissive. To be denied annual religious inspection would mean being labeled a Kirishitan, and this would seriously jeopardize one's social existence. For example, in 1792, An'yōin, a Jōdoshū temple in Miyashiro village of Suchi county in Tōtōmi, warned its seven danna families "not to be negligent in *practicing* nenbutsu *and in visiting the temple. . . . In the case of failing to do so, [we] would not exercise our right of religious inspection." Alarmed, the* danna *families had to bring the case to the government office for solution, even making the accusation that the head monk of their* danna *temple was not suitable for the job.[3] Similarly, in 1831, Jōshinji, a Nichirenshū temple in Ōyaguchi village of Higashikatsushika county in Shimōsa, refused to inspect a* danna, *Takebee, saying that he had been inattentive to annual ancestral rites, had not paid his fees, had not offered his labor to the temple, and had disregarded sectarian teachings and temple regulations. Jōshinji threatened to stop certifying his non-Christian status. Concerned village officials persuaded Takebee to write a letter of apology to the temple.[4] Clearly, religious inspection was a powerful weapon for Buddhist temples.*

However, this did not mean that Buddhist institutions were allowed to pursue their interests unchecked. The shogunate's 1665 decree, known as the "Law for Buddhist temples of all sects" (Shoshū jiin hatto), *maintained that the choice of a* danna *temple should rest with* danna *patrons themselves and that* danna *families should not be objects for which Buddhist monks compete with each other.[5] This decree made it clear that law-abiding residents had a choice regarding the Buddhist temple with which they would be affiliated for religious inspection. It also made it clear that the shogunate did not want the populace to be dragged into power games played by anti-Christian religious inspectors. When considered together, the shogunal edicts of 1665 and 1687 indicate that the* danka *system was a process of compromise and social construction.*

The danka *system was not an exclusive domain of any one party.* Danna *patrons, Buddhist temples, and public authorities all had vested interests in the* danka *system — interests that reflected, and were affected by, the mode of the* danna *relationship, family structure, the religious needs of* danna *households, competition between* danna *temples, state regulations, and local customs relating to funeral services and ancestral rites. Depending on these factors, the operational mode of the* danka *system could vary. The* danka *system was never a monolithic or unilateral institution, but rather a socio-religious practice in which households, temples, and the state were linked together and interacted with one another through the practice of funerary Buddhism — a practice that can be epitomized in the symbolic presence of a Buddhist household altar (*jibutsu *or* butsudan) *where tablets containing ancestral spirits were placed and to which rites of ancestral veneration were devoted.[6] In Part II, I discuss the social practice of the* danka *system in relation to death-related rituals, ancestral veneration, and the household institution.*

CR

FOUR

The Social Mode of the Danka System

With the establishment of the system of temple certification, all households, regardless of their social status, came to be officially affiliated with a *danna* temple of their choice. Once affiliated, the latter exercised an exclusive right to preside over the funerary and memorial services of the former. This was the framework within which the *danka* system was put into practice. Even the shogunal house, which stood above the law, was not excepted. When Tokugawa Ieyasu took over Edo in 1590, he soon designated Zōjōji, a Jōdoshū temple that was first located in Kaizuka village and later (in 1598) relocated to Shiba, as the funerary temple of his family.[7] After his death, his body was enshrined at Nikkō, where the third shogun (Iemitsu) was also buried; however, the second shogun (Hidetada) was inhumed at Zōjōji. When the fourth and fifth shoguns (Ietsuna and Tsunayoshi, respectively) were buried at Tōeizan Kan'eiji, this temple in Ueno seemed to replace Zōjōji as the new shogunal funerary temple. Zōjōji protested vigorously, and the shogunal house decided to alternate between these two temples.[8] Although, unlike other families, the shogunal house had two official funerary temples, it still fell within the framework of funerary Buddhism. The rule of *bodaiji* (funerary temples) was applied to all classes from top to bottom, and, as a result, family life in Tokugawa society could not be separated from *danna* temples and their religious services for the dead and ancestral spirits.[9]

The registers of sectarian inspection pertaining to Yotsuko village, a remote mountain village in Echigo, for example, show that the affiliation between *danna* households and funerary temples was thorough and persistent. This village did not have a single temple; however, according to the 1650 register, all seven of its households (with a total population of 67) were fully incorporated into the *danka* system: six households were affiliated with Shōkakuji (a Jōdoshinshū temple in a neighboring village) and one household was affiliated with Enmanji (a Sōtōshū temple located in another neighboring village). By 1696, the number of households increased to fourteen, but these two outside temples continued to serve as funerary temples for ten and four households, respectively. About 40 years later, in 1735, the situation remained basically unchanged. Of eighteen households with a total population of 116, eleven were affiliated with Shōkakuji while seven were affiliated with Enmanji. In all cases, not a single household was left without a funerary temple.[10]

We should clarify here how the household unit was defined within the *danka* system in terms of its composition, property, and social status. The 1868 register of Kashiwa village, for example, shows that one eleven-year-old girl formed a household (which possessed land yielding a mere 2.4 *to* [1 *to* = 4.765 gallons] of rice per year), as did a brother and sister with no land. Among 94 households listed on this register, 6 were landless and 5 were landless tenant households.[11] In contrast, several households on the 1696 register of Yotsuko village were quite large in both land size and membership: they included, within the same household unit, family members of three or four generations, relatives, bond servants, and hired laborers. The household of the village head, for example, consisted of his own family members, three male servants, and a female servant and her parents—fifteen people in all.[12] Households without land or consisting of only minor children certainly could not fulfill all aspects of their public duty, including paying the annual tax. In this sense, these social units were deficient and were thus excluded from village politics. However, within the *danka* system, these households—regardless of *kokudaka*, status, or family size—were all accepted as full-fledged *danka* units.

Indeed, the social modes of households were neither uniform nor static. This was particularly so in the urban areas, where a market economy was increasingly pushing many households to the social margins. Kanda Sakumachō yonchōme in Edo, which consisted of two subwards — the Motochi (original ward) and the Uramachi (rear ward) — is a case in point. Of the 42 households in the Motochi, more than 85 percent of them were either house-tenant (*tanagari*) or land-tenant (*jigari*) households, while only a few of them owned their own house properties (*iemochi*) or worked for the house-owners (*yamori*). In other words, a majority of the residents in this ward were without property. They formed a floating mass of urban poor — people who could barely eke out a living as street peddlers, day laborers, or entertainers.[13] Yet all of these people were regarded as independent, legitimate household units and were individually affiliated with *danna* temples. Even a 23-year-old single man who supported himself as a servant formed a household unit that was officially affiliated with a *danna* temple, as did a 43-year-old widower who sought a livelihood far from his home village.[14] The Uramachi's register shows that its economic situation was gloomier than was that of the Motochi: among a total of 44 households, only one owned property, two were managers of someone else's property, and the rest were all tenant-classes, either *tanagari* or *jigari*. Even so, there was not a single household that was not individually affiliated with a *danna* temple. In addition, migrant residents in the ward maintained their own *danna* temples. Altogether, the families of the Uramachi were served by 45 different funerary temples.[15]

As far as the *danka* system was concerned, the examples of Kanda Sakumachō yonchōme were not unusual. To be sure, many tenant households in Edo were unstable and transient, being vulnerable to dissipation and often ceasing to exist. But all of them remained within the purview of a *danna* temple. The system of temple certification, which had been introduced nationwide in the mid-seventeenth century, was still strong two centuries later.[16] This means that *danna* temples, which fared well even within the capricious urban environments, enjoyed long-lasting, binding relations with their *danna* patrons, who were not allowed to escape from the *danna* obligation. Tokugawa Japan's anti-Christianity policy transformed entire families into permanent patrons of Buddhist temples.

That said, however, it should be noted that the *danka* system had little to do with the religious faith or the free will of individual family members; rather, it was a system of binding affiliation that was inherited to the posterity generation after generation. In other words, once established, individual *danna* patrons could not arbitrarily choose or change, based on their own individual faith or religious orientation or free will, their *danna* temples. They just inherited the initial affiliation formed by their forebears and stuck to it. Freely switching to another temple was not in accord with the operational mode of the *danka* system.

To be sure, there were conflicts with the conventional mode of the *danna* relationship. When such conflicts occurred, they were accommodated only within certain conditions: for example, when a family moved to a distant place, when a family adopted a new member, or when a daughter or son married out to a new family or returned to her or his original family upon being divorced. On an individual basis, public authorities allowed a person to switch to a new *danna* temple or to return to their original temple as long as he or she secured a legitimate "certificate of religious sending" (*shūmon ninbetsu okurijō*) – a document that was drawn up by his or her village or ward head on the basis of temple certification (*teraukejō*). The *shūmon ninbetsu okurijō* contained such information on the person in question as name, age, family relationship, the village he or she left and the one to which he or she relocated, reason for relocation, sectarian affiliation, and *danna* temple.[17]

The purpose of *shūmon ninbetsu okurijō*, which was enforced by the shogunal law of 1716, was to ensure the identity of the transferee before adding him or her to the census register of sectarian inspection compiled at the new village.[18] The most important item to be checked in this documentation, which was exchanged between the village heads, was non-Kirishitan identification, which was to have been verified by the previous *danna* temple. If a *danna* temple refused to confirm the non-Kirishitan identity of a transferee, then the latter could not legally move to another village or town.[19] Similarly, in the case of adoption, the adoptee would ask his or her village head and *danna* temple to issue a "certificate of religious sending" addressed to the village head of the adopting family; upon receiving the certificate, the village head would officially accept him or her as its new resident and add him or her to the village's census register of sectarian inspection.[20] If a whole family moved to a distant location, then it was also allowed to switch to a new temple provided that its current *danna* temple acknowledged and agreed to issue a certificate of religious inspection that could be used in drawing up a *shūmon ninbetsu okurijō*. In all cases, *danna* temples affected by the "certificate of religious sending" exchanged "documents of temple transfer" (*tera okurijō, tera okuri shōmon,* or *shūshi okuri tegata*), often through the mediation of the village heads or officials involved. Without undergoing this procedure, switching to another *danna* temple could not be finalized.[21]

However, as may be seen in the census registers of sectarian inspection in Tsubuura (a village developed on reclaimed wastelands in Bizen), being relocated only a short distance did not usually affect the established *danna* relationship. More than ten Buddhist temples associated with Tsubuura's new settler households, whose number would increase to 120 by the end of the Tokugawa period, were all located outside Tsubuura.[22] In other words, even after having moved to a newly established village, all of these Tsubuura settlers continued to maintain their previous *danna* temples. It was not at all clear how far away someone had to move in order to qualify for a temple transfer. But what is evident is that *danna* temples, if they could, tried to keep their current *danna* relationships by retaining the right of religious inspection over their *danna* families.

What really made the association between a household and a *danna* temple so strong and enduring? The answer might be found in how Buddhist temples exercised the right of "religious judgment" over their *danna* patrons. From the late seventeenth century on, the head of a *danna* temple, when issuing non-Christian certificates, usually specified why the inspectees were not, or could not be, Kirishitan: "It is true that the person in question has been a *danna* of this humble temple generation after generation. . . . Based on this, I hereby conduct 'religious judgment' (*shūhan*)."[23] The phrase "generation after generation" implies that the "religious judgment" of the person in question was based on his or her enduring *danna* status. Buddhist temples began using the phrases "generation after generation" and/or "for generations" as a barometer for measuring non-Kirishitan status, and *danna* patrons took this very seriously.[24] Inspector-temples were never lax with regard to utilizing this new phraseology, and inspectee-patrons rarely questioned its validity. As far as the shogunate was concerned, because the wording was thought to promote social stability, there was no compelling reason to inveigh against it. Thus, *danna* relationships, once established, were a done deal.

As a matter of fact, however, the enduring relationship between a household and a *danna* temple was, in theory, supposed to be up to the former. As the 1665 *bakufu* law spelled out, how Household A was to be affiliated with Buddhist Temple B was the consequence of A's initial choice. Nevertheless, once that choice was made, power relations often shifted quickly in favor of the *danna* temple because it was the institution that wielded the authority of religious inspection. In other words, Household A, which activated Temple B's right of religious judgment in the first place, usually ended up being subjected to the enduring power of the latter's "religious judgment." Those born later into the bondage of a *danna* relationship could not do much about it. Descendants simply had to live with what they had inherited from their ancestors.

Furthermore, the binding relationship between *danna* patron and *danna* temple was quickly translated into the latter having supervisory power over death-related rituals, memorial services, and ancestral rites. Legally, the shogunate never specified that Buddhist temples should have a monopoly over the death-related rituals of their *danna* patrons, but this was what transpired. The temple indicated on the register of sectarian inspection as a household's *danna* temple proved to function as that household's permanent funerary temple.

Thus, the task of understanding the structure of the *danka* system, above all, comes down to the question of the genesis of each individual *danna* relationship. Tracing the history of each case, however, would not be easy, especially since (1) cases where all the households of a village were associated with the same temple were extremely rare and (2) the patterns of affiliation did not follow any given set of rules or conventions. Depending upon the social composition of a village or ward, as well as upon the availability of Buddhist temples in the area, the ways in which households were associated with funerary temples could vary considerably. Not only that, depending upon its origin, blood lineage, main-branch family relations, family tradition, social status, wealth or prestige, neighborhood, factional division, geography, social pressure, and religious orientation, the initial affiliation of a household with a funerary temple could go in any direction.[25] Worse yet, all these relatively predictable factors, which might have affected the initial formation of a *danna* relationship, were often untraceable due to having been corroded over time, to not having been recorded in the first place, to social mobility, to lack of interest, and so on. In particular, an urban society like Edo contained a large population of "rootless" households that rarely offered reliable clues regarding how their *danna* relationships had initially been established.

In spite of all these limitations, scholars have identified some noticeable patterns in the initial association between households and funerary temples. Morioka Kiyomi suggests that clan or quasi-clan relations played a decisive role.[26] According to him, it was almost customary for branch households to follow the lead of their main household. Since the member households sought protection and solidarity by venerating their common ancestors, it was natural to insist upon using the same funerary temple. This kind of pattern was most frequently found in the rural areas, where clusters of households belonging to the same clan or quasi-clan of kin and affines (*dōzoku*) dominated the village.

There were two types of *dōzoku* groups: one containing branch households organized within the economic perimeter of the main household, and the other consisting of branch households organized without the economic perimeter of the main household. The first type refers to the organization of the main household and its branch households established by its former bond servants (*nago* or *hikan*), who were able to rent land from, or were given it by, their master. Despite there being no blood connection between them, these branch households tended to bind themselves to their master household simply because, without the latter's protection and generosity, life was hard. On the other hand, the second type, which was a cognate organization and more prominent in more advanced regions, was formed when a big landholding household spent generations dividing its inheritance between its offspring and producing multiple branch households in the village.[27] Since these branch households owned land and functioned as autonomous units, they did not have to be economically submissive to, although they maintained a strong spiritual bond with, their main household.[28] In either case, what bound these *dōzoku* households together was land, over which the main household originally commanded suzerainty.

Although, over time, the land could not escape being partitioned, distributed, or rented out to individual branch households, as long as group solidarity was maintained the original mass of land was regarded, if only fictively, as communal property belonging to the *dōzoku* group—a property that was collectively placed under the divine protection of the *dōzoku*'s common ancestral deities.[29] For this reason the *dōzoku* group was likened to an extension of the main household; branch household members were likened to inseparable parts of the main household; and *dōzoku* members collectively venerated their common ancestors. In this context, when a branch household member died it was customary for the main household head to arrange a funeral for that person and to ensure his or her interment at the communal burial site—a practice that was dealt with communally by the entire *dōzoku* group.[30]

On the other hand, in a village where residents were divided along factional interests (or for other reasons), funerary temples often served to mark the separate group solidarity of each division. For example, in Higae village of Kuwada county in Tanba there were three temples: Saigenji, Tokujuan, and Seikōji. In medieval times, Saigenji had been a small *nenbutsu* hall erected beside the village cemetery; Tokujuan had been a branch hermitage of Saigenji; and Seikōji, an obscure Buddhist hall, had already ceased to function. In the early seventeenth century, the whole village was incorporated into shogunal land, but in 1665 a large part of it was given to Kajiinomiya *monzeki* of Sanzen'in in Kyoto. As the village was divided into shogunal and *monzeki* lands, and as village officials were separately appointed in each subvillage, the latent animosity between these two groups surfaced.[31] In the same year, when the shogunate imposed religious inspection nationwide, Saigenji, which was located in the shogunal land, tried to scrutinize all the villagers. The residents living in the *monzeki* land refused to be subject to Saigenji's inspection, quickly restored the dilapidated Tokujuan and Seikōji temples in their area, and associated themselves with them as *danna* patrons. Throughout the Tokugawa period, the division of the village was reflected in the *danna* affiliation.[32]

Similarly, in neighboring Nakae village, there were two funerary temples: Tōrinji and Rinshōin. Tōrinji, which had started as a private Buddhist hall for the Kobatake house (a powerful family in the village), came to include all households belonging to the Kobatake clan as its *danna*. In contrast, Rinshōin, which used to be a private Buddhist hall for the Kakigi house (another powerful family in the village), secured all anti-Kobatake residents as its *danna* and served as a rallying point for them. When there was an event in which all villagers had to participate, it was always held at Tōkōji, which was a sort of village hall that did not have any *danna* patrons and was not affiliated with any particular Buddhist sect.[33] In this way factional conflict in the village was often projected into the *danka* system, and, when this happened, the village often saw the proliferation of new funerary temples. During this process many private or dilapidated Buddhist halls were restored to the status of full-fledged *danna* institutions.[34]

The status of a temple also affected the pattern of the *danna* relationship. When there was a highly regarded temple in the village, then it was quite common for villagers to seek *danna* relationship with it. Ozaki village in Bizen, for example, had a well-known Shingonshū temple, Rengeji. According to the 1839 register, 99 households among 111 in the village were affiliated with it, while the remaining 12 households belonged to seven different minor temples located in other villages.[35] When a more prestigious temple was available in the vicinity, from the outset families often sought *danna* relationship with it beyond their village boundary. The 1868 register of Kashiwa village in Shimōsa clearly shows such a pattern. Among 94 families—all Nichiren followers—78 were associated with Hōrenji (of these families, 60 were the *danka* of its head subtemple, Jōkōin), and the remaining 16 were associated with Shōgyōji. Shōgyōji, which was erected in the village in 1254, was a very old temple, but Hōrenji, in the neighboring village of Ōno, was larger and had a better reputation.[36] Many families in the village opted for prestige over geographical convenience or hometown loyalty.

In cases when there was more than one temple and all of them were well established and available, village residents were often divided into discrete groups in *danna* affiliation. The 1741 census register of Oroshimo village in Kusatsu of Ōmi shows that, with regard to temple affiliation, 92 households in the village were basically divided into three groups: 41 households belonged to Entokuji, 29 to Saijōji, and 18 to Enshōji—all Jōdoshinshū temples. The only exception was four upper-class households, which were affiliated with an old Tendai temple, Raigōji, in Sakamoto across Lake Biwa.[37] This Tendai temple was considered to be more prestigious than were the Jōdoshinshū temples located in the village. Similarly, in Isoshi village in Muko county of Hyōgo prefecture there were two temples (one belonged to Jōdoshū, the other to Jōdoshinshū). The families of this village were divided into two groups in terms of *danna* affiliation: the families of older lineages and wealth were all affiliated with the Jōdoshū temple, and the remaining relatively new families, which formed a confraternity of their own against the established families, were all affiliated with the Jōdoshinshū temple.[38] This does not mean, however, that affiliation with a Jōdoshinshū temple always implied low social status. There were cases in which affiliation with a Jōdoshinshū temple represented the opposite, depending on the rank, history, and prestige of the temple in question. When there were multiple Jōdoshinshū temples in the same village, families were often hierarchically grouped according to the temples with which they were affiliated.

The point is that, under certain circumstances, *danna* temples could extend one's social status. One of these circumstances involved the case of *burakumin* (social outcasts). It is well known that *burakumin* in western Japan were almost all affiliated with Jōdoshinshū temples (with a few exceptions found in Bizen, Bitchū, Mimasaka [Shingonshū], and Hizen [Nichirenshū]).[39] Morioka Kiyomi suggests two reasons why most *burakumin* came to be affiliated with Jōdoshinshū temples: (1) they might have felt an affinity with the inclusive nature of the teachings of Shinran, who showed unfailing compassion to the lower classes and even embraced evil creatures; and (2) they might have been attracted to the promise of the next life, which, as Jōdoshinshū monks preached, was believed to compensate them for their current misery.[40] Many of the so-called *burakumin danna* temples that emerged in western Japan formed head-branch relationships with middle-rank *burakumin* head temples, which were put under the direct control of Honganji headquarters in Kyoto. The "four head temples" (Konpukuji, Mansenji, Kyōtokuji, Fukusenji, all located in the *jinaichō* [temple ward] of Honganji in Kyoto) were best known for their grip on local *burakumin danna* temples. Genshōji in Himeji and Honshōji in Kyoto were also prominent in this regard. The head-branch relationships between the *burakumin* temples were compiled into a register, which was treated separately from other "ordinary" temple registers.[41]

In the Kantō and Tōhoku regions, in addition to Jōdoshinshū temples, *burakumin* were usually affiliated with Buddhist temples that had had previous dealings with them. In most cases, these temples belonged to Zenshū, Jōdoshū, and Nichirenshū.[42] In these regions, the sectarian affiliation did not indicate much about the social status of *burakumin*; rather, discriminatory posthumous names played a visible role in marking their lowly status. When there were no temples available nearby, *burakumin* usually erected a temple in their village and invited a monk to practice there. Public authorities, however, rarely authorized this kind of makeshift temple, which was usually labeled an "unclean temple" (*eji*). The monk of an "unclean temple" had to obtain a temple seal from his head temple whenever he issued non-Christian certificates to his *burakumin danna*.

As we have seen, the factors that affected the initial formation of the *danna* relationship were complex and multidirectional. When factors such as clan lineage, faction, prestige, and social status were combined with factors such as temple marketing, local customs, religious interests, socio-economic conditions, and so on, *danna* relationships were fluid. This is seen in the census registers (1637–41) of Onomichi in Mitsugi county of Bingo. During these years the domain government intensified anti-Christian investigation, and the families of Onomichi, which numbered more than 2,000, were forced to be affiliated with Buddhist temples. There were about 50 temples in this prosperous port city. Among them Saikokuji (Shingonshū) and Jōdoji (Risshū) were the oldest and enjoyed the highest status. But the census registers show that the numbers of *danna* families affiliated with these two prestigious temples were extremely low: Saikokuji had 48, while Jōdoji had only four, most of whom belonged to the upper social echelon. In contrast, two relatively new temples, Jōsenji and Fukuzenji (both Jōdoshiunshū), which were established in 1543 and 1630, respectively, had the largest numbers of *danna* families (Jōsenji had 476 *danna*, while Fukuzenji had 411), most of whom belonged to the lower social echelon.[43] Initially, many of these *danna* families were affiliated with the high-status temples of their masters, but they later switched to Jōdoshinshū temples in search of independence and self-identity. They were attracted to these new temples that, with neither land nor prestige, aggressively preached the idea of salvation by "other power." In contrast, old temples, which insisted on the status and prestige of the past, remained rather detached from the ordinary residents and failed to adjust to the new environment of this anti-Christian age. With fewer and fewer *danna* families affiliated with them, their past glory and influence gradually diminished.[44]

Like this, in a situation where independent nuclear households kept proliferating, the social adaptability of both families and Buddhist temples affected the formation of *danna* relationships, temporally as well as spatially. It became increasingly so as the spectacular growth of Buddhist temples ushered in a period of competition over as well as opportunity for *danna* patrons. All this further dragged *danna* relationships into formats that defied any particular pattern.

According to Tamamuro Taijō's survey of the genesis of Buddhist temples in Mutsu and Noto, more than 90 percent of 318 temples in the region were established or restored between 1467 and 1665.[45] Similarly, Takeda Chōshū examined in detail a 1696 national survey of about 6,000 Jōdoshū temples. Among these temples he was able to identify the origins of 3,821 through their autobiographical chronicles, and he concluded that more than 90 percent of them had been established or restored between 1501 and 1696. Of particular interest was the fact that about 62 percent of them had been restored in the 70 years between 1573 and 1643.[46] Similarly, Ōkuwa Hitoshi, who surveyed temples belonging to the Higashihonganji subsect of Jōdoshinshū in Shinano, confirmed that the vast majority of them had acquired their official status in the seventeenth century.[47] On the other hand, the temple chronicles, known as *Jiin kaikichō* (Register of the origins of Buddhist temples), which was compiled by the Mito domain in 1663, show that more than 70 percent of the 1,735 temples in the domain were established between 1500 and 1650. In the case of the Kumamoto domain, a stronghold of Jōdoshinshū (440 of 955 temples belonged to this sect), more than 67 percent of its temples were erected between 1596 and 1654.[48] All current studies invariably suggest that, although there were some regional and sectarian variations, the growth of Buddhist temples and the formation of *danna* relationships followed a parallel course—one that complicated the *danka* system.

In retrospect, during the tumultuous years of the Sengoku period, when many temples fell into disrepair, many upper-class families began to revive or erect their own private Buddhist halls—religious facilities known as *jibutsudō* (halls enshrining a Buddha), or *ujidera* (clan temples)—in or near their residential compounds for the memorial repose of the spirits of their ancestors and relatives. With the increase in *danna* affiliations in the seventeenth century, most of these petty private religious facilities were converted into officially recognized *danna* temples. On the other hand, as has been mentioned, in those villages where ordinary residents could not find a *danna* temple, they often erected a communal Buddhist sanctuary, invited a monk to inhabit it, and affiliated the sanctuary with an established regional temple. Villagers also had the option of converting existing communal Buddhist halls (*butsudō*) known as *sōdō*, or "village halls" (*sondō*)—which provided public spaces for gatherings, meetings, religious rituals, or entertainment as well as a symbol of village solidarity and sanctity—into funerary *danna* temples. These communal religious facilities (often called Amidadō, Kannondō, Yakushidō, or Jizōdō, depending on the identity of the Buddhist deity enshrined), which were maintained by village communities and occasionally visited by peripatetic religious practitioners, were a fertile source of *danna* temples in the early Tokugawa period.[49] It goes without saying that, for their part, Buddhist monks, who were seeking new settlements during this transitional period, played a vital role in converting these religious structures (whether private or communal) into funerary temples. The monks developed a sectarian affiliation, secured official institutional status and rank, and eagerly responded to small-scale households that had broken away from the main-branch household nexus.[50]

All in all, the irregular increase of Buddhist temples and households complicated the geographical contours of the *danka* system. *Danna* relationships, which were rarely affected by the boundary-zoning of an administrative unit, often produced disorderly, even zigzagged, networks. As a result it was almost impossible to divide them into discrete temple-centered parishes, despite the fact that the registers of sectarian inspection were drawn up and kept by each administrative unit. If the government had really intended to use the *danka* system as a means of administration, then it would have forced all residents to be associated with the temple(s) located within each village or ward unit. But this was far from being the case. As long as the requirement of religious inspection was fulfilled, the matter of how individual *danna* relationships should be formed was left to the free will of each *danna* household. And this points to the fact that, before the system of temple certification was implemented nationwide, there had already been interactions, to one degree or another, between various families and Buddhist temples. The shogunate could not do much about this.

To what extent did *danna* relationships crisscross the boundaries of administrative units? In order to answer this question, one must examine the registers of sectarian inspection. This being said it should be remembered that, at least from the 1660s on, for over two centuries each administrative unit, whether it was a village or an urban ward, drew up a register of sectarian inspection annually. It should also be remembered that there were about 73,000 administrative units in Tokugawa Japan.[51] The daunting number of extant registers, and the fact that they appeared almost all over the country, deter one from examining them in any depth. And, really, it is not necessary to do so because, given that the shogunate tried to impose a standard procedure upon all of Tokugawa Japan, the format and content of all religious registers were not much different from each other.

It was rare for all the households of a village to belong to the same *danna* temple. There were, of course, situations (such as an isolated or cognate village where only one temple was available) in which the *danna* relationships of all households were contained within the same temple, but this was not common. Usually, families tended to seek *danna* temples located outside their own villages. Of course, when there was no temple available in the village, this was a necessity, as was seen, for example, in Kuroishi, a small branch village of Urata in Bizen, which had no temples in its territory. Its 1683 register shows that all but one of the village's 41 households were affiliated with Rengein, a Shingonshū temple in Urata. When the only household that maintained a different funeral temple later ceased to exist, Rengein remained the sole provider of funerary services for the villagers of Kuroishi until 1870.[52]

Even if a new temple were erected within their village, families usually chose to go outside. To be sure, once the *danna* relationship had been formed, it was not easily undone, so perhaps it is not surprising that villagers continued to go to outside temples with which they were already affiliated. However, even newly established village households, which, in theory, could choose to go to a newly erected temple within the village, almost always chose to go outside. For example, in 1643 wastelands near Kuroishi were reclaimed and families in the neighboring villages moved in and formed a new village called Tsubuura-shinden. More than half a century later, in 1706, when a census register of sectarian inspection was compiled, it was found that there were 11 *danna* temples associated with the village's 85 households (among these, Saimyōin in Tsubue village held 40 households, while Rengein in Urata village held 20). None of them was located in the village. Even though by this time temples had already been established within the village, villagers did not pay any attention to them. Another half century later, in 1757, there were 87 households in Tsubuura-shinden but there was no change in their *danna* affiliations. By 1870, despite the fact that there were now 116 households, there was basically no change in this pattern (except for a few new immigrant families who added their own outside funerary temples to the list).[53] Clearly, the tendency to seek *danna* temples outside the village persisted even when temples were amply available within the village boundary.[54]

With regard to the geographical contours of *danna* relationships, Fukuta Ajio suggests four patterns. The first pattern occurs when there is only one temple available in the village and all households are affiliated with it. The second pattern occurs when there is a great temple in the village and it embraces all local households as well as many others located in neighboring villages. These two patterns, which would have integrated nicely with the governing structure of the *bakuhan* system, were, however, extremely rare. The third pattern, which is more visible than the first two, occurs when there are multiple temples in a village and they divide the local households among them. The fourth and most dominant pattern occurs when multiple temples in neighboring villages divide the households in each village and form *danna* relationships with them.[55] There is no way to verify Fukuta's patterns on a nationwide scale, but current studies indicate that *danna* affiliations were dictated neither by political power nor by administrative convenience.

Given the crisscrossing patterns of *danna* relationships, which defied geographical sectioning or administrative zoning, it was almost impossible to spatially distinguish one *danka* cluster from another. *Danka* clusters were intermixed and sometimes seemed quite scrambled. This was especially true in urban areas, where a high degree of social mobility rendered the idea of *danna* parishes utterly meaningless. The 1857 census register of sectarian inspection for the Motochi ward of Kanda Sakumachō yonchōme in central Edo, for example, unambiguously demonstrates the complexity of *danka*-temple webs. In this ward there were 42 registered households (which had a total of 176 family members) and 14 migrant residents (such as servants, seasonal laborers, and co-inhabitants) who were allowed to maintain their *danna* temples but who were all enrolled under the name of the household that employed them. If we count these migrant residents as independent *danna* units, then altogether there were 56 of them. These 56 *danna* units were served by 53 *danna* temples. Among these temples, only 3 had 2 *danna* units each, and the other 50 each maintained only a single *danna* unit. The sectarian distribution of these temples was as follows: Jōdoshū (thirteen), Zenshū (ten), Jōdoshinshū (nine), Nichirenshū (eight), Shingonshū (seven), and Tendaishū (six). Their locations were scattered all over the city and included such areas as Shiba, Yotsuya, Ushigome, Komagome, Koishikawa,

Hongō, Shitaya, Yanaka, Asakusa, and the Honjo-Fukagawa district. Three temples were even located beyond the boundaries of Edo, one in Musashi and two in Shimōsa.[56] Thus, it would be futile to try to map the geographical distribution of *danka*-temple affiliations: these relationships cannot be defined simply as a "parish system" as conventional scholarship has habitually been doing. In short, the patterns of individual relationships between *danna* patrons and funerary temples were diverse, diffused, and haphazard.

So far, one might have the impression that a household unit was affiliated with one Buddhist *danna* temple only. This practice was known as the principle of one temple per household, or *ikka ichijisei*. However, given that the religious inspection that gave rise to the *danka* system was never designed to check the non-Christian identity of the household unit as a group, it was hardly expected that the principle of one temple per household would be implemented *in toto*. The system of temple certification did not operate so as to scrutinize the members of a household as a unit but, rather, so as to check each household member one by one. For this reason, when individuals were checked and recorded on the register of sectarian inspection, their names were arranged one by one and their temple affiliations were confirmed one by one, with each name stamped with a separate temple seal. Similarly, statistical summaries at the end of the register were also specified in terms of the totals of individuals affiliated with each Buddhist sect and temple rather than in terms of number of household units.[57] If the principle of one temple per household was strictly enforced, then there would not have been much need to conduct religious inspection on an individual basis. This suggests that governments, both local and central, recognized plural *danna* affiliations within the same household unit.

Nevertheless, some domains were quite pushy with regard to promoting the principle of one temple per household. For example, the Kaga domain government decreed in 1696 and 1697 that "when an adopted son or a son-in-law inherits the household, he should switch to the [*danna*] temple of his father-in-law."[58] Again, in 1711 it issued the following instructions, which would be repeated in 1723: "Wives and children should have the same sect and same temple to which their husbands and fathers belong and should not be associated with different sects or temples for reasons of religious faith or prayer purposes."[59] It continued: "In cases where there exists a compelling reason, those families who seek divisive *danna* relations should obtain approval from village officials, and the temples involved should follow the direction of superintendents of temples and shrines after reporting the matter to them."[60] Ōkuwa Hitoshi suggests that, through these measures, which would foster the lineal succession of the household institution, the Kaga domain tried to transform composite large-scale medieval-style household units into independent nuclear household units (which were more amenable to the early modern taxation system).[61]

With regard to Ōkuwa's suggestion, Hōzawa Naohide insists that he not only misunderstood the Kaga edicts but also failed to verify how these edicts could actually advance the institutional strength of petty agricultural households. Instead, Hōzawa argues that the Kaga domain primarily wanted to prevent the disorderly practice of plural *danna* affiliation, which often resulted in disputes and even lawsuits over the issue of change of *danna* affiliation.[62] Whatever the reason, the idea that all members of a household should belong to the same *danna* temple gained more and more dominance as time progressed, particularly in the agriculturally advanced regions where nuclear household organizations were widely established. Fukuta Ajio attributes this increasing popularity of one temple per household to the changing mode of *ie* (household) institutions rather than to government policy. He suggests that, increasingly, people in the late Tokugawa period longed to perpetuate their household institutions along the paternal lineage, and that this goal was sought by strengthening spiritual (religious) solidarity, which was best nurtured in the practice of one temple per household.[63] With regard to Fukuta's suggestion, Hōzawa Naohide counters that some domains actually tried to promote the principle of one temple per household upon the populace—a policy that was later endorsed by the *bakufu*. To be sure, Toyoda Takeshi is incorrect to suggest that the principle of one temple per household was a *bakufu* policy from the beginning that was unilaterally imposed upon the nation as law;[64] however, it is also incorrect to assume that this principle was all the time separate from the will of the *bakufu*.

By the mid-eighteenth century, the shogunate still did not officially recognize the principle of one temple per household as the norm. This may be seen in its 1749 response to the inquiries of the Takada domain on the issue of switching a *danna* temple.[65] However, from 1780 onward, it was clear that the shogunate began to lend its support to this principle when the superintendents of finance informed the *daikan* of the shogunal lands that (1) a married couple is expected to belong to the same temple, and (2) if spouses belong to two different temples, then their children should belong to the father's temple.[66] In 1827, under the endorsement of the *bakufu*'s magistrates of temples and shrines, the *daikan* office of Mizuhara, which bordered the Shibata domain in Echigo, issued an edict to its land and neighboring daimyo domains. This edict held that the situation in which each member of a couple belonged to different temples would be allowed to continue for only one generation; after that, all members of a household were to be affiliated with one temple only. By the end of the Bunsei era (1818–29) it became clear that the shogunate, which now regarded the principle of one temple per household as being "reasonable" (*sujiai*), gave it its full backing.[67]

No doubt, the principle of one temple per household was dominant by the end of the Tokugawa period; however, this does not mean that the custom of plural *danna* affiliations within the same household disappeared all together. Contrarily, this custom was, if not dominant, still quite visible in the underdeveloped regions and among families of lower status. Its persistence seemed to reflect the legacy of the extended household system, which was composed of multiple discrete sub- or quasi-family units.[68] At the same time, it should also be noted that plural *danna* affiliations were relatively prominent among the *danna* associated with temples belonging to Jōdoshinshū or Nichirenshū, all of which showed strong sectarian tendencies.

There were various forms of plural *danna* affiliations in which two or more temples (sometimes of different sects) served as the *danna* temples for different members of the same household. More specifically, according to Fukuta Ajio's classification, there were four types of plural *danna* affiliations. The first type involved bifurcatory *danna* affiliations in the same household split along gender lines, in which, upon marriage, sons-in-law and daughters-in-law would change their premarital *danna* affiliations and move to the patriline and the matriline, respectively. The second type involved multiple *danna* affiliations formed in line with the father's temple (to which all sons belonged) and the mother's temple (to which all daughters belonged). If a household were composed of three or more generations, then there could be three or more different groups of *danna* affiliations, since no members were supposed to change these affiliations even after marriage. The third type, a variation of the second type, involved separate *danna* affiliations between father and mother, although children all belonged to the father's *danna* temple. And the fourth type involved multiple but irregular *danna* affiliations where a couple had separate *danna* temples but without rules dictating the temple to which children and siblings were to belong.[69]

Among these four types of *danna* affiliation, the fourth was most rare. The second and third types, which reflected a strong parent-child relationship, were frequent throughout the seventeenth century. However, over time, the first type gained the most currency as the *ie* increasingly took precedence over the parent-child relationship. This type of *danna* affiliation, which was bifurcated along the gender lines, was often referred to as the household of *handanka* (half *danka*) or *fukudanka* (plural *danka*).[70]

Not surprisingly, the custom of plural *danna* affiliations as seen in these four types sometimes caused disputes between temples that stood either to gain new members or to lose existing members — disputes that came down to the issue of economic interests. When temples were threatened with losing their *danna* patrons through marriage or adoption, they fought back. Some temples insisted that all children, even if their mothers had already changed *danna* affiliation, must be associated with the original maternal *danna* temple.[71] As a way of solving the problem that put the maternal temple at loggerheads with the paternal temple, Buddhist head monks in some regions agreed upon a set of collective guidelines and tried to accommodate mutual interests.

In 1649, for example, Buddhist monks in Nanbokugō of Fugeshi county in Noto held a meeting at Guzeiji in Ōmachi village in an attempt to solve disputes over funerary *danna* patrons. They agreed upon a set of thirteen principles. The tenth principle reads:

In the case of a single child, whether it is a son or a daughter, or whether it is born between a couple or an adopted son, that child should be affiliated with the temple of the paternal line. When an only daughter marries and takes her husband to her household, the couple should visit the monk of her father. However, for example, when there are three children born between a couple, one of them should inherit the temple with which his or her grandmother is affiliated, provided that the head monk of the temple with which his or her grandfather is affiliated gives consent.[72]

In dealing with inheritance disputes, the Nanbokugō monks concurred that the household successor should inherit the temple of the previous household head. Since this status was passed down along the paternal line for the most part, it is understandable that the paternal temple was given preference over the maternal temple. However, in order to mitigate the devastation this wrought upon maternal temples, the monks came up with various forms of compromise. For example, when there were more than two children, at least one of them was to be assigned to the maternal temple; and, should the maternal temple lose all its patrons, it should be allowed to partially recover them in the third generation.[73]

Similarly, the *bakufu*, which was concerned about the problem of plural *danna* practice in some areas, warned in 1780 that this was attributable to the reluctance of some temples to issue the certificate of temple transfer, without which the switch to another *danna* temple would be illegal. Also, in order to compensate for loss, some temples often charged an exorbitant fee for issuing this certificate. Even though their official position was that of non-interference with *danna* affiliation, *bakufu* officials urged Buddhist temples to be lenient and to let married women switch their *danna* affiliation.[74]

Indeed, the uneasy tension surrounding plural *danna* affiliations sometimes led to odd situations, as is illustrated by an example cited by Nagura Tetsuzō that took place in Kakudahama village in Echigo. In the first month of 1847, the head monk of Ganshōji was invited by the Ichizō family to conduct the third-year memorial service for the deceased former household head. However, a female member of the family, who was affiliated with the Nichirenshū temple Myōkōji, invited its monk and proceeded to hold another memorial service for a deceased female family member. The two monks, who arrived at the family residence almost simultaneously, began to quarrel over seating. They failed to settle this issue, and the Ganshōji monk, who retreated to wait with a neighboring *danna* family, pressed Ichizō to drive the Myōkōji monk out of the house. This kind of trouble did occur, particularly when Jōdoshinshū and Nichirenshū monks, who tended to refute each other's rituals, encountered each other while attempting to serve the same family.[75]

In another twist of the institution of *danna* affiliation, some regions had the custom of dual *danna* patronage, in which a household unit was simultaneously affiliated with two temples, usually with a higher-ranking main *danna* temple located far from the village and with its branch or proxy temple located within the village. This custom, which was most prevalent among Jōdoshinshū temples in northern and western Japan, came about when the distance between the original *danna* temple and its patrons made frequent contact onerous. In this case, the main *danna* temple delegated the right of conducting both anti-Christian inspection and death-related rituals, or the latter only, to the local proxy temple (*enkaridera* or *enkadera* in the north and *keshōdera* in the Aki-Hiroshima region). With regard to *danna* patrons, this kind of arrangement was meant to allow them, for pragmatic reasons, to "borrow the blessing of the (Buddhist) Law" from a nearby temple.[76]

For example, many households in Shimofukagawa village, Taka-miya county, Aki were officially affiliated with Enryūji, a great Jōdo-shinshū temple located in distant Teramachi in Hiroshima. However, as far as religious services related to death and ancestral rites were concerned, *danna* households in Shimofukagawa were served by Yōtokuji, which was located in the village and functioned as a local proxy for Enryūji. Under this sort of arrangement, the head monk of the main *danna* temple usually visited its *danna* households once a year. During his visit he would conduct an annual commemorative service for Shinran, or *hōonkō* (the "confraternity for requiting the favor"), at an assembly that consisted of all *danna* patrons; exercise the "right of religious judgment"; and, in the name of a first-crop offering, collect annual fees. However, all other matters were dele-gated to the proxy local temple.[77]

Interestingly, in Monma village in Musashi, the distance between a main *danna* temple and its patron families gave birth to a further peculiar division of labor. Saikōin, a Shingonshū temple that had some trouble looking after the graves of some of its *danna* families due to their distant location, arranged to have its branch temples, Hōshōin and Iōin, take care of them. Likewise, Tankeiji, a Jōdo-shinshū temple in the village, also delegated some of its patron fami-lies to the care of Iōin, which was designated as their "grave" tem-ple.[78] In both cases, the main *danna* temples exercised all legal rights pertaining to religious inspection and funerals, even though the "grave" temples took care of the graves and were actually allowed to conduct certain minor roles in the funerary and memorial ser-vices.[79] For the patron families who paid fees to both temples, this amounted to having two *danna* temples simultaneously.

Understandably, despite its remoteness, the titular *danna* temple did not usually tolerate any attempt on the part of *danna* households or the proxy temple to dispense with its supervision.[80] When it felt that its influence was in danger, the titular *danna* temple tried to reclaim its position by asserting "direct service" over its *danna* households.[81] For example, Zenshōji in Teramachi in Hiroshima petitioned the domain government in 1830 to allow it to extend direct service over its *danna* households, which were scattered in several villages in Saeki county and all of which were entrusted to proxy local temples. Zenshōji argued that in a situation where "there are neither funerary rituals nor *danna* visits to the temple," it was very difficult to deliver "spiritual guidance." Zenshōji maintained that it should directly conduct not only the commemorative service for Shinran and various gatherings for Buddhist teachings but also religious inspection and all other forms of guidance.

With regard to this sudden move, the proxy temples and village officials reacted furiously, arguing that they had respectfully been carrying out all religious duties and that those duties had already become their right. They then pointed out that "every year when [the *danna*] received [anti-Christian] certificates [from Zenshōji], we the proxy temples send messenger-monks and, at the time of the collection of fees in the fall, deliver compliments [to Zenshōji] according to the numbers of people inspected." They suggested that if Zenshōji insisted upon direct service, then this change would entail an extra burden upon the *danna* members. Even though domain officials could not immediately ignore the legitimate demand of Zenshōji, over time they showed more sympathy toward the proxy local temples and let them be gradually transformed into full-fledged *danna* temples with increasing control over the consigned *danna* patrons in their vicinities.[82] *Danna* relations were never uniform, despite the fact that they all stemmed from the same *bakufu* policy of anti-Christian religious inspection.

The social mode of the *danka* system was multiple in its genesis, evolution, and operation; however, all in all, it was a socio-religious institution sustained by two cardinal elements: (1) the lasting affiliation between *danna* households and funerary Buddhist temples, and (2) the Buddhist monopoly on religious services related to death and ancestral spirits. Indeed, the shogunal policy of anti-Christianity came to ensure that all Japanese had to follow the path of Buddhist death. For the Tokugawa Japanese, this amounted to accepting the *danka* system as the only way of ensuring the spiritual well-being of their deceased family members and, by extension, the perpetuation of their household institutions. For Buddhist temples, however, it did not necessarily mean that their monopoly on the business of death rituals and ancestral veneration automatically guaranteed their stable subsistence. As we see in the following Appendix to Chapter 4, the number of *danna* households or patrons, which a Buddhist temple maintained, showed a wide range of variations and reflected the environments of tight competition and power relations. For survival, many temples often needed to diversify sources of their income beyond the perimeter of funerary Buddhism.

Appendix: Danna *Holdings by Buddhist Temples*

In examining the statistics of *danna* holdings by Buddhist temples, the *Kōzuke no kuni jiin meisaichō* (Detailed registers of Buddhist temples in Kōzuke province), collected in 1879 and compiled in 1880–81, provides a good example of comprehensive and thorough data.[83] Table 4, which is based on these registers, pertains to Kōzuke province only and is not directly related to the general situation during the Tokugawa period. Nevertheless, given that all *danna* patrons in Table 4 inherited their *danna* affiliation from their previous generation, and that this inheritance endured the years of anti-Buddhist storms during the early Meiji period, it offers some insight into the nature of *danna* holdings in Tokugawa society.

The *danna* are indicated as the numbers of individual *danna* patrons rather than number of *danna* households, so it would be difficult to determine how many of the latter were held by Buddhist temples. However, given that plural *danna* affiliations within the same household persisted, the data can offer a reasonably precise index of the strength of *danna* holdings within each temple. From Table 4 we know that, in the case of Tendaishū and Shingonshū, those temples with 200 or fewer *danna* patrons constituted close to 62 percent of all temples; that those with 201 to 500 *danna* patrons constituted about 23 percent; that those with 501–1,000 *danna* patrons constituted about 13 percent; and that those with more than 1,000 *danna* patrons constituted about 2 percent. In comparison, the Zenshū temples, like the Jōdoshū temples, did far better. For example, the approximate ratios of Sōtōshū temples that held *danna* patrons of corresponding ranges were 43 percent, 26 percent, 21 percent, and 10 percent, respectively. Temples belonging to Jōdoshinshū, Nichirenshū, Jishū, and Ōbakushū were relatively scant in Kōzuke province, but their *danna* holdings were not so different from those of Tendaishū and Shingonshū temples.

Table 4: *Danna* Holdings by Buddhist Temples in Kōzuke

Number of *danna*	1–100	101–200	201–300	301–400	401–500	501–600	601–800	801–1,000	1,001–3,000	3,001–	Total
					Number of temples						
Tendaishū	156	50	31	25	13	16	15	8	6	2	322
Shingonshū	171	76	50	31	16	22	25	13	10	0	414
Sōtōshū	73	74	42	26	20	17	32	22	33	2	341
Rinzaishū	14	6	4	7	3	3	1	2	5	0	45
Ōbakushū	3	1	0	1	0	0	0	0	1	0	6
Jōdoshū	16	17	10	5	11	4	9	2	4	0	78
Jishū	6	1	2	2	1	1	0	1	0	0	14
Nichirenshū	9	10	2	1	1	0	0	0	0	0	23
Jōdoshinshū	18	10	5	4	0	1	2	0	0	0	40
TOTAL	466	245	146	102	65	64	84	48	59	4	1,283
%	36.3	19.1	11.4	8.0	5.1	5.0	6.5	3.7	4.6	0.3	100.0

SOURCE: *Kōzuke no kuni jiin meisaichō* (Detailed registers of Buddhist temples in Kōzuke province).

It is hard to estimate how many *danna* patrons each Buddhist temple needed in order to sustain itself without supplementary income. What is clear is that those blessed with a large number of *danna* patrons were very rare in Kōzuke (only 4 out of a total of 1,283 temples had more than 3,000 *danna* patrons) and that variations in *danna* holdings were both wide and deep.[84] On the whole, those temples with 200 or fewer funerary *danna* patrons constituted about 55 percent of all temples, those with *danna* patrons ranging from 201 to 500 constituted about 25 percent, those with *danna* patrons ranging from 501 to 1,000 constituted about 15 percent, and those with more than 1,000 *danna* patrons constituted a bit less than 5 percent. It would be hard to imagine that those temples with no more than 200 *danna* patrons prospered on income from their funerary *danna* patrons alone. Many of these temples owned agricultural land that provided foodstuffs for them, and they also tried to tap other sources of income, such as prayer services (particularly so for Tendai and Shingon temples, which embraced *shugen* practitioners within their institutions), almsgiving, and the like. Nonetheless, as a whole, funerary *danna* patrons remained a most important source of income for the majority of temples in Kōzuke.

As Table 4 indicates, the patterns of funerary *danna* holdings showed a wide range of variations, depending on locality, sectarian strength, and the situation of individual temples. At a national level, how could these findings be compared? There are no comprehensive Tokugawa-period materials available for this purpose, but we do have an alternative source: the *Shaji torishirabe ruisan* (A classified collection of inquiries on shrines and temples), which contains data on the funerary *danna* holdings of Buddhist temples. This collection of materials, which was compiled by the Meiji government between 1870 and 1871, offers the best information on the patterns of Buddhist *danna* holdings not only because of its comprehensive cross-country data but also because of its temporal proximity to the Tokugawa period.[85] Based on this collection, we can get some ideas regarding the nature of *danna* holdings. For comparison, I have randomly chosen five different areas, from north to south (Kakuda in northern Honshū, Izu in eastern Honshū, Kurashiki in western Honshū, Ōzu in Shikoku, and Hita in Kyūshū).[86]

In Kakuda domain (currently part of Miyagi prefecture), where temples belonging to Shingonshū and Sōtōshū showed a strong presence (90 among 139 temples), those temples that had *danna* households ranging from 51 to 150 constituted about 48 percent of all temples, while those that had fewer than 50 *danna* households constituted almost 40 percent (see Table 5). In contrast, those temples having *danna* households ranging from 151 to 300 constituted about 9 percent of all temples, while those having more than 300 *danna* households constituted about 2 percent. In particular, many

Table 5: *Danna* Holdings by Buddhist Temples in Kakuda

Number of *danna*	1– 25	26– 50	51– 75	76– 100	101– 150	151– 200	201– 300	301– 600	601–	Total
					Number of temples					
Tendaishū	0	0	1	0	0	0	0	0	0	1
Shingonshū	13	˙10	7	1	7	0	0	0	0	38
Sōtōshū	2	14	14	8	6	3	2	2	1	52
Rinzaishū	1	3	4	4	4	0	1	0	0	17
Jōdoshū	0	3	2	1	1	2	0	0	0	9
Jishū	0	1	0	1	2	0	0	0	0	4
Nichirenshū	1	0	1	1	0	0	0	0	0	3
Jōdoshinshū	3	6	2	0	1	1	2	0	0	15
TOTAL	20	36	31	16	20	8	5	2	1	139
%	14.4	25.9	22.3	11.5	14.4	5.8	3.6	1.4	0.7	100.0

SOURCE: *Shaji torishirabe ruisan* (A classified collection of inquiries on shrines and temples).

Table 6: *Danna* Holdings by Buddhist Temples in Izu

Number of *danna*	1–25	26–50	51–75	76–100	101–150	151–200	201–300	301–600	601–	Total
					Number of temples					
Tendaishū	0	0	0	0	0	0	0	0	0	0
Shingonshū	5	2	2	2	0	0	0	0	0	11
Sōtōshū	32	33	37	14	9	8	3	0	0	136
Rinzaishū	28	32	17	9	7	3	2	0	0	98
Jōdoshū	10	11	9	2	1	3	0	1	0	37
Jishū	2	3	0	0	0	0	0	0	0	5
Nichirenshū	23	21	8	6	7	1	0	0	0	66
Jōdoshinshū	2	3	4	1	3	2	0	0	0	15
TOTAL	102	105	77	34	27	17	5	1	0	368
%	27.7	28.5	20.9	9.3	7.3	4.6	1.4	0.3	0	100.0

SOURCE: *Shaji torishirabe ruisan* (A classified collection of inquiries on shrines and temples).

temples, which embraced *shugen* practitioners, were *danna*-poor compared to Zenshū and Jōdoshū temples, which were relatively better off. However, the *shugen* practitioners of Shingonshū temples commanded another source of income: prayer ritual services, which contributed to the upkeep of their affiliated temples.

Izu, which did not have any Tendaishū temples, was dominated by Zenshū (136 Sōtōshū, 98 Rinzaishū) and Nichirenshū (66) temples, which combined to form more than 81 percent of all temples (see Table 6). In this situation, small-scale temples holding no more than 50 *danna* households constituted about 56 percent of all temples. In the case of Nichirenshū in particular, the ratio exceeded 66 percent. Across all sects, temples that maintained 51 to 150 *danna* households constituted about 37 percent of all temples. In contrast, those that maintained between 151 and 300 *danna* households constituted about 6 percent, while those that maintained more than 300 constituted only 1 percent.[87] Izu had more *danna*-poor temples than did Kakuda.

In Kurashiki, temples belonging to Shingonshū were the most numerous, accounting for 113 of 301 temples in total, whereas those belonging to Tendaishū (14) and Jōdoshū (8) were few (see Table 7). On the whole, those temples that held *danna* households of 50 or less constituted about 35 percent of all temples, whereas those that held 51 to 150 *danna* households constituted about 40 percent. *Danna*-rich temples were not so rare in Kurashiki. Temples that maintained

Table 7: *Danna* Holdings by Buddhist Temples in Kurashiki

Number of *danna*	1–25	26–50	51–75	76–100	101–150	151–200	201–300	301–600	601–	Total
	Number of temples									
Tendaishū	0	2	3	0	2	1	2	2	2	14
Shingonshū	11	12	18	13	11	10	22	15	1	113
Sōtōshū	20	16	14	7	9	2	1	0	0	69
Rinzaishū	7	6	1	2	1	0	0	0	0	17
Jōdoshū	1	1	3	2	0	0	1	0	0	8
Jishū	0	0	0	0	0	0	0	0	0	0
Nichirenshū	6	4	5	6	12	7	3	1	0	44
Jōdoshinshū	12	7	6	4	2	2	2	1	0	36
TOTAL	57	48	50	34	37	22	31	19	3	301
%	18.9	16.0	16.6	11.3	12.3	7.3	10.3	6.3	1	100.0

SOURCE: *Shaji torishirabe ruisan* (A classified collection of inquiries on shrines and temples).

151 to 300 *danna* households constituted about 18 percent of all temples, while those that maintained more than 300 *danna* households amounted to about 7 percent. Shingonshū temples exceeded all others: among its 113 temples, those holding more than 150 *danna* households constituted about 42 percent of the total, while those with 50 or fewer constituted only about 20 percent.

Ōzu was dominated by the Rinzaishū, with 84 temples, or more than 62 percent, out of a total of 134 temples. Shingonshū, which had 28 temples, followed Rinzaishū (see Table 8). In this situation of lopsided sectarian distribution, Rinzaishū temples were quite affluent in terms of *danna* holdings. Exactly one-half of its 84 temples maintained more than 150 *danna* households, whereas those that maintained 50 or fewer constituted about 10 percent. Myōōji, the Rinzaishū temple with the largest *danna* holdings, maintained 715 households. Across all sects, the approximate ratios of temples that maintained *danna* households of 50 or fewer, 51 to 150, 151 to 300, and more than 300 were, respectively, 12 percent, 41 percent, 39 percent, and 8 percent.

Hita showed a strong Jōdoshinshū presence (see Table 9). This sect had 190 temples, or about 48 percent, out of a total of 394 temples. Compared to Shingonshū, Sōtōshū, and Rinzaishū, which presented high ratios of *danna*-poor temples, Jōdoshinshū was relatively better off: 72 of the 190 Jōdoshinshū temples, or close to 38 percent,

Table 8: *Danna* Holdings by Buddhist Temples in Ōzu

Number of *danna*	1– 25	26– 50	51– 75	76– 100	101– 150	151– 200	201– 300	301– 600	601–	Total
					Number of temples					
Tendaishū	1	0	3	0	0	1	2	1	0	8
Shingonshū	1	1	4	3	6	6	5	2	0	28
Sōtōshū	0	0	0	0	0	0	0	0	0	0
Rinzaishū	4	5	5	6	22	15	19	7	1	84
Jōdoshū	0	0	0	0	0	0	0	0	0	0
Jishū	0	0	0	0	0	1	0	0	0	1
Nichirenshū	2	0	0	0	0	0	0	0	0	2
Jōdoshinshū	1	1	1	3	2	1	2	0	0	11
TOTAL	9	7	13	12	30	24	28	10	1	134
%	6.7	5.2	9.7	9.0	22.4	17.9	20.9	7.5	0.7	100.0

SOURCE: *Shaji torishirabe ruisan* (A classified collection of inquiries on shrines and temples).

Table 9: *Danna* Holdings by Buddhist Temples in Hita

Number of *danna*	1– 25	26– 50	51– 75	76– 100	101– 150	151– 200	201– 300	301– 600	601–	Total
					Number of temples					
Tendaishū	1	0	0	1	1	0	1	0	0	4
Shingonshū	5	3	5	3	2	0	0	0	0	18
Sōtōshū	31	18	7	11	9	7	1	1	0	85
Rinzaishū	11	3	2	4	7	3	1	0	0	31
Ōbakushū	3	1	0	0	0	0	0	0	0	4
Jōdoshū	5	7	9	5	9	7	2	1	0	45
Jishū	2	0	0	1	0	0	0	0	0	3
Nichirenshū	1	3	3	0	4	1	1	1	0	14
Jōdoshinshū	38	31	34	17	21	20	8	16	5	190
TOTAL	97	66	60	42	53	38	14	19	5	394
%	24.6	16.7	15.2	10.7	13.5	9.6	3.6	4.8	1.3	100.0

SOURCE: *Shaji torishirabe ruisan* (A classified collection of inquiries on shrines and temples).

maintained between 51 and 150 *danna* households; 49, or about 25 percent, maintained more than 150 *danna* households; and 21 maintained more than 300 *danna* households (among these, 5 temples maintained more than 600 *danna* households). The largest Jōdoshinshū *danna* holder was Eishōji, which had 6 subtemples and managed 1,397 *danna* households altogether. In Hita Jōdoshinshū stood out.[88] Across all sects, the approximate ratios of temples that held *danna* households of 50 or fewer, 51 to 150, 151 to 300, and more than 300 were, respectively, 41 percent, 39 percent, 13 percent, and 6 percent. The *danna* holdings of Buddhist temples in the five areas described above is summarized in Table 10, which indicates that about 41 percent of all temples had no more than 50 *danna* households and that about 40 percent maintained 51 to 150 *danna* households. This means that a majority of Buddhist temples survived with 150 or fewer *danna* households. Those that maintained more than 150 *danna* households constituted about 19 percent of the total, while those that maintained more than 300 did not exceed 5 percent.

Were urban areas different in the pattern of *danna* holdings from the rural areas discussed above? The data pertaining to the rural vicinities of Edo (various *honmatsu jigō sonota meisaichō* [1870–71] in the *Shaji torishirabe ruisan*) show that the number of *danna* households maintained by each funerary temple ranged from 1 to more than 900. In the Shinagawa area, for example, there were many small-scale funerary temples that had only a few *danna* households, whereas some relatively well-to-do temples—such as Konsenji (a Rinzaishū temple in Shinza county), Jōenji (a Nichirenshū temple in Toshima county), and Renchōji (a Nichirenshū temple in Musashi)—maintained more than 100 *danna* households (130, 150, and 160, respectively). Tōkaiji, a renowned Rinzaishū temple in Shinagawa,

Table 10: Summary of *Danna* Holdings by Buddhist Temples

Number of *danna*	1– 25	26– 50	51– 75	76– 100	101– 150	151– 200	201– 300	301– 600	601–	Total
					Number of temples					
Tendaishū	2	2	6	2	3	2	5	3	2	27
Shingonshū	35	28	36	22	26	16	27	17	1	208
Sōtōshū	85	81	72	40	33	20	7	3	1	342
Rinzaishū	51	49	29	25	41	21	23	7	1	247
Ōbakushū	3	1	0	0	0	0	0	0	0	4
Jōdoshū	16	22	23	10	11	12	3	2	0	99
Jishū	4	3	1	1	1	3	0	0	0	13
Nichirenshū	33	28	17	13	23	9	4	2	0	129
Jōdoshinshū	56	48	47	25	29	26	14	17	5	267
TOTAL	285	262	231	138	167	109	83	51	10	1,336
%	21.3	19.6	17.3	10.3	12.6	8.2	6.2	3.8	0.7	100.0

SOURCE: *Shaji torishirabe ruisan* (A classified collection of inquiries on shrines and temples).

oversaw 17 subtemples and 937 *danna* households. Among these subtemples, Hakuun'an was most privileged, with 519 *danna* households, followed by Shōrin'in (184), Shunhyakuan (84), and Seikōin (40). Sensōji in Asakusa was similar to Tōkaiji: according to a survey conducted in the early 1810s, Sensōji oversaw 20 funerary *danna*-holding subtemples and boasted more than 900 funerary *danna* households in total. Among the subtemples, Enmeiin far exceeded others with 256 *metsuzai* (annihilation of sins) *danna* households, followed by Henjōin (160), Hōzen'in (132), Tokuōin (123), and Kongōin (78).[89] With some exceptional cases such as Tōkaiji and Sensōji, a majority of temples in urban areas also had to be satisfied with relatively small numbers of *danna* holdings.

To be sure, the sheer number of *danna* households did not necessarily determine the level of economic well-being of a *danna* temple. Rather, the overall affluence and status of *danna* households often mattered more than their number, and the local customs and sectarian conventions that guided the ritual behavior of *danna* households could make a significant difference. Similarly, *danna* temples that were able to operate cemeteries and/or charnel houses could enhance income from the given pool of their *danna* households. Nevertheless, given that funerary Buddhism remained the financial mainstay of a majority of *danna* temples, and that the ways in which *danna* temples were involved in the death-related rituals of their *danna* households were by and large standardized throughout the country, the issue of how many *danna* households a temple was able to maintain could not be ignored. For this reason, temples usually paid the utmost attention to the task of securing as many *danna* households as possible.

Interestingly, in this game of competition over *danna* households, Jōdoshinshū temples, which lacked land endowments compared to those belonging to other sects, were often highly successful in securing a large number of *danna* households. Kodama Shiki, who examines the mode of *danna* holdings in Jōdoshinshū strongholds, offers some interesting findings, as may be seen in Table 11.[90] The table shows that the ratios of temples with no *danna* households were almost 14 percent in the Kaga domain and a bit less than 2 percent in the Chōshū domain. Temples that had 60 or fewer *danna* households reached as high as 19 percent in Kaga but only about 7 percent in Chōshū, whereas temples endowed with more than 300

Table 11: *Danna* Holdings by Jōdoshinshū Temples

No. of *danna*	0	1–30	31–60	61–150	151–300	301–600	601–
A. Kaga							
No. of temples	43	59	30	69	48	24	35
%	13.9	19.1	9.7	22.4	15.5	7.7	11.3
B. Chōshū							
No. of temples	8	34	64	172	137	50	12
%	1.7	7.1	13.4	36	28.7	10.4	2.5

SOURCE: All data in these tables, adapted from Kodama Shiki, p. 33, are based on temple registers in the *Shaji torishirabe ruisan.*
NOTES: Of the 308 Jōdoshinshū temples in Kaga, 279 belonged to the Higashihonganji subsect and 29 belonged to the Nishihonganji subsect. All 477 Jōdoshinshū temples in Chōshū belonged to the Nishihonganji subsect.

danna households amounted to 19 percent in Kaga but only 13 percent in Chōshū. In particular, ten temples in Kaga maintained more than 1,500 *danna* households, and among these temples, six had more than 3,000 *danna* households, and one nearly 6,000 *danna* households; in contrast, no temples in Chōshū maintained more than 1,500 *danna* households. Temples that maintained 61 to 300 *danna* households numbered about 38 percent in Kaga compared to about 65 percent in Chōshū. In sum, Kaga presented a high degree of disparity between *danna*-poor and *danna*-rich temples in comparison with Chōshū, whose temples were concentrated in the middle range.[91]

From these tendencies, and based on additional examples in other Jōdoshinshū areas, Kodama Shiki suggests two patterns of *danna* holdings: the Chōshū type and the non-Chōshū (or Hokuriku) type, seen in such areas as Hokuriku, Tōhoku, Aki, Iwami, Buzen, and Bungo.[92] Understandably, many small-scale temples in the non-Chōshū regions that lacked a self-sufficient *danna* base often served as local agents for those great temples that embraced a large number of *danna* households over a wide area. In contrast, a majority of temples in Chōshū maintained their *danna* households locally and exercised tight control over them, allowing them to remain highly self-sufficient and autonomous.[93]

As a whole, the *danka* system in which temples were able to secure *danna* households as a major source of income was firmly entrenched in Tokugawa society and has been transmitted to the present.[94] Although it does not mean that the subsistence of *danna* temples was all singularly determined by the financial contribution of their funerary *danna* households, the authoritarian monopoly with which the former dealt with death-related rituals for the latter was poised to serve as the central station of Buddhist power that penetrated deep into the life-world of the Tokugawa Japanese.

CҘ

FIVE

Buddhist Mortuary Rituals

For the Tokugawa Japanese, death signified more than the permanent cessation of biological life. They believed, as did other peoples, that death released the soul from the body, and that if the surviving family of the deceased provided good care for the soul, then it would travel to the other world and join its ancestors. The idea that the soul was an entity separable from the body was the starting point of all death rituals, whose goal was to smooth the soul's transition into the other world.

The duality of soul and body that enabled the soul's transition from the old life in this world to the new life in the other naturally led to other concerns about the process involved in the decomposition of the body. The Tokugawa Japanese inherited the age-old idea that the corpse emitted a destructive energy and was, therefore, a defilement, a source of pollution, disorder, and immorality. These beliefs continued to be evident in the ritualized handling of corpses in early modern times. The task of how to dispose of the corpse was an essential component of any mortuary ritual in Tokugawa Japan.[95]

A third challenge involved restructuring the social constellation that was disrupted by death. As cultural anthropologists have observed, a death is not simply a private matter: it is also a social incident that disrupts normal social life, attacks social cohesion, and disturbs social equilibrium.[96] The death of a person cannot be fully grasped without referring to the social context within which he or she once had a stake. The task of understanding how the Tokugawa

Japanese dealt with death, therefore, also involves understanding how they tried to restore order to social relations and to ensure their collective well-being.

In dealing with the death of a family member that entailed these concerns, the Tokugawa Japanese followed a series of ritual measures that can be grouped into four stages. The first-stage rite concerned the idea of the separation of the soul and the body. Based on the belief that, if the departing soul could be lured back into the body, then the dead could come back to life, the first action taken upon the death of a family member involved trying to bring his or her soul back to the body. This gave rise to a rite known as "calling back the soul" (*shōkon*), or "bringing back to life" (*sosei*). This first-stage rite, however, soon yielded to concerns with addressing feelings of loss, sorrow, uncertainty, defilement, fear, and distance. These were dealt with by the second-stage rite, which involved appeasing the soul, taking care of the corpse while it decomposed, and trying to protect survivors from the danger that death might pose. This rite, known as "appeasing the soul" (*chinkon*), or "cutting off the connection" (*zetsuen*), aimed to sever the worldly ties between the living and the deceased so that the latter might smoothly move to the other world. After the rite of severance, a funeral ritual was held in order to send the soul to the other world, where it would attain eternal life as a "Buddha" or *hotoke*. This constituted the third-stage rite: the rite of "transforming [the deceased] into a Buddha" (*jōbutsu*), or "sending off the soul" (*sōkon*). Once this rite was completed, the corpse was entombed or cremated and its ashes were buried. Even then, the rituals for disposing of the corpse and for transforming the soul into a "Buddha" were not complete. The fourth-stage rite, which took place over an extended period of time, was designed to facilitate the transformation of the deceased into an ancestral deity and was known as "making merit on behalf of the deceased" (*tsuizen kuyō*). Here, merit (acquired through ritual actions) refers to the virtue of effort (*kudoku*; *punya* in Sanskrit), which, in Buddhist theory, is believed to offset the bad karma of the deceased. The Tokugawa Japanese believed that through the power of these intercessory rites, the deceased would eventually be transformed into an ancestral deity in the other world.[97]

To one degree or another, death rituals in Tokugawa society all addressed the preceding four rites; however, it should be noted that these rites, which were composed of bits and pieces of many ideas, practices, and customs, were never free from local variations. They could be diffuse, redundant, overlapping, and self-contradictory. They could even be reversed. For example, in many regions families erected "breathing bamboo" (*ikitsuki take*) on the grave after performing a rite of separation, in the hope that the hollow bamboo stick that reached to the coffin and jutted out into the air might encourage the deceased to come back to life. In western Japan, while conducting memorial services for the deceased—who was, in theory, on his or her way to the other world—families still believed that his or her soul stayed at the roof ridge of the house, and they would make a symbolic gesture to attempt to bring him or her back to this world.[98]

Interestingly, these rites pertaining to death and postmortem care were collectively referred to as "Buddhist rituals" or *butsuji*, a term that attests to the fact that, in Tokugawa society, death did indeed occur under the aegis of Buddhism. In 1683 Tokugawa Mitsukuni of the Mito domain, in his seventeen-article admonition delivered to Kyūshōji (a temple erected as a prayer hall for his deceased mother), commented on Buddhism's involvement in mortuary rituals.[99] The seventh article reads: "These days a funeral has become the job of Buddhist monks who have learned how to conduct it and have turned it into their routine business. Lamentably, the death of a patron or *dan'otsu* has become their source of income. The Law of the Buddha has met its demise. What could be more terrible than this!"[100] Mitsukuni was highly critical of Buddhist monks for whom death rituals were a vehicle of sustenance. He was no less harsh in his assessment of the populace, as may be seen in the eighth article: "These days, in conducting Buddhist rituals for the deceased, family members pay attention to setting up their mortuary tablet at the Buddhist hall and to conducting memorial services by decorating the altar with incense, flowers, tea and cookies. All these material offerings do not fulfill even one-hundredth of what should really be offered to the Buddha."[101] Despite its critical tone, Mitsukuni's admonition never questioned why funerary rituals and ancestral rites should be conducted under the guidance of Buddhism. From top to bottom, rituals related to death and designed to produce ancestral deities, no matter how they were conducted, were under the sway of Buddhism.

The Rite of Calling Back the Soul

When a family member neared death, or right after he or she died, the remaining family members practiced the rite of calling his or her name. However, the manner in which this age-old spirit-beckoning rite, known as "calling the soul" (*tamayobi*), was conducted was not uniform. Most commonly, a family member would climb onto the roof of the house and, facing in the direction of the family gravesite, a mountain, the sea, the west, or the deceased, would shout something like "please come back [the name of the deceased]." This rite, designed to lure the spirit back into the body, was often accompanied by beating the lid of a kettle or a wooden measure (*masu*) or by waving a cloth, a ladle, or a winnowing basket. In the northern Musashi and western Tsugaru areas, a family member would stick his or her head into a well and call the name of the dying in order to bring back his or her soul.[102]

At the same time, when a death occurred, family members, relatives, and neighbors would commence wailing. They would do this not just out of sorrow but also in order to bring the departing soul back to the body. According to Akata Mitsuo, the custom of wailing, in which, during the seventeenth century, all family members and relatives participated, varied locally; and when a young person died, the weeping was especially intense. Over time, however, the custom of wailing for the purpose of bringing the deceased back to this world came to be dominated by women (female members of the family and female villagers), who were believed to be closer to *kami* than were men. Eventually, this custom was taken over by professional female wailers.[103]

With regard to professional female wailers, known as *nakime*, in the villages of Uonuma county in Echigo "[the family] hires a woman who can weep with a voice loud enough to create a mournful wailing. It is said that, depending upon the wealth of the family and upon her skills, the wailing can fetch one *shō* (= 0.477 gallon) of rice or two *shō* of rice."[104] In Awaji, families usually hired an old, experienced woman as a wailer.[105] Customs in the Mito domain were diverse, but professional wailing was still widely practiced in conjunction with the wish to revive the deceased: "Some peasant families have a custom of beating drums, and others hire a wailer. The wailer wails and speaks of the good things the deceased has done."[106] Overall, however, under the influence of Buddhist monks, who played a more and more active role in mortuary rituals, professional wailers became increasingly marginalized and many disappeared.[107]

The custom of wailing was on the decline, but this did not mean that the desire to resuscitate the dead had also declined. In fact, it remained strong throughout the Tokugawa period. Saitō Ryūzo describes an Edo custom: "On one's deathbed, family members and relatives gather and moisten one's lips. This is referred to as the water of last moments."[108] The action of dampening the lips of the dying or the dead with a brush or a chopstick wrapped in cotton was a last-ditch effort to keep his or her life from departing. This custom known as "water at the final moment" (*matsugo no mizu*) was based on the story of Śākyamuni, who was said to have sought water right before slipping into Nirvana.[109]

Indeed, there were many stories pertaining to the successful resuscitation of the dead, and these aroused much curiosity. In his *Mimibukuro* (A sack of ears), Negishi Yasumori (1737–1815) recounts several episodes: "In 1794 a man in the Shiba area, who had made a living by performing tedious manual jobs, was suddenly found dead. Members of the *nenbutsu* confraternity to which he belonged got together and buried him at a temple. But one or two days later, people could hear a groaning sound coming from the inside of his grave. The monk of the temple, who was frightened, informed the caretaker about the grave and dug it out. Alas, the man was alive!"[110] Stories like this encouraged many families to erect *ikitsuki take* on the grave so that the deceased might start breathing again and let friends and relatives know of his or her revival.[111] For the Tokugawa Japanese, it did not matter whether or not these events had actually occurred: what mattered was the possibility, however slight, of bringing their loved ones back to life. Thus the custom of calling back the soul lingered on.

Appeasing the Soul, or Cutting Off the Connection

"When one closes his or her eyes and dies, the family seals its household Shinto shrine [*kamidana*] in order to keep the defiled energy [of the deceased] from penetrating it. And then the family closes the front doors and hangs bamboo blinds at the entrance."[112] This was a typical scene when a family member died in Tokugawa Japan. Right after a person's death, the rite of calling back the soul was performed with great seriousness. However, as time passed and efforts to resuscitate the deceased continued to fail, the fear of the defiling nature of death set in. The family then took various steps to prevent the defiling energy or ritual pollution (*kegare*) of death from spreading.[113]

Traditionally, the "red impurity" caused by menstrual blood and the "white impurity" caused by the blood of childbirth were both feared; however, neither was feared as much as was the "black impurity" caused by death. With regard to death as an object of fear and danger, Edmund Leach's theory of taboo helps us understand the cultural matrix of "black impurity." Reasoning that "if A and B are two verbal categories, such that B is defined as 'what A is not' and vice versa, and there is a third category C which mediates this distinction, in that C shares attributes of both A and B, then C will be tabooed,"[114] Leach suggests that a new death (C), located at the transitional threshold between this world (A) and the other world (B), is tabooed because it violates the established order and confuses certain fundamental categories that give order to human life. In other words, a new death is an ambiguity in so far as it represents a state of transition and limbo, and ambiguity triggers intense feelings of curiosity and anxiety, as may be seen in a general abhorrence of supernatural beings of a highly ambiguous kind, such as ghosts, monsters, and the like, which do not clearly belong to either this world or the other world.[115] Death as an object of taboo is, therefore, not concerned so much with the deceased as with the living, who are poised to restore the status quo disrupted by death through the actions of taboo, prohibition, and abstinence. In Tokunoshima, Satsuma, when a family member neared death, all grain seeds were removed from the house out of fear of pollution and put in a safe place. If a family failed to take this measure, then it had to burn or dump all of the "contaminated" grain seeds, which were referred to as "troubled seeds" (*komaridane*).[116]

In other regions, peasants shunned using horses and cows that had been exposed to the pollution of death. It was not only things and animals but also "contaminated" time that had to be dealt with cautiously. When a death occurred on a day or in a month associated with special religious events, the Tokugawa Japanese believed that its defiled energy would gain extra strength and that therefore an extra effort would be required to eradicate it. For example, in the Iwaki region in Fukushima, a family that suffered a death between the first and the fifteenth day of the first month (known as the minor new year, *koshōgatsu*) buried the corpse in secret and at night. Only after the sacred period of the New Year had passed were they allowed to have a formal funeral procession (even though this involved the carrying of an empty coffin). Similarly, if only rarely and under special circumstances, memorial services for the dead could be tabooed in the first, fifth, and ninth months, during which Buddhist temples held special prayer rituals for the "three seasons" (*sanki*).[117]

Not surprisingly, the measure taken by the Tokugawa Japanese against the pollution of death contained cultural elements that were specific to Japanese religious tradition. For example, immediately after a death most families hung blinds over entrances and vulnerable spots in the house in order to protect them. Paper or bamboo materials were favored as these were the materials traditionally used to make a temporary lodging place for deities called *yorishiro*. Paper was believed to be an advanced form of *yorishiro* that had evolved from *sakaki* tree branches, which were commonly used in Shinto purification rites. And bamboo twigs were a common instrument used by a female shrine-shaman, or *miko*, when performing divine dances (*kagura*) and calling upon the deities for aid. The Tokugawa Japanese believed that these traditional *yorishiro* materials possessed special power capable of attenuating the defiling energy of the dead.

Within the overall context of spatial and temporal demarcation, as the mortuary ritual progressed, the effort to cleanse death pollution shifted to the behavior of those who were exposed to death. To begin with, family members were all expected to refrain from conducting routine business, and, in particular, adult males did not shave. The custom of leaving unshaven the usually shaved front part of the head (*sakayaki*) was a way of expressing grief and abstention.[118] Another custom involved hanging a lantern at the main entrance of the house along with the sign reading "in mourning" or "in the middle of abstinence" (*kichū*). The "abstinence" lantern served to inform the neighborhood of the occurrence of a death. Upon receiving notice of a death, those in the village whose age was the same as that of the deceased feared that they might also be taken to the other world. As a way of preventing this, they sealed their ears with glutinous rice cake and pretended as though they had not heard of the death. They would also eat fresh fish in order to strengthen their spirit. These precautionary customs stemmed from the belief that people of the same age belonged to the same spiritual community and that their cosmic fates, like their social lives, were bound together.[119]

A death affected not only the individual but also the community. In the name of communal abstinence, loud noises, excessive gestures, festive dining and drinking, recreational activities, and so on were all banned. In the rural areas it was customary for the abstinence lantern to be hung only after the village head had signed it. This was to ensure that death would be dealt with communally, with the full cooperation of all villagers. This rule was very strong, and no one was exempt, as is dramatically demonstrated by the system of village ostracism. Commonly known as *murahachibu*, village ostracism was designed to punish a household that had committed theft, violence, arson, or some other act that was deemed destructive to communal life. As the term *murahachibu* (literally "eight parts out of ten") indicates, an ostracized household was forbidden from participating in eight areas (or "parts") of social interaction (i.e., coming-of-age ceremonies, weddings, memorial services, births, sickness, floods, travel, and building and repairs [particularly roof thatching]). There were only two areas of social interaction—fire and funerals—in which they could be included.[120] In this scheme, when a death occurred in the ostracized household, all villagers were alerted and were expected to help out with the funeral. This offer of help was, of course, not out of sympathy; rather, it stemmed from need to expunge the danger that death might pose to the entire community.

Pollution never occurs in isolation: it is always part of a system. As Mary Douglas suggests: "Where there is dirt there is system. Dirt is the by-product of a systematic ordering and classification of matter, in so far as ordering involves rejecting inappropriate elements."[121] In expunging danger from, and restoring order to, a system disrupted by the death of one of its members, society as a whole engages in a collective effort of abstinence. At the national level, for example, the death of the shogun entailed two bans: one prohibiting the samurai class from shaving their *sakayaki*, and the other prohibiting among the general populace the use of all "things that make noise" (*narimono*). The ban on *narimono*, which refers to musical performances and entertainment, was usually accompanied by a ban on construction work (*fushin*).[122] For the samurai, leaving the *sakayaki* unshaven was a way of demonstrating their feelings of sorrow as well as their respect for the dead leader. Depending upon the distance from the deceased shogun, one's position, and one's family status, the length of the ban on *sakayaki* varied from a few days to nearly fifty.[123] As for the populace, maintaining tranquility and abstinence during the period of the ban on *narimono* (which could be as long as a month) was a way of participating in a nationwide effort to "restore order in the wake of the political crisis created by the death of the king."[124]

The ban on *narimono* was issued not only when the shogun died but also when the emperor, imperial family members, shogunal family members, or high *bakufu* officials died. The length of abstinence varied, with that for the shogun outdoing that for all others, including the emperor.[125] As Hayashi Yukiko suggests, here we see a sort of "hierarchy of death pollution" carefully constructed to underpin the political order of the *bakuhan* system, at the helm of which was Tōshō Daigongen (Tokugawa Ieyasu), the founder of the Tokugawa shogunate.[126]

The political utility of death pollution was systematically exploited when, in 1684, the shogunate introduced the "law of mourning and abstinence" (*bukkiryō*), a series of state regulations on how people should mourn and from what they should abstain when their parents and relatives die. According to this law, which had undergone numerous minor emendations until its abolition in 1874, children were required to engage in abstinence for 50 days and in mourning for 13 months following the death of a parent. During these periods, no one in the family was allowed to participate in a festival or to be involved in Shinto-related matters. The duration of abstinence varied, depending upon who died, how the living were related to the dead, and under what circumstances one came to know of the death.[127] In all cases, the mourning of a death, which had been a private family matter, was now subject to the whims of state law. By guiding and regulating the "innermost order of the household" in the name of "filial piety and etiquette," the shogunate strove to strengthen the ideological apparatus of the *bakuhan* system.[128]

No matter what measures were taken to suppress or preempt death pollution, the mortuary ritual had to deal with the task of handling the dead body. "The corpse is laid on a straw mat, with its head pointing in the direction of the north and the body facing the western direction, and is enclosed by a folding screen. A picture of the Buddha is hung in the room, and a fire is lit on small pieces of incense wood [a Japanese star anise] by the bedside of the dead."[129] The positioning of the dead body derives from the legend that, on his deathbed, Śākyamuni asked his disciple Ānanda to lay his body toward the west with the head facing north because he wished the Buddhist dharma to spread north after his death.[130] Whether people were aware of this story or not, placing the body in that particular direction became a well-established custom, due probably to the belief in the Western Paradise. In many regions "a short sword is then laid by the dead body in order to ward off malevolent spirits."[131] In some areas rice cake dumplings, known as "pillow dumplings" (*makuradango*), were offered to the dead on the grounds that they were powerful enough to counter the defilement of death and/or to return the departed to life.[132]

After this, the family began to receive mourners who came to offer their condolences or help. At the same time the family was required to report the death to its *danna* temple. Upon being notified, a monk, commonly referred to as *kōsori* ("shaven head"), would visit the family (often accompanied by village or ward officials), offer a brief recitation of a "pillow sūtra" (*makuragyō*), a Buddhist sūtra chanted at the "pillow-side" of the deceased, and then inspect the body in order to determine whether or not death had occurred naturally.[133] In the late 1890s, Ichioka Masakazu, who had served the Tokugawa *bakufu*, recalled in his *Tokugawa seiseiroku* (A record of Tokugawa prosperity): "When there is evidence of unnatural death for which a written explanation is not provided, [the *danna* temple] neither recognizes the death nor offers a funeral. [Even if there is] no hard evidence of unnatural death, when it is suspected [the *danna* temple] neither recognizes the death nor offers a funeral unless the relatives submit a cosigned document that invalidates the suspicion."[134] In the case of a natural death that passes *danna* inspection, village officials updated the village's census register of sectarian inspection. In the case of an unnatural or suspicious death, the government conducted an official investigation.

Once the death was declared legal, the relatives, members of mutual assistance groups (usually a *nenbutsu* confraternity), neighbors, and the *danna* temple were publicly involved in the tasks of laying the dead to rest and of restoring normalcy to the community.[135] The first tasks came with the arrival of night: relatives gathered and washed the body using a vessel in which hot water had been added to cold (a reversal of ordinary practice) and outfitted the deceased with a new robe known as a "sūtra garment" (*kyōkatabira*). This garment was made of hemp, cotton, or paper stitched using thread with no knots and was inscribed with lines from Buddhist scripture. A Buddhist monk from the *danna* temple then would chant sūtras and shave the corpse's head (often symbolically, by cutting a small clump of hair on the front part of the head). Shaving the head and shrouding the body in a "sūtra garment" were actions designed to prepare the deceased to renounce this world and to follow the path of Buddhist salvation into the other world.[136]

Around this time, as a token of initiating the deceased into the Buddhist path to salvation, "the head monk of the *danna* temple grants a posthumous Buddhist name to the deceased. A Buddhist name usually consists of four or six characters chosen from among Buddhist words that offer a eulogy to the deceased."[137] The name was then inscribed on two temporary white mortuary tablets (*ihai*): one of these was placed beside the deceased during the funeral and then taken to the grave, and the other was placed on the household Buddhist altar for memorial services. The Jōdoshinshū sect, which assured its followers of salvation without being mired in transmigration, insisted that there was no need to use mortuary tablets.[138] Nonetheless, as Ekū (1644–1721) observed in his *Sōrinshū* (1698), from the late seventeenth century many Jōdoshinshū followers belonging to the "temples in the barbarous peripheries" secretly adopted the custom of enshrining "spirit tablets" at the household Buddhist altar, particularly in the Tōkai, Kyūshū, Shikoku, and Tōhoku regions.[139]

A posthumous Buddhist name, or *kaimyō* ("precept name"), originally referred to a two-character *hōgō* or *hōmyō* ("dharma name") that was conferred upon those who had completed all procedures involved in renouncing the secular world and had entered the gate of the Buddhist *sangha* (i.e., those who were ordained as Buddhist monks).[140] This involved the official approval of the initiation of a Buddhist neophyte into the world of Buddhist dharma. In the context of mortuary ritual, however, the name was simply given to the deceased as he or she was undergoing a funeral — a ritual considered equivalent to the Buddhist ordination ceremony. Moreover, in Tokugawa society a posthumous name did not end with the two- or four-character *kaimyō* common to ordination; rather, it was usually accompanied by a titular suffix indicating the rank of the recipient in the hierarchy of Buddhist designation, such as (in order of descending rank) *koji*, *shinji*, *zenjōmon*, and *zenmon* for a man, and *daishi*, *shinnyo*, *zenjōni*, and *zenni* for a woman. Those who belonged to the upper echelon of the samurai class were often decorated with such an honorific prefix as *ingō* or *indengō* ("name of cloister"). In the case of a child, a suffix such as *dōji* (young boy) or *dōjo* (young girl) was attached to the posthumous name.[141] It was no secret that all these titular affixes hinged upon the deceased's lineage, wealth, social position, and status. In other words, everyone knew that these names were granted in accord with the financial contributions of the deceased's family to the *danna* temple.

After the conferral of a posthumous Buddhist name, the body of the deceased, shrouded in the "sūtra garment," was prepared to be placed in the coffin, usually purchased from a funeral house:[142] around its neck was tied a sack in which "six-courses coins" (*rokudō-sen*) and Buddhist amulets were deposited, a triangular hat was put on its head, gaiters were tied to its legs, straw sandals were attached to the front and back of its body, and a rosary of 108 beads was placed in its hands.[143] Details of this kind of adornment were largely a matter of local custom and manners; however, the common purpose was to prepare the deceased for the process of transition from this world to the other world.

The posture of the deceased in the coffin was that of a traveler who was about to embark on a long, "six-course" journey to the other world. The custom of providing "six-courses coins," which refers to a set of six copper coins (after 1636, mostly Kan'ei *tsūhō*), stemmed from a vulgar theory of Buddhist transmigration which held that, after death, the deceased would pass through six stages in the underworld.[144] More commonly, people believed that the "six-courses coins" would be needed when the deceased was ferried over the *Sanzu no kawa*, an underworld river (even though this river had nothing to do with the six-stages cosmology). From the early seventeenth century families followed the fad of burying coins along with the dead, and some daimyo families even buried small gold pieces. Being concerned that this was wasteful, the shogunate banned this custom in 1742 (to little effect).[145] On the other hand, amulets inscribed with Buddhist symbols and the 108-bead rosary were fetishes that were thought to protect the soul of the deceased from evil spirits during its journey, while the footgear was to ensure the comfort of the traveler.

Despite all the care taken with the deceased, the journey was supposed to be a one-way trip. Unlike the earlier stage at which the family called back the soul, at this stage the family paid much attention to ensuring that, once departed, the deceased did *not* return: the heels of straw sandals were threaded on a string and tied to the fingertips, or the body was tightly tied with a straw rope, to prevent the corpse from turning around.[146] The well-being of the deceased in the other world was strongly desired but, at the same time, his or her return to this world was feared. Wishing the deceased to lead a comfortable life, families often deposited things in the coffin that might be needed in the other world, including items such as grains, bowls, bottles, spoons, chopsticks, vessels, knives, needles, cosmetic articles, smoking pipes, and the like, along with his or her personal belongings. If a husband died, the wife cut a bit of her hair and placed it in his coffin to show that she would not "see" another man. In the case of children, toys and dolls were placed in the coffins.[147] Feelings of grief and fear collided during the ritual of severing ties with the deceased.

After laying the dead body in the coffin, family members and relatives kept vigil over it throughout the night. This was a wake, commonly known as *tsuya*, and it inherited some elements from the ancient custom of *mogari*, in which mourners "lived with" an encoffined dead emperor or aristocrat in a specially erected building or "mourning hut" (*moya*) for a certain period of time before burying or cremating the body.[148] In some regions, the surviving family members used to seclude themselves in a segregated hut, where they stayed with the deceased for a few days and observed a life of abstinence. The custom of *tsuya*, in which mourners shut themselves up (*komoru*), was originally an expression of the wish to revive the dead by sleeping with him or her in the same room.[149] In extreme cases, the family member who was considered closest to the dead hugged the corpse during the *tsuya* in order to resuscitate it. In other cases, it was only female family members who were allowed in the *tsuya* room; this was because it was believed that their nurturing power could bring the dead back to this world.[150] However, under the influence of Buddhism, *tsuya* was gradually transformed from a rite for reviving the deceased into a rite for protecting the soul of the deceased from evil spirits. During the *tsuya*, a monk from the *danna* temple usually chanted the *Amitābha Sūtra* in order to solicit Buddhist merit and ensure the departing soul's smooth passage to the other world.[151] The Tokugawa Japanese believed that the observance of *tsuya* would result in the soul of the deceased being safely separated from the body.

The Funeral Ceremony

The *tsuya* was followed by a funeral. The scale of preparations was determined by the status and wealth of the family. As we see in the records of a wealthy and influential farming family (the Kuramochi house) from Kutsukake village in Shimōsa in 1850, funerals could involve elaborate planning. This family organized a large number of relatives and helpers into several small groups in order to greet the

officiating monk from the *danna* temple and other monks (the officiating head monk was to arrive on horseback followed by a procession), escorting and treating mourners, setting up resting places for
mourners and monks, preparing food offerings for the deceased and
meals for the guests, receiving and recording "incense offerings" or
"incense money" (*kōden*), and so forth.[152]

In the rural areas the funeral was usually held at the house belonging to the family of the deceased. At this time the neighbors
would begin to visit the family and offer their condolences as well
as "incense offerings." In the Kantō area relatives usually brought
glutinous rice steamed with red beans (*kowameshi*), and neighbors
offered rice, grain, incense, candles, tea, noodles, cookies, fruits, and
the like. From the mid-eighteenth century these material items were
gradually replaced with currency that went directly toward defray-
ing funeral expenses. In return, the funerary family would treat their
callers with food and drinks and, after the funeral, thank them by
sending them handkerchiefs, paper, or money.[153]

In urban areas, which did not have the luxury of space, funeral
ceremonies were usually held at the *danna* temple. In Edo, for example, the family would dispatch a messenger to its *danna* temple
to post a sign on its gate announcing the upcoming funeral. Food,
drinks, and tea bowls, all prepared for the mourners who would
attend the funeral, were transported to the temple. The coffin would
then be carried by pallbearers in a procession. The mourners called
at the temple to pay their condolences, and, soon after the funeral
procession had arrived, the family treated them with glutinous rice
steamed with red beans wrapped in a bamboo leaf.[154] Although
rare, sometimes the coffin was carried directly to the gravesite for
a simple funeral. On the other hand, Jōdoshinshū families, which
practiced cremation, conducted funeral ceremonies at ritual halls
attached to crematoria.

There were two types of funeral ceremony, depending upon how
the deceased was related to the chief mourner: (1) a full-scale ceremony for grandparents, parents, and principal wife; and (2) a minor
ceremony for siblings and children. In the case of a full-scale funeral,
where the head monk and accompanying ritual monks were present,
it was customary to invite monks from other temples as well. In
Aki, for example, sons and daughters who had been adopted or
married out to other families, and who therefore did not have direct
funeral responsibilities toward the deceased, often brought the monks

of their *danna* temples to the funeral.[155] A minor ceremony was customarily presided over by a monk from the *danna* temple (sans accompanying monks), and the mourners were limited to close relatives and friends.

Despite wide variations in scale and magnitude, the setting for a funeral ceremony was not complex. When it was held at a house, the room containing the coffin was used as a stage. The coffin was usually half surrounded by a folding screen or curtains, and on both sides of it candles or lanterns were lit. Monks from the *danna* temple stood by the folding screen and led the ceremony. When a funeral was held at the *danna* temple, the ritual setting took full advantage of the Buddhist altar in the main hall. Terakado Seiken (1796–1868) observed of a funeral in Edo: "As soon as the coffin arrives at the temple, it is placed between central columns in the main hall. Family members take seats on the eastern steps, and guest mourners take seats on the western steps across the columns."[156] Then the ceremony would commence: "Amid the sounds of the clanging of a gong and chanting of a sūtra on the part of hired monks, who line up along both sides of the columns, the chief priest quietly enters, clearing his throat, and stands facing the coffin. He waves a ritual horsehair flapper (*hossu*) and leads the ceremony."[157]

Issac Titsingh (ca. 1740–1812), who lived in Nagasaki between 1779 and 1781 as the head of the Dutch East India Company's operations in Japan, collected information on the Japanese way of life, including wedding and burial customs.[158] His description of a funeral at a Jōdoshū temple is quite detailed:

As soon as the coffin has reached the temple where the priests are already assembled, it is set down before the image of the god, and the priests immediately begin to read hymns. The ihai [spiritual tablet] is placed before the coffin, and before the ihai are set some plates of sweetmeats, pears and flowers, and in the front of these the "burning-incense," or small box for burning incense. The eldest son steps up before the ihai, says his prayers, and burns some incense; when he has returned to his place all the relatives and friends do the same one after another. The priests having read hymns for about half an hour, the bells are struck, the drums beaten, the yamabushi [Shugen practitioners] sound their trumpets, and the komusō [mendicant monks], the flutes . . . After reading a hymn in this position, the coffin is taken up and carried to the grave.[159]

Titsingh's depiction summarizes the procedure of a Jōdoshū funeral featuring the chanting of sūtras and hymns and the offering of incense burning—ritual actions conducted amid the musical accompaniment of bells, gongs, drums, and the like. This was a scene one could commonly observe in Buddhist funerals in Tokugawa Japan.

Structurally, all Buddhist funerals were designed to send the deceased to the other world via the path of Buddhist salvation. In order to accomplish this, most Buddhist funerals (with the exception of those conducted according to Nichirenshū and Jōdoshinshū beliefs) incorporated two essential ritual components: the establishment of the deceased as a Buddhist disciple through the conferring of a set of Buddhist precepts, a sort of posthumous ordination (*jukai; upasaṃpad* or *upasaṃpanna* in Sanskrit); and the guiding of the deceased, now a newly anointed Buddhist disciple, to rebirth in the Pure Land, or Paradise (*indō; parikarṣaṇa* in Sanskrit). The first component could be started, depending on sectarian traditions, when the deceased was tonsured or encoffined, when a posthumous name was conferred, or during the *tsuya*; however, in all cases, the process had to be completed before or during the funeral ceremony so that the deceased would be ready to enter the path of Buddhist salvation as a newly committed Buddhist (*shibochi*). The ritual formula for the second component varied. For example, Shingon Buddhists tended to perform a *kanjō* ceremony (*abhiṣeka* in Sanskrit), which featured sprinkling water on the head of the deceased. In the case of Zen sects (Sōtō, Rinzai, and Ōbaku), the formula usually consisted of a brief sermon concerning the emptiness of attachments and desires.[160] As can be seen, in conducting the *jukai* and *indō* rites, each sect followed its own ritual tradition, even though the goal was the same: the smooth transition of the deceased from the world of desire and ignorance to the Buddhist world of bliss.

Being centered on ordination and guidance toward salvation, Buddhist funerals required ritual elements that would help extinguish the sins of the deceased. Since the deceased could not cleanse themselves, these ritual elements involved the indirect soteriological path of *ekō*, in which the bad karma of the deceased was offset by a transfer of merit from the living.[161] With the power of transferred religious merit, the deceased was believed to be reborn in the heavenly paradise. Given the karmic doctrine of self-responsibility and the inactive state of the deceased, the soteriological path of *ekō* was understandable. If we put aside doctrinal implications, the issue at stake in this stage of mortuary ritual is how to invoke the compassion of Buddhist deities and thereby generate the transfer of religious merit. Ritual strategies for this could be diverse, but sūtra chanting, *dhāraṇī* (spells or mantras), and hymns were most common.

Sūtra chanting, which constituted a liturgical means of learning the doctrinal truth and moral ideals of Buddhist scriptures (and, therefore, was held to be an effective form of merit-making), was a fixture of Buddhist funerals.[162] When one read or recited a sūtra it did not really matter whether or not one understood its discursive meaning. In some cases, only a few words or phrases — and in most cases, only one or two fascicles, or *gāthā* (verses epitomizing the teachings of the Buddha or praising the grace of buddhas and bodhisattvas) — of a sūtra were chanted. And in the case of Nichiren Buddhism, the title of the *Lotus Sūtra* was repeatedly chanted in the belief that it embodied the totality of the sūtra — a practice known as *daimoku*.

However, depending on sectarian traditions and ritual formulae, the sūtras favored for recitation could vary. In the case of Shingon-shū, the *Adhyardhaśatikā-prajñāpāramitā Sūtra* (*Rishukyō*) was preferred, and in the case of Tendaishū, the *Lotus Sūtra*, particularly its sixteenth chapter ("The Life-span of the Thus Come One"), was preferred. Jōdoshū funerals usually adopted the *Sukhāvatī-vyūha* or the *Prajñāpāramitā-hṛdaya Sūtra* (*Hannya haramitta shingyō*), and Zen sects favored the twenty-fifth chapter ("The Gateway to Everywhere of the Bodhisattva He Who Observes the Sounds of the World") of the *Lotus Sūtra*, commonly known as *Kannongyō*.

The chanting of *dhāraṇī* (*darani* in Japanese), which consisted of incomprehensible combinations of Sanskrit syllables and which were usually untranslatable, also constituted a major means for invoking the salvific compassion of Buddhist deities.[163] People believed that the chanted sounds of the *dhāraṇī* formula itself constituted the true words or sounds (*shingon*) of Buddhist deities and that by merely reciting them one could obtain merit from the buddhas, bodhisattvas, and gods in question. Each sect preferred particular formulae devoted to particular deities. The Shingon sect most often adopted the "mantra of clear light" (*kōmyō shingon*) and Amida *darani*, whereas the Tendai sect favored the "mantra of clear light" and the *gāthā* in the sixteenth chapter of the *Lotus Sūtra*. In the case of Jōdo sects (Jōdoshū and Jishū), besides *nenbutsu* chanting, Amida *darani* was frequently chosen. The Zen sects favored *daihishin darani* (also called *senju darani*, which praises the grace of the Thousand-Armed Kannon). It should be noted, however, that no matter what formula was adopted, it was believed that the miraculous power of Buddhist deities invoked by the sounds of *dhāraṇī* could cleanse the deceased of sins, lead him or her to eternal happiness, and liberate him or her from sufferings in hell. The modus operandi of *dhāraṇī* chanting is unambiguously illustrated in the ritual practice of the "mantra of clear light."

The "mantra of clear light" refers to the *dhāraṇī* that reads "*on abogya beiroshanau maka bodara mani handoma jinbara harabaritaya u-n*," and it is explicated in various esoteric scriptures and treatises.[164] This *dhāraṇī*, which was introduced to Japan during the Heian period as a magical spell for annihilating sinful karma or for being reborn in paradise, was believed to be the dharma body of the truth of the cosmos, or the true words of Dainichi *nyorai* (Mahāvairocana). Upon its introduction, this *dhāraṇī* was soon adopted for death rituals in the form of sand blessed by the grace of Mahāvairocana, in an esoteric ritual called *doshakaji* that aimed to help the deceased achieve rebirth in paradise through the cleansing and annihilating power of the medium of the incantatory sand.[165] Procedures for the *doshakaji* ritual involved collecting sand from a clean place and putting it in a bottle, placing the bottle in front of an image of Mahāvairocana, announcing a wish, performing *mudrā* hand gestures, and blessing the sand by repeatedly touching it with a small pestle while intoning the "mantra of clear light" 108 times. The ritual performer would then sprinkle the blessed sand on the dead body of a person or on the grave.[166] In addition to the *doshakaji* ritual, the words for the "mantra of clear light" were also often inscribed on the grave stupa (*sotoba*), the urn for ashes, the coffin, or other funerary items — the goal in all cases being the salvation of the deceased.[167] The "mantra of clear light" resembled the indigenous purification (*harae*) ritual, where sins were defined as "pollution" (*kegare*) and were believed to be removable through the divine spells of Shinto prayer — spells known as *kotodama*, or the spirit of words.[168]

In addition to chanting offerings, Buddhist funerals across all sects shared many other ritual elements, such as purifying the priests and funeral site; inviting, greeting, and feasting the Buddhist deities and praising, thanking, or offering worship to them; repentance; incense burning; and dedication of merits to the deceased and all sentient beings. On the surface, the ways in which these ritual elements were put into practice looked similar, but each sect maintained, to one degree or another, its own style and tradition. The differences mostly lay in such details as how these ritual elements were selected, arranged, and executed; which elements were highlighted or emphasized over others; and/or which deities were invoked. Furthermore, even within the same sect, ritual practices were not necessarily identical due to their localization and mélange with folk elements. Variations ran through locality, period, individual temple, and even individual head monk.

Given all this, the task of comparing the characteristics of death rituals between different sects requires us to generalize. Worse yet, it is still not easy to pinpoint these characteristics as there are few temple materials that specifically inform us about funerary rituals. The main problem is that, during the Tokugawa period, no sect maintained a standardized funerary ritual manual or *vade mecum* that could guide, or be enforced upon, its temples across the country or region.[169] In fact, funerary rituals almost seemed to be a private business run by each temple. To be sure, some *danna* patrons recorded the events of funerary rituals as a matter of diary keeping, but diary materials are too brief and too uninformed to use for information on the procedures and meanings of a funerary rite. The following discussion is limited to the most basic features of funerary rituals that have evolved into current forms.

In the case of Tendaishū, the funeral was premised on the teaching that all sentient beings possessed the innate nature of Buddhahood, so that when the deceased was awakened to this truth, he or she would be emancipated from the karma of transmigration. Accordingly, the purpose of funeral was to help the deceased to realize his or her Buddha nature, which had been contaminated by daily life.[170] In order to help the deceased get rid of the shades obscuring his or her Buddha nature, various ritual measures were taken during the funeral; among these, the chanting of sūtras—particularly the Lotus repentance, or *Hokke senbō*, of the *Lotus Sūtra*—was most favored. This was a formula of ritual chanting adopted from the daily disciplinary practices of monks at Mount Hiei.[171] Tendai followers believed that, by listening to the chanting of the *Lotus Sūtra*, the deceased would be purified and brought to the realization of Buddhahood. With regard to esoteric measures, the "mantra of clear light" ritual was most favored because it was believed that, once the blessing rays of Mahāvairocana had been poured into the deceased, he or she would be able to obtain Buddhahood. In other words, the funeral in the Tendai tradition was designed to annihilate the shades of carnal desires that clouded the deceased's innate Buddha nature and guide him or her to the "attainment of enlightenment in this very existence" (*sokushin jōbutsu*).[172]

Shingonshū funerals were initially based on the teachings of Kūkai (774–835), who advocated the ideal of *sokushin jōbutsu*. Later, Kōgyō (1095–1142) added to this aspects of Pure Land thought, and Myōe (1173–1232) added the "mantra of clear light," further complicating the ritual procedure.[173] The goal of the Shingonshū funeral was the union of the deceased with Mahāvairocana, which was believed to entail the eternal life of the deceased in the Pure Land of Tuṣita (Tosotsuten). In order to achieve this state, the ritual officiator conferred upon the deceased the Buddhist precepts and a posthumous name, which would establish him or her as a Buddhist disciple, and then conducted a series of rituals that featured the "three mysteries" of the Buddha, represented by the triad of body (*mudrā*), speech (*mantra*), and mind (*samādhi*). These mysteries were meant to facilitate the union of the deceased with Mahāvairocana.[174]

In the case of Zen, whether Sōtōshū or Rinzaishū, funerals followed the procedure known as *matsugo sasō*, in which, with the conferral of the Buddhist precepts and a posthumous Buddhist name, the deceased was ordained as a disciple and connected to the blood lineage (*kechimyaku*) of Zen masters.[175] As an ordained Buddhist disciple, the deceased was then blessed with incense burning, an offering of tea, the chanting of sūtras, the dedication of merits, and repeated bowing.[176] Sōtōshū, which based its funerary formula on the *Keizan shingi*, a collection of ritual manuals compiled by Keizan (1268–1325), paid particular attention to the elements of ordination, repentance, the vow of returning to the three jewels of Buddhism, merit-transference, and sūtra and spell chanting.[177] On the other hand, Rinzaishū, which did not maintain any guiding manual and which extensively incorporated local customs into its funerary formula, nevertheless by and large stayed within the *matsugo sasō* fomat.[178] In both sects the final words of guidance (*indō*) offered by the officiating priest (who usually spoke in his own words about the Buddha's teachings and the meaning of the posthumous Buddhist name conferred upon the deceased) were considered particularly important.[179]

Unlike the formula of Zen funerals, which was modeled after monastic traditions, the formula of Jōdoshū funerals was rooted in the ritual practice of *nijūgo zanmai* (twenty-five *samādhi*), which Genshin (942–1017), based on Tendai's constant *samādhi*, had articulated to the populace. Initially, on the fifteenth day of each month, the *nijūgo zanmai* featured a *nenbutsu* chanting practice conducted before an image of Amida Buddha by a group of 25 members in a secluded prayer hall. The purpose of *nijūgo zanmai* was to pray for rebirth of the deceased into the Western Paradise, to take care of the dying with deathbed prayers, and to provide mutual help in conducting funerals for the deceased.[180] Later, *nenbutsu* chanting, in combination with ordination and salvific guidance, evolved into a funerary rite for the followers of Pure Land Buddhism.[181] It is known that the current ritual formula goes back to the memorial service held at Zōjōji in 1614 for the deceased mother of Ieyasu—Denzūin—on the occasion of the thirteenth anniversary of her death.[182] In Jōdoshū, the funerary ritual basically focused on guiding the deceased to rebirth in the Western Paradise under the grace of Amida Buddha (albeit with many local variations).

As has been mentioned, the funerary rites of Nichirenshū and Jōdoshinshū followers were different from those of other sectarians. Nichirenshū adherents omitted the ordination rite on the ground that the deceased had already accepted the teachings of the *Lotus Sūtra* and, thus, would automatically be ushered into paradise. For this reason, there was no procedure in the Nichirenshū funeral for initiating the deceased into Buddhism through the conferring of precepts; instead, the deceased was granted a "dharma name" (*hōgō*)—as opposed to a "precept name" (*kaimyō*)—as evidence that he or she was already a follower of the dharma of the *Lotus Sūtra*.[183] Within this context, the role of ritual officiant was not so much to guide the spirit of the deceased directly to paradise as to introduce it to Nichiren, the founder of the sect, who would lead it to the paradise of Pure Land. Under the guidance of Nichiren, the deceased was firmly connected to the Buddha and the salvific world of the *Lotus Sūtra*, which would prevail through the three spans of past, present, and future.[184] The Nichirenshū funerary service, which was devoted to the *Lotus Sūtra*, featured the chanting of the title (*daimoku*) or the first few words from the chapter entitled "Expedient Devices" (Hōben) as well as the *gāthā* verses from the chapters entitled "Apparition of the Jeweled Stupa" (Kenhōtō) and "The Encouragements of the Bodhisattva Universally Worthy" (Fugen bosatsu kanbotsu)[185]

In comparison, Jōdoshinshū followers believed that all members of the sect had already been redeemed by the original vow of Amida Buddha, and therefore that the funeral service signified nothing more than the continuation of their usual expression of gratitude for Buddha's salvation. The funerary ritual differed little from the usual daily worship.[186] Based on this doctrinal framework, all religious services throughout the funeral period were primarily devoted to Amida Buddha rather than to the deceased: family members, relatives, and friends would give thanks for Amida's compassion and celebrate the salvation of the deceased. Neither ordination nor salvific guidance was needed. The funerary service was simply an occasion for all participants to give thanks that they had been given an extra opportunity to listen to the teachings of Shinran.[187] Within this context, all services were conducted in the spirit of "the practice of companions" (*dōbōgyō*) under the doctrinal dictum that there were no distinctions between monks and laypeople. There were even some cases in which the funeral ceremony was officiated by a layperson—a relative or a fellow believer.[188] It was Rennyo (1415–99), the eighth patriarch, who systematized funerary customs into a unified tripartite ritual format that featured the recitation of *shōshinge* (or *shōshin nenbutsuge*, which refers to the "verses of the *nenbutsu* of true faith" described by Shinran in his *Kyōgyōshinshō*), *nenbutsu* chanting, and the singing of hymns (*wasan*) composed by Shinran in Japanese, praising the teachings and activities of the Buddha, bodhisattvas, and great teachers.[189] In theory, the doctrinal stance of "other-power" (*tariki*) salvation was not compatible with such ideas as appeasement and purification of the deceased, but the lay followers of Jōdoshinshū in the strong lay-centered tradition were not free from local customs and often diverged into numerous ritual variations directed to the deceased.[190]

No doubt, a range of sectarian teachings and ritual orientations translated into diverse Buddhist funerary practices even though, in theory, they all shared the identical theme of Buddhist salvation of the deceased. What further complicated Buddhist funerary rituals was their continuous conflation with local customs, which were also not immune to change over time. Funerary rituals, no matter what their sectarian flavor and no matter where they were executed, did not remain static. But the real puzzle lay in the irony that the Tokugawa Japanese did not believe that one funerary rite could completely annul the sinful karma of the deceased. For them, the funeral constituted only the first stage of postmortem care.

Right after a funeral ceremony, family members, relatives, and close associates shared food, which also functioned as a farewell meal with the deceased. After that the coffin was carried to the gravesite for burial or cremation. In most regions, the coffin was taken out right after the ceremony, within 24 hours, or on the following day. Upper-class families in Kaga carried the coffin to the burial site two days after a death, and the middle- or lower-class families did so the day after the death.[191]

The manner of "removing the coffin from the house" (*shukkan*) varied according to local customs, which particularly focused on the concern that the departing soul, not being fully appeased, might return to the house and inflict harm upon the living. Such unfortunate happenings had to be prevented and the house, which the deceased had left behind, had to be restored to a "normal" state. An example from the Wakayama region shows the care and symbolism involved in the *shukkan* practice:

When it comes time to take the coffin out [of the room], the family puts fine bamboo stocks tightly along the inner rims of the door. This is to create a makeshift gate through which the coffin is to be passed; when taking the coffin out of the house, the one holding the rear of the coffin comes out first and then quickly moves around in order to reverse the position of the coffin; the family then scorch any traces that the coffin has passed with fire (called "gate fire"); this custom is observed not only among the commoners but also among the samurai families.[192]

The purpose of installing a temporary exit and changing the direction of the coffin was to confuse the deceased and so prevent his or her return. Scorching the trail of the coffin was meant to purify death pollution. There were many local variations on these customs, such as making a temporary exit through the wall (which would be sealed as soon as the coffin had been taken out) or through the rear door; spreading salt in the room right after having taken out the coffin; having a monkey tumble around in the room so that it could absorb any remaining defilement and then driving it out; spreading ashes in the room or putting a stone mill in the inner garden of the house in order to keep the soul from reentering; or smashing tea bowls in order to frighten away the soul.[193]

Once taken outside, the coffin was carried by pallbearers to the gravesite. Since, in the countryside, the gravesite was usually separated from the funeral site, the transport of a coffin involved a procession to "send [the deceased] to the edge of a wild field" (*nobe okuri*), representing the one-way journey of the deceased to the other world. In the Shirakawa domain, for example, "the heir holds the tablet;

all others, including relatives and acquaintances, carry various articles related to the Buddhist service and the altar; and women, who position themselves in front of the coffin, haul the cotton rope called 'the rope of connection' (*en no tsuna*) and queue up in a procession. At this point, not only the fellow villagers but also people from neighboring villages gather, and old people offer the chanting of *nenbutsu*. Amid the sounds of gongs and drums, they conduct *nobe okuri*."[194] The *nobe okuri* procession usually took a complicated route in order to ensure that the deceased could not easily find his or her way back home.[195]

In some regions, a separation ritual was performed at the village border, with the idea that the border constituted an entrance to the other world. In Tosa, when the funeral procession reached a bridge at the village limits, the participants extinguished and threw away all torches and lanterns, spread salt around the bridge, and recited separation spells.[196] Separation from this world was concomitant with entry into the other. Within this context, it was customary to mount a toy bird (made of paper, wooden panels, or vegetables [usually potato or radish]), or to hang a painting of birds on the head of the coffin or on the ridges of the roof of the house. Birds were believed to guide the deceased safely and surely to the other world.[197]

Before lowering the coffin into the grave, a Buddhist monk usually conducted a brief committal service. Nevertheless, even at the moment of burial, the Tokugawa Japanese tried to make sure that the deceased journeyed in only one direction and did not look back. In order to ensure this, it was quite common to put heavy rocks on the coffin, to turn one's back and throw rocks toward the grave after burial, and/or to tear rice cakes and throw them back toward the grave pit. In the Nagaoka and Shirakawa domains, it was customary after burial to arrange for a *shugen*, or mountain ascetic, to purify the house; or to cut a piece of cloth into strips and hang them on the gate as a sign of severance.[198] In other regions, people spread salt around the house right after returning from the burial, or they destroyed hoes, sickles, and straw sandals that were used in digging the grave. All these measures bespeak the strong feelings of the Tokugawa Japanese toward the persistence of death pollution while yet wishing the deceased a safe journey to the other world.[199]

When a funeral was held at the *danna* temple (which is where funerals in urban areas were most often held), the transportation of the coffin involved two stages: going to the temple for the funeral and going to the gravesite after the funeral. Most attention was paid to the former, with the latter often being a modest affair. What follows was a typical scene in Edo:

The funeral procession is headed by a carrier of a lantern (veiled by an all-white cloth) hung on a long pole, followed by a Buddhist monk, who ushers the procession; holders of other lanterns of hexagonal shape with dragon heads; and bearers of paper flags. The group leading the procession is followed by a bier carrying a coffin (the upper-class families use a palanquin, but ordinary people use a litter with trapdoors or a simple stand). The coffin is completely covered with spotless white cloth and canopied by a baldaquin. Behind the coffin is the chief mourner holding the spirit tablet of the deceased (*ihai*) in his hands, accompanied by other family members and relatives, who hold incense burners, torches, and flags.[200]

Factors that affected the scale and format of the procession included the status of the deceased within the family, the social status and wealth of the deceased's family, and local customs.[201] For those families who could not afford an elaborate procession, two or three pallbearers from the neighborhood carried the coffin on their shoulders, often at night; there was no accompanying monk; and the wooden coffin was bound with ropes to a long bar. It should be noted, however, that regardless of the scale of the procession, "it was the norm for the male heir, who wore ceremonial dress, to carry the spirit tablet of the deceased."[202]

Whether in the rural areas or in the urban areas, it is interesting that, despite Buddhist rhetoric, cremation was not widely practiced in Tokugawa society, even though some regions, such as Jōdoshinshū strongholds and Kinai, had a relatively high rate of cremation. In particular, the cemetery keepers (*sanmai hijiri*) in the Kinai region, who held the rights to dispose of corpses and to manage communal cemeteries known as *sōbo*, played a key role in keeping the custom of cremation in place.[203] Nevertheless, according to one 1897 estimate, the rate of cremation was a meager 26.8 percent even after the Meiji government banned the construction of new cemeteries in Edo in 1884 and strictly enforced the cremation of those who died of a contagious disease.[204] The Buddhist custom of cremation, which had been introduced to ancient Japan in 700, was still an alien custom in Tokugawa society, and even a number of Buddhist monks did not accept it. Even the imperial family, which had hitherto cremated their dead, abandoned the practice in the mid-seventeenth century because of the harsh criticism of Confucianists who regarded the destruction of one's parents by fire as an unforgivable violation of filial piety.[205] Cremation was used most often when there was an urgent need to promptly terminate the defilement associated with a violent death—a defilement that was believed to be much more persistent and malicious than that associated with a regular death. Reducing the body to ashes would ensure the annihilation of forms of defilement that might otherwise linger on.[206]

Besides associating it with malignant death, there was another factor that hampered the spread of cremation: the idea that the dead may be regenerated as another person or animal.[207] There were many fascinating stories of rebirth through reincarnation (*umarekawari*): a grandfather was reborn as a grandson, a commoner as shogun, a couple who had committed double suicide as a new couple, Takeda Shingen (1521–73) as Yui Shōsetsu (1605–51), a child as a bird, and a monk as a cow.[208] One very well known story, and one that impressed Hirata Atsutane (1776–1843), told of a boy named Katsugorō who was born in 1815 to a peasant couple in the Nakano village of Tama in Musashi. Apparently, when he reached the age of 8, Katsugorō revealed that he was the reincarnation of a boy named Tōzō who had lived in a neighboring village and who had died in 1809 at the age of 5. He added that all this was made possible by a mysterious old man who was clad in a gray robe, had a long white beard, and who appeared when Tōzō was buried in order to guide him to the womb of his current mother. Upon hearing this, Atsutane visited Katsugorō in 1823 and was convinced that the story of rebirth was true.[209]

To be sure, cremation—at least visually—ensured the complete removal of death pollution. However, this seemed to pose a new quandary: the removal was so complete that it not only posed an affront to the resurrection of the body but it also threatened to destroy all possibility of an afterlife. This kind of concern was especially acute at the funerals of young children, whose mortality rate reached as high as 70 to 75 percent during the Tokugawa period.[210] Funerals and "abstinence" were sometimes not provided for children under the age of 7. Their bodies were buried under the floor of their homes or in a separate "child tomb" in the hope that their spirits might soon return and be reborn.[211] It was customary in Mutsu "for a child who dies in the same year as his or her birth to be buried under the floor of the house, while a child at the age of 2 or above is sent to the *danna* temple upon death."[212]

In any event, families of high status or great wealth paid much attention to decorating burial facilities, including coffins, sepulchers, and gravestones. In contrast, those who lived in urban areas and were not blessed with wealth buried the coffin, usually a small wooden or ceramic casket quickly purchased from a coffin maker (*hayaokeya*), without erecting any significant structure at a cemetery. Coffins in Edo, for example, whether wooden or earthen, measured more or less 60 by 60 centimeters for commoner adults and about 30 by 30 centimeters for commoner children, indicating that the dead body was arranged in a fetal position.[213]

After the inhumation of the body, the family erected a grave stupa, known as a *sotoba*, at the gravesite. Grave stupa, often perceived as emblems of a family's social status and containing information on the deceased (e.g., posthumous Buddhist name and date of death), varied in material, size, shape, and decorations, ranging from elegant stone stupa called *hōkyōintō* (*karaṇḍa-mudrā* stupa) to ordinary gravestones to simple wooden boards. Despite their varieties, all of them featured the "five-wheel" (*gorin*) structure, which represented the five elements of the dharma in Esoteric Buddhism: earth, water, fire, wind, and air (from the bottom upward).[214] In Buddhist terms, erecting a five-wheel grave stupa symbolically returned the spirit of the deceased to the world from which it had originally come and, thereby, put him or her in harmony with the Buddha. The Tokugawa Japanese believed that a five-wheel stupa was one of the most virtuous and meritorious Buddhist offerings. At the same time, it was also commonly believed that the grave stupa would serve as a resting place of the spirit.[215] In the case of cremation, the ashes of the deceased were collected, put in an urn, and taken to the house. The urn was then placed on a special altar. Forty-nine days after death the urn was taken to the grave and the urn or a portion of the ashes therein were buried with a brief ceremony. The family then erected a stupa.

Grave customs differed throughout the country. It is known that Jōdoshinshū followers in some regions neither made a grave—a custom known as the *mubosei* ("no-grave" system)—nor erected a gravestone. For them, disposing of the corpse was not much different from disposing of waste in the wilderness.[216] For example, families in Kasasa island of Suō reserved some cremated bones to be sent to the Honganji's charnel house in Kyoto and then abandoned the remaining ashes in the wilderness; in the Asozu district of Izumo in present-day Shimane prefecture, families threw the ashes into

the lake after keeping some bones for enshrinement; and in the Kōzu-
hara area of Ibukichō in Ōmi, families threw the ashes into the nearby
forest after collecting some bones.[217]

Among a variety of burial customs, the *ryōbosei* ("dual-grave system") offers a unique structure that reflects the deep-seated ideas of
Tokugawa Japanese regarding the dead body and ancestral spirits.
In this grave system, which started in the Kinki area and later spread
to the Chūgoku-Shikoku region as well as to the Kantō, the family
established two graves, one at the actual burial site, which was usually outside or near the village boundary, and the other within the
village, which was used for ancestral veneration. The former was
called a burying grave (*umebaka*) or dumping grave (*sutebaka*), and the
latter was called a visiting grave (*mairibaka*).[218] Once the corpse was
buried at the *umebaka*, it was abandoned. In contrast, family members
tended the *mairibaka* and regularly visited it to pay their respects.

On the origin of this dual-grave system, Bitō Masahide suggests
that "because the actual burial site, which was associated with a state
of pollution, was not regarded as a suitable venue for the performance of such [ancestral] rites, separate ritual graves were eventually established."[219] Folklore scholars argue that before the emergence of gravestones, there were various substitutes that functioned
as *mairibaka*, including sacred mountains, forests, trees, spaces,
stones, Buddhist halls, memorial tablets, and the like. They suggest
that these sacred objects, where ancestral spirits were believed to
settle or reveal themselves after death, had, by early modern times,
transformed into the system of *mairibaka*.[220] No matter whether families practiced the single-grave system or the dual-grave system, the
spirit of the deceased, which was not easily separated from the
stigma of death pollution, had to be ritually cleansed and tended.

The conclusion of a funerary rite was not the end of ritual care
for the deceased; rather, it only signaled the beginning of the next
stage of ritual care. After a funeral, the focus of ritual care moved
from the gravesite to a newly built domestic Buddhist altar, where
a white spirit tablet (now a memorial tablet) for the deceased was
enshrined.[221] Despite its origin in Chinese Confucianism, the custom
of enshrining the memorial tablet, first in the family temple during
the medieval period and then in the household Buddhist altar
during the early modern period, was, in fact, not alien to Japanese
traditional culture, in which worshipping deities or spirits always
involved installing a lodging place (*yorishiro*) for their temporary

residence. The memorial tablet was very similar to the traditional Japanese lodging place (*tamashiro*) for the departed spirit.[222]

Once the memorial tablet was enshrined, the feelings of grief over the loss of a family member and fear of death pollution gradually subsided. In ritual terms, this marked the "clearance of funeral abstinence" (*kichū harai*). "After the funeral, the family treats, with food and drinks, those who have offered, or have been forced to offer, labor for the Buddhist ritual, and from the following day things return to business as usual. The period during which daily routines are suspended is rarely extended beyond the first seventh day [after death], even for a rich family."[223] In most cases, the date for the "clearance of funeral abstinence" for commoner families was set at the first seventh day after death (*sho-nanoka*). When a family's livelihood was threatened, this time span could be shortened by three or four days.[224] With release from funeral abstinence, the family moved to the next stage of religious care for the deceased.

CR

SIX

Memorial Services for the New Spirit

For a certain period of time after a funeral, posthumous memorial services were held at which follow-up offerings (*tsuizen kuyō*) were made to increase the merit of the deceased.[225] The rationale for these memorial services, which were often simply called "Buddhist rituals" (*butsuji*) or "dharma rituals" (*hōji*), was based on the belief that the deceased was still in the process of "attaining Buddhahood" (*jōbutsu*) and that, therefore, he or she needed further religious care. Understandably, the idea of these interim intercessory *butsuji* was eagerly embraced by monks, who saw in it an opportunity to expand their interests and to strengthen their influence over the populace. During this interim period, the folkloric ideas and ritual elements that highlighted the theme of "resuscitation" and "severance of connections" receded significantly, if not completely.

The period during which these memorial services were conducted consisted of two distinct stages: that which began after the burial and continued up to the "clearance of memorial abstinence" (*imiake*), the day on which the temporary white mortuary tablet was burned and a permanent spirit tablet (an upright wooden plaque, usually lacquered in black, standing on a flat base) was prepared and installed in the household Buddhist altar; and that which began after the "clearance of memorial abstinence" and continued up to the "conclusion of memorial services," or *tomuraiage* (a term that had rich local variations, such as *tomoraishimai, toiage, toikiri, matsuage, nenkiage*, and so on), the day on which the individual spirit tablet enshrined in the household Buddhist altar was either burned or sent to the temple repository.

Depending on local customs or family situations, the celebration of the "clearance of memorial abstinence" could take place on the seventh day (*hito-nanuka*), twenty-first day (*mi-nanuka*), thirty-fifth day (*itsu-nanuka*), or the one hundredth day after death. However, it took place most commonly on the forty-ninth day after death. Up to this day, Buddhist rituals (seven altogether) were offered at seven-day intervals. On the forty-ninth day, the family usually invited numerous relatives and Buddhist monks from its *danna* temple and offered a grand Buddhist ritual in honor of the deceased. During this seven-week period (the "seven sevens"), the spirit of the deceased was believed to progress through the stages leading toward rebirth and ancestral deification. With the completion of the seventh seven-day interval, the spirit of the deceased was transferred from a temporary home to the household Buddhist altar. If ashes had been preserved, the family then buried them or sent a portion of them to a Buddhist charnel house at Zenkōji, Kōyasan, Osorezan, Asamayama, or the like—places reputed to be entrances to paradise.[226] After this, free from the shadow of death pollution and mortuary obligations, the family began to eat usual food and to distribute mementos of the deceased to relatives and friends.[227]

The second stage of posthumous memorial services, which began after the "clearance of memorial abstinence" and ended with the "conclusion of memorial services," lasted far longer than did the first stage and was marked by longer intervals between memorial services. Usually, these services occurred on the one hundredth day and on the first, third, seventh, thirteenth, and thirty-third anniversaries of the person's death. This amounted to six memorial services. On rare occasions, two more services, held in the seventeenth and fiftieth year after death, respectively, were also conducted. The Tokugawa Japanese believed that, by the end of this second stage, the spirit of the deceased had been completely transformed into an ancestral deity who would thereafter remain a permanent source of godly help to its descendants. Herman Ooms suggests that the process of ancestral deification, which took time and required ongoing ritual care, structurally resembled the growth cycle of a person: death equals birth, *kaimyō* equals the naming of a child, the "seven sevens" equals the first visit to the tutelary Shinto deity (*hatsu miya-mairi*), the annual memorial services equal *shichi-go-san* (the festival marking the growth of children to 3, 5, and 7 years of age), and *tomuraiage* equals marriage.[228] On the whole, during the first and second stages of the interim period, thirteen memorial services were held. These were collectively referred to as the "thirteen Buddhist rituals" (*jūsan butsuji*).

But this was not the end of the story. In addition to these thirteen special occasions, less formal ritual offerings were also made on the monthly and yearly anniversaries of death, depending on local customs and family traditions as well as on the timing of regular annual events (such as New Year's, Higan, and Bon). It was also customary to make daily offerings of candles, tea, and incense, particularly during the first 49 days after death. Without this on-going ritual care the Tokugawa Japanese believed that the deceased would be doomed to a miserable fate in the other world.

Saitō Ryūzo describes the general features of post-funerary memorial services: "After the funeral, the family installs the tablet of the deceased in a new Buddhist altar, lights a lamp every day, and pays homage to it by offering incense, flowers, tea, and a meal."[229] Titsingh's observation focuses on the "seven sevens": "Every week, reckoning from the day of the death of the deceased, a priest attends, and in the night of that day and the morning of the next, reads hymns for an hour before the *ihai* (memorial tablet). He is each time supplied with refreshments, and money is given him to the amount of five or six *monme* [of silver currency]."[230] As is seen in the Sensōji diary, in the Tendai tradition the "seven sevens" performed for dignitaries involved various ritual formulae: the ritual of the "mantra of clear light" (the first seven), the Lotus repentance (the second seven), the chanting of the *Lotus Sūtra* (the third seven), the ritual of "good place" or *kōshō* (the fourth seven), the ritual of the store-house mandala (the fifth seven), the ritual of the "six courses" (the sixth seven), and the ritual of the diamond mandala (the seventh seven).[231]

It should be noted that no matter what formula was adopted, these Buddhist memorial services were all based on the premise that the spirit of the newly deceased did not completely depart the house where it had lived, even though it had presumably been sent to the other world through the funerary ritual. Ideas concerning the whereabouts of the spirit of the deceased were neither logical nor consistent, and they sometimes contradicted their own preaching. Buddhist monks often reinforced the idea that the new spirit would still be around even after the funeral meant to send it off. As the temporary Buddhist altar for the new spirit was called "an altar for the intermediate state" (*chūindan*), the Japanese believed clearly that during this period, the new spirit, represented by the tablet, still hovered about the house as a sort of in-between being.

The idea of an intermediate state (*chūin* or *chūu*; *antarābhava* in Sanskrit) presumes that the spirit of the deceased undergoes a transitional existence during the interim between death and birth.[232] Originally, the Abhidharma tradition suggested that there were four possible durations for this intermediate period: no fixed duration, 7 days, 49 days, and a short, non-specific time.[233] In Japan, the "seven sevens" gained almost universal currency. The time span of 49 days was then punctuated at 7-day intervals, and each segment was believed to mark the spirit's passage from one phase to the next in the intermediate realm. Based on this theory, which is further explicated in such scriptures as the *Yugashijiron* (*Yogācāra-bhūmi*), *Bonmōkyō* (*Brahma Sūtra*), and *Jizō hongankyō*, the Tokugawa Japanese believed that the deceased was destined to pass through these phases before eventually entering the second stage of the posthumous period.[234] A memorial ritual performed on every seventh day was, therefore, supposed to expedite the safe passage of the deceased through the various phases of the intermediate realm and to ensure an auspicious destiny.

To be sure, the theory of intermediate existence was expounded in Buddhist terms, but the idea itself was not foreign to the Japanese, who traditionally believed that, right after the funeral, the spirit of the deceased was still unstable and, therefore, needed to be further appeased and stabilized. The Japanese believed that the new spirit, called *aramitama*, or untamed spirit, was not completely liberated from the defilement and agony of death. Worse yet, they believed that, if the deceased were not further pacified through posthumous ritual care, he or she would inflict curses upon the survivors. In some regions, fear of the unstable new spirit, which underwent agonies in the transitional period and was prone to vengeance, led survivors to take countermeasures designed to bring the spirit back to its previous life. For example, for the spirit of a child, a special form of *nenbutsu* chanting, such as "chanting the Buddha's name one million times" (*hyakumanben nenbutsu*) was popular in the Kantō area. Repeating the Buddha's name in unison tens of thousands of times, the chanters prayed for the child's quick return to life.[235]

In medieval times, concerns with the new spirit, which resonated with age-old ideas of "vengeful spirits" (*goryō* or *onryō*), spawned a variety of local religious customs. These remained diffuse and fragmented until the early seventeenth century, when they converged to form a series of Buddhist rituals for the dead. The entrenchment of the *danka* system reinforced this trend. By the late seventeenth century, the Japanese commonly practiced the "thirteen Buddhist rituals" for the benefit of the deceased, believing, as Buddhist monks preached, that these rituals would generate religious merit and that these, in turn, could be transferred to the deceased. The overall ritual scheme followed the logic that, by the transference of merit, the karmic virtue of the deceased could be augmented so that he or she would eventually be reborn in the Pure Land, or heavenly paradise.

With regard to the suggestion that the transference of merit runs counter to the Buddha's teachings regarding self-responsibility and the principle of moral retribution, Richard Gombrich notes that "one's good actions build up a kind of spiritual bank account from which one can make payments to others."[236] Furthermore, as the Tokugawa Japanese understood, the action of transferring merit to others after conducting merit-accumulating activities was doubly beneficial: the acquisition of merit was good in itself, and transferring merit so acquired to others was also good.[237] In particular, in the Mahāyānic tradition it was expected that the monks would call on buddhas, bodhisattvas, or Buddhist saints to donate some of their immeasurable merit (acquired through many lives of altruism) to the dead. Indeed, the idea of merit transference, which had developed in early Buddhism under the rationale that it was "for the welfare and happiness of all beings" and/or "an act of veneration (*kuyō*; *pūjā* in Sanskrit) for one's parents," gained wide popularity across different schools throughout India, China, and Japan.[238]

Interestingly, criticisms of the idea of merit transference came from Confucians, who condemned it as an intolerable breach of filial piety. They argued that Buddhists treated their dead parents as if they were serious sinners. Patricia Ebrey notes: "Ssu-ma Kuang [1019–86] went on to argue that if perchance paradise actually existed, the good would be reborn there anyway. . . . Ssu-ma Kuang also made fun of the idea of transferring merit, as this implied that the Buddha could be bribed into treating sinners favorably and that the rich would fare better than the poor."[239]

From early on, however, Japanese Buddhists elaborated upon the idea of merit transference, presenting it as a major means of saving all sentient beings who were unable to act for themselves. This idea, which was embraced by all Buddhist sects, including Jōdoshinshū, was honed into a sort of cure-all solution during the Tokugawa period. In theory, the position of Jōdoshinshū, which categorically rejected the salvific path of "self-power" (*jiriki*) premised on one's own merit-making, was not compatible with the idea of the transference of merit; however, in practice, its followers were not reluctant to conduct merit-making *nebutsu* chanting for their deceased family members, particularly under the influence of Rennyo (1415–99), who recognized the ritual efficacy of memorial services for the deceased.[240] With regard to the wide reception of the idea of merit transference in Japan, Kajiyama Yūichi cites the role of the *Prajñā-pāramitā* sūtras, noting that in some of these sūtras the salvation of the deceased through the transfer of merit is portrayed as amounting to enlightenment.[241]

Once accepted, the idea of transferring one's merit to someone else was gradually tailored to suit the system of ancestral deification. Memorial services were not designed to facilitate the deceased's Buddhist salvation per se; rather, they were intended to appease, purify, and stabilize the newly deceased spirit so that it might transform into a benign ancestral deity. In the Tendai tradition, for example, meritorious activities such as the Lotus repentance (*Hokke senbō* or *Hokke zanmai*), the chanting of the "mantra of clear light" or *nenbutsu*, the erection of a stupa, and the dedication of copied scriptures or mandala paintings were favored for individuals of distinction.[242] For commoner families, things were far more simple: a monk from the *danna* temple would recite some lines from the *Lotus Sūtra* or the *Amitābha Sūtra* or chant *nenbutsu* before the altar. In all cases, these memorial actions merged with the logic of ancestral deification, which focused on the purification and stabilization of the new spirit.

The example of the Lotus repentance, also known as the Lotus *samādhi*, illustrates how this Tendai ritual was assimilated into the symbolism of postmortem purification when it was adopted as a memorial (or funeral) rite.[243] Originally, this penitential rite was expounded by Chih-i (538–597) in his famous treatise *Mo-ho chih-kuan* ([Treatise on] the great calming and contemplation) as a means for attaining the enlightenment of the Lotus. As Chih-i prescribed it, the Lotus repentance, which featured alternately walking and sitting, was programmed as a 21-day practice focused on intensive worship, recitation of the *Lotus Sūtra*, seated meditation, and the performance of a repentance ceremony.[244] It had two main religious components: to state one's former evil deeds and to correct the past through confession and thus to "extinguish sin and obtain purification" (*metsuzai*).[245] In Japan, the Lotus repentance was first introduced by Saichō (767–822), who wanted to promote it as a disciplinary practice for the Tendai monks. Not long after, under the leadership of Ennin (794–864), several Tendai institutions, including Kyoto Sanzen'in and Tōdaiji, began to set up separate halls for their monks so that they could devote themselves to this particular disciplinary practice.

However, when it was adopted as a ritual formula for posthumous memorial services, it was transformed into a simple rite that featured the recitation of the fourteenth chapter—"Comfortable Conduct" (Anrakugyō)—in the *Lotus Sūtra*.[246] During the Tokugawa period, the rite of Lotus repentance was typically conducted in the space of less than an hour, and all its disciplinary components were omitted. As a memorial service, it moved away from its original purpose (i.e., to enable one to repent one's sins and to achieve *samādhi*) and was condensed into a formula whose recitation was expected to appease and to purify the volatile nature of a spirit in transition. The rhetoric of repentance (washing away sin) had a psychological appeal that was associated with the imagery of purification. In ancient Japan, the rites of repentance devoted to buddhas or bodhisattvas were often mobilized "much like the Shinto purification rituals and harvest rites" to obtain material benefits or to overcome natural calamities or epidemics. In other words, repentance was likened to driving evil elements out of the community.[247] In this cultural tradition, the rite of repentance was believed to generate meritorious power that could cleanse those sins associated with defilement and death pollution.[248]

Traditional ideas pertaining to the defilement and instability of the new spirit set the context within which posthumous Buddhist rituals operated. The underlying functioning of these traditional ideas was revealed at the conclusion of the "seven sevens" on the forty-ninth day—a conclusion that was referred to as "clearance of memorial abstinence."[249] As has been discussed, throughout the mortuary period abstinence was key to countering the danger of death pollution. In traditional Japanese culture, as Gorai Shigeru notes, abstinence was understood as an act of "cleansing" (*imoi*), whether it was aided by the magical power of water, spiritual or physical retreat, Buddhist merit, or esoteric spells.[250] The path of the "seven sevens," through which Buddhist merit was accumulated during a 49-day period, indeed, constituted a process that involved purifying and pacifying the new spirit.

The idea of pacifying the new spirit could be seen even in Jōdoshinshū followers who, in theory, rebuffed the idea of salvation through ritual actions. Right after the "seven sevens," or the first Bon, many Jōdoshinshū followers brought the ashes of their loved ones to Kyoto and buried them at the cemeteries where Shinran's ashes were interred ([Higashi] Ōtani *sobyō* in the case of the Higashihonganji subsect, and [Nishi] Ōtani *honbyō* in the case of the Nishihonganji subsect). On the surface, this custom of "burying the ashes" (*nōkotsu*) near Shinran's resting place was an expression of the wish to send the deceased to the Pure Land, to which the burial site of Shinran was likened.[251] Upon closer inspection, however, we notice that this custom was also associated with the traditional belief that the other world, whether it was referred to as the Pure Land or as paradise, was not completely detached from this world. It should also be noted that entrance to this sacred and pure site was permitted only after the new spirit had completed the 49 days—a stage requisite to its appeasement and purification through memorial services. In this instance, it appears that the idea that absolute salvation through the grace of Amida Buddha should not require any intercessory ritual action was compromised.[252]

Interestingly, despite all the ritual measures that led to the "clearance of memorial abstinence," the new spirit continued to be subject to appeasement, purification, and religious nourishment, beyond the duration of the seven posthumous memorial services to the tenth, thirteenth, fifteenth, or even more rituals. It was paradoxical that the seven posthumous Buddhist rituals, which purported to ensure a safe and effective close to the intermediate existence of the new spirit, were extended to another series of memorial services, thus undermining the whole scheme of ritual efficacy.[253] Also, people remained quite fuzzy about the whereabouts of the new spirit after the seven memorial rituals of the first stage had come to a close. It could be in the Buddhist other world, in a mountain, over a paddy field, in the sky, under the ground, over the sea, at the gravesite, on a gravestone, in the *danna* temple, in the house, on the memorial tablet enshrined in the household Buddhist altar, or just nearby.

Customarily, with the completion of the seven posthumous memorial services, the tablet of the new spirit, which was now referred to as a "clean spirit" (*shōryō*) rather than a "dead spirit" (*shiryō*), was transferred from the temporary altar to the regular Buddhist household altar.[254] Since the new spirit was believed to be further undergoing the final stage of ancestral deification, it was treated like a semi-ancestral deity. When it was finally fully integrated into the cluster of ancestral deities, the occasion was celebrated as the "conclusion of memorial services" (*tomuraiage*). From this time on, the spirit of the deceased, which had discarded its negative nature, was believed to exist as a benevolent ancestral deity.[255]

In order to achieve this auspicious final result, a series of intermittent Buddhist memorial rituals had to be continued until (or beyond) the thirty-third year after the death of the deceased. Not only that, but, as was mentioned before, these post-seven posthumous memorial services were also supplemented by auxiliary rites conducted as part of regular ancestral veneration, including New Year, Higan, and Bon celebrations, which were directed at all extant ancestral spirits and deities, as well as deathday rites for the new spirit conducted on both a monthly (*maitsuki meinichi*) and a yearly basis (*shōtsuki meinichi*).[256] Among these auxiliary rites, a particularly important one was the first Bon in which the newly dead was pacified at a special altar installed separately from that for other ancestral spirits and deities. In some areas families loaded the new spirit in a boat made of straw or paper and floated it down the river or over the sea at the end of their first Bon.

In the seventeenth century, the custom of performing "intermittent Buddhist memorial rituals" during the second stage of ancestral deification showed a wide range of local variation in the number of times and schedules by which they were conducted. The exception seemed to be the first three rituals (the eighth through tenth after the funeral), which were offered on the hundredth day and on the first and third anniversaries of death, respectively. With the exception of these three rituals, there was no nationwide standard. For example, the twelfth service was conducted in the thirteenth year after death in Edo, Mutsu, and Wakasa, and in the seventeenth year after death in Echigo; the thirteenth service was conducted in the seventeenth year after death in Awa and Wakasa, in the twenty-fifth year after death among some Jōdoshinshū followers, in the twenty-seventh year after death in Echigo, and (if only rarely) in the forty-

ninth or fiftieth year after death in certain isolated areas.²⁵⁷ Moreover, wealthy and powerful families often extended these memorial
services to include fourteen, fifteen, or even more rituals.²⁵⁸

Despite local and sectarian variations, as the term "thirteen Buddhist rituals" indicates, a dominant pattern emerged: six more rituals
were added to the seven posthumous services conducted during
the first stage of Buddhist memorial services. These six additional
memorial rites were usually conducted after 100 days, 1 year, 3
years, 7 years, 13 years or 17 years, and 33 years after death. There
was no clear doctrinal explication for this schedule.²⁵⁹ Nevertheless,
with the entrenchment of the *danka* system, conducting "thirteen
Buddhist rituals" after a funeral almost became the norm in Tokugawa society.

In line with the establishment of the custom of thirteen memorial
rituals, Buddhist monks preached that the deceased might not be
saved unless all of these ritual requirements were fulfilled—a theory
that evolved from the ten courts of the underworld depicted in
a Kṣitigarbha scripture known as *Jizōkyō*. This scripture, which refers
to the *Jizō bosatsu hosshin innen jūōkyō*, is a Japanese version of a late
twelfth-century Chinese Buddhist apocrypha called the *Sūtra on the
Prophecy of King Yama* (*Yen-lo-wang shou-chi ssu-chung ni-hsiu sheng-ch'i
wang-sheng ching-t'u ching*) that expounds the ten underground courts
and the kings who control them.²⁶⁰ The *Jizōkyō*, with which late medieval Japanese were acquainted thanks to its popular vernacular treatise, the *Jūō sandanshō* (Extracts of admiration of the ten kings),
delivers the message of the compassion of Jizō bosatsu (the bodhisattva Kṣitigarbha), who manifests himself in many different forms,
including as King Yama and nine other Buddhist deities/kings, all
of whom are involved in the business of saving sentient beings from
hell. According to the *Jizōkyō*, after death one is destined to go through
the ten courts of the underworld, where one receives judgment; when
helped by these deities, one can eventually be led to the Pure Land
of Amitābha.²⁶¹

The *Jizōkyō* had only ten deities, but the "thirteen Buddhist rituals" were premised on thirteen deities. Where did these other three
deities come from? This is hard to pinpoint, but scholars suggest
that by the sixteenth century, a set of thirteen Buddhist deities had
gained currency as peripatetic esoteric Buddhists, *nenbutsu* practitioners, and Buddhist mountain ascetics (*shugenja*) preached an esoteric Pure Land Buddhist cosmology of thirteen deities. People in-

corporated these deities into their memorial services for "dead spirits," into "reverse rituals" (*gyakushu*) for the living, and/or into prayers for preventing unfortunate spirits from turning into grudging spirits.[262] With the rise of the *danka* system, in which mountain ascetics and other peripatetic religious practitioners were excluded from the realm of death rituals, the set of thirteen Buddhist deities was quickly incorporated into funerary Buddhism. Needless to say, along with the ten deities (kings), the thirteen posthumous memorial services that corresponded to the thirteen realms in the underworld had three additional Buddhist deities: Akṣobhya Tathā-gata (Ashuku *nyorai*), Mahāvairocana Tathāgata (Dainichi *nyorai*), and the bodhisattva Ākāśagarbha (Kokūzō *bosatsu*).[263] In this schema, the deceased was believed to receive the blessings of these deities in addition to the blessings of those mentioned in the *Jizōkyō*. The general cosmological structure of the thirteen Buddhist rituals fol-lowed by the Tokugawa Japanese is outlined in Table 12.[264]

Compared with the underworld of the *Jizōkyō*, where Jizō (literally, "the storehouse of earth") plays a leading role in guiding the de-ceased to the realm of Amitābha, the underworld of the thirteen Buddhist rituals concludes with Kokūzō (literally, "the storehouse of air or heaven"), a Bodhisattva who was believed to control the Para-dise of Mahāvairocana. Thus, with the positioning of Jizō (under-world) in the middle and Kokuzō (paradise) at the end, the thirteen realms constituted a vertical cosmology of the other world.[265]

In theory, the six additional memorial services, all posited within the framework of the thirteen Buddhist rituals, were supposed to generate Buddhist merit that would be transferred to the new spirit and ensure its salvation. However, as was seen in the case of the seven rituals conducted during the first stage of Buddhist memorial ser-vices, the Tokugawa Japanese treated these additional rituals as oc-casions for further purifying and stabilizing the new ancestral spirit. For them, the Buddhist deities of the underworld realms were not judges who would weigh the merit of the deceased but rather saviors who would exert the magical power of ancestral deification. The idea of ancestral deification through the thirteen steps spawned related religious customs concerning the deceased, including the perfor-mance of thirteen Buddhist *nenbutsu* (*jūsanbutsu nenbutsu*), a set of thirteen stupas (*jūsan sotoba*), a mandala of thirteen Buddhist deities (*jūsanbutsu mandara*), and a set of thirteen Buddhist scriptures (*jūsan-bukyō*).[266]

Table 12: The Cosmology of the Thirteen Buddhist Rituals

Time span	Underground kings	Buddhist deities
First 7 days	The Far-Reaching King of Ch'in	Acalanātha (Fudō)
8–14 days	The King of the First River	Śākya (Shaka)
15–21 days	The Imperial King of Sung	Mañjuśrī (Monju)
22–28 days	The King of Five Offices	Samantabhadra (Fugen)
29–35 days	King Yama	Kṣitigarbha (Jizō)
36–42 days	The King of Transformations	Maitreya (Miroku)
43–49 days	The King of Mount T'ai	Bhaiṣajya (Yakushi)
100 days	The Impartial King	Avalokiteśvara (Kanzeon)
1 year	The King of the Capital	Mahāsthāmaprāpta (Seishi)
3 years	The King of the Cycle of the Five Paths	Amitābha (Amida)
7 years	The King on the Lotus	Akṣobhya (Ashuku)
13 or 17 years	The King Who Eliminates Suffering	Mahāvairocana (Dainichi)
33 years	The King of Compassion and Grace	Ākāśagarbha (Kokūzō)

SOURCE: Compiled from Sano (1996), p. 89.

Despite sophisticated theories and numerous customs, the actual rituals performed for the deceased during the second stage of Buddhist memorial services were rather simple. Usually a monk from the *danna* temple chanted some lines from the *Lotus Sūtra* or the *Amitābha Sūtra* in front of the altar and family members burned incense and offered food. In the case of Jōdoshinshū followers, memorial rituals conducted during this period, like those conducted previously, were not originally designed for ancestral deification or veneration; rather, they were based on the doctrine of salvation by other power, and they usually featured vegetarian meals (*otoki*), which were offered to the monks of the *danna* temple in gratitude to the Buddha, the dharma, and the *sangha*. However, over time, as Genchi (1734–1813) observes in his *Kōshinroku* (1774), the Shinshū followers were also assimilated into customs pertaining to ancestral ritual: "[They] paint a portrait of the deceased, hang it in the Buddhist hall, and place it along with those of Buddhist patriarchs; completely ignoring the instructions of the head temple; they then use even more ornate ritual paraphernalia than they do for Buddhist patriarchs, and chant sūtras and *nenbutsu* exclusively for it. There are many laypeople who do this."[267]

No matter how they were conducted, the series of memorial rituals involved a process for transforming the deceased into an ancestral deity. Indeed, the Tokugawa Japanese often even went beyond the time frame of 33 years and conducted ritual services on the fiftieth, seventy-fifth, and one hundredth anniversary of the deceased's death. Not surprisingly, this continuous ritual practice eventually gave rise to the custom of "perpetual sūtra chanting" (*eitaikyō*), in which families paid fees to their *danna* temple to have it "perpetually" perform the ritual of sūtra chanting for the deceased. From the late eighteenth century on, even Jōdoshinshū followers began to succumb to the custom of *eitaikyō* (even though, in some regions, this did not happen until the mid-nineteenth century). This enterprising practice was first initiated by major head temples, and local temples soon followed suit.[268]

In any case, when the thirteen Buddhist rituals were completed upon the thirty-third year after death, the tablet of the spirit in question was then removed from the household Buddhist altar and was either burned, floated down the river to its imagined permanent residence, or taken to the *danna* temple for permanent enshrinement. Some affluent families sent the tablet to a prominent religious place such as Kōyasan or Zenkōji. The rite of sending off the tablet, which effectively concluded the whole series of memorial rituals, was a festive occasion.[269]

The celebration of the "conclusion of memorial services" signified that the new spirit had been completely purified, freed from the danger of death pollution, and elevated to the status of ancestral deity. With regard to the deification of the deceased, Yanagita Kunio comments: "In the thirty-third year after a person died (rarely, in the forty-ninth or fiftieth year), a final Buddhist ritual called *tomuraiage*, or *toikiri*, is held. It is said that on this day the person in question becomes an ancestor. . . . It means that [he or she] has been completely purified from the pollution of death so that descendants can now worship [him or her] as a *kami*."[270] In short, the rhetoric of Buddhist salvation, which justifies the involvement of *danna* temples and Buddhist monks, serves the process of *kami* making. In the final analysis, ancestors were neither buddhas nor Buddhist deities: they were *kami*.[271]

SEVEN

The Annual Veneration
of Ancestral Deities

The Tokugawa Japanese believed that, in the process of being deified, the spirit of the deceased would gradually lose its individuality.
With the development of "registers of the past [the dead]" (*kakochō*),
tombstones, and genealogical charts—in which deceased family
members were recorded—ancestors were, to some extent, individually remembered. However, as objects of ancestral veneration, their
individuality had no particular meaning. Ancestral deities, which
were collectively referred to as ancestral spirits (*sorei*), were treated
as a cluster of deified spirits.[272] With regard to traditional beliefs
concerning the whereabouts of ancestral deities, Yanagita Kunio emphasized two points: that ancestral deities stay connected to their
descendants, and that there are frequent contacts, both regular and
irregular, between ancestral deities and their descendants due to
their frequent visits to this world.[273]

In contrast to the transcendental world of the Western Paradise,
which Buddhists championed as the most sought-after destination
for the deceased, the Tokugawa Japanese believed that their ancestral
deities would stay in nebulous proximity for posterity. The dwelling
places of the ancestors could (often simultaneously) be in the sky,
in the mountains, under the sea, across the sea, or just nearby. In
some cases, such numinous mountains (*reizan*) as Kōyasan, Hakusan,

Ōyama, Asamayama, Higaneyama, Yamadera (Risshakuji), Osorezan, and the like were recognized as possible abodes of the ancestral
spirits.[274] Saitō Ryūzo notes: "The family often sends teeth or hair
of the deceased to Kōyasan and enshrines them at a charnel house
on the mountaintop in order to pray for the posthumous well-being
of the spirit and to wish it to be connected to Daishi [i.e., Kōbōdaishi
(Kūkai)]."[275] Kōyasan was the burial site of Kūkai, and families believed that by keeping some remains of their loved ones near that
sacred place, the karmic status of the deceased could be improved
and rebirth in Amitābha's Pure Land could be achieved. In the case
of Jōdoshinshū followers, the preferred abode of deceased family
members was near the grave of Shinran in Kyoto.[276] Despite the evidence of traditional Buddhist cosmology in these customs, however,
the Tokugawa Japanese were not precise when it came to determining
the resting place of their ancestral deities.

Furthermore, the Tokugawa Japanese believed that ancestral deities appeared as formless, colorless, collective manifestations. Traditionally, ancestral deities were vaguely understood to appear as the
deity of the paddy field (*ta no kami*), the deity of the mountain (*yama
no kami*), the deity of the estate (*yashikigami*), the deity of the house
(*ie no kami*), the deity of the new year (*toshigami* or *toshitokujin*), or
just as ancestral spirits.[277] The vagueness of such manifestations provided people with a convenient source of frequent contact with their
ancestors.

Contact between ancestors and descendants was usually initiated
by the latter, who made food offerings to the former on the occasions
of annual observances (*nenchū gyōji*). Unlike the Buddhist ritual offerings made during the transitional period — offerings that were
directed toward a specific individual spirit on specific dates — these
regular ancestral offerings were based on an annual schedule and
were made collectively. The date of an individual family member's
death (*kinichi* or *meinichi*) did not have any particular bearing on annual ancestral veneration.[278] However, it should be noted that schedules for the annual observances of ancestral veneration during the
Tokugawa period were not uniform: they differed slightly from region to region, or from one status group to another. Much of these
variations had to do with local calendars, which were developed by
religious institutions, local scholars, or other groups. Among them,
the Ise calendar, produced by the Grand Shrine of Ise and distributed
by its religious promoters (known as *onshi* or *oshi*), garnered nation-

wide popularity. In addition, peasants in the countryside sometimes maintained their own calendars, which were designed to accommodate the agricultural cycles and seasonal changes of their regions.[279] Nevertheless, the shogunate made efforts to unify the nation's calendrical system by imposing an official calendar: the Senmyō calendar was in effect until 1684, followed by the Jōkyō calendar, which was first devised by Shibukawa Harumi (1639–1715) and modified in 1754, 1798, and 1843. These efforts continued until the Meiji government adopted the Gregorian calendar in 1873.[280]

On the whole, these multiple calendrical systems complicated the schedule of annual ancestral rites. For example, in Edo alone there were four different traditions with regard to greeting and celebrating the New Year and with regard to conducting the rituals of ancestral veneration.[281] In order to prevent the confusion and financial waste associated with a flood of "private" calendars, which were often exploited by diviners and quasi-astrologers, the shogunate designated eleven official engravers and authorized them to print official calendars in 1718. These were sold while the circulation of "private" calendars was banned.[282] However, private calendars continued to appeal to the populace, who were not much bothered by the overlapping of annual observances.

The annual observances of ancestral rites were also symmetrical. The year was evenly divided into two symmetrical cycles (i.e., the first and second half of the year) that basically repeated themselves. The calendar was set out as follows: celebrations in the first month of the first half of the year began on the first day, with an offering of veneration to ancestral deities who were invited to the New Year altar (*toshidana*), and they concluded with an event known as "minor first month" (*koshōgatsu*), which lasted from the fourteenth to the fifteenth or sixteenth day. Celebrations in the first month of the second half of the year (i.e., the seventh month) began on the first day, with the installment of an altar (*shōryōdana*) at which ancestral deities were venerated, and concluded with the Bon festival (*matsuri*) from the thirteenth to the fifteenth day.[283] Similarly, in the second month of the first half of the year, as in the second month of the second half of the year (i.e., the eighth month), one week, designated as Higan, was dedicated to celebrating the equinox and venerating the ancestors. On the last day of the last month of each cycle—the sixth and twelfth months, respectively—major purification rites were conducted in preparation for the upcoming ancestral rites. All in all, the symmetrical structure of ongoing annual ancestral rites ensured that the contacts between ancestral deities and descendants remained close and perpetual.

The *Bingo no kuni Numakumagun Urasakimura fūzoku toijō kotae* (Answers to the questionnaires on the customs and manners of the Urasaki village of Numakuma county in Bingo) provides a typical example of how these contacts took place. In the New Year "at a separate altar, [families] offer celebratory rice cakes to the deities of shrines, including the Ise Grand Shrine, which they worshipped, as well as to the main image and the tablets of ancestors in the household Buddhist altar; and [they] also send celebratory rice cakes to their tutelary shrine (*ujigami*), *danna* temple, main household, and relatives. . . . From the dawn of the first day of the year all family members visit their tutelary deity (*ubugami*), *danna* temple, and the graves of their ancestors."[284] On the sixteenth day of the first month "[families] pay veneration to the tablets of ancestors and the sacred spirits of relatives in the Buddhist altar."[285] During the Higan period of the second (and seventh) months "[families] offer rice dumplings to the Buddhist altar on the first, middle, and last day [of the period] and visit their *danna* temple."[286] For the Bon festival, "On the thirteenth day, a monk from the *danna* temple visits and offers sūtra chanting. . . . From the thirteenth day to the eighteenth day [families] pay homage to ancestral spirits in the Buddhist altar. . . . [Families] also offer a bundle of flowers at their family graves, spread lotus leaves in front of it, and offer rice, chestnuts, cucumbers, green beans, and water, and they burn incense."[287] These observances, which were centered on ancestral veneration, were ubiquitous in Tokugawa Japan, although the details of their ritual performance could vary slightly from region to region or from family to family.

Ancestral veneration during the New Year observance usually started with a ritual offering for the new spirits of those who had died in the old year (referred to as "dead spirits" or *shirei*) as well as for other wandering spirits. This custom, which aimed at separating new spirits from the older ancestral spirits, stemmed from the belief that the former were still volatile and prone to be malicious. A ritual offering for new spirits was usually made at the gravesite on the last day of the old year or at an altar temporarily erected outside the house.[288] By making a special ritual offering, families hoped to expedite the process of ancestral deification, and at the same time, to safely greet and venerate established ancestral deities.

In order to greet ancestral deities and celebrate the New Year, families erected a pair of pine trees or bamboo stalks stuck with pine branches (known as *kadomatsu*) at their gate on the last day of the old year. The *kadomatsu* signified the start of an auspicious new year, with the pine symbolizing 1,000 years and the bamboo symbolizing 10,000 years, respectively.[289] In many regions, a straw festoon stuck with beanstalks and pods, charcoal, seaweed, and dried persimmons was also hung over the gate. Thus, with a pair of pine trees and bamboo stalks festooned by straw bundles, which taken together looked like the archway to a Shinto shrine (*torii*), a sacred space for greeting and accommodating New Year deities was created. In popular understanding, the nature of the "New Year deities" or "deities of New Year fortune" (*toshitokujin*) to which the household head, as chief priest, made offerings as "man of the year" (*toshiotoko*), was rather vague.[290] In some regions they were likened to the deities of paddy fields, and in other regions to the deities of agriculture. By and large, however, it was commonly believed that they were none other than ancestral deities who, in different manifestations, returned en masse to visit living family members. In all cases, New Year deities were associated with wishes for a good harvest, prosperity, and good life.

After erecting pine trees at the gate, each household installed a New Year altar (called *toshidana*, *toshitokudana*, or *ehōdana*) that faced the direction from which the New Year deities would visit. The altar, temporarily set up on a table or on a board in a drawing room, was decorated with pine trees, bamboo branches, straw festoons, paper, lanterns, and the like. On the altar were placed food offerings such as mirror-shaped rice cakes (*kagamimochi*), sake, rice, dried persimmons, dried fish, and so on. These were all for the New Year deities, who would stay around the altar until it was dismantled at the end of the New Year celebration. Among these food items, *kagamimochi* were particularly important as they were specifically regarded as a divine New Year's food for ancestral deities. After having made food offerings, family members usually visited the graves of their ancestors, and then sent such New Year offerings as glutinous rice cakes of various kinds, fruits, and the like to their *danna* temple, where the ancestral tablets were enshrined. In return, monks from the *danna* temple made their rounds of their *danna* families for sūtra chanting.[291]

Another event integral to the New Year observance was a communal meal that all family members were supposed to share with their ancestors. After a ritual had been performed for the New Year deities, some of the food items used were taken and made into a meal featuring rice-cake soup (*zōni*). The collective eating of *zōni* on the first day of the year was considered a solemn occasion—one that strengthened the spiritual unity between ancestors and descendants. This communal meal resembled a traditional Shinto feast known as *naorai*, in which the priest and all ritual participants, along with the deity they had just venerated, shared the divine food.[292] This divine food was also believed to nurture and strengthen the spirits of living family members.

Later on the fourth, sixth, fourteenth, fifteenth, or sixteenth day, depending on local customs, each household took down its New Year altar and all other decorations and burned them or floated them down a river, thus symbolically sending its ancestral deities back to their imaginary resting place.[293] This concluded the New Year's ancestral rite. The tripartite nature of this rite—greeting ancestral deities at the altar, venerating them and joining them in a communal meal, and then sending them back to their dwelling—was more pronounced in certain rural areas where various customs of seeing in the New Year (*toshikoshi*) were practiced. Believing that ancestral deities would appear during the night, family members quietly sat around in front of the New Year altar or shut themselves up in a shrine (*toshigomori*) during the entire night of the last day of the year. Their purpose was to greet the arrival of the New Year as well as the descent of the ancestral deities. It was commonly believed that, the more sincerely family members devoted themselves to ancestral veneration, the more likely they would have a good harvest.[294]

Compared to the New Year celebration, the Higan ceremonies, observed for a week during the vernal and autumnal equinoxes in the second and eighth month, respectively, were more directly associated with ancestral veneration, except for some Jōdoshinshū followers who paid more attention to sermons about Shinran's teachings and vegetarian meals at their *danna* temple.[295] The *Ryori saijiki* (A record of yearly events of villages), which details annual observances in the Takasaki area of Kōzuke in the late eighteenth century, describe typical Higan activities: "During the period of seven days of Higan in this month [the second month], families venerate ancestors, pay homage to graves, and visit temples."[296] During this week-long period of ancestral veneration, families decorated their household Buddhist altar, offered food to their ancestors, paid homage to their family graves, and visited their *danna* temple with rice offerings. For their part, monks visited their *danna* households for sūtra or *nenbutsu* chanting. On the whole, ancestral veneration during the Higan also featured a tripartite structure — welcoming ancestral deities to the house, making food offerings to them, and sending them back. It was common for each part of this structure to be celebrated with offerings of initial rice cake dumplings (*hairidango*) on the first day, rice cake dumplings covered with bean flour (*botamochi*) on the equinoctial or middle day (the day known as *jishō* on which people eat simple food and clean themselves), and concluding rice cake dumplings (*akedango*) on the last day.[297]

Along with ancestral rites, other Higan activities are outlined in the *Ryori saijiki*: "Rituals and gatherings pertaining to Buddhist preaching are held at Jōdoshū temples. In the evening of the middle day, old men and women gather at Buddhist halls at the outskirts of town, loudly chant the Buddha's name, and pray for the day of their death. This is called the *nenbutsu* of heavenly way."[298] This custom was based on the belief that, because the sun enters the eastern gate of paradise on this particular day, those who want to make connections with the Buddha should chant his name and pray for their future salvation. Almost everywhere people attended confraternity meetings to chant the Buddha's name, and temples offered special sessions of Buddhist preaching or storytelling.[299] All these activities were, to one degree or another, related to the religious wishes of Higan, which literally means the "other shore" — Buddhist nirvana.

During this period, visiting a set of six temples famous for Kannon, Jizō, or the Amida Buddha was also believed to be especially meritorious. Interestingly, however, religious visits were not confined only to Buddhist temples. Visiting a set of seven Shinto shrines with stone *torii* gates was also popular in Kantō. The folk belief had it that making a round of visits to these Shinto shrines would free one from chronic disease.[300] Mountains and temples, which were reputed to be good places for ritual practice related to the Western Paradise, also attracted visitors, who prayed toward the west when the sun was setting in order to express their longing to enter paradise.[301] Shitennōji in Osaka was especially popular as people believed that its western gate would surely lead them to the Western Paradise if they prayed at it during the week of Higan.[302] It is said that the custom of worshipping the sun during the equinoxes was based on a theory found in the Buddhist treatise *Kuan-wu-liang-shou-*

ching shu (Commentary on the Meditation Sūtra) authored by Shan-
tao (613–681). It states: "On these days the sun rises from the due east
and sets in the due west. The Land of the Amitābha corresponds
to the very place the sun sets."[303]

Despite the Buddhist rhetoric associated with various customs
observed during the period of Higan, these nonetheless remained
peripheral to the business of ancestral veneration. Indeed, Higan,
which was firmly established as an annual observance during the
Tokugawa period, is unique to Japan. Some scholars suggest that it
evolved from the custom of sun worship, which had been popular
since ancient times. But this theory falls far short of explaining how,
by the Tokugawa period, it had developed into a custom featuring
ancestral veneration.[304]

The importance of ancestral veneration is again emphasized in
the observance of Bon (Bonku), which was held on the thirteenth
through the sixteenth day of the seventh month. As Kitagawa Morisada (1810–?) described it in 1867, the Bon celebration was primarily
an occasion for venerating ancestral deities: "In Edo, the people,
instead of using the household Buddhist altar to conduct ancestral
rites, install a temporary altar. For this, they erect green bamboo
branches in each of the four corners, hang a straw festoon around
them in the upper part, spread out a rush mat on the frontage below
the stage, and fence around the stage with Japanese cedar leaves.
Then, they transfer the tablets in the household Buddhist altar to this
temporary altar."[305]

Although the shape of the Bon altar and the materials used to
construct it varied both locally and according to family, it was always
set up so that it was clearly separate from the household Buddhist
altar. Families usually hung lanterns on the entrance gate during
the Bon period. Some families, as was seen in the Nagaoka domain
in Echigo, erected bamboo branches in front of tombstones, set up
a *torii*-style arch with eulalia and rice straws, lit lanterns, and offered
food or flowers.[306] Those families that had suffered a recent death
usually either erected another altar in addition to the Bon altar or
hung a lantern and other decorations high under the eaves of the
house in order to accommodate the new spirit.

After having set up the Bon altar, each family greeted ancestral
spirits that included spirits under ancestral deification (*shōryō*) and
ancestral deities (*sorei*).[307] This was done in the evening of the thirteenth day by lighting their way to the altar with fire or lanterns—

a ritual known as "welcoming fire" (*mukaebi*), or "welcoming pine torch" (*mukaetaimatsu*). For this ritual, family members would burn bundles of hemp stalks, firewood taken from pine trees, rice or wheat straws, or bean plant bundles in front of the main gate of their house, in the garden, on the road or border of the village, in front of the grave or (rarely) on a riverbank, beach, or mountain. Those families concerned with performing the full ritual procedure often escorted their ancestral deities, placing lanterns inscribed with their family emblems along the streets from the gravesite to the house. When the leading lantern arrived at the house, the household head personally greeted his ancestors at the gate and ushered them in to the altar.[308] In some areas of Echigo, family members went to a nearby river because they believed that ancestral deities would travel over the water; they would call out the names of the ancestors and then return to their home, making gestures that signified they were carrying their ancestors on their backs. The remaining family members greeted the arrival of their ancestors at the gate with pine torches in hand.[309] In almost all cases, for the next three days or so ancestral deities enshrined at the altar were treated to select food offerings, which usually featured the first crops of the year, including sake, rice, grains, vegetables, fruits, and seafood.[310] With this, an element of thanksgiving was also incorporated into the ancestral veneration of Bon.

The only exception to this custom was Jōdoshinshū. As Nagura Tetsuzō notes, on the occasion of Bon, Jōdoshinshū followers in Kakudahama village in Echigo gathered in groups at their *danna* temple, brought donations of rice and salt as Bon gratuities, chanted *shōshinge* and *wasan*, listened to guest preachers speak of Shinran's teachings and other Pure Land parables, and enjoyed a vegetarian meal (*otoki*); or monks from the temple visited *monto* families, chanted sūtras and *nenbutsu*, and preached about Shinran's teachings. In either case, Jōdoshinshū followers did not conduct the ritual offering designed for their ancestors on an individual basis; for them, the Bon festival was an annual occasion for expressing their deep-felt gratitude toward the Amida Buddha, who had already saved them and their ancestors. Nevertheless, it should be noted that, on the fifteenth day, most *monto* families visited their ancestral graves in the village or at their *danna* temple.[311]

With the exception of some Jōdoshinshū followers, then, it was customary for families to pay a visit to the graves of their ancestors and to their *danna* temple during the Bon period. From the four-teenth day, monks from the *danna* temple made a round of their patron families in order to chant Buddhist sūtras in front of the Bon altar—an annual ritual known as "altar sūtras" (*tanagyō*)—and to collect service fees.[312] In Wakasa, Jishū monks, who usually formed a group of three (two carried drums and one carried a gong), visited their patron families and chanted *nenbutsu* to the beat of gongs and drums at the gate of each household; sometimes they performed dancing *nenbutsu*.[313] In addition to venerating ancestral deities, fami-lies often set up a small altar outside the house for wandering ghosts with no descendants (*muenbotoke*) and made food offerings in order to appease them.

When Bon worship offerings concluded on the evening of the six-teenth (in some regions, fourteenth or fifteenth) day, families sent their ancestral deities back to their permanent dwelling place under the guidance of fire: this rite was known as "sending fire" (*okuribi*). Fire, which marked the commencement as well as the closing of the Bon festival, was believed to facilitate the transport of ancestral deities and to connect this world with the other world.[314] In the early morning of the following day, families dismantled the Bon altar and other decorations, wrapped all of the pieces in a rush mat, and threw them out or floated them away on the river or sea. In some regions, families cut watermelons or eggplants into the shapes of horses or cows and sent them away, or made boats with rush mats, loaded them with ritual offerings, and floated them away while chanting *nenbutsu*—a spectacle that often attracted crowds of onlookers.[315] Ac-cording to Kitagawa Morisada, many families in Edo relinquished their wrapped paraphernalia, along with a fee of twelve copper coins, to collectors who rowed small boats around the canals and rivers, shouting, "Welcome, *shōryō-sama!*"[316]

The Bon celebration provided descendants with an occasion to communicate directly with their ancestors. This tradition was even kept by those—like servants, shop workers, or seasonal laborers—who were employed away from their home village. During the Bon period, they were often granted a few days off from their daily work to visit their hometown family, to engage in ancestral veneration, and to take a rest. This custom was known as "entering a thicket" (*yabuiri*). As the word "thicket" (*yabu*) implies, the custom of *yabuiri* symbolized moving from culture, city, and order to nature, the coun-try, and disorder. It was a way of returning to the origin of life.[317]

Those who could not afford a visit to their hometown usually took a day off and spent it at temples or at scenic places. During this time, temples that housed images of King Yama (Enma), the ruler of the underworld, were crowded with visitors. It was a common belief that a visit to King Yama on the sixteenth day would ensure the well-being of one's deceased family members and ancestors.[318]

Ancestral veneration was at the center of the Bon celebration, to be sure, but it should be noted that the festival was also an occasion for celebrating the spirits of one's living parents. Custom had it that, on the fifteenth day, grown-up sons and daughters treated their parents to a meal that featured salted mackerel and steamed rice prepared on a lotus leaf. People believed that this special meal would strengthen the living spirits (*ikimitama*) of their parents and thereby ensure their longevity and health.[319] It is known that treating parents on the fifteenth day originated from a Chinese ritual found in the Taoist pantheon known as honoring the "Middle Primordials" (Chung-yüan). In China, this ritual took the form of repentance and was based on the belief that Primordials would descend from heaven to earth to judge people for their conduct in this life. However, in Japan this annual ritual, which was added to the Bon observance, somehow developed into an occasion for celebrating the spirits of living parents. In addition, in order to celebrate Bon, relatives or friends sent each other mackerel and noodles. To those families that had suffered a recent death, instead of celebratory items people in Nagasaki (for example) sent a white lantern along with incense sticks and cookies.[320]

Although some scholars suggest that the term "Bon" was derived from a Chinese Buddhist festival known as Yü-lan-p'en, the practice of Bon in Tokugawa Japan had little to do with this festival, either contextually or theologically.[321] The Yü-lan-p'en in China, which was conducted on the fifteenth day of the seventh month, was represented by a "bowl" (*p'en*) in which one would place offerings for Buddhist monks in the hope that the Buddhist merit so acquired would rescue one's parents from the fate of "hanging upside-down" (*yü-lan*) in hell. The Yü-lan-p'en festival took making offerings to the monastic community very seriously, emphasizing that this would produce a stock of Buddhist merit for the benefit of one's parents.[322] The Japanese Bon was not driven by Buddhist beliefs.

The basic functioning of the Bon festival, which was not bound by Buddhist ideas, was clearly revealed in the rite dedicated to hungry ghosts (*segaki*), a sacrificial ritual conducted at Buddhist temples on the fifteenth day. For their part, in conjunction with the Bon observance, lay families often made a food offering to hungry ghosts at an altar set up under the eaves of their dwelling. The ritual of *segaki* evolved from an episode involving Ānanda, one of the Buddha's ten disciples. Legend has it that, while Ānanda was in the middle of meditating on the Buddha's dharma, hungry ghosts (*preta*) appeared before him and warned that, three days hence, he would become prey to the same fate that had befallen them. They told him that the only way to avoid this fate and to ascend to the highest ladder of the six courses would be to make a food offering to all beings associated with the six courses as well as to the Three Jewels of Buddhism. Ānanda followed their instructions and, as a result, was saved.

When the Ānanda story was transformed into the *segaki* ritual in Japan, its Buddhist merit-accumulating theme was much diluted. In the early nineteenth century, officials of the Mito domain reported on how the monks of Gionji understood the rationale of the *segaki* ritual: for them, it was a means of countering evil spirits, whether alive or dead, which were believed to inflict sickness.[323] The rite of *segaki* was employed to pacify wandering or grudge-bearing spirits, which were believed to be the source of most things that went awry in human life. Since the Sengoku period, when innumerable violent deaths resulted due to war and when epidemics swept the land, people began to worry about the whereabouts of these unfortunate souls and turned to the *segaki* ritual in order to pacify them.

In Tokugawa Japan, Buddhist temples, with the exception of those belonging to Jōdoshinshū, conducted the *segaki* ritual according to their sectarian traditions, local customs, and ritual specialties.[324] By and large, *segaki* was held in front of a specially installed altar in the main hall and usually attended by *danna* members; the ritual itself was composed of various elements, including the recitation of Buddhist sūtras and hymns or mantras, offerings of food, and transference of merit.[325] This was followed by the second, more important stage of the ritual: *nagarekanjō*, a rite that combined traditional purification by water (*misogi*) and the esoteric ceremony of sprinkling water on the head (*kanjō*). "People erect paper banners at the riverside. Beating gongs, wooden bowls and drums, monks and laypeople form a crowd. Getting on board a boat, they chant sūtras and *nenbutsu* and drop wooden boards or flat stones, upon which sentences from Buddhist scriptures are inscribed, into the water."[326] This was a typical scene from the *nagarekanjō*, or the "flowing kanjō," which was observable throughout the country. This ritual, also called river *segaki* (*kawa-segaki*), was particularly targeted at those who had drowned. Apparently, the *kawa-segaki* was designed to pacify vengeful spirits with the purificatory power of water and esoteric spells and prayer. Cleansing, rather than Buddhist soteriology per se, loomed large in the *segaki* ritual.

The Bon observance, although bifurcated into ancestral veneration at the level of individual households and the appeasement of wandering spirits at the level of Buddhist institutions, was always concerned with taking care of the spirits of the deceased for the sake of the living. With regard to ancestral deities, close and frequent contacts were to be sought through offerings; with regard to wandering spirits, negative elements were to be washed away through purification. When all of these measures were regularly conducted according to an annual schedule, family members could convince themselves that they were united with their ancestors in harmony. This spiritual unity that would continue through generation after generation was a Japanese version of the idea of rebirth.

To one degree or another, Buddhist monks and *danna* temples were all involved in mortuary rituals, memorial services, and ancestral rites. Their multifaceted involvement in the household institution through the *danka* system ranged from officiating rituals, to chanting Buddhist sūtras, to taking care of graves, to responding to the special needs of *danna* patrons. Nevertheless, it should be noted that these Buddhist rituals were not strictly "Buddhist" in either content or structure. Traditional ideas and customs related to death pollution, purification, temporary lodges of deities, deification processes, ancestors, calendars, the other world, grudge-bearing spirits, and so forth were all inseparable from the context within which these "Buddhist" rituals were practiced. This was the religious context of Buddhist death, which contributed to the merging of funerary Buddhism and the *ie* society of Tokguawa Japan.

ℭℨ

EIGHT

Funerary Buddhism and Ie Society

"One should not be neglectful of respecting and venerating ancestors. Ancestors are the root of the blood lineage out of which one comes into being; they are the foundation of one's household. Thus, on their anniversary, one should purify oneself, make offerings to them, visit their tombs, and fulfill all 'Buddhist rituals' for them."[327] This is what Ise Sadatake (1717–84), a low-ranking official of the shogunate, set out in his family precepts (*kakun*) in 1763. In Tokugawa society, ancestral rites were the norm not only for the samurai class but also for commoners. In 1808, Onuki Man'uemon (1762–1837), the head of Onuki village and a follower of National Learning (*kokugaku*), insisted that one was expected "to get up early in the morning, to venerate the Shinto deities and Buddhas as well as the tablets of ancestors, and to work with might and main for the family business and the harmony of all family members."[328] Tejima Toan (1718–86), a Shingaku scholar who was seriously engaged in child education in Kyoto, emphasized in *Zenkun* (Admonitions for children) that children should pay homage to the household Buddhist altar in order to express their deep gratitude to the ancestors for their daily food.[329] This kind of admonition stressing the daily, seasonal, and yearly conduct of ancestral rites, homage to the Buddhist altar, and the practice of filial piety was a cross-class fixture in family precepts and childhood education.[330]

Takeda Chōshū notes that by the Genroku era (1688–1703), each household came to take care of its own ancestral deities. This stood in contrast to the previous period, when death rituals and ancestral rites were a collective enterprise of the clan group, or *dōzokudan*. Under the *danka* system, which developed in tandem with the proliferation of nuclear households, each family member was given full individual attention upon death. Funerary and ancestral rites were no longer avenues by which the main household of a clan group could sanctify and strengthen its claim to the exclusive privilege of the lineage. Before the late seventeenth century, it was still not a universal practice to commemorate the individual deaths of branch household members through such emblems as gravestones, tablets of spirits, and death registers. However, this changed as individual households increasingly began to assert their own right with regard to the posthumous well-being of deceased family members and to claim ancestral lineages of their own.

The gravestones (*hakaishi*) upon which individual posthumous names are inscribed are a good indicator of how ancestral veneration and the nuclear household developed with the entrenchment of the *danka* system. Numerous archaeological finds suggest at least three trends: (1) from the late seventeenth to the early eighteenth century, the practice of erecting gravestones began to spread from the Kansai and Kantō regions to outlying areas; (2) the shapes and sizes of gravestones changed in tandem with the proliferation of independent nuclear household units; and (3) the number of posthumous Buddhist names inscribed on the same gravestone increased in the late Tokugawa period, eventually giving rise to ancestral graves in which several generations of a family might be interred (*senzo daidai no haka*).

Tanigawa Akio studied 336 gravestones in the Takataki and Yōrō districts of Ichihara in Chiba, as well as the gravesites of Jishōin (a Tendaishū temple converted from Nichiren Fujufuse in 1665) and Kan'eiji Gokokuin in Tokyo, and found that gravestones erected before the eighteenth century were few (only 26 out of 336 in the case of Ichihara, and 17 out of 211 in the case of Jishōin). He suggests that in the Kantō region, the Kyōhō era (1716–35) represented a turning point in the popularity of the custom of erecting gravestones.[331] His other archaeological surveys took into account approximately 2,800 gravestones in twelve cemeteries in Akishima, Tokyo, 935 gravestones in the cemetery of Hokekyōji in Ichikawa, Chiba, and 189 gravestones in two cemeteries in Funabashi, Chiba. The findings from these surveys are all similar: the custom of erecting gravestones began to spread in the late seventeenth and early eighteenth centuries.[332] In Kantō, this trend was confirmed by Shintani Takanori, who surveyed more than 1,500 gravestones in the Ōwada area in Niiza, Saitama, and by Sekiguchi Norihisa and others, who examined gravestones in Tokyo and the Tama area.[333] With regard to the Kansai region, a comprehensive survey of about 15,000 gravestones in Ōsakasayama revealed—as did surveys in Nara of the Nenbutsuji cemetery in Tenri and the Gokurakuji cemetery in Shinjōchō—that the custom of erecting gravestones started spreading between the Kanbun (1661–72) and the Kyōhō eras (1716–35).[334]

To be sure, local variations should be taken into account, and, in particular, the Tōhoku region as well as areas dominated by Jōdoshinshū deviated from the general trend. In some regions, the number of gravestones decreased after the mid- to late eighteenth century. This was due not only to the new custom of inscribing multiple posthumous names on the same gravestone but also to the stagnation of population growth.[335] Nevertheless, it was apparent that from the urban areas in the Kantō and Kansai regions to remote rural areas, the custom of erecting gravestones for deceased family members was spreading steadily. Based on this general trend, which, by and large, ran parallel with the development of independent nuclear households, scholars relate the popularity of gravestones to a move away from clan collectivism toward an appreciation of the individual household lineage, as expressed through independent posthumous care and ancestral veneration.[336]

Indeed, changes in the shape of gravestones testified to how they served as a repository of rising "household consciousness" (*ieishiki*). In the Kantō region, in the early to late seventeenth century, a dominant form of gravestone took the form of a five-wheel stupa (*gorintō*) or an elegant stone stupa (*hōkyōintō*), which used to be devoted to monks and upper-class individuals. This was soon replaced with a boat-shaped stone that had a Buddhist image chiseled on its flat front face and a simple, single-sided stone slab, the top of which was cut into the shape of a triangle. These two types of gravestones prevailed until the mid-eighteenth century. At that time, however, they yielded to a rectangular, flat, four-sided stone post ending in a dome; and in the late eighteenth to the early nineteenth centuries, this gave way to a rectangular, four-sided stone post culminating in a pyramidal, flat, or platform-shaped top.[337] Changes in the shape of gravestones (marked, of course, by much local variation) defy a universal cross-country pattern. Nonetheless, extant studies suggest that, over time, gravestones were made to be suitable for the inscription of multiple posthumous names, along with brief information such as date of birth and death, age, and common names.

Gravestones consisting of a rectangular, four-sided stone post contained neither a Sanskrit letter nor a Buddhist image (i.e., a magical symbol that had previously been used to convey a strong wish for Buddhist salvation), but rather a family crest—an insignia that denoted a rising household consciousness.[338] Concurrently, from the early to mid-eighteenth century, some families arranged to have the same gravestone serve more and more members of the family. This trend eventually led to using the same gravestone for multiple generations.[339] The emergence of these sorts of gravestones was first visible among commoner or declining families who, for economic reasons, were forced to accommodate as many members as possible in a tight space, but this trend gradually spread.[340] The gravestone was a powerful symbol of familial unity—a symbol that each household, or *ie*, tried to maintain.

In Tokugawa society, the term *ie*, which, etymologically, derives from "hearth," signified the matter of managing a corporate unit of living by establishing a residence rather than a house building or a family unit. The term *kazoku*, which is rendered as "family," was not used until the Meiji period. The term most commonly used in Tokugawa society was *setai* (or *shotai*, which is usually rendered as "household" in English), a term that had originally stood for offices at the court and had widely been used in medieval times when referring to manorial properties. For the Tokugawa Japanese, *setai* (or *shotai*) signified the management and subsistence of a residential unit. The terms *kazoku* and *ie* are, therefore, different in both origin and connotation: the former signifies the members of a consanguineous or quasi-consanguineous unit regardless of whether or not they live under the same roof, whereas the latter signifies members of a residential unit who conduct the business of life together regardless of their blood relationship. In fact, during the Tokugawa period, many great farming and merchant families employed "peasants who offered labor for subsistence" (*kakaebyakushō*), servants, or workers, all of whom lived in the same residential unit and shared the same activities related to production and consumption. Thus, the term *ie* represents "something that was much larger and more important than the family."[341] It is for this reason that I render *ie* as "household" rather than as "family."

Many scholars suggest that the household institution consisted of at least three essential elements: (1) household property (*kasan*), household salary (*karoku*), or household occupation (*kagyō*), which generated household income; (2) social status in the form of household status (*kakaku*) or social standing (*mibun*), which was publicly recognized by the community and the state and defined in terms of statutory rights, privileges, and public obligations, as well as entitlement to membership of an organization, confraternity, or community; and (3) a house-name (*kamei*), which referred to the title (often the hereditary name of the household head) that publicly represented the household unit in question.[342] To these elements some scholars add two more: (4) family members, both dead and living; and (5) family ritual facilities that included a Shinto altar (*kamidana*), a Buddhist altar, and a family grave.[343] Interestingly, even if it had no family members, the household unit was held to exist as long as the first three elements were sustained and a related household continued to take care of its dead members through religious offerings. When the related household provided the nominal household with living members, the latter could be fully resurrected.[344]

On the whole, the elements constituting a household institution can be grouped into two separate yet interdependent categories: a material base represented by means of production and labor (in the case of a peasant household, for example, these would be a farm field, a homestead, and able-bodied family members); and a non-material base represented by status, family title, and lineage. Depending upon how these elements were practiced, combined, acquired, or granted, the social modes of the household unit could go in various directions.

However, regardless of how a household unit was acquired or composed, what was taken most seriously was preserving the unit as a social institution. And this involved ensuring the continuity of the household lineage through its ancestors, its current members, and its future descendants.[345] Without both the recognition of the ancestors and the potential of future generations, the household could not realize its collective goal of continuing subsistence.[346] "If we do not treat our ancestors with due respect, not only shall our offspring face decline, but our own fate will also eventually sink into jeopardy," warned Ise Sadatake.[347] Perpetuity was the ultimate raison d'être of the household institution and the primary duty of its living members, and this goal could only be realized if the household ensured the well-being of its deceased members. It was within this context that Miyaoi Sadao (1797–1858), the head of Matsuzawa village in Katori county of Shimōsa and a follower of National Learning, wrote in his *Minkan yōjutsu* (A handbook for families) in 1831: "When one dies, one's spirit enters the other world and becomes a benevolent god. . . . And then, without fail, it protects and blesses its descendants for their happy life when they venerate it. When there are no offerings of veneration, the ancestors shall be destitute in the other world, and this will make them unable to protect their descendants in this world."[348]

Indeed, for the Tokugawa Japanese, the well-being of a household as a corporate body—in fact, the household was the smallest social grouping with the greatest corporate function—was ensured when its ancestors provided it with divine protection. By the same token, they also believed that the posthumous welfare of the ancestors was contingent upon the care of their descendants. If the living household members did not care for their ancestors, then the latter were believed to suffer from "malnutrition and starvation" and, eventually, to lose their godly power. The paramount nature of a household's lineage was often represented by an unchanging household name. According to this custom known as "inheriting the name" (*shūmei*) or "common name" (*tsūmei*), when an heir inherited the headship of a household he discarded his own name and assumed the "common name" of the household.[349] The common household name, which consisted of a single given name, represented the household in the person of its current head. Although the custom of inheriting a given name generation after generation stemmed partly from the fact that most commoners were not allowed to freely adopt a surname, it also clearly reflected the increasing growth of household consciousness and lineage.[350] Once adopted, this permanent name functioned as though it were the surname of the household.

The custom of "inheriting the name" was widely practiced by the late eighteenth century, and the government officially recognized it. The common household name was used in public documents and functioned as the legal title of the household in question.[351] According to a survey pertaining to the households of Yamaguchi village in the Murayama region of Tōhoku, for example, the ratios of those households that practiced the custom of "inheriting the name" had increased from 16 percent in the case of established households and from 13 percent in the case of the tenant households in 1712–51 to 46 percent and 16 percent in 1752–86, and to 79 percent and 64 percent in

1787–1843, respectively.[352] When the new heir assumed his household name, all he had to do was to request officials to correct an entry pertaining to the age of the household head on the land and census register.[353] Once this procedure was taken care of, all the legal rights pertaining to household properties were lawfully transferred to the new heir, and this person, who was now empowered and sanctioned with the household name, was obliged to work hard for the perpetual subsistence of the corporate household. For this reason, the Tokugawa Japanese often referred to the household name as the "name of public authority" (*kōgimei*).

Indeed, the Tokugawa Japanese regarded household properties as something that belonged to the household institution itself rather than to the current household head or to its members. Thus, Miyaoi Sadao warned: "The farms and household belongings are properties temporarily entrusted to the charge of descendants; they all come from the ancestors and parents; they are not possessions of one's own."[354] The household properties were a communal asset that came into being as a result of collective sacrifices and endeavors; therefore, they belonged to the collective body made up of all household members—past, present, and future. As someone who was temporarily given an opportunity to manage them, the household head had a solemn obligation to transmit them to the next generation "by taking care of what is entrusted, no matter what, by making up items whenever they are damaged or lost, and by preserving all items, not losing even one."[355] Whether it was a family business or farmland, those who squandered it for whatever reasons could not escape what Onuki Man'uemon referred to as "heavenly punishment."[356]

In Tokugawa society what was expected of descendants was always clear: "Protect the 'household occupation' more than anything else. . . . You do not have to sweat more than usual in order to increase properties. Protect the properties and farmlands entrusted to you by your ancestors from being diminished, and be frugal in all matters."[357] This is what Yoda Sōzō (1708–84), a wealthy farmer in Katakura village of Saku county, told his descendants in his *Kakun zensho* (A collection of family precepts) in 1760. Yokoōji Katsuoki, another peasant in Kaminofu village in Chikuzen, believed that "if misfortune continues to force spending, and, as a result, if it gradually becomes harder and harder to make a living, then try to devise ways to fix the problem early on without considering giving up farmlands. . . . Even though you may be forced to sell your house and household belongings, it is important to try to find ways not to sell your farmlands."[358] Similarly, when Enomoto Yazaemon, the head of a great merchant family in Kawagoe, handed the family business to his son in 1681, he stated: "Filial piety starts by devoting oneself to the family occupation and conducting business without negligence. This is the most important [responsibility]."[359] Irie Hiroshi, who examines a wide range of family precepts found in Tokugawa society, sums up the virtues that merchant families cherished most: respect for public authority, simplicity and frugality, devotion to family occupation, diligence, and filial piety. These are all values that function, above all, to preserve the family business.[360] Given all this, to lose household properties was not only to bring shame to the household name but also, and more seriously, to betray ancestral trust.

For ancestors, the household was a place where their spirits could find peace and tranquility. Yanagita Kunio captures the deep-seated wish of the Japanese people: "When asked what could compensate for all the hardships farmers go through in this world, their answer is a guarantee that their household will perpetually continue."[361] The household itself was regarded as an altar where descendants conducted rites of veneration for their ancestors so that the latter could have peace and comfort in the other world. In this context, Yokoōji Katsuoki advised: "Every morning burn incense and offer flowers to buddhas and deities, and at night light the lamp and nurture the mind of faith; one should not be lazy in keeping the annual Buddhist services for ancestors."[362] In fact, each household maintained a Buddhist altar that served as a vehicle for ancestral veneration throughout the year. The Buddhist altar was the spiritual epicenter of a household institution that brought its members into unity through generations.

The Buddhist altar, which was common by the late seventeenth and early eighteenth centuries, featured a cabinet-style miniature shrine and was usually set up on a shelf or table in the drawing room or bedroom, along with the *kamidana* for Shinto deities.[363] Some wealthy Jōdoshinshū families often transformed an entire room into a "Buddha room" (*butsuma*) and set up an altar in its front part. Although sectarian affiliation dictated, to some extent, the altar's size and how it would be decorated, the setting was quite similar everywhere: a main image (a Buddhist statue, a portrait of the sectarian founder, or a hanging scroll of letters used for chanting) in the upper center, ancestral tablets arranged below the main image, a register of the deceased and a Buddhist scripture placed side by side, and a small table, flanked by candles, attached at the bottom of the altar, upon which flowers, food, and drinks were offered. Family members, particularly the household head, paid homage to their ancestors every morning by lighting candles, offering food and tea, and bowing toward the main image and ancestral tablets.[364]

Beyond being the domestic ritual center of ancestral veneration, the Buddhist altar was also a sort of gateway connecting the household to its *danna* temple. Whenever a monk from the *danna* temple visited his *danna* household, it was the Buddhist altar that served to justify his presence: the monk was to stand before it and chant either a few lines from a Buddhist sūtra or the Buddha's name. As far as the *danna* temple was concerned, the Buddhist altar offered evidence that its household patron was in compliance with *danka* requirements. In fact, as the Tokugawa Japanese often dubbed the annual Bon visit of a *danna* monk an "inspection of the Buddhist altar" (*butsudan aratame*), the Buddhist altar functioned as a constant reminder that death rituals and ancestral veneration were an integral part of the *danka* system.[365]

At the same time, the Buddhist altar was also the household lodge (*yorishiro*) for ancestral spirits. The absence of a Buddhist altar would mean that one's ancestral spirits would wander in the wilderness of the other world as "buddhas without attachment or affiliation" (*muenbotoke*). There were many circumstances that resulted in the spirit of the deceased not being cared for at the Buddhist altar. For example, an adult family member who did not marry and who therefore died without children was not treated as a full-fledged ancestor and could be forgotten. When children who had been married or adopted out returned to their natal family after being divorced or disowned, they were treated as "burdensome cohabitants" (*yakkai*). After death, they were usually not cared for at the Buddhist altar, and thus were condemned to be *muenbotoke*.[366]

Those spirits that were removed from, or lost, their household connection were destined to face a grim fate after death. Those who fared worst were "people dying on the street" (*yukidaore*) such as beggars and the homeless, people who had drowned and been left uncared for, and entire families who perished by fire, accidents, or other natural disasters. These unfortunate souls, having no caring descendants, were believed to join the world of vengeful spirits and were accused of causing all kinds of disasters, from floods to droughts to plagues of insects.[367] As a way of countering the curse (*tatari*) of these drifting spirits, people made extra food offerings at Bon or took other collective measures at the village level. One such collective measure was a ritual known as "driving insects away" (*mushiokuri*), with "insects" representing vengeful, drifting spirits.[368] Spirits with no place to which to return—that is, with no household Buddhist altar—symbolized a shattered household institution.

When ancestors were well nourished through ancestral veneration, they would, in return, bless the household of their descendants with divine protection. The household institution was a joint enterprise whose success depended on both the deceased and the living. In this sense, ancestors and descendants were eternal partners who depended upon each other for their respective well-being, even though, in practice, it was the current household head who took responsibility. Nothing was more important than preserving the household institution and passing it down to posterity. To the Tokugawa Japanese, this task was a solemn obligation—an obligation that was tied up with the idea of filial piety.

"Never, ever assume that the official position of the household will remain safe from generation to generation, no matter how affluent the household. Farmers are supposed to concentrate on agriculture. That is what is called showing 'filial piety' towards parents. . . . Never forget the painstaking efforts by which the founding ancestors of the household have enabled you to be where you are in the present."[369] So spoke Muramatsu Hyōzaemon (1762–1841), an agriculturalist in Machii village of Hakui county in Noto in the early nineteenth century. His words echo in those of an anonymous farmer in Chikuzen: "In particular, if the homestead or farmlands are turned over to others, this amounts to perpetrating great violence on one's duty to show filial piety toward one's ancestors. No shame could be greater."[370] Ōtō Osamu aptly captures the essence of filial piety as understood by the Tokugawa Japanese: "to preserve the household property inherited from ancestors, to devote oneself to the household business or occupation, and to keep up the household name and ancestral veneration."[371]

In Tokugawa society, filial piety focused upon the household institution rather than upon individual members of the household. It affected people from all walks of life; it even affected the Jōdoshinshū followers of Shinran whose teachings did not embrace filial piety. In the mid-seventeenth century, the head of the Nishihonganji subsect (Ryōnyo, 1612–62) enthusiastically promoted filial piety—along with compassion, diligence, honesty, thrift, and endurance—saying that these values were essential for preserving the household institution.[372] In line with this, Ninsei (1657–1724), a well-known Jōdoshinshū preacher in Kaga, suggested in his *Nōmin kagami* (Mirrors of farmers) that when one devoted oneself to the household and to agriculture to the extent that one's bones were crushed, then one would be freed from the cycle of transmigration.[373]

Thus, it comes as no surprise that failure to adequately manage the household sometimes resulted in the forced retirement of the incumbent head.[374] A diary kept by the head of the Takiguchi family in the remote mountain village of Yamanoshiri in northwest Suruga relates certain episodes that explain how a household head was "forced to retire" when he was judged unsuitable for the task of filial piety. This diary, which covers the period between 1773 and 1855, is one of the few writings detailing the daily concerns of Tokugawa peasants.[375]

In the evening of the twenty-fourth day of the eleventh month of 1774, Yamanoshiri village officials and fellow residents held a meeting and decided to replace as head of household a villager named Wauemon with his son because "loans have increased, and the relationship between father and son has deteriorated." They not only decided to remove Wauemon as household head but also specified how his household properties were to be divided between him and his son: all properties, except the collateral pawned for loans and a portion of the farmland allocated for taxes, were to be divided in half; a storehouse was to be given to Wauemon as his new residence, along with half of the rice remaining in the household, one straw bag (*tawara*) of *mochi* rice, two straw bags of barley, two *to* (1 *to* = 4.765 gallons) of wheat, tatami, tools, and some vegetables.[376] Similarly, the Tōjiemon family had some financial trouble that led to a family dispute between father and son. These problems were all attributed to the household head, who was accused of unspecified "misbehavior." Fellow village residents and relatives intervened to force him out and to install his son as household head.[377] This custom, known as the "abdication [of headship] by force" (*oshikome inkyo*) was not unusual in Tokugawa society.

The head of household had the power to "exercise the household seal" and was more than a private member of society. If he failed to live up to expectations, he could be forcibly removed from his position; but when he was challenged without justifiable reason, he was protected. In the second month of 1781, a villager named Seikichi who had ongoing disputes with his father-in-law asked his fellow villagers to intervene. Siding with Seikichi, the villagers decided that the father-in-law, who had already turned over the household to his son-in-law but had been living in the same house, should be removed to a separate "retirement house," and they provided details regarding how this separation should be arranged.[378] The cause of the problem was that the retired father-in-law attempted to exercise some of his former power and thus came into conflict with his son-in-law. The villagers, who determined that the conflict must stop for the sake of the household, decided to empower the son-in-law.[379]

According to *bakufu* law, parents were supposed to wield absolute authority over their children. When there were conflicts between parents and their children, the latter were not allowed to bring the case to the public authorities. In fact, if children were bold enough to bring a case to the public authorities, they were subject to punishment for a "crime of unfilial action," unless their parents' alleged wrongdoings were clearly proven to be serious or chronic.[380] However, legal parental authority was often bypassed when the smooth running of the household was at stake. For example, in the eighth month of 1775 in Yamanoshiri village, Riemon got drunk and punched his father San'emon. A neighbor reported the incident to the village head. Shocked, the village head ordered "all nearby members of the [five-man group] association, without exception, to hold a meeting and to try to solve [the problem] internally" in order to prevent the father from going to the government. Under pressure from his fellow villagers, San'emon agreed to accept their collective suggestion of settlement, which was that Riemon pledge not to drink any more and to submit a letter of apology to the head of the five-man association.[381] The rationale for pardoning Riemon was that the tranquility of the household organization was more important than anything else. It is striking that a son, for whatever reason, could hit his father and escape punishment.

This is what sharply distinguished Tokugawa society from Chinese and Korean society. As Confucius taught in the *Hsiao-ching*, which exerted enormous influence upon both Chinese and Koreans, "the duty of children to their parents is the foundation whence all other virtues spring, and also the starting-point from which we ought to begin our education." Only after "paying careful attention to every want of his parents" could a son "serve his government loyally" and then "establish a good name for himself."[382] Filial piety toward one's parents was the foundation of all other ethical norms, and it was believed to nurture all other virtues, including self-discipline, household management, state government, and universal peace.[383] Following this, for example, education in Chosŏn Korea was primarily devoted to the Confucian value of filial piety: the government exhorted the populace to filial piety through the publication of various Confucian writings. Of these, the *Tongguk sinsok samgang haengsildo* (A new follow-up edition illustrations of the conduct of three cardinal ethical norms in the eastern country), a collection of stories about the individuals who practiced filial piety, loyalty, and chastity, remained influential in public brainwashing to the late Chosŏn period.[384] This text was very clear on what filial piety entailed: "obeying, serving, and protecting one's parents—no matter what sacrifice or price one has to pay; nursing parents' sickness with special food; curing wholeheartedly the wounds of one's parents even if this might involve cutting one's own flesh or finger."[385]

Unconditional obedience to and veneration of parents was the starting point of filial piety, as the *Hsiao-ching* declared: "The first duty of a son is to venerate his parents."[386] Even when one's parents committed a crime, the Confucian position was clear: "In serving his parents, a son may gently remonstrate with them. When he sees that they are not inclined to listen to him, he should resume an attitude of reverence and not abandon his effort to serve them. He may feel worried, but does not complain."[387] Within this belief system, which holds that "[one's] body and hair and skin are all derived from [one's] parents and [that] therefore [one has] no right to injure any of them in the least," parenthood could not be violated under any circumstances. In particular, the father, who in premodern Korean society exercised absolute power over his children, remained the sole authority of the household until death. There was not, and could not be, any notion of "retiring" him from his household leadership. If children behaved badly toward their parents, then they were subject to punishment by law (not to mention public condemnation). Given all this, striking one's father would be an unthinkable and absolutely unforgivable crime. When such an act occurred in Chosŏn society, the one responsible was not only beheaded but the administrative status of his or her village was demoted and all its residents were shamed for generations.

It should also be noted that in China and Korea, filial piety had to do with the bond between parents and children who were directly linked by patrilineal blood. It began at home, with the veneration of one's parents, and it continued after their death in the form of ancestral sacrifice. In Chosŏn society, "A descent line, once established, was under pressure to perpetuate itself, if only for one reason—to continue the observance of rites for the ancestors of the line."[388] Adoption was not prevalent in Chosŏn society, but when it did occur, the adoptee was usually chosen from among paternal nephews sharing the same blood lineage. Someone not related by blood was never adopted because no ancestor could receive worship from persons bearing different clan-names. The principle of descent and communion between ancestors and descendants was at the core of traditional Korean family life.[389] Within this context, filial piety had no direct relevance outside the relationship constituted by "me" and "my" parents; therefore, the foundation of this "my-ism" was the starting point of the ethical value of filial piety that was extendible and applicable both vertically (toward one's ancestors, the lord, the heavens, and the earth) and horizontally (toward siblings, relatives, neighbors, and society in general).[390]

By comparison, having a household in Tokugawa society meant "having an obligation not only toward one's ancestors but also toward one's village community dictated by the system of *murauke* in which tax payment was the joint responsibility of the village unit as a whole. The household head was therefore a 'public man' who participated in the management of the village as the representative of his household."[391] Indeed, the survival of individual households was inextricable from a system of mutual support, the communal usage of natural resources (such as water, firewood, and pastures), and the governing structure of inclusion and exclusion. When a household head caused trouble or was found unsuitable, whether inside or outside his household, his community could remove him.[392] With regard to the collective expulsion of the household head, the government did not interfere: it was an act left to the collective will of household members, relatives, and the community.

Even in the daimyo household (a form of extended household organization featuring a lord-vassal relationship), vassals (household members) could unseat the incumbent daimyo (household head) without serious consequences. This occurred when the whole daimyo household organization was considered to be in jeopardy because of the daimyo's personal mischief (e.g., excessive indulgence in pleasure, thus causing the depletion of the domain treasury, and consequently, heavy taxation upon the domain; illegal, cruel, or immoral behavior that could invite shogunal punishment; an ongoing inability to get along with his own vassal households; or involvement in disputes over internal succession).[393] In the name of loyalty to the "honorable household" (*goke*), the vassal household members (*kashin*) could "rebel" against their master. This is a samurai version of "filial" action, and it is justified by the rationale that domain residents and lands were not the personal possessions of the lord. The troublesome lord who kept ignoring constructive advice and was thought to be ruining the household organization could be brought down. The samurai believed that the "honorable household" was both transcendental and eternal, and that it took precedence over the personal authority of an individual leader.[394] Abdication by force was a final (albeit treasonous) resort that could save the household organization from obliteration. When such revolts occurred, the shogunate feigned ignorance on the understanding that such action was essential to the survival of the daimyo household in question. For the Tokugawa Japanese, filial piety was a virtue that had to be honored even if this meant rebelling against the household head.[395]

Again, unlike the case in China and Korea, filial piety in Tokugawa society was practiced within the framework of Buddhist death rituals and ancestral rites—a framework that entailed distinctive social implications. Professional Buddhist practitioners, except those belonging to Jōdoshinshū, were required to abandon ordinary family life, and for that reason, they were commonly referred to as renunciants (*shukkesha*), or "those who left the family." Anti-Buddhist critics charged that it would be ludicrous to delegate filial piety to those who rejected their parents, had no descendants, and only contributed to terminating the family lineage.[396] Paradoxically, however, under the *danka* system, temples and monks offered the Buddhist blessing of filial piety to their patron households.[397] Even more paradoxically, all households were not equal with regard to receiving the Buddhist blessing of filial piety, for though it was claimed to be a universal blessing, in fact it was distributed according to the social status, wealth, or political power of each household, as we see in the conferral of posthumous Buddhist names.[398]

Before the mid-eighteenth century, despite heavy local variations, the most usual posthumous names for commoners consisted of two characters to which titles of varying rank were suffixed. High-ranking titles such as *koji* or *daishi* were rarely added.[399] However, as time progressed, more and more households sought such titles as *koji* or *daishi* (which would be suffixed to two- or four-character names), or such titles as *zenjōmon* or *zenjōni* (which would be suffixed to four-character names). Some families even sought such highest titles as *ingō* or *indengō* in order to additionally attach them before names, which were already suffixed with *koji, daishi, shinji, shinnyo, zenjōmon,* or *zenjōni.* Amid this trend, two-character names suffixed with *zenmon* or *zenni* became quite scarce in many regions by the late eighteenth or early nineteenth century, and many families had to offer more and more donations to their *danna* temples in an attempt to dignify themselves with higher posthumous titles.[400]

All this escalating attention to the social status of one's household gained more force amid the increase of households made up of social outcasts—such as those described as "much filth" (*eta*) and "nonpersons" (*hinin*)—who could not escape discrimination even after death.[401] Funerals for these members of the underclass were usually conducted at a temple not associated with other classes, and the posthumous names given to them, whether they were registered in a separate or in a collective death register, were visibly distinguished from the entries for ordinary *danna* household members. Most commonly, their outcast or unusual status was, directly or indirectly, indicated in the Chinese graphs used to show their two-character posthumous names, which were usually suffixed with *zenjōmon* (*zenjōni*) or *zenmon* (*zenni*).[402] Underclass households tried to cast off the image of low, pollution-stricken status through the acquisition of elevated posthumous names, but this sort of Buddhist blessing was hardly within their reach.[403] Their efforts were blocked not only by other classes, which tried to maintain their relatively high social standing through class segregation, but also by Buddhist monks who could not see much benefit in the universal application of Buddhist compassion.

For the Tokugawa Japanese, ancestors, who were deified and cared for by Buddhist rituals, signified the purity and dignity of the household—and it was this purity and dignity that had to be protected from the increasing presence of social outcasts. In other words, the competition for household status, which could be represented by the posthumous Buddhist names of ancestors deified through Buddhist blessing, ended up reinforcing social discrimination. It is ironic that ancestral veneration via Buddhist rituals, which were cherished under the *danka* system, contributed to excluding social outcasts from their alleged universal salvation.[404]

But the discriminatory nature of ancestral veneration was not confined to the household institution; it often extended into the village community where the ancestral deities of individual households constituted village deities at a collective level. People believed that a village's tutelary deity (*chinjugami* or *ubusunagami*), which was worshipped at the tutelary village shrine and served to bind them into the village community, was inseparable from their own ancestral deities. According to Yanagita Kunio: "In order to worship ancestral spirits with abstinence and free of pollution, [villagers] designated a place outdoors. This is the origin of hundreds of thousands of Shinto shrines in the country."[405] The tutelary village shrine, as the collective seat of the purified ancestral spirits of all village households, did not tolerate social outcasts within its territory. The segregation of social outcasts was built into the religious mindset of Tokugawa Japanese. Within this context, the communal worship of a tutelary village deity amounted to the veneration of all the ancestral spirits of each individual household, and individual household members, who were connected to each other through the communal worship of the village deity, formed a kind of extended family that was free of pollution.[406]

The logic of this type of expansion was applied to other forms of household organizations as well. For example, the Mitsui merchant family, which had come to encompass 220 stores in Kyoto, Osaka, Edo, and Matsusaka by the early 1720s, developed a multilayered system of management that granted a high degree of autonomy to each unit. Each store unit was like a separate household. However, when employees died, they were collectively buried and honored as a whole through annual memorial services held on the occasion of Bon and other annual events. For this purpose the Mitsui family maintained "collective cemeteries" (*sōbo*), at its *bodaiji* temples located in Kyoto (Shinnyodō, a Tendaishū temple), Osaka (Saihōji, a Jōdoshū temple), and Edo (Shinseiji, a Tendaishū temple). All employees, no matter the branch at which they worked, were treated as legitimate members of the same extended Mitsui household.[407] Similarly, individual samurai households were also connected to a larger community through the lord-vassal relationship. At the domain level, they were incorporated into the daimyo household, and at the national level they were incorporated into the *bakuhan* system, which was led by the shogunal household. In other words, the *bakuhan* system, which was under the leadership of the Tokugawa house, functioned as the extended household of the samurai estate. It is no wonder that branches of Tōshōgū, where the spirit of Tokugawa Ieyasu was enshrined, were set up throughout the country to bring the samurai estate under the *bakuhan* system through communal worship.[408]

No matter how ancestors were venerated on a collective level, this did not much affect the social outcast class. The hamlet of social outcasts was the only space in Tokugawa society where ancestral veneration had little meaning. Given that these outcasts, whether *eta* or *hinin*, had nothing for which they should be thankful, it is understandable that ancestral veneration was not a big part of their religious life. Nevertheless, this did not mean that they were free from the constraints of the *danka* system. For them, the religious benefits that the *danka* system was supposed to bring simply receded into the dark mists of a discriminatory social order. Ironically, social outcasts, who did not benefit from the salvific path of Buddhist death, ended up absorbing all the elements pertaining to dirt and defilement into themselves and their hamlet community. This laid the foundation for a society structured around status, with the lowest class allowing all the others to be free of pollution. For its part, the *danka* system of funerary Buddhism further strengthened a "household" society based on status by arranging the deceased family members and ancestors of each household along a scale that ranged from pollution to salvation.

Conclusion

Buddhism was involved in every stage of death-related rituals and ancestral rites, both of which were underpinned by such indigenous ideas as death pollution, purification and abstinence, volatile spirits, temporary dwelling places of spirits, regeneration, divine protection, the other world, and seasonal observances. The interaction between Buddhism, traditional religious ideas and practices, and local customs enriched the ritual procedures of Buddhist death and ancestral veneration in Tokugawa household society.

In understanding the paradigm of Buddhist death and ancestral veneration, which gained universal currency in early modern times, it should be remembered that a majority of Buddhist temples were established between the sixteenth and early seventeenth centuries in response to the rise of independent nuclear households and their increasing demand for ancestral veneration. These relatively new temples, which in most cases were a result of the recreation, revival, or expansion of existing religious facilities and prayer halls, laid the foundation for funerary Buddhism, which would be institution-alized into the *danka* system under the nationwide imposition of anti-Christian policy.

The trend that saw nuclear households coming to function as inde-pendent agents of ancestral veneration was represented by the Bud-dhist altars that were a feature of each household. This altar was called by many different names, including *jibutsu* in Wakayama and the Shirako area of Ise, *jibutsudan* in the Fukuyama area of Bingo, and *jibutsudō* or *butsudō* in the Nagaoka area of Echigo. As these examples show, the household Buddhist altar was, in effect, a con-densed version of a village hall enshrining the Buddha (*jibutsudō, ujidera, sōdō*, and *sondō*).[409] When the Buddhist village hall was moved into the household in this miniature form, it became a household Buddhist altar—and in rare cases, a "Buddha room" (*butsuma*). When the hall was expanded into an official religious institution, it became a funerary Buddhist temple.[410] Thus, the trajectory along which Bud-dhist facilities moved testifies to how Buddhism came to dominate death-related rituals and ancestral rites.

In medieval times, many households maintained *kamidana*, where a variety of deities were enshrined and worshipped, and where amulets or talismans acquired from Ise *oshi* (*onshi*) or other Shinto shrines and temples were deposited. The *kamidana* was the household center of religious activities, where ancestral spirits were also often enshrined and venerated along with other deities.[411] During this period, the in-volvement of Buddhism in death-related rituals and ancestral venera-tion was partial, and at best complemented local folk customs that emphasized communication between ancestors and descendants.[412] However, as Buddhist altars were installed in households, changes began to occur: ancestral spirits were separated from the pantheon of spirits enshrined at the *kamidana* and were put into the Buddhist altar. As a result, many early modern households had two separate religious altars: a Buddhist altar for ancestral spirits and a *kamidana* for all other deities not related to the deceased or the ancestors. The separation of the Buddhist altar and the *kamidana* also signified the dominance of Buddhist funerary and ancestral rites, and this domi-nance was put into practice within the *danka* system.

As Buddhism was associated with the collective well-being of the family, the medieval Buddhist worldview, which had been represented by the cosmology of "six courses" and had been primarily directed toward individual salvation, lost much of its appeal. Buddhism became a religion whose function was to further the continuance of the household institution rather than the salvation of individual family members. The soteriology of individual-centered Buddhism gradually gave way to the soteriology of family-centered Buddhism, which appropriated the conventional notions and practices of deification and ritual veneration—an appropriation of ritual dominance that was played out among households, funerary temples, and the state and complicated their power relations within the *danka* system.

꧁

PART III

The Cultural Politics
of the Danka System

In *1780, a* danna *household in the Shirakawa domain in northern Japan
had its temple's* danna *affiliation revoked because it failed to pay seasonal
fees and to offer gifts, or* tsuketodoke.[1] *As the annual religious inspection
approached, the* danna *household, to no avail, petitioned the temple to
cancel its decision to terminate their affiliation. Finally, the household asked
the temple to issue a document for "sending" (*okuri*), as was required
by law, so that it could switch to another temple. But the temple responded
that it would do this only if the other temple would agree to bring compliments (*aisatsu*).*

Amid this bickering over the danna *affiliation, a household member
suddenly died of illness. Because it no longer had a funerary* danna *temple,
the household could not properly "bury" its dead. It did not have any other
choice but to temporarily inhume the corpse. Panicked, the family brought
its predicament to the domain government; however, domain officials found
that the legal issue of "leaving the* danna *affiliation" (*ridan*) was outside
their jurisdiction.[2] In order to seek shogunal direction, domain official
Kusakabe Takeemon forwarded to the* bakufu *the documents related to
the dispute.*

The bakufu *responded that it had neither issued regulations nor established guidelines that would justify a temple revoking its affiliation with
a* danna *household because the latter neglected to pay its fees. It then*

emphasized that a dispute over danna *affiliation should not affect the requirement of annual religious inspection.*[3] *Clearly, the shogunal response, which followed the principle of minimum interference in individual* danna *relationships, did not provide an answer to the questions posed by the Shirakawa case. It is not known how the Shirakawa domain government dealt with the dispute, although it is likely that, as was usual in Tokugawa society, it opted for a private out-of-court settlement* (naisai).

Despite the murky nature of this matter, we do know for certain that an irreconcilable dispute surrounding the termination of a danna *affiliation, whether it was initiated by a* danna *temple or by a* danna *household, could be brought to the nation's highest authority. This had to do with the fact that* danna *disputes were, in the final analysis, inseparable from the state policy of anti-Christianity, which, in the form of annual religious inspection, had developed into a nationwide system of population surveillance. The parties involved in the* danna *dispute could never be free of the anti-Christian framework adopted by the shogunate.*

For Buddhist danna *temples, annual religious inspection was a source of power, a publicly sanctioned monopoly. As the* danka *system bound the populace to the requirement of* tsuketodoke, *Buddhist temples were able to secure their income while increasing their social influence. Although* tsuketodoke *implies voluntary donation, in fact it was imposed upon* danna *households in the form of a series of annual dues. Buddhist temples insisted that in return for funerary and memorial services, their* danna *households had to pay* tsuketodoke, *which ranged from ritual fees and thanksgiving presents to occasional almsgiving and labor services. For the general populace, annual* tsuketodoke *dues were often not much different from an extra tax burden, and for the government, they were like a source of extra revenue that they were unable to tap. For this reason, Kumazawa Banzan criticized the imposition of* tsuketodoke *as a "drain on the state's resources."*[4]

As time went on, criticism of tsuketodoke *became harsher and more widespread. When the Shirakawa daimyo, Matsudaira Sadanobu (1758–1829), was appointed as senior councilor of the* bakufu *in 1787, he sought advice from Nakai Chikuzan (1730–1804), a Confucian scholar from the Kaitokudō academy in Osaka. In his* Sōbō kigen *(Critical words of the grassroots), which maintained that Buddhist religious inspection was depleting the dignity and integrity of shogunal sovereignty, Chikuzan contended that some monks were abusing the system in order to pursue their own financial gains. He seemed particularly bothered by the behavior of some* danna *temples, which seemed to be indiscriminately issuing non-*

Christian certificates to wanderers and seasonal laborers without checking their backgrounds.[5] As a matter of fact, as Ogyū Sorai (1666–1728) pointed out in his Seidan *(Discourses on government), this kind of irregularity was already visible in the early eighteenth century, when social mobility had begun to increase. He complained that bogus religious inspection was particularly rampant in Edo. Although Sorai agreed that it would not be easy to trace the religious affiliations of the large and fluid population of Edo, he did not believe that this was any reason to vindicate Buddhist temples of the crime of producing counterfeit citizenship.[6]*

Despite such criticisms, the real problem was that the government simply did not have the administrative capacity to verify all danna *affiliations. The shogunate delegated to the Buddhist temples the authority to approve and administer changes in affiliation, stipulating that it was legal to switch to a new* danna *temple if the old one consented and issued the person in question a "document for sending" (*okuri tegata).[7] *If the old* danna *temple refused to issue the document, then a new* danna *relationship could not be established, and the family involved could find itself in trouble. And for a family that had just suffered a recent death, this kind of situation spelled double jeopardy. Before burying the dead, the law required that a monk from the* danna *temple verify the death before deleting the deceased from the population register. Without such an official inspection, death had no legal meaning.[8]*

What bothered families even more than the legal status of a death was the fate of the deceased, whose posthumous well-being was believed to hinge upon the religious care offered by his or her danna *temple. In Tokugawa society, people believed that if a new spirit was denied access to Buddhist death rituals and postmortem services, then it was doomed to be a wandering ghost, unable to attach itself to its descendants and forever flitting about in the wilderness of the other world. Furthermore, when deprived of the divine protection of ancestral deities, a household was believed to run the risk of losing its divine wall of protection and eventually ceasing to exist.*

The danka *system, leveraged by the shogunal policy of anti-Christianity, had far-reaching ramifications. For Buddhist temples, it provided a major source of income and socio-religious influence; for* danna *households, it provided assurance of religious welfare and continued prosperity; and for the state, it provided an institutional apparatus for socio-religious control and political maneuvering. Within this triangular structure, no one party could fully control the whole system — not even the* bakufu. *Matsudaira Sadanobu, the shogunate's top official, agreed with Nakai Chikuzan that*

Buddhist monks were useless, even harmful, to society.[9] *But Sadanobu, who was forcefully pushing through his Kansei reforms, knew better than anyone that the* danka *system was not something that could be tampered with: it was a system rooted in the inviolable political will of the founding fathers of the Tokugawa regime. As such, the* danka *system persisted throughout the Tokugawa period as a site of dispute and contention for* danna *households, funerary temples, and the state.*

ɔ⅗

NINE

Danna *Patrons, Buddhist Death,* and *Funerary Temples*

In 1613, the eighteenth year of the Keichō era (1596–1614), Tokugawa Ieyasu issued a shogunal decree variously entitled "Gojōmoku shū-mon danna ukeai no okite" (Itemized regulations for confirming *danna* of the sect), "Tōshōgū jūgokajō" (Fifteen articles of Tōshōgū [Tokugawa Ieyasu]), "Shinkunsama gojōmoku jūgokajō" (The Fifteen-article law by the Holy Shogun), and so on.[10] This document was so treasured that there were virtually no Buddhist temples that did not possess a copy of it. Many scholars cite this document in order to illustrate the manner in which the *danka* system operated, with particular focus on what obligations and duties Buddhist temples imposed upon their *danna* patrons.[11] The copy I cite is one found at Kōanji in Yushima, Tokyo, a small Jōdoshū temple established in 1606.[12]

This decree is bogus, even though its skillful fabrication fooled Meiji legal scholars, who included it in their compilations of Tokugawa laws entitled *Tokugawa kinreikō*.[13] The document predates the actual prescriptions that it lays out: the nationwide ban on Christianity was not in full swing until 1638, the alleged prohibition of the Nichiren Fujufuse sect (including the Hiden subsect) was not completely enforced until 1691, and the *bakufu* policy on the switching of *danna* affiliations was not articulated until 1729.[14] These inconsistencies suggest that the decree was probably forged in the early eighteenth century.

Despite the fact that it was an obvious forgery, this document exerted tremendous influence over the relationship between Buddhist temples and their funerary patrons. And probably because it did not pose any direct threat to the stability of the relationship between quasi-official Buddhist agents of anti-Christianity and the target population, *bakufu* officials did not attempt to take it out of circulation. On the contrary, this Tōshōgū decree contained articles that strongly defended the "divine country" of Japan by condemning "evil" religious elements that dissented from shogunal authority. One of these articles defined Kirishitan as religious maniacs who would not fear death even if they were thrown into fire or water, who would regard themselves as being "enlightened" when they bled to death during punishment. Similarly, another article condemned the Fujufuse and Hiden subsects as promulgating wicked teachings that had no place in the divine country.[15] These bogus articles sanctified Buddhism as the legitimate religion of the divine country while condemning those defiant sects that the shogunate already regarded with suspicion.

But the real intention of the Buddhist monks who forged, and capitalized upon, the Tōshōgū decree was to remind the populace that their "ill behavior" would only serve to prove their deviant religious status. The second article specified how the wicked followers of Christianity could be identified: they would be the people who resisted obeying the Law of Śākyamuni and who tried to avoid their *danna* duties.[16] According to the third article: "with regard to a [*danna*], even the head *danna*, who fails to visit [his or her funerary temple] on the days of the sect founder's memorial service, Bon, Higan, and the memorial services of his or her ancestors, [the *danna* temple] will cancel its seal [on the anti-Christian certificate], refuse him or her entry to the place of religious inspection, and bring him or her for strict investigation."[17] At the same time, *danna* patrons were expected to pay generous fees and to offer presents to the Buddhist monks of their *danna* temple. This was portrayed as being no different from paying for "favors received from heaven." If people did not do this, then they were suspected of being Fujufuse adherents.[18]

While strictly warning against taking death rituals and memorial services to another temple, the Tōshōgū decree also emphasized that the head monk of the *danna* temple was entitled to verify any given death and to confirm that it had nothing to do with the evil sects of

Christianity or Fujufuse. Upon completing this procedure, the head monk was supposed to provide "a knife for cutting the hair of the dead" and was eventually "to confer upon him or her a Buddhist posthumous name."[19] Even those who were physically incapable of walking were expected to attend their *danna* temple to witness all Buddhist rituals pertaining to their ancestors. After laying out the inviolability of *danna* duties (*dan'yaku*), the Tōshōgū decree went so far as to declare that, as a way of ascertaining a *danna*'s devotion to his or her temple, monks from the *danna* temple were entitled to visit their *danna* households during the Bon festival in the name of inspecting the household Buddhist altar.[20]

Each year, under the shield of anti-Christianity and Buddhist funerary services, the head monk of a *danna* temple would remind his *danna* household of their duties by reading the articles of the Tōshōgū document to all members of the household before renewing their non-Christian certificates. In the case of Jōdoshinshū temples, which relied heavily upon funerary *danna* households for sustenance, the Tōshōgū document was like a gift from heaven. They posted it in their main hall, read it to their *monto* whenever events were held there, and stressed the importance of practicing its articles. It is also well known that many Jōdoshinshū temples swiftly transformed the Tōshōgū articles into their personal regulations regarding the behavior of *danna* members. Needless to say, these regulations invariably emphasized that the *monto* were expected to be faithful and generous in their support of *danna* temples through observing the requirements of funerary Buddhism.[21] Indeed, across sects, the Tōshōgū document was utilized in many different ways. Even Buddhist monks who were involved in education at "temple schools" (*terakoya*) made use of it, exploiting it as a textbook for young children who would be their future funerary patrons.[22] It is well known that, by the end of the Tokugawa period, about 30,000 to 40,000 *terakoya* schools were established throughout the country and that, particularly in the countryside, many Buddhist monks served as teachers at such schools.[23] The Tōshōgū document must have been a perfect text with which to conduct reading and writing practice. In this way, the decree's unmistakable message, which echoed in every corner of the country, was inscribed deep into the minds of the populace.

Should a *danna* household neglect to send "donations" to its funerary temple, the latter, in theory, could revoke the household's *danna* affiliation. This course of action, which would involve refusing to verify the *danna*'s non-Christian status, could bring the *danna* under suspicion of being a Kirishitan, and accordingly lead to "removal from the register [of sectarian inspection]" (*chōhazure* or *chōgai*). The punishment of *chōhazure*, which would terminate the citizenship of the involved (including any right of inheriting properties) and transform him or her into a social outcast, was obviously the worst thing that could happen to someone living in Tokugawa Japan. Tamamuro Fumio tells of an episode that took place in Iiyama village of Aikō county in Sagami. In 1846, a villager named Sajirō, who had been warned of his imminent *chōhazure*, wrote a letter to his *danna* temple Shōrenji, begging for leniency. He admitted that over the past three years, he had failed to "make any contribution to the events commemorating the birth of the Buddha, conduct any annual memorial services for [his] parents and ancestors, and heed the temple's instructions."[24] Apparently, the head monk of Shōrenji made several unsuccessful visits to Sajirō's place to collect donations. It also appears that the temple had long wished to repair its main hall, a project that required extra donations from its *danna* patrons. However, Sajirō again seems to have ignored such solicitations. After confessing his "sin," he made a pledge: "From now on I will be a different person deep in my heart, I will keep the law of the temple as well as the law of the state, and I will never disobey the temple."[25] Facing the peril of removal, Sajirō, under the auspices of the representative of his five-man group, appealed to the head monk not to erase his household from the temple's *danna* roster.

According to the law, the punishment of *chōhazure* did not fall within the jurisdiction of Buddhist monks. The *Jikata hanreiroku*, a collection of rules and procedures regarding local administration, specifies the two circumstances under which this punishment could be handed down: (1) when, despite repeated advice and warnings, a person continued to engage in misbehavior and cause trouble for the village community; and (2) when, despite a continuous search, a person was missing for more than six months.[26] In the first case, the relatives and village officials would agree to *chōhazure*; if there were no relatives with whom to consult, then village officials were required to work with the five-man group. In the second case, the village officials would report the missing person to their district government administrator and then erase his or her name from the population register of sectarian inspection. In either case, the person was supposed to be dropped from the register kept at the village administration office, not from the *danna* roster kept at the Buddhist temple. Yet somehow Buddhist monks managed to maneuver the system of *chōhazure* so that it served their own purposes.

In particular, as far as financial matters were concerned, *danna* temples were insistent. The 1687 "Shojiin jōmoku" (Regulations on all temples), which contains some bogus articles, tells us of the course followed by Buddhist temples.[27] One of the articles reads: "*Danna* members should fulfill their assigned contribution not only in erecting Buddhist halls but also in repairing them when the head monk cannot afford to do so."[28] Another article advised that when the head monk stood to receive a higher rank, the *danna* patrons should financially contribute to this event. When a *danna* refused to cooperate, the decree warned, he or she would be reported to the public authorities and be strictly investigated.[29] It did not really matter whether or not people were aware of the spurious nature of this shogunal decree, as it reflected much of what was commonly practiced in Tokugawa society.

When it came to the matter of funerary fees, some *danna* temples were occasionally out of touch. A dispute at Chōsenji in Hayakawa village in Sagami offers a good example of this. In 1819, the temple's *danna* members got tired of being goaded by Gyokutan, the head monk, into accepting overly expensive funeral rites. They were also tired of his unacceptable behavior (e.g., adultery, self-indulgence, and violence) and so appealed to Chōsenji's head temple, Seigen'in, in an attempt to sever their ties with Chōsenji. In their letter of petition, the *danna* members enumerated the ways in which Gyokutan had abused the *danka* system: demanding excessive fees and donations, particularly on the occasion of a new death; imposing extravagant funeral procedures, even upon poor families; harassing bereaved families by charging 200 copper coins, two *shō* of rice, plus vegetables, for a post-ritual meal; posting notices in public to urge donations at the time of an annual memorial service; and insisting on a full-fledged funeral and memorial services even for a baby who died within seven days of its birth.[30] Gyokutan vigorously refuted these accusations; however, the head temple, which realized the seriousness of the matter, expelled Gyokutan from Chōsenji.[31]

As the Chōsenji case indicates, *danna* households did not always have to acquiesce to the demands of their *danna* temples. Usually, *danna* households would cooperate with their *danna* temples; however, when necessary, the former stood up to the latter, cast aspersions upon monks who fell afoul of convention, and took action. The manner in which *danna* households dealt with their funerary temples and monks was not always uniform, of course. For example, a powerful *danna* household that established its own *danna* temple (known as a founding *danna* or *kaiki danna*) could virtually control it by supervising its head monk and paying its operating costs. The shogunate honored the special status of *kaiki danna* households, which in most cases belonged to powerful local dignitaries. A 1665 decree relating to Buddhist temples specified that "the matter of installing a head monk to a temple founded by a *danna* patron lies with the wish of that *danna*. It should follow the *danna*'s intention so long as the head temple is consulted."[32]

Although not comparable to high-handed *kaiki danna*, ordinary *danna* households were able collectively to fend off untoward priestly influence and to keep their temple in check through supervising its properties. The shogunate acknowledged the households' right vis-à-vis temple property on the grounds that the latter should be managed as a communal asset rather than as the personal asset of the head monk. The third article of the 1687 decree on Buddhist temples required that upon the transfer or replacement of a temple's head monk, the former head, the new head, and the *danna* representatives should check all property items to see that they matched those on the list.[33] Temple properties included not only real estate and *danna* households but also such movable items as Buddhist images, treasures, cash, and (sometimes) personal effects. If a new debt had wrongfully occurred, or if a fund for commercial lending (*shidōkin*) had been mismanaged during the period of the former head, then the transition to a new head could be bumpy. There were even cases where temple properties were sold or pawned as collateral without the endorsement of the *danna* representatives. It was the responsibility of the *danna* households to prevent this kind of problem.[34]

The right of *danna* households to supervise the properties of their *danna* temple was naturally extended to the process of selecting and installing a new head monk. Although the matter of choosing a new head monk usually rested with the incumbent head or the head temple, the process required that monks consult and gain the endorsement of *danna* members.[35] To be sure, the transfer of temple headship in Jōdoshinshū took place from father to son and was almost a family business. However, *danna* members were still expected to keep an eye on prospective householder cleric successors and to ensure that they were a proper fit for the position.[36] In most sects, a typical procedure for choosing and installing a new head monk went as follows: the incumbent head designated a candidate, consulted the *danna* representatives on his choice, and finalized it; all concerned parties inspected the temple's property; the incumbent head then submitted the decision, along with a letter of endorsement from the *danna* representatives, to the head temple for approval; upon screening all relevant documents, the head temple officially appointed the new head.

The following example occurred in Edo: in 1782, the head monk of Fudōin (a subtemple of Sensōji), who had been appointed to his position only two years previously, requested retirement on the grounds of illness and recommended Jūjōin as his successor. The head monk emphasized that Jūjōin, who belonged to his dharma lineage, was trustworthy and highly qualified for the position. To his letter of recommendation he attached a list of temple properties and income sources, including 56 funerary *danna* households, an annual donation box (*saisen*) income of eight *kanmon* in copper coins, income from various prayer services, tax income from the temple-owned land, annual funerary fees that consisted of one *koku* of rice and twelve *kanmon* in copper coins, an Inari shrine that generated an annual income of fourteen *kanmon* in copper coins, and rent income from the front district. All these documents were endorsed in separate letters by the representative of the temple association to which the Fudōin monk belonged as well as by three representatives of its *danna* members. In addition, colleagues of Jūjōin added their support, saying that their fellow member would quickly move to repair decayed buildings upon his appointment. All these supporting documents reached Kan'eiji, the head temple of Sensōji, and Jūjōin was soon officially appointed as the head monk of Fudōin.[37] As may be seen, the endorsement of *danna* members was a precondition for the installation of a head monk.

Thus, head monks needed to be careful not to be too confrontational or abrasive. If they were too greedy in squeezing donations from their *danna*, then they could invite state punishment or run the risk of a collective *danna* revolt. Having said this, however, it should be emphasized that *danna* households usually perceived their temple as a communal asset and supported its financial well-being, as this was seen to enhance their own collective religious well-being.[38] In fact, outright confrontation between the *danna* temple and its collective patrons was a rare occurrence. The state's anti-Christian policy discouraged both parties from straying too far beyond the workable structure of the *danka* system. If any trouble occurred, it was generally at the individual level and was usually solved on a case-by-case basis. In a situation where *danna* affiliation, once established, was difficult to change, it is not surprising that there were numerous obstacles associated with withdrawal. Furthermore, the shogunate took an obscure and sometimes even self-contradictory position with regard to whether or not an individual *danna* household had the freedom to choose or change its own *danna* temple. All this led funerary *danna* temples to insist that *danna* affiliation, once formed, had to remain in place.

In its 1665 decree, the "Shoshū jiin hatto" (Law for Buddhist Temples of All Sects), the shogunate allowed the *danna* to choose their funerary temple, and this suggests that it would also be permissible to switch to a new temple.[39] Nevertheless, as temples grew increasingly bogged down in competition for the same pool of *danna*, the shogunate, in collaboration with the head temple of each sect, cautioned that poaching the *danna* of other temples would not be tolerated.[40] Still, the shogunate appeared to imply that individual households were basically entitled to change their *danna* affiliation. However, the shogunate began to take a harder position in 1722 with regard to collective action: in a decree entitled "Shoshū sōryo hatto" (Law for Buddhist Monks of All Sects), it prohibited *danna* households from arbitrarily withdrawing in groups from their existing *danna* relationships. The last sentence of the last article reads: "If *danna* conspire together and try to cut their ties with their funerary temple, [then the matter] should be reported to its regional sectarian supervisors (*furegashira*) and judged by the higher jurisdiction."[41] Apparently the shogunate decided to prevent Buddhist patrons from engaging in a large-scale desertion of their existing *danna* affiliation. At the same time, *bakufu* officials were quite wary of Buddhist corruption (e.g., some head monks, through the leverage of the *danka* relationship, had enticed female *danna* to their temples and held all-night drinking parties).[42] The *danna* relationship was a delicate phenomenon that required a balanced approach.

Six or so years later, probably between 1728 and 1729, the shogunate stepped up its effort to discourage *danna* households from leaving their current *danna* relationships. This policy was promoted through guidelines co-signed by the magistrates of temples and shrines, the treasury, and Edo city. It attempted to alleviate the financial distress of funerary temples in remote rural areas by stabilizing *danna* relationships.[43] This situation was quite different from the urban areas, where a relatively abundant and concentrated population offered a fertile source of *danna* households. For example, *bakufu* officials figured that in remote areas, the withdrawal of as many as 100 *danna* patrons from their current *danna* relationships to freely choose their new *danna* temples could cause "any temple in the area to plunge into a state of hardship."[44] Thus the shogunate declared that it would not allow arbitrary changes of *danna* affiliation. Only if the change had occurred a long time ago and had been brought before the public court would the shogunate favorably consider it and try to minimize its impact.

A case in point is a dispute in Sagami over *danna* membership brought to the highest shogunal court in 1728. The Sōtōshū temple Gensanji in Kagawa village, Kōza county sued a villager named Rihee, who had been its *danna* patron for generations, accusing him of recently, and without notice, converting to the Nichiren sect and becoming a *danna* of the Nichirenshū temple Jōkyūji in a nearby village. Rihee countered that four years ago, when he had been gravely ill, he had asked a Nichiren priest to pray for him, and that thanks to his prayers, he had fully recovered. Out of gratitude he had converted to Nichirenshū and had become a *danna* of Jōkyūji. Rihee claimed that he had reported all of this to Gensanji. However, the shogunal court found Rihee guilty on two counts, saying that he not only abandoned, without reason, the *danna* temple that had served his household for generations, but that he had also forced his wife and children to switch to Jōkyūji. Nor could Jōkyūji escape shogunal denunciation as it had received Rihee as a *danna* without gaining consent from Gensanji and had arbitrarily used its stamp of religious inspection. Despite its scolding tone, however, the shogunal verdict was rather conciliatory: Rihee was allowed to stay with Jōkyūji, his family members were all ordered to return to Gensanji, Jōkyūji was pardoned, and everyone was exhorted to honor the *danka* system. Obviously, in dealing with *danna* disputes, *bakufu* officials paid the utmost attention to maintaining the stability of the *danka* system, constantly urging cooperation and compromise.[45]

Another *danna* dispute brought before the shogunate involved a group action. In 1729, the Tendaishū temple Daishōji in Ōyama village, Shimōsa appealed to the shogunal court because three of its *danna* suddenly left without due procedure in order to return to their previous Jōdoshinshū *danna* temple, Kōtokuji. According to Daishōji's accusation, the dispute had a somewhat complicated history. Six years previously, in 1723, eighteen *danna* households belonging to Kōtokuji in the neighboring Shinchi village had switched their *danna* affiliation to Daishōji. However, they had continued to send fees and presents to the former while having their non-Christian status certified by the latter. In 1729, in another twist, six of the eighteen *danna* households changed their minds, left Daishōji "without any reason," and reverted to Kōtokuji. Soon after, however, three of the six admitted that their decision had been ill-considered and restored their relationship with Daishōji. Then Daishōji claimed that the remaining three *danna*, who were now with Kōtokuji, would serve as a bad example by flying in the face of the social custom that treasured the stability of the *danna* relationship, and it sued for the shogunate to correct the situation. The three villagers in question countered that although they had originally left Kōtokuji, this was due to the collective action of fifteen other villagers and was not what they had really wanted. They contended that for generations they had been faithful followers of Jōdoshinshū, and that since being coerced into switching their *danna* affiliation in 1723, they had made constant efforts to return to Kōtokuji. The shogunal court decided to side with these three villagers because they had been faithful *danna* of Kōtokuji for such a long time. They were allowed to stay with Kōtokuji.[46]

As these two cases demonstrate, the *danna* relationship was not completely immune from change. It was not impossible for a *danna* household to sever its ties with its current funerary temple and switch its *danna* affiliation to a new one. Similarly, as the Shirakawa case shows, a funerary temple could, if only rarely, terminate its relationship with a *danna* household. In either case, the shogunate did not intervene as long as what occurred was a matter of mutual consent. Only when a *danna* dispute was brought to the court did the shogunate attempt to settle it. Even in dealing with contentious *danna* disputes, shogunal officials still encouraged the parties involved to solve their problems peacefully.

However, when a dispute was deemed to have political implications, the shogunate was unwavering. Consider, for example, a case involving a high-ranking samurai, Tanaka Sahei, and his *danna* Sōtōshū temple Zenjōji in Kumamoto. In 1738, Tanaka Sahei, the third highest-ranking official in the Kumamoto domain government, with land holdings of 4,000 *koku* in rice, attempted to switch his temple affiliation from Zenjōji to Honmyōji, a well-known Nichirenshū temple that had previously served as the *danna* temple for the Katō daimyo house of the Kumamoto domain. Sahei's action stemmed from the "miraculous" cure of his chronic disease—a cure that he attributed to a Honmyōji monk. Sahei had been so sick for so long that he could not properly carry out his duties as the magistrate of temples and shrines in the domain. One day, he happened to meet a monk from Honmyōji, who cured his disease through prayer. Out of gratitude, Sahei decided to switch to Honmyōji, and he informed Zenjōji of his intention. Even though Sahei assured Zenjōji that all his other family members would remain with it, the temple did not accept this; rather, it brought the case to the domain government, arguing that Sahei's attempt to leave was so abrupt and arbitrary that it could spoil the well-established custom of the *danka* system. Caught in the dispute between one of its own most powerful officials and an influential temple, the Kumamoto government forwarded the case to the shogunal court. The shogunal court ruled that Tanaka Sahei must be stripped of his position and sentenced to house arrest.[47] The shogunal government did not like the fact that a high domain official, who was supposed to stabilize the *danka* system, was, in fact, disrupting it.

As society became more complex and fluid, the shogunate was becoming more critical of the irregularities of the *danna* relationship. During the Kanpō era (1741–43), for example, it specified the circumstances under which withdrawal from the current *danna* affiliation might be allowed: when the *danna* temple was found to be too greedy; when one deeply wished to be affiliated with a different temple for the period of one's generation only; when it was the dying wish of one's father; when a few years had passed since one had departed one's temple or when one had relocated one's family tombstones to a new temple; and when, in the case of a *kaiki danna*, the death register indicated that one's family was previously affiliated with a different *danna* temple.[48] Although these articles make it sound as though the shogunate had become more flexible with regard to the issue of withdrawing from one's existing *danna* relationship, they did not mean to make it easy for, or encourage, *danna* households to change their *danna* affiliations.

Nevertheless, in the urban areas it seemed hardly practical to block all residents from switching their *danna* affiliations, especially given that more and more people were moving to the cities from rural areas in search of job opportunities and settlement. An analysis of Kyoto's population registers of sectarian inspection, which contain information on the original and new *danna* temples of the residents from 1843, shows that more than one-third of the new residents who moved from somewhere else switched their *danna* and sectarian affiliations.[49] Although these registers still reveal that the extant residents rarely changed their *danna* temples, at the social margins of urban mobility the principle of fixed *danna* affiliation seemed to undergo some readjustment across all Buddhist sects. To be sure, the abundance of temples available in Kyoto probably made it much easier for the new settlers to abandon their old *danna* temples and to find new ones, but this trend also indicated that the vigor of the *danka* system was beginning, however slightly, to wear.

Amid new opportunities posed by heightened social mobility, Buddhist temples paid more and more attention to acquiring new *danna* patrons in search of an additional source of income and prestige. As far as the income structure of the *danka* system was concerned, there were three areas of death-related business from which income could be generated: funerary rituals and burial sites, the conferral of posthumous names, and memorial services. However, it is not easy to estimate how much *danna* temples in any given area earned from these businesses. And it is useless to look at them in terms of a seller's or a buyer's market because *danna* fees were not determined by the market; rather, they were determined through a "mutual understanding and agreement" between a funerary temple (which provided services) and a *danna* household (which received them). The level of fees varied depending on precedent, local customs, period, social status, the quality of the Buddhist services in question, sectarian customs, public regulations, and so on.

One source that sheds some light on the business of funerary Buddhism is *Asakusa komemise yorozu hikaechō* (A notebook of memoranda of an Asakusa rice dealer), a record kept by an affiliate of the Osaka-based Sumitomo merchant house between 1823 and 1869. The Asakusa store was a member of the group of Edo rice merchants (*fudasashi*) entitled to handle rice stocks belonging to the *bakufu*. Located in Suwachō and run by a manager who traditionally assumed the name Sen'oku Jinzaemon, the store usually employed fifteen people.[50] When these workers died while employed, the store arranged funerals for them. Its memoranda notebook contains six such cases, and these provide some data on funerals and memorial services.

A series of entries from 1842 details how much was spent for the funeral of a senior employee named Naojirō. The ceremony was held at the funerary temple, Gyokusen'in, and was presided over by one of its monks.[51] As the record indicates, it was a grand-scale ceremony that involved more than ten priests and cost a bit more than twenty gold pieces (20.68 *ryō* in gold *koban*). In mid-nineteenth-century Edo, a lower-class family of three or four needed at least thirteen or so gold pieces to cover a year's living expenses; twenty gold pieces, worth about eighteen *koku* of rice at that time, was certainly a large sum of money.[52] The cost of Naojirō's funeral can be categorized as follows (in converting non-gold currencies into *ryō*, the exchange rates of 1 *ryō* = 60 silver *monme* = 6,503 copper coins, all calculated based on the record, are applied):[53]

- 3.45 *ryō* for a funeral ceremony. 3 *ryō*, paid to the temple in a lump sum, were to cover wages for temple personnel who were involved in the ceremony (altogether more than twenty people, including the ritual officiator, who was paid 300 *hiki* [3,000 copper coins, 1 *hiki* = 10 copper coins], temple officials, assistant priests, monk apprentices, a monk-shaver for the dead, servants, and guards) as well as expenses for decorating the funeral altar. In addition, 0.125 *ryō* was paid to each of three helpers who washed the dead body, and 50 *hiki* were paid to the monk who kept vigil overnight for the wake.

- 3.64 *ryō* for cremation and for the laying of the ashes. Interment was common in Edo, but the Sumitomo house, like many other merchant houses that hired employees from far-away villages, opted for cremation. After the funeral ceremony, the dead body was laid in a casket and kept for a wake, after which it was laid in a palanquin and carried in procession to a crematory. The Sumitomo house spent 0.125 *ryō* and 100 copper coins for a casket, 248 copper coins for an urn for the ashes, 0.25 *ryō* and 648 copper coins for transporting the casket to the crematory, and 50 *hiki* for the monk who received the casket. A cremation fee of 1.5 *ryō* and 1,000 copper coins was paid to the crematory. In addition, a bit more than 1.42 *ryō* was spent for treating mourners and workers at the crematory as well as for procuring sundry items.

- 0.77 *ryō* for memorial services. The Sumitomo store arranged in advance to have the Gyokusen'in temple conduct eight memorial services in total for the spirit during the period of "intermediate darkness" as well as on the one hundredth day. The Sumitomo house paid 200 *hiki* to the Gyokusen'in temple and 300 *hiki* to its head monk.

- 7.76 *ryō* for erecting a tombstone. 3 *ryō* were paid to the Gyokusen'in temple for providing a lot for burying the ashes and for erecting a tombstone; 4.75 *ryō* and 0.6 *monme* of silver were paid to Ichigorō, a mason, for making the tombstone (3.25 *ryō* and 9.5 *monme*), a pair of doors (0.25 *ryō* and 4.5 *monme*), nine paving stones (0.5 *ryō* and 8.6 *monme*), and four incense stands (0.25 *ryō* and 8 *monme*). In paying for these items, the Sumitomo house used all of the *kōden* offerings it had received—a total of 0.75 *ryō* and 11.5 *monme*.

- 5.06 *ryō* for other expenses. This category included 0.75 *ryō* and 7.45 *monme* of silver spent to purchase clothes (white robes, cotton cloth for the dead, and three sets of waistcloth for those who wash the dead);[54] 1 *ryō* spent to treat 60 guests with boiled rice and tea; 2 *ryō* and 765 copper coins spent to buy 12 boxes of cookies, 12 cases of tea, and 30 packs of tile-shaped rice cake, which were sent to Sumitomo-affiliated stores and other associates in order to thank them for their help; 0.75 *ryō* and 1,402 copper coins were spent in sending Naojirō's personal belongings and ashes to his native home in Kansai; and 700 copper coins were given to Matsuemon, the head of "non-persons" (*hinin*) in the area.[55]

On the whole, all expenditures directly related to the mortuary ritual and the burial site amounted to 53 percent of the total, and more than two-thirds of the money ended up in the coffers of Gyokusen'in and the crematory. In particular, the Gyokusen'in temple was able to attain a handsome income of 6 *ryō* for presiding over the funeral ceremony and for lending the Sumitomo rice store a lot for Naojirō's tombstone. Funeral rituals and gravesites were a good source of income for funerary temples. *Danna* households found that sending their dead to the other world on the Buddhist path was a costly undertaking. Of course, they could significantly reduce this cost by scaling down the magnitude of the funeral and by not erecting a tombstone. In the case of the Sumitomo rice store in Asakusa, funerals for low-ranking employees were relatively simple and therefore relatively inexpensive. In contrast to the costly funeral of Naojirō, the funeral expenses for five other salesclerks were modest: the Sumitomo memoranda notebook shows that none of them were buried in an individual grave marked by an independent tombstone.

No matter how much they were scaled down, however, all funerals incurred some basic expenditures in one way or another: a gratuity fee to the head monk of the funerary temple; ritual fees for priests involved in the ceremony; and expenses for dressing and cremating or burying the dead, bedecking the altar, and treating, paying, or thanking those involved in the labor of the funeral. As in the case of Naojirō, the Sumitomo house paid a lump sum to Gyokusen'in at the time of the funeral and arranged posthumous memorial services

Table 13: Funeral Costs for Sumitomo Salesclerks

Year	Salesclerk	Funeral	Cremation	Memorial	Others	Total
1833	Shōzaburō	1.37	4.96	0.50	2.62	9.45
1836	Kōshirō	1.32	3.54	0.42	1.46	6.74
1838	Tokumatsu	1.33	3.76	0.43	1.11	6.63
1846	Jūzō	1.00	3.03	0.50	0.82	5.35
1847	Tsunejirō	1.51	3.16	0.50	1.72	6.89

SOURCE: Sumitomo shiryōkan, ed., *Sumitomo shiryō sōsho: Asakusa kometen yorozu hikaechō (jō).*
NOTES: All expenses are converted to gold *ryō* according to the following exchange rates: 1 *ryō* = 60 *monme* of silver = 4,702 copper coins (1836), 4,666 copper coins (1838), 4,000 copper coins (1846), 3,987 copper coins (1847). These differing exchange rates for copper currency were calculated based on the monetary records available in the *Hikaechō*. In case the exchange rate cannot be identified (e.g., for 1833), the standard rate of 1 *ryō* = 6,000 copper coins is applied. The category of "Others" includes expenses spent in procuring cloth and other sundry items as well as in treating and thanking funeral helpers and guests. Money paid to Matsuemon (the head of "non-persons" of the area), which ranged from 300 to 800 copper coins, is also included in this category.

for its deceased employees up to the one hundredth day after their death. Table 13 shows the funeral costs for the five Sumitomo sales-clerks.[56] The numbers indicate that expenses related to cremation usually accounted for more than half of the total cost of funerary services. In particular, a fee for using an independent chamber of the crematorium, as in the case of Naojirō, was 1.5 *ryō* (with the exception of Shōzaburō, which was 1.94 *ryō*). When it was combined with fees for a funerary ceremony and memorial services, the monies directly paid to Buddhist temples usually reached approximately 3 *ryō*, or 50 percent of the total. The rest was spent for items such as cloth, a casket, presents, and food and drinks for mourners and workers.

Fees for cremation were high, with the result that the family could save money by having the deceased interred. However, in this case, a burial lot was needed, and free lots were not easily attainable in urban areas. Even when a household already owned a family burial lot, it still had to spend extra money when it erected a tombstone for the deceased. For example, the great merchant house Shirokiya had four branch stores in Edo. When its Nihonbashi branch manager Morioka Tashichi died in 1853, he was buried at Tōhokuji in Shibuya. The total cost of the funeral was 10.62 *ryō*.[57] Among these costs, 4.9 *ryō* (or almost half of the total cost) were paid to Tōhokuji; 3.4 *ryō* went for expenses for the funeral ceremony; and 1.5 *ryō* served as an advance for posthumous memorial services. Despite the advance, the Shirokiya also pledged to donate rice, sake, and soy sauce to the temple each time a memorial service was held. And how were the remaining 5.72 *ryō* spent? Shirokiya had a burial site at the temple that it could use without extra cost, but the entombment of Morioka Tashichi cost 1.39 *ryō* for labor, an additional 1.5 *ryō* for the erection of a tombstone, and 2.83 *ryō* for treating mourners and helpers and procuring sundry other items.[58]

For samurai families, particularly those belonging to a lower echelon, a Buddhist funeral and subsequent memorial services posed a financial hardship. The *Kanpu gosata ryakki* (A brief record of public instructions), a diary kept by Ono Naokata (a retired Edo Castle guard who received a rice salary of 40 *koku*) between 1745 and 1773, shows what Edo's lower-class samurai families paid their Buddhist temple for funerals and memorial services.[59] The diary indicates that when Ono Sōemon (probably a relative of Naokata) died in 1746, 2 *ryō* were paid to the family's *danna* temple (Seiunji, located in Asakusa) as a funeral fee, and another 2.25 *ryō* were spent on the erection of a tombstone. It is not known how much the family of Tachino Kyūen, who died in 1753 and who was the stepfather of Naokata's second son, paid to its *danna* temple (Kōgakuji, located in Koishikawa); however, it did pay 3 *ryō* in advance for posthumous memorial services (up to the one-hundredth day after the initial service).[60] The diary details other posthumous services as well. For two memorial rituals held for the deceased wife of Naokata's son (in the third year [1741] and the seventh year [1745] after her death), the family sent 0.5 gold *ryō* to Seiunji, along with rice and other foodstuffs, for each ritual. On the other hand, for his deceased father, Naokata arranged grander memorial services. For the one held in the seventeenth year (1745), he sent 0.5 *ryō*, 2,000 copper coins, and 0.1 *koku* of rice to Seiunji; for the one held in the twenty-third year (1751) he sent 0.75 *ryō*, 0.1 *koku* of rice, and some silver pieces; and for the one held in the twenty-seventh year (1755) he sent 0.75 *ryō* and 0.1 *koku* of rice. In addition, Naokata held a fiftieth-year memorial service for his grandmother and a one-hundredth-year memorial service for Jōshin *koji* (probably an important ancestor of the extended Ono family). On both occasions he sent 0.5 *ryō* and some rice to Seiunji.[61] On the whole, each memorial ritual cost at least half a gold piece.

The Inoyama family, a minor samurai family that served the Kaga domain government as a hereditary accountant house, left a detailed record of monthly household expenditures from 1842 to 1879 (the portions between the mid-third month of 1845 and the mid-fifth month of 1846 are missing). During this period, the family incurred expenses

Table 14: Funerary Expenses of the Inoyama Family, 1842–67

Year	Relationship	Total expenditure	Incense money	% of self-burden
1849	father	16.40	6.48	43%
1849	grandmother	12.05	8.81	27%
1852	mother	7.45	1.55	79%

SOURCE: Isoda Michifumi, *Bushi no kakeibo: "Kagahan osan'yōmono" no bakumatsu ishin.*
NOTES: For consistency, all expenses are converted from *monme* of silver to rice to gold *ryō* according to the following price indexes of rice in Edo: 1 *koku* of rice = 1.60 *ryō* in 1849; and 1 *koku* of rice = 1.49 *ryō* in 1852. Relationship is to the record keeper (who was also the household head).

for three funerals and postmortem rites, as outlined in Table 14.[62] Even though the burden of a funeral was greatly alleviated by "incense money" contributions from various sources, the expenses up to the forty-ninth day after death could easily gobble up as much as about one-fourth of the household annual income.[63]

On the other hand, commoners in rural areas also dealt with the issue of cost and effect related to funerals in their own way. Consider, for example, the Maruya household, a wealthy agricultural family from Tajii village in Takata county, Aki. In his *Kagyōkō* (A reflection on household occupation, probably written in the Meiwa era [1764–71]), Maruya Jinshichi, the head of the household, specified how many monks should be invited, how much they should be paid, what items should be prepared, and how memorial services should be conducted. In the case of a major funeral for grandparents, parents, and principal wives, he advised that the family should invite the head monk, two ritual monks, and eleven servants from Chōrakuji (its *danna* temple, which belonged to Jōdoshinshū), as well as the head monk, a ritual monk, and two servants from Kyōzenji (another temple located in the same village). With regard to fees to be paid to these temple personnel, his advice was as follows: 8 *monme* of silver to the head monk of Chōrakuji, 6 *monme* to the head monk of Kyōzenji, 2 *monme* to each of the ritual monks, and 1 *monme* to each of the servants from these two temples—a total of 33 *monme* of silver (equivalent to a bit more than 0.5 gold *ryō*). In addition to these ritual fees, it was expected that the family would spend more than 2 or 3 *ryō* to procure necessary items and to treat funeral helpers, mourners, and itinerant blind musicians.[64] For the first seven-day posthumous service after the funeral, the Maruya family was also expected to pay 6 *monme* of silver to the head monk of Chōrakuji, 2 *monme* to its retired head monk, 1 *monme* to each of the ritual or novice monks, and 0.5 *monme* to each of the temple servants. For the remaining seven-day rituals, Jinshichi recommended that 6 *monme* should be paid to the head monk; for the third, seventh, thirteenth, twenty-fifth, and fiftieth-year memorial services, a fee of 8, 6, or 4 *monme* was to be paid to the head monk.[65]

For the Maruya family, which traced its lineage to the powerful Kikkawa house of Aki, a funeral was not only a procedure for dealing with a deceased family member, but also an occasion for displaying social status and wealth. In order to aggrandize the deceased, the Maruya family usually invited many monks from other temples and hired four or five carpenters, who would make a decorative coffin in the gabled house-style (*karahafu*). After the funeral, the family usually prepared enough food to treat 150 to 160 mourners, including relatives, confraternity members, and helpers.

To be sure, many families tried to reduce unnecessary funeral expenses and to maximize ritual effect. In the case of the Maruya family, the number of Buddhist monks invited for a minor funeral for siblings, children, uncles, and aunts was usually halved or even reduced to four or two; total ritual fees paid to Buddhist monks rarely exceeded 10 *monme* of silver, which was less than one-third of the cost of a major funeral. In his *Kagyōkō*, Jinshichi also admonished that, with regard to all posthumous memorial services except the first one, no monks from other temples should be invited; rather, the head monk of the *danna* temple was to take care of everything.[66] As far as funeral expenses were concerned, many households in the rural area, including the Maruya household, had free access to a family burial site and to the help of neighbors. They also had access to less costly funeral items than did urban dwellers. All these resources helped rural *danna* households to save on funeral costs.

The situation in the urban areas was quite different from that in the rural areas. In particular, it was not easy to acquire a free burial lot. In fact, most families had to purchase a burial lot at their *danna* temple. Once a lot was secured, the family was forced to allow its *danna* temple to supervise the conduct of posthumous memorial services according to whatever schedule it chose. Obviously, for funerary *danna* temples in urban areas, the scarcity of land guaranteed a steady flow of income from their *danna* patrons.

It should therefore come as no surprise that when a burial site appeared to no longer generate income, the *danna* temple often removed the grave in question and replaced it with that of a new client.

Archaeological finds at two temples in Edo, Ennōji (an Ōbakushū temple) and Hasshōji (a Sōtōshū temple), both of which were located at Yotsuya Samegabashi, reveal that temple cemeteries were commercial properties and that they were dedicated to making a profit. Ennōji, which was founded in 1666, had a mixed group of *danna* households during the seventeenth century, and these included some influential and generous samurai patrons. However, the rapid decline of these samurai patrons resulted in hardships for the temple during the Meiji period, and Ennjōji merged with Kaizōji in Aoyama in 1874. On the other hand, Hasshōji, which was founded in 1667 thanks to a donation from a *hatamoto* family, survived until the end of the Tokugawa period due to the support of tens of *danna* households.[67] Burial sites excavated at both temples reveal two unusual features: a very high density of graves within a small area (many of them were laid out shoulder by shoulder and overlapped, while some were located on top of older ones) and burial pits that were so shallow that some caskets were almost touching the surface of the ground.

Burial sites function as an archaeological shorthand for determining how the living treated the remains of the dead. In the case of Hasshōji, it is quite obvious that after a lot had been used up, the temple "re-buried" its occupant by laying some dirt on top of it in order to create a new burial space. Scholars have found that at an interval of every 30 to 60 years, a new layer had been added to the cemetery until the end of the Tokugawa period, and that this vertical expansion had created four different plumb layers at the cemetery of Hasshōji.[68] On the other hand, Ennōji, where two different types of cemeteries coexisted—one in the inner precinct and the other behind the Main Hall on the backyard slopes—offers another example of how urban cemeteries operated. Graves located in the inner precinct were low-density and were arranged in a neat and orderly fashion. Not only that, but many of those buried in this frontal cemetery were also laid to rest in expensive earthenware caskets. All of this indicates that those buried here either belonged to the samurai class or were well-to-do townspeople. In contrast, those buried in the rear cemetery were mostly laid out in cheap wooden caskets, and their burial sites, which bear no grave-posts, were quite disorderly due to overlapping reburial. In addition, the burial accessories of these two groups show clear status-related discrepancies. About 60 percent of the graves of the former group were found to have contained such items as copper coins, dolls, battledores (*hagoita*), ceramics, tobacco pipes, and small *shamisen*; in contrast, fewer than 10 percent of the graves of the latter contained burial accessories.[69]

It seems outrageous that some Buddhist temples went so far as to destroy old graves in order to create new ones. A document contained in the Obama Sakai family library notes: "Because temple cemeteries in this area are limited and cramped, those graves that nobody tends are demolished because they cannot generate an adequate income. At the cleared sites new burials take place."[70] For many temples in Edo, where burial lots were at a premium, graves were a precious commodity that guaranteed financial contributions from *danna* households. According to the Sakai family document, "if graves have not generated financial contributions for three years, then, at the entrance of their cemeteries, Buddhist temples often post a notice of their upcoming removal."[71] During the Kyōhō era (1716–35), many Buddhist temples often petitioned a sympathetic shogunate to allow them to transform their newly acquired adjacent lands into cemeteries in an attempt to expand the base of posthumous income.[72] However, from the early nineteenth century on, the expansion of burial lots in the inner city became next to impossible due to the increase in the number of residents, many of whom began to inhabit the city's heretofore empty spaces. The situation in Edo was more acute than that in Osaka or Kyoto, where suburban cemeteries were undergoing development.

Not surprisingly, when burial pits failed to generate income for whatever reason, Edo temples proved to be unforgiving: they decimated them for the sake of new "tenants." These "murdered graves" (*korosareta haka*) were obviously those that belonged to poor families living in cramped tenement houses — people who barely made a living as peddlers, petty artisans, day laborers, or entertainers. When their households were discontinued due to lack of descendants, epidemics, natural disasters, or other misfortunes, their ancestral graves also ceased to exist.[73] In the *Shisō zōshiki*, we find that an anonymous official who had probably worked at the office of the magistrate of temples and shrines commented on why Edo had very few tombstones that were more than 200 years old: "On the entrance door of an old temple cemetery it is written that in cases where there has been no presents or fees (*tsuketodoke*) for a long time, tombstones will be torn down. I also hear that some temples give out neglected tombstones to masons, who then rework and sell them."[74] Buddhist temples rarely bothered trying to extend their religious services to the poor or marginalized.

Not only the ancestors of defunct households but also those of poor migrants and seasonal laborers were often abandoned after burial. In 1843, a ward head reported the following to the city magistrate office: "Migrant seasonal workers are temporarily registered at their broker's or guarantor's temple. . . . When they die, they are temporarily buried there."[75] It was a custom in Edo that when a bond servant or a laborer with no immediate family died, the person (a personal guarantor or job agent) who had mediated his or her employment was responsible for taking care of him or her after death.[76] In theory, the spirits of those who were temporarily interred at the alien temple ground of their guarantors was supposed to be transferred to their own *danna* temple. But this rarely happened. In late Tokugawa Edo, tens of thousands of poor migrant workers from the Kantō and beyond remained unmarried and unaffiliated with any Edo *danna* temple. When they died, it was very likely that they would become wandering spirits.[77]

In 1805, Negishi Yasumori (1737–1815), a *bakufu* official, was very moved when he heard a story about the death of a drifting laborer. According to his *Mimibukuro* (A sack of ears), this man, who had once worked for a samurai family, died alone. "His dead body was supposed to be taken care of by his guarantor. Upon hearing that his body was about to be dumped, she [a prostitute who had once lived with him] made a donation to the monk of Ekōin, whom she had known for some time, and insisted that her connection to the deceased could not be ignored. It is said that he was eventually buried through a funerary ritual conducted by the Ekōin monk."[78] Yasumori was apparently drawn to the compassion and chastity of the prostitute, who herself was symbolic of the gloomy fate of Edo's increasing number of poor and marginalized. The prostitutes of the Yoshiwara existed outside the early modern institution of the household; when they died, they were taken care of by Jōkanji, a temple known as a "place for throwing in."[79]

The well-being of an ancestral spirit hinged upon the continuance of its household, which was supposed to have a stable relationship with a funerary temple. And the health of ancestral graves reflected the degree of harmony in the relationship between a household and its ancestral spirits and funerary temple. This was why Tokugawa households paid a great deal of attention to the resting place of their ancestors, which they marked by a tombstone that, in the form of inscribed posthumous Buddhist names, symbolized their socioreligious standing. But as has been discussed, obtaining posthumous Buddhist names was hardly separable from financial transactions. Within this milieu, from the late seventeenth century on, status-conscious families readily paid a hefty price to acquire a laudatory high-ranking Buddhist name and so enhance their social standing.

Buddhist death was a booming market. Jutokuji in Egasaki village, Musashi was straightforward about the market values of posthumous names. In 1661, it specified price tags, adding that one could acquire a title even without any Buddhist merit: 7.5 gold *ryō* for the titles of *koji* and *daishi*, and 3 gold *ryō* for those of *shinji* and *shinnyo*.[80] Jikōji in Nakauri village in Mikawa was also not shy about selling honorific titles. In 1796, the price of an *ingō* title was set as high as 20 gold *ryō*, while those for the titles of *koji, angō, shinji,* and *zennyo (zenjōni)* were set at 3, 1.5, 0.5, and 0.25 gold *ryō*, respectively—all newly adjusted discount prices. When this temple was at the height of a fundraising campaign a few years earlier, it set fees for the titles of *koji, anshu* (equivalent to *angō*), and *shinji* at 5, 3, and 1 gold *ryō*, respectively.[81] In 1831, a Sōtōshū temple in Kantō was very clear about how much its *danna* households should pay in order to acquire the various brands of posthumous Buddhist names: 5 or 3 gold *ryō* for a name at the rank of *in, ken,* or *an* (all referring to cloister names—the highest honor); 1 *ryō* for a name at the rank of *koji* or *daishi*; 2,000 copper coins for a name at the rank of *shinji* or *shinnyo*; 1,000 copper coins for a name at the rank of *zenjōmon* or *zenjōni*; and an unspecified sum for a simple name of two characters with no affix indicating rank.[82] To be sure, there was no standardized system of pricing, but *danna* households had a tacit understanding regarding how much they should pay when they asked for a posthumous name. A price range for posthumous names was subject to local customs, the status and sectarian affiliation of an individual temple, the demand of *danna* households, economic conditions, and so on. It ranged from tens of gold pieces or thousands of copper coins to a bag of rice.

Those commoner *danna* households that could afford to pay the hefty prices of Buddhist names could elevate (albeit only on paper) their social status as high as that of the *hatamoto* class. The death register of the Ōbakushū temple Kaifukuji in Fukagawa, Edo shows that several prominent Nihonbashi merchant families acquired names at the rank of *ingō*, which was usually granted to upper-rank vassals of the daimyo or to *hatamoto* families. Four-character names at the rank of *shinji* or *shinnyo*, which were usually granted to lesser daimyo retainers or to low *hatamoto* families, were also granted to many merchant families as long as they could pay for them. In contrast, in the death register of Manshōji, another Ōbakushū temple in the same area—but one whose *danna* patrons consisted mostly of the lower echelons of the townspeople class—two-character names were most common. Many of these two-letter name holders were migrant workers, servants hired by samurai families, petty merchants, or artisans.[83]

The death of a family member offered a household an opportunity to assert its social standing, but this opportunity did not come for free. Surrounding the issue of cost and effect, *danna* households and funerary Buddhist temples were engaged in the process of producing markers of social status and distinction that increasingly defied the ground rules of Tokugawa feudal society.

C3

TEN

Danna *Temples, the State,*
and Anti-Buddhist Criticism

In 1644, three temples designated as administrative supervisors (*furegashira*) for the Kantō region circulated a memorandum to the Sōtōshū temples under their supervision, informing them of the shogunal decision concerning a dispute over funeral rights between two temples in Hachiōji: the Sōtōshū Eirinji and the Shingonshū Gyokusenji. This memorandum confirmed that "prayer practitioners" were to be prohibited from involving themselves in funerals as ritual priests, pointing out that Tokugawa Ieyasu had already rendered their funerary role illegal.[84] Here, "prayer practitioners" refer to practitioners of Shugendō (*yamabushi* or *shugenja*) and itinerant quasi-monks who had their own religious facilities or who were affiliated with Buddhist temples (mostly Shingonshū or Tendaishū). At that time, their involvement in funerals consisted of conducting "prayers" that supplemented rituals for the "transference of merit," which were officially conducted by Buddhist clergy. The boundary of funerary "prayers" was, however, both wide and porous, and these *shugenja* were aggressively expanding their roles from performing rituals for purifying funeral dates, funeral places, and death pollution to providing prayer services designed to smooth the transition of the deceased from this world to the other world. Buddhist monks tried to stop the intrusion.

Before Ieyasu established his political base at Edo, the Kantō region had been a stronghold of *shugenja* belonging to the Shōgoin sect. Under the protection of the Hōjō house, many of these practitioners settled in local villages as "village *shugen*" (*satoshugen*), and secured patrons through offering funerary services. In 1595, however, when a dispute over funerary rights broke out in Kazusa between a Zen temple and a Shingon temple run by Shugen practitioners, Ieyasu sided with the former and ruled against the latter, who were closely associated with the old regional lord, the Hōjō house. Ieyasu figured that his new regime needed the backing of the orthodox Buddhist sects.[85]

Despite Ieyasu's ruling, conflicts between Shugen practitioners and Buddhist monks continued. The problem was that funerals were a lucrative source of income, and neither side could afford to dispense with them. Furthermore, since funeral customs in the Kantō region contained a mixture of heterogeneous ritual elements, both sides could claim their legitimacy as funerary priests. The Shugen practitioners tried to increase their influence through the "way of prayer worship" (*saidō*). Meanwhile, the Buddhist clergy, led by Zen monks, tried to expand their influence through conducting a rite of "salvific guidance" (*indō*). By cleansing funerary rites of Shugen "prayer" elements, the Buddhist monks tried, under the protection of the new regime, to bring the region into line with funerary Buddhism. The increasing rivalry between both sides soon developed into conflicts and often escalated into vandalism and violence that ended up in the destruction of ritual paraphernalia and even in the desecration of graves.[86] As the 1644 memorandum indicates, the shogunate emphasized that the *satoshugen* and peripatetic prayer priests should surrender their funerary rights to Buddhist monks; but disputes lingered on, if less virulently, into the mid-eighteenth century. These prolonged disputes stemmed from mixing "prayer worship" and "salvific guidance" as well as from the fact that many Shingonshū monks and, to a lesser extent, Tendaishū monks in the region inherited Shugendō lineages. Nevertheless, the shogunate maintained that as far as funeral rites were concerned, elements of "prayer worship" were to be eliminated.[87]

Why was the government so negative toward including elements of "prayer worship" in funeral rites? It was because these elements were associated with itinerant religious practices and did not neatly fit into what was expected in transparent institutional Buddhism. The Tokugawa regime, which tried to reorganize society into a transparent social order, did not want to see obscure religious practitioners blending into local society through the offering of petty ritual services. At the same time, *bakufu* leaders strove to control Buddhism, which had been at the epicenter of socio-political havoc in medieval times, by tightening up ordination procedures, apportioning religious functions and privileges, and streamlining sectarian institutions. As a whole, these goals were pursued through institutionalizing funerary Buddhism and by suppressing the creation of petty prayer temples. The control of obscure practitioners, itinerant religious vagabonds, and quasi-religious riffraff, on the one hand, and the goal of institutionalizing funerary Buddhism, on the other, constituted two sides of the same coin. As *bakufu* officials figured it, the best way to achieve these goals was to control the business of death-related rituals and, concomitantly, to ban the disorderly erection of new temples.

Indeed, since the medieval period, death-related rituals had occupied the minds of a wide range of itinerant religious practitioners, including tea-whisk peddlers (*chasen*), donation-soliciting mendicants (*kanjin hijiri*), burial mendicants or cemetery keepers (*sanmai hijiri*), Kōya mendicants (Kōya *hijiri*), and gong beaters (*kaneuchi*). The livelihoods of these religious vagabonds, who were sometimes engaged in entertainment or peddling, depended heavily upon their skills in *nenbutsu* chanting for the dead.[88] For example, the *chasen* "cremated or buried those impermanent souls found dead on the roadside and ushered them into the grace [of the Buddha] and prayed for their next life."[89] These peddlers, who belonged to a low stratum of society, justified their religious profession by claiming that it had originated with Kūya (903–972), who was known as the father of popular Pure Land Buddhism.

However, in the seventeenth century, as ordained Buddhist monks came to monopolize death-related religious services through the leverage of anti-Christian temple certification, these itinerant mendicants were gradually driven out of their traditional profession. Since the Kan'ei era (1624–43), both central and local governments, which endeavored to bind the population to the land, pushed these evasive sojourners to settle in one place as ordinary residents, made it illegal for them to establish religious facilities (through the ban on new temples), and tried to cut them off from the religious arena of death-related rituals. At the same time, government officials ordered local residents to stay away from these people.[90] For example, in 1660, the Hagi domain government instructed village officials as follows: "[religious] itinerants such as street preachers, quasi-*yamabushi*, and peddler-exorcists should not be allowed into villages under any circumstances." It cautioned that "the [fact] that itinerants in plain dress, who call themselves street-preachers of Ikkōshū, conduct rituals for the dead and sermonize the people is a serious violation of the law."[91]

In particular, it was during the Kanbun era (1661–72) that the *bakufu* established its system of temple certification and that shogunal officials stepped up their efforts to curb the influx of itinerant religious entrepreneurs into Edo — the nation's urban center and a magnet to all kinds of transient populations. In 1662, the shogunate informed Edo residents that "only when a document, issued by a head temple, proves their status as [legitimate] disciples, and [only] when a guarantor endorses them, will *shukke* [wandering monks and nuns], *yamabushi*, *gyōnin* [wandering ascetics based in Mount Kōya], and *gannin* [vagabond-monks] be allowed to stay at a secular house. Renting a place to those who are not [officially] affiliated with a head temple is prohibited."[92] Edo officials tried to keep the rented domiciles of these evasive religious mendicants under check through instituting registration requirements and guarantorship via the head-branch relationship, adding that Buddhist temples should not harbor them even for a night. "In cases where wandering monks and *yamabushi* have already set up a 'temple' in the ward," stated the edict, "ward officials must immediately report them."[93] Four years later, in 1666, the shogunate mobilized officials from the magistrate of temples and shrines and the city police to destroy Buddhist altars and wooden Buddhist images that itinerant prayer monks had erected in secular houses.[94]

The shogunate continued to try to cleanse institutional Buddhism of unruly elements, and thereby, to integrate Buddhist practitioners into the sedentary structure of funerary Buddhism. For example, the *bakufu* demanded in 1673 that landlords and ward officials be jointly responsible for any religious practitioner who was accommodated at a secular house.[95] In 1684, the shogunate once again made an effort to stem the tide of "vagabonds who sneak into the city, set up Buddhist altars under bright lanterns, and induce crowds to attend their *nenbutsu* or *daimoku* chanting events, which are held in the name of fund-raising for the Buddha" while also trying to suppress the burgeoning of abodes outfitted with religious standards, altars, signboards, and iconography.[96] Despite the strenuous efforts to keep peripatetic religious entrepreneurs from slipping into Edo, the problems related to phony exorcism, street preaching, and financial swindling (all committed in the name of Buddhist pietism) did not easily disappear.[97]

The shogunate also pushed to bring Buddhist temples under its authority, starting with its 1631 ban on building new temples—a ban that demarcated "old-tract temples" from "new-land temples." Prior to this edict, *bakufu* officials had tried to control institutional Buddhism through the head-branch organization of temples, as was seen in the temple laws addressed to the nation's major sects and temples in 1615 and again in 1622. The 1631 edict, which helped incorporate Buddhist institutions into the *bakuhan* governing system, still fell far short of fulfilling the shogunal intention, as was seen in the incomplete Kan'ei head-branch registers.[98] It was not until the Kanbun era that shogunal control of Buddhist institutions was pointedly achieved. Through its leverage of the system of anti-Christian temple certification, the shogunate banned the erection of new temples in 1663 and two years later made it illegal to turn secular houses into "places containing Buddhist altars." These actions enabled the shogunate to secure control of "religious inspection" temples, effectively making them public agents whose function was to carry out state policy. Throughout the remaining years of the seventeenth century, the shogunate continued to stem the proliferation of Buddhist temples built on new land. In 1692, the *bakufu* recognized those temples that had been erected between 1631 and the current year, and that had acquired funerary *danna* patrons, as de facto "religious inspection" temples and treated them as though they were "old-tract temples."[99] In this way, Buddhist temples were by and large contained within the institutional framework of funerary Buddhism.

Following the lead of the shogunal government, many domain governments also joined the effort to establish the institutional framework of funerary Buddhism. For example, the Kaga domain banned the erection of new temples in the early 1660s, and in 1678–79 directed the *furegashira* temple of each sect to draw up and to submit a list of all the temples under its control. Again, in 1685, Kaga officials ordered all temples in the domain to submit their chronicles of origin through their *furegashira* temples. After that, those temples not listed on these documents were prohibited from conducting anti-Christian religious inspection whether they had *danna* patrons or not.[100] Similarly, the Mito domain's policy of "temple retrenchment," conceived in 1663, crystallized the hostile attitude of the Tokugawa establishments toward those petty prayer preachers who tried to tap into death-related rituals. In 1666, Tokugawa Mitsukuni ordered his senior councilor Kawasumi Yukitaka to destroy "puny" temples that had been newly erected by obscure monk-preachers and that were trying to take *danna* patrons away from (and depleting the financial bases of) "legitimate" temples. After these temples were demolished, their lands and *danna* patrons were to be returned to legitimate funerary temples, and those unqualified monks who were left with no temples were to be defrocked and made into tax-paying commoners.[101]

In adopting this ham-fisted temple retrenchment policy, Tokugawa Mitsukuni presented his officials with nine articles explaining his decision to take this draconian measure—a measure that would result in the removal of more than 1,000 temples along with 3,088 other petty religious facilities (run by *yamabushi*, vagabond-monks, exorcists, shamans, *kami* preachers, and the like) and defrock 344 monks who had transgressed the Buddhist commandments.[102] In the first article, Mitsukuni made it clear that "the original duty of those who have renounced the secular world lies in annihilating the sins of the people," a reference to saving the dead through Buddhist rituals within the framework of the *danka* system.[103] He then indicated which temples were most likely to shirk this duty: the temples of Zenshū, Jōdoshū, and Nichirenshū, which specialized in prayer only or were solely engaged in the business of "preventing disaster"; temples exercising the right of religious inspection without offering funeral services; temples with no funerary *danna* households; and temples that were set up at secular houses. After reminding the officials of other illegal operations performed in these temples, Mitsukuni emphasized that his instructions were all based on the "regulations of Gongensama [Tokugawa Ieyasu]," which refer to the role of Buddhist temples as agents of anti-Christian religious inspection, which gave birth to funerary Buddhism and the *danka* system.[104] As a result of this temple retrenchment policy, which was implemented over a period of 30 years, Buddhist temples in the Mito domain were streamlined and incorporated into the institution of funerary Buddhism.

By pushing policies designed to suppress elusive religious elements, the Tokugawa regime recognized funerary Buddhism as a socio-religious institution inseparable from its governing structure. In this line, funerary Buddhist temples were given privileges and protection and, in return, were expected to carry out the "public duty" of anti-Christian religious inspection. As part of this responsibility, Buddhist monks were obligated to investigate the death of each citizen. In its 1687 edict, the shogunate specified: "If you find something suspicious when a *danna* has died of disease, or if you hear something bad about your *danna*, strictly investigate his or her family members and relatives. If you still find something suspicious, report it to the government office and ask for an official examination, and then conduct a funeral and bury the person according to government instructions. If it is found later that you have hidden something, you [the *danna* temple] will be punished."[105] Buddhist monks were indeed like government agents who served as anti-Christian caretakers of the spiritual well-being of the people from birth to death.[106]

Further punishments awaited Buddhist monks who would defy the prescribed procedure of death inspection. The fifty-fourth article of the *Kujigata osadamegaki*, a compendium of criminal laws compiled between 1740 and 1742, calls for the following penalty: "A Buddhist temple that secretly buries a *danna* who has died an unnatural death [shall be subject to] house arrest for 50 days."[107] The shogunate held Buddhist temples responsible for scrutinizing their *danna* from registration to death, and any failure to do so was punishable. For example, in 1791, the city magistrate of Kyoto sentenced Keimyō (a caretaker monk at Myōganji in Tai village, Gamō county, Ōmi) to house arrest for 30 days. Keimyō was at that time temporarily in charge of the temple while its head monk was traveling to Kyoto, and he was found guilty of cremating a villager named Sakuemon without inspecting the body. He did this because two village officials indicated that Sakuemon had died of disease; however, it had been rumored that the villager had, in fact, been murdered, thus making it incumbent upon Keimyō to conduct a full inspection.[108] Similarly, temples that offered funerals to non-*danna* members were also subject to punishment on the grounds that they were performing bogus inspections. Consider, for example, the case of Gokurakuji, a Jōdo-shū temple in Edo. It was found that in 1797, Gokurakuji had issued a "cremation slip" to a non-*danna* resident, and when that resident later brought the slip back and asked for a funeral for a deceased family member named Tōshichi, the temple offered one without inspecting the *danna* status of the dead. The head monk of Gokurakuji was sentenced to house arrest for 50 days.[109]

Some Buddhist temples were punished for not being discreet enough when responding to the request for a funeral, even if this was due to a simple technical error. In 1779, for example, the head monk of the Jōdoshū temple Zensōji (a branch temple of the famous Chion'in) in Kyoto was asked to conduct a funeral for a child of Kaihiya Saburōbee, who brought a "document for sending" from Jōshūji, his *danna* temple. But he noticed that the document contained incorrect information indicating that Zensōji belonged to Jōdoshinshū rather than to Jōdoshū. The head monk demanded that Saburōbee obtain a new document from Jōshūji. The man promised to do so if the monk would first handle the urgent matter of his child's funeral. The Zensōji monk conducted the funeral but felt uneasy about it because he suspected that his action might not be legal. He soon sought the advice of the head temple on the matter. Chion'in officials instructed Zensōji to bring the "document for sending" to them so that they could investigate it; however, probably out of fear, Zensōji instead returned the document to Saburōbee, thus nullifying the latter's wish to switch his *danna* temple. Consequently, the funeral for the child turned out to be illegal. Upon hearing the case, the magistrate officially reprimanded Zensōji for its wrongful conduct.[110] The whole case was the product of incorrect information concerning the sectarian affiliation of Zensōji, probably amounting to nothing more than a careless conflation of Jōdoshū with Jōdoshinshū. But even such a minor mistake could not escape official scrutiny.

Under the aegis of protection and responsibility, anti-Christian religious inspection served to incorporate Buddhism into the Tokugawa governing system and entrench the *danka* system in Tokugawa society. In theory, the *danka* system was justifiable only so long as Buddhist temples carried out the task of identifying Christian elements for the state. By the late seventeenth century, however, all Kirishitan had been terminated and there were no more Kirishitan to be inspected. However, this did not mean that the power of the temples was accordingly terminated. On the contrary, Buddhist temples never relinquished the right of religious inspection; rather, they reinforced their power by gripping their *danna* patrons ever more firmly. With regard to this odd situation, Kumazawa Banzan questioned the necessity of non-Christian inspection (which had already been hollowed out) in the early 1680s, asserting that the system of temple certification was only used to exploit a perplexed and impoverished people and therefore proved "useless and nothing but an unnecessary waste of the [central and local] governments."[111] He pointed out that "with regard to anti-Christian inspection by

Buddhist temples, poor people are annoyed and those who are to some extent enlightened feel miserable. This is because poor people cannot get temple inspection unless they bring gold and silver to the monks."[112] Banzan went on to argue that if religious freedom were granted, then most people would abandon their *danna* temples; therefore, the system of temple certification should be abandoned.[113]

In a similar vein, in the early seventeenth century Ogyū Sorai argued in *Seidan* (Discourses on government) that temple certification was increasingly tainted with deception. He observed that the situation in Edo, with its large transient population, was almost out of control:

Then the world changed and the military houses came to live in Edo, where they lost their hereditary servants and hired temporary servants on contract. Because these servants serve all the time in Edo, without anyone knowing their origins, they use a guarantor's temple as their *danna* temple. Likewise, many daimyo retainers have become used to living permanently in Edo, and when masterless samurai from all over are employed [by these retainers], they have their *danna* temples set up there. Consequently, the words [on their religious certificates] have become a great lie.[114]

As far as Sorai was concerned, some Buddhist temples casually distorted the system of religious inspection itself by issuing false certificates. In order to stem such a deceptive practice, he proposed that all temporary servants be guaranteed by the landlords of their native villages rather than by their recruiters or temples in Edo.[115]

For Muro Kyūsō (1658–1734), on the other hand, the "exploitative practice" of Buddhist inspection came down to the problem of the materialistic indulgence of funerary Buddhism: "the Law of the Buddha in all sects is already decayed and is no longer able to lead people to good. Buddhist monks, who are suffused with the favor of laypeople, only nourish their mouths and stomachs. They take control of funeral rituals and are satisfied with being guardians of graves."[116] Annoyed by these complaints, Shogun Yoshimune (r. 1716–45) is said to have once given serious thought to the suggestion that the whole system of temple certification should be scrapped.[117]

The rationale for temple certification indeed thinned out as time progressed, and the Buddhist death-related rituals that it safeguarded were subjected to further criticism. However, critical comments pertaining to funerary Buddhism, no matter how negative, could never break out of the confines of a discursive polemic. Buddhist inspection and funerary Buddhism remained an integral part of the Tokugawa system. Instead of attempting to challenge the legitimacy of Buddhist involvement in Tokugawa governance, *bakufu* officials tried to amend the ways in which Buddhist institutions enacted their privileges. Not surprisingly, from the late seventeenth century on, the shogunal policy toward Buddhism gradually moved from protecting and encouraging its practices to checking and controlling them.[118] At the crossroads of the system, where temple certification and funerary Buddhism merged and were institutionalized into the *danka* system, Buddhist temples now saw the "good old days" of protection dissipating.

The shogunal attempt in the late seventeenth century to tame Buddhist temples was spearheaded by a crackdown on Fujufuse monks and their followers. It was an object lesson warning all Buddhists that the Law of the King took precedence over the Law of the Buddha, no matter what. From the beginning of the Tokugawa period, the Fujufuse sect maintained that it neither took donations from, nor gave its teachings to, those who did not accept the *Lotus Sūtra* as the sole scripture of the Buddhist truth and faith. This stance signified disengagement from the Law of the King and had made the sect the target of persecution. However, unlike earlier times, when suppression was directed solely at Fujufuse preachers, *bakufu* crackdowns were more comprehensive and more thorough from the 1660s. In response to this trend, in 1665 three covert Fujufuse temples in the Kantō area (Tanjōji in Kominato village, Nagasa county, Awa, where Nichiren was born; Hokkeji in Himon'ya village, Ebara county, Musashi; and Yanaka Kannōji in Edo) joined forces to form a faction known as the "Lands of Compassion" subsect (Hidenshū). This subsect distinguished itself from Fujufuse fundamentalists after having accepted shogunal lands on the assumption that these properties were "lands of compassion" for the people rather than material offerings donated by the secular authorities.[119] In 1669, the shogunate put Fujufuse followers into the same category as Kirishitan and began to sharpen its watch on the sect.[120] Then, in 1691 the shogunate moved to force the three Hidenshū temples to eliminate the suspicious *hiden* elements in their beliefs and to officially change their sectarian stance to Jufuse ("take, no give," which would signify submission to the Law of the King). They yielded to the shogunal demand and accepted the Jufuse label, but they were found seven years later to be still functioning in secret as local hubs of the Fujufuse faith.[121] Heavy punishment ensued, and under duress Kannōji and Hokkeji changed their sectarian affiliations from Jufuse to Tendaishū. Thereafter, in 1707 and again in 1715, the shogunate continued to capture and exile groups of surreptitious Fujufuse preachers and their followers.

The problem of Fujufuse Buddhism persisted, however, and again surfaced in Namegawa village, Isumi county, Kazusa in 1718. Attracted by the story of a villager who claimed that his serious illness had been cured thanks to the divine power of Fujufuse Buddhism, more than 200 people secretly switched their allegiance to the clandestine Fujufuse temples Myōsenji and Honjakuji. According to non-Fujufuse temples in the village, these underground Fujufuse followers neither visited their *danna* temples nor brought donations to them after their conversion. Upon receiving this report, the shogunate immediately arrested and punished preachers and lay leaders. Four monks and seven lay followers eventually vanished into Edo prison cells, five monks were exiled to remote islands, and the laypeople were ordered to discard their faith.[122] In 1742, the shogunate detailed in the *Kujigata osadamegaki* the type of punishment that would be applied to Fujufuse violators: depending on the status of violators in the Fujufuse organization and the degree of their involvement in the spread of Fujufuse Buddhism, punishments ranged from severe (banishment to a remote island, various types of expulsion) to relatively light (dismissal from office, payment of a fine).[123] This Kyōhō legal code prompted nationwide Fujufuse suppression. In particular, clandestine Fujufuse followers in their stronghold of Okayama had to endure at least twelve large-scale repressions from the mid-eighteenth century until 1876, when the Meiji government finally set them free.[124]

Fujufuse suppression, which was limited to regional pockets, did not have direct impact on "legitimate" *danna* temples. Furthermore, it was often triggered by other factions of Nichirenshū, who competed with Fujufuse followers over the limited pool of Nichiren adherents, and thus tried to exploit the illegality of their Fujufuse opponents. Nevertheless, the shogunal message, delivered through the punishment of Fujufuse followers, broadly defined to include the Hidenshū, was clear: the Law of the Buddha serves the Law of the King. In placing the Law of the King over the Law of the Buddha, the shogunate did not question the right of Buddhists to perform the public duty of religious inspection; rather, it simply decided which Buddhists had the right to perform that duty. Those who were classified as not having that right—Fujufuse and wandering prayer Buddhists or semi-monks—were scrutinized and denied. The shogunate did not tolerate religious practitioners who refused to submit to the *bakuhan* governing system. With regard to those working within the prescribed system of the Law of the King, the shogunate imposed upon them its own regulations and codes of behavior.

In particular, the shogunate was sensitive to Buddhist behavior, both individual and institutional, that put excessive pressure upon *danna* patrons. A 1722 shogunal edict declared: "From now on, no matter how cordial, the number of dishes [for treating priests of the *danna* temple after a ritual] should be limited to one soup and two or three dishes, and the amount of sake to three cups. Even though a *danna* family offers a special invitation [to priests of their temple], a meal should be limited to two kinds of soup and five dishes, and sake to three or five cups."[125] On the occasion of a funeral, it was quite common for a *danna* family to treat ritual priests from the *danna* temple with sake and all kinds of fine dishes. This bothered government officials, who often struggled to come to grips with the economic hardships suffered by a nation steeped in famines and chronic fiscal deficits. Sumptuary laws, imposed repeatedly throughout the late Tokugawa period, were also applied to death-related rituals and ancestral rites. Admonished by the shogunate, each Buddhist sect set up its own guidelines for lessening the financial burdens of funeral *danna* patrons and for maintaining quality ritual services regardless of the level of financial contribution.[126]

Nevertheless, wasteful rituals and the lavish treatment of *danna* priests were not the only problems. The trouble seemed to run deep, as is suggested by the aforementioned 1722 edict: "Stop disgraceful customs such as selling talismans to the lay attendants at the time of a ritual, or circulating an empty bag among them to collect donations. . . . Offerings for a sūtra chanting or merit-making ritual should first be directed to the attending priests, and then, if something is still left, it can be used for the repair of buildings."[127] This article implies that under the aegis of the *danka* system, Buddhist monks tended to put pressure upon their *danna* patrons to make donations for the upkeep of temple buildings. Temple maintenance was, in fact, a problem with which the shogunate had been wrestling since the early eighteenth century in an effort to dissuade the monks from pursuing material gain.

A 1718 shogunal decree addressed to the temples in Edo, many of which had been lost or damaged due to two massive fires in the preceding year, reads: "Repair of temple buildings that have been damaged by fire should be kept to a minimum. Keep in mind that the restored building [should] be smaller than the one lost to fire. . . . For such repairs, financial contributions may be asked of the *danna* patrons, but they should not be imposed on them. Each temple should keep this in mind."[128] While giving temples permission to repair their damaged buildings, the shogunate warned that the costs entailed should not fall to the *danna* households. In order to make sure that repairs were conducted in a proper manner, the shogunate ordered that they be reported, along with charts showing the size of each building (both before the fire and after repairs) and floorplans.[129] For Buddhist institutions, building maintenance was, in fact, a major source of financial drain because public grants-in-aid had been in steady decline since the late seventeenth century. In particular, those temples that could not raise enough funds from a relatively small pool of *danna* households had no option but to seek alms from the public. In order to lessen the hardships of those temples, the shogunate announced in 1729 that it would allocate to them an annual public fund of 1,000 gold pieces.[130]

Despite its seeming sympathy, the shogunate was not really ready to hand out public grants for the upkeep of temple buildings (as it had done in the earlier years) in the name of protecting the nation's spiritual strength. Shogunal support for Buddhist temples and Shinto shrines was limited to a handful of prominent institutions, and declined over time in magnitude and in frequency. For most temples, building repair became a private task to be taken care of through recourse to landed property, *danna* patrons, public fundraising, or other business operations. Interestingly, as may be seen in an administrative directive circulated among officials of the magistrate of temples and shrines in the late 1740s, the shogunate was not entirely opposed to these options: "Do not encourage temples to repair their buildings with [income from] their lands or with the help of the public. . . . In case they attempt to repair their buildings [through public fundraising], the *bakufu* might consider providing some grants and lumber in accordance with their rank and status, but do not let this policy be known to the temples and shrines."[131] This was a Catch-22. The shogunate recognized the importance of maintaining temple buildings, but it wanted to keep it at a minimal level. At the same time, by funding temple maintenance, the shogunate hoped to justify its claim that the Law of the King prevailed over the Law of the Buddha. However, the *bakufu*'s deteriorating finances did not readily allow for such a graceful gesture. Given the circumstances, the best strategy was to discourage or limit building repairs and to ban the construction of new buildings.

When construction became unavoidable, the government allowed temples to collect special donations from the public—a system in which temples solicited donations by exhorting the Buddha's teachings (*kange* or *kanjin*).[132] Such efforts helped many temples and shrines raise the funds necessary for their building repairs. Among several gradations of *kange* campaigns, the "honorific permission" fundraiser (*gomen kange*) was the most prestigious: it required approval from senior councilors of the shogunate. When a religious institution obtained *gomen kange* permission, it could, for a certain period of time, almost "impose" contributions upon people beyond its *danna* circle; and those who were asked to assist could hardly reject the shogunal suggestion that they make "Buddhist merit-accumulating" donations.[133] Under the shadow of the *kange* campaign system, some temples occasionally ventured to launch their own "private *kange*" campaigns.

The *kange* campaign in general, despite its original purpose, gradually developed into another brand of compulsory fundraising to which all villagers were compelled to comply. It became customary for an upper-rank temple to assign a share of its *kange* goal to each of its branch temples, which, in turn, passed it down to their *danna* members. Or when donation collectors appeared in a village under a banner bearing the emblem of shogunal permission, villagers had no choice but to prostrate themselves and to present their contributions. The problem was that the demand was too frequent and too costly. In the period between 1815 and 1830, for example, the 308 residents and 63 households of Hazawa village in Musashi had to deal with 70 *kange* solicitations (on average, 4.6 solicitations per year), 11 of which were *gomen kange* campaigns.[134] In order to deal with enforced donations, which came relentlessly one after another, some villages had to put aside a certain amount of money from their regular budgets, and upon notification, send a lump-sum donation to the *kange* temple, which often did not even bother visiting them.[135]

However, as *kange* campaigns increased and became disorderly, the shogunate realized that they were depleting the economic surplus of Tokugawa society—a surplus that might otherwise have ended up in government coffers. The shogunate began to take action as early as 1750: "In recent years too many applications for *kange* campaigns have been submitted. Those applications from institutions that were erected with shogunal support, or with due reason, are excepted. But others shall not be approved."[136] Restrictions on *kange* campaigns grew over time, as may be seen in the *bakufu*'s repeated issuance of anti-*kange* regulations in 1757, 1758, 1759, and so on.[137] From 1758 onward, religious institutions were obliged upon receiving permission for building repairs to report such repairs (along with detailed illustrations) to the magistrate's office of temples and shrines.[138]

Despite various efforts to restrict the access of Buddhist temples to *kange* donations, the shogunate found their insistence difficult to ignore. The perplexed *bakufu*, which viewed itself as the final bastion of the nation's spiritual welfare, could not be impervious to the temples' demand for financial help. Along with *kange* campaigns, *bakufu* officials also had to deal with such avenues for public solicitation as exhibitions of secret deities or treasures for fundraising (*kaichō* or *kaichō kanjin*), and lottery games (*tomitsuki*).[139] In 1790, the shogunate commented: "In recent years, fundraising drives such as *kange* and lottery games have become too numerous. Among these, lottery games are especially numerous, causing societal unrest. This practice should be suppressed."[140] At the same time, it advised religious institutions to refrain from requesting permission for *kaichō* in the name of building repairs, suggesting that such requests would probably be unnecessary if small problems in the building were taken care of whenever they occurred. In fact, the matter of public fundraising, diverse in method and often elusive in operation, remained a bone of contention between Buddhist temples and the government. In an anti-Christian society, where Buddhism assumed a vital role and where Buddhist funerary rites were cemented into the *danka* system, no single party could gain full control over the issue of revenue allocation—although it was, in the final analysis, *danna* households that bore the cost.

In a book entitled *Jinsuke banashi* (A story of Jinsuke), which was compiled in the Kansei era (1789–1800), an official in the Kumamoto domain named Shimada Katsuji (1755–1819) lamented:

In this region, too, when monks thrive, the people fall into poverty. A donation is often referred to as a little token of gratitude, but it is none other than an additional expenditure for the people. Once all little tokens of gratitude are collected, [the monks] soon begin to collect materials from the people all over again with the excuse of having to restore a Buddhist hall or purchase a new Buddhist image. I also hear that, when it comes to monks, people extend their hands to help and also add an extra token of gratitude. Apparently, the practice of donating a little token of gratitude is not for the lord; it is simply an unnecessary expense. Year after year, the construction of buildings and spendthrift monks translate into poverty for the people. Furthermore, the current practice of donating a little token of gratitude, no matter how little, amounts to nothing more than robbing the lord.[141]

Donations to Buddhist temples, whether for repairing buildings or for paying the expenses of the monks, eroded the pockets of both people and government. No doubt, as Shimada Katsuji observed, the prosperity of the temples came at the expense of the people.

Nevertheless, the temples' thirst for fundraising did not stop with "little tokens of gratitude." In order to maintain and enhance the symbols of their religious power—Buddhist halls and pagodas— many Buddhist temples undertook other business ventures. During the late Tokugawa period, a usury business aimed at raising "money for ritual halls" (*shidōkin*) prospered.[142] This scheme was simple: a temple would get wealthy *danna* members to contribute to a fund by promising them a high rate of interest on their contribution. Then, once the funds had been raised, the temple would operate a loan business, lending money to its *danna* members and others who were in need of it. The annual interest, after paying what was promised to those who contributed to the fund, was deposited in the temple's coffers.[143] In most cases, the *shidōkin* loan business was endorsed by the government, which saw in it a solution to its ever-worsening fiscal situation. By allowing the *shidōkin* loan business, which offered a leeway for amassing savings, the government could, to some extent, excuse itself from the burden of directly subsidizing the temples. As for the temples, by operating a loan business under the sanction of the government, they could alleviate the danger of people's defaulting while compounding the value of income from moneylending.

When borrowing temple money, peasants usually mortgaged their farmlands to the temple. But these peasants, who were easily trapped in a spiraling debt load, often had to see their land forfeited to the temple, and they were then forced to cultivate it as tenant peasants. Now their burdens intensified further as they were under a dual obligation to pay the monks as well as to pay the annual rice tax to the government. Many peasants were pushed into a vicious cycle of poverty, having to borrow additional temple money in order to pay existing debts. This situation would be exacerbated by bad crops or natural disasters.[144] There were many bankrupt villagers, and entire villages would then be bound to their temple landlords.

The creeping Buddhist ownership of farmlands chipped away at the tax base of the *bakuhan* landlords as those lands, once registered under the name of a temple, could be exempted from taxation. Particularly when a tract of newly acquired land was used as a site for relocating temple buildings or as a space for a cemetery, the temple's claim to tax exemption was hard to ignore.[145] In an attempt to expand the status of tax-exemption, some temples even conspired to forge documents for land entitlement. Temple lands, once classified as tax-exempt lands (*jochi*), were immune from the annual rice tax owed to the samurai landlords. Meanwhile, those who cultivated temple lands and paid their temple landlords a "rent for tenancy" (usually set at a level not below that of the annual tax rate), were further subjugated to the temples. All in all, an increase in temple lands meant for the *bakuhan* landlords a decrease in their own tax revenues as well as a diminution of their control over peasant cultivators. The tax system of the Tokugawa regime was cracking from within.

But this problem was not something that could be attributed to the "greed" of Buddhist temples alone. It was, in a sense, the inadvertent result of the shogunate's own strategy, which lacked consistency and a long-term vision. As was evidenced by the edict of 1775, the shogunate first sought to avoid directly contributing to the upkeep of Buddhist institutions. Nevertheless, in this edict, the shogunate promised:

If it is really for generating expenses for building repair, and if [the money] cannot be left idle, then the Buddhist temples may deposit all the money they have with the government. Officials will then loan the money to wards or villages according to the terms of interest and the loan period set by the magistrate's office or a shogunal deputy. When a temple in question needs this money, the government office will collect it and transmit it to the temple.[146]

However, 44 years later in 1819, the shogunate had grown weary of the ever-troublesome loophole created by the *shidōkin* business. "From now on," the shogunate warned, "new loans shall not be approved so easily." And if a temple already had a *shidōkin* fund in operation, then it would be "allowed neither to add a new fund to its pool nor to raise interest rates."[147] Concurrently, the shogunate announced that it would no longer be involved with any loan defaults. Buddhist temples, which saw their loan business stripped of its previous "public" sanction, concentrated more and more on accumulating lands.

Buddhist temples were pushed into a defensive position vis-à-vis the state, although it had been the *bakufu* that had first empowered them. As time progressed, shogunal control became increasingly identified with iron-fisted regulations. But Buddhist temples did not easily succumb to administrative pressure. On the contrary, they seemed to be mushrooming in a random manner and to be vigorously expanding their religious businesses. In 1794, the shogunate attempted to "weed out" new temples that seemed to have sprung up from nowhere: "Among the temples in the remote domains, there are those with neither *danna* nor head temples. Their head monks belong to no particular sect. Those who want the job are casually installed as head monks regardless of their sectarian affiliation. . . . Those temples which are not indispensable for the local community should be abolished."[148] There is no evidence, however, that many of these "illegal" temples were actually eliminated; in fact, Tamamuro Fumio has compared the numbers of temples in the Kumamoto domain between 1715 and 1871 and found that some sects saw an increase in temples during this period. According to his estimate, for example, more than 6 percent of the temples belonging to the Nishihonganji subsect were erected during this period.[149]

Despite the fevered pitch of regulatory rhetoric from the *bakufu*, Buddhist institutions, which were already entrenched within the daily life of the people, remained almost unscathed and prospered even more than they had before. Senior councilor Matsudaira Sadanobu heeded the advice of government officials and Confucian thinkers. Nakai Riken (1732–1817), the younger brother of Nakai Chikuzan, bemoaned that temples were squeezing "sweat and blood from the people" and that monks were "bewildering the minds of the people."[150] His suggestion was radical: "demolish all new temples in and around the Three Cities [Kyoto, Osaka, and Edo] that had been erected since the Kyōhō era [1716–35]. . . . In the case of old ones, merge three or five of them into one."[151] Although Sadanobu was sympathetic to Riken's frustration, he knew that as chief administrator of the shogunate he needed to be practical. As he correctly understood, Buddhist temples were more than administrative agents of the *bakufu*'s anti-Christianity policies: they were also part of the imperial institution. Any attempt to modify Buddhist institutions in too extreme a manner could invite a political backlash that would implicate the emperor—a dormant figure who was, nonetheless, the ultimate source of national authority.

As a matter of fact, *bakufu* leaders in the mid-eighteenth century were increasingly aware of imperial authority. In 1788, Sadanobu even reminded the young shogun Ienari (r. 1787–1837) that "Japan's 60-odd provinces are entrusted [to the shogun] by the imperial court."[152] But in the following year, when Emperor Kōkaku tried to honor his father Prince Sukehito by investing him with the title of "retired emperor" (*dajō tennō*) even though he had never assumed the throne, Sadanobu blocked the attempt and managed to punish the courtiers behind the plot. The Title Incident, as it was known, dragged on until 1793 and later contributed to Sadanobu's resignation from the position of senior councilor.[153] In snubbing the court, Sadanobu was apparently affected by the previous two political mishaps involving the status of the emperor: the Hōreki Incident and the Meiwa Incident. The Hōreki Incident of 1758 stemmed from dissension among the courtiers, but the shogunate decided to scapegoat Takenouchi Shikibu (1712–67), charging that he had told a number of courtiers that the emperor should be revered and that the decrepit imperial court could be restored through learning. On the other hand, the Meiwa Incident of 1767 unfolded dramatically as the shogunate determined that the crime of Yamagata Daini (1725–67) and Fujii Umon (1720–67) amounted to an act of *lèse majesté*. In particular, the shogunal verdict stated that Yamagata Daini had said "that imperial tours of the provinces no longer take place and that the emperor is a virtual prisoner."[154] Both of them were judged to have been guilty of "extreme disrespect and the utmost insolence" and were sentenced to death. Unusually harsh punishments aside, the shogunate's swift censure of pro-imperial idealists left the impression that "the emperor [was] unjustly being kept at bay, like a prisoner."[155]

Not surprisingly, these highly publicized incidents contributed to animated public discourses among both National Learning scholars and some conservative political critics on the "theory of the [imperial] delegation of power" to the *bakufu*. To be sure, these discourses invariably emphasized the harmony between the court and the *bakufu*, but the hidden message was quite obvious: the existence of the imperial sovereign should not be entirely forgotten.[156] Within this context, it would not have been wise for the shogunate to come out and insult the imperial court. For its part, the imperial court began to express concerns over worldly matters, as seen in its 1787 message to the *bakufu* regarding the emperor's and ex-emperor's wish that the shogunate take measures to save the people from starvation.[157] These political discourses had implications for Buddhism.

As Tokugawa Ieyasu himself acknowledged in the 1615 "Laws of the Imperial Court and Courtier Households," Buddhism had been considered part of the imperial institution from the early years of the Tokugawa regime. Articles 14 to 17 addressed regulations pertaining to the granting of honorable Buddhist titles to monks from the imperial and upper-class courtier families, head monks of "purple robe" temples, and great scholar monks (*shōnin*).[158] It is not surprising that those regulations pertaining to monks from imperial and courtier families were included in this law. But the fact that the imperial court was expected to control other high Buddhist monks (i.e., purple robe and scholar monks) indicates that the shogunate admitted that Buddhism belonged in the sphere of the Kyoto court. In contrast, the Laws of Military Households did not mention anything about Buddhism. In fact, through the leverage of titles and ranks, not only upper-class monks but also ordinary head monks were joined with the imperial court—a liaison that would help to protect Buddhism from the whims of shogunal power.

The association between Buddhist monks and the imperial court was basically one of exchange: Buddhist monks acquired prestige from the imperial court, while the latter collected financial contributions from the former. Buyō Inshi, in his *Seji kenbunroku* (An account of events seen and heard), touched upon this exchange relationship:

The supreme head temple of the Sōtōshū is Eiheiji in Echizen province. These days, it is said that it would be difficult to become abbot of this head temple without stashing away 2,000 gold pieces, of which 1,000 gold pieces are needed for expenses for preparing to enter the temple, and another 1,000 gold pieces for gifts and other items when visiting the imperial court. . . . For lesser temples as well, the head monk position is traded for gold and silver, in accordance with the rank of the temple and the number of its *danna*.[159]

According to Buyō Inshi, the abbacy of Eiheiji was a commodity that could be purchased from the imperial court with 1,000 gold pieces. This is, in fact, no exaggeration. Based on documents found in Eiheiji and Dōshōan in 1822 and in 1848, respectively, Tamamuro Fumio ascertains that a candidate seeking the head monk title of Eiheiji actually spent far more than 2,000 gold pieces to obtain a purple robe from the imperial court.[160] The whole procedure was extraordinarily costly. The candidate first had to pay a visit to the shogun, which involved a grand procession from Eiheiji to Edo Castle, in order to obtain a shogunal letter endorsing his candidacy. After returning to Eiheiji, he then went through a series of ceremonies and rituals designed to celebrate the fact that he had obtained shogunal approval. He then set out for Kyoto in order to pay a visit to the court with the mediation of the Kajūji house (a courtier family that served as an official go-between between the emperor and abbacy candidates), to receive the head monk title from the emperor upon presenting him with the shogunal letter along with a donation of 1,000 gold pieces, and to thank high-ranking courtiers and Kajūji.[161] Clearly, his expenditures far exceeded those suggested by Buyō Inshi.

It was not only through the selling of purple robes that the imperial court wielded influence over religious institutions but also through the selling of lesser titles. In the case of the Sōtōshū, which boasted of its adherence to strict Zen practice, the 1611 sectarian law stipulated that no member would be promoted to retreat elder until he had completed at least 20 years of disciplinary practice, and that no member would be promoted to resident abbot until he had completed at least 30 years of practice.[162] As far as Buyō Inshi was concerned, this was a lie: nothing seemed impossible if one had money, and a bribe of ten gold pieces seemed enough to produce a temple head: "These ten gold pieces would go to Kyoto. By offering five gold pieces to their head temple [Eiheiji or Sōjiji], accompanied by a false report that they have completed 20 years of Buddhist practice, they obtain a letter of endorsement. They then visit Kajūji [in Kyoto] and offer another five gold pieces. Upon its recommendation, an imperial appointment is issued without any objection. [With this] they are promoted to the status of an elder and further to that of a great abbot."[163]

The conferral of Buddhist titles and ranks, regardless of a person's sectarian affiliation, was often turned into a matter of monetary transactions between individual monks and the imperial court. These transactions amounted to a sort of "extraterritorial" shortcut that nullified the official hierarchical ladder of Buddhist titles and ranks, which were supposed to be granted according to the quality and length of one's education and disciplinary practice. One might wonder how these career-conscious monks raised the slush funds needed to obtain an imperial sanction. The example of a monk from Unryūji, a Sōtōshū (now Rinzaishū) temple in Izusawa village, Chichibu county, Musashi, is illustrative. In 1858, this monk sought to replace his black robe with a colored robe that would give him the status of abbot.[164]

For this he raised a total of 18.625 gold *ryō* and 55 copper coins. About 60 percent of this money came from his "neighboring temples," and the rest came from his funerary *danna* patrons. With this money, he first visited Eiheiji, presented 5.5 gold pieces, and received a ceremony endorsing his application for abbotship. After that, he traveled to Kyoto and presented 5 gold pieces to Dōshōan, which forwarded 98 percent of the money to the court and took the rest as its commission. Then with 3.1875 gold *ryō*, he purchased a ceremonial robe suitable to his new title. While staying in Kyoto for two weeks, he followed the procedure for promotion by visiting the court and obtaining an imperial letter of appointment. When he returned to his temple, two months had passed. The official documents show that he spent a total of just over 18 gold pieces.[165] In the late Tokugawa period, the imperial court could garner at least 5 to 10 gold pieces from each candidate seeking an abbotship, no matter how low the temple's status within the head-branch hierarchy.

Buddhist institutions enjoyed imperial sanction in return for financial contributions until 1869, when the imperial house ceased authorizing Buddhist titles and ranks through its three go-betweens (Ninnaji, Daikakuji, and Kajūji).[166] How many endorsement letters had the imperial court issued to Buddhist monks, and how much income had those letters generated? It is hard to determine exact figures across all sects; however, as far as the Sōtōshū was concerned, the imperial court authorized, on average, a little more than 450 applications for titles related to abbotships and pocketed more than 4,500 gold pieces each year between 1650 and 1868.[167] If examples of other sects are added to the Sōtōshū figures, and if endorsements for purple robes, which brought at least 2,000 gold pieces per case, are taken into account, then it is clear that the imperial court reaped a yearly windfall from Buddhist institutions.

It should be noted that the entire imperial-Buddhist nexus was, in the final analysis, sustainable due primarily to the auspices of the *danka* system in the sense that most of the donations from Buddhist temples to the imperial court were acquired from funerary *danna* patrons. With the emperor authorizing them from above, and with their *danna* patrons supporting them from below, Buddhist institutions were able to survive and prosper. When they were harassed by shogunal authorities or other critics, Buddhist institutions had no difficulty fighting back. When they fought back, their revenge could be deadly, as was demonstrated by the punishment that fell upon

Tokugawa Nariaki (1800–60), the Mito lord who was regarded as one of the most influential and outspoken players in *bakuhan* politics in the 1830s and early 1840s.

Tokugawa Nariaki touched the lethal poison when, in the name of reforms, he ruthlessly destroyed Buddhist temples and defrocked their monks in the late 1830s. The cries for help from the Buddhist temples in the Mito domain could be heard all the way to the imperial court. Buddhist forces that joined their desperate effort included powerhouses such as Kan'eiji (the head temple of the Eastern Tendai sect, whose abbot, Rinnōji no miya, was appointed from among imperial princes), Zōjōji (the head temple of the Pure Land sect in eastern Japan, which served along with Kan'eiji as a shogunal funerary temple), and Daijōji (a Nichirenshū temple in Komagome of Edo, which was a branch temple of Kyūshōji in Hitachi, which had connections to the Mito Tokugawa house).[168] Summoned to the *bakufu*, Nariaki, under interrogation, vigorously defended his "destruction of temples" and the "laicization of monks," but not with much success. In the fifth month of 1844 the shogunate handed down its verdict: "Hereby [the punishment of] abdication [from the headship of the family] is issued. Limit [your] dwelling to the residence of Komagome and keep [yourself] in abstinence quietly and strictly. Tsuruchiyo [Tokugawa Yoshiatsu, Nariaki's eldest son] will take over the headship of the family."[169]

Political pundits came up with a number of theories as to how Nariaki's house arrest came about, including internal strife and power struggles among his vassals and retainers. Outsiders seemed quite certain about what had really caused Nariaki's sudden fall. Kurimoto Joun (1822–97), a *bakumatsu* luminary, summed it up as follows: "Mito Nariaki earned punishment from the *bakufu* because he had arbitrarily abolished temples, melted Buddhist bells into cannons, removed Buddhist stone images and used them as cornerstones of bridges, brought down the name-plaques of temples granted by the imperial court, and expelled monks from honorable prayer halls. Those [who were expelled] secretly appealed to Kyoto. It is said that Kyoto delivered secret orders [to the *bakufu*]."[170] It seems that the imperial court had intervened in one way or another. Katsu Kaishū (1823–99) put Kyoto's intervention in perspective.

The most serious matter was his destruction of Buddhist temples. To begin with, generation after generation, Buddhist temples had been erected under the protection of the imperial court. The institution that was the head temple of each sect was generally led by an imperial prince who was installed as abbot, and many of these temples served the wishes of the imperial court. From medieval times temples such as Hieizan or Honganjii resisted the king and even commanded military power (if only temporarily). Oda Nobunaga took weapons from them and weakened them to some degree, but they remained basically unchanged. Tokugawa Ieyasu set up rules and regulations and tried to control the arrogance and rudeness of Buddhist priests, but he rarely went beyond what had been done in ancient times. All the Buddhist temples, down to branch temples in the local areas, were under the command of head temples, and all were in communication. Given this, how could one abolish them overnight? How on earth could their destruction be called the will of the public? The temples affected were totally dumfounded, and naturally appealed to their head temples. When [the imperial court] demanded of the Kantō [the *bakufu*] through the head temples that an explanation be given, how could the *bakufu* have answered to it?[171]

Concerned with the adverse effects that open suppression of Buddhist temples might invite, the shogunate directed its attention more and more to containing the unruly sprawl of marginal "illegal" temples without touching the institution of funerary Buddhism. Shogunal Buddhist policy was a delicate business, and it was best to negotiate it carefully lest one risk encroaching upon the imperial-Buddhist alliance or destabilizing the *danka* system rooted in the system of temple certification. Even the most sarcastic critics of Buddhism during the *bakumatsu* period could not but continue to accept the status quo as the "great law of the realm."[172] For the shogunate, which faced mounting problems of its own, confronting imperial authority with the aim of controlling Buddhist temples was not worth it.

In short, within the Tokugawa governing structure, Buddhist institutions were to be embraced rather than denied. That was why the escalating anti-Buddhist regulations during the late Tokugawa period were, for the most part, rhetorical. And even when they were implemented, this was done superficially. What became salient was a polemical tug of war between anti-Buddhists and pro-Buddhists that often bore neither direct impact upon, nor much relevance to, reality. The verbal confrontations between them intensified from the early eighteenth century, particularly over issues relating to the *danka* system; however, these clashes did not really do much more than slake the thirst of mutual dislike.

For example, Ogyū Sorai questioned in his *Seidan* the two underlying rationales for the *danka* system—the Buddhist monopoly on rituals for the dead and anti-Christian temple certification. In his criticism of Buddhism both as a religion and as an institution, Sorai first argued that it made no sense for Buddhist clergy to monopolize death-related rituals and rites of ancestral veneration: "Annual memorial services for the dead are not mentioned in the Buddhist sūtras. The Law of the Buddha teaches neither the bestowal of a posthumous name after a mortuary ritual nor the burial of the dead in the temple ground."[173] On the other hand, with regard to temple certification, Sorai insisted: "People called Kirishitan no longer exist in any part of Japan, so it no longer makes sense to investigate Kirishitan families and relatives. . . . There is no one who reads books on Christianity, so there is no one who can talk about that religion."[174]

About half a century later, Nakai Chikuzan ridiculed the system of temple certification, which had become an administrative method for collecting national census data: "A village head compiles a population register of his villagers simply based on one-page religious certificates issued by temples. He usually does not check the actual number of households [in his village] and simply delegates everything to the temples. The fact that administrative rights over the nation's households belong to Buddhist monks bespeaks nothing but the loss of governing principles."[175] According to Chikuzan, by relegating much of the task of taking a national census to "house-leavers," the government encouraged unreliable data collection, and this benefited Buddhist temples. He observed that monks habitually issued non-Christian certificates without actually checking their *danna* households and that they arbitrarily accepted seasonal workers and servants without removing their names from the registers in their previous hometowns. He also argued that the only way to redress the problem of double counting and other abuses was to have secular officials take over the duties of religious inspection.[176] Only when monks were deprived of the power of temple certification, Chikuzan believed, would the government be able to subdue what he referred to as "all other Buddhist ills."[177]

Not surprisingly, Chikuzan's calls for the abolition of temple certification were echoed by his faithful disciple, Yamagata Bantō (1748–1821), a merchant-scholar in Osaka. In his treatise *Yume no shiro* (A period of dreams), Bantō proposed that the conduct of funeral rites be handed over to Confucianism and that religious inspection be handed over to Shinto priests.[178] In the 1840s, the Mito scholars Fujita Tōko (1806–55) and Aizawa Seishisai (1782–1863), who were fiercely anti-Buddhist, persuaded their lord, Tokugawa Nariaki, to proceed with anti-Buddhist reforms.[179] But their push stopped far short of convincing Nariaki to abolish the system of temple certification. Almost every Confucian ideologue seemed to have something, whether imaginary or practical, to say about Buddhism, but things remained unchanged. As Fujimori Kōan (1799–1862), an Edo Confucianist who was sympathetic to Nariaki's anti-Buddhist reforms, concluded: "given that [temple certification] is already firmly in place as a political instrument, Buddhism cannot easily be destroyed."[180] Even when returning monks to membership in the laity, Nariaki's language was political and protective: they were never forcibly "defrocked" but, rather, were allowed to "return to farming" (*kinō*) or "return to the secular" (*genzoku*). The language used suggests that Buddhist monks were not stripped of their priesthood but, rather, were guided back to "a more socially and ontologically natural status" — one that fit with a society run according to what Confucian ideologues loved to call agrarian ideals. Similarly, in demolishing temples Nariaki rarely used the term "demolition" (*hakyaku*), preferring the terms "disposition" (*shobun*) or "amalgamation" (*gappei*), which gave the impression that he was talking about a simple managerial adjustment.[181] In 1855, Kōan suggested a compromise: temple certification should be taken over by a secular administration, while Buddhist monks should be guaranteed the right to conduct prayer and death rituals.

No matter what alternatives were suggested, the system of temple certification was firmly locked into the structure of the Tokugawa regime itself. Instead of trying to bring the system of temple certification down, many anti-Buddhist critics concentrated on bringing to light what they branded as "Buddhist corruption" — almost as though determined to pick a grain of sand out of a bowl of rice. Again, Buyō Inshi exercised his acid tongue in depicting how Buddhist monks were capitalizing on the "public power" of religious inspection and, as a result, enjoying a "fixed salary" from their *danna* patrons.[182] He pointed out that, "when a *danna* does not comply with what monks say, or speaks against their wrongdoings," then the monks may refuse to sign documents relating to religious inspection, refuse to issue documents for marriage, fabricate a pretext for refusing to perform funerals, or simply refuse to perform funerals altogether.[183] It was no longer a secret that too many monks were ignorant of Buddhist teachings yet amazingly arrogant with regard to performing rituals or interacting with poor *danna* patrons. Buyō Inshi concluded that the manner in which monks provided their religious services was contingent upon how much a *danna* could pay, and he pointed out that some of them went so far as to display the ancestral tablets of high-status families in their temples in order to attract new customers.[184]

In 1840, Shōji Kōki (1793–1857), a wealthy merchant in Arita in Hizen, likened Buddhist monks to a "group of professional exploiters of *danna* households and spoilers of the public treasury" in his *Keizai mondō hiroku* (A private record of an inquiry into managing the world and governing the people): "Although the people are children of the lord, they never expect a piece of their residential plot to be exempted from taxation. In contrast, temple lands are exempted from taxation, and those temples with no tax-exempted lands force their *danna* to pay annual taxes. Monks do not give any thought to the hardships of the people."[185] To Shōji Kōki, this was grossly unfair. Matsuoka Yukiyoshi (1794–1848), a samurai in the Kurume domain, agreed that "many Buddhist monks neither paid taxes nor provide any corvée service. [They were, in fact] totally useless to the country."[186] Among many "solutions to this problem," Kōki proposed: "Temples in the countryside should be relocated in a temple district of one *ri* (2.44 miles), which should be allocated near a post station or in the corner of a town, like Kyoto or Osaka, where they should be arranged sect by sect. And each temple's space should be limited to five *se* (118.611 square yards)."[187] He also proposed that Buddhist monks should be banned from traveling around and that each domain should limit its number of monks.

In 1849, no less determined than Shōji Kōki, Hirata Atsutane, a National Learning scholar, poked fun at "monks who seem to believe that their duty is to dupe the people for material gains."[188] He was particularly harsh with regard to the Jōdoshinshū and Nichirenshū monks and temples. In his *Shutsujō shōgo*, Atsutane extended the critical tone of *Shutsujō kōgo* (Talks after having left meditation [*samādhi*]), an influential treatise on the doctrinal developments of Buddhism in India and China by Tominaga Nakamoto (1715–46).[189] *Shutsujō kōgo*, completed in 1744, has a somewhat enigmatic title: "shutsujō" means "leaving meditation or concentration" and "kōgo" means "talks thereafter."[190] On the other hand, Atsutane's *Shutsujō shōgo*, which mimics Nakamoto's title, can be translated as "laughable talks," or a "laughing discourse," on the *shutsujō*. In both works, the main thread of the polemic revolves around the "realities of Buddhism in the secular world" — realities that were both laughable and pejorative.[191] And, indeed, Atsutane "laughed":

According to Matsushita, because monks cannot make a living when the people are experiencing neither grief nor misfortune, they pray, particularly when they run out of gold and silver, that their *danna* may die so that they can make money from memorial services.[192] This reminds me of something comparable: "non-persons" (*hinin*) are like monks in that they, too, walk around begging. But since "non-persons" can beg anywhere and anytime, whether the occasion be one of celebration or mourning, they can at least pray that something good may happen. In contrast, monks only pray for deaths to occur in their *danna* households.[193]

Hirata Atsutane was especially cynical with regard to such Buddhist ideas as *nenbutsu, daimoku*, paradise, hell, and the like, all of which were related to death, rebirth, and funerary rituals. He suggested that a sort of last-moment salvific sweepstakes of *nenbutsu* or *daimoku* chanting would only encourage evil deeds among the populace and goad people into squandering their possessions in search of the rewards of paradise.[194]

On the whole, as far as the *danka* system and temple certification were concerned, the promoters of anti-Buddhist discourses can be categorized into two groups: Confucian ideologues who blamed Buddhism for damaging the Tokugawa governing structure and who tried to restore the ideals of the *bakuhan* system, and National Learning scholars who derided Buddhism as a religion of foreign origin and juxtaposed it with Shinto—Japan's original and autochthonous faith. Among these two groups of ideologues, the first group, which included Kumazawa Banzan, Ogyū Sorai, Nakai Chikuzan, Buyō Inshi, Shōji Kōki, and Aizawa Seishisai, was especially eloquent regarding "the evils and harm of Buddhism."[195] Nakai Chikuzan and Shōji Kōki claimed that Buddhist monks who did not fit into the status order of "four classes" were nothing more than "wandering people" (*ryūmin*) who were detrimental to the well-being of the state. They were particularly harsh with regard to the Ikkōshū temples, which refused to enshrine Shinto deities yet "embraced many peasants as *danna* households and depended upon *danna* relationships for survival due to the lack of temple lands and, as a result, were only weakening the tax-payment capacities of the peasants who should support the feudal economy."[196]

In his four-volume magnum opus, Tsuji Zennosuke (1877–1955) summed up all of these anti-Buddhist criticisms, whether imaginary or factual, in the theory of Buddhist "decadence" (*daraku*). In the fourth volume, Tsuji concluded: "Buddhism had almost fallen into a state of paralysis; temple monks could preserve their status in society simply by relying on the force of indolent habit."[197] His contention that Buddhism in the Tokugawa period lost its vitality and moral righteousness has exerted a significant impact upon scholarship. Tokugawa Buddhism has been understudied and, too often, subjected to blind criticism, despite the fact that Buddhist influence over the populace actually peaked during this period. Ōkuwa Hitoshi notes that, "in the past four decades or so scholars in the field have strained every nerve in order to overcome the 'decadence' theory of Tsuji Zennosuke, but without much success."[198] Given that the *danka* system and temple certification were at the epicenter of Tsuji's "decadence" theory, the context in which his anti-Buddhist criticism unfolded could be related to the anti-Buddhist discourses that were rife in the Tokugawa period.

First of all, it should be noted that the idea of "decadence" is premised on the assumption that there is a pure, original mode of Buddhism. Has "pure" Buddhism ever existed? As L. S. Cousins reminds us: "It is an error to think of a pure Buddhism, which has become syncretistically mixed with other religions, even corrupted and degenerate in later forms. Such a pure Buddhism has never existed. Buddhism has always coexisted with other religious beliefs and practices."[199] The various types of Buddhism that have evolved in different directions at different places and at different times seem to indicate that what we collectively refer to as "Buddhism" has never existed: there have been "Buddhisms" but no "Buddhism." Furthermore, as far as institutional degeneration is concerned, one might argue, for example, that Buddhism in the medieval period, which was mired in all kinds of conflicts and disputes, was no better than Buddhism in the Tokugawa period.[200] It would be erroneous, indeed ignorant, to try to distill a pure form of Buddhism for the sake of critique. In evaluating Tokugawa Buddhism, Tsuji was operating from within a totalizing mindset: he encapsulated Buddhism into its imaginary purity, overlooked the sectarian variations and diversities in Buddhist culture, and generalized all this into a theory of degeneration.

More problematically, Tsuji's criticism inherited much of the ideological legacies of the anti-Buddhist critics of the Tokugawa period. Borrowing this hackneyed anti-Buddhist rhetoric, which had been around much earlier in China, Tokugawa ideologues refuted Buddhism by claiming that it was antisocial, otherworldly, and, therefore, inimical to family values.[201] What can one say to this? In fact, the opposite is true. Buddhist institutions were an integral part of the governing apparatus of the Tokugawa regime, and Buddhist monks were the indispensable agents of family values, as was evidenced in their role in death rituals and ancestral rites.[202] Far more than any other religious tradition, Buddhism was socially oriented and family-centered. As William R. LaFleur suggests, we cannot discard the impression that the invective of Buddhism's critics was a product of frustration: "Buddhism's critics were disturbed by the continued worldly tenacity of an institution they judged should already have been relegated to history's slag heaps."[203] For Confucian ideologues, seeing that their claim to ideological hegemony could not be supported, the sustained prosperity and social influence of Buddhism must have been a pill too bitter to swallow. To their consternation there was no way for them to cover the box of Buddhism with the lid of Confucianism.

Many Buddhist monks simply ignored the anti-Buddhist criticism that often accompanied empty charges. Fujii Manabu notes that since the collapse of Ikkō *ikki* and the ban on the Fujufuse, Buddhists never again attempted to prioritize the Law of the Buddha over the Law of the King; rather, they simply submitted themselves to secular authority.[204] Head-on confrontation with anti-Buddhist critics, as well as the claim to autonomous religious authority, had to be avoided if Buddhist institutions, which had had a rough ride in the sixteenth century, were to survive.[205] For them, the best strategy was to take the benefits that the *danka* system offered and to bypass hollow, ideological attacks. They were convinced that, no matter how critics tried to discredit Buddhism, their verbal attacks alone were not going to undo the system of temple certification and funerary Buddhism.

This does not mean, however, that all Buddhists remained immune to anti-Buddhist assaults, which at times amounted to an almost daily festival of abuse. Some monks tried to mollify anti-Buddhist critics with pro-Buddhist publications, while others emphasized the compatibility between Shinto, Confucianism, Daoism, and Buddhism. The key point of these counterarguments was that these religious traditions complemented each other in "promoting the ethics of good and evil and providing services for the well-being of the people."[206] Their rather languid approach, which was often tried in China, could not stem the tide of anti-Buddhist sentiment.

Some monks admitted that there were some problems in Tokugawa Buddhism and proceeded to provide specific and practical suggestions. In his 1666 *Kaijō monogatari* (A tale of the sea), the Sōtō-shū monk Echū (1628–1703) lamented: "All Buddhist sects have forgotten the Way of the Buddha and have ceased to be the treasure of the state. Contrarily, they often make themselves the enemy of the state."[207] Many followed Echū's lead and called for serious reflection on problems related to the *danka* system. Among these people, Jiun (1718–1804), a Shingonshū monk, endeavored to reform Buddhism by urging not only Buddhist monks but also laypeople to practice daily the "ten good precepts" against killing, stealing, adultery, lying, frivolous language, slander, equivocation, greed, anger, and wrong views. Jiun's preachings were typical of those of Buddhist leaders involved in self-regeneration movements during the late Tokugawa period.[208] Even in Jōdoshinshū, which embraced "precepts of non-precepts" (i.e., no precepts at all) and allowed its monks to marry and pass on temple properties to their descendants, some leaders urged their monks to conduct self-discipline and to respect the spirit of Buddhist commandments.

Amid the deepening national crisis of "disaster from without," or the intrusion of foreign powers, from the early nineteenth century onward many leaders of Buddhist reform aggressively tried to present Buddhism as a spiritual vehicle that could protect the nation. This represented a new trend in which the previous pro-Buddhist polemic, which had stressed the unity between secular ethics and Buddhist teachings, was replaced with the argument that Buddhism could protect people from wicked religions and subversive ritual practices.[209] These "protecting-the-nation and repelling-the-evil" campaigns helped, at least to some extent, to assuage hard-line Buddhist critics and nativists, whose anti-Buddhist attacks had been sharpened against a backdrop of increasing foreign intrusion into Japan. In this atmosphere, with slogans such as "revere the emperor, expel the barbarians," and "revere the emperor, protect the dharma," these campaigns produced (particularly among Jōdoshinshū adherents in western Japan) what were known as "monks loyal to the king" (*kinnōsō*).[210]

Among these loyal monks, a case in point is Gesshō (1817–58), a Nishihonganji subsect leader in Suō.[211] He exerted pro-Buddhist influence over many Chōshū loyalists, including Yoshida Shōin (1830–59) and Rai Mikisaburō (1825–59), and motivated other pro-imperial monks, such as Chō'nen (1793–1868), Mokurin (1824–97), and Shimaji Mokurai (1838–1911). In his book *Buppō gokokuron* (A thesis on the Way of the Buddha and national protection), which was widely circulated after its publication in 1856, Gesshō integrated the Law of the Buddha, national well-being, and the defense of the "country of the gods" (*shinkoku* or *shinshū*) against Western barbarism (represented by Christianity) into the following Buddhist mandate: "Stupid people along the shorelines are now befriended by [Western] barbarians. Bewitched by their wicked teachings, the people have become like dogs and sheep. Today, for maritime defense, there is no more urgent task than using Buddhist teachings to prevent this kind of tragedy. Who is going to take this responsibility? The Buddhist monks of [the nation's] eight sects."[212] Thus, Gesshō created a space of Buddhist revival, and his effort furthered the idea that "the two aspects of the essential and the secular" (*shinzoku nitai*) should be united into one—a key strand of Jōdoshinshū thought that had been suggested by Shōkai (1765–1838), a Jōdoshinshū monk, in the early nineteenth century and was put into full practice in the Meiji period.[213] The ultimate goal of this thought was, as Gesshō expounded, to help people realize Buddhist truth by merging Buddhist faith (the essential) and the protection of the state (the secular) into one. In the long run, this nationalistic thought, officially embraced by Jōdoshinshū leaders in the early Meiji period as the guiding principle of their denomination, exerted tremendous influence over Meiji political leaders from the Chōshū domain, who later played a key role in advancing Japanese imperialism.[214]

In the *bakumatsu* period, many Jōdoshinshū monks and laypeople in Chōshū who understood that the tenor of the times was tilting in favor of the imperial court enlisted in the "irregular brigade" (Kiheitai) organized by Takasugi Shinsaku (1839–67). This force, made up of foot soldiers, peasants, merchants, and priests, joined regular soldiers in battles against the *bakufu*. The Law of the King now shifted toward the emperor, and the Law of the Buddha offered its service to the King in the name of defending the "divine country" under the care of the imperial court.[215] Once again, and shrewdly, Buddhist leaders who were trying to restore the vigor of Buddhism resorted to attacking Christianity—an alien religion that had brought the boon of the *danka* system in the first place. Indeed, anti-Christian sentiments had proved to be of great benefit to Buddhism, and they remained as such well into the Meiji period.

౮

ELEVEN

Funeral Practice, Public Authority, and Social Control

The *danka* system, which subjected the entire populace of Tokugawa Japan to funerary Buddhism, perpetuated a social order based on anti-Christianity. Compliance with Buddhist death rituals ensured that a household was a lawful social entity and that the well-being of its members would be safeguarded after death. Through Buddhist death rituals, the Tokugawa Japanese were held accountable to the sovereign authority of the Tokugawa shogunate. For its part, the Tokugawa regime mobilized these rituals—which were practiced in the form of mortuary rites, memorial services, and ancestral veneration—as a tool of social engineering.

This does not mean, however, that Buddhist funerary rites were always enforced to the full satisfaction of public authorities. Even though everyone was subject to these rites, the ritual handling of death on the part of individual families was not an easy thing to control due to its private nature. The elements constituting the practice of death ritual and ancestral veneration, being essentially symbolic and diffuse, were often barely detectable and, hence, hard to monitor closely. Furthermore, changing social environments were not conducive to the effective control of ritual. Particularly in the urban areas, class lines were becoming blurred; new forms of social networks, groups, and associations were on the rise; and the economy was evolving away from the static principles of the agrarian *kokudaka* system. The religious handling of death through ritual performance was not unaffected by these changes. Clinging to physiocratic social engineering in spite of the increasing ascendancy of a commercial economy, *bakufu* leaders insisted on their hereditary mandate, which held that the samurai class should rule over all others, "not only in their functions, but also in the quality of their dress, food, and housing, in behavior and speech, and in intellectual and cultural activities."[216] As far as shogunal authorities were concerned, rituals and ceremonies were occasions for reinforcing the social order and should remain coterminous with social hierarchy and status. But the theory did not match the practice. For example, many wealthy commoners often used the death of a family member as an occasion to assert their "real" social status and to show off their social influence through conducting splashy funeral services.

This chapter examines why and how the state tried to control the rituals pertaining to Buddhist death. Why was the shogunate so concerned that "excessive" death-related rituals would be damaging to the design of Tokugawa social order? Given that the state was so wary, particularly during the late Tokugawa period, one may wonder how death rituals affected the health of society. From the late eighteenth century on, *bakufu* leaders were convinced that the *bakuhan* system was in crisis, as may be seen in their frequent reference to "troubles within and disaster from without" (*naiyū gaikan*). For them, the problems posed by funerals and memorial services were an unequivocal reflection of this general crisis. The issue of funerary practices was part of a larger concern with social customs and manners in general, not an isolated object of scrutiny.

In the mid-1810s, senior councilor Matsudaira Sadanobu summed up in his *Kantei hisetsu* (Secret words in the bottom of the box) the crises that kept the Tokugawa system in trouble: foreign threats and social disorder. In his view, the threat posed by "southern barbarians" was linked closely to peasant rebellions and urban dissent.[217] It was with these troubles that *bakufu* officials were attempting (with little success) to grapple. Why were the people prone to staging uprisings and spoiling the social order, thus bringing the whole governing system into crisis? Sadanobu insisted that this had to do with the tendencies of "the low [to] outshine the high," as was most graphically demonstrated by the "hauteur and solecism" of Edo rice dealers who belittled the samurai class.[218] There were many problems, to be sure; however, as far as Sadanobu was concerned, the solution had to involve restoring dignity and authority to the ruling samurai class. The deterioration of the social hierarchy was at the heart of all the troubles.

In fact, the issue of status was a chronic problem for *bakufu* leaders. When he launched the Kansei reforms, Sadanobu paid utmost attention to the deteriorating hierarchy of status. Amid the reforms that were already under way, in 1789 he delivered to the shogunal vassals and retainers his views on what should be done in order to restore the spirit of the besieged samurai class:

> Despite the repeated issuance of sumptuary regulations since the Kyōhō era (1716–35), the people do not heed them. There are no distinctions in clothing between those above and those below. People mistakenly think that wearing hemp or cotton cloth will fulfill the requirement of frugality and thrift. For this reason, the samurai, townspeople, and peasants are all alike in appearance. Because of this, our country is losing good customs. Even within the samurai class, since status is differentiated, dress style should also be differentiated. If both those above and those below wear the same clothes, how can status distinctions be made![219]

What an unbelievably trite statement! Was this "serious" warning actually issued by the highest official of the shogunate? One might laugh; however, for Sadanobu, this was very serious business. He was bothered by two interrelated trends: sumptuary regulations that went unheeded and clothing that flouted status distinctions.[220] In emphasizing the importance of the hierarchical separation of classes, he focused on the issue of clothing (e.g., its material, colors, patterns, and design) on the grounds that it constituted "the most useful body of material on which to base qualitative and social distinctions."[221] For Sadanobu, the customs and manners of clothing, which functioned as an index of key social values and practices, reflected concrete social and political relations.

About half a century later, in 1841, Mizuno Tadakuni (1794–1851), the senior councilor of the shogunate, had just launched the Tenpō reforms. He warned government officials that,

> Since the Bunsei era (1818–29) the trend of frivolity and overindulgence has become extreme. If we could reverse it on this occasion and clean it up at once, all aspects of society would be rejuvenated. This should be kept in mind in the next thirty or forty years. Even if [this reform effort] were to cause the castle town [Edo] to wither and were to ruin the livelihood of commoners and devastate the merchants, one should not mind in the slight-

est. If the edict on simplicity and frugality is kept strictly for the next two or three years, the status hierarchy will be rectified.[222]

Tadakuni, like Sadanobu, was also frustrated with the messy state of the status hierarchy and attributed it to a lack of frugality or austerity. Upon closer inspection, however, we notice that these two men were not in full agreement with regard to how strictly austerity measures should be enforced. Sadanobu cautioned that these measures should be put into practice lest the livelihood of the commoners become jeopardized. He argued that the effort put into restoring the status hierarchy would benefit the whole population by ensuring a trickle-down economy.[223] In contrast, Tadakuni contended that the trend towards a sumptuous lifestyle had already spread to the entire population and had caused the impoverishment of the samurai class to the benefit of some segments of the merchant class and wealthy peasants. As a result of this, the status hierarchy had been plunged into further disorder. He argued that the only practical way to save the dignity of the samurai class would be to depress the lifestyle of the commoner class, particularly the merchants, through imposing strict austerity measures. He believed that even if these measures paralyzed the merchants, this was of no consequence. As far as Tadakuni was concerned, the current topsy-turvy state of the status hierarchy cried out for radical surgery.

To be sure, status order, premised on hierarchical distinctions in power, economic well-being, and privilege between the samurai class and the commoner class, was the backbone of the Tokugawa governing system. This requisite gap between the two classes, however, not only gradually narrowed but also, in some cases, was even reversed. Too many samurai families were indebted to wealthy merchants and traders, and the dignity associated with their status was at a low ebb. In order to rescue these samurai families, both central and local governments often took draconian measures (such as debt moratorium, cancellation of debt, regulation of commodity prices, and so forth) against the merchant class, but these measures, which were both unilateral and anachronistic, could not be a long-term solution within this ever-expanding commercial economy.[224] In this situation, sumptuary regulations, which were easy to enforce and had tangible effects, were frequently enacted in the name of stemming the "out-of-bounds" expressions of wealth and social influence that were rampant among commoners. These expressions ranged from violation of clothing regulations and the performance of excessive rituals to the practice of cultural activities that called into question the superior status of the samurai class.[225] In pressing for an austere lifestyle, Tadakuni charged that the "evil customs and manners" of townspeople were contaminating the entire society and despoiling social ethics and values. He therefore prescribed repressing them with full force.

In the world of Confucian social engineering to which both Matsudaira Sadanobu and Mizuno Tadakuni subscribed, the issue of "customs and manners" (*fūzoku*) was key to governance because the control of *fūzoku* amounted to "an educative and regulatory process by which the unruly nature of the people was subjected to state control and brought into harmony with the universe."[226] The term *fūzoku* as it was understood by Confucian ideologues denoted the hierarchical harmony that existed between the ruling and the ruled (which was likened to the harmony of the universe): "*fū*" (wind) denoted the "civilizing influence" of the ruling class, whereas "*zoku*" (vulgarity) indicated "the people's habits," which needed to be exposed to the civilizing wind of the ruling class.[227] With regard to the sociopolitical matrix of *fūzoku*, Sadanobu was a man of conviction: "The people, although without being ordered, follow what the lord cherishes. For this reason, it is called wind (*fū*). When the wind blows, it naturally becomes the learning of the times and comes to shape a habit (*zoku*) of the people. Therefore, one can notice what the lord cherishes or does not cherish just by taking a look at the customs and manners of the country."[228] Following this line of thinking, the wind, which represents the virtue of the ruler, should blow down so that the people, who are prone to vulgar desires and egoistic interests, may be guided. When this hierarchy is reversed or distorted society is destined to plunge into a mess—a mess that is manifested in "evil customs and manners."

Amid this deepening cultural crisis, *bakufu* leaders were pressed to take action. As Ogyū Sorai suggested, customs and manners were both a product and a constituent part of social and political processes. For him, the governance of people should start with rectifying their customs and manners: "The matter of changing extant customs and manners is like redeeming the people of the world—a job of unsurpassable significance."[229] By the same token, Hirose Tansō (1782–1856), a Confucian educator in Bungo, summed up what should be done in order to reinvigorate the failing *bakuhan* system: "The *fūzoku* is the root of the country. The rise and fall of a country is contingent upon the beauty or ugliness of *fūzoku*."[230] Tansō focused on customs and manners, which he perceived to be the foundation of society as well as a channel through which people could nourish their innate moral potential and thus reinforce the *bakuhan* social order.

In trying to restore the health of the social order through establishing good customs and manners, the shogunate turned its eyes toward Edo, a melting pot of "social ills." During the late Tokugawa period Edo was a huge problem for the shogunate. The city seemed to be deviating from rule by class division, a tendency that was reinforced by the constant influx of poor peasants from the Kantō and Tōhoku regions. As statistics attest, the continual absorption of poor rural peasants into Edo's social margins epitomized the serious nature of the problems facing the Tokugawa system. For example, between 1721 and the time of the Tenmei famines in 1786, the population of Shimotsuki decreased from 560,000 to 435,000 (22.3 percent) and that of Hitachi from 710,000 to 515,000 (27.7 percent). The situation in the Mito domain was not much different: it lost approximately 30 percent of its population over a period of four or five decades, beginning in the mid-eighteenth century. The trend of population decrease in Edo's hinterlands continued through to the mid-nineteenth century.[231]

In 1838, before launching the Tenpō reforms, Mizuno Tadakuni sought opinions from the intendants (*daikan*) who administered the shogunal lands on how to "increase the populations of rural areas while decreasing the population of Edo." Tadakuni asked for their views on the question of why so many people were abandoning their home villages and heading for Edo. He received responses from 34 intendants.[232] Teranishi Zōtai of Hita in Bungo suggested: "It is because in Edo, no matter how little talent one has, one can quickly elevate one's low status and raise a fortune. [This kind of story] has spread throughout the whole country so that people think that once they move to Edo, they will be able to secure a living."[233] The intendant of Ōtsu in Kansai, Ishihara Seizaemon, responded: "These days the villagers easily forget their status, mimic the customs of the city, indulge in luxury that is beyond their station in life, and, as a result, fall into poverty. Even village leaders forget what they are supposed to do, and people from poor peasants down to seasonal servants rush to adopt the frivolous lifestyle [of urban centers]. People increasingly forget the differences between root and branch."[234] Intendants in the Tōhoku region all had similar takes on the problem.

Soeda Ichirōji of Shibahashi in Dewa observed that young people, once exposed to the lively environment of Edo and other urban centers, find it very difficult to return to a life of rural privation.[235] "Edo is like a lamp that attracts all kinds of bugs from all directions," and, once attracted, these "bugs" (i.e., migrants) "begin to lose a sense of their social station and pursue desires and dreams that are totally frivolous and meaningless."[236]

When villagers moved to urban centers, and when they abandoned agriculture and adopted a way of life focused on commerce, entertainment, or casual labor, they crossed a boundary—one that defied the class system that buttressed the Tokugawa system. Fluid social margins were a serious threat to the Tokugawa system. What was even more alarming was the fact that the problems of Edo were no longer confined to Edo: they were to be found throughout the country and were affecting peasants, rural villages, the samurai class, and, by extension, the entire social system. Buyō Inshi fumed: "The whole country has become the world of townspeople: in appearance people mimic the townspeople, and in manners they follow the style of townspeople; the courtesy and etiquette that used to be solid have all been lost; all has fallen into decrepitude."[237] For government officials and social critics, Edo embodied the failure of the Tokugawa system: the term "townspeople" became an epithet for social disorder and moral decadence. It is no wonder that the *bakufu*'s social reform efforts were concentrated on the problems of social fluidity and the deteriorating status order in Edo. Order implies restriction and tight boundaries; disorder implies freedom and porous boundaries. The government's concern with the inappropriate practice of death-related rituals came about at a time when the governing system appeared to be being called into question. The stakes were very high.

Until the mid-Hōreki era (1751–63), it was common to see many women in Edo taking part in a funeral procession that consisted of a long line of lacquered palanquins: "They made a flamboyant procession as if boasting of their family status with a cavalcade of 30 or 50 palanquins that proceeded one after another."[238] It must have been quite a spectacle. A few men in ceremonial dress (*kamishimo*, the formal dress tunic and trousers worn over the kimono) usually led such a funeral procession. After the Hōreki era, however, due to a government crackdown, female palanquin riders disappeared from the scene. In their stead a large number of male participants, all in ceremonial dress, made a colorful funeral procession. These men, most of whom were related to the funeral family through membership in the same confraternal organization, were at the center of transforming the funeral procession into an event full of pomp and circumstance—at least until the shogunate suppressed them through the issuance of sumptuary edicts in the Kansei era (1789–1800).[239]

The changing style of funeral processions showed how death rituals partook of larger historical processes, responded to the circumstances of the times, and represented cultural ambitions as well as conflicts. In the above two examples we see two forces working against each other: the townspeople trying to raise themselves up through funerary ceremonies and the government trying to keep them in their place by suppressing "excessive" ritual expression.

As part of the Kansei reforms, the *bakufu* implemented a sumptuary law in 1791 with the purpose of redressing the incongruity between status assigned and status asserted. The edict starts by reminding people that, in the third month of 1668, the shogunate had already stipulated that Buddhist funeral services must be conducted in a modest manner, no matter how wealthy a family might be.[240] It continues:

Is it because a long time has lapsed that people do not heed this stipulation? We hear that many families conduct [funeral ceremonies] in a lavish manner that does not correlate to their status. From now on, at the time of a funeral, only family members and close relatives [of the deceased] will be allowed to wear hemp ceremonial dress. Neighbors and confraternity members are strictly forbidden from attending [the funeral] in great numbers.[241]

The edict concluded that, unless there were special circumstances, no more than four or five people (outside of family members and relatives) could attend a funeral.

In 1821, the shogunate said that many families were continuing to conduct lavish funerals in recent years: "[The shogunate] hereby again hands down the same edict. Keep this without exception. In the case of violation, the ward officials as well as the persons in question will be punished."[242] The fashion for holding extravagant funerals persisted among urban residents, and the government continued to make efforts to stem it (albeit without much success). Two decades later, in 1842, the shogunate repeated the same warning, reminding people that the twice-issued edict of 1791 and 1821 remained in force.[243] The government's ongoing warnings and its reissuing of the same edict only denote that Buddhist funeral ceremonies remained a site of conflict between the state and commoners. What was at stake was how the most important component of the *danka* system — funerary rites — should be conducted in the interest of public order.

Why was the shogunate so bothered? This question might be answered by the story of the Nakai family. A funeral ceremony was conducted in 1787 by the Harimaya Nakai money-exchange merchant family for its third head, Takaaki, who died at the age of 25.[244] This prospering merchant family held an exorbitant funeral for Takaaki at its *danna* temple, Jōkenji, assembling more than 40 monks. The ceremony was officiated by the head monk of Jōkenji, who arrived sitting on a sedan chair carried in a procession. In the ceremony, he was assisted by the head monks of ten different temples, each of whom was escorted by a parasol bearer and followed by a sandal-carrier. In addition, the family hired another five head monks and their assistants as well as thirteen other monks who chanted sūtras during the ceremony as a kind of informal addendum. For this funeral ceremony, the Nakai family spent more than 40 gold pieces; and for a round of posthumous services to be held over the next 49 days, it committed more than 4 gold pieces in advance.[245] Not only did the Nakai family pay for the tens of Buddhist priests but it also paid mourners and the workers who set up an altar, carried the coffin to the crematory temple, and handled sundry other jobs.

After the fifth service, the family sent thank-you presents of glutinous rice steamed with black beans wrapped in bamboo leaves to all mourners, who, for their part, had brought incense monies and other obituary offerings to the ceremony. These mourners, who numbered more than 200, included landlords, ward elders, caretakers of the Nakai family's real estate holdings, merchants and artisans affiliated with the family through business, and its branch-store managers.[246] The Nakai family was never loath to take advantage of the occasion of a funeral to flaunt its wealth and social influence. As old social boundaries lost their vigor, the lavishness of a funeral, which served as an index of the deceased's social status, expressed a family's aspirations for a higher rank.

In contrast, many samurai families watched helplessly as their status crumbled. When they fell into financial difficulties, they found themselves dependent upon the mercy of wealthy townspeople; when they were unable to honor the terms of their loans, they had to give up their last remaining bits of dignity in order to avoid further suffering. The commercial wealth that sparkled so brightly during the spectacle of a merchant's funeral served as a cold and painful reminder of the corrosion of the social hierarchy. The splendor of these funerary rites was an insult to what the Tokugawa system most cherished. It was easy for the regime to condemn these funerals; however, bringing them to an end was another matter. After all, a funeral was hardly a premeditated political conspiracy. In a society that so treasured ethical decorum, harassing a family in mourning — even if in the name of shogunal authority — would have been both mean and risky. Instead of engaging in a direct assault, the shogunate resorted to delivering public edicts aimed at restraining sumptuous extravagance.

Death offered a social space in which the organization of authority was not only conveyed in the body politic but also constructed in the body social through ritual expression and performance. When the shogunate repeated its edict on funerary restraint in 1821, the ward elders of Edo did indeed feel the heat. They held a meeting, discussed the matter, and adopted a seven-point program for self-regulation. First, they decided to organize a surveillance network in which landlords, real estate managers, and five-man associations were collectively accountable to their ward elder. For example, when a day laborer living in a tenement house died, his or her landlord or real estate manager was required to immediately report the death to the deceased's ward elder so that the latter could supervise the upcoming funeral. Second, pointing out that funerals often became too boisterous when confraternities are involved — particularly, the "wooden-fish" (*mokugyokō*) confraternity, whose members beat fish-shaped wooden blocks — the ward elders decided to ban them from involvement in its members' funerals. Third, the ward elders decided to limit the number of monks present at funeral ceremonies to one per *danna* temple. Fourth, such ostentatious practices as setting up tents and holding musical performances at funerary *danna* temples were prohibited. Fifth, the great merchant families and landlords, who often forced the people under their influence (e.g., branch-store employees, suppliers, and tenants) to attend their family funerals, had to pledge, in writing, not to do this. Sixth, labor agents, contract workers, and firefighters (all of whom maintained a strong sense of group solidarity and tended to hold funerals for their members) were also forced to sign written pledges not to force others to attend their family funerals. Seventh, the funeral family was neither to invite too many guests nor to offer them treats (e.g., rice cakes, cookies, and sake). If the issuing of such treats was unavoidable, then the number of guests should be limited to four or five at most.[247]

However, the restraint program of the Edo ward elders was not realistic. For many townspeople who could afford what they desired, a funerary rite offered a chance to vent their frustration with the rigid Tokugawa social system. Sharp-tongued Buyō Inshi could not believe what was happening: "These days a commoner's funeral is extravagant. Everyone related to the family dresses up in ceremonial costume; the coffin is beautifully decorated; sake, food, dumplings, cakes, glutinous rice, and the like are prepared for as many as 2,000 or 3,000 guests who attend the ceremony; and 200 or 300 *tawara* [1 *tawara* = two-fifths of a *koku*] of rice are squandered as honoraria for the monks."[248] To be sure, Buyō Inshi was second to none when it came to excessive social criticism. As far as the trend of commoners' funerals was concerned, he seemed to be truly incensed:

Thus, [temples] choose a wealthy town family over numerous upper samurai *danna* families. They are busy looking after such commoner *danna* with great care, and conferring upon them the highest posthumous Buddhist names, such as *koji*, *daishi*, or *ingō*, treating them like high-ranking samurai officials. For this reason, for example, a samurai family at the rank of 500 or 1,000 *koku* of rice is far less significant than is a wealthy town family. Not surprisingly, the samurai at the rank of 30 or 50 bags [12 or 20 *koku*] of rice are less significant than are the firefighters (*tobi*).[249]

The firefighters belonged near the bottom of the social hierarchy (and were made up mostly of construction workers, low-class laborers, and scoundrels), yet in funerals they seemed to be better off than did some segments of the samurai class. Joining forces with *bakufu* officials and Buddhist critics, Buyō Inshi called for the urgent restoration of rule by status.

Problems with rule by status, however, did not stem solely from the deterioration of conventional social distinctions. There emerged a new challenge posed by new forms of social organization, both business-related and faith-related. With regard to the former, there were head-branch or landlord-tenant networks and labor organizations, while with regard to the latter, there were religious confraternities. All kinds of new social groupings were springing up and rapidly penetrating the lifeworld of commoners, presenting them with a new mode of being that was antithetical to what government officials liked to refer to as "good customs and manners." When the members of these new gemeinschaft-type associations were involved, a funeral could easily be transformed into a social occasion in which they could express their sense of honor and identity, their commitment to group solidarity, and their views of dignity and authority. New social forces were pushing up from the bottom—forces that were expressing themselves in the form of new rituals and behaviors.

To be sure, the organizational principles of Tokugawa society were safeguarded by the political monopoly of the samurai class and were not something that any individual commoner could challenge. But when commoners acted as a group, they came to see that this offered them an outlet for feelings that could not be honored within the Tokugawa system. In a society where ritual was taken very seriously, government officials knew what it meant when thousands of people gathered, of their own initiative, to express themselves through a funeral procession. The problem for the *bakufu* was how to strike at this collective form of "private mourning," which was apolitical and under the protective shield of Buddhism, without provoking too much antagonism.

In 1847, senior councilor Abe Masahiro (1819–57), who was concerned with the diminishing effect of the Tenpō reforms on social customs and sumptuary regulations, alerted the two city magistrates of Edo, Tōyama Kagemoto (Kinshirō, 1793–1855) and Nabeshima Naotaka (in office, 1843–48), of his concerns about the funerary practices of wealthy commoner families in Edo: "On the occasion [of a funeral], not only the ward residents and the person's relatives but also those who are loosely connected to the family (or to its branch stores) hang blinds over the entrance of their houses, saying that it is an expression of mourning for someone who is associated with the family."[250] Abe Masahiro pointed out that when a death occurred to a family of influence, the funeral was arranged by the residents of the ward and that the family's relatives and *danna* temple seemed to play a secondary role. He continued: "In some cases, the ward residents put their children in ceremonial dress and send them to the funeral procession; in return, the funeral family thanks them with glutinous rice, sake, rice cakes, cookies, or the like. When the members of voluntary associations to which the family belongs are added, the funeral ritual is easily elevated to a great spectacle."[251] As can be seen, the collective power of extended social networks and associations was certainly worrisome.

Along with Abe Masahiro's concerns, the two city magistrates conveyed their own views on the problem: "Wealthy [commoner] families own tens of blocks of city land and employ tens of agents in order to manage their real estate. In particular, those who are granted a favor or who have been extended a loan are eager to attend the funeral of the family, saying it is their obligation to repay the favor despite the latter's courteous refusal."[252] City officials figured that the magnitude of funeral attendance was a reflection of the wealth and social influence of the townspeople. The expansion of a commercial economy during the late Tokugawa period resulted in wealth being concentrated within a small group of successful merchants and financiers, and these wealthy families, which were shut out of the political arena, were thirsty for social recognition. The networks of wealth and social influence—stratified according to relationships between landlords and real estate managers, main stores and branch stores, moneylenders and borrowers, employers and employees, and house owners and tenants—were wide, closely knit, and penetrating.[253]

Nevertheless, wealthy townspeople, no matter how influential, could not ignore the watchful eye of the public authorities. In particular, they took extra precautions during periods of reform, often to the extent of conducting a funeral at midnight or just before dawn in order to avoid unnecessary trouble. However, as government officials observed, the problem seemed to be deeper than they had thought: "Even though the family may announce that a funeral will be held at 10:00 A.M. and they actually conduct it as early as at 7:00 A.M., mourners quickly gather around and form a crowd."[254] In an endeavor to tackle the problem, the city magistrates adopted various measures: for example, limiting the maximum number of ritual monks tending the funeral to ten, limiting the size of a tombstone to four *shaku* (approximately four feet), and swiftly investigating and punishing any family that has too many mourners at its funeral.[255] It is not known how effective these measures were in deterring excessive funerals: probably they were not effective at all.

Indeed, ordinary residents, who were organized into religious confraternities, held religious gatherings and demonstrated their group solidarity. In 1842, officials in the magistrate's office of Edo's northern district reported: "Despite repeated injunctions . . . townspeople gather in great numbers at the time of a funeral, saying [that they are members of] Fujikō, *daimokukō*, or *mokugyokō*. Members of the latter raise a clamor as they beat fish-shaped wooden blocks and chant *nenbutsu* with loud voices while walking around."[256] Religious confraternities, which mushroomed throughout the city, were organized under different names but were all similar in purpose: the members would gather on a regular basis to conduct rituals and to chant; they would raise funds for communal purposes; and when something happened to a member, they would deal with it collectively. Especially when it came to a death in a member's family, it was usual for all members to excuse themselves from their daily routines and to take part in the funeral.[257] The occasion of "mourning" offered an opportunity for the confraternity members to reinforce their solidarity.

Furthermore, as officials noticed, some groups that presented themselves as religious confraternities were dubious: "Artisans, day laborers, or petty peddlers form a confraternity, dress up like mountain ascetics, carry priest-like staffs with them, chant together while walking, and stop in front of houses and ask for alms."[258] Although they posed as *yamabushi* and even carried a big Bonten image on their shoulders, their "religious" services were ridiculous: "When they were asked to pray for the sick, they would gather together and burn rice straw, saying that it was *goma* burning [a reference to the Buddhist rite of burning cedar sticks], and chant sūtras in a loud voice.... They walk around the wards in great numbers, slip a piece of cloth into the gate of each house, and then ask for the first crop offering (*hatsuho*)."[259] In the late eighteenth and early nineteenth centuries, those who introduced themselves as Fujikō members were especially notorious for forcing residents to purchase their religious products after a display of incomprehensible sūtra chanting and cedar-stick burning. They were banned in 1775 and 1795, more strictly in 1802, and again in 1847.[260]

From the mid-nineteenth century onward, *mokugyokō* and *nenbutsukō* confraternities caused much trouble through unwanted solicitations. There even appeared street villains, who roamed around, feigned being members of a religious confraternity, and forced donations from residents through coercion and threat. When they thought a donation too small, they often humiliated or harassed the donor.[261] Deeply annoyed, the shogunate issued a decree in 1852 and cracked down on all illegal soliciting. This time the major target was *mokugyokō*, which was now out of control. Whenever religious events (such as *kaichō* or *ennichi* festivals) were held somewhere in the city, the members of *mokugyokō* would gather in great numbers on the streets, carry big fish-shaped wooden blocks that were wrapped in a bed quilt, and make a loud noise by beating gongs and chanting sūtras in the name of welcoming deities.[262] As *bakufu* officials noted (and as was mentioned earlier), the trouble was that a majority of those joining these confraternities were young construction workers, petty artisans, firefighters, peddlers, and street ruffians, all of whom belonged to the lowest rungs of society. It was these people who formed big crowds at funerals, rejoiced in deviating from social rules, and gave vent to their suppressed energy while promoting mutual connections.[263]

An 1852 episode described in the *Fujiokaya nikki* (Diary of Fujiokaya) illustrates how these lower-class inhabitants of the back streets of Edo could transform the occasion of a funeral:

On the same day [the seventeenth day of the third month] a funeral was held for the deceased mother of Kihachi, a tenant firefighter in Hongō. . . . This funeral [procession], led by the members of two subgroups of the *moku-gyokō*, was followed by eight people carrying the coffin, six people bearing palanquins, thirty-six mourners, and all the captains of ten firefighting brigades and their lieutenants, without exception. [The family] prepared *kowa-meshi* [steamed rice with red beans] for 1,200 people.[264]

Twelve hundred mourners for the deceased mother of a firefighter? This does not seem like a credible number. But what is certain is that Edo townspeople, both high and low, were increasingly organized into voluntary social networks or associations. In particular, two groups of people excelled at developing tight self-help networks: firefighters (mostly construction workers) and day laborers and servants, including coolies, seasonal workers, and petty artisans, who were more or less within the sphere of influence of labor agents known as *hitoyado*.

Until 1717, when Edo city magistrate Ōoka Tadasuke (1677–1751) ordered the ward elders to organize a fire brigade (*machihikeshi*) in each of their wards, firefighting had been the corvée duty of all ward residents. With the establishment of more systematic fire brigades, professional firefighters were poised to take over the job. Since firefighting in Edo was mainly a matter of preventing a fire from spreading rather than of trying to extinguish it, what was needed was a professional labor force capable of quickly clearing inflammable houses, buildings, and structures surrounding the fire. Understandably, most of the firefighters were hired from among construction workers, who were good at demolishing buildings and who were also known for being tough and fearless. These construction workers, collectively known as *tobi*, came to dominate Edo's fire brigades, and by 1797 were all organized into thirteen divisions that transcended ward boundaries.[265] The *tobi* members of these fire-fighting divisions were prone to defy traditional values and the status order. Their defiant attitude, steeped in a strong sense of brotherhood and cocky hedonism, was mirrored in their opulent dress and accessories, in their manners and behavior (which was violent and pompous), in their style of speech, and in their lavish gatherings and drinking parties. When they gathered in great numbers for festivals, rituals, funerals, memorial services, or celebratory events, they often exacted financial contributions from merchants and ward residents.[266]

Similarly, labor agents (*hitoyado*)—who procured temporary or seasonal laborers and servants for the daimyo, *hatamoto*, temples and shrines, and the families of well-to-do townspeople—also carved out a cultural space of their own. The demand for skilled laborers, seasonal workers, servants, and other casual labor in Edo was high, as may be seen upon looking at the records for 1840: in this year 35,143 workers found employment through labor agents. These labor agents, whose services were officially sanctioned by the *bakufu* in 1710, maintained self-governing associations: in 1710, there were 13 associations with 370 labor agents; in 1730, there were 11 associations with 202 agents; after that, the number of agents fluctuated, increasing to 245 by 1816, to 482 by 1851, and then decreasing to 412 by 1859, and to 408 by 1864.[267] It is well known that these tough-mannered labor agents, whose resources stretched from rural poor migrants, casual laborers, and street rascals to coolies and vagrants, indulged in a culture that thrived on festivity tinged with outlaw behavior and street violence.[268] When a funeral was held for a fellow member of one of their associations, for example, these people formed a big crowd and demonstrated their solidarity as though they belonged to one big household.

On the whole, Edo society during the late Tokugawa period was losing a force that once bound all classes to a hierarchical order. Defying their given social stations, ordinary people easily assumed the roles of ritualists or healer-magicians simply by changing their clothes into religious robes and carrying exotic ritual paraphernalia. Once they joined a confraternity in which low-class samurai, peasants, merchants, peddlers, and day laborers mingled, people were no longer bound by the principles assigned to their individual social status. This was especially visible when they were engaged in "collective demonstrations" of a religious nature, which were fraught with social tension.[269] As networks became more and more horizontal due to the proliferation of new forms of social organizations, Edo society seemed to be developing a new mode of social existence, possibly even a reverse class structure.

For example, kabuki actors in the seventeenth century were considered a lowly bunch of street entertainers and used to run their shows at the social margins; however, by the nineteenth century, they occupied the central stage of Edo culture. The funeral for the beloved kabuki actor Nakamura Utaemon IV (1796–1852), who died in Osaka in 1852, illustrated their vastly improved status. The *Fujiokaya nikki* describes this funeral in detail. It was held twice: first in Osaka and then in Edo. The Osaka funeral, which was conducted at Jōenji, concluded with a grand procession consisting of 7 head monks, 4 oblong chest carriers, 4 samurai, and some 60 kabuki actors. The coffin was placed on a portable shrine, a spiritual tablet was carried by the deceased's son, 15 or 16 disciples flanked the coffin, and 30 or 40 more disciples followed it.[270]

When the second funeral for Nakamura Utaemon IV was held in Edo, its purpose was neither to bury his body nor to send his spirit to the other world; rather, it acted out the public identity of his life through staging a high-toned funeral procession. The procession started at Saruwakamachi, where the Nakamuraza theater (also known as the Saruwakaza) was located, and then proceeded through the front streets of Asakusa Kannon, finally ending up at Chōenji. The magnitude of this funeral parade went beyond everyone's imagination: 45 dancers, 300 disciples in colorful dress, 20 kabuki actors wearing large straw hats, the bearers of an exorbitantly decorated portable shrine, a tablet carrier, and Nakamuraza managers and workers. Altogether around 400 people took part. The spectacle that swept through Edo's bustling cultural center caused a citywide sensation. It is said that the Nakamura family prepared a huge number of bean jam-filled buns, enough to treat 6,000 mourners at the funeral temple.[271] In the year following the funeral procession, *ukiyoe* paintings were dedicated to the life of Utaemon. These paintings inundated the streets of Edo: "Paintings dedicated to the Buddhist merit of Utaemon, who had died in Osaka, were sold on the streets. Altogether, 63 different printings came out, and when duplicate or facsimile editions were added to these, they numbered 82. It is said that 33 publishing houses were involved."[272] The death of Utaemon demonstrates just how far the funeral of a commoner could transgress the prescribed status order in late Tokugawa society. Commoners who watched these types of spectacles played out in the city streets must have registered the upsurge in the status of such icons of commoner culture.

It was not only urban residents but also peasants who were keen to assert their social status through funerals. Wealthy farmers, in particular, who often served as village elders or officials, utilized funerals as a sort of public platform upon which to create or claim their "esteemed" lineages. A shogunal decree from 1831 describes the phenomenon:

Recently, it is heard that villagers and townspeople, beyond the boundary of their status, conduct grand-scale funerals, erect large tombstones at burial sites, and obtain *kaimyō* [for the deceased] at the ranks *ingō* and *kojigō*.[273] What audacity! From now on, villagers and townspeople, even those of wealth and distinction, may not have funerals conducted by more than ten priests. They must also donate fees and offerings appropriate to their positions, limit the height of a tombstone to four *shaku* (approximately four feet) or less, and should not seek *kaimyō* of the ranks *ingō* and *kojigō*.[274]

Public regulations on how the deceased should be buried were never in short supply, but families often flouted shogunal edicts and conducted elaborate funerals not only to assert status but also to honor their deceased family members in the name of filial piety. As we will see in the next chapter, however, the ways in which families practiced filial piety beyond funerary exercises were not necessarily in rapport with the *bakufu*'s exhortation on this ethical value—one that was also treasured as a tool of social engineering.

CR

TWELVE

Filial Piety, Feudal Ethics,
and Wandering Spirits

As we have seen, Buddhist death rituals did not end with the interment of the deceased. The funeral was only the first step in a series
of ancestral rites that highlighted the issue of filial piety—an issue
that went far beyond the confines of funerary Buddhism. For traditional Confucianists, filial piety was "the root of all virtue and the
source of all teachings." Human values desirable for a good society,
such as goodness, propriety, righteousness, and sincerity, "all lay
in reverent, persistent service to parents and cautious behavior that
avoided bringing shame on them."[275] For *bakufu* officials who held
the Confucian vision of an orderly society, the issue of filial piety
could not be dismissed.

In this context, when a sense of crisis set in beginning in the late
eighteenth century, *bakufu* leaders began to pay a great deal of attention to the ethics of filial piety. Matsudaira Sadanobu, with the coun-
sel of the Confucian ideologue Shibano Ritsuzan (1736–1807), ordered
as part of his Kansei reforms of 1787–93 that government officials and
Confucian scholars should collect and publish stories relating to the
exemplary practice of Confucian virtues.[276] Sadanobu wanted "these
exemplary stories to move people's minds when they read or [were]
taught them so that [the populace in general] could be enlightened."[277] His intention was put into practice with the promulgation

of the *Kankoku kōgiroku* (Official records of filial piety and righteousness), which was published in 1801 and distributed throughout the
country.[278]

The *Kōgiroku* collection contains the stories of 8,614 people whom
central and local governments rewarded with rice or money (or on
rare occasions, with a tax reduction or a grant of land) for their virtuous conduct. This conduct was classified into eleven categories
(though some of them are not clearly distinguishable): filial conduct,
righteousness, loyal filial behavior, female chastity, harmony between siblings, harmony in the household, harmony between relatives, compliance with good customs and manners, purity, benevolent deeds, and diligence in agriculture. The people cited in the
collection are listed in chronological order, stating name, occupation
or social status, age, reasons for receiving the citation, and home
domain or village/ward. The stories took place between the years
1602 and 1798 (although most stories occurred in the late eighteenth
century) and encompassed examples from all provinces except
Hida.[279] Among those cited, the collection focuses on 894 stories and
discusses their virtuous deeds in detail. As the title of the collection
indicates, those deeds pertaining to the category of filial piety were
"taken most seriously" and, therefore, "given preference." Such stories made up more than 60 percent of the collection.[280]

Those who were praised for their filial conduct can be categorized
into four groups: (1) those who, despite difficulties, earnestly conducted memorial services for their ancestors, prayed for the spirits of
their parents, visited their tombs to pay homage, and preserved their
keepsakes; (2) those who, through their own efforts, toiled to maintain their household, to restore it, or to reestablish its livelihood; (3)
those who wholeheartedly nourished their parents, parents-in-law,
and/or family members and took good care of the sick; and (4) those
who devoted themselves to practicing family morality, obeyed their
parents, and kept or fostered harmony in the household.[281] Among
these four, the last two, particularly taking care of old parents, are
the ones most commonly emphasized in traditional Confucian scriptures. But most relevant to this discussion are the stories belonging
to the first two categories—stories that were not necessarily set out
in Confucian terms but rather those related to funerary Buddhism,
the *danka* system, and the ideals of the "household" institution.

The story of a potter living in Amagi post station in Chikuzen,
Kurasaki Kauemon, and his sister, Haru, shows how government

officials understood the virtue of filial piety and how they wanted to see it practiced. The brother and the sister, who had already lost their mother, had to deal with the death of their father, of whom they had been taking good care for some years. For three years after his death, without skipping even a single day, they visited his tomb and made food offerings (such as rice cake, dumplings, and tea) to his tablet at home. In conducting Buddhist memorial services at the first and third anniversary of their father's death, they always did whatever they could to make the memorial services more meritorious. For many years they never ate meat and fish, and before the tablet of their father they always behaved as if he were still alive. As a way of praying for the well-being of his spirit, they wished to transcribe the *Lotus Sūtra* but found that they could not afford to purchase paper for this purpose. A doctor in their neighborhood, who came to know of their pitiable situation, gave them some paper. The brother and the sister asked the former head monk of their *danna* temple to copy the sūtra. Moved by their devotion, he accepted their request and completed copying the sūtra several months later. The merit-making conduct of transcribing a Buddhist sūtra for their deceased father was a culminating moment of their filial piety. The lord Kuroda of Chikuzen, upon hearing their pious story, commended them and awarded them with rice. This occurred in 1631.[282]

The story of Kuno, the wife of a blind merchant from Sakata Sannōdōchō in Akumi county, Dewa, also tells how filial piety was practiced in Tokugawa society. Kuno was always pious toward her mother-in-law. Even after her mother-in-law died of disease in 1760, Kuno continued to devote herself to praying for her spirit. In 1766, when the seventh anniversary of her mother-in-law's death was approaching, Kuno and her husband were saddened because they could not afford a memorial service. In deep despair, Kuno said to her husband, "Not offering memorial services for a deceased parent is not the way of human beings. I will cut my hair, make a wig, and sell it to raise the money [to pay for the memorial service]."[283] Kuno was able to make two wigs with her hair, and she asked her daughter to sell them in the market. She earned 150 copper coins from the sale of these two wigs. Realizing, however, that the money was still not nearly enough to finance a memorial service, Kuno pawned whatever she could find. Eventually, she was able to acquire 260 copper coins—an amount of money that could just pay for a Buddhist service: 200 copper coins were paid to the *danna* temple as a ritual fee, and 60 were spent for a feast after the ritual. At that time she was 28 years old.[284]

A case reported from the Odawara domain in Sagami conveys a similar message with regard to the practice of filial piety. Tōemon, who lived in Itabashi village in Ashigarashimo county, dedicated himself to taking care of his old mother, who had lost all of her teeth. He always prepared soft food for her and tried to provide her with amenities of all kinds, constantly showing her blind obedience. After his mother died, Tōemon always got up early in the morning and, in a loud voice, chanted the title of the *Lotus Sūtra* in order to pray for the well-being of her spirit. In the beginning, his neighbors were annoyed at his unusually loud voice and complained about his chanting. But their complaints eventually gave way to admiration for his unremitting devotion. When he visited his *danna* temple, his chanting became even louder. Attributing the prosperity of his household to the help and protection of his ancestors, Tōemon never stopped practicing meritorious Buddhist rituals. In 1772, the lord Ōkubo granted him a permanent tax exemption on his farmland, which was estimated to yield 5.12 *koku* of rice per year.[285]

In Confucianism, filial piety was treasured not only as a way of keeping families and, by extension, society in harmony, but also as the springboard of all other social virtues (such as sincerity, propriety, compassion, neighborly love, and loyalty).[286] The fact that more than 60 percent of the *Kōgiroku* stories pertained to filial piety indicates the seriousness with which government leaders clung to Confucian morality in their attempt to correct the wayward direction that Tokugawa society seemed to be taking. This meant that social ills were diagnosed and treated in terms of individual ethics rather than in terms of social systems. This new approach matured within the socio-ethical ambit of Neo-Confucian thinking, which stressed the importance of public education.[287] The sweeping reform measures during the Kansei era, which featured a ban on all heterodox teachings, the promotion of Confucian teachings, the suppression of disorderly religious beliefs and practices, and the publication of the *Kōgiroku* for the purposes of public education, were all responses to calls for the "edification of people's minds" (*minshū kyōka*).[288] Emphasis on filial piety was at the center of these reforms.

Interestingly, however, this Confucian virtue of filial piety was promoted within the religious framework of Buddhism—a framework that had been subjected to criticism precisely because of its "anti-family" and "anti-social" orientation. Confucian ideologues, almost without exception, were anti-Buddhist, regarding Buddhism as a heresy that promoted the ideal of "no-self" and labeling Buddhist monks as "vagabonds" living in comfort at the expense of hardworking people. Citing Chu Hsi's admonition that "households should 'never' employ 'Buddhist monks,' offer sacrifices to the Buddha, or make extravagant display at funerals,"[289] Confucian ideologues argued that Buddhist services for the ancestors violated the virtue of filial piety because they misled people with the promise of being reborn in paradise without having to make the effort to engage in serious moral training. Nonetheless, the three stories discussed above illustrate the importance of Buddhist rituals such as memorial services and transcribing or chanting sūtras. These stories, along with many more found in the *Kōgiroku*, offer a point of entry into the ways in which filial piety was praised within the religious framework of the *danka* system. In short, *danna* temples and Buddhist monks came to be arbiters of "Confucian" filial piety.

In addition to the fact that the ritual practice of filial piety was dictated by Buddhism, it should be noted that the ethical exhortation of filial piety was tied up with the well-being of the household institution: "The awards for filiality and the publicity concerning them served the primary purpose of shoring up the *ie* as a key social institution."[290] A late seventeenth-century example that took place in Shirakawa village, Aso county, Higo, illustrates the association between filial piety and the maintenance of household property. Myōki, the daughter of the village elder Shichiemon, had lost her mother at the age of 13 and had been left with her sick father and two younger brothers. She took over the household, which was slipping into trouble. Over many years, with endurance and hard work, she was eventually able to restore economic stability and to reestablish for the household the status associated with a village elder. When her father died at the age of 80, she was already 53 years old and still single. She had fulfilled the duty of filial piety by resuscitating the household, but she had lost her chance to marry. So she tonsured, renounced the world, and became a nun. Myōki was her Buddhist name. Thus Buddhism was the final solace for her perseverance. Recognizing her dedication and sacrifice as a dutiful daughter, the lord Hosokawa rewarded the nun Myōki in 1685, one year after her withdrawal from the secular world.[291]

The late eighteenth-century story of Shōsuke, the son of a poor tenement-house dweller in Kanda Hanabusachō, Edo, also demonstrates how the maintenance of household property was recognized as an act of filial piety. In Shōsuke's neighborhood there lived a lumber merchant, Chōemon, who was ill and who had a young son named Kichijirō and a grown-up daughter. Shōsuke arranged to marry the daughter and inherited the household as a son-in-law, under the new name Hanshichi. Shōsuke proved to be a dutiful son-in-law to Chōemon, a caring brother-in-law to young Kichijirō, a capable manager of the lumber business, and a respected civil servant for the ward. But Chōemon's daughter died seventeen years later, and Shōsuke then arranged to marry the niece of Chōemon's wife. When Kichijirō was old enough to be able to manage the household business, Shōsuke adopted Kichijirō (who was his brother-in-law) as his own son in order to bequeath to him the household. After having bequeathed both the household business and his name to his adopted son, Hanshichi reassumed his previous name Shōsuke, moved to a new residence in Kanda Hanabusachō, and opened a new business (selling bamboo). The parents-in-law, who were moved by the filial piety of Shōsuke (who was now the former husband of their daughter), wanted to divide the household property and give half to him; however, he refused to accept it, saying that the property of the main household should not be depleted. Shōsuke continued to look after his former parents-in-law and his adopted son as before. In 1796, the city magistrate of Edo commended his exemplary filial piety and rewarded him with silver.[292]

In Tokugawa society, Shōsuke's life exemplified the Confucian virtue of filial piety. However, if the events of his life had occurred in traditional China or Korea, Shōsuke would have been regarded as being outlandish in at least two respects: (1) in the continental Confucian world, filial piety was a virtue whose primary focus was the relationship between parents and children, not the relationship between parents and their children-in-law; and (2) the action of adopting a brother-in-law as a son-in-law would have been a grave violation of Confucian ethics, which was founded on the notion of genealogical hierarchy (it was absolutely unimaginable to adopt a brother as a son). Far from being considered a proponent of filial piety, Shōsuke would have been condemned and probably removed from society. However, in Tokugawa Japan, Shōsuke's conduct was seen as reinforcing the proper management of the household institution and was, therefore, considered to be virtuous. The *Kōgiroku* includes many stories that feature good household management, and all of them serve as examples of filial piety. The message that *bakufu* leaders wanted to put out was unequivocal: a household in trouble could, and should, be restored through individual effort.

In fact, after the publication of the *Kōgiroku*, *bakufu* leaders continued to further sift through the local examples of "filial piety and righteousness," distilled and adapted those that were deemed useful, and foisted these virtues upon the people as a way of keeping their household institutions in order during difficult times. In 1807 and again in 1810, the *bakufu* ordered the nation's administrators to collect stories about individuals who had been known for their filial piety and righteousness. The stories so collected, though not immediately printed, were later (in 1848) compiled by Hayashi scholars into 100 fascicles.[293] Similarly, the *Gofunai bikō* (Reference notes on the inner districts [of Edo]), published in 1829, contains 135 examples of Edo residents who were cited for their virtuous conduct between 1757 and 1828. Even though most of these had already been cited, this repetition testifies to the importance government officials placed on the relationship between Confucian morality and social engineering.[294] In 1843, while wrapping up the Tenpō reforms (which focused on Edo's problems), the office of the city magistrate again circulated a similar publication, this one entitled *Chūkōshi* (A chronicle of loyalty and filial piety), in order to disseminate examples of proper filial conduct. The protagonists in these stories were portrayed as role models who held the solution to the predicaments faced by Edo society.[295]

Among the 261 Edo stories introduced in these three new collections, 162 (approximately 62 percent) feature people who, in spite of difficult circumstances, excel at filial piety. The primary focus of the government was on enduring, sacrificing, and working hard to venerate deceased parents; caring for parents or parents-in-law; and restoring the economic foundation of the household. The idiosyncratic character of Tokugawa filial piety is clearly represented by the life story of Katsu, a former maid for a samurai family, who was awarded five pieces of silver by the city magistrate during the height of the Tenpō reforms. Katsu married Tashichi, the adopted son of Heiroku from Hakozakichō, and later gave birth to a son. But Tashichi was no good: he casually stole clothes from the family and pawned them for cash, and he frequently caused all kinds of trouble.

Irritated, Heiroku disowned him and adopted Katsu as his daughter, then marrying her to his newly adopted son, Ihei. But Ihei's family life did not last long as, for some unknown reason, Heiroku soon disowned him. Heiroku then adopted another man, Tadasuke, and married Katsu to him. Like those before him, Katsu's third husband could not survive Heiroku's whims, and he was soon disowned and ousted from the family. Katsu, who did not remarry, took good care of Heiroku until he died. Even after her stepfather's death, Katsu visited his grave at least three times a month, and whenever a Buddhist priest was preaching in the neighborhood, she always carried her stepmother to this event.[296] Katsu's marriages were chosen not by her but by her stepfather, but she never complained and remained devoted to him even after his death. This was the type of filial piety that the Tokugawa shogunate was eager to propagate.

The emphasis on individual ethics during the "filial piety and righteousness" campaign served to suppress a discussion of structural problems, and this opened up opportunities to Buddhist monks who were thirsty for loyal followers. Echoing shogunal propaganda, they produced a series of publications known as "biographies of those reborn in the Pure Land" (*ōjōden*), in which they trumpeted the "filial piety" of their patrons and linked it to Buddhist rituals. Understandably, Pure Land Buddhists were most active in compiling this didactic literature, but their readership was not necessarily confined to Pure Land followers. *Ōjōden* had an aura of factuality despite many of them being fictitious. These stories, which highlighted the positive karmic effects of *nenbutsu* chanting and practicing a virtuous life, conveyed a message that was not so different from that being delivered by campaigners of "filial piety and righteousness." Public authorities never discouraged Buddhists from publishing, circulating, or preaching these parables, which encouraged "obedience and submissiveness in expectation of deferred rewards in Paradise."[297] These *ōjōden* stressed not only obedience and submissiveness but also working hard (especially in agriculture) and chanting *nenbutsu* from morning until night whenever possible.[298]

The *ōjōden*, which were published under various titles and in hundreds of editions, typically put forth two types of morals: a religious one, which espoused the merit of the Buddhist practice of *nenbutsu*, and a secular one, which espoused the virtue of ethical conduct in daily life.[299] For example, the *Kinsei ōjōden* (Biographies of rebirth in the Pure Land in recent times) introduced the life stories of 46 people

(2 more were later added by the publisher) who were believed to have achieved rebirth in the Pure Land. Its editor, Myōshun, stated that he had wanted to "rejuvenate the mind of the public." Kōken, the publisher of the volume, was deeply moved by Myōshun's loyal spirit: "By spreading this book widely to all people, we are trying to connect them [to the compassion of Amida Buddha] through *nenbutsu* so that they may be reborn in the Pure Land. [If we could do this, then] that would enable us to honor both the lord and the Buddha."[300] What should the mind of the public be filled with? To Myōshun and Kōken, the answer was honesty, harmony, compassion, selflessness, filial piety, diligence, and hard work.[301]

To be sure, Pure Land monks were not engaged in promoting ethical conduct for the sake of the Tokugawa regime; rather, their concern was to promote edifying tales of ideal lay Buddhists that could serve as models to their *danna* patrons. Consider, for example, the main theme of *Nikka nenbutsu tōshukuhen* (An edition of lodging in daily *nenbutsu*), compiled in 1800 by Butsujō (1734–1800), the head monk of Sennenji in Kyoto. On the surface, many of its stories highlight a range of exemplary feudal ethics. Each of the four classes (samurai, farmers, artisans, and merchants) was expected to live according to its assigned station in society: a samurai should show filial piety to his parents and lord, and never forget the favor his ancestors have bestowed; a farmer should get up early and work hard until late evening; an artisan should train his posterity through education; and a merchant should care for his employees with compassion.[302] When emphasizing the virtues of filial piety, loyalty, sincerity, and so on, Butsujō is never ambiguous: the same ethical virtues should be applied to the relationship between Buddhist patrons and their *danna* temples. Thus, within the context of *nenbutsu* Buddhism, these "Buddhist" virtues, which were propagated by *ōjōden* but had little to do with conventional Buddhist teachings, were seamlessly incorporated into "the morality that political power and society demanded."[303]

How should one practice Buddhist virtue in the secular world? The answer is given in the *Kinsei awaumi nenbutsu ōjōden* (Biographies of rebirth in the Pure Land by freshwater sea *nenbutsu* in recent times), compiled in 1822 by Butsujō's disciple Ryūen (1759–1834). The story of Nishikawa Tokuzō, a faithful Buddhist in Hachiman-shinmachi, Ōmi, presents him as a picture of virtue: "[He] was frugal and simple, not self-oriented at all, not sumptuous, but modest and sincere, and very warm-hearted. He worshipped the three treasures of Buddhism [i.e., the Buddha, the dharma, and the *sangha*], always chanted *nen-butsu* out of deep faith, disciplined his mind as far as he could, strictly observed the schedule of monthly memorial rites for his ancestors, and never stayed away from the seat of the Buddha on the days of affinity [*ennichi*]."[304] The diligent practice of Buddhist memorial services and funerary rites — the merits that enabled Tokuzō to be reborn in the Pure Land — was what was expected of good citizens.

Similarly, the six-fascicle *Myōkōninden* that contained biographies of exemplary faithfuls of Jōdoshinshū also shows how the ideals of feudal ethics were woven into Buddhist didacticism. Stories of these admired believers and practitioners of *nenbutsu* (*myōkōnin*), which were compiled and published between 1842 and 1858 by three Honganji monks, illustrate why one should show gratitude to the Buddha, Shinran, one's lord (shogun and daimyo), and one's parents.[305] In particular, these stories invariably stressed the virtues of obedience and public responsibility as ways of repaying the favors one has received from the state and Tōshōgū (Tokugawa Ieyasu): "One must respect the orders of the lord and land stewards, fulfill the details of annual tax obligation, and keep all edicts and regulations."[306] Whether one was happy in this world or not, these stories constantly reiterate that one would surely be able to attain the rank of *myōkōnin* (the highest honor in Jōdoshinshū) if one kept one's faith in the Amida Buddha, fulfilled one's filial duty to one's parents, and practiced loyalty to one's lord.[307]

In fact, the overall religious orientation of Jōdoshinshū since the eighteenth century had moved away from being "above the secular world" to becoming increasingly conciliatory toward secular power. For example, the neighborhood confraternities in the Aki region, known as *koyorikō*, would invite a monk once a month and hold a gathering to hear his sermon. However, such a gathering was usually more than a religious occasion: the confraternity members discussed how to fulfill the government's wishes, learned the "instructions and directions" issued by public authorities, and encouraged each other to lead an ethical life.[308] Secular ethics, preached and studied repeatedly, were an integral part of the religious lives of Jōdoshinshū *monto*. Of these ethical imperatives, filial piety was the most important because it was believed that "practicing filial piety and nourishing parents is grounded in the bondage of filiation formed before one decides his or her [Buddhist] faith."[309] Instead of promoting Buddhist precepts, which were different for different sects, Jōdoshinshū preachers began to assert that lay followers should embrace the virtues of impartiality, righteousness, and the "Five Relationships" (*gorin*). All of these virtues were taught within a Confucian framework. To be sure, there were still some religious elements that distinguished the Jōdoshinshū faithful from other Buddhist sectarians, but the overall trend was to cherish ethical behavior and self-responsibility, and this resonated with the feudal ethics of the Tokugawa system.[310]

The emphasis of Jōdoshinshū on secular ethics was strongly pronounced in the letters (*shōsoku*) that the head (*hossu*) of each subsect delivered to its entire congregation, as well as in the "rules to keep in mind" (*kokoroe*), which many *danna* temples imposed upon their *monto*. For example, the temple Jōrenji in Yoshida village, Yoshiki county, Hida, forced its approximately 300 patron families, which were scattered over fifteen different villages, to sign a pledge in 1831 detailing the obligations of its *monto*—obligations spelled out under the warning that Kirishitan had just been arrested in Kyoto and were under investigation. The items in the pledge, which carried the authority of fearsome shogunal names such as Tōshō Gongen (Ieyasu) and Gen'yūin (Ietsuna), were all too familiar: keep the law of public authority and the ban on gambling; visit the *danna* temple on the occasions of hōonkō (the death anniversary of Shinran), New Year, Higan, and Bon; observe all rites for deceased parents and ancestors; pay attention to all announcements coming from the *danna* temple and visit it in person when there is a need to consult; practice frugality on all occasions except when showing gratitude to the temple; and keep the family in harmony and work hard for the household.[311] The content of the pledge was not much different from what the government had stressed all along. Within this environment, the Jōdoshinshū *monto* emerged as exemplary agents of feudal ethics. The family precepts (*kakun*) of some Jōdoshinshū patrons, which featured hard-work, ancestral veneration, and frugality, conveyed the spirit of a time when secular and religious interests were being merged into one.[312]

The populace was being exhorted from all sides. And when these exhortations were related to the *danka* system, people knew exactly what they implied. Given that, from 1687 on, each domain maintained a special register of Kirishitan descendants, people could easily be haunted by the specter of Christianity. Under shogunal law, Kirishitan descendants, even if they had nothing whatsoever to do with Christianity, were subjected to prolonged and painful surveillance.[313] The familiar saying "even a drop of Kirishitan blood will turn one's blood from red to black" was a harsh reality. The system of registering Kirishitan descendants led the populace to believe that once their family line had been contaminated by Christianity, they would need an unimaginably long period of time to purify their blood from its taint. Purification was possible only through the unfailing performance of Buddhist rituals and the fulfillment of one's *danna* obligations.[314]

Still, we should not assume that the populace blindly complied with the Tokugawa regime's ethical exhortations. Changing socioeconomic realities helped people to realize the structural problems inherent within the Tokugawa system. Moral impositions from without, designed to reinforce the status-bound feudal order, did not seem to make much sense when it came to economic issues. Instead of being swayed unilaterally, commoners tried to find their own way of comprehending and overcoming their daily realities, as was seen in their efforts to survive within a moral framework that made sense to them.[315] This trend was especially evident in Edo and Kantō, where the magnitude of commercial enterprises gave the lie to the trickle-down economics espoused by government officials. More and more, the economy was moving forward according to its own logic, defying the feudal principles of Confucian fatalism that, for example, defined economic well-being as predetermined by the will of Heaven. For Edo townspeople, this was not the case. They figured that anything wrong with their "given" economic position had more to do with the social structure around them than with individual ethical failures. In contrast, *bakufu* leaders and Confucian thinkers continued to insist that social stability, based on the karma inherent within an immutable, class-based moral hierarchy, could be achieved and secured only when each social class dutifully carried out its own designated assignments. Who should be blamed for the crumbling of the households of the urban poor? *Bakufu* leaders maintained that this problem was the fault of household family members. People needed to change their bad habits, work harder, and endure more; in other words, they had to practice ethical virtues at the individual level.[316] To be sure, the *Kōgiroku* and other similar publications were widely circulated and read, but their logic ran counter to how commoners were now perceiving society and their position within it.

In the rural areas, too, the frequent occurrence of *ikki* uprisings in the effort to gain tax relief strengthened a tendency on the part of peasants to make direct and collective efforts to remedy socio-economic ills.[317] As far as the peasants were concerned, the hardships and troubles they faced were more than what the government's ethical prescriptions could possibly solve. For them, it was ridiculous that the problems for which they were held accountable (e.g., poverty, desertion, social disorder, and the deterioration of village communal spirit) could be so easily attributed to a lack of Confucian (or Buddhist) ethical virtues, or to their feeble-mindedness or laziness, or to their indulgence in luxury and leisure. These phenomena were what Buyō Inshi referred to as "evil things," and he characterized them as being "townspeople-like, merchant-like";[318] however, this labeling was preposterous. The peasants believed that the real problem was to be found in excessive taxation. Indeed, the county intendant Teranishi Zōtai of Hita pinpointed this in his report to the *bakufu* at the time of the Tenpō reforms. In suggesting measures for preventing peasants from deserting their villages and migrating to Edo—and thereby restoring agricultural communities in the Kantō and Tōhoku regions—Teranishi Zōtai was straightforward: "There is no other way but to reduce annual land taxes."[319] As far as he was concerned, rural privation had already become a problem that could no longer be covered up with edifying ethical discourses. The villagers were not persuaded by the government's cure-all prescriptions of "filial piety and righteousness."

The tendency for the peasant class to rebuff ethical exhortations ran parallel with their growing sense that their relationship with their tax-collecting lord should be reciprocal. In his article on rebellion and peasant consciousness in Tokugawa Japan, Irwin Scheiner quotes a petition from a group of peasants in Aizu domain who staged an uprising in 1720: "We wish to ever serve as 'honorable peasants' (*onbyakushō*) and we petition with reverence so that we may pay taxes (*omononari*). If we are aided by your mercy, we the lower, will respectfully and thankfully accept your aid."[320] The peasants held that since they, as *onbyakushō*, were willing to pay taxes, the lord should, in his turn, provide them with aid. Here, the peasants' self-styled identity as "honorable peasants" reflected their perceptions of themselves as tax-paying, "honorable" people. In their view, tax payment should not be a one-way street; rather, it should be balanced by "aid" (*osukui*), a term that refers to the government's responsibility to care for them during times of hardship. They envisioned a government that emphasized benevolence. Traditionally, *osukui* included the distribution of money or grain, the operation of soup kitchens, the lending of rice or money at low rates, and tax reduction or exemption. Among these measures, what the peasants were most concerned with was low taxation, which was regarded as the cornerstone of "benevolent rule" (*jinsei*). The sense of reciprocity that led to the Aizu rebellion was based on the understanding that, as long as tax obligations were fulfilled, the "honorable peasants" were entitled to "benevolent rule."[321] The payment of taxes within a framework of benevolent rule gave rise to what Scheiner terms a "covenant paradigm," and this was supposed to be the ruling paradigm of the Tokugawa system.[322] Within this framework, the peasant class expected their lord to perform in the manner set out by Kumazawa Banzan in the late seventeenth century: "The lord of a domain has a heavenly mandate to be the parent of the people of the domain, and the lord of the realm has the heavenly mandate to be the parent of the people of the realm."[323]

Too often, however, reality betrayed expectations. When famines caused by the volcanic eruption of Mount Asama and cold rain hit the Kantō and Tōhoku regions in 1782–84 and devastated many villages, the shogunate quickly moved to implement measures for restoring them. However, these measures actually turned out to involve increasing the tax base as well as tightening government control of these regions. These measures (which included strict application of taxation, reclamation of waste land as a source of taxation, conversion of newly developed tax-exempt lands into taxable lands, the streamlining of the tax collecting agency, containment of tax-paying villagers, and the imposition of sumptuary regulations) were integrated into the core programs of the Kansei reforms. The thrust of this tax policy, which was pushed in the name of restoring agricultural villages, remained in force until the end of the Tokugawa period.[324] Mizuno Tadakuni, who commanded the Tenpō reforms for the purpose of dealing with the devastation brought on by the famines in the 1830s, was both ambitious and insistent. In 1843, he launched a sweeping tax policy known as the shogunal land reforms (*goryōsho kaikaku*), directed at agricultural villages that were already reeling. His aim, however, was to increase taxes to their past levels. In order to do this, Tadakuni ignored the skepticism of some officials and ordered the shogunal deputies to implement rigorous eleven-point tax-collecting measures and to strictly enforce Confucian ethical standards.[325] Did the ruling class really believe that impoverished villages could be restored by increased tax collection? It seemed that the covenant between the ruling and the ruled, even if there had ever been one, was utterly lost.

In this situation, the villagers, who fulfilled their tax-payment obligations and other duties and, in return, expected benevolent rule, felt that their collective actions (including the *ikki* uprisings) against the excessive demands of a new tax policy were not without ethical justification. Though it cost many lives, the increase in collective actions during the late Tokugawa period further encouraged the peasants to try to expand their own self-reliance and independence through "the ethical effort of industry, thrift, familial harmony, and the like."[326] Given this, it would be ludicrous to construe people's practice of filial piety and ancestral veneration as a matter of their intent to strengthen the Confucian social order of the Tokugawa system; rather, they practiced these things in order to achieve autonomy, dignity, self-reliance, and, above all, the survival of their households.

Conflict between households and the state over social order was not confined to the realm of family members and ancestral deities: it extended to the realm of spiritual beings who were without descendants or households: namely, the wandering ghosts (*muenbotoke*) who did not have familial caretakers and who therefore were outside the *danka* system. On the occasion of Bon *matsuri*, individual households were involved in pacifying wandering ghosts by making the *segaki* food offering. For its part, the government was more systematic in dealing with the wrath of wandering ghosts. For example, whenever large-scale disasters occurred, the government funded a select group of Buddhist temples to conduct grand *segaki* rituals in the name of protecting the nation and the people. It is interesting to see how spiritual beings who were believed to roam outside the *danka* system were understood and dealt with.

Let us take the example of the 1657 Meireki Fire, which brought destruction to large sections of Edo (including most of the shogunal castle's buildings, some 500 daimyo mansions, 779 *hatamoto* residences, 350 temples and shrines, and more than 400 blocks of commoner neighborhoods) and killed over 100,000 people, perhaps one of every five city residents.[327] Immediately after this unspeakable catastrophe, the shogunate buried the victims of the blaze at a place in the Motomachi area of Honjo, erected a "connectionless" (*muen*) stupa, and ordered Jun'yo, the head monk of Zōjōji, to perform a seven-day ritual (which involved chanting 1,000 sūtras) in order to

appease these unfortunate souls. For this ritual, the shogunate provided Jun'yo with 300 gold pieces. After the ritual, Jun'yo erected a
temple at the same place and named it Muenji, "a temple of no affiliation"; later, this temple was renamed Ekōin, "a Buddhist hall for
the transference of merit." From that time forward, Ekōin served as
a temple where *segaki* rituals were held for the spirits who had no
caring descendants, including the spirits of criminals who died in
prison or who had been executed.[328] The increasing number of transients in Edo posed endless challenges to the shogunate, one of them
being the ceaseless production of nameless deaths.

The shogunate was systematic in dealing with the deaths of the
homeless—deaths that could not be contained within the *danka* system. In 1685, the city magistrate instructed the ward elders on how
to deal with "people [found] dead on the street" (*yukidaore*). When
someone died on the street and his or her family could not be identified, the responsible ward elder had to adhere to procedure: immediately report the matter to the city magistrate's office, inspect the
corpse and send it to the Ekōin's branch temple (Jōgyōan in Kotsukappara) for cremation, and then forward the death report to Ekōin
for a *segaki* ritual.[329] Now charged with the task of taking care of
all the homeless deaths in Edo, Ekōin performed a grand collective
segaki ritual on the seventh day of the seventh month in order to
placate the unhappy spirits and erected stupas to pray for their well-
being in the other world.[330] Upon shogunal request, Ekōin also offered its ritual services to those who had met unnatural deaths in the
Kantō area. For example, in 1791, when many residents in the Susaki
and Gyōtoku seashore areas of southern Fukagawa were swept
away by a tsunami, the shogunate asked Ekōin monks to pay a
round of visits to the affected villages and to appease the spirits of
the victims. Through special arrangements, Ekōin monks held *segaki*
rituals at Eitaiji in Fukagawa for the Susaki victims, at Tokuganji in
Gyōtoku for the Ibaragi village victims, and at various local temples
in Tachibana county in Musashi for the victims in that area.[331]

By extending its religious care to the unfortunate souls who were
cut off from the institution of the household, the shogunate was
demonstrating its control over both this-worldly and other-worldly
order. Indeed, it asserted its authority over all beings in the realm
and tried to set itself up as the ultimate arbiter of their destinies. As
was seen in its frequent issuance of orders to major temples around
the country regarding the performance of *segaki* rituals, the sho-

gunate was careful to ensure that the nation's religious institutions got rid of the misfortune inflicted by grudging spirits, thus restoring peace, safety, and prosperity.[332] The *danka* system was supposed to deal with the world of spirits, but its parameters were rather limited. It was not structured to deal with those spiritual beings who had no descendants to whom to turn for religious care. It was the shogunate that, through its manipulation of religious institutions, took care of this situation. As far as *bakufu* leaders were concerned, all beings, including ghosts and underground creatures, were subject to their assigned space; wandering spirits, unappeased, malignant, and prone to vengeance, should not be left unchecked. These creatures lived in a gloomy world of disorder and destruction, and if not contained, could adversely affect the social order.

That is why public authorities were uneasy with a new trend that was emerging in the mid-eighteenth century: commoners, particularly townspeople, were beginning to celebrate the notion of the existence of vengeful spirits. In Edo, theatrical presentations of ghost stories captured the imagination of ordinary people by offering an alternative worldview to that propagated by the Tokugawa system. Through acts of vengeance and betrayal, all of which were played out in the "billingsgate theater" (*akutai shibai*), heroes and heroines in the form of vengeful spirits ridiculed the social establishment and ethics of the ruling class, twisted and reversed allegedly immutable social realities, and ushered the viewers into a world of alternatives. Wandering ghosts were similarly depicted in popular prose and *ukiyoe* prints: they focused their anger on the order of things, incited fear and turmoil, and engaged in back-street fighting and terrorism.[333] These artistic genres enabled the citizenry to question assumed social realities and provided their audiences with a sense of uplift, comfort, and catharsis. Those who were fascinated with these creatures (all of whom were antithetical to the social givens of the day) were freed, at least in spirit, from the binary structure of ruled and ruler. They could now slake their thirst for an upside-down society. Indeed, it is within this world of fantasy, which was filled with newly fashioned creatures, that Edoites were awakened to their plight.

Oiwa, the protagonist in the form of a vengeful spirit in the *Tōkaidō Yotsuya kaidan* (Tōkaidō Yotsuya ghost stories), written by Tsuruya Nanboku (1755–1829) as a kabuki script in 1825, illustrates how images of vengeful spirits were newly constructed during the late Tokugawa period. It is known that Tsuruya Nanboku created the character of

Oiwa based on the old ghost story of Kasane, a well-known vengeful female spirit from the seventeenth century.[334] The original story of Kasane can be summarized as follows.[335] In Hanyū village, Okada county, Shimōsa there lived an ugly girl named Kasane, who was expected to inherit land from her father. In 1647, a villager named Yoemon hatched a scheme to rob Kasane of her land: he married her, drowned her in the Kinu River, and took possession of her land. Yoemon then took a new wife, but she was soon driven to death by Kasane's vengeful spirit. Undeterred, Yoemon took wives one after another, but all of them were driven to death by Kasane's vengeful spirit. However, Yoemon's seventh wife survived and gave birth to a daughter, Kiku. However, when Kiku turned thirteen, her mother also succumbed to Kasane's vengeful spirit. Yoemon adopted a young villager, Kingorō, as the future husband of Kiku. After this arrangement, Kiku, who suddenly fainted, professed that she was actually the incarnation of Kasane. She tried to kill her father but to no avail. Upon hearing of this, Yūten Shōnin, a famed Pure Land Buddhist monk, successfully pacified Kasane's grudging spirit through prayer. But this did not last for long.[336] Kiku was possessed by another spirit, and Yūten Shōnin pressed her to reveal her real identity. She finally disclosed that she was actually a reincarnation of the spirit of Suke, a five- or six-year-old boy. Upon hearing this, an old villager recalled that Suke had been the son of a woman who had come to marry Kasane's father-to-be, whose name was Yoemon—the same name as that of Kasane's husband-cum-murderer. According to the old villager, Kasane's father-to-be, Yoemon, hated the boy (now his stepson) so much that the boy's mother was driven to kill him in order to please her new husband. The year after the murder of the boy, a disfigured daughter, later named Kasane, was born as the offspring of Yoemon and the dead boy's mother. Thus Suke, once murdered, was reborn as Kasane, and Kasane, who was also murdered, was reborn as Kiku. Yūten Shōnin appeased the spirit of Suke—the spirit who had originally possessed Kasane.

Oiwa, who appears in Nanboku's *Tōkaidō Yotsuya kaidan*, has a destiny quite unlike Kasane's.[337] Oiwa's husband, a handsome masterless samurai named Tamiya Iemon, kills Yotsuya Samon, Oiwa's father. Oiwa chooses her husband over her father and gives birth to Iemon's child. But Iemon soon betrays Oiwa and falls in love with Oume, the daughter of his rich neighbor. Oiwa is then poisoned by Oume's father, who wants to destroy her and then marry his daughter to

Iemon. As a result of the poison, Oiwa's face becomes horribly dis-figured. Iemon returns home and sees the terrifying appearance of his wife. He turns cold toward her and treats her harshly, hoping that she will leave him voluntarily. Iemon's faithful servant Kohei begs him for medicine for Oiwa. Angered by this, Iemon ties Kohei up, locks him in a cupboard, and leaves the house. Oiwa, who can no longer stand the torment, kills herself with a sword. When Iemon comes back, he discovers Oiwa's body. Realizing that Kohei is the only witness to all these happenings, Iemon kills him. He then ties the two corpses to either side of a wooden door (*toita*) and hires a gang of ruffians to throw the door into a nearby river.

The house is then set for the wedding of Iemon and Oume. The new bride arrives in full dress, but when Iemon lifts her head cover-ing, he sees Oiwa's deformed face. Panicked, he pulls out his sword and slashes Oiwa's head: when it drops to the floor, it turns out to be that of his new bride. Totally unnerved, he rushes out and en-counters Kohei. He beheads the man on the spot, only to find that he has actually killed Oume's father. In despair, Iemon wanders along the riverbank like a man who has lost his mind. There he sees something rising from the river. It is Oiwa, attached to the wooden door, and she calls him in her ghostly voice. Frightened, Iemon tries to sink the wooden plank in the water, but the other side of it rises to the surface. Then it is Kohei who cries beseechingly: "Master, medi-cine!" — the exact words he had uttered when begging help for Oiwa. Iemon, in despair and confusion, throws himself into the river. The story of Oiwa, which was first staged at the Nakamuraza in 1825, was a huge success. Since then the *Tōkaidō Yotsuya kaidan* has became one of the most famous kabuki performances and has remained a source of inspiration for many great *ukiyoe* artists, TV dramas, films, and modern stage productions.[338]

In creating new images of vengeful spirits based on the story of Kasane, Tsuruya Nanboku replaced an ugly Kasane with a beautiful Oiwa. For Nanboku, the story of Kasane was unfathomable: Kasane is in agony from the beginning and is forced to suffer one life after another without reason or release. Suke, who was killed by his step-father Yoemon, was reborn as his murderer's daughter-cum-stepsister Kasane; Kasane married a villager, also named Yoemon, who killed her; yet the murdered Kasane was destined to be reborn as the daughter of her murderer husband Yoemon. Before being murdered, the persons reincarnated through the same spirit of

Kasane (literally, "overlapping" – a nounal derivative from the verb *"kasaneru"* [to overlap]) were always faithful and obedient – as son (Suke), as wife (Kasane), and as daughter (Kiku). For some unknown reason, the spirit involved in these "overlapping" reincarnations never took revenge on Yoemon; rather, five innocent women were inexplicably victimized. Worse yet, by driving these innocent women to death, Kasane in fact ended up helping her husband take new wives, creating ever more innocent victims. For Nanboku, all of this, which was presented as a "working out of retribution," was irrational, incomprehensible, and outrageous. This was not how vengeful spirits should behave. So he changed all this. He injected rationality and justice into the stories of vengeful spirits through presenting the life story of Oiwa. Oiwa's vendetta was solely directed at her culpable husband, Iemon, and his accomplice – never at anyone else.[339]

Kabuki audiences held their collective breath when they followed Oiwa's dramatic, yet tragic, transformations, from a girl who chose her lover over her father, to a wife betrayed and deformed, to a woman driven to suicide, and to a vengeful spirit. They were then thrilled by the vengeance wreaked upon Iemon. Compared to Oiwa, Kasane was subservient and helpless, even conspiring to ensure her own cruel fate. Kasane was a fitting symbol of feudal society, where women – and, by extension, the ruled – were forced to accept their destiny as the state presented it to them. Kasane was the image of women who choose to remain victims, "faithful and blind" to the endlessness of their own suffering as their personal catastrophes "pile up" (*kasanaru*) one after another.[340] In creating new images of vengeful spirits, Nanboku rejected this image. Victims had their vengeance, and members of the audience were relieved to see the feudal values imposed upon the weak subjected to the anger of wandering spirits. They began to realize that there were alternatives to the way things were presented by the Tokugawa authorities. It is no wonder that Oiwa, whose spirit was pacified at Myōgyōji, was soon deified as Oiwa Inari and enshrined in Yotsuya, where it received much veneration from the populace.[341]

The anti-feudal strain unveiled in the world of wandering spirits gained wide popularity as social unrest continued to grow. Outside the framework of funerary Buddhism and the *danka* system, these newly bred spirits satiated the thirst of a populace who had for too long been subjected to feudal regulations. The Tokugawa system demanded the ruled accept their apportioned "karma" and "retribution"—just as Kasane did—no matter how inscrutable, inexplicable, or unjust. For *bakufu* leaders, this new appreciation of wandering ghosts was an alarming sign. How were they to rein in people's sentiments and emotions, their desire for another way of being? The Tokugawa regime could not tolerate Oiwa. From the late eighteenth century onward, under the rubric of Sadanobu's "ban on heterodoxy" (*igaku no kin*), the government began to increase its censorship of popular culture and push for a return to Confucian orthodoxy. However, this only increased people's yearning for fresh air. The world of wandering spirits, which was supposed to be contained within the framework of the *danka* system, catapulted the populace into a new way of seeing.

Conclusion

The *danka* system, which oversaw funerary rituals and ancestral rites, required that there be a spirit of cooperation between *danna* households and funerary temples. However, when conflicts occurred— whether due to excessive demands and/or poor service on the part of funerary temples, or a failure to meet financial obligations and/ or to cooperate on the part of *danna* households—both sides had ways of reaching a settlement: funerary temples exercised the right of anti-Christian certification or refused to provide ritual services, while *danna* households resorted to petitions, collective action against the incumbent head monk, a refusal to pay fees, or the instigation of lawsuits. Avenues for addressing the conflicts between funerary temples and *danna* households were various, but all occurred within the overall framework of the *danka* system. To be sure, the administrative clout of anti-Christianity, which empowered funerary temples, often overwhelmed *danna* patrons; however, when the latter were united in undertaking a particular action, the former had to take heed.

It should be noted, however, that whatever happened, power relations merged within the *danka* system with the logic of differential posthumous salvation—a logic that was amenable to particularist doctrines of funerary Buddhism rather than to the universalist doctrines of Buddhism in general. This logic of salvation was supported by an economy that traded in death rituals, memorial services, and posthumous Buddhist names, and it was in accord with the hierarchical social order of Tokugawa Japan. Indeed, at a collective level, the hierarchical structure of Tokugawa society was confirmed, reinforced, and perpetuated by the differential salvific principles of familial funerary Buddhism. The death-related beliefs and rituals that shaped the *danka* system functioned by merging Buddhism, as an agent of social order, with the Tokugawa governing system.

By incorporating Buddhist temples into the administrative apparatus of anti-Christian policy, the Tokugawa regime tried to contain them within the overarching rubric of institutional Buddhism. As a result, those Buddhist or quasi-Buddhist facilities and practitioners who stood outside the orbit of institutional Buddhism were controlled, suppressed, or denied. But this did not mean that institutional Buddhism was left unchecked. As Buddhist temples and monks wielded more and more power over the populace, the shogunate began to institute a series of nationwide regulatory measures. Within this milieu, contentious economic issues related to the business of death rituals and fundraising often pitted Buddhist temples against the government. Beginning in the early to mid-eighteenth century, as the Tokugawa governing system itself was called into question, public attempts to control Buddhist institutions further intensified.

Acquiescence to the Law of the King was the norm. Nevertheless, amid the rise of anti-Buddhist criticism, which gradually became the fashion of the times, Buddhist temples endeavored to preserve themselves and gain more influence over the populace. Ironically, however, it should be noted that the anti-Buddhist rhetoric with which various social critics vented their wrath was often premised on excoriating a type of Buddhism that did not exist in Tokugawa society. To be sure, some elements of Tokugawa Buddhism were vulnerable to criticism in one way or another. In particular, as national crises set in with the appearance of foreign powers, which exacerbated the deteriorating social order, Buddhist leaders began to heed the cacophony of anti-Buddhist discourses. Some of them tried to address the issue of a degenerate Buddhism, while others tried to formulate a revised Buddhism in order to address the pressing needs of the time. The latter were most vividly represented by the movement known as "protecting the country," which was spearheaded by Gesshō and his followers in Chōshū. But as far as the *danka* system was concerned, the protestations of anti-Buddhist critics amounted, at best, to no more than empty echoes within the Tokugawa system.

As a whole, the *danka* system persisted to the end of the Tokugawa period and instituted a social order dependent upon funerary Buddhism through the mandate of anti-Christianity. For this reason, when the social order showed symptoms of disarray or instability, government authorities tended to look at how the *danka* system was operating and to measure funerary rituals and rites of ancestral veneration against the ideal of good customs and manners. For the *bakufu*, rituals and ceremonies were essentially a vehicle of social engineering. What particularly troubled government officials was that a number of new social groups seemed to stray from the Tokugawa social order by utilizing these rituals. The many religious confraternities that mushroomed in Edo, for example, casually resorted to religious events in order to build solidarity among their members, and they demonstrated their collective strength through massive gatherings. In particular, large-scale funeral processions, which countenanced the bluster of the parvenu, posed an embarrassing puzzle for, and threat to, established samurai privileges. The game of hide-and-seek, or of violation and crackdown, that was played out over the mode of death rituals embroiled both the government and the people in what one might term a cultural politics of death.

Over time, in dealing with the excessive bounds of death rituals, public authorities were naturally drawn to the issue of filial piety within the paradigm of funerary Buddhism. Filial piety was an ethical value that contributed to invigorating the household institution; as such, the shogunate exhorted the populace to practice it. However, as it turned out, the unilateral imposition of edifying ethical values upon the people was accompanied by the growing awareness of the idea of "benevolent rule," which justified the demands of "honorable peasants." The crisscrossing spheres of filial piety and benevolent rule further colored the time leading up to the demise of the Tokugawa system—a time that was often imbued with notions of wandering, uncontrollable spirits. It is interesting to see how people strove to justify their place in society through attempting to establish a balance between their service to the state and the state's service to them—a balance that, when death rituals and wandering spirits were infused with new imaginative possibilities, sometimes looked as though it might tip. No matter what possibilities were available for creating a new balance, however, they all fell far short of destabilizing the *danka* system. A more serious challenge to this system was to come from Shinto priests, who pushed for Shinto funerals.

CB

PART IV

Funerary Buddhism and Shinto Funerals

*The religious climate in the late Tokugawa period was in transition. Uncon-
ditional submission to Buddhist death rites began to unravel from within
as Shinto activists launched a movement challenging the fundamentals of
the danka system. To be sure, it was still unthinkable for ordinary people
to question the danka system, which was locked into the governing framework of anti-Christian policy; however, some Shinto priests endeavored to
free themselves from the shackles of funerary Buddhism by starting a movement to realize Shinto funerals (shinsōsai, shintō sōsai, or shinsō, all sig-
nifying "Shinto funeral rites").*

*Some local governments were sympathetic to the Shinto priests engaged
in the Shinto funeral movement. In 1841, the Owari government announced
that the head priests of Masumida Jinja, the principal shrine (ichinomiya)
of the domain, as well as the prominent shrine Atsuta Jingū, could conduct
Shinto funerals, provided their danna temples consented. This announce-
ment prompted the head priest of Atsuta Jingū, Chiaki Kijō, to ask his
danna temple (Hōjiji, a Sōtōshū temple) to allow his release from the
danna affiliation, but to no avail. Upon hearing this, the Owari government, which was sympathetic to Chiaki Kijō, put pressure upon Shōgenji
(the head temple of the Sōtōshū temples in Owari) and Eiheiji (the head
temple of the entire Sōtōshū sect), saying that going "without Buddhist
danna affiliation has already been approved by the bakufu and by public
authority (kōgi)."[1] It is not clear whether or not the bakufu had actually
taken such a position with regard to the danna relationship between Buddhist temples and Shinto priests. Eiheiji instructed Shōgenji to avoid un-*

necessary trouble while trying to block Chiaki Kijō. The dispute dragged on for a few more years.

During this dispute, Chiaki Kijō retired and was succeeded by his son, who was more assertive than was his father about the cause of Shinto funerals. The danna temple Hōjiji held that danna affiliation and temple certification had been a tradition for hundreds of years and that terminating it would constitute a violation of the "regulations of the Keichō era" — a reference to the policy that carried the signature of Tokugawa Ieyasu.[2] Hōjiji also argued, with the full support of Shōgenji and Eiheiji, that the arbitrary termination of danna affiliation would strike a serious blow to the economic well-being of Buddhist temples. With regard to the economic issue, the Owari government advised that the Chiaki family would not only continue to fulfill all its previous financial obligations but that it would also make additional contributions to Hōjiji in order to offset any possible loss.

In 1846, Hōjiji eventually yielded to mounting pressure, declaring that "from now on, only the current chief priest and his heir might leave the [Buddhist] sect."[3] Based on this, the chief priest of the Chiaki family and his heir were exempted from danna affiliation with a Buddhist temple and could conduct Shinto funerals. It is not known how the Owari domain government managed to skew the shogunal mandate of anti-Christian temple certification integral to funerary Buddhism. Nevertheless, the Chiaki case seemed to presage the dawning of a new age — an age in which the rigidity of the Tokugawa religious order was called into question.

In the long run, the goal of the Shinto funeral movement was to undermine the universal imposition of Buddhist death rites. And the Chiaki case was certainly an encouraging one. However, as Part IV shows, people would not be free from Buddhist death rites as long as the Tokugawa system continued. Even under the Meiji Restoration, which gave its full support to Shinto, the Shinto funeral movement did not go as smoothly as expected. Here we examine the historical trajectory of Shinto funeral movements from the late Tokugawa to the early Meiji periods in order to understand the socio-religious matrix of Buddhist death and funerary Buddhism.

THIRTEEN

Shinto Funeral Movements
in the Bakumatsu

In early 1773, twenty-eight Shinto priests from the Tsuchiura domain in Hitachi province joined forces, petitioning the domain magistrate of temples and shrines to allow them to conduct Shinto funerals for themselves and their family members. Their petition soon developed into a group dispute between Buddhist monks and Shinto priests. After several months of consideration, the Tsuchiura domain government decreed that Shinto funerals could be allowed under three conditions: that Shinto priests should first secure consent from the Buddhist monks in the domain, that a funeral permit from the Yoshida Shinto house should be presented, and that even if the preceding two conditions were met, Shinto funerals would be offered only for the Shinto priest himself and his male successor, not for any other family members. This was the Tsuchiura domain government's decision. Nevertheless, it should be noted that it reflected, albeit indirectly, the newly emerging opinions of some *bakufu* officials. At that time, the lord of the Tsuchiura domain, Tsuchiya Atsunao (1732–76), was serving as both the magistrate of temples and shrines and the master of ceremonies (*sōjaban*) for the shogunal government.[4] The Tsuchiura case, which spurred the movement for Shinto funerals, posed a challenge to the *danka* system at a national level.

In retrospect, however, Shinto funerals were not an entirely new custom that came into being in the late eighteenth century. Their origin goes back to the late sixteenth century, as may be seen in the diary of Yoshida Kanemi (1535–1610), where he describes the funeral of his father, Yoshida Kanemigi (1516–73).[5] From this record, we know that the Yoshida Shinto house clearly switched from Buddhist funerals to Shinto funerals for its deceased family heads.[6] This new brand of Shinto funeral, allegedly based on a theory about the destiny of one's spirit after death articulated by Yoshida Kanetomo, featured several characteristics: Buddhist monks were not allowed to attend the funeral, the funeral was held in the middle of the night, a small spirit-shrine (*reisha*) was constructed over the burial site, a separate tomb was erected at the Buddhist temple in order to bury relics of the dead, and Buddhist and Shinto memorial rites were conducted concurrently.[7] At the turn of the sixteenth century, the Toyotomi house adopted the Yoshida funerary formula in order to deify the spirit of Hideyoshi, who would be worshipped at the Toyokuni Shrine as Toyokuni Daimyōjin — a Shinto posthumous name (*reishin-gō* or *reigō*) of the *myōjin* title within the tradition of Yoshida Shintō. When Tokugawa Ieyasu died in 1616, the Yoshida house and its leader Bonshun once again tried to apply its ritual expertise in order to deify Ieyasu's spirit with a *myōjin* title; however, it had to be satisfied with conducting a private mortuary ritual and burying his body. Tenkai, the founder of eastern Tendai (Tōeizan), who prevailed over Bonshun with the argument that a *myōjin* title should be avoided, succeeded in applying a *gongen* title in accordance with Sannō ichijitsu Shintō (or Sannō Shintō — a Shinto formula from the Tendai tradition) and apotheosized Ieyasu as Tōshō Daigongen at Nikkō.[8]

Despite a political setback in the beginning of the Tokugawa period, the Yoshida house, which had somehow managed to keep conducting Shinto funerals for its chieftains, tried to promote its ritual tradition beyond the confines of its family circles. Unlike the Yoshida house, which enjoyed an exceptional status with the government, the general populace and other Shinto priests were not allowed to perform Shinto funerals. It was not until the An'ei era (1772–80) that some Shinto priests took action. Amid frustration over the fact that even their own posthumous well-being was to be delegated to the care of Buddhist clergy, they were encouraged by the rise of nativist movements and anti-Buddhist discourse. They began to fight for

Shinto funerals by acquiring Yoshida house funeral licenses. Seizing this opportunity for expanding its influence over Shinto families, the Yoshida house quickly moved to issue funeral permits to Shinto priests who sought to break away from funerary Buddhism. Shinto funeral permits, accompanied by the Yoshida house's funeral manual, *Shintō sōsai ryaku shidai* (Synoptic procedures of Shinto funeral rites), suddenly became much sought-after items.[9]

However, the acquisition of a Yoshida permit and ritual manual did not automatically result in the performance of Shinto funerals. In order to conduct such funerals lawfully, one had to obtain consent from the *danna* temple as well as the government, and this was not easy.[10] Nevertheless, it is significant that from this time on, the shogunate reluctantly moved to open a door that would allow the practice of Shinto funerals. Shinto funerals were now possible, at least in theory, when they were authorized by the Yoshida house, the funerary *danna* temples, and the government. Of these conditions, the hardest to come by, of course, was the authorization of the *danna* temple. By insisting that *danna* temples were entitled to exercise the right of refusal, public authorities were able to avoid directly confronting Shinto priests. Here, one might ask why the shogunate dragged the Yoshida house into the dispute over Shinto funerals in the first place.

The answer goes back to the 1665 edict *Shosha negi kannushi hatto* (Laws on all shrines, deputy priests, and head priests), the third article of which reads: "shrine personnel (*shanin*) holding no ranks should wear white robes, other [ceremonial] robes are allowed only when they acquire the permission of the Yoshida house."[11] This edict officially authorized the Yoshida house, which had served as a sort of deputy of the imperial house in administering Shinto affairs, to issue ordination licenses to the Shinto priests of local shrines through bestowing colored ritual vestments.[12] Traditionally the imperial house controlled, through its proxy houses (*shissōke*), the head priests of the 22 highest-ranking shrines and the chief provincial shrines (*ichinomiya*). The Yoshida house was one of these imperial proxy houses, which numbered 10 in 1702 and 22 in 1794.[13] Among these proxy houses, the Yoshida house was singled out and empowered to issue its own sacerdotal licenses to local Shinto priests.[14] Taking advantage of this privilege, the Yoshida house began aggressively to issue, along with sacerdotal licenses, court rank and title certificates (*sōgen senji*) to the main deities of local shrines, which were mostly managed by Buddhists, villagers, or other religious practitioners.[15] For example, between 1691 and 1738, the Yoshida house granted at least 1,998 court rank and title certificates to local Shinto shrines. After 1738, the issuance of court rank certificates was almost halted due to the opposition of the imperial court, which saw its traditional prerogatives on the conferral of court ranks being eroded, but the Yoshida house still managed to keep issuing certificates bearing the title of *daimyōjin* or *daigongen* to local Shinto deities.[16] All this resulted in a tremendous increase in the influence of the Yoshida house over national Shinto shrines and their functionaries, particularly in the Kantō region.[17] The shogunate, noting the increasing religious clout of the Yoshida house, chose to direct dissatisfied Shinto priests seeking Shinto funerals to their spiritual master. Using the influence of the Yoshida house helped to streamline Shinto funeral petitions to a great extent, thus allowing the public authorities to avoid the issue as much as they could.[18]

However, when a dispute was brought to the public authorities, the local government usually sought guidance from the shogunate, and the latter usually applied the precedent set by the Tsuchiura case. For example, the lord of the Matsumoto domain in Shinano asked for shogunal advice regarding a problem in his domain. According to the 1785 report, a Shinto priest who had acquired a funeral permit from the Yoshida house sought to dissociate himself and his family from his *danna* temple. The Matsumoto lord feared that he lacked the authority to deal with this issue. The shogunate replied that, regardless of obtaining consent from the *danna* temple and a funeral permit from the Yoshida house, a Shinto funeral could be allowed only to Shinto priests and their successors.[19] The shogunate gave the same answer for similar cases in the Sanuki domain in Kazusa (1788),[20] the Tsu domain in Ise (1791),[21] the Obata domain in Kōzuke (1802),[22] and the Ōtaki village under intendant Ina Hanzaemon (1826).[23]

Despite the hurdles, it seems that by the early nineteenth century some Shinto priests were indeed able to have Shinto funerals. The *Shintō shūmon shokoku ruireisho* (A book of similar examples on the Shinto sect in all domains), a collection of Shinto documents compiled in 1805, alleges that in many parts of the country Shinto funerals were, although still far from the rule, at least on the rise.[24]

Interestingly, as time went on, freedom from funerary Buddhism was sought not only by Shinto priests but also by some *shugenja*.

In 1827, for example, Daijōin, a *shugenja* living in Ishibashi village, Tajima, successfully petitioned the domain government to allow him and his family to be buried according to a Shugendō funerary service. The domain government granted permission on the condition that the *shugenja* obtain consent from his *danna* temple and that other residents in the village do not raise any objection to the Shugendō funeral.[25] The *Tokugawa kinreikō* cites one more example of unknown date in which a *shugenja* and his family were exempted from funerary Buddhism: the magistrate of temples and shrines allowed Sanpōin and his family in Shimozawa village, Tone county, Kōzuke to sever its *danna* relationship with Jumyōin, a Shingonshū temple in Tsukiyono village. The rationale was that the temple, which was located across the river from the family, was too far away. The result of this decision involved more than the termination of Buddhist funerary services. This *shugenja* family no longer had to be inspected by the *danna* temple; instead, the *shugenja* was allowed to ascertain his family members' non-Christian religious identity through self-inspection.[26]

A number of Shugendō documents went one step further, arguing that *shugenja* were indeed allowed to conduct anti-Christian self-inspections as well as their own funerary rituals. It appears, although this is difficult to authenticate, that the head temple Shōgoin issued regulations in 1722 advising its Honzan Shugen practitioners that hiring Buddhist monks to perform funerary services was against its principles, and urged its followers to adopt their own funeral practices. The Tōzan sect under the control of Daigoji Sanpōin also reminded its *shugenja* not only that all members were supposed to conduct their own funeral rituals but also that they were to issue their own anti-Christian certificates.[27] Other documents allege that, from 1804, all Shugen sects were authorized to apply religious self-inspection not only to active practitioners but also to their family members.[28] Despite all these claims, it seems that, as far as religious inspection was concerned, most Shugen practitioners were still under the control of Buddhist monks and that Shugen funerals, which were referred to as "self-guidance" (*jishin indō*), were rarely practiced.

All in all, no matter how eagerly Shinto priests or *shugenja* sought non-Buddhist funerals, a significant hurdle remained: the consent of their *danna* temples. Understandably, Buddhist *danna* temples resisted giving up their funerary privileges, because Shinto funerals signified a return to "the old way that had existed before the arrival of Buddhism" and were, therefore, poised to nullify the practice of Buddhist religious inspection.[29] That is why public authorities had to be cautious in dealing with disputes over Shinto funerals. In 1819, the chief priest of Shingū Myōjin in Taima village, Yamato Iwami, petitioned for Shinto funerals for himself and his successor. In granting permission, the domain government had to be clear on the issue of religious inspection: "The priest Iwami and his heirs are allowed to conduct Shinto funerals and, accordingly, they shall be exempted from religious inspection by Gokurakuin [the *danna* temple]. But his wife and other family members will continue to receive religious inspection from the same temple, and the matters of burning incense and memorial services will remain unaffected."[30]

For funerary Buddhist temples, anti-Christian religious inspection was not only the object of a power struggle but also a matter of survival. When the petition for a Shinto funeral was settled through an agreement with a *danna* temple, the Shinto families in question were often forced to pledge ongoing support to their *danna* temple regardless of the status of their official *danna* relationship. Either that or they were to pay a lump-sum severance fee in order to defray the temple's potential loss in income.[31] In 1793, Shinto families belonging to Akagi Jinja in Miyosawa village, Seta county, Kōzuke succeeded in settling their petition for Shinto funerals with their *danna* temple Ryūseiji, in an agreement endorsed by the Kawagoe domain government in 1798. The terms of agreement that would result in dissociating incumbent priests and heirs from the temple and allowing them to conduct Shinto funerals included continued financial support for the temple, continued fulfillment of *danna* obligations, and continued donation of customary funeral fees. Officially, the priests and their heirs had nothing to do with the *danna* temple; financially, however, they continued to support it.[32]

Compromise could be struck in one way or another, but it should be remembered that in most cases the petition for Shinto funerals usually escalated into a long, bitter dispute, exhausting all parties involved. A classic example of such a prolonged dispute occurred between a group of Shinto priests known as the Masudagumi and the Shingonshū temple Shōtatsuji in the Hamada domain of Iwami in the mid-nineteenth century. The Masudagumi was one of several regional associations into which Shinto priests in the domain were organized, and Shōtatsuji was the *danna* temple of some of its members. The death of Horie Buzen, the head priest of Sahimeyama Jinja in Otone village and a member of the Masudagumi, triggered a conflict over Shinto funerals between the Masudagumi and Shōtatsuji that lasted from 1838 to 1845.[33] This conflict, commonly known as the Hamada episode, illustrates the intricate chemistry involved in the challenge to the dominance of funerary Buddhism.

When Buzen died in 1838, his death was immediately reported to Shōtatsuji so that his funeral service could be arranged. Upon receiving the report, the deputy monk of the temple (at that time the head monk was in Edo on other business) came to inspect the death, as was required by law. When he opened the casket he found that Buzen's hair had not been shaved. The deputy monk declared that a Buddhist funeral service could not be offered to someone who had not been initiated into Buddhism. It was commonly understood that the act of shaving the hair was the first step of Buddhist initiation, but the Horie family argued that this custom had never been applied to Shinto priests in their village. Despite the strong protest of the Horie family, the deputy monk proceeded to shave the hair of the deceased, conducted a brief Buddhist rite, conferred a posthumous Buddhist name upon the deceased (even though he was clad in Shinto robes with his hands folded together holding a priestly scepter), and then left. The villagers, who witnessed an odd combination of half-Buddhist, half-Shinto postures, made fun of the deceased Buzen, saying that he had been transformed into a chimera (*nue*) — a legendary evil bird that Minamoto no Yorimasa (1104–80) had allegedly killed.[34] The Horie family felt humiliated.

The following year, another member of the Masudagumi, Masuno Sahee, died on the third day of the second month. His *danna* temple was also Shōtatsuji. The Masuno family asked the head monk of the temple to conduct a funeral service for Sahee, but he refused. The head monk noted that Sahee did not deserve a Buddhist funeral because he had served his *danna* temple poorly while he was alive. Sahee's alleged "poor service" was a reference to an episode that had occurred in the previous year. In 1838, Shōtatsuji was in the process of recompiling its death register, many parts of which had been damaged by vermiculation. For this task, Shōtatsuji circulated a list of *danna* households and asked its patrons to provide the posthumous names and dates of death of their ancestors and deceased family members. Upon receiving the list, Sahee found that his name was placed after those of townspeople — an indication of the inferior status of his family.[35] Gravely insulted, he ignored the request and replied that he would not forgive Shōtatsuji's maltreatment. Shōtatsuji did not react immediately to Sahee's indignation. However, when Sahee died, Shōtatsuji displayed its weapon—the funeral service. The Masuno family, which did not have any other option under shogunal law, repeatedly entreated the temple for a Buddhist funeral for Sahee. Shōtatsuji finally responded that a Buddhist funeral rite could be offered on one condition: the dead man's hair must be shaved before the funeral could be held. The Masuno family and Masudagumi members rebuffed the demand and appealed to the domain government for a solution. The domain government allowed the Masuno family to bury the corpse with a Shinto funeral.[36] Two months later, the office of temples and shrines summoned the head monk of Shōtatsuji and reprimanded him for his apathy toward the Masuno family. Afterwards, Shōtatsuji reluctantly agreed to make the death official, and in lieu of inspecting the corpse, offered a brief Buddhist rite at the Masuno residence and then conferred a Buddhist posthumous name upon the deceased.[37]

A few weeks later, representatives of the Masudagumi, led by Horie Inaba and Tanaka Daizen, visited a high-ranking official in the office of temples and shrines of the domain government. They argued that in light of the two previous unpleasant incidents, the best way to prevent similar troubles in the future would be to allow them to sever their *danna* relationships with Shōtatsuji. But the domain official advised them to negotiate directly with Shōtatsuji, suggesting that changes in the *danna* relationship should be based on mutual consent. Following the government's advice, a meeting between the Masudagumi and Shōtatsuji was held. The head monk of Shōtatsuji explained that his insistence upon shaving the corpse had been a matter of special circumstances, and he assured the Masudagumi that it would not occur again. Not convinced, the Shinto priests expressed their deep concerns, particularly about the offensive behavior of the deputy monks, and insisted that the head monk's words be put in writing and signed. The head monk refused to accede to this demand, and instead promised that he would strictly educate his deputy monks.

But Horie Inaba's father, Horie Hitachi, died seven months later and the Shōtatsuji's promise was not carried out. Shōtatsuji dispatched a deputy monk to the Horie house, but he refused to conduct a funeral service because the hair of the deceased was not shaved. Horie Inaba cited what the head monk had pledged and explained why the custom of shaving had not been applied to Shinto priests in the region, but the deputy monk was unmoved. Horie Inaba, along with Tanaka Daizen and other members, rushed to the office of temples and shrines and entreated a Shinto funeral for his deceased father. Horie Hitachi, clad in Shinto robes and holding a scepter, was eventually given a Shinto funeral. Afterwards, as with Masuno Sahee, a monk from Shōtatsuji reluctantly visited the Horie house and conducted a simple Buddhist service before Hitachi's spiritual tablet. With this, Hitachi's death was brought to its official conclusion.

The following month, representatives from the four associations of Shinto priests in the area (Masudagumi, Misumigumi, Hikimi-gumi, and Jōkagumi) submitted a joint petition to the domain office of temples and shrines. In it they claimed that from ancient times the customs of "the way of the age of gods" had been applied to the burials of Shinto priests; however, since Buddhist temples were given the right to perform anti-Christian inspections, the old customs had been replaced with Buddhist ones.[38] They further argued that "[under] the Kantō regulations, issued in the second year of the Tenna era (1682), whether a funeral was to be Shinto-style or Confucian-style was subject to one's own wishes. Based on this edict, [some families] in the domain of the Mito lord switched to Confucian funerals, while in other domains many Shinto priests were allowed to conduct their Shinto funerals."[39] But the domain officials remained silent with regard to this obscure claim.

A year later, in the tenth month of 1840, a death occurred that would again pit Shinto priests against the *danna* temple—that of Tanaka Daizen's mother. Daizen's *danna* temple, Enfukuji, flatly refused to provide a funeral service for his deceased mother, saying that the Tanaka family had served it very poorly. Daizen protested vigorously that he had never been negligent in sending rice donations and gifts to the temple at the New Year, Bon, and the memorial anniversaries of his ancestors.[40] Enraged by the temple's continued rejections despite his repeated appeals, Daizen threatened to bring the case to the domain government, along with information on the misdeeds of the head monk of Enfukuji. Upon receiving the threat, Enfukuji yielded and agreed to offer a Buddhist funeral service. Soon after, Daizen was shocked to find that the posthumous name conferred upon his mother was totally unacceptable. This name was "Denkō fuchū shinnyo," which seemed to make little sense but which included a word meaning "infidelity" (*fuchū*).[41] When the head monk of Enfukuji came to conduct a Buddhist funeral service, Daizen raged against the name and demanded redress. The head monk promised to compose a new name later, but he never did.

Immediately after the funeral for Daizen's mother, the representatives of the four associations of Shinto priests once again submitted a joint petition to the domain government for the right to perform Shinto funerals. For more than a year, the government did not react. In 1842, the four associations resubmitted the petition. In the twelfth month they finally received a response from the government, but to their disappointment it was a negative one. Undeterred, these Shinto priests resolved to push further: if the domain government maintained its current stance, then they would appeal the matter directly to the shogunate. While this appeal was under way, no member was to be negligent in fulfilling tax duties and in performing Shinto rituals and ceremonies; and all costs related to the petition efforts were to be shared equally by all members. In the sixth month of 1843, each association once more simultaneously sent a petition for Shinto funerals to the domain government. The petitioners first detailed how abusive *danna* temples were when conducting funeral services, while noting that Shinto funerals had been traditionally practiced in the past. In justifying their argument for Shinto funerals, the petitioners highlighted two particular "evil deeds" committed by the monks of *danna* temples: intoxication and fornication (*nyobon*, literally "violations involving women").[42] Adding that the former head monks of Enfukuji, Saifukuji, and Tōdenji had all been expelled due to their unacceptable behavior, the petitioners asked why they should entrust them with funeral services.[43]

In the ninth month of 1843, the Shinto petitioners received a reply from the domain office of temples and shrines, but it was again a disappointing one: Shinto funerals would be contingent upon two conditions—consent from the *danna* temple and the acquisition of a funeral permit from the Yoshida house. At the same time, under no circumstances could any family members other than the priest (former and present) and priest-in-waiting be exempted from Buddhist funerals and annual religious inspections. Based on this response, the associations of Shinto priests moved to negotiate with their *danna* temples. This did not go well. In the sixth month of 1844, the head monk of Myōgiji, who represented a group of *danna* temples, stated that *danna* temples would allow Shinto priests to "leave the *danna* relationship" only if the government legalized Shinto funerals. The negotiations were over.

Frustrated again, the Shinto priests remained defiant. They decided to make one more try. In their petition submitted to the domain government late in the sixth month of 1844, they pushed their case by arguing that the monks of *danna* temples were "deeply addicted to all kinds of wrongdoing." Nevertheless, the local government was very slow to respond and claimed that it had to consult with the central government. In the eleventh month of 1845, the domain office of temples and shrines summoned the representatives of the Shinto petitioners and delivered its final decision: Shinto funerals would now be allowed for current priests, their heirs, and former priests but not for other family members. It is not known if this decision was based on consultations with the shogunate, but the requirement of obtaining consent from the *danna* temples— which had been the main sticking point—was finally dropped. It was a victory, if not a sweeping one, for the Shinto priests who had fought tirelessly for the past seven years. They were extremely pleased with this official approval. All of them visited the Hamada castle and expressed their gratitude to the domain officials.[44]

When the lord of their home domain was anti-Buddhist, Shinto priests could take some solace even though Shinto funerals were not fully legal. In 1842, the staunch anti-Buddhist daimyo of Mito Tokugawa Nariaki is alleged to have "tacitly encouraged" the domain residents to adopt Shinto funerals.[45] A year later, he launched his notorious anti-Buddhist campaign: about 190 temples were abolished and their monks defrocked and returned to agricultural occupations, temple bells and bronze objects were confiscated and used for cannons, temples attached to shrines were abolished, and the shrine-monks were forced either to return to lay life or to become Shinto priests.[46] Anti-Buddhist hatred ran extremely high in Mito under the tenure of Nariaki, but it is not known to what extent his abrasive policy "encouraged" Mito families to switch to Shinto funeral; in fact, it is probable that only a very few families actually proceeded to adopt Shinto funerals. No matter how determined he was to suppress Buddhism, Nariaki did not dare go so far as to scrap the entire *danka* system and stamp out funerary Buddhism. As it turned out, Nariaki's radical anti-Buddhist campaign did not last long: in the fifth month of 1844, the shogunate placed him under house arrest and brought forth seven charges against him, two of which pertained to his religious policy: that he had ruthlessly destroyed too many temples and that he had arbitrarily converted the Tōshōgū on Mount Tokiwa into a Shinto shrine.[47] Although Nariaki was gone, his legacies foreshadowed what would eventually befall the *danka* system during the Meiji period.

Something similar occurred in the Tsuwano domain, Iwami, a *tozama* domain known as a stronghold of National Learning. Encouraged by the Hamada case and Mito's anti-Buddhist suppression, the Shinto priests in the domain resumed their "Shinto funeral" movement in 1846 under the leadership of Oka Kumaomi (1783–1851), a well known National Learning scholar-cum-Shinto priest.[48] Thirty-five years earlier, when Kumaomi launched a petition for Shinto funerals, the domain government was quite indifferent; this time, however, it observed that the much more powerful *fudai* domain of Hamada had taken action. The emboldened Tsuwano government accepted the petition for Shinto funerals without much hesitation in 1847, a year after it had been submitted.[49] Nevertheless, the Tsuwano domain government knew that, under the shogunate's anti-Christian policy, the matter of Shinto funerals was still a delicate political issue that had to be handled with caution. It did not dare go so far as to allow Shinto funerals to the domain's general population. For this, it had to wait until 1867, when the Tokugawa shogunate was almost helpless.

Given that they had to be subordinated to Buddhism even after death, one can understand why Shinto priests fought so hard for Shinto funerals. Despite persistent efforts, their wish to be liberated from funerary Buddhism was never fully realized during the Tokugawa period, their prolonged fight for Shinto funerals garnering only a partial victory.[50] The wishes of these Shinto activists remained largely unfulfilled, and they (with the exception of those priests who were allowed Shinto funerals) had to die Buddhist. Ironically, however, they need not have been too disappointed, for their spirits were, in the final analysis, deified within the parameters of indigenous, rather than Buddhist, ideas and beliefs. As discussed in Part II, what Buddhist rites for the deceased attempted to ensure was not at odds with what the advocates of Shinto funerals attempted to ensure. Buddhist death rituals were designed to elevate the spirit of the deceased to the status of an ancestral *kami*, a goal more or less in line with Shinto funerary beliefs.

The compatibility between Buddhist and Shinto funerals was evident in the theories of spirit deification articulated by National Learning scholars who, to no small degree, inspired the Shinto funeral movements. For example, Motoori Norinaga suggested that although most of the spirit was destined to go to the netherworld (*yomi no kuni*) after death, some part of the spirit would remain in this world, become a household deity, and protect the descendants and the country of Japan. In order to ensure the divine help of ancestral deities, Norinaga stressed that their descendants should venerate them on a regular basis even though the largest part of their spirits resided in the unclean subterranean land.[51] Hirata Atsutane, who was not happy with Norinaga's notion of the netherworld, put forward a new theory: after death, the spirit would stay in this world much as the deities in the *Kojiki* and the *Nihon shoki* stayed in Shinto shrines. They would "dwell amongst us, eating, dressing, and living just as we do." They would contact and protect the descendants and the country of Japan, and would have "reunions around its shrine or family plot with those who had gone before."[52] For his part, Oka Kumaomi, under the strong influence of Hirata Atsutane, devoted his entire life to promoting Shinto funerals in the Tsuwano domain. Combining the theories of Norinaga and Atsutane, Kumaomi argued that even though half of the spirit would disappear into the netherworld after death, it would remain at the gravesite, and upon receiving proper care and veneration, provide divine protection to its descendants.[53] Buddhist death rituals, as the Tokugawa Japanese understood them, were to fulfill all these expectations.

Why, then, did Shintoists insist on replacing Buddhist death rituals with Shinto ones? It is interesting that they rarely spoke against how Buddhist mortuary and memorial services dealt with the spirit of the deceased. Indeed, they raised no strong objection to the ritual procedures of death-related Buddhist rites, which featured the appeasement of the newly deified ancestral spirit, ritual measures designed to ensure intimate contact between ancestral deities and their descendants, and the evocation of the divine protection extended by ancestral deities. It is true that Shinto funeral advocates endeavored to expand the scope of the ancestral deities' divine help beyond the boundary of family to include the emperor, the divine country of Japan, and even the cosmos.[54] But generally speaking, at least in terms of their ritual goals, there were no fundamental differences between Shinto and Buddhist funerals.

What really bothered and hurt the advocates of Shinto funerals was the fact that their pride and dignity were subjected to Buddhist monks who, in their view, were corrupt and greedy. It was outrageous to have to endure yet one more round of Buddhist intervention when having to deal with death.[55] The problem was that without a Buddhist funeral, nobody could legally conclude his or her life cycle. If this could be accomplished through a Shinto funeral, then all these troubles would be resolved at once. Amid the increasing influence of National Learning and through the networks of the Yoshida house, which called for the restoration of the dignity and pride of Japan's indigenous religious tradition, Shinto advocates sought to redress the *danka* system. At the same time, by trying to avoid the control of Buddhist temples and village officials by establishing a formula for anti-Christian Shinto certification, they were trying to recuperate their position in a society that had become unstable.[56] In Tokugawa society, the religious format of a funeral implied far more than a simple choice of religion.

The Shinto funeral movement involved a challenge, if not a threat, to one of the cardinal systems that buttressed the Tokugawa social order and status system. For that reason, even if they were sympathetic to petitions for Shinto funerals, local domain governments had to be cautious when taking unilateral action. When pressed, domain authorities first attempted to persuade both sides of the dispute to come to an agreement, and only when this did not happen did they intervene. As we have seen, the decision in the Tsuchiura case of 1772 favored the Shinto petitioners. The Hamada case, on the other hand, was concluded only after the petitioners had put up a struggle that lasted from 1838 to 1845. In both cases, the Shinto petitioners garnered only a partial victory.

To be sure, the mandate of anti-Christianity remained unchallenged; nonetheless, from the late eighteenth century onward, some changes began to occur in the margins. This was seen in the cases of Kazusa and Izumi, where public authorities ended up allowing, if only partially, the self-certification of anti-Christian identity. In a situation in which Kirishitan had been wiped out, it would have been unrealistic to insist upon the original rigidity of anti-Christian scrutiny. Anti-Christian rhetoric seemed to shift to reflect the changing social order, and this, in turn, brought with it a more flexible approach to social control.

In 1790, a feud erupted in Urakami village, Hizen between the villagers and their head Takaya Eizaemon. The village head asked for donations from all villagers in the hope of erecting a Buddhist image at the village's tutelary Shinto shrine; however, nineteen of the villagers, all relatively well-off, refused to contribute. Upset at their refusal, Eizaemon accused them of being followers of a heretical sect (*ishū*), by which he meant the Kirishitan religion, and denounced them to the shogunal representative in Nagasaki. The Nagasaki office immediately arrested all of them and put them under investigation. Despite intensive interrogation, the Nagasaki officials failed to detect any solid evidence of their Christian faith; five months later, the accused were all released from jail. Eizaemon and his backers were charged with making false accusations and were dismissed from their village positions. But Eizaemon did not give up: he went on to search for signs of heresy. A year later, he submitted another report, denouncing the same villagers to the Nagasaki shogunal office. This time the office ignored him. However, based on someone else's information, Nagasaki authorities arrested five villagers in early 1792, including Fukahori Yasuzaemon, who had helped the nineteen villagers get out of jail two years earlier. In 1793, frustrated at the government's imprisonment of Yasuzaemon and four other fellow villagers for more than a year without official charges, Kumejirō, a family associate of Yasuzaemon, secretly traveled to Edo. He made a direct appeal to finance magistrate Kuze Hirotami (1732–?), who had previously been a Nagasaki shogunal deputy. Kumejirō's petition to a high-ranking *bakufu* official prompted the shogunate to take an official look into the matter of the heretical sect in the Nagasaki area. Despite a presumably thorough two-year investigation, the Nagasaki deputies reported to the shogunate in 1796 that they could not find any evidence of the existence of a heretical sect in that region.[57]

The problem of *ishū* again broke out in the Amakusa area in 1805, this time implicating around 5,000 people. The Amakusa *kuzure* hit four villages (Ōe, Sakitsu, Imatomi, and Takahama), all of which had been involved in the Amakusa-Shimabara Rebellion of 1637. The incident was triggered by the head of Imatomi village, Ueda Engoemon, who secretly informed the Shimabara domain government that he had discovered some suspicious signs indicating the existence of underground Kirishitan in his village. Engoemon's report soon leaked to the Nagasaki shogunal deputies, who then officially directed the domain government to conduct an investigation. Alarmed by this unintended development, the Shimabara domain government swiftly moved to look into the matter and reported back that there did indeed seem to be some followers of a heretical sect in the domain. The investigation confirmed the existence of about 5,000 *ishū* followers who admitted their faith in "heretical law" (*ihō*) and surrendered some of their religious paraphernalia, including "heretical Buddhist images" (*ibutsu*). Deeply shocked, the domain government promised the shogunate that it would take immediate action to root out this sect. As it turned out, however, the domain government decided to forgive the "crimes" of these *ishū* followers after converting them to Buddhism—a decision probably taken in order to prevent the eruption of a massive peasant rebellion.[58] Surprisingly, the shogunate gave tacit approval to the domain's ruling; worries of possible peasant rebellions seemed to override the issue of Christianity.

Furthermore, when a group of about 280 peasants from Imatomi village wanted to get rid of their village head in 1811, the domain government went along with them and pressured him to resign. Despite the fact that core members of this peasant group had once been suspected of being "underground Kirishitan," the domain authorities decided not to risk antagonizing the villagers. While social stability was deteriorating, public authorities were careful not to provoke unnecessary "village disturbances" (*murakata sōdō*). In this milieu, the existence of Kirishitan could be ignored and even pardoned as their suppression would risk instigating a collective disturbance.

However, toward individual Kirishitan who did not pose any threat of a collective disturbance, the shogunate was harsh. In 1827, a female soothsayer in Settsu named Sano was accused by her landlord of swindling him through fortunetelling. Upon hearing this complaint, city official Ōshio Heihachirō (1793–1837) interrogated Sano and her associates and found, through the confession of Sano's master Kinu (who lived in Osaka), that their divination business was rooted in a Kirishitan sect. Further interrogation of Kinu led to the arrest of her master in Kyoto, Toyoda Mitsugi, who confessed that he had learned his divination skills from Mizuno Gunki. Gunki was already dead, but Ōshio Heihachirō was able to arrest his former disciples, including Fujita Kenzō (who was found to possess "forbidden books" on Christianity) and over 50 other associates. In the twelfth month of 1829, 6 people, all of whom were indicted as Kirishitan, were put to death by crucifixion (4 of these people had died in prison, and their exhumed bodies were crucified); the rest received less harsh punishments.[59]

It was never clear to what extent those accused of being Christian followers and who were punished accordingly were actually "Kirishitan." This was up to the public authorities: once they decided to label the suspects as "Kirishitan," the ensuing punishments were brutal. With the exception of Fujita Gunki, who maintained a comfortable life as a physician, the others were all petty diviners and prayer practitioners, poorly educated and socially marginal; they drew not only on vague ideas about Christianity but also on various other religious ideas (e.g., Buddhism, Shinto, Daoism, and folk religion) for their prayer business. It seems that these people had derived some knowledge from two illegal Christian books—*Tenshu jitsugi* (The true meaning of the lord of heaven), published in 1601 in Beijing, and *Kijin jippen* (Ten paradoxes of eccentric people), a treatise on heaven and hell published in 1608 in Beijing—authored by Matteo Ricci and smuggled into Japan from China.[60] But it would be too naïve to think that exposure to Christian books automatically converted people to Christianity; rather, their attraction to Christianity stemmed from their religious curiosity and adventurism. For these petty prayer entrepreneurs, the image of Jesus or the Virgin Mary would have been an appealing source of magical power, exotic and, indeed, heretical. Nonetheless, public authorities decided that they should be classified as Christian followers and therefore punished as evildoers.[61] After the tragic conclusion of the Amakusa-Shimabara Rebellion, Kirishitan had invariably been portrayed as incarnations of demons who would seek every possible chance to inflict misfortune upon innocent people and who would eventually destroy the country of the gods through their wicked preaching and tricks. Whether or not one could prove that someone was really Kirishitan often did not matter. The category "Kirishitan" was used as a way of vilifying anything alien or threatening, whether it was a person, a group, a form of behavior, a theory, or a thing. When someone was identified as a "Kirishitan" and punished, the populace cheered.

The Tokugawa regime categorically demonized Kirishitan as the most dangerous social species. Yet ironically, its brutal anti-Christian policy ended up creating a form of "Christianity" (i.e., the *ishū*) that could be tolerated, as was seen in the Urakami and Amakusa incidences. As long as they did not deviate from the order of the *bakuhan* system and did not assert their religious identity, the *ishū* Kirishitan were not blackballed.[62] Clearly, the politics of anti-Christianity was losing much of the relevance and vigor it had once enjoyed. For the underground Kirishitan, if any, who had somehow been able to preserve their religion, the *ishū* label could be seen as indulging their religious crime. In 1842, it was again revealed that Urakami village contained many *ishū* followers, but the problem was resolved without much fuss and the authorities decided not to pursue it.

Another revelation occurred in 1856. This was known as the third Urakami *kuzure*, and it involved secret information, investigations, arrest and imprisonment, and the eventual release of the accused without the laying of any formal charges. The Nagasaki shogunal deputies at this time feared that the spread of the *ishū* would be aided by the foreign ships that frequently docked in their city and were secretly collecting information on underground Christian followers. Upon receiving a tip from an unknown informant, the Nagasaki shogunal office discovered that there were many followers of the *ishū* and that they were organized into a tight network. Thanks to the confession of an upper-level member named Kichizō, the Nagasaki authorities realized that the *ishū* network was extensive, embracing hundreds of followers: "[They believe that] those who have faith will be blessed with good harvests in the paddy and dry fields and with good news in all other matters, including happiness and longevity in this world and that they will be ensured of rebirth — as will their parents, wives, children, brothers, and sisters — into Paradise in the next world after death."[63] The Nagasaki authorities also found out that the *ishū* faith, based on the knowledge of Jesus and Christmas, was by and large focused upon the Virgin Mary. All the evidence pointed toward Christianity. Again, the authorities determined that this religion, which was inherited from their ancestors, belonged to a "heretical sect different from the sect of Jesus [which is] under the ban [of the shogunate]."[64] In late 1860, the Nagasaki deputies finally reported to the shogunate that a group of *ishū* followers had been uncovered in their jurisdiction but that none of them had been found to be Kirishitan.

However, when the same group of *ishū* followers resurfaced seven years later in 1867, the shogunate reversed its previous position and struck back at them. It found that some of them were in contact with foreign Christian missionaries, who had entered Japan when it was forced to open its doors to the West. In a sense, the Tokugawa regime's final confrontation with these clandestine Kirishitan in Kyūshū, known as the fourth Urakami *kuzure*, was something that had been presaged ever since the *bakufu* had yielded to the West. The United States forced Tokugawa Japan "to open its trading ports" in 1853. When that demand materialized in the United States–Japan Treaty of Amity and Commerce in 1858, Christianity was declared legal in the extraterritorial sections of foreign residents. The eighth article of this decree reads: "Americans in Japan shall be allowed the free exercise of their religion, and for this purpose shall have the right to erect suitable places of worship. . . . The Americans and Japanese shall not do anything that may be calculated to excite religious animosity. The Government of Japan has already abolished the practice of trampling on religious emblems."[65] Before long, the Tokugawa shogunate was forced to include similar articles in the treaties with Holland, Russia, Great Britain, and France. Once Christianity was permitted in the foreign settlements, Christian missionaries entered the treaty ports (Hakodate, Yokohama, and Nagasaki) with an ambition that encompassed more than simply shepherding foreign residents.[66] In 1862, a Roman Catholic church was erected in Yokohama by two French missionaries, Prudence-Séraphin-Barthélémy Girard and Pierre Mounicou, who belonged to the Paris Society of Foreign Missions (Société des Missions Étrangères de Paris). Three years later, in the first month of 1865, Louis-Théodore Furet and Bernard-Thaddée Petitjean built a church in Nagasaki with the name Nihon Nijūroku Junkyōsha Tenshudō (Church of the Twenty-Six Martyrs of Japan). It was at this church, which was commonly known as Ōura Tenshudō or Furansu Temple, that a dramatic encounter took place between French missionaries and Urakami Kirishitan, who had been in hiding for more than two centuries.

One day, in the second month of 1865, three middle-aged women visited the church disguised as spectators and quietly knelt down beside Father Petitjean. One of them, holding her hand on her chest, spoke softly to him: "All of us here have the same heart as you do." When Father Petitjean asked her where they came from, she replied that they were from Urakami. She then asked him, "Where is the image of Santa Maria?"[67] Once it was known that Roman Catholic fathers had returned to Nagasaki, the Kirishitan from the areas of Urakami, Imamura, Sotome, Amakusa, Hirado, and Gotō secretly visited the Nagasaki church and confessed their faith. The Kirishitan residents in Urakami village, who were emboldened by the establishment of the Ōura Tenshudō not far from their village, actually dared to practice their religion openly in violation of the "great law" (*taihō*) of the state.[68]

In the third month of 1867, nine months before the declaration of Meiji Restoration and the fall of the Tokugawa regime, a resident of Urakami village named Sanpachi had lost his mother. He refused to invite a priest from his family's *danna* temple, Shōtokuji, to conduct a funeral, even though the village head had already informed the temple of her death. Instead, Sanpachi openly buried his mother's body at a Christian funeral service.[69] This was, in fact, the third time that year the shogunal law had been violated. The first time was when a villager named Mokichi died. His family successfully schemed to provoke the Shōtokuji monk who was sent to officiate the funeral rite so that he would return to his temple. Afterwards, Mokichi underwent a Christian funeral. The shogunal law was violated for the second time when Kyūgorō gave his son a Christian funeral and failed to report his death either to the village head or to Shōtokuji. The Nagasaki shogunal office knew about these two violations but decided to disregard them, with the improvised rationale that these two families were so poor that they could not afford a Buddhist funeral rite. However, Sanpachi was "number three" in rank in the village, according to the village head. The Nagasaki officials summoned Sanpachi before them and strongly reprimanded both him and his fellow villagers.[70]

Nevertheless, other Kirishitan residents soon began to follow Sanpachi's lead and publicly declared their faith. Some of the defiant Kirishitan even notified their village head that they would terminate all ties with their *danna* temple. The document, signed by them and submitted to the village head, was unequivocal: "Even though we receive funeral rites offered by the *danna* temple, this cannot be of any help or use for the life after death. For this reason, from now on, when death occurs, we will conduct our own funerals."[71] They believed that if their faith in "Deus" remained firm, then they would be reborn into eternal life. Their collective action, which snubbed the national policy of anti-Christianity, shocked the government. Deeply annoyed, the Nagasaki shogunal officials took action, even though they were under mounting pressure from the West to show more tolerance toward Christianity. In the sixth month of the same year, the authorities arrested 68 Kirishitan in the village and confiscated all Christian images and artifacts. These were enshrined at four locations where Christian chapel-like structures had been erected (later the confiscated items were returned because the Kirishitan argued that they had borrowed them from foreigners). Then, through torture, the public authorities successfully forced the Kirishitan to abandon their religion—but only temporarily. Their Christian faith soon revived, and surveillance and punishment ensued.[72] As the crackdown on the Urakami Kirishitan became known, foreign ministers began to protest, and the Tokugawa shogunate promised lenience. However, until the very end, the Tokugawa regime did not really loosen its anti-Christian position, and its anti-Christian legacies were passed on to Meiji Japan.

CB

FOURTEEN

Shinto Funerals in Early Meiji Japan

From the outset, the Meiji regime stood firm against Christianity and decided to perpetuate the Tokugawa *bakufu*'s policy: "Until regulations are established, in scrutinizing the Kirishitan sect, follow what the old *bakufu* has laid down and investigate the whereabouts of suspicious people."[73] Indeed, one of the earliest religious edicts of the Meiji government was a ban on Christianity. This was posted on public bulletin boards throughout the country in the third month of 1868: "The Kirishitan sect is strictly prohibited. Suspicious persons should be reported to the proper [government] office. Rewards will be granted."[74]

At its incipient stage, the Meiji regime had to overcome the deep political and ideological divisions among its diverse socio-political groups and classes; it badly needed an "enemy" that could unite them all in a common cause. This enemy was Christianity, an alien religion that, for centuries, had been demonized by ideologues and political activists of all stripes. Against this backdrop of anti-Christianity, Meiji leaders swiftly moved to unite Shinto ritual and government (*saisei itchi*), a move that would eventually manifest itself as State (*kokka*) Shinto. The only difference in belief between the Tokugawa and Meiji governments about the threat of Christianity was that the hostility of the former was unsubstantiated while that of the latter was not. Unlike Christianity in the *bakumatsu* period, which existed only as an imagined evil lingering in fading memories of the Amakusa-Shimabara Rebellion, Christianity in early Meiji Japan—thanks to the emergence of Kakure Kirishitan—could be seen as a genuine diplomatic "menace."[75]

The first anti-Christian strike in Meiji Japan victimized the Kirishitan in Kyushu, starting with the banishment of 114 Kirishitan leaders from Urakami to the Tsuwano, Hagi, and Fukuyama domains. Two further blows to the Kirishitan came in the middle of 1868. The Kurume domain government forced Kirishitan in Imamura village to convert to Buddhism even before the central government started its campaign: only two Kirishitan refused to promise to conduct Buddhist funerals, and they were jailed for a short time. Then the Meiji government imprisoned more than 220 Kirishitan in the Gotō islands who came out of hiding when their leader, Domingo Matsugorō, arranged with Father Petitjean to invite the French missionary Jules Cousin to the islands. Upon being imprisoned, the Gotō Kirishitan had to endure torture and hunger along with unspeakably cramped and filthy quarters. Many of them died in prison.[76] And those who escaped arrest were far from safe as hatred toward Kirishitan boiled up in the ruling establishments.

One evening during the first month of 1870, four local samurai of the Fukue domain in the Gotō islands stopped by a house to get some drinking water on their return from martial practice. They found that the people who lived there were followers of the so-called heretical sect. Displeased, they pressed these Kirishitan to abandon their religion, but to no avail. They retreated for the moment but returned to the house at night, determined to force the Kirishitan to discard their faith. This led to a verbal scuffle, and the short-tempered samurai finally acted. Condemning Christianity as the "unpardonable vice of the imperial country," they pulled out their swords and murdered five helpless Kirishitan, including three women and a child. Only a 5-year-old child was spared.[77] Under vigorous protest from foreign ministers, particularly from the British foreign minister Harry S. Parkes, the shogunate ordered the domain government to release the Gotō Kirishitan still held in prison. By 1872, when their leaders were finally released, 42 Kirishitan had perished in jail cells.

What happened to the remaining Urakami Kirishitan who had lost their leaders in 1868? From the beginning, the stance of the Meiji government was clear: if it did not treat these people harshly, then anti-government groups might exploit its inaction for their own purposes by contending that it had caved to pressure from the West.[78] Already in the twelfth month of 1869, the Meiji government deported more than 3,300 Urakami Kirishitan to twenty different domains—a punishment known as "total banishment."[79] The Urakami persecution was soon developed into a focal point of Western pressure. In the first month of 1870, foreign ministers from Great Britain, France, the United States, and North Germany held a conference with a delegation of Japanese leaders led by Iwakura Tomomi; the diplomats presented their governments' displeasure and demanded redress. But Iwakura replied: "What the people of the Christian sect say is that since Japan's *kami* and Buddhas are all born out of the Christian sect, it would be of no benefit to believe in those *kami* and Buddhas. For this reason, [they] are in unspeakable discord with the people of our sect."[80] As far as Iwakura was concerned, national unity was the most critical issue for his incipient government, and anything that might disturb it had to be dealt with resolutely. He continued:

> The native Christians of Urakami have given much trouble to their neighbors through their hostile and overbearing conduct. If this were allowed to continue unchecked, then serious disturbances would ensue, and this would prove prejudicial to foreign trade. We therefore consider it necessary to remove them to another place. We do this not for the single reason of their being Christians but, rather, because they have become ungovernable.[81]

Iwakura was firm in his conviction that "Japan is at present constituted of one uniform faith, and this is essential to good government; the sudden introduction of a foreign religion would give rise to the most serious troubles."[82] British foreign minister Parkes reported to his government: "I endeavored in vain to persuade those [Japanese] officers to delay their proceedings."[83] Nevertheless, Meiji leaders increasingly felt that their anti-Christian position might derail their efforts to revise unequal treaties, and by extension, to build a modern country—a country of "civilization and enlightenment."

Despite the fact that Christianity was kept in check, the system of temple certification began to lose its power. The first omen of this already occurred in the third month of 1868, when an anti-Buddhist movement spread with lightening speed. It was ignited by the government's official separation of Shinto and Buddhism (*shinbutsu bunri*), which was implemented through a series of edicts and ordinances with the purpose of cleansing Shinto of Buddhist elements.[84] Vandalism and pent-up resentment drove the nationwide campaign "to reject the Buddha and destroy Śākyamuni": temple buildings were destroyed or burnt down, small temples were forcibly merged into bigger ones, statuary and ritual implements were destroyed or melted for cannons, and other temple properties were confiscated or looted. Many Buddhist monks were defrocked, returned to a secular life, and/or expelled from their temples.[85]

In a show of trying to divest imperial rites and ceremonies of any Buddhist character, Emperor Meiji conducted Shinto-style memorial services for his father, Emperor Kōmei (r. 1847–66), who had previously been buried with a Buddhist service. After this, the imperial house no longer conducted Buddhist funerary rites for its members.[86] In the fourth intercalary month, the Meiji government moved to order all Shinto priests to conduct Shinto funerals for their family members, effectively freeing them from the bondage of the *danka* system.[87] At the same time, it encouraged the populace to leave their *danna* temples voluntarily and to switch to Shinto funerals. This anti-Buddhist, pro-Shinto atmosphere began to take a heavy toll on the *danka* system. As Zōryū, the head monk of Kōyasan Myōōin, put it, "leaving the *danka* relationship, harassing the Buddha, destroying temples, and switching to Shinto funerals" were actions poised to paralyze, if not to expunge, Buddhism's cherished religious function—the performance of death-related rituals and memorial services.[88]

Understandably, those who were involved in designing and executing much of this anti-Buddhist, pro-Shinto policy were Shinto advocates and nativist scholars who had been active in, or sympathetic to, the Shinto funeral movement in the late Tokugawa period. A key figure (among many) was Kamei Koremi (1825–85), lord of the Tsuwano domain and vice-minister of the Department of Divinity (the Jingikan, a government organ vested with broad authority over religious affairs), who had already forced Shinto funerals upon the residents of his domain in 1867.[89] Kamei was a staunch patron of Oka Kumaomi, who had spearheaded the Shinto funeral movement in Tsuwano since 1846. It is said that no sooner was the Meiji government formed than Kamei enforced Shinto funerals in his domain, along with submitting to the Meiji leaders three Shinto ritual manuals: one on memorial services, one on funeral rites, and one on funeral oration.[90] Assisted by his former vassal Fukuba Bisei (1831–1907, undersecretary for the Department of Divinity, instructor of Emperor Meiji in Shinto ceremonials, and faithful follower of National Learning) and Ōkuni Takamasa (1792–1871), Kamei pushed for the nationwide adoption of Shinto funerals. James E. Ketelaar discusses why Kamei and Fukuba were so keen on instituting Shinto funerals:

By defining funerals—which by their very nature involved every person, members of every sect, and most of the deities in Japan—the state sought the right to define death, including the possibilities thereafter, and thereby reflexively to order life itself. It was assumed, in short, that those who controlled death controlled life. [Kamei and Fukuba] . . . perceived Buddhist-style funerals to be the central axis of the Buddhist institutional framework as well as of its social organization. To take full legislative control over the operation of funerals down to the smallest details on the national level would, they reasoned, serve the dual purpose of removing a prominent source of Buddhist influence from all levels of society from the Imperial household to the general populace.[91]

At the local level as well, Shinto priests, government officials, and village elders who were supportive of National Learning or late Mito-gaku (a school of Shinto-Confucian syncretic thought) promoted Shinto funerals. They argued that they were introducing a new custom for a new age. Some daimyo were extremely enthusiastic about promoting Shinto funerals. For example, the daimyo of the Matsumoto domain, Toda Mitsunori, abolished his family's Buddhist temple and adopted the Shinto style of funerals in 1869. The next year he forced Shinto funerals upon all residents of his domain and distributed such Shinto funeral manuals as the *Sōji ryakki* (Synopsis of funerals). The Matsumoto domain's pro-Shinto funeral policy continued until 1871, when all daimyo domains were replaced with new national prefectures.[92] The people, who had endured the dominance of Buddhist monks and the high cost of old-fashioned Buddhist funeral services, seemed to respond (albeit slowly) to calls for Shinto funerals, which were hailed as a symbol of "civilization and enlightenment."[93]

Nevertheless, the long-held custom of Buddhist funerals did not go away as easily as Shinto proponents had hoped. The populace remained quite uneasy about the new custom of Shinto funerals; many Shinto priests were worried that if they performed funeral rites, they would contract the pollution of death; and there was still no standardized format or manual for the performance of Shinto funerals. Moreover, the idea of enforcing Shinto funerals among the entire populace did not seem to be compatible with the Meiji government's ambition to construct State Shinto, which should stand above all religions and maintain the highest spiritual standards. In 1870, the Meiji government surveyed all shrines in the nation, organized them hierarchically, and redistributed land to them. A year later, in 1871, it banned Shinto priests and families from inheriting their positions according to blood lineage.[94] These measures were intended to improve the qualifications of Shinto priests and institutions, and to incorporate them into the governing structure of State Shinto. But to their frustration, government officials soon realized that once State Shinto was established and Shinto funerals were fully put into place, the private citizens of the country were to be buried with funeral services officiated by priest-officials of the state. This meant that the nation's Shinto priests—many of whom were ill-educated, self-serving, and factionalized—would, without exception, have to be made into state officials with the right to oversee the private family rituals of the populace. Given the overall state of Shinto priests and their shrines, this was too ambitious a vision to be realized.

Despite a flood of various ideas and efforts, anti-Christianity remained a contentious issue. Even if the populace was encouraged to terminate their *danna* relationships with Buddhist temples and to conduct Shinto funerals, government officials were not sure whether these changes could ensure the prevention of Christianity. Shinto funerals, which were still vague in format and in procedure, were often indistinguishable from "private funerals" (*jisō*) that were neither Buddhist nor Shinto and that were conducted by laypersons without clerical or administrative supervision. For the most part, Kakure Kirishitan could have their own way simply by saying they were conducting "private funerals." For this reason, even the Jingikan was very cautious in handing out permission to families seeking independent Shinto funerals. For instance, in the eighth month of 1868, a family in Kyoto associated with the Yoshida Shinto house petitioned the government to allow it to conduct Shinto funerals. In approving the petition, the Shinto policy bureau attached the condition that "the family should submit a pledge written in blood, certifying that its members are not members of the wicked sect [i.e., Christianity]."[95]

Some Meiji leaders were uneasy with the aggressive attitude of Shinto fanatics and were not enthusiastic about enforcing Shinto funerals among the entire population. Local governments, with the exception of such pro-Shinto domains as Satsuma, Tosa, Naegi, Matsumoto, Tsuwano, and the like, were also rather guarded when it came to dealing with issues related to Shinto funerals and tended to consult the central government on delicate situations.[96] This ambivalent atmosphere continued at least until the fourth month of 1871, when a new law pertaining to family registration was passed. Based on this new legislation aimed at establishing "a homogenous national structure for determining the number of households, the size of the population and other census information," the central government ordered local governments in the second month of 1872 to conduct a census and to draw up a register of all residents under their jurisdiction.[97] Taking the Chinese zodiacal name of the year it was established, the Jinshin *koseki* system replaced the previous population register of sectarian inspection.

This was a sweeping administrative overhaul, and it officially terminated the age-old system of temple certification that had gripped Japanese society for more than two centuries. The new family registration system, which introduced a new way of obtaining non-Christian certification (*ujiko shirabe* or *ujiko aratame*), was designed to work as follows.[98] The nation's entire population was to be organized into tutelary "*ujiko* parishes"; every household was to register its members as parishioners (*ujiko*) at its tutelary shrine and was to receive protective talismans (*mamorifuda*) as proof of their non-Christian identity (at death, the talismans were to be returned to the tutelary shrine); and every six years, at the time of renewal of household registration, officials were to check the residents under their jurisdiction for possession of non-Christian talismans.[99] In order to ensure that control of this new household registration system remained in the hands of public officials rather than in the hands of Shinto clergy, the government stipulated that parents first report new births to the village or ward head or registrar, acquiring from him a certificate assigning the child to the parents' shrine parish, and then present the certificate to the priest of the shrine. Upon receiving this, the priest was required to register the child as a parishioner of his shrine and to present the household with a tutelary talisman.

Despite all the work that went into this new system, government officials realized that Shinto shrines and priests were not ready to be involved in the important task of nationwide population registration, which was linked to the covert agenda of anti-Christian surveillance.[100] Too many Shinto shrines were without qualified Shinto priests, and too many Shinto priests were themselves in need of reform. As a result, shrine registration was quickly abandoned in May 1873. Nevertheless, the Jinshin *koseki* system deprived the *danka* system of its most formidable weapon—temple certification. Buddhist priests, who were now disconnected from the anti-Christian administrative apparatus of the government, were, along with Shinto priests, all registered under a separate category in the Jinshin *koseki* system and were put under state supervision.[101]

With the introduction of the Jinshin *koseki* system, the Meiji government had to counter Christian elements without the effective tool of temple certification.[102] On top of that, the Western countries continued to complain about Japan's ongoing hostility toward Christianity. A few days before his departure for the United States and Europe on a mission to, among other things, revise unequal treaties, Iwakura Tomomi had a meeting with British acting foreign minister F. O. Adams. Iwakura repeated his government's anti-Christian stance: "It was absolutely necessary that the people of Japan should believe that His Majesty the Tennō was descended in an unbroken line from the Goddess Tenshōkō Daijin and was therefore of divine origin. The Christian religion was directly opposed to this article of faith, for it taught its disciples not to believe in any God save one."[103] However, once he and his team arrived in the West, they immediately realized how Japan's anti-Christian policy could easily complicate their efforts to revise the "humiliating" unequal treaties. Wherever they went, whether Washington, London, Paris, or the Hague, the Japanese envoys were met with harsh criticism, incessant protests, and mass demonstrations.[104] Iwakura reported to the Tokyo government that as long as Japan held on to its anti-Christian stance, it would be very hard to get the unequal treaties revised.[105]

The Meiji government did not easily relinquish its deep-rooted dislike of the followers of Christianity. Those who complicated the politico-religious battlefield for the imperial government included not only the old Kirishitan but also the new followers of Roman Catholicism, the converts to Protestantism, and the followers of the Russian Orthodox Church.[106] Under intense Western pressure, the government officially advised local governments to refrain from harassing Christians too aggressively. In the sixth month of 1872, it issued two decrees that clearly harbored hidden agendas: the first prohibited families from conducting private funerals, obliging them to entrust this task either to a Shinto priest or to a Buddhist monk; the second instructed Shinto priests to tend to all matters related to funeral services when so requested by their parish members.[107] The first decree, which banned private funerals, specified that only two religions—Buddhism and Shinto—could lawfully be involved in conducting funerals. The second decree took the first a step further, insisting that Shinto priests play a more active role in dealing with the deaths of their parishioners.[108] The real purpose—to make Christian funerals illegal—was not explicitly stated. This was a covert anti-Christian strategy, and it was contrived specifically to appease Western pressure while continuing to suppress Christianity.

In a situation in which outright suppression of Christianity was no longer a wise option and Shinto funerals were still alien to most of the populace, the Meiji government opted to revive Buddhist funerals as a tool of anti-Christian surveillance. Once this strategy was back in place, the Meiji government proclaimed in February 1873 that: "From now on, the existing clauses [concerning the prohibition of Christianity] on the public bulletin board are to be obliterated."[109] With this decree, the anti-Christian regulations were removed from the nation's public bulletin boards, supposedly bringing to an end the prohibition of Christianity. Diplomatically, the Meiji government was off the hook; however, it should be noted that the populace was still unable to conduct Christian funerals freely.[110]

While the authorities kept Christianity in check through the ban on private funerals, Meiji officials stepped up their efforts to promote Shinto funerals. In the process, they noticed that there were two specific stumbling blocks that required immediate attention. One was that the populace did not seem to have a clear idea about how to practice Shinto rites. Shinto funerals differed from locality to locality, ritual manuals were difficult to come by, and when they were available they were almost incomprehensible. In order to solve these problems, the government studied various ritual formulae, then published and distributed a standard ritual manual entitled *Sōsai ryakushiki* (Synopsis of [Shinto] funerals).[111] However, this funerary manual was too brief to offer detailed guidelines, and it soon led to the publication of numerous supplementary ritual texts that reflected the characteristics of various traditions and schools.

The other obstacle had to do with the method of disposing of the corpse. For Shinto funeral advocates who reviled Buddhist cremation as being "barbaric and cruel" and "unfilial," the only option was burial.[112] However, this posed a problem, particularly in urban areas where high population density had already produced an acute shortage of burial space. Cremation, on the other hand, was not free from trouble either: an awful stench tormented the densely populated neighborhoods of Tokyo, where most crematoria were located. The government was inundated with complaints about this, and it took the opportunity in 1873 to outlaw cremation throughout the country.

However, this seemingly pro-Shinto measure did not do much to disrupt the custom of Buddhist funerals. In areas where the practice of cremation was deeply rooted, the edict had little effect, and Buddhist temples that possessed cemeteries were not much bothered by it.[113] The real problem lay in the shortage of new burial spaces, particularly in big cities such as Tokyo and Osaka. The situation quickly worsened as families were increasingly encouraged to adopt Shinto funerals.[114] Unlike Buddhist temples, Shinto shrines dared not set up cemeteries within their precincts. As a way of addressing this predicament, Tokyo began to allocate new burial sites in the metropolitan area that were to be used exclusively for Shinto funerals (originally, two places in Aoyama and Shibuya Hanesawa, and then an additional four places in Aoyama, Zōshigaya, Komagome, and Fukagawa).[115]

Despite this effort, the government's insistence on burial soon created a more serious problem—the unsanitary conditions caused by "spillover" and rotting corpses. The shortage of burial grounds was rapidly becoming a serious problem. Government officials came to understand that cremation, which had gained popularity in the West on sanitary grounds, was a banner of modern "civilization"—the very banner they were looking to hoist.[116] Heeding the arguments of the pro-cremation side, the government reversed its previous decision on cremation in 1875, banned burial in Tokyo's inner-city area, and relocated all crematory facilities to the outskirts of the city. At the same time, new burial spaces were allocated in the outer city and were to be used exclusively by families practicing Shinto funerals.[117] The adoption of Shinto funerals was strongly promoted, but government officials also felt that they could no longer remain blind to the mounting demand for burial space among the general public. After a series of trials and errors, the government eventually gave up all of its attempts to establish exclusive burial sites for those families practicing Shinto funerals and decided in 1880 that cemeteries would be open to any family, regardless of its religious affiliation. Shinto funerals were incorporated into the public cemetery system; thus, the recipient of a Shinto funeral usually ended up being buried in a public cemetery far away from the domain of Shinto.[118] The lifting of the ban on cremation meant that the legal maneuvering that had fueled the campaign for Shinto funerals was losing much of its impetus.

More important, in building an empire upon the idea that State Shinto should transcend all religions, the Meiji government could no longer afford to be selective when mobilizing potential spiritual support. As long as they fell within the larger frame of Japanese cultural tradition, minor sectarian differences, whether Shintoist, Buddhist, or Confucian, were to be tolerated and mobilized for a grander cause. In fact, the Meiji government had already in 1872 reconstituted the Department of Divinity into the Ministry of Doctrine, which would lead the Great Promulgation Campaign (*taikyō senpu undō*) — a nationwide campaign begun in 1870 that aimed to create a state religion by indoctrinating the populace and preventing the spread of Christianity. Beginning in 1872, the Ministry of Doctrine reorganized "proselytizers" (*senkyōshi*), who had been involved in the indoctrination campaign from the outset, and incorporated a wide range of additional instructors (including Shinto priests, Buddhist monks, Confucian scholars, ministers of new religions, preachers of National Learning, and even kabuki actors and storytellers) into the newly minted position of "instructors of doctrine" (*kyōdōshoku*).[119] A corps of doctrinal instructors assigned to nationwide teaching institutes launched a full-force campaign to inculcate in the populace the Three Principles of the "Great Teaching": revere the *kami* and love the country, illuminate the principle of Heaven and the Way of Man, and respect the emperor and serve the will of the imperial court. The Three Great Teachings, which were not particularly Shinto in character, were eventually molded into a tool for constructing State Shinto.[120]

Amid the promotion of the Great Promulgation Campaign, some zealous officials at the Ministry of Doctrine made efforts to increase Shinto funerals by resorting to the ongoing ban on private funerals. However, progress lagged far behind expectation. It seemed that many Shinto priests, who fashioned themselves as state ritualists, remained by and large ignorant of the procedural details of Shinto funerals and were still quite wary of death pollution — the notion that Hirata National Learning had tried to repel through its funeral manuals.[121] In an attempt to widen the pastoral base of Shinto funerals, the Ministry of Doctrine moved in 1874 to allow all doctrinal instructors, regardless of their religious affiliation, to conduct Shinto funerals. The official rationale for this policy was that, through the active involvement of all doctrinal instructors, people could be guided "to orient their life and so to arrive, after death, at a place where their soul could rest without regret."[122] Whatever the rationale, the ministry's real intention was to provide a way for Shinto priests to conduct Shinto funerals as doctrinal instructors rather than as Shinto priests. It was hoped that this would enable them to bypass the death taboo while also raising much-needed revenues for the Three Great Teachings campaign. By following this policy, Shinto priests could, at their convenience, adopt a "second identity" when it came to conducting Shinto funerals. Already in 1872, soon after Shinto priests had been co-opted into the Great Promulgation Campaign, the Ise Grand Shrine (Ise Jingū) created the Jingūkyō church as a teaching institute for doctrinal instructors. This institute was separate from the shrine so that religious activities (including the promulgation of "great teaching") other than state rituals could be promoted without violating the sanctity of State Shinto. By 1875, the Jingūkyō had developed into a nationwide network of 1,600 preaching stations located in local shrines, and these, in turn, were organized into 31 districts. Many Shinto shrines were now equipped with separate religious halls or churches (*kyōkai*), where funerals could be held without contaminating the dwelling places of *kami*. Under the protective shields of a second identity and separate church facilities, Shinto priests-cum-doctrinal instructors could enter into "a subterfuge that allowed them to adopt both ritualist and pastoral roles but also permitted them to keep the roles separate whenever their conflation would conflict with traditional notions of pollution."[123] The government hoped this would serve to preempt the occurrence of "private funerals," by which it meant Christian funerals.

Despite various efforts to mitigate them, many problems broke out over "private funerals." For example, in August 1874, a military physician named Nagase Tokie was indicted for giving his wife's grandmother a Christian funeral. The Tokyo court found Nagase guilty of violating the edict on private funerals and fined him two *yen* and fifty *sen*.[124] In December of the same year, the government charged three Christians in a much publicized trial with violating the ban on private funerals. Those indicted were: Itō Jōuemon, who had given his deceased mother a Christian funeral; and two of his fellow Christians, Ogawa Yoshiyasu and Okuno Masatsuna, who had attended the ceremony. The story has it that on her sickbed, Itō Jōuemon's mother, who was a "*danka*" (a Buddhist term used to refer to members of the Christian church) of a Yokohama church, asked her non-Christian son to provide her with a Christian funeral. Upon her death, Itō asked the head monk of An'yōin in Meguro, where the family grave was located, to bury his mother according to her wishes, but the monk refused for fear of punishment. Pressed by time, Itō purchased a public burial ground in Yanaka and through

Ogawa and Okuno was able to arrange a Protestant-style funeral conducted by an American missionary, David Thompson (Scottish missionary Henry Faulds also attended). Ogawa and Okuno, prominent figures in the slowly growing Christian community in the Tokyo-Yokohama region, were arrested for their involvement and were interrogated under torture.[125] Upon hearing this news, the disheartened Christian community quickly moved to save these two men by appealing to the government and by soliciting help from foreign missionaries and ministers. The petitioners contended that Ogawa and Okuno had not been directly involved in the funeral, but rather had simply happened to be present. They also pointed out that these men had never before violated the "national law of Japan." They also argued that both men were entitled to exercise freedom of faith, a reference to the decree of February 1873 that led to the removal of anti-Christian statements from public bulletin boards.[126] As things were getting complicated, the government decided to delay the trial permanently.

As long as the ban on private funerals was not repealed, Christian funerals were, in theory, still illegal. But that did not seem to matter. In June 1875, less than a month after the removal of the ban on cremation, the Meiji government again encountered a case that involved Christian defiance of the proscribed private funerals. Takahashi Ichiemon, a resident of Shikahama, Tokyo, became a Christian upon the recommendation of his younger brother (who had converted to Christianity the previous year) and relinquished all paraphernalia pertaining to his previous religious life. He burned Shinto talismans, ancestral tablets, Buddhist images, and the like, then asked the city government for permission to practice "private" (i.e., Christian) funerals. The city government, perplexed by this defiant request, asked the central government for guidance. What most disturbed officials of the central government was that Takahashi had thrown away the "paper amulet, or *taima*, that was the spiritual symbol of the Great Divine Shrine of Amaterasu."[127] But they knew that they could not do much about Takahashi's "right of belief" for fear that, should it be suppressed, Japan might face difficulty in building good relations with the Western powers. In August, the central government directed the city authorities to "exhort" Takahashi, and by extension, all Christians, not to get involved in such offenses—a vague instruction that did not really mean anything.[128] Local provinces sought guidance for similar cases involving Christian funerals; however, due to mounting

pressure from the West, the central government was not able to provide satisfactory solutions. Takahashi Ichiemon got his way. From
this time on, the government seemed to give up trying to criminalize
Christian funerals. In the face of reports that new Christian converts
in Sundō county, Shizuoka were destroying Ise amulets and ancestral
tablets, the Meiji government again proved to be helpless.[129]

Worse yet, government officials grew more and more concerned
that the instructors of doctrine, being heterogeneous in origin,
might taint the divine stature of Shinto. In particular, they felt that
high-ranking Shinto priests of imperial-sponsored (*kanpei*) and state-
sponsored (*kokuhei*) shrines—the principal liturgists of state rites—
should be distinguished from the lowly hybrid priest-instructors.
Furthermore, with the abolition of the Great Teaching Institute in
1875 and the withdrawal of Buddhists from the Great Promulgation
Campaign that followed, the Ise Grand Shrine assumed de facto leadership of the campaign and imbued it ever more aggressively with
the character of Shinto. In 1877, the government decided to close down
the Ministry of Doctrine itself, which had been the driving force of the
campaign, and transferred religious affairs to the Bureau of Shrines
and Temples (*shajikyoku*) under the Ministry of Internal Affairs. Under
the leadership of the Ise Grand Shrine, however, the Great Promulgation Campaign did not go well: it was plagued with sectarian profi-
teering and factional disputes, culminating in what came to be known
as the Pantheon Dispute (*saijin ronsō*).[130]

While the campaign was bogged down in factional rivalries, public opinion calling for the separation of religion and government
was gaining more and more support, and the thesis that "Shinto
is not a religion" began to creep into government discourse. In 1882,
the government decided to separate Shinto priests from doctrinal
instructors and banned them from being directly involved in any
pastoral religious service, including Shinto funerals.[131] This edict,
which initially forbade all Shinto priests from conducting funerary
rituals, was soon amended and applied only to those serving at im-
perial- and state-sponsored shrines. The purpose of this amendment
was to prevent the disruption of the income base of lesser shrines.
Nevertheless, as a reaction against this edict, many Shinto instructors
withdrew from the Great Promulgation Campaign.[132] By 1884, the
Meiji government ended the almost defunct promulgation campaign,
which had now completely lost its popular appeal. Soon afterward,
the government lifted the ban on private funerals, proclaiming that

all matters pertaining to funeral rites should be free from government regulation.[133] In its attempt to guard Japan against Christianity, the Meiji government first opted for utilizing funerary Buddhism and later endeavored to replace it with funerary Shinto. Both these efforts now ceased.

It is hard to know to what extent the populace actually switched to Shinto funerals during the Meiji period. Two decades into the Meiji era, Western scholar Arthur Hyde Lay observed that, out of 754,000 deaths in one year, Shinto deaths numbered roughly one-third (224,500), Buddhist deaths two-thirds (526,500), and Christian deaths 3,000.[134] Despite the fact that the imperial family and the upper classes had adopted Shinto funerals at the beginning of the Meiji period, Lay found that "the bulk of the nation—and in particular the country people—have, however, clung tenaciously to their old belief, and most of the burials among the middle and lower class are still carried out with Buddhist rites."[135] However, comprehensive data that might illustrate the overall trend of funeral practices during the Meiji period are not available.

In measuring the popularity of Shinto funerals, local variations should be taken into account. Clearly, the residents in the areas most strongly influenced by National Learning and Shinto activists were easily compelled to adopt Shinto funerals. On the other hand, the residents in the areas under the rule of pro-Shinto lords were often forced to switch to Shinto funerals, as is seen in the example of Satsuma. It is said that, until the mid-nineteenth century, all Shimazu lords of Satsuma faithfully lived up to the dictum of its fifteenth authoritarian chieftain, Shimazu Takahisa (1514–71), who had warned: "He who believes not in Buddhism is no descendant of mine."[136] But the last two lords, Nariakira (1809–58) and Tadayoshi (1840–97), quickly turned antagonistic toward anything Buddhist. Tadayoshi buried his wife with "the ceremony of the divine country, or *shinkoku*" in 1869 and then transferred all of his clan's memorial services from the Sōtōshū temple Fukushōji, which had served as the clan's *danna* temple for the last seven or so centuries, to the newly erected Tsurumine Shrine in the Sengan'en Garden.[137] Not only that, he also moved to impose new Shinto posthumous names upon all of his deceased ancestors, who, as devout Buddhists, had been blessed with Buddhist names. He carved these "revised names" (*kaigō*) into "each and every one of the clan members' gravestones, often over the freshly chiseled-away Buddhist name."[138] Given the thoroughness and insistence of their lord, the residents of Satsuma had no other options. Similar mass conversions occurred in other domains such as Kanazawa, Tannan, Naegi, Matsumoto, Tosa, and Kawara.

Similarly, the families living in the anti-Buddhist Ise, Miyazaki, and Yamagata areas were forced to switch to Shinto funerals. In these areas, many Buddhist temples were abolished or were stripped of serving monks (or were merged with Shinto shrines, with the result that Buddhist monks were forced either to defrock or to transform themselves into Shinto priests). In villages under the heavy influence of the Ise Grand Shrine and its branches, Shinto funeral movements were spearheaded by local leaders who were determined to overhaul the much-troubled *danna* affiliations with Buddhist temples. As demonstrated by the examples of Uji, Yamada, Takihara, and Nohara villages, pro-Shinto village leaders and "instructors of doctrine" joined forces and succeeded in converting all residents to Shinto funerals.[139] Likewise, in Fukuoka and Iwate, where Shinto propagandists were active, Shinto funerals were adopted rapidly among the populace.[140]

The rapidity and ease with which families switched to Shinto funerals varied considerably by region. The earliest example in the Kantō area occurred in the second month of 1869, in the Naegashima (more than 100 families) and Kashiwagura villages of Kazusa. The most active conversion took place in Iwahana (part of present-day Gunma and Saitama prefectures) between summer 1869 and spring 1870, where local officials sympathetic to National Learning as well as Shinto priests spread the anti-Buddhist movement.[141] In all villages, mass conversion to Shinto funerals was justified "as a response to the restoration of imperial rule" or "as a way to pay back the favor of being born in the imperial land." For example, the residents of Seki village, Kodama county, Musashi stated in their petition that with the arrival of a new age ushered in by the imperial restoration and the abandonment of Buddhism, "we wish to return to the past preserved for more than a thousand years by quickly switching to Shinto funerals [and moving] away from the guidance of enterprising Buddhist monks."[142] When their wish was realized, the villagers speedily moved to get rid of Buddhist paraphernalia and to build Shinto-style spirit halls in their houses as well as to install spirit tablets decorated with *sakaki* trees.[143] Similarly, the residents in Enoshima, Ōyama, and Hasugesan in Kanagawa, who had maintained *danna* relations with *shugenja*, all swiftly switched to Shinto funerals by 1872 in a situation where these hybrid-practitioners were either transformed into Shinto priests, expelled from their shrines, or prohibited from engaging in religious activities.[144] On the other hand, the residents of Sekioka village in Fukushima universally adopted Shinto funerals in February 1873, when five funerary temples in the village were reduced to one.[145] By and large, the adoption of Shinto funerals, which came about through both force and persuasion, peaked in the sixth month of 1872, when the Meiji government banned private funerals and ordered Shinto priests to take a more assertive role in conducting rituals for the deceased.

Against the increasing dominance of Shinto funerals, Buddhist temples fought back in an alliance with their pro-Buddhist followers. The case of Naegi domain—a small domain of 10,000 *koku* in Ena county, Mino—is a good example. In 1869, the governor of Naegi (most of the former daimyo of the nation's domains were appointed as governors in the sixth month of 1868) charged Aoyama Naomichi, an ardent follower of Hirata National Learning, to carry out a sweeping religious reform. Aoyama wasted no time in declaring that National Learning should be the principal teaching and that all Buddhist temples should be abolished, their monks defrocked, and their lands confiscated. And then, in 1870, he ordered all domain residents to abandon their *danna* temples and to change to Shinto shrines.[146] Fifteen temples (most of them Rinzaishū) in the domain were completely abolished, and all residents were forced to adopt Shinto funerals. However, the Jōdoshinshū followers of Shiomi village, whose *danna* temple Hōseiji was in the neighboring Owari domain, resisted and petitioned against the order. Amid the tension, the governor was on a tour of inspection and was staying at the home of the village elder, when he discovered that the village elder's family had not yet dismantled their household Buddhist altar. Displeased, the governor ordered the village elder and the head of the village association to bring the Buddhist images and all their other Buddhist paraphernalia to the yard in front of the room in which he was staying. The next day, before the eyes of the governor all those Buddhist items were burned, despite the entreaty of the village elder who said that this would break the heart of his septuagenarian uncle. At that time, the wife of the association head was so disheartened that she had to be held back from jumping into the flames in an attempt to "burn herself to death along with the main Buddhist statue." The governor then ordered the officials to collect and destroy all Buddhist objects that could be found within the village.[147] After this episode the villagers were forced to pledge that they would keep to the order of Shinto. The domain officials encountered pockets of resistance, including an appeal staged by Hōseiji's head temple in Kyoto, Higashihonganji, but eventually they achieved their goal.[148]

Buddhist temples began to grow desperate. In the tenth month of 1871, Yuigyō, head monk of the Jōdoshinshū temple Renkyōji in Iwami, joined forces with lay followers who were disgruntled over "unfair" tax burdens. Armed with bamboo spears and intending to "kill officials involved in the *ujiko* registration" as well as "the enemies of stone Buddhist statues" (referring to those who knocked down stone Jizō statues on the roadside), they conspired to stage an uprising. Sadly for them, their hastily cobbled together plan produced only prisoners.[149]

Interestingly, the resistance of Jōdoshinshū followers to the Meiji government's pro-Shinto policy was often fueled by their deep-rooted anti-Christian sentiments. The Meiji government's policy on the separation of *kami* and buddhas was never meant to constitute a friendly gesture toward Christianity, yet some Jōdoshinshū followers saw in it a pro-Christian scheme. Early in the third month of 1871, about 3,000 Jōdoshinshū followers in Mikawa decided to interpret the enforcement of Shinto prayer at shrines, the abolishment and consolidation of Buddhist temples, and the elimination of Buddhist religious inspection as being the result of pro-Christian pressure. As they surrounded the residence of the village head, officials dispatched from the government tried to negotiate with them. When the officials emerged from the residence without much success, the protesters attacked them, shouting that "Yaso [Jesus] has come out!" One official was killed with bamboo spears.[150] Similarly, Jōdoshinshū followers and monks in Tsuruga and Echizen were rattled by a series of anti-Buddhist policies and rose in the name of protecting the Law of the Buddha, arguing that "the affairs since the Restoration are all Christianity's asking. . . . The imperial court became fond of Christianity, and [Western-style] haircuts and Western-style dress are Christian customs. The teaching principles of the three articles are Christian teachings, and the Western letters taught at school are Christian letters."[151] For ardent Buddhist supporters and monks, who suddenly found themselves confronting a very bleak situation, the early Meiji period was certainly a time of trauma. Still, it is ironic that their frustration, despair, and anger were assuaged when their loyalty to their traditional worldview was again pitted against Christianity — an alien religion against which they had been well-indoctrinated — rather than against Shinto. Buddhist fanatics even argued that Shinto funerals had been introduced by Christian enemies who wanted to destroy Buddhism.

Anxiety about Shinto funerals ran deep not only for Buddhist temples poised to lose everything but also for the people who were suddenly pressured into abandoning generations-old customs and norms. Many families who had switched to Shinto funerals tried to switch back to Buddhist funerals once they realized how uneasy they were with the former and once the government gradually eased its aggressive policy.[152] In the seventh month of 1872, some 107 residents of Seki village petitioned the domain government to allow them to revert to Buddhist funerals, arguing that their 1869 conversion to Shinto funerals had been made under duress because the monks of their *danna* temples had all been eliminated. Their petition also had a legal point: according to the 1872 ban on private funerals, Buddhist funerals were perfectly lawful. The petition was approved, but the domain government warned the people that they should not be swayed by "a wicked teaching of misguided origin," adding that the 1872 legislation was intended to promote Shinto funerals as a symbol of "enlightenment."[153] In 1877, the dozens of residents in Sekioka village who had adopted Shinto funerals "upon the recommendation of officials" in 1873 appealed to the local government to allow them to return to performing Buddhist funerals. They argued that: according to the 1874 legislation, conversion to a religion should be a matter of free choice; they were still deeply attached to Buddhist funerals; senior family members had a particularly hard time in understanding why they should follow the new custom of Shinto funerals; and ancestral graves and tombstones were all located in their previous Buddhist *danna* temples.[154] Their appeal was accepted.

Many families were very nervous about having to move their ancestral tablets (which were enshrined in Buddhist altars) once they adopted Shinto funerals. They feared that the removal of ancestral tablets from the ancestral *danna* temple or household Buddhist altar might irritate their ancestors and invite misfortune. The government eased its stance on Shinto funerals to the point where, in 1878, it announced that "the [religious] format of a funeral should rest with the desire of each person" and that this rule should apply even to the families of Shinto priests and instructors. The Matsumoto domain was one of the most anti-Buddhist domains. In fact, the lord Toda Mitsunori forced all residents—from his vassals, foot soldiers, and peasants to his servants—to adopt Shinto funerals immediately after the Meiji Restoration. In order to make sure that every single resident abandoned funerary Buddhism and practiced funerary Shinto, Toda dispatched officials to each village to conduct an inspection.[155] But here, too, most of the domain residents gradually switched back to Buddhist funerals once the domain was abolished in the seventh month of 1871.[156] Throughout Japan, many families reverted to Buddhist funerals. By the year 1884, when the government lifted the ban on private funerals, instantly transforming funerary Shinto into merely one type of funerary ritual among many, funerary Buddhism regained much of its previous dominance.

The system of temple certification had already become a relic of the past, but the *danka* system weathered the pro-Shinto era of Meiji. The Buddhist framework of funerals and ancestral rites in Meiji Japan no longer had its previous legal (or semi-legal) clout, but it did persist. Given that most of the populace did not really dispense with the customs of funerary Buddhism, one might wonder how it was eventually incorporated into the governing structure of the state. Meiji leaders were preoccupied with the task of building a powerful modern nation-state; as part of this effort, ancestral veneration, which was firmly entrenched in the family life of the populace, could not be ignored whether it manifested itself in Buddhist or in Shinto terms. It was understood that ancestral veneration, which was now often termed ancestor worship (*sosen sūhai*), spiritually buttressed household institutions that were to be integrated into the nation-state. Furthermore, Meiji leaders envisioned the nation-state as one big family headed by the emperor. And this family, both structurally and spiritually, resembled that of the individual household. This vision of state rule is known as the family-state (*kazoku kokka*).

Meiji leaders endeavored to mobilize the spiritual source of ancestor worship for the construction of a family-state according to a hierarchical logic. The ancestral deities of each household were to be linked to the tutelary Shinto deity (*ujigami*) of the village in which those members lived, and the collective body of tutelary deities at the village level was to be linked to a supreme tutelary deity at the national level—the Sun Goddess (Amaterasu, the ancestral deity of the imperial family), who was enshrined at Ise Jingū. In this chain of connection, the acts of ancestor worship conducted at individual households were all to converge upon the Sun Goddess of the state via the channel of the tutelary deities of local villages. The Sun Goddess was the ultimate object toward which the people of the entire nation were, as members of the single big family, to pay their homage and worship.

In actuality, however, ancestor worship at the household level was channeled to veneration toward the emperor, who, as the head of the family-state of Japan, personified the Sun Goddess, through the institution of household heads and village organizations. In this structure, the members of a household were expected to direct their veneration to their household head, who personified and represented their household institution toward the village community. The act of venerating the household head, which was stressed as constituting filial piety, was then extended to the communal well-being of the village. At the national level, the collective action of filial piety in each locality was then loyally directed toward the emperor himself. Loyalty to the emperor could not be established without the channel of filial piety to the household head.[157]

In order to ensure that filial piety toward the household head converged with loyalty to the emperor, the Meiji state tried to strengthen the status of the household head and to guarantee his rights and power, which were to be inherited through the principle of primogeniture. This was promoted through legislation: first by the Family Registration Law of 1871, which incorporated each family (as represented and controlled by the household head) into the governing structure of the state, and then by the Civil Law (*minpō*) of 1898, which put the finishing touches to the power and right of the household head.[158] The absolute "right of pater familias" (*kafuken*) or "right of household head" (*koshuken*) featured in the 1898 Civil Law accommodated what Hozumi Yatsuka (1860–1912) had advocated in his critical treatise on the ill-fated first draft of that law from 1890. In his treatise (entitled *Minpō idete chūkō horobu* [Loyalty and filial piety collapse with the legislation of this civil law]), which denounced the original draft for downplaying the rights of the household head, Hozumi clearly stated why and how this position should be strengthened: "The household head represents the spirits of ancestors, and his right is sacred and inviolable in the same manner in which the spirits of ancestors are sacred and inviolable. All household members, old and young, male and female alike, must comply with the authority of their household head and seek his protection in unity."[159]

According to Hozumi, showing filial piety to the household head amounted to practicing the solemn virtue of ancestor worship. The same logic applied to the emperor, who was declared in Article 3 of the Meiji Constitution of 1889 to be "sacred and inviolable." Thus, being filially pious and loyal to the head of the family-state of Japan was considered to be a virtue, sacred and inviolable, that could neither be questioned nor subordinated to any other virtue. The 1890 Imperial Rescript on Education was specific on this point and so became "the pillar of prewar Japan's ethics and morality."[160] It declared: "Our Imperial Ancestors have founded Our Empire on a basis that is broad and everlasting, and they have deeply and firmly implanted us with virtue; Our subjects ever united in loyalty and filial piety have from generation to generation illustrated the beauty thereof. This is the glory of the fundamental character of Our Empire, and herein also lies the source of Our education."[161] It was the vision of the emperor system (*tennōsei*) that grew within the cocoon of the family-state, where filial piety and loyalty toward the emperor became the "morality of the people" (*kokumin dōtoku*).[162] In this way, filial piety and loyalty, two aspects of the same virtue, became the ideological bedrock of the family-state.

It should be noted, however, that at first it was not easy to integrate the people into a family-state mega-system through the leverage of ancestor worship, which after all, was a custom that was by nature both individual and apolitical. The psychological gap between traditional individual households (which had their own logic of survival and their own value systems) and the body politic of a modern nation-state (which was being constructed within the framework of the emperor system) seemed insurmountable.[163] In bridging this gap, Meiji leaders opted to mobilize household heads because they knew that trying to integrate individual citizens directly into the governing apparatus of the state would be almost impossible. They figured that by assigning each household head (the parent of each family) the task of bringing his family members to the parent of the state (i.e., the emperor), they could achieve their goal. As it turned out, the nation's populace eventually accepted the sacrosanct imperial leadership of Amaterasu's descendant, agreeing to become his "children." In this way, ancestor worship gave a shape to the ideological contours of the emperor system of Meiji Japan.

Conclusion

The ideology of family-state rested upon two cardinal elements: the household institution and ancestral veneration. And these elements had been fostered by funerary Buddhism throughout the Tokugawa period. The Shinto funeral movement attempted to place these two elements under the control of Shinto through the leverage of anti-Christianity. However, this endeavor, which was designed to deprive Buddhism of its monopoly on death-related rituals and household institutions, did not succeed as expected. Meiji leaders, who came to realize the political utility of funerary Buddhism, eventually decided to integrate it into the ideal of family-state.

Within the family-state design, each household was to be firmly melded into the state through ancestral veneration, which had been entrenched under the *danka* system. Over time, the household institution and the state, which were heterogeneous both in nature and in function, were indeed integrated into a unique Japanese-style modern nation-state, which would dictate the course of Japanese history until 1945. Ancestral veneration, which was practiced through the household head at the individual household level and by the emperor at the state level, played a key role in this process. Sanctified in funerary Buddhism and empowered in Meiji civil law, the household head brought individual households into the collectivity of the state, which was represented by the emperor.

According to the *Kojiki* and *Nihon shoki*, which attracted much attention in the Meiji period, the ancestral spirits of individual households originated from the same ancestral lineage as did the imperial household. Based on this, the people were exhorted to believe it was not only natural but also obligatory to direct their filial piety and loyalty to the emperor, who personified the ancestral lineage of Japan. According to this logic, the emperor, at the collective level, was the head of all individual households. For Inoue Tetsujirō (1855–1944), who in 1891 wrote an official treatise on the Imperial Rescript on Education entitled *Chokugo engi* (A commentary on the Rescript), filial piety was the ethic of individual households while loyalty was the ethic of collective households. Both of these ethical values were indispensable for the polity of Japan: "When [one] expands the spirit of filial piety for the household to the state, it becomes loyalty for the emperor. The ethic of loyalty is not different from that of filial piety because the emperor holds the household headship of the Japanese people."[164] The unity of filial piety and loyalty, which was integral to the idea of the family-state, was an ethical imperative that came into being within the tradition of ancestral veneration as preserved in the household institution under the *danka* system — and against a backdrop of anti-Christianity.

In the late Meiji period, Yanagita Kunio was alarmed by the phenomenon of domicide — the "killing of households" — which was clearly on the rise. Households could be disintegrated or cease to exist, and he regarded this as a form of "killing": in a sense, when a household no longer existed, its ancestors would lose their dwelling place and perish. For Yanagita, who was concerned with the whereabouts of ancestors, the discontinuance of a household amounted to the crime of "killing" one's ancestors.[165] Ancestors were at the center of the household institution, and the continuance of the household was ensured when its ancestors were venerated through proper ritual care. Furthermore, as has been said, ritual care for ancestors integrated individual family members into their household institution and individual household institutions into the state. This was the spiritual foundation of the Japanese nation — a foundation that had been laid within the framework of funerary Buddhism and the *danka* system.[166] Meiji leaders tried to rework the functioning of household institutions by replacing funerary Buddhism with funerary Shinto, but to no avail. The *danka* system, which weathered the anti-Buddhist storms of the Meiji period, was eventually integrated into the apparatus of the family-state.

CR

CONCLUSION

For more than two and a half centuries leading up to the Meiji period, anti-Christianity was the cornerstone of Tokugawa Japan's statehood. The weapon of anti-Christianity helped the Tokugawa shogunate not only to consolidate its governing structure but also to hold sway over its people and all political entities of the country. Kirishitan, denounced as the enemies of the *kami* and buddhas, were the perfect scapegoat and were manipulated by the regime for the purposes of social control and dominance.[1] In cementing the social order of anti-Christianity, Tokugawa leaders utilized Buddhist institutions, through the system of temple certification, to keep the entire population under surveillance. The utilization of Buddhist institutions as de facto agents of the state was the product of political calculations that underwent a prolonged period of trial and error. As it turned out, putting Buddhist institutions at the forefront of the "divine country" was an effective move: the institutional apparatus of Buddhism kept the entire populace away from the alien teachings of Christianity, and it entrenched a social order of anti-Christianity by subjugating the entire populace to Buddhist death.

Buddhist funerary services were tied up with anti-Christian scrutiny and enabled the state to control people without directly supervising their ritual lives. At the same time, Buddhist death, which was structured around ancestral veneration, helped reinforce the household institution and converted people's search for otherworldly salvation into a search for order and prosperity in this world. In this way, Buddhist death set its mark upon the lifeworld of the Tokugawa Japanese. Furthermore, in the long run, the anti-Christian element in Buddhist death contributed to nurturing a conceptual framework that would ingrain narcissistic notions of evil, otherness, and social disorder into the puristic self-image of the Japanese.

The prominence of Buddhism in Tokugawa Japan was, however, not entirely a result of the efforts of Buddhists and shogunal policy: it owed much to the inability of other religious traditions to deal with the ritual issues related to life and death. For the Tokugawa Japanese, the most common wishes were for "peace in this world" (*genze annon*) and a "good place in the next life" (*goshō zensho*). They knew that these wishes could only be fulfilled through Buddhism, which was accessible within the framework of the *danka* system. In comparison, Confucianism was remote from the religious lives of the people and failed to provide a way of realizing these wishes. The Confucianists, who were too often bogged down in an ideological agenda, did not show much interest in providing anything of substance to deal with people's religious concerns.[2] For their part, Shinto priests tended to the issues pertaining to this world; however, they were largely uninvolved when it came to matters in the other world. Despite its inherent proximity to the polity of anti-Christianity, Shinto could not help people in their quest for well-being after death, particularly because of its notion of death pollution. Thus it was Buddhism to which people turned when they desired a "good place in the other world" as well as "peace in this world," and Buddhist institutions and their monks were quick and active to respond. Beyond satiating the religious wishes of individuals, the Buddhist mode of death also helped foster ethical values and ritual practices that buttressed the survival of the household institution in the Tokugawa social order.

Moreover, the social order of Buddhist death enabled the Tokugawa regime to frame its governance as a battle between the divine principles of the *kami* and the buddhas and the alien cosmology of Christianity. Whereas the Confucian paradigm of *yin* and *yang*, or energy and principle, prevailed in China and Korea, the social order of Tokugawa Japan was inseparable from the divine world of the *kami* and the buddhas and depended on their godly protection. Rule by divinity, within the spiritual perimeter of traditional deities and against a backdrop of anti-Christianity and funerary Buddhism, was sublimated into the collective self-image of the divine country in juxtaposition with the outside world.

Prior to the arrival of Portuguese traders and Christianity in the mid-sixteenth century, the Japanese worldview was "largely a Buddhist one that perceived the world as composed of three entities: Japan (Honchō), China (Shintan), and India (Tenjiku)."[3] Although Christianity was eventually accused of promulgating "evil teachings" that threatened the country of the gods, it also played a decisive role in expanding the horizon of the Japanese worldview beyond the Buddhist outlook. In this process, Christianity was co-opted into the collective psychology of an "us vs. them" dichotomy, and in turn, this dichotomy led the Japanese to reinforce a collective identity of double-edged divinity that would justify and sanctify not only their polity of domestic governance but also their system of foreign relations. This ideological juxtaposition of "us" and "them" did not remain in abstract terms; rather, it was put into daily practice in the form of anti-Christian temple certification and funerary Buddhism.

Once the *danka* system was entrenched, Tokugawa leaders did not pay much attention to people's religious lives. All rites for the dead and ancestral spirits were to be practiced according to the dictates of funerary Buddhism, but other sorts of religious activities were relatively unchecked as far as they did not cross the boundaries of social order. People enjoyed many forms of popular religious culture, which offered moments of catharsis and relief for those seeking divine help or just a break from daily routines. Religious destinations famous for prayer, pilgrimage, and sightseeing were bustling with visitors and religious practitioners of various types. Annual festivals and seasonal religious events were fixtures in villages and towns throughout the country.

Ironically, however, within funerary Buddhism itself there was no religious freedom: once a *danna* relationship was established, it persisted from generation to generation. The *danka* system had little to do with the personal faith of individuals, who were bound by the generational *danna* relationship regardless of their own religious beliefs. In other words, the *danka* system was not geared to foster individuality and freedom in religious life; rather, it was structured to keep individuals from moving from one religious affiliation to another according to their will. As a result of this, the Tokugawa Japanese naturally settled into practicing familial funerary Buddhism within the framework of the generational *danna* relationship, which emphasized form over content. Thus, within the arena of familial Buddhism, the individual quest for Buddhist salvation did not count for much—it was given and ensured. By the same token, in a situation in which the status quo ruled, Buddhist monks did not bother to nurture the religious faith of their *danna* patrons, who were, after all, obliged to stay on within the confines of the *danna* relationship.

All of these tendencies overwhelmed even the Jōdoshinshū followers, who tended to stress the supremacy of individual belief and had even attempted to establish their own autonomous Buddhist community in medieval times. In Tokugawa society, various elements of individual faith receded into the backstage of funerary Buddhism and those elements devoted to the household institution and ancestral spirits came to the fore.[4] Indeed, as long as the Tokugawa system persisted, the survival of familial funerary Buddhism, locked into the *danka* system, was ensured across all sects.

It should be noted, however, that the anti-Christian framework of funerary Buddhism was vulnerable to criticism whenever its social role was called into question. Beginning in the early eighteenth century, political pundits began to complain that the religious life of the people as dominated by funerary Buddhism bore some responsibility for an increasing sense of crisis. The country's economic and social woes were handily attributed to the state of mind of a people in spiritual disarray. During the period of the Kyōhō reforms, for example, Confucian-minded Ogyū Sorai and Dazai Shundai maintained that the populace should be brought under the strict spiritual supervision of the state so that they could be steered away from "immoral rituals" (*inshi*) and guided toward a state of harmony with supernatural beings. *Inshi* is a metaphor referring to the "disorderly state" of religious beliefs and practices that "thrive when people stray from the path of normative ethical principles and religious practice."[5] When the people strayed in this way, Sorai and Shundai were quite convinced that nothing could go right. This was a strong accusation: Buddhism, so privileged and so dominant, was now failing miserably to point the hearts and minds of the populace in the right direction.

In line with this skepticism, *bakufu* leaders urged Buddhism to play a more aggressive role in guiding the people and become less complacent in the *danka* system. In retrospect, we understand that the *bakuhan* system of the Tokugawa regime was founded on the categorical denial of Buddhist politics, as may be seen in the annihilation of the Ikkō *ikki*, and that the Law of the Buddha was kept well away from the realm of state ideology, which was often framed in abstract Confucian terms. Yet the Tokugawa regime still expected Buddhism to exhort the populace to the proper path, and Buddhist leaders such as Suzuki Shōsan were eager to remold Buddhist monks into promoters of the public good through the concept of "obligation" (*yaku*). Perceptions of Buddhism's socio-political role were sometimes ambivalent and even self-contradictory; however, the Buddhists were always held accountable when things did not go well.

As time went on, debates over the guiding role of funerary Buddhism intensified as critics became more and more agitated by the proliferation of what they viewed as strange prayers and incantations, haughty talk of paradise and hell, nonsensical exorcisms, wasteful pilgrimages, mushrooming confraternities, faddish forms of worship, and so on.[6] When national woes were further deepened by the threats from the West that emerged in the late eighteenth century, reform-minded critics raised their voices. Discourses on the dangers of Christianity (which was associated with foreign powers) came to the fore. Aizawa Seishisai (1782–1863), author of the influential treatise *Shinron* (New theses), suggested that in order to avert "troubles from within, disaster from without," the hearts and minds of the people should be guided toward a belief in the inextricability of religion, government, loyalty, and filial piety. Within this context, he denounced any heterodox ideas that might be detrimental to the achievement of this goal, including magic, divination, Ikkōshū, and Christianity. The disintegration of people's hearts and minds was Seishisai's biggest worry, and the most feared perpetrator of this state of affairs was the "religion of barbarians" or Christianity: "They may deceive stupid commoners with it. . . . The great majority of people in the realm are stupid commoners; superior men are very few in number. Once the hearts and minds of the stupid commoners have been captivated, we will lose control of the realm."[7]

Obviously, as far as Aizawa Seishisai was concerned, the danger Christianity posed to the country of the *kami* was inseparable from the problems of funerary Buddhism, which amounted to "a serious defect in our array of official shrines and rituals." Instead of relying upon Buddhist clerics, who have "ruined our powers of moral suasion and depraved our folkways," he proposed that the state "revive rituals that have fallen into disuse, reinstate rituals now missing . . . and tacitly convey their didactic value to the people. By thus inducing all people in the realm to be loyal and filial, to be sincere in their reverence for forbears, to feel gratitude and indebtedness to rulers for blessings bestowed, to hold the spirits in awe, and to respect the deities, we will make them submit [to the Way]."[8]

In fact, under the sway of Buddhist critics, such domains as Mito, Chōshū, Satsuma, and Tsuwano took measures to remedy the social disintegration that authorities blamed on the disorderly state of people's religious lives. Buddhism was hit hard: many temples were demolished and many monks were defrocked. Criticism of Buddhism's monopoly of funerals and memorial services ran high in many parts of the country, amid charges that the *danka* system was dull and possibly even corrupt and that it was not really of any help in empowering people's hearts and minds.

No matter how strongly anti-Buddhist attacks were pushed, they were never powerful enough to dislodge the *danka* system, which was firmly built into Tokugawa governance and its anti-Christian mandate. For *bakufu* leaders, the *danka* system remained the best option available for binding people to the Tokugawa social order. To be sure, some anti-Buddhist critics insisted that anti-Christian temple certification could be replaced with Shinto certification, arguing, albeit falsely, that it would work better than the former because all of Japan's districts and villages were neatly partitioned into the separate parishes of tutelary Shinto shrines. However, the idea of overhauling the system of temple certification was neither practical nor realizable. The shogunate did not want to divert its already dwindling energies toward changing something that, by and large, seemed to be working fine. Buddhism, anti-Christianity, and the *danka* system formed a triangle that bolstered the social order throughout the era of Tokugawa Japan. The task of reform was left to the Meiji regime.

Initially, the Meiji government did not want Buddhists, who were regarded as the target of reform, to meddle with its policy toward Christianity; instead, Meiji leaders decided to build up the supremacy of Shinto. Within this context, *kami* were separated from the pantheon of Shinto-Buddhist hybrids, and all foreign religious ideas and customs, including Buddhism, were pushed aside. However, in a situation in which it was necessary to establish a sustainable rapport with the West while at the same time fending off the intrusion of Christianity, Meiji leaders soon realized that an insistence upon Shinto purism was unrealistic. They thus switched to making use of all available spiritual resources as long as they were not antithetical to the ideal of State Shinto. Taking advantage of this opportunity, Buddhist leaders quickly refashioned themselves as the vanguard of those concerned with "protecting the country" (*gokoku*) against Christianity, while their lay followers reignited the deep-rooted anti-Christian antagonism inherited from the previous period.[9] Buddhists took advantage of the prevailing tide of anti-Christianity and succeeded in restyling themselves as keepers of the divine country; by doing so, they were able to recoup many of the previous privileges of the *danka* system despite the challenges posed by Shinto funerals. Legally, the system of anti-Christian temple certification was now a thing of the past; however, its lingering psychology was quick to absorb the legacies of funerary Buddhism.

For the Meiji regime, the age-old *danka* system passed on the legacies of the custom of ancestral veneration that proved to be instrumental in strengthening the household institution and *kami* rites — elements that would lay a key foundation for the family-state and State Shinto. In the process by which household institutions were structured into the hierarchy of the family-state, each household's ancestral rites were incorporated into rites for tutelary Shinto deities, and the latter were further incorporated into rites for Amaterasu at the apex of State Shinto. Even though the original idea of State Shinto did not directly materialize from the *danka* system, the tradition of funerary Buddhism, which had nurtured ancestral rites for centuries, was absorbed into the ideology of a "family state" — an ideology that was in full force as Meiji Japan endeavored to streamline its emperor system. Buddhism, reconfigured under new circumstances, once again found itself to serve as a spiritual bulwark for a state fraught with the zeal of overcoming the "Christian" West.

CR

Reference Matter

∾

Notes

For complete author names, titles of works, and other publication data, please see the Works Cited list.

Introduction

1. It is almost impossible to give even a ballpark figure, never mind an exact one, with regard to how many temples existed during the Tokugawa period. On six different occasions (1632 [Kan'ei era], 1692, 1744, 1781–1800 [Tenmei-Kansei eras], 1834, and 1839), the shogunate ordered the nation's head temples to submit a list of their branch temples. But there are only two extant registers of head-branch temples (*jiin honmatsuchō*) available for calculating nationwide statistical data—those pertaining to the Kan'ei and Tenmei-Kansei eras, respectively. According to Tamamuro Fumio's analysis of these surviving registers, the Kan'ei register lists around 12,000 temples, while the Tenmei-Kansei register lists around 40,000 temples. Both registers, however, are incomplete and fall far short of reflecting the whole picture of the times. (For a detailed analysis, see Tamamuro Fumio [1981], pp. 15–26.) On the other hand, there are mysterious reference figures—between 460,000 and 500,000—that were often cited, if indiscreetly, as the total number of Buddhist temples in Tokugawa Japan (e.g., see Yoshida Nobuyuki [2002], p. 30). These figures indeed appear in the *Shinron* (New thesis) of Aizawa Seishisai (1825), the *Kasshi yawa* of Matsura Seizan (1821–41), and the *Suijinroku* (edited by Katsu Kaishū in 1890). It is said that these figures were based on a fundraising campaign at the turn of the eighteenth century in which Shitennōji in Osaka was alleged to have "successfully" solicited donations from 459,040 of the country's temples when it had appealed for assistance to rebuild its destroyed buildings. There is no basis to this story. Interestingly, however, the *Shaji torishirabe ruisan*, an early Meiji-period collection of documents, reiterates that there were 465,049 temples in Tokugawa Japan. (For more details, see Monbushō shūkyōkyoku, ed., "Daijusshū," pp. 30–36

and Tamamuro Fumio [1981], p. 19.) In 1925, the Ministry of Education, which gathered statistical data on the nation's Buddhist temples (*jiin*) and halls (*butsudō*), found that there were 70,012 temples and 33,824 halls. Adding to these figures the estimated number of temples destroyed during the time of the anti-Buddhist movement in the early Meiji years (at least 20 percent to 30 percent of the total), the report indicates that, during the Tokugawa period, there were more than 90,000 temples (excluding Buddhist halls, which, according to the report, did not have serving monks in residence). But it is unlikely that all of these "Buddhist halls" had no serving monks in residence during the Tokugawa period. (For more details, see Monbushō shūkyōkyoku, ed., "Dairokushū," pp. 1–3 and Monbushō shūkyōkyoku, ed., "Daijusshū," pp. 38–44.) Taking into account an additional set of factors — that many monks voluntarily opted to abandon their Buddhist status, to transform their temples into secular residences, and/or to leave their temples in a dilapidated state during the early Meiji period — I suggest that the total number of Buddhist temples in Tokugawa Japan exceeded 100,000. The figure of between 200,000 and 250,000, which includes all subtemples, is Tamamuro Fumio's.

2. For a discussion of the demography of Tokugawa Japan, see White, pp. 9–18 and Hayami (1997), pp. 78–81 and (2001), pp. 56–58. And for a reference for the number of village units, see Kodama Kōta, pp. 496–508. The shogunal government's 1834 nationwide cadastral survey on the capacity of rice production (*kokudaka*) informs us that there were 63,480 village units in the country. There are no reliable statistical data on the total number of the nation's urban wards, but it is estimated that there were about 10,000 of them. See Yoshida Nobuyuki (2002), pp. 32–33. According to government statistics, the total number of village and ward units in 1884 was 71,137. See Murata (1999), p. 33.

3. This register refers to a compilation of branch temple registers submitted by head temples to the office of temples and shrines by the tenth year (1633) of the Kan'ei era (1624–43). Among them, only 45 registers survive. For a more detailed account of how the Kan'ei register was compiled, see Tamamuro Fumio (1981), pp. 8–12.

4. Ibid., pp. 20–21.

5. For the list of temples and shrines, see Asakura Haruhiko, pp. 3–88. It should be noted that there were hundreds of petty Shinto shrines in Edo erected in the corners of residential districts, on the sides of streets, or attached to other buildings. These small-scale shrines, collectively referred to as *shōsha* or *shōshi*, were not usually tended by priests in residence. For an account of these petty shrines in Edo, see Inoue Tomokatsu, pp. 22–25.

6. Originally, the *bakufu* conducted a survey of wards and religious institutions as part of the *Gofunai fūdoki* (Records of customs and land of the inner districts [of Edo]), a would-be reference book completed in 1829 containing basic data regarding the shogunal castle town (that would supplement the previously edited *Shinpen Musashi fūdoki* [A new edition of the records of customs and land of Musashi]). Among the survey results, those pertaining to religious institutions (which were primarily obtained from

temple/shrine reports) were compiled as a separate compendium under the title *Gofunai jisha bikō* (Reference notes on temples and shrines of the inner districts [of Edo]). Although the volumes of the *Gofunai fūdoki* were destroyed in an 1872 fire, *Gofunai jisha bikō* has survived in its entirety and enables us to examine the mode of existence of Buddhist temples in Edo.

7. Nittō (1998), p. 4.

8. In this book, I refer to the True Pure Land Sect as Jōdoshinshū, and, on rare occasions, as Ikkōshū, or the Honganji sect. During the Tokugawa period, this sect was usually called Jōdoshinshū, and, less often, Ikkōshū, Gomonto-shū, Shinshū, or simply Jōdoshū. However, the name Shinshū was not officially recognized by the government until 1872. See Nagura (1995), p. 172.

9. Monbushō shūkyōkyoku, ed., "Daijusshū," pp. 1–3.

10. In understanding the incipient forms of what were later officially recognized as Buddhist institutions (*jiin*), Tamamuro Fumio's analysis of a 1633 temple survey pertaining to Kōshi county in the Kumamoto domain is helpful. According to him, even in the early decades of the seventeenth century, many Buddhist "temples" were still nothing more than semi-private prayer halls attached, or adjacent, to the main residential building of a family. They were not managed by ordained monks and they did not have official temple names. These religious facilities, which were run by semi-religious or peripatetic figures or were maintained by wealthy farmers or village officials, were later developed into independent, self-sustaining, publicly recognized Buddhist temples. Tamamuro Fumio, *Edo jidai no Sōtō-shū no tenkai*, pp. 27–40.

11. For an overall discussion of the relocation history of temples in Edo, see Nittō (1995), pp. 181–83. There are many case studies pertaining to the formation of temple districts in early modern Edo. For the Asakusa, Shitaya, Yanaka, and Ushigome temple districts, see Komori, pp. 90–96 and Itō Take-shi (1995), pp. 13–18.

12. Reproduced from the work of Nittō (1998), p. 11. In this illustration, the vermilion line refers to the city boundary set in 1818 by the *bakufu*, which wanted to confirm the areas under the jurisdiction of the offices of inspector general and of the magistrate of temples and shrines. At this time, the city magistrate's office indicated the areas under its jurisdiction with a black line.

13. Tōkyōto Bunkyōku kyōiku iinkai, ed., p. 586.

14. All this gave rise to a perennial scene, as Saitō Gesshin (1804–78) described in his *Edo meisho zue* (Illustrations of famous places in Edo) and *Tōto saijiki* (A record of annual observance in the eastern capital), in which Edo residents strolled in the temple precincts marked by the spectacle of exotic buildings and pagodas, while being thrilled by many kinds of rituals and events held throughout the year.

15. Konchiin in Shiba was granted a land of 700 *koku*.

16. For a more detailed statistical analysis of the temple lands, see Nittō (1995), pp. 183–88.

17. For more details, see Hur, pp. 14–21.

18. For example, well-known prayer temples (with names of enshrined Buddhist images in parentheses) in Edo included Nishihonganji (Amida), Shōdenji (Bishamonten), Genkakuji (Konnyaku Enma), Fukagawa Fudōdō (Fudōmyōō), Yūtenji (Amida), and Ryūsenji (Meguro Fudō). For a detailed account of Edo's popular Buddhist (and Shinto) deities, which attracted large crowds, see Niikura, pp. 12–243.

19. Instead of the term *danka seido*, some scholars adopt the term *jidan seido* (temple-patron system). This is because they believe that the former does not properly represent the reality of the relationship between funerary temples and *danna* patrons in two respects. The first is that the term *danka seido* assumes that *danna* affiliations were all formed between Buddhist temples and household units rather than between Buddhist temples and individual patrons. This being the case, the assumption of one *danna* temple per household fails to adequately explain the multifaceted affiliations between temples and individual *danna* patrons, as is seen in what is commonly known as *handanka* (half *danna* households) or *fukudanka* (multiple *danna* households). The second is that the term *danka*, which was rarely used in official documents in Tokugawa society, did not gain wide currency until the Meiji period. For these reasons certain scholars prefer the term *jidan seido*. See Fukuta (2004), p. 120 and Hōzawa (2004), pp. 158–60. However, the fact is that we find ample use of the term *danka* in temple documents as well as in local archival materials during the Tokagawa period, especially during the late Tokugawa period. Furthermore, the term *danka* is so familiar that it does not make sense to stop using the term *danka seido* simply for the sake of accommodating a minor stream of *handanka* or *fukudanka* households. Here, I follow established convention and use the term *danka seido*.

20. The term *tetsugitera* (a temple of mediation) in Jōdoshinshū denotes that its *danna* temples mediated between the sectarian head (*hōshu*) and *danna* patrons (*monto*). The services the head monk of a *tetsugi danna* temple provided for his patrons were regarded as something delegated from, and therefore conducted on behalf of, the head of the sect. Within the same context, the *monto* believed that they were the *monto* of the sectarian head rather than of their *tetsugi danna* temple.

21. For more details on the survey, see Ushiki, vol. 1, pp. 3–11, 37–42.

22. The data on funerary *danna* were indicated in terms of the numbers of individual *danna* patrons, not *danna* households, affiliated with temples. Though quite rare, this kind of data offers a precise indicator of the actual number of funerary patrons held by each temple.

23. These data are based on Ushiki, vols. 1–8.

24. See *Shiiyahan honmatsu jigō sonota meisaichō* (1870). The *meisaichō* documents, including the present one used in this book, are all from Professor Tamamuro Fumio's collections. I am grateful for his generosity in allowing me to use his materials.

25. Arimoto Masao groups Buddhist sects in Tokugawa Japan into three clusters, according to their religious orientation and ritual behavior: Shingonshū, Tendaishū, and Nichirenshū, which stressed both individuality and

communality; Zenshū and Jōdoshū, which emphasized communality over individuality; and Jōdoshinshū, which denied the efficacy of votive prayer. He then illustrates, based on the statistical data collected by the Meiji government in 1877, how the three clusters of Buddhist sects were distributed in three geographical regions (Kantō, Kinki, and the traditional strongholds of Jōdoshinshū). In the Kantō and its vicinities (Suruga, Tōtōmi, Izu, Kōshū, Shinano), about 49 percent of all temples belonged to Shingonshū, Tendaishū, and Nichirenshū; about 46 percent belonged to Zenshū and Jōdoshū; and the remaining 5 percent belonged to Jōdoshinshū. In the Kinki and its vicinities (Wakasa, Inaba, Hōki, Bizen, Bitchū, and Mimasaka), about 30 percent of all temples belonged to Shingonshū, Tendaishū, and Nichirenshū; about 40 percent belonged to Zenshū and Jōdoshū; and about 30 percent belonged to Jōdoshinshū. In the Jōdoshinshū strongholds, which encompassed Echigo, Etchū, Echizen, Noto, Kaga, Hida, western Mino, western Owari, Aki, Iwami, Sūō, Nagato, Chikuzen, Chikugo, Higo, and western Buzen, about 57 percent of all temples belonged to Jōdoshinshū; about 13 percent belonged to Shingonshū, Tendaishū, and Nichirenshū sects; and about 30 percent belonged to Zenshū and Jōdoshū sects. See Arimoto (2002), pp. 375–76. For a further detailed geographical distribution of Jōdoshinshū strongholds, see Arimoto (1997), pp. 55–58, 61–63, 66–67.

26. Arimoto (2002), pp. 12–13.

27. Ibid., pp. 168–72.

28. For details, see Nagura (1995), pp. 170–73.

29. Nagura (1994), pp. 250–53.

30. See Fukuishi, p. 426. Other rules included: keep the regulations of the Law of the King as well as those of the Law of the Buddha; devote all energies to the family occupation and agriculture; do not forget the favors one receives from the state; respect the head monk of the *danna* temple; keep the ethics of the five relationships; practice frugality and sincerity; and so forth. Interestingly, there was no single article mentioning the core religious teachings of Shinran; what was primarily stressed was the fulfillment of *danka* obligations, ancestral rites, and other feudal ethics.

31. Arimoto (2002), pp. 304–5.

32. Here, Christianity invariably refers to Roman Catholicism, at least until 1859, when the first Protestant missionary, John Liggins of the American Episcopal Church, arrived in Nagasaki.

33. Gonoi, pp. 2–4.

34. Miyazaki Kentarō suggests that those who had been associated with Christianity until 1873 — the year the anti-Christian ban was lifted and Roman Catholics reappeared in Japan — should be "Kirishitan." Based on this, he contends that those Kirishitan who went underground between 1644 and 1873 should be called "underground Kirishitan" in order to distinguish them from Kakure Kirishitan — those Kirishitan who continued to keep their religion even after 1873. See Miyazaki Kentarō, "Roman Catholic Mission in Pre-Modern Japan," p. 5. During the Tokugawa period, the term "Kirishitan" was written with various characters: initially, it was written 幾利紫旦, 貴理

志端, 記利志旦, or 吉利支丹; however, after it had been banned, it was changed to 鬼利至端 or 貴理死貪. When Tokugawa Tsunayoshi 綱吉 assumed the shogunal post, the character 吉 was no longer used in the term "Kirishitan" because the character appeared in the shogun's name; thereafter, it was usually written 切支丹, きりしたん, or キリシタン. See Gonoi, p. 2.

35. For more details, see Gonoi, pp. 5–12. According to Gonoi, before Toyotomi Hideyoshi had banned Christianity, there were about 200,000 Kirishitan, 200 churches, and 22 missionary facilities in Japan. The number of Kirishitan increased to about 300,000 by 1601 and again to about 370,000 by 1614, when the shogunate issued the anti-Christian edict. After the edict, most of the Kirishitan abandoned their religion, but missionary activities did not cease so soon. From 1614 to 1629, the Jesuits were able to gain more than 20,000 followers, and the Franciscans more than 26,000 in the Tōhoku region.

36. Ikuo Higashibaba notes that the uncritical use of the terms "converts" or "conversion" might be misleading, as these labels could give "the impression that all Japanese followers' religiosity was as uniform as the theological definitions of these terms imply." See Higashibaba, pp. xv-xvi.

37. Morioka (1962), pp. 24–26. Similarly, we need to use the terms "monk," "clergy," or "priest" with caution. Within Buddhism, a monk is generally understood to be a member of a community of religious renunciants who has undergone a formal ordination ceremony conducted by a quorum of fully ordained monks; the clergy is the body of all persons ordained for religious duties in a Buddhist institution; and a priest is an ordained monk or nun who is authorized to perform certain rites and to administer certain rituals.

38. For an account of the relationship between the imperial court and the *bakufu* during the early decades of the seventeenth century, see Tsuji Tatsuya, pp. 57–94.

39. LaFleur (1983), p. 26.

40. Ibid., p. 29.

41. According to William R. LaFleur, paths to salvation that were commonly undertaken in medieval Japan were personal and faith-based, whether they featured devotion to buddhas or bodhisattvas, reliance upon the mystic power of *nenbutsu* (chanting the name of Amida, the merit of which was believed to lead one to the Western Paradise of Amida), or an attempt to reconstruct the *rokudō* system through the metaphor of "play" (*asobi*). In particular, LaFleur suggests that when the entire *rokudō* system was conceived as an arena of play, people could display "a remarkable capacity for enjoyment — one that over the centuries produced much humor, festival, spoof, the pleasures of a 'floating world,' the lyrics of an Ikkyū or a Ryōkan, and the comedy of *kyōgen*." In addition to the ludic mode of overcoming the pain of transmigration, LaFleur cites the practice of dancing *nenbutsu* (*odori nenbutsu*) as an example of "a mode of salvation through play." See LaFleur (1983), pp. 54–58.

42. Barbara Ruch is critical of the term "Kumano *bikuni*," which, according to her, "cannot be found in documentation prior to the seventeenth century." She notes that this composite term, which is rather vague and even pejorative, in no way represents a wide array of itinerant or mendicant nuns

belonging to different orders and professions. See Ruch, pp. 540–41, 557–60. Nevertheless, a majority of Japanese scholars still employ this term to refer to a representative group of painting-recitation nuns. According to them, at the end of each year Kumano nuns used to retreat into Kumano, where they performed ascetic practices; and beginning in the fourth month they traveled to eastern Japan along with Kumano *oshi* and *sendatsu* in order to distribute Kumano talismans while preaching about the scroll of hell. For example, see Hayashi Masahiko, pp. 313–17 and Yamamoto Shigeo, pp. 49–53.

43. In Edo, there appeared commercial houses where Kumano nuns engaged in entertainment activities. These houses, known as *nakayado*, were located in Izumichō, Shiba, Kyōbashi, and Kayabachō. When the public authorities cracked down on these entertainment houses, the nuns, who had been engaged in prostitution, turned to street solicitation. When the crackdown eased, they soon returned to their entertainment businesses. See Sone, pp. 37–38 and Nei, pp. 167–68.

44. Asai, p. 57. Cf. Ruch, p. 547. As Engelbert Kaempfer, a German physician, of the Dutch trade factory at Nagasaki observed in 1691, "Kumano nuns" were no longer viewed as serious religious practitioners. See Kaempfer, pp. 275–76:

Among them are some who have been trained in houses of prostitution and have bought their freedom after having served their term to spend the remaining part of their youth in this fashion. These *bikuni* move in groups of two or three, walk daily one or several miles from their home, and approach genteel travelers who pass in *kago* or on horseback. Each of them attaches herself to one particular traveler, starts up a rustic tune, and as long as it is to her advantage, she accompanies and amuses him for several hours. . . . So I can hardly exclude them from the category of loose women and prostitutes, however much they adopt religious tonsure.

For a brief discussion of the transformation of Kumano nuns in early modern times, see also Faure (2003), pp. 250–54 and Sone, pp. 32–33.

45. Sone, pp. 34–35.

46. See *Buke genseiroku*, pp. 116–17 and Kikuchi Takeshi, pp. 48–49.

47. Sone, pp. 35–36. According to a 1727 document, there were seven "temples of the original vow" with which Kumano nuns were supposed to be affiliated. These "temples of the original vow" were religious centers authorized to collect donations from the public for the construction, maintenance, and repair of the buildings and facilities of the Kumano Sanzan ("Three Mountains of Kumano," referring to Hongū, Shingū, and Nachi). In return, those affiliated with these "temples of the original vow," including *shugen*, *yamabushi*, monks, and nuns, were entitled to distribute and to commercialize Kumano talismans and other religious products throughout the country. When Kumano nuns drifted away from these "original vow" organizations, they ended up having to survive on their own, and this often meant turning to the street. See Nei, pp. 168–71.

48. For a detailed discussion of how Kumano nuns were gradually transformed into street entertainers, see Kikuchi Takeshi, pp. 51–53. On top of this,

the Kumano Sanzan, which had been under Buddhist control and had served as the religious bases of the Kumano nuns, lost their right to distribute talismans when the Shinto families of the region took them over. See Yamamoto Shigeo, pp. 50–51.

49. Suggesting that there were still many active painting-recitation nuns, as seen in the pictorial evidence, Barbara Ruch implies that hell scrolls still commanded much popularity even in the late Tokugawa period. However, among the evidence she cites, items that pertain specifically to the "scroll of hell" are a very few, and even these belong mostly to what Ruch calls "gendered hell paintings," which pay far more attention to such religious themes as female defilement and childlessness than to the cosmology of hell and the afterlife in general. For more details, see Ruch, pp. 566–75. But the overall trend, as we see in Part II, was moving toward the entrenchment of death rites, bypassing the issue of hell.

50. The term *sorei* was not commonly used in the Tokugawa period even though some National Learning scholars and Shintoists adopted it to refer to the spirits of ancestors (particularly when attempting to launch a Shinto funeral movement). The common use of this term in folklore is attributable to Yanagita Kunio, who highlighted it in his "Senzo no hanashi" (1946).

51. According to Yanagita Kunio, the word *hotoke* was derived from *hokai* or *hotoki*, the "vessel" used in making offerings to the buddhas as well as to the spirits of the dead. From the medieval period, people began to indicate both the buddhas and the spirits of the dead by the word for the vessel (*hotoki*), which was somehow transformed into *hotoke* and was eventually misconstrued as the term for Buddha. In any case, the essence of ancestral rites for Yanagita lay in offering food to the deified ancestors. See Yanagita, "Senzo no hanashi," p. 84; Bernier, p. 61; and Smith (1974), p. 53. On the other hand, Aruga Kizaemon, who is critical of Yanagita Kunio's speculation and draws attention to the fact that in the *Nihon shoki*, the term *butsu* was already being referred to as "Tonarinokuni no kami," hypothesizes that the ancient Japanese erected clan (*uji*) Buddhist temples and worshipped Buddhist images in addition to *ujigami*. These images were called *hotoke* (as the tutelary deity of the *uji* group), and ancestors who were venerated at these *uji* temples as tutelary deities were also known as *hotoke*. For this reason, Aruga contends, Buddhist images and memorial tablets, which were all placed at the household Buddhist altar, came to be referred to as *hotoke* without distinction. For more details, see Aruga, pp. 63–88.

52. Yasumaru, "Sōron: rekishi no naka de no kattō to mosaku," p. 28.

53. For more details, see Vesey, pp. 14–15 and Nagura (1995), p. 173.

54. LaFleur notes that the negative images of monks portrayed within the purview of "funerary Buddhism" included the directors of funerals, the chanters of requiems, and the collectors of donations. See LaFleur (1992), p. 81.

55. Ōkuwa (1986), pp. 69–70. There are two Japanese terms that can stand in for "ancestor": *senzo* and *sosen*. Of these two terms, according to Fukuta Ajio, *senzo* was widely used in ancient Japan and was particularly popular in the Tokugawa period. In contrast, although Confucian and National

Learning scholars sometimes used it during the Tokugawa period, the term *sosen* was quite alien to the Tokugawa Japanese and only gained popularity in the Meiji period, when it was officially adopted as the Japanese counterpart of the English word "ancestor." See Fukuta (2004), pp. 6–9. In this book, I use the term *sosen* when it refers to "ancestor" or to compound words containing the word "ancestor" (such as *sosen saishi* or *sosen sūhai*) because it is more widely used within the academic Japanese context than is the term *senzo*.

56. Ōkuwa (1986), p. 67.

57. Fujii Masao (1983), p. 126. For a detailed discussion of the ancient custom of dumping dead bodies in the Kyoto region, see Katsuda (2003), pp. 36–47.

58. For an introduction to these two ancient chronicles, see Sakamoto Tarō, pp. 141–54, 169–86.

59. For examples, see Katsuda (1987), pp. 40–46; Ury, p. 183; and Morrell, p. 105. Based on a detailed examination of records, Katsuda Itaru makes a comprehensive list of the number of times abandoned corpses were found in Kyoto in the twelfth and thirteenth centuries. See Katsuda (2003), pp. 252–64. Bitō Masahide suggests that the legacy of disposing of the dead by abandoning their corpses was apparent in the custom of the "burying grave" (*umebaka*). Indeed, in some regions, the *umebaka* was referred to as the "dumping grave" (*sutebaka*). Corpses were generally placed in shallow pits, and after only a short interval the ground was often dug up and used to bury another corpse. See Bitō (1991), p. 378.

60. For example, in the eleventh century, the cemetery of the glorious Fujiwara family in Kohata was abandoned on a desolate mountain hill, and its descendants seemed to have no idea where their ancestors had been buried. When the dead were cremated, family members were not usually in attendance; instead, family servants or monks collected the ashes and deposited them in a sepulcher. See Tanaka Hisao (1979), pp. 183–204.

61. Bitō (1992), p. 130.

62. Yanagita, "Senzo no hanashi," p. 144.

63. Takeda Chōshū (1996), pp. 211–13.

64. Kuroda Toshio (1990), pp. 328–31.

65. For a comprehensive treatment of Sūden and Tenkai, see Tsuji Zennosuke (1953), pp. 26–173.

66. For an account of *jiin seiri* in these three domains, see Tsuji Zennosuke (1953), pp. 331–36.

67. Fujii Masao, "Nihonjin no senzo kuyōkan no tenkai," pp. 99–101.

68. For a theoretical discussion of how society is constructed through the working of force and discourse, see Lincoln (1988), particularly the Introduction, pp. 3–11.

69. As Glenn Jordan and Chris Weedon (p. 14) note, "social power manifests itself in competing discourses. Discourses are more than ways of giving meaning to the world, they imply forms of social organization and social practices which structure institutions and constitute individuals as thinking,

feeling and acting subjects." Following the definition of power suggested here, I attempt to illuminate the cultural politics of funerary Buddhism and to show how they determined the socio-religious meaning of death in Tokugawa society. For a theoretical discussion of cultural politics, see Jordan and Weedon, pp. 3–17.

70. For an account of the history of disputes over Shinto funerals, see Tsuji Zennosuke (1954), pp. 115–39.

71. Yasumaru, " 'Kindaika' no shisō to minzoku," pp. 438–39.

72. Ōhashi Yukihiro, "New Perspectives on the Early Tokugawa Persecution," pp. 46–47: "The established view holds that the Christian threat was twofold: firstly, there was the fear of the 'colonization' of Japan through the military might of Portugal and Spain on whom the Christian missionaries were seen to rely, and secondly, there was fear of the outbreak of popular uprisings inspired by Christians."

73. Kenneth A. Marcure's "The Danka System," particularly pp. 40–47, is informative to some extent, but his heavy reliance upon secondary English materials (which neither represent original studies on, nor are fully devoted to, the *danka* system) and his tendency to jump to simplistic conclusions render it not only sketchy but also outdated and erroneous.

Part I

1. Kinryū Shizuka, pp. 82–85. For a detailed account of the Ishiyama Honganji battle, see McMullin, pp. 145–51.

2. Ishige Tadashi, pp. 178–80.

3. Ishige further suggests that Nobunaga ethicized *gekokujō* by prioritizing military power over imperial authority. Nobunaga's *tenka*, in Ishige's view, was none other than the military principle that took precedence over imperial authority and justified "the dictatorship of benevolent rule." Ibid., pp. 182–83.

4. Berry, pp. 85–87. Berry attributes Hideyoshi's conciliatory gestures toward Buddhism to his desire to win adulation, and she refers to it as "a show of generosity that displayed his self-consciousness as a unifier, in more than military terms, and his concern with laudable government." But it would be naïve to explain away Hideyoshi's policy on Buddhism solely in psychological terms. As it turned out, Hideyoshi had hoped that, once he had domesticated them, he would be able to incorporate Buddhist legacies into a political strategy for legitimating his military hegemony.

5. Quote from Berry, p. 102.

6. Honda, p. 350 and Ishige, pp. 187–91.

7. Berry, p. 187.

8. Quote from Lu, p. 197.

9. Kirishitan bunka kenkyūkai, ed., *Kirishitan kenkyū*, vol. 17 (1977), pp. 268–69. For an example of the Kirishitan destruction of Buddhist temples, the domain of Ōmura Sumitada, who was baptized in 1563 with the name Bartolomeu, stands out. In this domain, whose residents converted to Christian-

ity en masse in the mid-1570s, "Temples were either changed into Christian churches or demolished. Two hundred Buddhist monks at about fifty monasteries received baptism in exchange for the lord's protection of their social and economic status. Many of the former Buddhist monks and priests thus became local lay ministers of Kirishitan churches." See Higashibaba, p. 15. Nevertheless, Hideyoshi's anti-Kirishitan ban was promulgated too abruptly and without a clear justification. The reasons scholars give for this are largely speculative and include: the cession of Nagasaki to the Jesuits, similarities in grouping between the Kirishitan and the members of the medieval Ikkōshū, Hideyoshi's inclination toward the ideology of the country of the gods, the refusal of Portuguese merchants to cooperate with Hideyoshi, the provocative and destructive activities of Kirishitan, and Hideyoshi's political needs. According to George Elison: "[The anti-Kirishitan ban] was part of Hideyoshi's program for the restructuring of Japan under central authority. It cannot be overemphasized that the step was essentially a matter of internal policy." See Elison, p. 117. For more discussions, see Higashibaba, pp. 127–33; Gonoi, pp. 147–56; and Neil S. Fujita, pp. 117–25.

10. For the puzzling evolution of events after the ban, see Hosotani, pp. 23, 26–27. For more details on the San Felipe incident, see Elison, pp. 135–41; Elisonas, pp. 363–65; and Neil S. Fujita, pp. 133–43. Interestingly, the presence of Franciscans in Japan (62 until 1632) began in 1593, when Hideyoshi, due to his interest in trade with Manila, permitted the Franciscan Pedro Bautista and his three companions from the Spanish Philippines to stay in Kyoto. By the time of the mass execution, there were eleven Franciscan missionaries in Japan; of these, six were crucified and the remaining five were expelled to Manila in the same year.

11. There were 152 characters inscribed on the bell. Ieyasu fabricated charges pertaining to two particular characters, 家 (*ie* or *ka*) and 康 (*yasu* or *kō*), which were included in the phrase 国家安康 (*kokka ankō*), meaning national stability and peace. Accusing Hideyori of attempting to curse him by intentionally separating two characters that, together, spelled "Ieyasu," Ieyasu made three demands and told Hideyori that he had to agree to one of them: (1) "alternate attendance" to Edo; (2) submit his mother, Yodo, as a hostage; or (3) withdraw from Osaka Castle. When none of these demands was accepted, Ieyasu used his military might to demolish Hideyori.

12. Fukaya (1988), pp. 99–100.

13. For a detailed discussion of "Regulations for the Imperial Court and Courtier Households," see Butler, pp. 525–41.

14. For details, see Fujii Jōji (1992), pp. 112–23 and Tsuji Tatsuya (1991), pp. 77–80.

15. Murakami Naojirō, *Ikoku ōfuku shokanshū*, pp. 91–92.

Chapter 1

16. Massarella, pp. 79–80 and Ross, p. 80. Ieyasu was particularly interested in Spanish mining experience as he wished to develop Japan's mineral

resources. However, the entry of Franciscans ignited a rivalry with the Jesuits, who claimed a monopoly of the mission in Japan based on the 1494 Treaty of Tordesillas. The treaty, however, did not deter the eager Spanish friars in the Philippines from attempting to expand their mission to Japan.

17. "The disastrous loss of the ship (and cargo which was worth more than 400,000 ducats) placed both the Jesuits and Portuguese in Nagasaki in severe financial straits. When Rodrigues Giram first went up to court in 1604 . . . Ieyasu was informed of the loss and spontaneously offered the Jesuits an outright gift of 350 taels, as well as a loan of a further five thousand to be repaid at the missionaries' convenience." Cooper (1974), p. 203.

18. For an account of Ieyasu's diplomatic strategy, see Fujii Jōji (1994), pp. 34–49.

19. Massarella, p. 45.

20. In 1600, the "De Liefde," one of five vessels of a fleet Holland had dispatched to explore the sea route to East India, drifted into the port of Usuki in Bungo. The ship's chief navigator was the Englishman William Adams, whom Ieyasu received favorably. Ieyasu soon replaced his diplomatic advisor, the Portuguese Jesuit João Rodrigues Tcuzzu (1561–1633), with Adams. With Adams's help, the commander of a vessel of the East India Company, John Saris (ca. 1579–1643), sailed into Hirado in 1613 and opened an English trade post.

21. Fujii Jōji (1994), p. 50.

22. Higashibaba, p. 9. Buddhist terms initially adopted to express Christian religious concepts included Dainichi (Mahāvairocana), *jōdo* (Pure Land), *jigoku* (hell), *tennin* (heavenly persons), and *tamashii* (souls). These Buddhist terms were the only reasonably acceptable Japanese counterparts to Christian religious and philosophical concepts. Later, in order to avoid misunderstanding, missionaries stopped using "Dainichi" and began using the Latin term "Deus" for God.

23. In 1601 Bishop Cerqueira ordained two Japanese Jesuits (Kimura Sebastião and Niabara Luís) to the priesthood, promoting them from the rank of brother to the rank of padre. After that, twenty more Japanese were ordained as padres. On the other hand, of 109 Japanese brothers, 36 left their positions and 18 could not be traced. See Boxer, p. 211; Moran, p. 161; and Gonoi, pp. 2–3.

24. The *dōjuku* and *kanbō*, who might be likened to "priestly interns" and "lay ministers," respectively, provided various services essential to missionary activities. The *dōjuku*, who were not officially clergy but were involved in teaching the catechism and preaching, lived with the padres and brothers and engaged in any necessary chores. The *kanbō* managed those churches not attended by padres and coordinated local believers. When the *dōjuku* were most numerous, they belonged to four orders and numbered between 400 and 500, while the *kanbō* numbered around 200. For more details, see Boxer, pp. 211–25; Neil S. Fujita, p. 74; Gonoi, p. 4; Moran, pp. 2–4; and Nosco (1993), pp. 5–8.

25. Boxer, pp. 268–83; Massarella, pp. 85–86; Cooper (1974), pp. 264–67; and Fujii Jōji (1992), pp. 146–47.

26. Elisonas, p. 366.

27. For a detailed account of the Okamoto Daihachi scandal, see Cieslik and Ōta, p. 203.

28. One of the well-known victims was the Korean woman Otaa Juria. In 1592, when she was 5 years old, she was taken captive by Konishi Yukinaga and brought from Pyongyang to Japan. Under the influence of Yukinaga's Kirishitan wife, Otaa was educated and grew up as a Kirishitan. When Yukinaga was executed after the Sekigahara battle, Otaa was transferred to the women's harem of Ieyasu's Sunpu Castle and worked there as a serving maid. In 1612, officials tried to force her to abandon her religion and to convert to Buddhism, but she refused. Her unyielding faith prompted her exile, first to Izu Ōshima, then to Niijima, and, eventually, to Kōzushima, where she died in the mid-seventeenth century.

29. Shimizu Hirokazu (1981), p. 101.

30. Massarella, p. 80.

31. Murakami Naojirō, *Ikoku ōfuku shokanshū*, pp. 65–66.

32. Asao, "Higashi Ajia ni okeru bakuhan taisei, pp. 116–17.

33. Berry, pp. 234–35. For a detailed discussion of the function of divine punishment in the traditional *kishōmon*, see Satō Hiroo, pp. 98–109.

34. For more details on the changing role of *kishōmon*, see Chijiwa, pp. 33–41.

35. Nakamura Kōya (1960), pp. 662–66.

36. Ibid., pp. 681–87. It is true that the Tokugawa documents omitted the usual long lists of deities that should be invoked by the oath takers. However, as Ieyasu claimed in his 1612 letter to New Spain, the lord-vassal relationship was founded upon the tradition of the divine pledge.

37. In fact, the second and third articles of the 1612 pledge were incorporated into the third and fourth articles, respectively, of the Laws of Military Households, which were promulgated in 1615. Thus, the 1612 oaths of loyalty were a key element in the most important law of the military estate in Tokugawa Japan. See Nakamura Kōya (1961), pp. 21–22.

38. For a detailed discussion of the practice of the divine pledge in the Tokugawa regime, see Matsudaira Tarō, pp. 82–92.

39. *Gotōke reijō*, p. 206.

40. Murai (1989), pp. 221–24.

41. Shimizu Hirokazu (1981), p. 111. Nevertheless, it should be noted that, at this time, the anti-Christian law mainly targeted missionaries and the warrior class rather than the general Kirishitan population. In a situation where local gentry-type warriors were not completely separated from the local peasants, the shogunate feared that the Kirishitan warriors might influence the peasants to follow Christianity and to use the Christian faith to bolster their authority. See Ōhashi Yukihiro, "New Perspectives on the Early Tokugawa Persecution," pp. 53–54.

42. See *Tsūkō ichiran*, vol. 5, pp. 154–55. This document, written in classical Chinese, was somewhat unusual in form and style for a *bakufu* law. Scholars such as Nakamura Kōya question its quality and content and suggest that

it must have been a treatise that Sūden (who did not have a clear understanding of Christianity) composed overnight. See Nakamura Kōya (1965), p. 649. Although the literal rendering of the title of the edict should be "Statement on Expelling Padres," it should be noted that the word *bateren* was used to refer to Christian followers in general. Takagi Shōsaku (1992), pp. 24–25. For the English translation of this document by Joseph Jennes, see Ross, p. 93.

43. See Takagi Shōsaku (1992), pp. 6–7 and Gonoi, pp. 202–7. At the same time, this edict had a covert purpose, which was to warn the Western daimyo and military remnants that remained sympathetic to the Toyotomi forces.

44. *Tokugawa kinreikō*, vol. 5, p. 122.

45. Ibid., p. 122.

46. Ibid., pp. 122–23.

47. Ibid., p. 123.

48. Ibid., p. 122.

49. The translation is from Hurvitz, p. 288.

50. For more accounts on Yoshida Kanetomo, see Hiromi Maeda (2003), pp. 31–49 and Matsunaga, pp. 282–83.

51. Takagi Shōsaku (1992), pp. 11–13 and Grapard (Spring 1992), pp. 45, 48–53.

52. Yoshida Kanetomo, p. 649. Cf. Grapard (Summer 1992), p. 153.

53. Grapard (Summer 1992), p. 155. Thus, Kanetomo concludes in verse form: "The Exoteric Teaching makes of the buddhas the Essence; / this superficial teaching establishes bonds between buddhas and human beings. / The Esoteric Teaching considers the *kami* as the only Essence; in the secret transmissions of this teaching the truth can be found." (p. 155)

54. Quote from Takagi Shōsaku (p. 15), who summarizes the content of a chapter concerning the "matter of the Buddha who was conceded the task of helping life from the gods" in the *Jingi seishū*, pp. 67–68.

55. Kuroda Toshio (1975), pp. 305–6.

56. Varley, p. 49.

57. Ibid., p. 78.

58. Zuikei Shūhō, pp. 2–5.

59. Takagi Shōsaku (1992), pp. 15–17.

60. Ōhashi Yukihiro, "New Perspectives on the Early Tokugawa Persecution," p. 46.

61. Takagi Shōsaku (1992), p. 23.

62. For more details, see Ooms (1985), pp. 50–62.

63. *Tokugawa jikki*, vol. 1, p. 646.

64. For details, see *Tsūkō ichiran*, vol. 5, pp. 35–39. There remained only 45 missionaries who disregarded the order and went underground, including 18 Jesuit padres and 8 *irmãos*, 6 Franciscans, 7 Dominicans, 1 Augustinian, and 5 Japanese priests.

65. For more on Takayama Ukon's Christian faith and his connection to Hideyoshi, see Hosotani, pp. 270–72.

66. Shimizu Hirokazu (1981), pp. 114–18.

67. For a detailed discussion of the Kokura inspection, see Tamamuro Fumio (1998), pp. 4–25. For more details about Hosokawa Garasha, see Johannes, pp. 21–26 and Endō Shūsaku, pp. 47–69.

68. See Toyoda Takeshi (1982), p. 117.

69. Tamamuro Fumio, *Edo jidai no Sōtōshū no tenkai*, pp. 1–3.

70. Cieslik and Ōta, p. 232.

71. The effect of the *bakufu*'s decision with regard to *korobi* Kirishitan was immediate. Those areas heavily populated with Kirishitan or former Kirishitan saw a rapid increase in the construction of new temples.

72. For Ieyasu's experience of an Ikkō *ikki*, see Atsuta, pp. 42–43.

73. For the texts of these laws, see Umeda, pp. 246–53, 259–66.

74. For detailed analyses of Ieyasu's temple laws, see Tamamuro Fumio (1987), pp. 5–26 and (1999), pp. 14–27.

75. Tamamuro Fumio (1987), pp. 5–6.

76. Gonoi, pp. 11–12.

77. *Gotōke reijō*, p. 110.

78. Ibid., p. 110. But Hidetada indicated that Chinese ships could call at any port they wanted to choose.

79. With this new policy, which was closely tied to his larger strategy for political consolidation, Hidetada took control of foreign trade, particularly the buying of high-quality lead (needed to make bullets) from British and Dutch traders. Hidetada lifted the order confining Chinese trade to Nagasaki, which his father's lieutenants (e.g., Honda Masazumi, Sūden, Hasegawa Fujihiro, and Miura Anjin [William Adams]) had imposed three months earlier. After that, diplomatic affairs were handled by Hidetada's advisors (e.g., Doi Toshikatsu and Soga Hisasuke).

80. Herman Ooms interprets the deification of Ieyasu as a process of "legitimation that entailed a distortion and veiling of the real nature of domination." Ooms (1985), p. 61. However, throughout the Tokugawa period, the Nikkō Shrine remained the rallying point of ritual politics, and the Tōshō Daigongen played an indispensable role in sustaining the *bakuhan* system, which Ieyasu himself had established. This was especially so in the formative years of the Tokugawa sovereignty.

81. For more details on the origin of this remuneration measure, see Shimizu Hirokazu (1979), pp. 264–67.

82. Higashibaba notes that missionaries often avoided arrest by concealing themselves in holes under floor boards, the holes being covered over with planks and mats, and "others stand all day long in a small space behind the privy, in dirt and filth wherein one would not expect to find a beast, let alone a man." Higashibaba, p. 142.

83. Ibid., p. 142. By 1643, about 100 missionaries had secretly entered the country and all of them, except for 23 who voluntarily left the country, were expelled, executed, or forced, under terrifying torture, to commit apostasy. After the martyrdom of *irmão* Konishi Mancio (1600–44) there was no longer a single missionary left in Japan.

84. Matsuda (1997), vol. 3, p. 47.

85. *Tokugawa jikki*, vol. 2, p. 175. The number of victims suggested in the *Tokugawa jikki* (i.e., more than 60) is not correct. For detailed accounts, see Matsuda (1997), vol. 3, pp. 56–61 and Kataoka (1979), pp. 326–36.

86. For detailed accounts of this affair, see Massarella, pp. 275–77, 292–98 and Kataoka (1979), 272–79.

87. Shimizu Hirokazu (1981), pp. 138–40 and Neil S. Fujita, pp. 174–76.

88. For details, see Kataoka (1979), pp. 353–62.

89. Previously, the *bakufu* put Kirishitan in the prison of Kotenmachō and then executed them at Asakusa. However, after Iemitsu was enthroned, the execution site was transferred to Shiba, which was adjacent to the Shinagawa post station in the south. This served to show the final destination of Kirishitan not only to the public at large but also to domain lords (who regularly visited Edo from western Japan).

90. *Tokugawa jikki*, vol. 2, p. 307.

91. Takagi Kazuo, pp. 88–91.

92. Shimizu Hirokazu (1981), p. 145.

93. Endō Shūsaku, pp. 75–77.

94. For more details, see Nosco (1996), pp. 148–49 and *Tsūkō ichiran*, vol. 5, pp. 214–18. Due to the problem of durability, the material used to draw or carve Christian symbols was changed from paper to wooden boards and then, by 1669, to copper plates. With regard to how the *fumie* shook the Kirishitan, Miyazaki Kentarō notes: "When they returned after having trodden on the image it is said that they repeatedly recited the *conchirisan* (*contrição*, a prayer expressing contrition) and *orashio* (*oratio*, prayers) expressing repentance for their sinful deed. Gradually the faith of the underground Kirishitan tended to move away from a God who was a strict father and judge and focus on a forgiving motherly God of infinite tenderness, Mary." Miyazaki Kentarō, "The Kakure Kirishitan Tradition," p. 21.

95. Shimizu Hirokazu (1981), p. 145.

96. Ibid., pp. 145–48; Boxer, pp. 351–53; and Ross, p. 100.

97. For a detailed account of the English departure from Japan, see Massarella, pp. 314–28. The Hirado factory was closed partly due to the Hirayama affair, which prompted the *bakufu* to restrict English trade. In 1621, the *bakufu* forbade the English and Dutch from taking Japanese laborers out of the country for any reason, from bringing military-related goods (such as armor, swords, spears, firearms, gunpowder) into Japan, and from interfering with Japanese, Chinese, and Portuguese vessels on Japanese water. With the institution of these regulations, the English were deprived of their trade-cum-military base at Hirado.

98. Fujii Jōji (1994), pp. 57–58.

99. Umeda, p. 65 and Butler, pp. 524–34.

100. See the sixteenth article of this law in Butler, p. 535.

101. See Bitō (1991), pp. 413–14; Tamamuro Fumio, *Edo jidai no Sōtōshū no tenkai*, pp. 68–74; Williams (2000), pp. 30–33; and, for the terms of the regulations, see Umeda, pp. 68–70, 72–79.

102. For details, see Saitō Natsuki, pp. 3–6.

103. For detailed discussions of the "Purple Robe Incident," see Tsuji Zennosuke (1953), pp. 237–75 and Murai (1987), pp. 152–65. By 1633, the *bakufu's*
governance of religious affairs was under the supervision of Kochiin Sūden.
Following his death in 1633, the task of regulating religious institutions
passed into the secular hands of temple and shrine magistrates.

104. Udaka, *Edo bakufu no Bukkyō kyōdan tōsei*, pp. 38–39. For an account
of the head-branch system through the example of the Sōtōshū, see Williams
(2000), pp. 41–49.

105. Nishiwaki, "Kinsei Bukkyōshi kenkyū no dōkō," p. 50. For a detailed
discussion of the *furegashira* system, see Vesey, pp. 157–79.

106. Tamamuro Fumio (1987), pp. 44–46 and Vesey, pp. 116–56. For a discussion of the *bakuhan* framework into which the head-branch system was
incorporated, see Chiba (1967), p. 51.

107. For more information on how the shogunal order was transmitted
to head temples, see Tamamuro Fumio (1987), pp. 47–51.

108. The number of temples listed in the extant Kan'ei registers is 10,818.
For an introduction to the Kan'ei register, see Tamamuro Fumio (1981), vol. 3,
pp. 5–26.

Chapter 2

109. The measures that Iemitsu took in 1632–33 in order to establish his
own authority (independent of Hidetada) and to staff the shogunal government with his own advisors included putting the military corps under his
direct command, rearranging Hidetada's lieutenants so that they occupied
minor positions, and reshuffling daimyo domains. The latter was manifested
by removing Katō Tadahiro (Kumamoto), transferring his brother Tadanaga
(Sunpu), and dispatching shogunal inspectors to the local domains. For
more details on Iemitsu's schemes of power restructuring, see Yamamoto
Hirofumi, pp. 13–36.

110. For more details of the operation of the *ito wappu* system, see Nagasaki kenshi henshū iinkai, pp. 81–96, 159–61.

111. Of the four articles related to anti-Christian policy, Article 7 ("In the
case of southern barbarians who promulgate Christianity, or in the case of
the discovery of evil persons, put them into the prison of Ōmura [domain]
as has been done before") and Article 8 ("Pay close enough attention to the
matter of Christianity to inspect the interior of a ship") contained nothing
new. See *Buke genseiroku*, p. 97.

112. Ibid., p. 97.

113. In fact, when Kirishitan brothers were discovered in the Satsuma
domain held by the Shimazu house, Nagasaki magistrates dispatched two
officials to bring them to the Nagasaki prison. Satsuma officials were ordered to take a hands-off position. See Shimizu Hirokazu (1981), p. 154.

114. *Buke genseiroku*, p. 97.

115. Shimizu Hirokazu (1981), pp. 172–76. In 1622, Kirishitan followers in
Nagasaki reported: "After the authorities announced an excessive amount

of cash reward for information about *bateren* and their lodges, greedy and evil-minded rogues have been searching for the monks day and night, utilizing various means. When they find a place even a little suspicious, they immediately intrude and investigate it: this is incessantly happening. Therefore, there no longer is any method of hiding the monks." Letter of the members of the Confraternity of the Rosary in Nagasaki, 23 January 1622, in Matsushida Kiichi, *Kinsei shoki Nihon kankei Nanban shiryō no kenkyū*, Tokyo: Kazama shobō, 1967, pp. 1172–73. Quoted in Higashibaba, pp. 143–44.

116. For the capture of Ferreira and his entourage, see *Tsūkō ichiran*, vol. 5, pp. 92–98. For a detailed account of his life in Japan after conversion, see ibid., pp. 99–112 and Endō Shūsaku, pp. 106–18.

117. Elison, p. 185. For more details on Ferreira, see Neil S. Fujita, pp. 193–96.

118. For more details on the biography and work of Inoue Masashige, see Elison, pp. 191–208.

119. For more on this group of padres, often known as the Rubino group, see Neil S. Fujita, pp. 201–3 and Elison, pp. 198–203. In particular, see Endō Shūsaku, pp. 129–36 for a detailed account of Chiara's life after apostasy.

120. Among the documents identified, this one is considered to be the oldest register and the closest to the "register of sectarian inspection" (*shūmon aratamechō*) in both format and content. However, the extant oldest register carrying the title of *shūmon aratamechō* is the *Mino Anpachigun Nirematamura shūmon ninbetsuchō* of 1638, which was organized by five-man group. See *Gifu kenshi: Shiryōhen kinsei 9* (Gifu: Gifuken, 1973), pp. 504–10.

121. Based on the data in *Kyūshū shiryō sōsho 37: Nagasaki Hiradomachi ninbetsuchō*, pp. 1–30.

122. It is true that in the late 1620s, temples or village officials in domains such as Akita and Ōmura issued religious certificates stating that "[the person in question] has accepted [Buddhist] scriptures" to non-Kirishitan residents. However, at that stage, this practice was not comprehensive.

123. Tamamuro Fumio, *Sōshiki to danka*, pp. 38–49 and Ōhashi Yukihiro (2001), pp. 110–11.

124. In the Kan'ei era (1624–44), many local governments still had difficulty enforcing the system of temple certification. In this case, they often substituted temple certification with secular certification (*zokuuke*), which entailed a secular certificate being drawn up by the village head or elders. The secular certificate included information on the religious status of villagers along with information on residents, households, and farm animals. The earliest examples of secular certification are found in the Fukui, Hiroshima, and Yonezawa domains. Over time, this practice gradually gave way to temple certification.

125. Nagazumi (1969), p. 202.

126. *Tsūkō ichiran*, vol. 5, pp. 39–40. Interestingly, however, children born of a Japanese father and a "barbarian" mother were allowed to live in Japan, even though their mothers were not.

127. *Ofuregaki Kanpō shūsei*, p. 628.

128. Upon Sakai Tadakatsu's order, Obama officials began to draw up a religious register that covered the entire domain populace. See Fujii Manabu (1963), p. 148. By the same token, Buddhist temples began to list all funerary patrons, whether or not they had surnames, in their roster of the dead (*kakochō*). For more details, see Fukuta (1992), p. 52.

129. *Nanzenji monjo*, vol. 2, pp. 17–20.

130. Cieslik and Ōta, pp. 232–33.

131. For more details, see Okada Akio (1953), pp. 157–59.

132. For some examples of the pledge document, see *Nanzenji monjo*, vol. 2, pp. 21–27. Okada Akio suggests that the "vow of the southern barbarians" was aimed at converting faithful Christian followers, those who took very seriously the matter of being punished by their deities and who, subsequently, were very effective when it came to forcing others to abandon their faith. See Okada Akio (1953), p. 162.

133. In Hiroshima (in 1635) and Nagasaki (from 1641 onward) as well, the *korobi* Kirishitan were subjected to the pledge of divine punishment and were listed on a *korobi* roster. In particular, the 1642 roster contained a brief "conversion" history of each enrollee. For details, see Ōhashi Yukihiro (2001), pp. 118–19 and *Kyūshū shiryō sōsho 37: Nagasaki Hiradomachi ninbetsuchō*, pp. 54–186.

134. *Tokugawa jikki*, vol. 3, p. 73. See also Yamamoto Hirofumi, pp. 67–68.

135. See in the *Kan'ei nikki* (Diary of the Kan'ei era) the entry for the ninth day of the twelfth month of 1637.

136. For more details on the hardships faced by the peasant population in the area during this period, see Nakamura Tadashi (1988), pp. 163–65 and Fukaya (1988), pp. 82–85.

137. For an account of "exploitative government" in Shimabara, see "Doarute Korea no shuki," pp. 12–28.

138. For more details on the role of Amakusa Shirō, see Okada Akio (1960), pp. 21–29 and Elison (1973), pp. 220–21.

139. The term *konfurariya* was derived from the Portuguese phrase "Confraria de Misericordia," which means "confraternity of compassion, martyrdom, or Santa Maria." When famines hit the Yamaguchi area hard in 1554, Kirishitan lay leaders, under the guidance of padres and brothers, attempted to succor those who were starving. After having achieved some good results, they began to systematically organize "confraternities of compassion" in various regions. Their proclaimed missions were to help the weak — including the poor, the sick, orphans, widows, social outcasts, and prisoners — and, at the same time, to promote Christian values (e.g., neighborly love, mutual help, chastity, and monogamy) and to fight theft, abortion, the slave trade, extortion, and so on. However, some of those confraternities that managed to survive the severe anti-Christian suppression of the early seventeenth century went underground. These covert organizations, which often formed a large geographical network, were instrumental in preserving the Christian faith of their members, in resisting persecution,

and in sustaining their clergy. For more details, see Ōhashi Yukihiro (2001), pp. 208–17; Neil S. Fujita, pp. 170–71; Miyazaki Kentarō, "The Kakure Kirishitan Tradition," p. 20; and Ross, pp. 89–90.

140. Murai (1987), pp. 12–21. Those who returned to Christianity were called *tachikaeri* Kirishitan. For the organization and role of *konfuraria*, see Taniguchi Keitarō, pp. 60–62.

141. For an account of Dutch participation in the expedition, see Nagazumi (1981), pp. 167–74.

142. For a detailed account of the events leading to the fall of the Hara fortress in 1638, see *Tokugawa jikki*, vol. 3, pp. 83–93.

143. Yamamoto Hirofumi, pp. 77–84. It is well known that just one person survived the attack on the Hara fortress—Yamada Emosaku (?–1655?), an artist who was a group leader during the rebellion but who later defected and provided information to the *bakufu* forces. For an account of Yamada Emosaku's treachery, see Shimura, pp. 108–11.

144. *Ofuregaki Kanpō shūsei*, p. 628. For more details on the national adoption and practice of this remuneration system, see Shimizu Hirokazu (1979), pp. 277–88.

145. Tamamuro Fumio, *Sōshiki to danka*, pp. 61–62. The estimation is based on the following exchange rates: a piece of silver currency equals 43 *monme* of silver; the exchange rate for one *ryō* of gold (which is worth approximately one *koku* of rice) is 60 *monme* of silver; and the rice consumption of one person for one year is, on average, 1.8 koku. However, Tamamuro notes that documentary evidence showing that these shogunal rewards were actually paid to informants has yet to be found.

146. The term *bateren monto* (or *bateren shūshi*), which meant followers of *bateren*, was also sometimes used when referring to Kirishitan. See Ōhashi Yukihiro (2001), pp. 19–20.

147. For more details, see ibid., pp. 15–18.

148. Harufuji Hiroshi, p. 85.

149. For a comprehensive list of the experiments of religious inspection in the 1630s, see Ōhashi Yukihiro (2001), pp. 103–6.

150. Tamamuro Fumio, *Sōshiki to danka*, pp. 62–63.

151. Ibid., pp. 64–66.

152. It was apparent in some areas that the system of universal temple certification turned out to be a long-term project requiring at least two preconditions: the conversion of the entire population to Buddhism (albeit in name only in some cases), and an adequate number of Buddhist temples to cover all the villages and wards of the nation. In particular, the shortage of Buddhist temples in some remote, mountainous areas was a problem that would take much time and many resources to solve. Where Buddhist institutions were not easily available, villagers often created their *danna* temples by elevating existing prayer halls to the status of official temples, by inviting in ordained priests, by organizing a Buddhist confraternity, or by building a new religious hall and installing a layperson or itinerant practitioner as

danna priest. Sometimes itinerant religious specialists took the initiative in establishing new temples. For details, see Tamamuro Fumio (1987), pp. 52–61.

153. *Ofuregaki Kanpō shūsei*, p. 628.

154. Ibid., pp. 628–29.

155. For more details on the coastal defense arrangements, see *Tsūkō ichiran*, vol. 5, pp. 28–29 and Yamamoto Hirofumi, pp. 102–16.

156. *Tokugawa jikki*, vol. 3, p. 193. See also *Tsūkō ichiran*, vol. 5, pp. 33–34; Boxer, pp. 383–89; and Cooper (1965), pp. 401–3.

157. For details, see Nagazumi (1969), vol. 4, pp. 492–95 and (1981), pp. 197–205.

158. Shimizu Hirokazu (1981), pp. 168–69.

159. Miura Shumon (1978), pp. 48–49. For a biographical account of Inoue Masashige, see Miura Shumon (1967), pp. 19–47. Miura suggests that Masashige promoted anti-Christian policies as a *korobi* Kirishitan, which means that he had been a Christian follower. Miura further shows that Masashige had a strong appetite for Western-style dress and food and that he sometimes asked Dutch traders to bring cheese and wine. Indeed, an entry in the Dutch diary kept at the Nagasaki trade factory even indicates that Masashige abandoned his Christian faith in 1625 when he turned 40. See Nichi-Ran gakkai, ed., p. 279. However, based on the theory that when he was young, he was a homosexual, and given that homosexuality was not tolerated by the Roman Catholic Church, Nagazumi Yōko dismisses the suggestion that he had been a Roman Catholic. In addition, by 1625, Christianity had already been prohibited for at least twelve years. See Nagazumi (1975), p. 17.

160. Nagazumi (1969), vol. 4, p. 209.

161. This story is recounted in pp. 647–48 of the *Kirishitoki* (A record of Christianity), a collection of documents relating to anti-Christian policies, compiled by Hōjō Ujinaga between 1652 and 1662.

162. Murai (2002), pp. 33–34.

163. The Kirishitan *yashiki*, also known as *yamayashiki* (mountain residence), was originally built in 1640. In 1646, it was expanded in order to accommodate storehouses and offices as well as prison cells. The entire edifice was surrounded by high walls. Due to the decreasing number of Kirishitan prisoners, the residence of Inoue Masashige was scaled back in 1700 and finally closed down in 1792. For more details, see *Tsūkō ichiran*, vol. 5, pp. 189–93.

164. Anesaki, pp. 76–78.

165. Ibid., p. 87.

166. For more details on the Kan'ei famines, see Fujita Satoru (1982), pp. 39–54.

167. Fujii Jōji (1992), pp. 287–88.

168. See Shimizu Hirokazu (1977), p. 318 and Nishiwaki, "Kinsei jidan seido no seiritsu ni tsuite: bakufu hōrei o chūshin ni," pp. 31–32.

169. *Gotōke reijō* (vol. 2), pp. 154–55. For a detailed discussion of shogunal policy measures, see Fujita Satoru (1983), pp. 45–56.

170. About the recalcitrance of Kirishitan followers, Inoue Masashige observed: "*Bateren* teach Kirishitan that, even though there are officials who are wise and capable of judging good and evil in a clear manner, their wisdom will become darkened and their speech will become paralyzed once they begin to interrogate Kirishitan; and [they further teach] that, thanks to the empowering blessing of Deus, those Kirishitan [under interrogation] will become wiser and will come to have more fluent tongues even though they may sound inarticulate and unwise." See Hōjō, p. 637. Thus, in dealing with Christianity, Masashige suggested that Japan needed a wiser and more rational strategy than that involving crude suppression. He urged officials to be innovative: "Tendencies to rely upon torture alone are not helpful. No matter how laborious, it would make more sense to investigate earnestly, to interrogate in detail, to apply various kinds of ideas, to devise means, and to explore better ways." See Hōjō, p. 632.

171. For an overview of the Buddhist pacification in the post-rebellion era, see Kashiwahara (1967), p. 125.

172. Boxer, p. 392.

173. *Tsūkō ichiran*, vol. 5, p. 210.

174. Elison (1973), pp. 232–33.

175. For detailed discussions of Fabian and his works, see ibid., pp. 142–84 and Neil S. Fujita, pp. 203–22. George Elison also provides an English translation of Fabian's *Ha Daiusu* (pp. 257–91). For a collection of anti-Christian treatises, see Ebisawa et al. (1970).

176. For the full text, see Elison, pp. 295–318.

177. Gonoi, pp. 237–38.

178. For more details, see Kudamatsu, pp. 285–300.

179. See Nagura (1994), pp. 229–30.

180. Elison (1973), p. 379.

181. For more details, see ibid., pp. 223–31. For a translation of *Ha Kirishitan*, see ibid., pp. 375–89.

182. For more details, see Murai (1987), pp. 167–76.

183. Elison (1973), p. 232.

184. Murai (1987), p. 177.

185. Elison (1973), p. 213. For the text of *Kirishitan monogatari*, see ibid., pp. 319–74.

186. *Tokugawa jikki*, vol. 3, p. 492.

187. Ibid., p. 492.

188. Hōjō, p. 637.

189. For example, even the well known Buddhist propagandist Sessō Sōsai was not an exception. In Nagasaki, his preaching would usually start with an attack on Christianity and then move to a discussion of the need to discredit the teachings of the Pure Land sects or Nichirenshū. His messages were not so much concerned with refuting Christian doctrines as they were with promoting sectarian doctrines that stressed Zen meditation, *nenbutsu*, and the keeping of precepts.

190. Hōjō, p. 637.

191. Ibid., p. 637.

192. For example, the five-man group system of controlling Christianity had shown signs of promise since the shogunate introduced it in 1642. If a Kirishitan were discovered within the group, then all group members would be subject to heavy punishment. A 1643 entry in a Dutch diary discussed the kinds of punishment that were meted out when a member of a five-man group was found to be a Kirishitan. These ranged from the execution of all group members to the deaths of the family heads of the members' households to imprisonments and fines (See Shimizu Hirokazu [1981], pp. 193–94). Although in a back-up capacity, this system remained effective throughout the Tokugawa period. Similarly, the reward system was put into practice throughout the country, as was the system of trampling on Christian pictures and images.

193. Hōjō, p. 637.

194. Ibid., p. 637.

195. Murai (1987), p. 47.

Chapter 3

196. Ōishi Manabu, pp. 420–23.

197. Of course, this does not mean that all *bakufu* elders favored civil arts over martial arts. But the advocates of the former, represented by Abe Tadaaki, won over those of the latter, represented by Sakai Tadakatsu.

198. Shimizu Hirokazu (1981), pp. 178–79.

199. For examples, see *Buke genseiroku*, pp. 112–13, 120.

200. Kataoka, "Ōmurahan Koori kuzure ikken kaidai," p. 710. For more details, see ibid., pp. 711–59 and Shimizu Hirokazu (1994), pp. 63–71.

201. *Tokugawa jikki*, vol. 4, p. 266.

202. Shimizu Hirokazu (1981), pp. 205–6.

203. Ibid., p. 207.

204. Ibid., pp. 207–8.

205. Ibid., p. 208.

206. *Ofuregaki Kanpō shūsei*, p. 631.

207. Ibid., p. 631. In addition, Article 3 reads: "It has been some time since the ban on Christianity was posted on the bulletin board in the first year of the Meireki era (1655). [Due to weathering] the writing [on the bulletin board] is hardly readable. Replace it with new text."

208. Tamamuro Fumio (1987), pp. 76–77.

209. For statistics on the arrests, see Anesaki, pp. 269–70.

210. On the grounds that the search for underground Kirishitan was conducted simultaneously at various places and under different circumstances, Murai Sanae suggests that the Bungo *kuzure* was a shogunate scheme rather than a natural revelation. In particular, she pays close attention to the practice of *fumie*, which was uniformly enforced upon the whole population (including non-Kirishitan) in Bungo, an area that used to be heavily Christian. See Murai (1987), pp. 70–72.

211. Ōishi Shinzaburō, pp. 321–23.

212. See Matsudaira Tarō, p. 707. However, at the local domain level, the system was not uniform. For example, in the case of the Okayama domain, it was not until the Kansei era (1789–1800) that the Kirishitan magistrate came to concurrently assume the responsibility of inspecting muskets and cannons. See *Ikedake rireki ryakki*, vol. 1, p. 313.

213. Shimizu Hirokazu (1981), pp. 206–7. Through the end of the Tokugawa period, inspectors of Roman Catholicism served concurrently as magistrates of construction. This post, which was called Tenshukyō *kōsatsu* this time around but was commonly known as *shūmon aratameyaku*, was also variously called Kirishitan *shihai*, Kirishitan *aratame*, Kirishitan *bugyō*, and Kirishitan *ruizoku aratame*. For a full list of inspectors of Roman Catholicism, see Shimizu Hirokazu (1976), pp. 48–53.

214. *Ofuregaki Kanpō shūsei*, p. 8.

215. All quotes below pertaining to these articles are from ibid., p. 633.

216. Upon shogunal order, for example, the Okayama domain government in 1665 appointed a vassal, Igi Tanomo, to the newly established position of Kirishitan magistrate. Before this appointment, the task of religious inspection had been handled by the magistrate of temples and shrines. See *Ikedake rireki ryakki*, vol. 1, p. 313.

217. *Ofuregaki Kanpō shūsei*, p. 633.

218. Shimizu Hirokazu (1981), pp. 210–11.

219. Murai (1991), p. 83 and (2002), pp. 49–50.

220. Nagoyashi kyōiku iinkai, p. 189.

221. For more details, see Ōhashi Yukihiro (1992), pp. 51–53.

222. *Gotōke reijō*, p. 185.

223. *Ikedake rireki ryakki*, vol. 1, pp. 348–49.

224. The shogunal inspection of the country, which was conducted whenever a new shogun was installed, survived until 1838. In its regular format, the country was divided into eight regions along fixed routes, and the focus of inspection was on the lives of local residents and the governance of local lords. However, as time progressed, the inspection gradually faded into a ceremonial formality, particularly in the early nineteenth century, when the domain governments began to assert their local autonomy.

225. Tamamuro Fumio (1987), p. 95 and (1968), pp. 28–34.

226. Tamamuro Fumio (1987), pp. 97–98.

227. Tsuji Zennosuke (1954), pp. 92–93.

228. *Ofuregaki Kanpō shūsei*, p. 608.

229. Ibid., pp. 608–9.

230. Ibid., p. 609.

231. Kumazawa Banzan, p. 446.

232. Tsuji Zennosuke (1955), p. 59. See also Hur (2000), p. 116.

233. Tamamuro Fumio (1987, p. 86) notes that, due to the superficial and lax training offered at local educational temples, many monks did not acquire even a basic knowledge of the doctrines and ritual procedures of their own sects. Thus, "ignorant" monks carried with them a doctrinal man-

ual (*shōmono*), which contained the basic teachings of the founders of their sects, and a ritual manual, known as "scrap paper" (*kirikami*), for performing death-related rituals.

234. *Ofuregaki Kanpō shūsei*, p. 609.

235. Ibid., p. 609.

236. For a useful introduction to this policy, see Tsuji Zennosuke (1953), pp. 331–36.

237. In the case of the Aizu domain, when Hoshina Masayuki died in 1672, he was buried with a Shinto-style funeral. But the domain government soon began to retreat from its anti-Buddhist stance, and by 1679, it fully restored the system of temple certification despite strong resistance on the part of Confucian scholars and Shinto priests.

238. Tamamuro Fumio (1987), pp. 104–7.

239. Ibid., pp. 107–11.

240. Ibid., p. 109.

241. Ibid., pp. 116–21.

242. Ibid., p. 122.

243. Kumazawa Banzan's anti-Buddhist sentiments were later compiled in his *Daigaku wakumon*, a treatise published in 1686. See Kumazawa Banzan, pp. 446–68. Another of his treatises, the *Shūgi gaisho*, which also delivers his unambiguous anti-Buddhist stance, was not published until 1679. For this reason, it is hard to prove to what extent Banzan directly influenced Ikeda Mitsumasa's religious policy. See Wakao, p. 222. For example, in 1654–55, the Okayama domain suffered greatly from massive famines, which resulted in 3,684 deaths and affected more than 80 percent of the domain population. Being desperate, Mitsumasa lowered taxes in order to alleviate the hardships and borrowed relief funds in order to purchase food for the starving. Amid the crisis, Mitsumasa was utterly disappointed to witness monks continuing to maintain a luxurious lifestyle, trying to collect more fees and donations from laypeople, and remaining indifferent to the government's relief efforts. All of this had happened before Kumazawa Banzan rose to prominence in domanial politics.

244. *Ikedake rireki ryakki*, vol. 1, p. 324. Wakao Masaki's close examination of the *Ikeda Mitsumasa nikki* shows the escalation of Ikeda Mitsumasa's anti-Buddhist stance from the 1650s to the 1660s. For more details, see Wakao, pp. 223–38.

245. Tamamuro Fumio, *Sōshiki to danka*, pp. 119–20. The *Ikedake rireki ryakki* tells us that out of 1,044 temples, 313 Fujufuse and 250 Tendaishū/Shingonshū temples were demolished, and that 847 monks (585 Fujufuse, 262 Tendaishū/Shingonshū) out of 1,557 were defrocked, while 1,110 survived. However, statistics pertaining to the numbers of monks do not match. See *Ikedake rireki ryakki*, vol. 1, p. 325.

246. See the entry for the fifth day of the eighth month of 1666 in *Ikeda Mitsumasa nikki*, p. 569. For a similar format, see *Ikedake rireki ryakki*, vol. 1, pp. 320–21. Here it should be noted that this new system of Shinto certification was implemented only after a vast number (10,527) of petty

Shinto shrines had been demolished. Those shrines that were involved in issuing anti-Christian certificates numbered less than 700. See Wakao, pp. 237–38.

247. Tamamuro Fumio, *Sōshiki to danka*, pp. 108–9.

248. Nagura (1994), pp. 231–32. In particular, Nagura Tetsuzō suggests that the unease of state councilors and other *bakufu* officials about Ikeda Mitsumasa's Shinto-centered policy had to do with their confidence in Buddhism, which was already entrenched in the lifeworld of the Tokugawa Japanese. See ibid., p. 233.

249. *Ikedake rireki ryakki*, vol. 1, pp. 326–27 and see the entry for the tenth day of the fifth month and the sixth day of the sixth month of 1667 in *Ikeda Mitsumasa nikki*, p. 578, 580.

250. *Ikedake rireki ryakki*, vol. 1, pp. 321–23.

251. Tamamuro Fumio, *Sōshiki to danka*, pp. 107–8.

252. It is well known that Shinto scholars rarely discuss the subject of the afterlife, never mind funeral ceremonies. Moreover, their views on the existence of spirits after death were not only varied—ranging from immortality to a limited lifespan—but also vague and even self-contradictory. See Asoya (1989), pp. 291–312.

253. Nagura (1994), pp. 233–34.

254. Tamamuro Fumio, *Sōshiki to danka*, p. 112.

255. *Ikedake rireki ryakki*, vol. 1, p. 330.

256. Until 1709, religious inspection by Buddhist temples was conducted on a monthly basis; thereafter, it was conducted on a semi-annual basis (spring and autumn). Active Shinto priests, including chief priests (*kannushi*), lesser priests (*negi*), female shrine shamans (*miko*), and low-level priests (*jinnin*), were still allowed to obtain non-Christian certificates from the Yoshida Shinto family.

257. Tamamuro Fumio (2003), p. 2.

258. Ibid., p. 22. The number of villages in the domain is based on the *Genroku gōchō* (Register of villages of the Genroku era), which was compiled between 1700 to 1702 for taxation purposes.

259. The *Chinjuchō* of the Genroku era contains information on the images of deities, types of buildings, landholdings, and managers of the domain's shrines. In order to keep track of how Buddhist images were replaced with Shinto images, the *Chinjuchō* uses three different symbols, one of which would be placed above each entry, as appropriate: a "circle" for a Buddhist image replaced with a mirror, a "triangle" for a Buddhist image replaced with cloth, and a "square" for an existing image that has been put in a new container. For more details, see Tamamuro Fumio (2003), pp. 7–22.

Buddhist management of Shinto shrines continued during the Tokugawa period. Helen Hardacre, who surveys in detail the institutional entanglements of Buddhist temples and Shinto shrines in Kōza county of Sagami and in the western Tama area in the early nineteenth century, finds that "shrines were pervasively influenced by Buddhism and maintained by a variety of connections with temples." For details, see Hardacre (2002), pp. 76–80.

260. See *Tsūkō ichiran*, vol. 5, pp. 124–36. Arai Hakuseki (1657–1725), who interrogated Sidotti four times in 1709 to 1710 and authored the *Seiyō kibun* (Tidings of the west), also concluded that Christian countries did not have territorial ambitions. However, in his recommendation for the continued ban on Christianity, Hakuseki reminded us that Christian activities had attributed to the collapse of the Ming Empire. See Elison, pp. 237–38 and Neil S. Fujita, pp. 227–37.

261. *Ofuregaki Kanpō shūsei*, pp. 633–34.

262. *Tokugawa kinreikō*, vol. 3, p. 279.

263. Ibid. p. 279. Given the importance of compiling an annual census register of sectarian inspection, which was indispensable to administration and tax collection, government officials visited each village and guided village officials with regard to the procedures of "religious inspection." Initially, this kind of instructional visit by government officials was taken very seriously; however, gradually it became routinized. See Narimatsu, pp. 149–51.

264. "Hōnen zeisho," pp. 723–24.

265. For an example, see Narimatsu, pp. 145–48.

266. For more details, see Nagura (1999), pp. 63–64.

267. For more details, see Kinoshita, pp. 4–5.

268. Hayami (2001), pp. 72–74.

269. At the shogunal level, anti-Christian inspections were originally supervised by the *shūmon aratameyaku*. But from the Enpō era (1673–80), the job was taken over by the magistrate of temples and shrines. See Shimizu Hirokazu (1976), p. 47.

270. *Ofuregaki Tenmei shūsei*, pp. 684–85.

271. Kinoshita, pp. 4–5.

272. Hayami (2001), p. 50.

273. Ibid., pp. 52–53.

274. Hayami (1997), pp. 63–65.

275. Ōishi Shinzaburō, pp. 366–67. Between 1721 and 1846, based on the merging of *shūmon aratamechō* and *ninbetsu aratamechō*, the shogunal government was able to conduct a nationwide census every six years.

276. Although most domains compiled the census register only sporadically or not at all (as it was merged into the census register of sectarian inspection), the Nihonmatsu domain compiled it annually from 1685 to the end of the Tokugawa period. This was exceptional. Some of the Nihonmatsu census registers contain detailed information on seasonal workers and their employment.

277. Shimizu Hirokazu (1981), p. 227.

278. Higashibaba, p. 158.

279. *Ofuregaki Kanpō shūsei*, pp. 634–35.

280. In fact, by the mid-seventeenth century, all residents regardless of Buddhist sect came to conduct memorial services for their parents in order to prove their religious innocence and to distance themselves from past Kirishitan family legacies. According to Nagura Tetsuzō, who examines documents on the *korobi* Kirishitan families in Bizen, some Jōdoshinshū

temples in the mid-seventeenth century, for doctrinal reasons, still resisted offering memorial services for the dead. Even in these cases, their *danna* patrons sought to perform memorial services for their Kirishitan parents at other sectarian temples. See Nagura (1995), pp. 170–73.

281. How seriously the matter of Christianity was handled was clearly demonstrated when a *korobi* Kirishitan died. The prescribed procedure was as follows: the corpse was to be salted in the casket and carried to his or her *danna* temple; two men (one from among the *danna* members of the temple, the other from among domain officials) were to guard it around the clock; domain officials were to report the matter to the *bakufu*, detailing the history of the deceased and the cause of his or her death; the *bakufu* was to issue permission for the burial; and the temple was to conduct a funeral and to bury or cremate the corpse. The whole process usually took around three months, and, during this period, family members were prohibited from approaching the deceased. See Tamamuro Fumio, *Sōshiki to danka*, pp. 165–66. For an example of *ruizoku* death that illustrates the salting of the corpse, local reporting, and *bakufu* inspection in the Kōriyama domain in 1732, see Ebisawa (1966), pp. 78–81.

282. *Tsūkō ichiran*, vol. 5, p. 213. For example, in 1693, Nagasaki officials made a list of Kirishitan *ruizoku* in the city, packed the registers in six wooden boxes, and sent them to Miyagi Kazumi, the Nagasaki magistrate (in office from 1687 to 1696), who was staying in Edo. He, in turn, was to submit the registers to the *bakufu*. See *Tsūkō ichiran*, vol. 5, p. 213.

283. Shimizu Hirokazu (1981), pp. 230–31.

284. Local officials experienced some confusion with regard to how far the category of Kirishitan *ruizoku* should be applied. In some areas, male descendants were treated as *ruizoku* for five generations and female descendants for three generations. On the Kōriyama domain in Yamato in the early 1700s, see Ebisawa (1966), pp. 83–85. In order to clarify the generational and relational range of *ruizoku*, the shogunate distributed a unified diagram of Kirishitan *ruizoku* (*ruizoku keizu*) in 1724. See Tamamuro Fumio, *Sōshiki to danka*, pp. 173–76.

285. See Ebisawa (1966), pp. 86–89, 92–94. For an example of registers for the Kirishitan *ruizoku* in Tennōji village, Higashinari county, Settsu, which were compiled in the Kyōhō era, see Fujiwara, pp. 49–94.

286. For example, in 1718, after declaring that Kirishitan *ruizoku* could be subject to ostracism, the shogunate ordered that local officials report twice a year on Kirishitan *ruizoku*: whether they died, were put to death, vanished, or were released from *ruizoku* status due to divorce or to the termination of the status of adopted son. In 1766, senior councilor Matsudaira Yasuyoshi (1719–89) warned that some officials were being negligent with regard to scrutinizing Kirishitan *ruizoku*, and he ordered that *ruizoku* inspection be conducted and reported twice a year, in the seventh and twelfth month, while regular religious inspection be conducted and reported in the tenth month. See *Tsūkō ichiran*, vol. 5, pp. 213–14.

287. For background on the ban on the Fujufuse, see Ooms (1985), pp. 189–93.

288. *Tokugawa kinreikō*, vol. 5, p. 125.

289. Ōishi Kyūkei, vol. 2, p. 97. Far before this measure was enforced, many villages had already specified strict, sometimes very detailed, anti-Christian rules in their five-man group register. For an example, see the rules adopted in 1662 by Shimosakurai village in Shinano, as quoted in Ooms (1996), pp. 356–57:

Christians. Following the investigations of the past, each and every one, down to the last person, has been thoroughly examined: not only house owners, [but also] men, women, children, servants and semi-independent branch houses (*kadoya*), renters, fully established branch houses (*kakae*), down to Buddhist monks, Shinto priests, *yamabushi*, ascetics, mendicant monks with flutes or bells, outcasts, common beggars and *hinin*, and so on—to make sure that there is not a single Christian in the village. If villagers see or hear about Christians, regardless of whether they are in the village or somewhere else, they must report them to the authorities at once and receive the appropriate reward. If intentionally no report is made and then someone else reports it, not only the headman and the five-man group but the entire village will be punished.

290. For missionaries who did not allow underground faith and who cherished martyrdom, the religious lives of these underground Kirishitan represented apostasy even if they were disguising their faith in order to avoid anti-Christian measures. In theory, the underground Kirishitan were all associated with funerary Buddhist temples and regularly underwent anti-Christian inspection. Higashibaba notes: "Were they apostates or were they still Kirishitan? The hidden Kirishitan themselves certainly believed that they were still Kirishitan. Hiding Kirishitan faith by external apostasy was reasonable for them, because it enabled them to continue their faith in this world. Whichever they might choose, whether apostasy or martyrdom, they could no longer continue to practice Kirishitan faith. Therefore, they created another option for themselves—to apostatize but not to abandon their faith—in order to live and continue their Kirishitan faith and practice." Higashibaba, p. 154.

291. Miyazaki Kentarō notes: "For example, according to interrogations of Urakami faithful recorded at the end of the *bakufu* regime some professed to consider the image of Maria Kannon to be the *honzon* (the principal image) and that of Jesus to be a *wakibutsu* (a companion Buddhist figure on the side)." Interestingly, even after 1873, when there was no longer any need to hide one's Kirishitan belief, many of the former underground Kirishitan did not return to the Roman Catholic Church but continued to keep their faith in the manner to which they had become accustomed during the Tokugawa period. These Kirishitan are Kakure Kirishitan and should be distinguished from the "underground Kirishitan" of the previous period. Miyazaki continues: "In the early 1990s many of the surviving Kakure Kirishitan disbanded their religious organizations and turned to other religions. . . . For instance, most of the former members of these Kirishitan groups in Ikitsuki, Hirado and Sotome became Buddhists. On Gotō they also turned to Shinto. The number of those who turned to the Catholic Church was surprisingly small." See Miyazaki Kentarō, "The Kakure Kirishitan Tradition," pp. 19–22, 30–32.

292. Based on the assessment that the threat of Christianity had ceased to exist by the 1660s, some scholars, including Murai Sanae, suggest that the reason behind the *bakufu*'s execution of nationwide anti-Christian inspection lay in its desire to tighten up its control over the nation's daimyo and peasant population. For their part, the domain governments faithfully followed shogunal policy in order to strengthen their own authority to carry out their domestic reforms. See Murai (1991), pp. 85–86 and (2002), pp. 36–43.

293. Shimizu Hirokazu (1981), pp. 214–18.

294. Ravina, p. 14.

295. For more details, see Bolitho (1991), pp. 202–3.

296. Hall, p. 150.

297. Takano, p. 166.

298. For more details, see Somada, pp. 316–20.

299. For more discussion, see Ōhashi Yukihiro (2001), pp. 56–65.

Part II

1. *Ofuregaki Kanpō shūsei*, p. 634.

2. Ibid., pp. 634–35.

3. *Shizuoka kenshi: shiryōhen 12*, p. 226.

4. *Matsudo shishi: shiryōhen 1*, p. 123.

5. *Ofuregaki Kanpō shūsei*, p. 609.

6. Gorai Shigeru (1992), pp. 607–8.

Chapter 4

7. It is generally accepted that there were three factors affecting Ieyasu's choice of Zōjōji as the funerary temple of his family: it was a Pure Land temple, just as his family's previous funerary temple, Daijuji in Mikawa, had been; it was the oldest and greatest of all Pure Land temples in Edo; and its then head monk was a disciple of the head monk of Daijuji. See Naitō Masatoshi, pp. 85–86.

8. In total, there were six shoguns buried at Zōjōji (the second, sixth, seventh, ninth, twelfth, and fourteenth shoguns), with the same number buried at Kan'eiji (the fourth, fifth, eighth, tenth, eleventh, and thirteenth shoguns).

9. See Ichioka, p. 226. For example, as far as the daimyo class was concerned, according to a Tenpō era (1830–43) survey, more than 60 percent of the nation's 266 daimyo households were affiliated with Zen temples (83 households with Sōtōshū, 70 with Rinzaishū, and 12 with Ōbakushū). Jōdoshū was next on the list with 65 households, followed by Tendaishū with 19, Nichirenshū with 11, and Shingonshū with 2. See Takeda Chōshū (1996), p. 210. Most daimyo were buried at their domain *danna* temples, but when they died in Edo, they were often buried at their auxiliary *danna* temple in Edo. For example, see Haga (1980), pp. 149–51.

10. All data are from *Niigata kenshi shiryōhen 7*, pp. 257–71.

11. All data are from *Ichikawa shishi*, pp. 331–55.

12. *Niigata kenshi shiryōhen 7*, pp. 262–63.

13. Hur, pp. 162–63. For more details on the general changes of the composition of commoner households in Edo, see ibid., pp. 123–33.

14. *Shinpen Chiyodaku tsūshi shiryōhen*, pp. 345–46, 349.

15. Ibid., pp. 350–59.

16. For another example, see the *shūmon ninbetsuchō* of Yotsuya Shiochō itchōme, published by the Edo-Tokyo Museum. It contains one of the most comprehensive collections of data on the household-temple relationship, providing census information from 1857, 1861–63, 1865, 1867, 1869, and 1870. See Tōkyōto Edo-Tokyo hakubutsukan toshi rekishi kenkyūshitsu (1998–99).

17. Narimatsu, pp. 115–18 and Gotō Haruyoshi, pp. 2–3, 7–9.

18. This law refers to the regulation "banning those who are omitted from the census register of sectarian inspection from being accepted (as new residents)." See Shimizu Hirokazu (1977), p. 406.

19. Gotō Haruyoshi, pp. 12, 55–56. In addition to anti-Christian identification, the *shūmon ninbetsu okurijō* was also used to check whether the person was involved in criminal activities, was respectful of the law, or was delinquent in paying taxes.

20. For an example of this custom, see ibid., pp. 10–11 and *Zenkoku minji kanrei ruishū*, pp. 304–5.

21. Gotō Haruyoshi, pp. 57–58, 63–64.

22. *Kurashiki shishi*, pp. 387–95.

23. Taki, p. 4.

24. For more examples of the wording, see *Kurashiki shishi*, pp. 408–20 and *Ichikawa shishi*, pp. 356–58.

25. Takeda Chōshū (1994), p. 160.

26. Morioka (1967), pp. 214–16.

27. However, it should be noted that, in order to curb the custom of partitioning family-landholdings among its members—a custom that had produced many unsustainable peasant households—the shogunate issued an edict in 1673 prohibiting "the division of land into holdings of less than 10 *koku*" (in the case of village headmen, less than 20 *koku*). In the long run this law discouraged those not inheriting the household property from parents from forming their own independent households; as a result, such individuals often chose to make their living as tenant peasants or to seek employment in towns or cities. In the end, this proved to be successful in halting the increase in the number of titled peasant households. For more details, see Ooms (1996), pp. 53–57, 189.

28. Ōtō (1990), pp. 95–96.

29. Takeda Chōshū (1976), pp. 75–78. In this case, members of the *dōzoku* group usually believed that they were all cultivating the same rice plant (*ine*) and that its growth hinged upon the care of their common ancestral spirits. Based on this shared belief, they adopted the same surname or *myōji* (literally, "letter of rice seedlings"). The same *myōji* signified that the same pedigree shared the same rice plant. The word *dōzoku* was often substituted for the word *dōmyō*, or "same seedlings." In the traditional *dōzoku* village it was

customary for the head of a *dōzoku* group to take care of rice seeds and to distribute them to member households in the spring, the time of rice planting.

30. For examples, see Mori (1992), pp. 260–310. In the Tōhoku region, for example, where *dōzoku* consciousness was especially strong, branch households associated themselves with a *danna* temple that was affiliated with their main household. In this region, many *dōzoku* customs persisted into the Meiji period. In contrast, in more advanced regions, by the late seventeenth century most of the *dōzoku*-type branch households had been gradually severed from the main household and had grown into independent nuclear households. Yet, their initial *danna* affiliation tended to persist. See Ōtō (1990), p. 96.

31. Factional disputes in Tokugawa society often stemmed from a conflict of interests among proprietors, landlords, or village elders; and such conflicts were sometimes traceable to medieval times.

32. Takeda Chōshū (1975), p. 269. For example, the 1872 survey shows that all of the 31 households in former shogunal lands belonged to Saigenji, and 33 households in former *monzeki* lands belonged to Tokujuan and Seikōji, who had 19 and 14, respectively.

33. Ibid., pp. 269–70.

34. Takeda Chōshū (1994), pp. 160–61.

35. *Kibi gunshi gekan*, pp. 2923–26.

36. *Ichikawa shishi*, pp. 331–55.

37. *Kusatsu shishi*, pp. 682–83. For another example, see the 1845 register of Kokeyama village in Bitchū, in which 32 households were almost evenly divided into three groups and were affiliated with the three temples in the village. *Kibi gunshi gekan*, pp. 2956–57.

38. Morioka (1962), p. 153.

39. For example, An'yōji in Takara village, Shingū domain, Kii had 515 *danna* households, and Honshōji in the Matsumura domain had 7 *danna* households. The *danna* households of these Jōdoshinshū temples all belonged to the *eta* class. See *Shingūhan shoshū honmatsu jigō sonota meisaichō* (1870) and *Matsumurahan shoshū honmatsu jigō sonota meisaichō* (1871), respectively. According to a survey conducted in 1932, about 85 percent of the *burakumin* population were still associated with Jōdoshinshū. The ties between *burakumin* and Jōdoshinshū were particularly strong in western Japan, except for Okayama prefecture, where some of the *burakumin* were affiliated with Shingonshū and Nichirenshū. See Morioka (1962), p. 155. Even today about 70 percent to 80 percent of the *burakumin* population, which is estimated to number around 3 million people residing in around 6,000 *buraku* (hamlets), belong to the Jōdoshinshū. See Sōtōshū jinken yōgo suishin honbu, p. 163.

40. Morioka (1967), pp. 215–17 and Ooms (1996), pp. 284–85.

41. In western Japan, there were also nineteen middle-class head temples besides these "*buraku*" head temples that controlled both *buraku* branch temples and other "ordinary" branch temples. Andachi Itsuo argues that the emergence of the "*buraku*" head temples was a result of the efforts of these geographically well positioned temples, which were, as latecomers, aggressively engaged in expanding their religious influence by bringing

local *burakumin* temples into their orbit. On the other hand, Yamamoto Nao-moto, who is critical of Andachi's view, suggests that the *buraku monto* first established Buddhist halls in their villages and then sought a head-branch relationship with the *"buraku"* head temples. The hope was that these head temples would serve as an intermediary when their Buddhist halls tried to acquire official status from the Honganji headquarters. For more details, see Andachi (1980), pp. 221–42 and (1984), pp. 56–63; Yamamoto Naomoto (1981) and (1982); and Sōda, pp. 108–10, 127–28.

42. Andachi (1984), p. 64.

43. Wakisaka, pp. 77–78.

44. Ibid., pp. 80–83 and Naganuma, pp. 40–41.

45. Tamamuro Taijō (1961), pp. 20–27.

46. Takeda Chōshū (1994), pp. 204–13.

47. For more details, see Ōkuwa, *Jidan no shisō*, pp. 57–66.

48. Sōtōshū jinken yōgo suishin honbu (2002), pp. 127–38. Based on the Honganji documents, which show how head temples (both the Nishi and Higashi) incorporated local prayer halls (*dōjō*) into their organization (i.e., through conferring wooden Buddhist images, temple titles written on paper, and/or portraits of Shinran to the local *dōjō* in return for payment of often hefty fees), Tamamuro Fumio shows that the number of Jōdoshinshū temples in Kumatomo drastically increased from the early to the mid-seventeenth century. For the local *dōjō*, the acquisition of sacred items from the Honganji head temples was meant to confer official recognition of their status as a temple. See Tamamuro Fumio, *Sōshiki to danka*, pp. 83–98.

49. For more discussions of the communal character of village Buddhist halls in the late medieval period, see Akata (January 1971), pp. 31–35; Fujiki, pp. 4–20; and Takeda Chōshū (1994), pp. 157–59. In some regions, the *sōdō* was erected at the village boundary in the expectation that it could prevent evil spirits from entering the village and keep it as an inviolable space of sanctity and purity. However, it should be noted that during the Tokugawa period, many villages in the Kinki region continued to maintain a communal prayer Buddhist hall (referred to as *sōji* and rooted in the tradition of *sōdō*) in addition to funerary *danna* temples affiliated with individual households. It was the custom for the village community as a whole to be responsible for supporting its *sōji*, where people offered prayer rituals for good harvests, security, and the well-being of the village community. For a detailed discussion, see Fukuta (2004), pp. 64–76.

50. For details on the transformation and functions of *butsudō* within the context of the rise of death rituals and ancestral rites in Ōmi during the late medieval and early modern periods, see Akata (March 1971), pp. 62–74.

51. The approximate number of villages can be estimated based on the *Tenpō gōchō* (Village registers of the Tenpō era), a nationwide survey of annual rice yields compiled for taxation purposes in 1831–34 by the office of the shogunal treasury. The shogunate compiled this kind of village register (*gōchō*) three times in the course of the Tokugawa period. The first one

(compiled in 1655–58) is no longer extant, but the second one (compiled in 1700–3) has partially survived. The third one, *Tenpō gōchō*, currently preserved intact in the Cabinet Library (Naikaku bunkō), indicates that there were 63,480 villages in the early Tempō era. Unfortunately, there is no comprehensive survey that informs us of the total number of urban wards at any given time during the Tokugawa period; however, it is estimated that there were about 10,000 wards. For more details, see Kanzaki Akitoshi, pp. 496–508.

52. All data are from *Kurashiki shishi*, pp. 636–50.

53. Ibid., pp. 387–405.

54. We can consider two reasons for this tendency. One is that, when a temple in the village wielded power as the *bodaiji* for the entire village, thus becoming the center of its religious life, it could easily become too powerful. The villagers might not have wanted to see this happen. The other is that, by forming *danna* relationships with temples in the neighboring village, households could have maintained a balance of power between themselves and their *danna* temples.

55. Fukuta (2004), pp. 151–52.

56. All data are from *Shinpen Chiyodaku tsūshi shiryōhen*, pp. 340–50.

57. See "Hōnen zeisho," p. 723 and Fukuta (2004), pp. 136–38.

58. Ōkuwa, *Jidan no shisō*, pp. 111–12.

59. Ōkuwa (August 1968), p. 28.

60. Ibid., p. 28.

61. Ōkuwa, *Jidan no shisō*, p. 112 and Yoshihara (April 2000), pp. 27–28. In fact, by the late seventeenth century, the distinction between landed peasants (*honbyakushō*) and tenant "water-drinking" peasants (*mizunomi byakushō*) had become firmly established in western Japan. By the early eighteenth century, it was gradually expanded and systematized throughout the country, forming the foundation of the Tokugawa *bakuhan* system. Mizubayashi, pp. 207–13.

62. For more details, see Hōzawa (2001), pp. 525–26.

63. Fukuta (2004), p. 145.

64. See Hōzawa (2001), pp. 526–27. For Toyoda Takeshi's view, see Toyoda (1982), pp. 123–27.

65. For more details, see Hōzawa (2001), pp. 527–29.

66. Despite the instructions that the *bakufu* set out in 1780, there was still some confusion in the shogunal lands with regard to disputes over the issue of switching one's *danna* temple. This indicates that the principle of one temple per household was not yet firm. See ibid., pp. 529–30.

67. For more details, see ibid., pp. 543–47, 555–57.

68. For a good example that shows the persistence of plural *danna* relations, see Ōkuwa (February 1986), pp. 24–29. Using the census registers of sectarian inspection from 1814, Ōkuwa examined the case of Shiriuchi village in the Kōriyama domain (in present-day Nara) and found that 34 out of 84 village households were in *handanka* relationships, and the remaining 50 households complied with the principle of one temple per household.

69. For more details, see Fukuta (2004), pp. 158–61.

70. The term *handanka*, which was commonly used, conveys the impression that two *danna* temples divided a household and that each possessed half of it. The term *fukudanka*, which is gaining currency as an academic term, stresses the standpoint of *danna* households rather than that of *danna* temples. For a discussion as to why gender played a decisive role in plural *danna* relations, see Takeda Chōshū (1976), pp. 129–32. For various examples of plural *danna* customs, see Fukuta (1992), pp. 59–66 and Ōkuwa (July 1968), pp. 27–34. For a bibliographical note of various studies on these customs, see Noguchi (1980).

71. Ōkuwa (August 1968), pp. 22–25.

72. Ōkuwa, *Jidan no shisō*, pp. 44–54.

73. Ōkuwa (July 1968), pp. 30–32.

74. Takeda Chōshū (1996), p. 353–56.

75. Nagura (July 1992), p. 19. Nagura suggests that it was due to this kind of antagonism between the followers of *nenbutsu* chanting and those of *daimoku* chanting that many *monto* families in Echigo, which embraced plural *danna* affiliations, tended to hold memorial services for their ancestors at their *danna* temple.

76. See Nakata, pp. 126–28; Kodama Shiki, pp. 207–8; and Morioka (1967), pp. 217–20.

77. Yamanaka, pp. 140–42.

78. For details, see Yoshihara (February 2000), pp. 73–86.

79. Ibid., pp. 86–91.

80. When a proxy temple took over the right of religious inspection from its titular *danna* temple, it frequently inherited its *danna* patrons as well. In some cases, as was seen in the dispute between Jōkōji (a titular *danna* temple) and Hōzōji (a proxy temple) in the Kaga domain, the proxy temple took care of the titular *danna* temple's patrons, regarded them as its own possession, and vigorously resisted when the titular temple tried to reclaim its patrons for the purpose of conducting funerary rituals. For details, see Nakata, pp. 116–23.

81. In 1821, a household in Fukagawa village, Aki that was a *danna* of Enryūji located far away in Teramachi, Hiroshima attempted to cut its ties with Enryūji and to switch to its proxy temple, Yōtokuji, located in the same village. Enryūji countered by petitioning the domain government, arguing that it should retain the right to conduct "direct service" for its *danna* in order to prevent "warm relationships [with them] from thinning out." Both sides were insistent, but it is not known how this dispute was solved. Compare with households in the Ōgaki village in Saeki county, which numbered 197 in 1755, and were affiliated with temples of head-temple status (Enryūji and Chōsenji in Teramachi of Hiroshima, and Kōjakuji in Hijiyama ward), all located far from their village. In 1755, all of these households successfully switched to Jōenji, a proxy temple in their village. See Yamanaka, pp. 140–42.

82. Kodama Shiki, pp. 132–35.

Appendix to Chapter 4

83. A collection of these temple registers is now available in print. See *Kōzuke no kuni jiin meisaichō* (1880–81), 8 vols., edited by Ushiki Yukio (Maebashi: Gunmaken bunka jigyō shinkōkai, 1993–98).

84. These *danna*-rich temples included Zenshōji (Tendaishū, Haga village), with 3,500 *danna* patrons (*Kōzuke no kuni jiin meisaichō*, vol. 1, p. 137); Ryūtakuji (Tendaishū, Momonoi village), with 3,210 *danna* patrons (ibid., vol. 2, p. 204); Sōrinji (Sōtōshū, Shirosatoi village) with 3,334 patrons (ibid., vol. 2, p. 227); and Jōrinji (Sōtōshū, Naganohara ward), with 3,900 *danna* patrons (ibid., vol. 4, p. 158). Interestingly, Hōdōji (Tendaishū, Furumaki village) did not have any funerary *danna* patrons but had 4,000 prayer *danna* patrons (ibid., vol. 2, p. 199).

85. The *Shaji torishirabe ruisan* contains two collections of data: the *jiin meisaichō*, which contains data on the sectarian affiliations, lands, and *danna* households of Buddhist temples; and the *Kyōbushō shiryō*, which contains various reports, government directives, correspondence between government offices, and inquiries concerning Shinto institutions. For a classified index of these collections, see Tamamuro and Nemoto (1984), pp. 1–140; for an introduction to these collections, see Tamamuro Fumio (1984), pp. 540–48.

86. All data pertaining to these areas are from *Kakudaken shoshū honmatsu jigō sonota meisaichō* (1871), *Izu no kuni honmatsu jigō sonota meisaichō* (1871), *Kurashikiken honmatsu jigō sonota meisaichō* (1871), *Ōzuhan shoshū honmatsu jigō sonota meisaichō* (1871), *Hitaken shoshū honmatsu jigō sonota meisaichō* (1871), respectively. All are included in the unpublished *Shaji torishirabe ruisan* collections.

87. The situation in Izu was quite similar to that in the Shingū domain in Kii—a Zenshū-dominant area (about 88 percent) with 72 Sōtōshū temples and 64 Rinzaishū temples out of a total of 154 temples. The ratio of temples holding no more than 50 *danna* households was about 57 percent, and those with more than 300 *danna* patrons was about 6 percent. See *Shingūhan shoshū honmatsu jigō sonota meisaichō* (1870).

88. In the Kumamoto domain Jōdoshinshū temples far exceeded those of any other sects in terms of their grip on funerary *danna* households. Out of a total of 807 temples in the domain, temples belonging to Jōdoshinshū numbered 443 (357 temples belonged to the Nishihonganji subsect, and 86 temples belonged to the Higashihonganji subsect). Many of them were well endowed with *danna* households, and 3 of them held more than 2,000 *danna* households. See Tamamuro Fumio (2000), pp. 85–89.

89. For a full list of *danna* for the "annihilation of sins," see Matsudaira Kanzan (1813), vol. 2, pp. 212–88.

90. All data in these tables, taken from Kodama Shiki, p. 33, are based on temple registers in the *Shaji torishirabe ruisan*.

91. For details, see Kodama Shiki, pp. 31–36.

92. Ibid., pp. 34–36.

93. Ibid., pp. 124–28.

94. See Tanabe Takafumi, pp. 25–29.

Chapter 5

95. For examples in premodern times, see Ōyama, p. 397; Takatori, p. 196; and Yoshie, p. 144.

96. For a classic observation of the social impact of death, see Radcliffe-Brown, pp. 285–87.

97. These four themes have been suggested by a number of scholars, including Akata (1986), pp. 35–36.

98. Ibid., pp. 88–89.

99. Kyūshōji refers to a Nichirenshū temple that was established by Mitsukuni at Inagi in Mito. In 1677, on the seventeenth anniversary of his mother's death, Mitsukuni transferred Kyōōji (located in the suburbs of the Mito castle) to Inagi and renamed it Kyūshōji after his mother's posthumous name Kyūshōin. The temple had eight branch temples and held land yielding 300 *koku* of rice per year.

100. Tsuji Zennosuke (1955), p. 346.

101. Ibid., p. 347.

102. The custom of *tamayobi*, premised on the belief that there was a possibility the dead could revive, was cited in the chapter on Emperor Nintoku in the *Nihon shoki*. In the Heian and medieval periods, we find more and more such examples in literary works, in collections of Buddhist tales (such as *Nihon ryōiki* and *Konjaku monogatarishū*), and in legends and religious tracts.

103. For details, see Akata (1986), pp. 41–47.

104. *Shokoku fūzoku toijō kotae*, "Echigo no kuni Nagaokaryō," p. 556. This 1817 document refers to a survey report compiled by the Confucian scholar Akiyama Keizan and submitted to the *bakufu*. In 1813–15, a group of Edo scholars represented by the *bakufu* official Yashiro Hirokata launched a nationwide survey of local customs and manners. They asked the domain governments to collect and report information on their local customs and manners according to questionnaires prepared under the title of *Shokoku fūzoku toijō* (Questionnaires on the customs and manners of all domains). These questionnaires were mostly concerned with events, rituals, celebrations, taboos, and observances that were practiced on a regular basis (e.g., customs pertaining to childbirth, coming-of-age, weddings, funerals, memorial services, etc.). Many domains cooperated in this endeavor. These reports, which offer nationwide information on the lifeworld of ordinary people, provide first-rate, comprehensive data for the study of Tokugawa customs. In particular, given that almost no comparable national data on death and ancestral rites are available, these survey reports are particularly useful.

105. *Shokoku fūzoku toijō kotae*, "Awaji no kuni," p. 788.

106. Ibid., "Hitachi no kuni Mitoryō," p. 538.

107. Inoguchi Shōji, who examined 35 examples of *nakime* in the areas from Iwate to Okinawa, found that the custom of hiring a professional female wailer had mostly survived in isolated fishing villages or islands where Buddhism held relatively little influence. For more details, see Ingochi Shōji (1954), pp. 209–13.

108. Saitō Ryūzō (1925), p. 993.

109. Fujii Masao (1977), pp. 121–22, 164–65; Matsuura Shūkō (1969), pp. 23–24; and Inoguchi, pp. 33–38.

110. Negishi, vol. 2, pp. 266–67.

111. For examples, see Inoguchi, pp. 149–59 and Akata (1986), pp. 62–63. Resuscitation tales had it that the dead were able to return to this world either because they could hear people's voices or because somebody called their name.

112. Saitō Ryūzō, p. 994. Cf. see Terakado, p. 121.

113. Okada Shigekiyo emphasizes the association of death pollution with social disorder and chaos, whereas Emiko Ohnuki-Tierney pays more attention to the loss of identity caused by death. For details, see Okada Shigekiyo (1989), pp. 446–54 and Ohnuki-Tierney, pp. 51–74. However, neither takes seriously the flip side of pollution — that it also functions as a source of "potential for good" or "creation." See Douglas, pp. 159–79.

114. Leach, pp. 39–40.

115. Hugh-Jones and Laidlaw, vol. 2, p. 229. All margins are considered dangerous and vulnerable because they threaten the established order. Taboo categories are anomalous with respect to clear-cut category oppositions. That is why, as Leach and Douglas suggest, anything that exudes from the orifices of the body (e.g., spittle, blood, feces, urine, semen, hair clippings, nail parings, body dirt, mother's milk, etc.) becomes an object of taboo. See Leach, p. 38 and Douglas, p. 121.

116. Akata (1986), p. 82.

117. Ibid., p. 83.

118. Ōtō (1996), p. 358.

119. Inoguchi, pp. 205–8.

120. Smith (1961), p. 525 and Ooms (1996), pp. 216–17. In extreme cases, the *murahachibu* household was punished through expulsion from the village, removal from the population register, demolition of household buildings, religious curse and harassment, confiscation of properties, prohibition of free movement, and even death through beating, drowning, or being buried alive. See Haga (1998), pp. 236–37.

121. Douglas, p. 35.

122. Kuroda Hideo, pp. 42–44.

123. For more details, see Hayashi Yukiko (1997), pp. 91–93.

124. Nakagawa, p. 47. In the early decades of the seventeenth century, when the Tokugawa shogunate still struggled to strengthen its power structure, *bakufu* leaders took nationwide abstinence imposed at the time of shogunal death as an occasion to remind the people of where power rested.

125. Hayashi Yukiko (1997), pp. 93–94.

126. Ibid., pp. 112–13.

127. For a collection of edicts on mourning periods that were revised several times during the Tokugawa period, see *Gotōke reijō*, pp. 269–82. As a matter of fact, notes Harold Bolitho, some Confucianists took abstinence during mourning very seriously: "The scholar Itō Jinsai shut himself away

for three years when his parents died, even though his relations with his father had been strained at best. So, too, under similar circumstances, did the 35-year-old Rai San'yō (1780–1832), who abstained not only from sake and meat, but, for good measures, from his newly acquired teenaged bride as well." Bolitho (2003), p. 17. For a detailed discussion of how the *bukkiryō* was actually applied, see Hayashi Yukiko (1998), pp. 124–47.

128. See Mizubayashi, p. 333 and Hayashi Yukiko (1997), pp. 116–17. Interestingly, however, the populace did not pay much attention to the Confucian undertone of the edict. For them, the law did not mean much other than that customs related to death pollution were legally sanctioned.

129. Saitō Ryūzō (1925), p. 994.

130. Matsuura, pp. 37–38.

131. Saitō Ryūzō (1925), p. 994.

132. Since "pillow dumplings" were believed to absorb the defilement of death, they were thrown away outside the boundary of the village after the ritual. Namihira (1985), pp. 60–62.

133. For local variations in reporting a death to the *danna* temple and local authorities, see *Zenkoku minji kanrei ruishū*, pp. 150–53.

134. Ichioka, p. 229.

135. For examples of how such groups took initiative to render assistance for a village funeral and to display proper funerary behavior, see Haga (1980), pp. 160–61.

136. Despite the apparent Buddhist symbolism, *kyōkatabira* was also treated as an efficacious fetish capable of preventing evil spirits from interfering with the passage of the dead to the other world. See Matsuura, pp. 31–32, 39.

137. Saitō Ryūzō (1925), p. 997.

138. Gamaike, *Shinshū to minzoku shinkō*, pp. 10–11.

139. Ekū, p. 255. According to a nationwide survey conducted by the Nishihonganji in 1983, a bit more than 60 percent of a sample of 1,407 *monto* families maintained memorial tablets in their household Buddhist altars. Those *monto* families that did not maintain memorial services were most numerous in the Hyōgo, Aki, Nara, and Tōhoku regions. See Gamaike, "Monto mono shirazu: Shinshū no sōsō girei to datsuraku shita shūzoku," pp. 25–27.

140. Jōdoshishinshū followers used the term *hōmyō* rather than the term *kaimyō*, thus sticking to their stance regarding the "precepts of no precepts." See Blum, pp. 183–84.

141. Fujii Masao (1977), pp. 40–41, 48–53; Tamamuro Fumio, *Edo jidai no Sōtōshū no tenkai*, pp. 191–92; and Williams (2005), pp. 27–29.

142. Funeral stores in the Tokugawa period were called *hayaokeya* (fast coffin makers, literally "stores of fast tubs") or *hayamonoya* (stores of fast items). The term *hayamono*, which refers to funeral paraphernalia in general, including the coffin, indicates that funeral items were usually not available for rent but that they could be quickly made and sold upon order.

143. Saitō Ryūzō (1925), p. 994.

144. Koizumi (1990), p. 43.

145. Suzuki Kimio, p. 374.

146. Tamamuro Taijō (1963), p. 83. For local variations of the custom, see *Shokoku fūzoku toijō kotae*, "Mutsu no kuni Shinobugun Dategun," p. 476; "Mikawa no kuni Yoshidaryō," p. 616; "Bingo no kuni Numakumagun Urasakimura," p. 768; and "Awaji no kuni," p. 788.

147. Saitō Ryūzō (1925), p. 995 and Titsingh, pp. 260–61.

148. For a detailed discussion of the custom of the "mourning hut," see Akata (1986), pp. 53–63. During the period of *mogari* (a custom never followed by commoners), the spirit of the dead was believed to be pacified and purified, as seen in Yamaori (1986), pp. 329–31. And for a detailed discussion of the practice of *mogari* at the imperial court in ancient Japan, see Ebersole, pp. 123–70.

149. Tamamuro Taijō (1963), p. 83.

150. Akata (1986), pp. 52–53.

151. In this connection, Buddhist monks often referred to the night of *tsuya* as *taiya*, or "great night," the implication being that the deceased would be made into a disciple of the Buddha once it was over.

152. See Kadomae, pp. 151–53.

153. Based on the "incense offering" records kept by the branch house of the Tomizawa family in Renkōji village, Tama county, Musashi between 1758 and 1865, Shishiba Masako suggests that with enhanced awareness of the household institution and the development of networks between households, many families kept records on the exchanges of "incense offering" beginning in the mid-Tokugawa period. For an example of items exchanged in the Tomizawa family in 1849, see Shishiba, pp. 42–43. For comparison, see Narimatsu, pp. 164–66 and *Fukui shishi shiryōhen 9: kinsei 7*, pp. 770–85.

154. Terakado, p. 122.

155. For a discussion of the scales of funerals, see Ōtō (1996), pp. 309–10, 317.

156. Terakado, p. 122.

157. Ibid., p. 122.

158. Although he was trained as a physician, Titsingh served as chief factor of the VOC outpost in Nagasaki three times in the late eighteenth century. His first spell of duty began in 1779 and lasted for about fourteen months, during which time he was received by Shogun Ieharu in Edo. A brief return to Europe was followed by a second spell of duty beginning in 1781, which included another visit to Edo. During his two journeys to and from Edo and his stay in Nagasaki, he collected material and wrote a book, which was divided into two parts: the first part dealt mainly with the shogun, his pedigree, and the way of life at the shogunal quarters; the second part described various wedding and burial customs. The English edition of this work, which was translated from the French in 1822 by Frederic Shoberl, has an exceedingly long title: *Illustrations of Japan: Consisting of private memoirs and anecdotes of the reigning dynasty of the Djogouns, or sovereigns of Japan: a description of the feasts and ceremonies observed throughout the year at their court: and of the ceremonies customary at marriages and funerals: to which are subjoined, observations on the legal suicide of the Japanese, remarks on their poetry, an expla-*

nation of their mode of reckoning time, particulars respecting the dosia powder, the preface of a work by confoutzee on filial piety, &C. &C. by M. Titsingh.

159. Titsingh, pp. 240–41.

160. Faure (1991), pp. 193–94 and Rowe, p. 358.

161. Fujii Masao (1983), pp. 155–57.

162. For a general discussion of chanting practice in Japanese Buddhism, see Shimizu Masumi, pp. 53–55.

163. In east Asian Mahāyāna Buddhism, the word dhāraṇī (darani in Japanese), which means "to hold," or "to support," was more or less interchangeable with the word "mantra" (shingon in Japanese, zhenyan in Chinese). Originally, the two were distinguished: dhāraṇī referred to memory aids used to hold, support, or maintain something in the mind, while mantra referred to syllabic formulae, spells, and incantations.

164. The Sanskrit equivalent is "om amogha vairocana mahāmudrā mani padma jivala pravarttaya hūm." For its meaning, see George J. Tanabe, p. 137. For further reference, see Fukūkenjaku jinben shingonkyō (T. 20), Fukūkenjaku Birushanabutsu daikanjō kōshingonkyō (T. 19), and Birushanabussetsu kongōchōgyō kōmyōshingon giki (T. 76).

165. Here, kaji refers to the "grace" of Mahāvairocana. According to Kūkai, "The compassion of the Buddha pouring forth on the heart of sentient beings, like the rays of the sun on water, is called ka [adding], and the heart of sentient beings which keeps hold of the compassion of the Buddha, as water retains the rays of the sun, is called ji [retaining]." Quote from Haketa, p. 92.

166. See Yokota and Kobayashi, pp. 218, 227. The sand sanctioned through the doshakaji ritual was also used for such purposes as healing disease, driving away evil spirits, or praying for longevity and health. For information on the ordinary "mantra of clear light" ritual, commonly known as kōmyōku, see "Kōmyō shingonhō," pp. 117–27 and Fujii Masao (1978), pp. 357–63.

167. Yokota and Kobayashi, p. 220.

168. For a discussion of the structural similarity between these two ritual traditions, see Sekiguchi Masayuki, pp. 18–31. For the concept of sin as a subcategory of kegare in traditional Japanese culture, see Aoki, pp. 269–90.

169. For example, the current funeral manual of Jōdoshū is the Jōdoshū hōyōshū (first published for circulation in 1953), which is based on the 700th memorial service for Hōnen that was conducted in 1911. See Fujii Masao (January 1993), p. 26. As for the Zen sects, they had no funerary ritual manuals whatsoever for their lay followers until 1960. In the case of Nichirenshū, the current manual is modeled upon the Jūgōen raijugiki, a collection of Nichiren ritual formulae, which was compiled by Nichiki (1800–59) in the late Tokugawa period. See Akahori and Fujii, p. 26.

170. Murakami and Fujii, p. 49.

171. Ibid., p. 48.

172. Ibid., pp. 44–45.

173. Yamada and Fujii, p. 26. For more information on the role of Myōe in spreading the "mantra of clear light" ritual, see Unno, pp. 167–79.

174. For more details, see ibid., pp. 26–27.

175. See Tamamuro Taijō (1933), pp. 180–81 and Williams (2005), pp. 41–45. In theory, the newly ordained deceased was believed to be linked, through the unbroken "blood lineage" of Zen masters, all the way back to Śākyamuni. The name of the newly ordained deceased was recorded in the lineage book, sometimes with ink made from the abbot's blood. The names in the lineage book were connected by a red line, which graphically symbolized the "blood lineage" of Zen masters. Bernard Faure notes that an important element of the ordination in death rituals was the transmission of a lineage chart, which, as a magical talisman, provided salvation for the dead by allowing them to join the "blood line of the Buddha." See Faure (1991), p. 201.

176. Traditional full-scale Zen funerals for monks were first systematically explicated in the *Ch'an-yüan-ch'ing-kuei* (*Zennen shingi* in Japanese), a Song period compilation of ritual manuals and regulations for the monastic life of monks. For accounts of these funerals, see Tamamuro Taijō (1963), pp. 100, 122–28 and Faure (1991), p. 193.

177. Takai and Fujii, pp. 42–43.

178. Ibid., pp. 46–47.

179. Ibid., p. 45.

180. For a detailed discussion of the rise and development of *nijūgo zanmai* practice at the turn of the tenth century, see Yamaori (2004), pp. 305–22.

181. Tamamuro Taijō (1961), pp. 35–37.

182. For more details, see Fujii Masao (January 1993), p. 26.

183. Akahori and Fujii, pp. 25–26. During the Tokugawa period, dharma names were often conferred upon Nichirenshū followers while they were alive.

184. Ibid., pp. 23–24.

185. For the standard ritual formula of the Nichirenshū funeral service, see Fujii Masao, *Bukkyō sōsai daijiten*, pp. 186–88. Nichiren Buddhists believed that chanting "Namu Myōhōrengekyō" (Homage to the *Lotus Sūtra*) was a necessary and sufficient means for relating the truth of the sūtra to the individual believer. This was because the title bore the salvific power of the entire scripture.

186. Tanaka and Fujii, p. 32.

187. Ibid., pp. 34–35.

188. Fujii Masao, *Bukkyō sōsai daijiten*, p. 179.

189. Tanaka and Fujii, p. 36. It should also be noted that, by the early sixteenth century, Jitsunyo (1458–1525), the ninth patriarch, had reorganized the ritual elements of daily service into another simplified format—one that featured the recitation of lines from the three Pure Land sūtras (*Muryōjukyō* [*Larger Sukhāvatīvyūha Sūtra*], *Kan muryōjukyō* [the Sanskrit original is not known], and *Amidakyō* [*Smaller Sukhāvatīvyūha Sūtra*]), *nenbutsu* chanting, and the transference of Buddhist merits. However, Rennyo's formula was more orthodox even though the Nishihonganji subsect leaned toward that systematized by Jitsunyo. For more details, see Fujii Masao (1977), pp. 318–25.

190. Sasaki, p. 134.

191. Ōtō (1996), pp. 343–44.

192. *Shokoku fūzoku toijō kotae*, "Kii no kuni Wakayama," p. 774.

193. Akata (1986), p. 76.

194. *Shokoku fūzoku toijō kotae*, "Mutsu no kuni Shirakawaryō," p. 489. For a wide range of local customs related to *nobe okuri*, see Inoguchi, pp. 96–131. In particular, the funeral procession in Jōdoshinshū usually included the chanting of *nenbutsu* amidst the beating of gongs.

195. For an example, see Kadomae, pp. 153–54. Similar measures designed to prevent the deceased from returning to this world included sealing the doors of the houses along the procession route with an X made of crossed bamboo sticks, as well as not stopping at any households on the way to the burial site. See Akata (1986), p. 77.

196. Ibid., p. 77.

197. For an example, see *Shokoku fūzoku toijō kotae*, "Awa no kuni," p. 811.

198. See ibid., "Mutsu no kuni Shirakawaryō," p. 489 and "Echigo no kuni Nagaokaryō," p. 556.

199. In many regions, it was customary to hold a postfuneral ritual on the night after the deceased had been buried. This ritual was designed to ensure the safe journey of the deceased to the Western Pure Land (or Western Paradise) and featured the chanting of *nenbutsu* or the singing of Buddhist hymns and intercessional prayers.

200. Saitō Ryūzō, p. 996. In most regions, however, the holder of the spirit tablet (usually the male heir) walked before the coffin.

201. For example, Titsingh offers a detailed description of a Jōdoshū funeral procession, which has the following components: two men carrying trestles upon which the coffin would be placed once it reaches the temple; a man who goes before the coffin with a large bundle of straw for the purpose of making torches to light the road during the night; six flags; four small white cases, nearly a foot high, and about four inches square, each containing a flower of water-lily, cut out of white paper; a small box for burning incense; the spirit tablet of the dead; priests striking small bells and reading hymns aloud; the coffin; the eldest son; the family; the intimate friends of the deceased, his colleagues, acquaintances, and servants of both sexes; and palanquins for the eldest daughter, wife, younger sister, nearest female relative of the deceased, other females in the family, and the wives of his friends (in that order). See Titsingh, pp. 239–40. Titsingh also describes the funeral processions of a civil officer of distinction and of the Nagasaki magistrate Tsuchiya Morinao, who died in 1784. Ibid., pp. 246–51.

202. *Zenkoku minji kanrei ruishū*, p. 154. It was commonly understood that the person who held the spirit tablet was the undisputed legitimate heir of the deceased and was entitled to claim the right of inheritance. In cases where the tablet was not used, the heir publicized his status by holding the coffin at its hindmost position.

203. These *sanmai hijiri*, who belonged to the underclass, lived in a separate hamlet near the cemetery and maintained their own regulations and organizations, which were designed to protect their exclusive rights pertain-

ing to cremation and the cemetery. In return for providing services related to cremation and the cemetery, they collected annual fees from the surrounding villages. These *sanmai hijiri* hamlets, which numbered about 500 in the Kinai region, were all under the control of Ryūshōin of Tōdaiji. For more details, see Yoshii, pp. 116–25 and Yoshida Eijirō, pp. 147–57.

204. For more details, see Okuno Yoshio, pp. 25–40. After the Meiji period, the rate of cremation increased steadily from 43 percent in 1925 to 54 percent in 1950 to 89 percent in 1977. This was due mainly to government regulations on sanitation and burial spaces, particularly in the cities, rather than to religious reasons. See Arai, pp. 341–55.

205. Saitō Tadashi, p. 230.

206. According to Namihira Emiko's study of funeral customs in contemporary Japan, the body of a person who died of unnatural causes is usually cremated, even in areas where the custom of interment dominates. Namihira (1988), p. 142.

207. For comparison, people in Chosŏn Korea invariably thought differently about burial. Burying the body was to preserve the "mind-matter" (*ki*) of the deceased, which circulated between the living and the dead. This "mind-matter" was likened to a tree: if the tree's roots are burned, then its branches and leaves will wither away and have no chance to prosper and to grow. In order to preserve the "mind-matter" of the deceased, families used heavy and tight coffins to ensure that the corpse did not rot too fast, and they dressed it in thick shrouds. Still concerned that this might not be adequate, they put cereal in the coffin so that invading vermin would eat it instead of the body. Deuchler (1992), p. 197.

208. For examples of customs intended to help deceased young children be reborn as another person, see Inoguchi, pp. 239–41.

209. Based on this story, Hirata Atsutane argued that there was no such thing as hell or paradise as Buddhists taught, and that the old man who had guided the soul of Tōzō was none other than *ubusuna-gami*, the life-creating deity of Shinto. Rejecting the Buddhist conception of the afterworld, Atsutane emphasized that it was not on the other shore but in this world, stating that "the spirits of the dead do not go to Yomi . . . but rather dwell amongst us, eating, dressing, and living just as we do." See Bolitho (2002), p. 409.

210. Nakajima, pp. 10–11.

211. For examples, see *Sensōji nikki*, vol. 3, p. 540 and *Shokoku fūzoku toijō kotae*, "Mutsu no kuni Shinobugun Dategun," p. 476.

212. Ibid., p. 476.

213. For more detailed studies of burial facilities in the Edo period, see Tanigawa (1991), pp. 80–110 and Koizumi (1990), pp. 31–57 and (2001), pp. 143–44.

214. Fujii Masao (1983), pp. 127–28. The name of *hōkyōintō* was derived from *karaṇḍa-mudrā dhāraṇī* —the *dhāraṇī* of 40 incantations cited in the *Hōkyōindaranikyō*, which states that if one invokes this *dhāraṇī* one can bring the deceased up to Paradise—even from hell—and can also prolong the lives of the sick and give much wealth to the poor.

215. In this sense, erecting a grave stupa was not so different from the old custom of planting a tree at the gravesite as a "lodging place" (*yorishiro*) for the spirit of the deceased.

216. Doctrinally, the Jōdoshinshū rejected any material symbol that might be used to commemorate the deceased; however, this does not mean that all Jōdoshinshū *monto* ignored gravestones or stupas. In the late seventeenth century some *monto* families began to erect stone stelae for their deceased family members around the head temple's charnel house in Kyoto, and this custom gradually evolved into a trend that saw some *monto* families begin to erect individual gravestones for their ancestors at their *danna* temple cemetery or even on their own gravesite. See Gamaike (March 1993), pp. 221, 226.

217. For more examples, see ibid., pp. 228–31.

218. For a comprehensive survey of the geographical distribution of dual-grave customs, see Shintani (1993), pp. 274–97.

219. Bitō (1991), p. 384. As Bitō Masahide notes, one puzzling question is why "the dual-grave system was most commonly practiced in the Kinki region and less frequently in outlaying regions." He suggests that "both the *umebaka* and *mairibaka* were originally communal in nature" and that "the dual-grave system emerged in conjunction with the maturation of the communal structure of the village," which was more prominent in the Kinki region. See ibid., pp. 384–85. According to Shintani Takanori, who surveyed 1,533 gravestones in Niiza city, Saitama, the dual-grave system in this area spread from the 1630s and was firmly entrenched by the 1660s and 1670s. For a bibliographical survey on the dual-grave system, see Shintani (1993), pp. 306–20.

220. Gamaike (1997), pp. 220–23. Indeed, many scholars have wrestled with the issue of the origin of the dual-grave system. For example, according to Kokubu Naoichi, there was an old custom in the islands Okinawa and southern Kyushu in which bones that had been buried for a certain period of time were dug up, washed, and cleaned and were then reburied at another place. He suggests that this reburial custom later evolved into the dual-grave system. For his part, Harada Toshiaki suggests that under the influence of Buddhism, a stone stele that had been erected to venerate the deceased was moved into the temple precincts and that this relocated stone stupa was further transformed into a grave for death rites.

221. Like the spirit tablet, which was buried or burned with the deceased, the memorial tablet had written on its face the person's posthumous name and the date of death. The obverse side usually bore the deceased's name in life, age at death, and the relationship of the deceased to the household head.

222. For a detailed discussion of the origin of the tablet and its evolution in Japan, see Gorai (1992), pp. 603–10 and Sudō, pp. 333–34.

223. *Zenkoku minji kanrei ruishū*, p. 172.

224. Ibid., pp. 172–82. For a detailed discussion of local variations of funeral abstinence, see Ōtō (1996), pp. 345–58.

Chapter 6

225. The term *kuyō* refers to those merit-making acts of ritual, worship, and offering through which Buddhists express their respect for the Three Treasures of Buddhism.

226. In particular, the residents of the Wakayama and Ise domains believed that on this day the dead spirit would move from the house to the *danna* temple where it might gain a new life. In order to facilitate this process, the families sent two kinds of rice cakes (one consisting of a set of 49 small cake balls, the other consisting of a large umbrella-shaped cake) to their *danna* temple. See *Shokoku fūzoku toijō kotae,* "Kii no kuni Wakayama," p. 775 and "Ise no kuni Shirakoryō," p. 625.

227. Akata (1986), p. 97.

228. The Japanese believed that a newborn life, which was considered fragile, unstable, and polluted, had to be ritually nurtured and protected through a series of rites of passage all the way up to marriage. Marriage would qualify a person to form a household of his or her own as an independent member of society and to produce the next generation. It could therefore be likened to the ceremony of *tomuraiage,* which completed the process of transforming the deceased spirit into an ancestral deity. This process, like that for a deceased family member, started with the naming of a newborn baby. This name was to be written on a slip and enshrined at the household *kamidana,* usually on the fourteenth day after birth. For more details, see Ooms (1987), pp. 96–101.

229. Saitō Ryūzō, p. 1001.

230. Titsingh, p. 245.

231. *Sensōji nikki,* vol. 14, pp. 405–7. This series of rituals conducted from the second day of the third month to the fifteenth day of the fourth month of 1820 was for Prince Arisugawa, *monzeki* of Kan'eiji. Each ritual was preceded by the "mantra of clear light" ritual, which was performed on the previous night.

232. Originally, the idea of an intermediate state referred to a process in which the deceased transmigrated according to the principles of karmic causation: it did not refer to an existing being or entity. However, when this idea was incorporated into death rituals in Japan, people understood the intermediate state figuratively: they saw it as a spiritual entity in transformation. See Yoshida Tokkō, p. 40.

233. Poussin, vol. 2, pp. 393–94 and Watanabe Shōgo, pp. 120–21.

234. Watanabe Shōgo, pp. 132–33.

235. For examples in the Kantō area, see Hiraide Kōjirō, vol. 3, p. 30. For a discussion of the contemporary practice of *hyakumanben nenbutsu* in Jōdoshū, see Narita Shunji, pp. 389–90.

236. Gombrich, p. 204. On the development of the idea of merit transference in Sinhalese Buddhism, Gombrich reasons: "The original doctrine of karma solved the intellectual problem of evil, but the solution was too perfect for emotional comfort, because it makes all suffering one's own fault"; and, for this reason, the acts of transferring merit and thereby acquiring merit "in turn solve, or at least alleviate, this emotional problem by mitigating

the rigor of the original doctrine and, in particular, by making it possible to improve one's karma after death; at the same time, they solve, by reinterpreting them, the intellectual problem of justifying surviving rituals for the dead." Ibid., p. 219.

237. Malalasekera, p. 86.

238. Schopen, pp. 36–41.

239. Ebrey, *Confucianism and Family Rituals in Imperial China*, p. 89

240. Tamamuro Taijō (1963), p. 183.

241. For more details, see Kajiyama, pp. 162–84.

242. For example, see *Sensōji nikki*, vol. 2, pp. 726–27.

243. The Lotus repentance draws its name from the *Lotus Sūtra*, "the main scriptural source around which its cultus is organized and to which it is directed as an object of ritual veneration." See Donner and Stevenson, pp. 261. For the history of *samādhi* practices that were adopted for funerary rituals in the Tendai tradition, see Tamamuro Taijō (1933), pp. 175–78.

244. For more details on the Lotus *samādhi* explicated by Chih-i, see Donner and Stevenson, pp. 261–69 and Stevenson, pp. 67–68. Regarding the centrality of the *Lotus Sūtra* in this rite, Stevenson notes: "According to Chih-i's manual for the Lotus samādhi, *Fa-hua san-mei ch'an-i*, the twenty-one-day Lotus repentance is to be performed alone in a hall consisting of a central sanctuary with an adjoining room for seated meditation. A high throne is set up in the sanctuary, on which a single copy of the *Lotus Sūtra* is enshrined. No other images, relics, or scriptures of any kind may be added." Stevenson, p. 68.

245. Dumoulin, pp. 84–85.

246. Compared to the highly structured ritual repentance that lasted for 21 days, this simple format was fluid in form and open-ended in duration. Donner and Stevenson, p. 263.

247. Matsunaga, pp. 156–57.

248. Hori, p. 162. In traditional China as well, the populace often applied the performance of repentance ritual to ancestor worship, believing that this would expiate "the sins of the living and of the dead," thereby establishing "harmony between the world of the living and the dead" and eliminating "the threat of possibly harmful acts by unappeased souls." See Reis-Habito, p. 49.

249. About this ritual Titsingh observed: "At the expiration of the seven weeks, he is at liberty to shave and to cut his nails: he then lays aside his mourning, opens the door of his house, and goes in his ordinary dress to inform the government that the time of his mourning is over. He next visits and pays a compliment to each of those who attended the funeral, and who came to pray at the grave." See Titsingh, pp. 245–46.

250. Gorai (1992), pp. 945–46.

251. For more details on this custom, see Gamaike (March 1993), pp. 216–19. The Ōtani *honbyō* was established at the current location in 1603, and the Ōtani *sobyō* was established in 1670.

252. Sasaki, pp. 251–53. In addition, scholars note that traditionally the popular Higashiyama site in Kyoto was believed to be a place where dead souls gathered and settled.

253. Concerned with the contradiction inherent in this extension of ritual schedules, the eminent Shingon monk Myōhen (1142–1224) refused to conduct posthumous rituals for his father after seven services, arguing that, if he were to do so, it would be in conflict with the Buddhist doctrine of seven services as well as of the transference of merit. Kokan, pp. 93–95.

254. Fujii Masao (1983), pp. 178–79.

255. Yanagita, "Senzo no hanashi," pp. 94–96.

256. In the case of Jōdoshinshū followers, the perennial offering of memorial services, which featured perpetual sūtra chanting (*eitaikyō*), gained increasing currency during the Tokugawa period. In addition, Jōdoshinshū followers used the *hōonkō* ceremony as an occasion for ancestral veneration. The *hōonkō* ceremony, which was dedicated to commemorating Shinran, was primarily supposed to increase a sense of community among the Shinshū *monto* through practice sessions and lectures; however, offerings made at the ceremony were also collectively directed to the ancestors of participants. On the communal nature of ancestral veneration at the *hōonkō* ceremony, Mark L. Blum notes: "Since this event occurred at the end of the year, the sense of gratitude toward the Buddha and the Founder Shinran was inevitably combined with a sense of gratitude for the harvest, which in turn brought on a sense of gratitude toward the ancestors for ensuring the harvest. The combination of all these emotive forces created powerful urges to give something back to one's parents and grandparents." Blum, p. 201. For a similar view, see Sasaki, p. 262.

257. Fujii Masao, "Nihonjin no senzo kuyōkan no tenkai," pp. 99–101.

258. Even though such prolonged "purificatory" rituals might, in theory, imply that the new spirit was particularly vengeful and defiled, people regarded them as indicators of privilege and high social status.

259. The *Shōsōrin shingi* suggests that the numbers 7, 13, and 17 might derive from combinations of 3 and 7 (which are important numerals in Buddhist scriptures) or the first number after the twelve honorary signs. See T. no. 2579, 81.711c–712a. On the other hand, Fujii Masao suggests that they might be combinations of 7 (based on 7 rituals), 13 (the 7th from 7), and 17 (the first number containing the numeral 7 after 7). See Fujii Masao, "Nihonjin no senzo kuyōkan no tenkai," p. 98. The choice of the thirty-third year is also unclear, but among various interpretations, the theory that the number 33 is derived from the 33 manifestations of Avalokiteśvara Bodhisattva (Kannon Bosatsu) is most well known. See Tamamuro Taijō (1963), pp. 172–73.

260. The most clear evidence that the *Jizōkyō* is a Japanese apocryphon is found in the term *yomi no kuni*, which is used to refer to the kingdom of King Yama. For a discussion of the origin of the *Jizōkyō*, see Ishida, pp. 215, 338. For accounts of the belief in courts of Ten Kings in medieval China and the *Sūtra on the Prophecy of King Yama* as well as for its translated text, see Teiser (1988), pp. 168–95 and (1994), pp. 152–62, 196–219.

261. In particular, Jizō Bosatsu appears in six different manifestations and takes care of each of the six paths of transmigration when delivering salvation to beings in the underworld. Thus, compared to the *Sūtra on the*

Prophecy of King Yama, which "deals only with the purgatorial aspect of the underworld and not with its lower paths of rebirth, the hells" (Teiser [1988], p. 184), the *Jizōkyō* places more emphasis on the salvific aspect of the underworld.

262. For more details, see Sano (1996), pp. 97–99.

263. It should be noted, however, that this does not mean that this set of three Buddhist deities was dominant from the beginning. In medieval times, other sets of deities were more popular. The current set of thirteen deities gained wide popularity only in the late sixteenth century. Sano (1996), p. 89.

264. Sano (1996), p. 89.

265. For details, see Sano (1991), pp. 351–73.

266. Tamamuro Taijō (1963), p. 172.

267. Genchi, p. 477. In fact, based on the daily records of annual events kept by the head monk of Ganshōji from 1846 to 1866, Nagura Tetsuzō provides us with detailed information on the religious lives of Jōdoshinshū followers in Kakuhama village, Kanbara county, Echigo in the late Tokugawa period. According to him, the Jōdoshinshū followers in this area all conducted post-funeral rites for their deceased family members up to the seventeenth year after their death. Nagura divides postfuneral rites in this area into three categories: (1) full-scale rites, in which a *monto* borrows an Amida or Shinran portrait from the temple and invites monks from the temple to his house, and the monks chant all three Amida sūtras for two days; (2) medium-range rites, in which one or two members from a *monto* family visit the temple and conduct a ritual for the deceased at the main hall; and (3) light rites, in which a group of *monto* families get together, set a date, and collectively conduct a ritual at the temple, and then for several days a monk from the temple visits three or four *monto* families a day and offers a ritual to each of them. Those *monto* families that conducted full-scale or medium-range rituals increased to 10 percent of all the *monto* families during this period, but the majority of families remained in the third category. For details, see Nagura (July 1992), pp. 4–17 and (1994), pp. 250–53.

268. Genchi, pp. 487–88. Genchi, who was critical of this custom, ridiculed the minor temples eager to promote the business of *eitaikyō*, saying that it would be impractical to expect these unstable temples to keep the obligation of "perpetual" chanting services.

269. Sakurai Tokutarō, "Sōron: seichi to takaikan," p. 5.

270. Yanagita, "Senzo no hanashi," pp. 94–95.

271. In relation to the deification of ancestral spirits, Robert J. Smith observes: "In many parts of the country the stupa or memorial tablet is replaced by an evergreen branch planted on the grave. This practice is doubtless pre-Buddhist and suggests that originally both the gods and the ancestors were summoned by means of a living tree branch, the classic vehicle for the passage of spirits into and out of this world." Smith (1974), p. 96.

Chapter 7

272. Yanagita, "Senzo no hanashi," p. 95.

273. Ibid., p. 120. In addition, Yanagita Kunio emphasized two more traits of ancestral deities: that the dying wish of the living would be carried out in his or her posterity, and that one would be reborn again and again to carry on one's life's work. Yanagita hoped, as scholars suggest, that these two traits, under the guise of ancestral veneration, could console young Japanese soldiers who faced death on foreign soil in the closing days of the Second Word War. See Kamishima and Itō, pp. 222–29.

274. Satō Yoneshi, p. 137–39. For a discussion of Asamayama as a place of the dead, see Sakurai Tokutarō, "Sanchū takaikan no seiritsu to tenkai," pp. 351–56.

275. Saitō Ryūzō (1925), p. 998.

276. Many Jōdoshinshū families divided the remains of the deceased between the Shinran mausoleum or Honganji complex in Kyoto and a gravesite close to the family residence. Along with this increasingly popular custom, many faithful also made the trip to Honganji as a "pilgrimage to the Pure Land" (*ojōdo mairi*). See Blum, pp. 195–96.

277. For discussions on worldly manifestations of ancestral deities in Japanese folklore, see Yanagita, "Senzo no hanashi," pp. 32–33, 38–41, 54–56 and Akata (1986), pp. 112–13.

278. This represents a major difference from what was practiced in traditional China and Korea, where the annual memorial service offered to the individual dead spirit on his or her deathday remained an important ritual (along with annual services).

279. Miyata (1984), pp. 9–18.

280. For more details, see Watanabe Toshio, pp. 51–70, 118–39.

281. The first day of the New Year in each tradition was the first day of the first month (called *ōshōgatsu* [major first month]), which was the official New Year; the fifteenth day of the first month (called *koshōgatsu* [minor first month], or *hyakushō shōgatsu* [peasants' first month]), which was celebrated by commoners; the twentieth day of the first month, known as *shigoto hajime* (the beginning day of work), which was celebrated by carpenters; and the fourth or fifth day of the second month, known as *risshun* (beginning of spring). See Miyata (1981), pp. 6–8.

282. *Ofuregaki Kanpō shūsei*, p. 991.

283. For more details, see Tanaka Sen'ichi, pp. 102–17.

284. *Shokoku fūzoku toijō kotae*, "Bingo no kuni Numakumagun Urasakimura," p. 761.

285. Ibid., p. 763.

286. Ibid., p. 763.

287. Ibid., p. 765.

288. Akata (1986), pp. 111–12.

289. On the origins of erecting *kadomatsu*, see *Minkan jirei*, pp. 78–81.

290. According to Yanagita Kunio, the "toku" of Toshitokujin (the deity of New Year fortune) was derived from the "toku" of *katoku* (a household fortune or the headship of a household). As Yanagita suggests, the etymology of Toshitokujin implies that for the head of a household, the most important

duty was to maintain the household's fortune (estate and fields) as well as to venerate its ancestral deities. Yanagita, "Senzo no hanashi," pp. 38–41.

291. For example, see Hirayama (1984), p. 317. Hirayama Toshijirō introduces a diary kept by the Yamamoto family, a low samurai household in Yamato. The head of this family kept a diary from 1676 to 1720 that contains useful information on customs related to religious life and annual observances. For details, see ibid., pp. 312–14.

292. For the original feature of *naorai* in *matsuri*, see Kurahayashi Shōji, pp. 31–32.

293. In 1667, the shogunate attempted to shorten the New Year's holiday by ordering that all decorations be dismantled by the early morning of the seventh day. Before then, families in Edo traditionally extended the New Year celebration to the fourteenth or the fifteenth day. Kitagawa, vol. 2, pp. 247–48.

294. Yanagita, "Senzo no hanashi," pp. 31–33.

295. Nagura (1999), pp. 40–41, 127–29. For example, in the Echigo region, those Jōdoshinshū families that kept memorial anniversaries for their deceased family members visited their *danna* temple in groups and conducted a collective memorial service featuring the chanting of *shōshinge* and *nenbutsu*.

296. *Ryori saijiki*, p. 340.

297. Nakamura Kōryū, pp. 105–6.

298. *Ryori saijiki*, pp. 340–41. For a similar practice, see *Minkan jirei*, p. 112.

299. For examples, see *Shokoku fūzoku toijō kotae*, "Mutsu no kuni Shirakawaryō," p. 481; "Dewa no kuni Akitaryō," p. 497; "Hitachi no kuni Mitoryō," p. 535; "Echigo no kuni Nagaokaryō," p. 545; "Ise no kuni Shirakoryō," p. 620; "Tango no kuni Mineyamaryō," p. 662; "Bingo no kuni Fukuyamaryō," p. 686; "Bingo no kuni Fukatsugun Honjōmura," p. 733; "Bingo no kuni Shinaharugun," p. 746; "Bingo no kuni Numakumagun Urasakimura," p. 763; "Kii no kuni Wakayama," p. 771; "Awaji no kuni," pp. 779, 798; and "Higo no kuni Amakusagun," p. 823.

300. Hiraide, vol. 2, pp. 105–6.

301. *Shokoku fūzoku toijō kotae*, "Echigo no kuni Nagaokaryō," pp. 545, 571. For an example of six Amida temple sites in Edo, see *Minkan jirei*, p. 112.

302. For more details, see Kitagawa, vol. 2, p. 252 and Iwasaki Takeo, pp. 174–78.

303. *Kuan-wu-liang-shou-ching shu* (T. no. 1750, 37.261c).

304. For example, Gorai Shigeru ([1982], pp. 37–39) suggests that the term Higan is a phonetic equivalent of the term *hi no gan* (wish to the sun), referring to a worship of the sun. However, there are scholars who maintain that Higan was based on a Buddhist theory concerning the efficacy of prayer rituals in relation to the equinoxes. See Uranishi, p. 66.

305. Kitagawa, vol. 2, p. 284. For a custom in the Kōzuke region, see *Ryori saijiki*, p. 353.

306. For a variety of local customs related to Bon altars and lanterns, see Hanzawa, pp. 636–41, 661–82.

307. The term *shōryō* was clearly distinguished from the term *shirei* (dead spirits). The Tokugawa Japanese believed that it would take one to three years for *shirei* to turn into *shōryō*, and that this is the state in which they would remain until they were deified and became *sorei* (ancestral deities).

308. Kikuchi Kiichirō, pp. 167–68.

309. *Shokoku fūzoku toijō kotae,* "Echigo no kuni Nagaokaryō," pp. 549–50. For other local customs, see Hanzawa, pp. 642–61. It should be noted that in some areas the residents also burned Bon torches as a communal event in the village, at a temple, or on a mountain slope. The Daimonji fire in Kyoto is one such event.

310. For more details with regard to local customs related to Bon offerings, see Hanzawa, pp. 682–94.

311. For more details, see Nagura (1990), pp. 26–29; (1994), pp. 251–53; and (1999), pp. 90–97, 111–17.

312. *Ryori saijiki,* p. 354 and *Minkan jirei,* pp. 155–56.

313. *Shokoku fūzoku toijō kotae,* "Wakasa no kuni Obamaryō," p. 649. For more details on local customs, see Hanzawa, pp. 598–629.

314. In addition, when being kept clean and for long, fire was believed to strengthen the perpetual existence of the household institution. See Gōda, pp. 216–18.

315. For more details on local customs related to sending ancestral deities back, see Hanzawa, pp. 694–97.

316. Kitagawa, vol. 2, p. 287.

317. Miyata (1990), pp. 62–64. For a discussion of the origin of *yabuiri*, see Anno, pp. 46–89. In a similar context, daughters-in-law, who were otherwise segregated from their natal family, were given a few days off from married life and allowed to return to their natal parents. In the Kinki region, this kind of *yabuiri* vacation was given twice a year, beginning on the sixteenth day of the first month and the sixteenth day of the seventh month, respectively. See Hirayama (1984), pp. 320, 328.

318. Mitamura, p. 180.

319. See *Shokoku fūzoku toijō kotae,* "Echigo no kuni Nagaokaryō," p. 550; *Ryori saijiki,* p. 351 and *Minkan jirei,* p. 156. For customs in Edo, see Saitō Gesshin (1970), vol. 2, pp. 171–76 and Miyata (1981), pp. 83–88.

320. Hanzawa, p. 604.

321. Yanagita Kunio emphasizes that from the beginning, Japanese Bon had nothing to do with the Chinese Yü-lan-p'en. According to him, a fire for greeting or sending ancestors in Bon was originally called *hōkai*, which referred to a "food" offered to wandering spirits, or to an "earthenware" container in which the food was kept.

322. Teiser (1988), pp. 3–4.

323. *Shokoku fūzoku toijō kotae,* "Hitachi no kuni Mitoryō," pp. 536–37.

324. An example is the ritual formula of *segakie* in the Shingon tradition. See the translation of "An Abbreviated Ritual for Feeding the Hungry Ghosts" in Payne, "Shingon Services for the Dead," pp. 162–65.

325. In some areas the *segaki* ritual held at Buddhist temples was a public occasion for *danna* members, who sat in hierarchically organized seats (*segakiza*), to demonstrate their status in the community. For this reason, when the established hierarchy of *danna* members was put into question due to socioeconomic changes, those members who had gained new status and influence (e.g., due to large financial contributions to the temple) sometimes challenged the sitting order of the *segakiza* and demanded a new arrangement. This would cause a dispute that would easily develop into a collective tug of war between different local factions. For examples in Tōtōmi in 1759 and, again, in 1857, see Suzuki Masaharu, pp. 304–16.

326. For details, see Sasaki, pp. 340–61.

Chapter 8

327. Ise, p. 93.

328. Onuki, p. 12.

329. Tejima, pp. 162–63.

330. In his annotated collection of family precepts, Yamamoto Shinkō shows that all families emphasized the importance of ancestral veneration in maintaining their household institutions. For examples, see Yamamoto Shinkō, pp. 254–55, 320, 332, 343–44, 363–64.

331. Tanigawa (1989), pp. 5, 10–11 and Jishōin iseki chōsadan, pp. 159–63.

332. Tanigawa (1987), p. 188.

333. For details, see Shintani (1991), p. 139.

334. For details, see Ichikawa, pp. 4–9.

335. Ibid., pp., 4–12.

336. For discussions of the correlation between the practice of erecting gravestones and the enhanced consciousness of the household, see Bernstein (1999), pp. 32–36; Tanigawa (1989), pp. 6–7; and Yoshizawa, p. 163. In contrast, Sekiguchi Norihisa surveyed the gravesites of the Ōmuro Suzuki family in Iwate and found that the increase in the number of gravestones had little to do with the "household" institution. He suggests that it seems to have been affected by other socioeconomic situations, such as material well-being, famines, and other environmental factors. See Sekiguchi Norihisa, "Kinsei Tōhoku no ie to haka," pp. 481–82.

337. For examples, see Tanigawa (1987), p. 190 and Shintani (1991), pp. 147–58. For a Kansai example, see Yoshizawa, pp. 163–67, 170–74.

338. Shintani (1991), pp. 156–58. Regarding the disappearance of Buddhist symbols and the emergence of family crests, Shintani suggests that gravestones underwent a paradigmatic change in their religious role: from an object of offering or a symbol of prayer for Buddhist salvation to a *yorishiro* for ancestral spirits, who would protect people from nearby.

339. For examples in the Kantō region, see Shintani (1991), pp. 157–58 and Tanigawa (1989), p. 6; for examples in the Kansai region, see Sekiguchi Norihisa, "Kaimyō, hōmyōkō," pp. 127–40 and Ichikawa Hideyuki, pp. 12–17.

340. Ichikawa, pp. 22–24. The custom of the family grave was eventually popularized throughout the country from the mid- or late Meiji period. In contrast, samurai families and wealthy peasant or merchant families who could afford spacious family cemeteries continued to erect individual gravestones and did not pay much attention to this new trend.

341. Kinoshita, pp. 157–59.

342. Ōkuwa, *Jidan no shisō*, p. 54.

343. Takeda Akira, p. 8 and Takeda Chōshū (1976), pp. 15–19.

344. Akitoshi Shimizu, p. 88.

345. Nakane, pp. 4–8. In this regard, Murakami suggests four elements as the "main sociological characteristics common to all household groups" that functioned to ensure the perpetual subsistence of the household institution: the "kin-tract" principle, stem linearity, functional hierarchy, and near-independence. Murakami Yasusuke (1979), pp. 302, 306–8.

346. Itō Mikiharu (1991), p. 373.

347. Ise, p. 93.

348. Miyaoi, p. 265.

349. *Zenkoku minji kanrei ruishū*, p. 390.

350. For more details, see Kinoshita, p. 169; Ōtō (1996), pp. 227–32; and Nagura (1980), pp. 47–50.

351. Toyoda Takeshi (1971), p. 139. At the same time, the person whose given name was adopted as the "household name" was usually venerated as the household founder. In the case of branch houses, the name of the person who was instrumental in establishing an independent branch house was adopted as the household name. However, in cases where a household fell into a state of decline, household names were often abandoned.

352. See Kinoshita, p. 169.

353. For this reason, there was no need to replace the name of a legal owner of household properties, registered on legal documents, each time an inheritance occurred. The custom helped to reduce ownership disputes pertaining to real estate. See Ōtō (1996), pp. 232–333.

354. Miyaoi, p. 308.

355. Irie, p. 408. Indeed, in the early modern period, *tankon shōkazoku* households, which enjoyed a high degree of independence and self-reliance, were a tremendous achievement—one made at the cost of long struggles and painful sacrifices. In a similar context, Kōnoike Shinroku (Shin'emon, 1570–1650), who operated a hugely successful brewery business in Kansai, insisted that the family business represented the "collective virtues of ancestors that have been accumulated over generations and what parents have nourished" and that it should "be transmitted to posterity no matter what." Failure to do this, warned Kōnoike, would amount to a "grave violation of filial piety, which heaven and earth can not forgive, and [the culprit] will surely meet punishment." See Kōnoike, pp. 383, 385–86. Story has it that Kōnoike stipulated that his family precepts be read before the Buddhist altar twice a year—the first month (New Year) and the seventh month (Bon)—when all family members gathered for annual ancestral rites. Those mem-

bers who did not keep this stipulation, advised Kōnoike, would be expelled from the family. See Ōkuwa (1986), p. 76. For discussions of the Kōnoike family precepts, which stressed devotion to the family occupation, see Kōnoike, p. 383; Yamamoto Shinkō, p. 254; and Kōmoto (1997), p. 107.

356. Onuki, pp. 61–62.

357. Yoda, p. 273. Yoda Sōzō's puzzling remark—"you do not have to sweat more than usual in order to increase properties"—reminds one of the family admonitions of Tamura Yoshishige (1790–1877) in the village of Shimogamō in Kawachi county, Shimotsuke: "Attempting to increase the household income a little constitutes filial piety toward the ancestors. But if one tries to increase it excessively and heaps up monies and bequeaths them to one's descendants, it could be, despite the achievement of great filiality, a poison for the descendants, for the descendants could fall into excessive comfort and forget the family business and indulge themselves in entertainment, excursions and luxury. One should understand that this could eventually bring the household to ruin." See Irie, p. 408.

358. Yokoōji, p. 72.

359. Nagura (1980), pp. 51–52.

360. For more details, see Irie, pp. 32–44.

361. Yanagita, "Nihon nōminshi," p. 218.

362. Yokoōji, p. 66.

363. Nozawa and Yagi, pp. 190–91.

364. Takeda Chōshū (1976), pp. 37–41.

365. Hirayama (1979), p. 225.

366. Ōtō (1996), pp. 153–54, 369–70. As a measure designed to save a dead child from the fate of *muenbotoke*, people practiced a custom that featured arranging a marriage for that child by holding a fictive wedding ceremony. For example, in Tsugaru, when a dead child reached a marriageable age, his or her would-be spouse was constructed in the form of a doll, and family members and relatives gathered and held a wedding ceremony. In Yamagata, a shaman played a role in finding a marriage partner for a dead child from among the unmarried dead and offered a congratulatory prayer at the ceremony. After the ceremony, the family usually dedicated a votive painting (*ema*), depicting the scene of a shaman in prayer, to a temple or Shinto shrine. Cf. Smith (1974), pp. 41–50.

367. Ōtō (1996), pp. 153–54, 369–72.

368. Asano, pp. 53–56. Of course, the early modern Japanese did not believe that these miserable *muenbotoke* were the only homeless spirits to haunt the world. Even ancestral deities, too long forgotten, could be transformed into *muenbotoke*.

369. Muramatsu, p. 254.

370. *Nōgyō yokoza annai*, p. 128.

371. Ōtō (1996), p. 21.

372. For more details, see Arimoto (1995), pp. 151–72. Shinran believed that all sentient beings were the result of transmigration and thus were parents and siblings to each other; that for this reason, everyone should make an

effort to become a buddha in the next life and to help others be saved; and that *nenbutsu* should be chanted not just for the well-being of parents but also for the well-being of all sentient beings.

373. Ibid., pp. 118–20.

374. In the beginning, the custom of retirement in Tokugawa society showed local variations. For example, in the Kinai region the household head who retired usually moved out to a separate branch residence, where he continued to work and to raise children until they established their own branch households. However, as the single inheritance of household properties began to dominate, the retired household head remained in the same residence or moved to a separate building on the same residential plot. He supported himself by tilling land allocated to him as a "retirement fee" through an arrangement with the household successor. Although the retired household head was not directly involved in the management of the household, he usually offered his experience and wisdom to the successor and played a key role in the household's religious affairs, including ancestral rites and annual observances. In some regions it was considered the primary duty of the retired household head to pray to *kami* and buddhas for the prosperity and peace of the household as well as for his own well-being in the other world after death. See Ōtō (1996), pp. 150–52.

375. Yamanoshiri village in the Odawara domain had around 60 households and about 300 residents during this period. For more detailed statistics on the village, see ibid., p. 404.

376. *Yamanoshiri mura no nanushi nikki*, p. 58.

377. Ibid., p. 52.

378. Ibid., p. 88. Upon agreement, the father-in-law was allowed to keep "eight straw bags of rice, two straw bags of beans, one straw bag and five *to* of barley, one straw bag and five *to* of millet—altogether twelve straw bags of grains." In addition, the villagers decided that the son-in-law should give his father-in-law "one-third of the tea available, one-third of the miso, some salt, one-third of the soy sauce, one straw bag of rice, one straw bag of millet, and some potatoes." Seikichi was advised that "since cookpots and all other utensils are already available at the retirement house, [he should] hand them over as they are." After all these arrangements had been executed, Seikichi "took over" all power pertaining to the household.

379. In a similar case, the villagers of Yamanoshiri held an emergency meeting in the second month of 1838 at which they decided to remove two fellow villagers, Tōemon and Fujiyatōkichi, from their household-head positions because they had been deemed unfit. After being forced to withdraw, Tōemon was replaced by his wife, and Fujiyatōkichi by his son. Ibid., pp. 316–18.

380. Kobayakawa, pp. 646–47.

381. *Yamanoshiri mura no nanushi nikki*, p. 61.

382. Chen, pp. 16–17. For a detail discussion of this phrase, see Michibata, pp. 18–37. The *Hsiao-ching* is divided into eighteen short chapters. The first half consists of an introduction followed by five chapters describing the filial piety that is to be observed by the five ranks of society and three chapters

describing filial piety as the basis for cosmic and human activity. The second half gives concrete examples of filial behavior and develops ideas mentioned in the first nine chapters. Throughout the text, the emphasis is twofold: filial piety (i.e., towards one's parents) and societal piety (i.e., towards one's lord and the official hierarchy).

383. For reference to how much Chosŏn Koreans cherished the ethical value of filial piety, see Cho, pp. 260–62, 267–68.

384. For example, the first eight fascicles in the *Tongguk sinsok samgang haengsildo* pertain to filial piety, whereas just one fascicle, the ninth, was devoted to the subject of loyalty. The tenth to the seventeenth fascicles contain a collection of short stories pertaining to chastity, while the eighteenth deals with exemplary individuals listed previously in the volume. For more details, see Shibu, pp. 65–74.

385. Cho, p. 261. This resonates with the first three mandates of the *Hsiao-ching*, which preached about the filial duty of a son: "He must venerate his parents in daily life; he must try to make them happy in every possible way, especially when meals are served; and he must take extra care of them when they are sick." Chen, p. 25.

386. Ibid., p. 24.

387. Quote from Chan, p. 28. More directly, Confucius discusses this issue when he addresses the question of what a son should do when he knows that his father has stolen a sheep: "The father conceals the misconduct of the son and the son conceals the misconduct of the father. Uprightness is to be found in this." Quote from Chan, p. 41. For a detailed discussion of the issue of filial piety between father and son in the Confucian tradition, see Whitlock, pp. 115–24.

388. Deuchler (1987), p. 36.

389. Ibid., pp. 36–39. With regard to this agnostic principle in traditional Korean society, Martina Deuchler aptly states: "Ancestors and their descendants, Chu Hsi remarked, consist of the same mind-matter (*ki*). Although a man's *ki* dissipates upon his death, its substance is preserved in his descendants. If they exert their utmost sincerity and reverence, they can call back their ancestors' *ki* during rituals (*chesa*). This is the reason that people unrelated by blood to the dead cannot perform ancestral sacrifices for him. Chu Hsi likened the succession of generations to the relentless forming and breaking-up of waves; although no one wave is the same as the one that came before or will come afterward, all waves consist of the same water. Similarly, the same *ki* unites the ancestors and their descendants in the ritual process." Ibid., p. 31.

390. Watanabe Hiroshi, pp. 140–47.

391. Ōtō (1998), p. 412.

392. In contrast, as Amino Yoshihiko notes, during the medieval period homesteads were regarded as a sort of asylum, where the principle of extra-territoriality was publicly acknowledged. Even government tax collectors could be blocked when the house was sealed with fences. For a detailed discussion, see Amino, pp. 225–35.

393. Kasaya, pp. 132–34.

394. Ibid., pp. 149–50, 168–69 and Tahara, pp. 73–74.

395. Merchant households also practiced the custom of forced retirement. According to Nakada Kaoru, a wealthy merchant family in Hongō of Edo exemplified the collective management of family business. Branch households, which shared the same shop curtain (*noren*) of the head household, were all required to keep the rules and regulations set by the latter in running business. If a branch household forgot the favor of the head household or committed a wrongdoing, stipulated the family precepts, the head household, "without hesitation, [would] confiscate the household name from the former and take strict measures against it"—a castigation known as *kyūri*, which, in effect, would cut it off from the extended family relationship. The head of the main household, who was expected to preserve the household property inherited from the ancestors and to pass it down for posterity, was also subjected to this rule: "If the head commits a serious wrongdoing, branch houses, store employees, relatives, and all other associates should hold a meeting and discuss [the matter] with sincerity. The head, who has committed the misconduct, should then be given a minimum allowance and forced to retire." This kind of collective action involving retirement by force was justified as a filial action "for requiting the favor and protection of ancestors." Likewise, the heir of the household headship, who was deemed unsuitable due to misbehavior or bad health, was to be replaced with an adoptee. According to the family precepts, in this case the adoptee could be chosen from among capable outsiders "rather than from among those who are related by blood but have no competency," all in order to ensure the perpetual subsistence of the household. For details, see Nakada, pp. 369–72.

396. Another common accusation was directed toward the custom of shaving as practiced by Buddhist monks. It was suggested that this act violated the cardinal injunction of filial piety with regard to one's body. In fact, *Hsiao-ching* and other Confucian classics invariably emphasize that the starting point of filial piety is to preserve one's body as given by one's parents, the logic being that body, skin, and hair are gifts received from one's father and mother and are therefore extensions of the parents themselves.

397. The *Fu-mu en-chung ching* (Sūtra on repaying the kindness of parents; *Bumo onjūgyō* in Japanese), a piece of Chinese apocrypha that was very popular in China and that spread to Korea and Japan, occupied the central position within Buddhist propaganda pertaining to the virtue of filial piety. This Buddhist scripture describes all the hardships that parents must bear in giving birth to, and raising, their children. It insists that children must return that favor through filial devotion, adding that, no matter how hard they try, they might not be able to do enough. For more details on this scripture, see Michibata, pp. 93–104.

398. For example, based on the *Ketsubonkyō* (The blood pool sūtra), Buddhist monks often committed sexual discrimination, preaching that women were destined to the "blood pool hell" after death due to the evil karma of

red pollution accrued from their menstrual and childbirth blood, and that the only way to save them was to recite the *Ketsubonkyō* or to perform rituals related to this scripture. For more details, see Bodiford (1993), pp. 206–7; Takemi, pp. 229–46; and Williams (2005), pp. 50–58.

399. It is almost impossible to trace changes in posthumous names over time across Japan. The conferral of posthumous names upon the deceased was not separable from other local customs, sectarian affiliation, the household institutions, economic development, social pressure, and the like. According to Sekiguchi Norihisa, who examined about 23,000 posthumous names in the Nara and Kyoto area, local variations were indeed wide and erratic. In Nara and its vicinities, for example, the style of posthumous names slowly changed from *zenmon* and *zenni* (in the mid-seventeenth century) to *shinji* and *shinnyo* (in the mid-seventeenth to the early or mid-nineteenth centuries) to *zenjōmon* and *zenjōni* (in the early or mid-nineteenth century). However, in the case of Nichirenshū, many families had not followed the custom of conferring posthumous names until the late eighteenth century, when some of them began to seek the titles of *shinji* and *shinnyo*. For details, see Sekiguchi Norihisa, "Kaimyō, hōmyōkō," pp. 126–44.

400. Tanigawa (1989), pp. 6–10 and Kobayashi, pp. 194, 223. As a way to upgrade the social standing of their household, many parents instructed their children on viable methods for conducting funeral rites and erecting grave facilities upon their death. See Gotō Shigemi, pp. 34–42. Similarly, *kakochō* records show a drastic increase in posthumous names beginning in the 1660s, providing ample evidence that households increasingly attempted to augment their social status by seeking a higher standing in the Buddhist soteriological hierarchy. For examples, see Sōtōshū jinken yōgo suishin honbu, pp. 151–52, 199–208, 255–58.

401. Underclass households increased in the seventeenth century as previous bond servants (*nago*) and subordinate peasants (*hikan*) began to form their own independent households.

402. For example, "brush strokes were omitted or extra strokes were added; lexical elements indicating 'servant' or 'leather' were inserted into seemingly innocuous Chinese graphs; the whole name was replaced by *sendara*—the Japanese transliteration of the Sanskrit word *candāla*, which refers to those who are beneath any caste classification." Bodiford (1996), p. 9. For more details and examples, see Kobayashi, pp. 280–303; Sōtōshū jinken yōgo suishin honbu, pp. 165–68, 210–16; and Williams (2005), pp. 30–31.

403. Ōtō (1996), p. 376. For example, Duncan Williams notes: "In 1778, for example, at the Sōtō Zen temple Chōfukuji [in Maruko village, Shinshū province], a certain Matsuemon who was upset because his parents had received the discriminatory posthumous name 'boku' (servant), donated a warehouse to the temple in order to have the name changed." Williams (2000), p. 65.

404. For a discussion of the issue of why ancestral veneration, which was associated with the continuance of households, exploited social outcasts and their pollution, see Ariizumi, pp. 219–24.

405. Yanagita, "Senzo no hanashi," pp. 103–4.

406. Yanagita, "Nihon no matsuri," p. 311.

407. Hayashi Reiko (1992), pp. 188–89. For a detailed discussion of how Mitsui employees were treated by the "collective cemetery" system, see Tanaka Yasuo, pp. 393–411.

408. For a list of major Tōshōgū shrines that have been preserved to the present day, see Takahashi, pp. 112–13.

409. Takeda Chōshū (1994), pp. 162–64. In contrast to the *jibutsudō* theory on the origin of *butsudō*, Yanagita Kunio thinks that the Bon altar gave birth to the household Buddhist altar. The weak point of Yanagita's theory is that despite the alleged conversion of the Bon altar to the Buddhist altar, each family still sets up a Bon altar separately from its Buddhist altar during the Bon festival. Arguing that only upper-class households could afford *jibutsudō*, Jeroen Bokhoven contends that, given that both the household Buddhist altar and the Bon altar basically function as an "altar of spirits" where memorial tablets are enshrined, the Buddhist altar must have evolved from a container for memorial tablets, or a *yorishiro* for spirits. See Bokhoven, pp. 357–58.

410. Kōmoto (1997), p. 106. In medieval times, *jibutsudō* were multipurpose quasi-Buddhist facilities: they were a place for conducting prayers, disciplinary practice, death rituals, or offering rites to ancestral spirits.

411. Cf. Smith (1974), pp. 86–91.

412. For the involvement of Buddhist practitioners in death rituals during medieval times, see Ōhashi Shunnō, pp. 48–49.

Part III

1. This episode is from *Shoke himonshū*, pp. 413–14. The *Shoke himonshū*, published between 1772 and 1802, refers to a six-volume edition (preserved in the Naikaku bunko) of the administrative manual known as *Tera-machi-kan himonshū*. This administrative manual contains questions and answers pertaining to late eighteenth-century administrative issues of concern to the central magistrate offices of temples and shrines (*jisha*), the city (*machi*), the treasury (*kanjō*), and local governments or lesser *bakufu* officials.

2. Ibid., p. 413.

3. Ibid., p. 414 and Tsuji Zennosuke (1954), pp. 114–15.

4. Kumazawa, p. 445.

5. Nakai Chikuzan, pp. 469–71.

6. Ogyū, *Seidan*, pp. 269–70, 404–5.

7. *Okuri tegata* consisted of a few lines such as: "The person in question has, without doubt, been a *danna* of ___ sect and ___ temple for generations but is now released from this temple. So please add him or her to your register."

8. See *Zenkoku minji kanrei ruishū*, pp. 150–53 for information about how death inspections were conducted.

9. Tsuji Zennosuke, (1955), pp. 390–91.

Chapter 9

10. More directly, even the word "Kirishitan" was used in one such title: "Kirishitan gojōmoku" (Articles on Kirishitan). See Ebisawa (1960), p. 55.

11. For example, see Tamamuro Fumio (2001), pp. 262–70.

12. *Kōanji monjo*, pp. 75–79. For Kōanji, see *Gofunai jisha bikō*, vol. 3, p. 454.

13. *Tokugawa kinreikō*, vol. 5, pp. 120–22. The *Tokugawa kinreikō* is a collection of Tokugawa laws compiled by legal scholars during the Meiji period.

14. For the dating of this document, see Tamamuro Fumio (2001), p. 265. Tamamuro suggests that the stated date of 1613 might have to do with the edict "Statement on Expelling Padres," which was issued in the twelfth month of 1613. For details on the Hidenshū, which was formed in 1665, see Miyazaki Eishū, pp. 201–12. In addition, this document consisted not of fifteen articles but of fourteen. For a typical text of the fourteen articles, see *Tokugawa kinreikō*, vol. 5, pp. 120–22.

15. *Kōanji monjo*, p. 75, 77.

16. Ibid., p. 75.

17. Ibid., p. 75.

18. Ibid., p. 76.

19. Ibid., p. 77.

20. Ibid., p. 78.

21. See Chiba Jōryū (1967), pp. 224–25 and Arimoto (2002), pp. 306–7.

22. Tamamuro Fumio (1972), pp. 31–38 and Bodiford (1996), p. 8.

23. For a detailed discussion on *terakoya* education, see Dore, pp. 252–70.

24. Tamamuro Fumio, *Sōshiki to danka*, p. 201.

25. Ibid., p. 202.

26. Ōishi Kyūkei, p. 125. The *chōhazure* was not a punishment handed down by the government but a check conducted at the village community level. Nonetheless, the government saw its usefulness and recognized it as a legitimate action. See Tsuji Mayumi, p. 6. However, at the same time, the system of *chōhazure* was also used by poor villagers who wanted to leave their village to find employment during the non-agricultural season. In 1780 and again in 1836, in an attempt to halt the degradation of farming lands, the *bakufu* issued edicts prohibiting peasants from leaving their farming villages and drifting into urban areas for seasonal employment. In this situation many poor peasants made use of the punishment of "dropping from the register," which allowed them to leave their villages. Once they returned from seasonal employment, their status was restored through the procedure of "communal pardon and acceptance." For examples, see Tezuka, pp. 722–31.

27. This "shogunal decree" is included in the *Tokugawa kinreikō*. However, it is not included in the *Ofuregaki Kanpō shūsei*, the first volume (containing the laws issued between 1615 and 1743) of the *Ofuregaki shūsei*, a multivolume collection of shogunal laws that, between 1744 and 1841, was four times collected and compiled by the highest shogunal court. It is almost certain that Buddhist monks fabricated some articles and inserted them into this 1687 shogunal decree.

28. *Tokugawa kinreikō*, vol. 5, p. 35; see also Date, p. 380.

29. *Tokugawa kinreikō*, vol. 5, p. 35.

30. See *Atsugi shishi*, pp. 964–65; see also Willams (2005), pp. 34–35.

31. For more details, see Tamamuro Fumio, *Sōshiki to danka*, pp. 219–23; Tamamuro Fumio (2001), pp. 289–92; and Williams (2000), pp. 68–69. This is not directly related to the *danka* system, but the accusations also included a head monk demanding one and a half gold pieces for the pacificatory ritual of *nagare kanjō*, which was performed on the occasion of a miscarriage or stillbirth, no matter how poor the woman in question might be. See *Atsugi shishi*, p. 965.

32. *Ofuregaki Kanpō shūsei*, p. 609. For an example of the power of *kaiki danna* in appointing a head monk, see Morioka (1967), pp. 221–22.

33. *Tokugawa kinreikō*, vol. 5, p. 34. See also Vesey, p. 362. Residents of the Kantō region in particular regarded their *danna* temples as being communal places for their ancestors, and accordingly had a strong voice in the management of temple properties (as was seen in the detailed temple regulations on abbatial succession and *danna* obligations and rights). See Arimoto (2002), p. 14.

34. Toyoda (1982), pp. 129–30.

35. Ibid., pp. 130–31 and Vesey, p. 363.

36. For more details on the collective involvement of the *danka* in the process of abbatial selection, see Vesey, pp. 362–71 and Morioka (1967), p. 223.

37. *Sensōji nikki*, vol. 4, pp. 620–23.

38. Narimatsu, p. 177.

39. *Ofuregaki Kanpō shūsei*, p. 609.

40. For examples of how each sect handled this matter, see Date, pp. 402 (Konchiin), 405 (Kōyasan), and 409 (Daitokuji).

41. Umeda, pp. 102, 297.

42. Ibid., pp. 101–2, 297.

43. As there is no date on the document, it is not clear exactly when this shogunal law, listed in the *Tokugawa kinreikō*, vol. 5, was promulgated. However, based on its signatories—including the identifiable magistrates of temples and shrines, the treasury, and the city of Edo—the document seems to have been issued between the seventh month of 1728 and the twelfth month of 1729. See Tamamuro Fumio, *Edo jidai no Sōtōshū no tenkai*, p. 179 and Sōtōshū jinken yōgo suishin honbu, pp. 156–57.

44. *Tokugawa kinreikō*, vol. 5, pp. 43–44.

45. Hiramatsu, pp. 243–44.

46. Ibid., pp. 284–85.

47. For details about this episode, see *Shin Kumamoto shishi: shiryōhen*, pp. 861–70; Tamamuro Fumio (2001), pp. 278–81; and Williams (2005), pp. 36–37.

48. Date, p. 278.

49. For more details, see Hamano, pp. 59–61, 64–65.

50. For more details on the operation of this store, see Sumitomo shūshi-shitsu, pp. 27–42.

51. Sumitomo shiryōkan, pp. 187–88.

52. For examples, see Nishiki (1999), pp. 121–24.

53. Sumitomo shiryōkan, pp. 187–90.

54. The family of the deceased and all females associated with the store wore white robes. See Nishiki (1999), p. 149.

55. Edo's *hinin* population, which numbered around 3,000 in total and was geographically divided into several subgroups, was controlled by Kuruma Zenshichi. Matsuemon was the head of the *hinin* subgroup residing in the Shinagawa area. *Hinin* made their living by engaging in "dirty" jobs related to the punishment and execution of criminals and to the maintenance of shogunal prisons. In return, they were allowed to collect a fee of one copper coin per day from each of the city's front-street stores, which numbered around 50,000 in the late Tokugawa period. In addition to this income, they solicited money from families in their territory on the occasion of a childbirth, marriage, or funeral. On such occasions, a group of three area representatives for the *hinin* would dress in cotton *haori* (half-coats) and call on the family in order to "collect" 100 copper coins or more (the actual amount of money collected depended upon the status and wealth of the family). In return, the *hinin* were expected to protect the family from beggars and street children who often attempted to exploit its members by demanding money or food. See Shiomi, pp. 38–42, 48–58, 68. In fact, on the occasion of funerals, marriages, or childbirth, well-to-do families usually exercised compassion (by distributing grains or money) to the impoverished in their village or ward. The blending of *hinin* spaces with the spheres of ordinary residents, including the samurai class, accentuated the division of social functions marked by the hierarchy of compassion. See Narimatsu, p. 167. For an example of a *hatamoto* family (the Fuse house) paying money (200 copper coins) to the *hinin* on the occasion of a funeral, see Ogawa, p. 50.

56. Sumitomo shiryōkan, pp. 96–97, 126–28, 135–37, 246, 250–52.

57. When an employee at an Edo branch store was cremated, his ashes were usually divided and part of them were carried to Kansai and laid in his family grave.

58. Hayashi Reiko (1982), pp. 105–8.

59. For an introduction to this diary, see Kitahara (1990), pp. 104–5. The fourteen volumes of this diary are available in a facsimile edition: Ono Naokata, *Kanpu gosata ryakki*. 14 vols. Tokyo: Bunken shuppan, 1992–94.

60. Kitahara (1991), pp. 117–18.

61. Ibid., pp. 120–22.

62. Isoda, pp. 129–31. After the seven-seven memorial services, the family still had to make additional payments for ongoing memorial rites. For example, those for Inoyama Nobuyuki, who died in 1849, incurred 12 *monme* (= 0.24 gold *ryō*) on the 100th day, 238 *monme* (= 4.82 gold *ryō*) on the first anniversary, and 119 *monme* (= 2.41 gold *ryō*) on the third anniversary, respectively.

63. For example, "incense money" for Inoyama Nobuyuki's funeral came from both his colleagues at the domain government and his relatives. In Kaga it was customary that the natal family and relatives of the daughter-in-law provide food and drinks during the funeral period, particularly at the wake.

64. On the occasion of a major funeral, the Maruya family offered alms of 1 *monme* of silver to old itinerant blind musicians (who were social outcasts) and 0.5 *monme* to young blind musicians. This custom, which spread from top to bottom, was intended to gain Buddhist merit, which could be acquired by showing compassion to the socially weak, and to transfer it to the deceased. It is well known that the shogunal house offered alms to social outcasts, including *hinin* and blind street musicians, whenever it held Buddhist rituals. See Ōto (1996), p. 322.

65. Maruya, pp. 157–62, 166–67.

66. In comparison, Maruya Jinshichi advised that branch families conduct a funeral on a scale that should be one-fifth or even one-tenth of that conducted for the main house.

67. For more details, see Nishiki (1997), pp. 34–35, 38. In particular, for Ennōji's history and its major patrons, see Nishiki (1993), pp. 76–81 and for Hasshōji, see *Gofunai jisha bikō*, vol. 5, pp. 358–60.

68. Nishiki (1998), p. 30.

69. For a detailed analysis of the burial accessories found at Ennōji, see Tanigawa (1993), pp. 109–12.

70. Quote from Nishiki (1997), p. 42.

71. Ibid., p. 42. Although the unknown author of the Sakai document condemned the act of demolishing old graves as the "malevolence of Buddhist monks," he agreed that the problem was a structural one that had been caused by the increase of Edo's population. As a solution, he suggested that more than ten spacious public cemeteries should be developed on the outskirts of the city.

72. For specific examples, see *Shisō zōshiki*, vol. 1, pp. 154–57.

73. Nishiki (1998), p. 33 and Ikegami (1973), pp. 158–60.

74. *Shisō zōshiki*, vol. 2, p. 621. The *Shisō zōshiki* (currently 72 fascicles) is a collection of administrative documents, legal records, chronicles, observations, and the like related to the matters of temples, shrines, religious practitioners, and social outcasts. It was compiled in 1834 by a vassal of Manabe Akikatsu (1802–84), who worked for the shogunate as magistrate of temples and shrines from 1831 to 1837.

75. Quote from Nishiki (1998), p. 31.

76. For more details on the role of mediator, see Nishiki (1999), pp. 68–72. When the mediator could be neither located nor identified, the deceased was usually sent to the Kotsukappara crematory under the control of Ekōin for cremation.

77. In his *Uge no hitokoto* (Words of a person under heaven), Matsudaira Sadanobu indeed worried that an increasing number of migrant workers were straining the social order. Sadanobu examined the domain census registers of 1780 and 1786 and found that the population in the Kantō domains had decreased by as many as 1.4 million during this period. He attributed this decrease to the fact that many people were deleted from the census registers after having drifted to Edo. Those who were not registered were believed to end up as wandering spirits after death. See Nishiki (1999), pp. 60–61.

78. Negishi, vol. 2, pp. 416–17.

79. Watanabe Kenji, pp. 192–93.

80. Sōtōshū jinken yōgo suishin honbu, p. 229; for another example in Musashi, see Vesey, pp. 376–77.

81. Vesey, pp. 195–96, 230.

82. Tamamuro Fumio, *Edo jidai no Sōtōshū no tenkai*, pp. 187–88 and (2001), pp. 275–76.

83. For a detailed analysis of the death registers of these two temples in relation to the social function of Buddhist temples, see Endō Hiroaki, pp. 14–30.

Chapter 10

84. Udaka, *Tokugawa Ieyasu to Kantō Bukkyō kyōdan*, pp. 143–44.

85. For more details on circumstances surrounding Ieyasu's religious policies on this particular matter, see ibid., pp. 136–42; Ozawa, pp. 34–40; and Udaka (1999), pp. 135–47.

86. Ozawa Masahiro documents cases of conflict brought to the shogunate that occurred in 1602, 1612, 1621, 1630, and 1632. See ibid., pp. 40–50.

87. In the early seventeenth century, most disputes were between Zen monks and village *shugen*, and, thereafter, between Zen and Shingon (and, to a lesser extent, between Zen and Tendai) monks who had adopted a variety of religious practices dear to the Shōgoin Shugen sect, including ritual techniques of purification and prayer. Zen sects, particularly the Sōtōshū, which emphasized the "initiation" dimension of funeral rites based on the principle of self-power, endeavored to overwhelm Shingonshū by eliminating elements of esoteric prayer from funeral rites. For its part, the Jōdoshin-shū, which did not have many followers in the Kantō, was rarely involved in the dispute, and the Jōdoshū and Nichirenshū were somewhat tolerant of *shugen*, for they were receptive to elements of "prayer worship" in funerary rites. See Udaka, *Tokugawa Ieyasu to Kantō Bukkyō kyōdan*, pp. 146–47.

88. Takano, p. 102.

89. *Shisō zōshiki*, vol. 2, p. 920.

90. In fact, itinerant religious practitioners had been suppressed from the time of Oda Nobunaga, who was said to have "arrested 1,383 Kōya *hijiri* traveling around in the Kinki area and executed them at three places — Azuchi, Shichijōgawara of Kyōto, and Kumozugawara of Ise." Toyotomi Hideyoshi continued to suppress popular exorcists who had abandoned agriculture to make a living through divination or prayer, saying that they "neither provide service for the public nor till farming fields." Similarly, Tokugawa Hidetada condemned these religious practitioners who, after deserting their jobs, would "wander around, loathe to return to agriculture in the village or to work at the samurai house, [and who would] become disciples of *yamabushi* and conduct prayers or exorcisms, or learn several sentences of prayer from Ise and Atago, and try to make a living by sermonizing the people." For more details, see Takano, pp. 103–04.

91. Umeda, p. 140.

92. Here, *gannin* refers, in Gerald Groemer's words, to "monkish figures who executed proxy pilgrimages, engaged in midwinter cold-water ablutions, produced and distributed riddle prints and talismans, and marched around town with small shrines or monstrances of Enmaō, the Buddhist god-king of the underground, or Awashima Daimyōjin, a Shinto deity reputedly efficacious in preventing women's diseases. . . . By the eighteenth century, *gannin* often abandoned their Buddhist pursuits and turned to street performances of the 'Sumiyoshi dance' (Sumiyoshi *odori*), a largely secular genre vaguely associated with the Osaka Sumiyoshi shrine." See Groemer, pp. 42–43.

93. Tōkyōto kōbunshokan, vol. 6, pp. 95–96.

94. For more details, see *Tokugawa jikki*, vol. 4, pp. 549, 552–53. At this time the shogunate, however, allowed those who had been settled in the ward for some time and had secured prayer customers to conduct prayer rituals by hanging pictorial images on a temporary basis. However, they were not allowed under any circumstances to hang a sign outside the house that might give the public the impression that they were running a temple.

95. Tōkyōto kōbunshokan, vol. 7, pp. 132–35. In order to do this, they had to secure a temple document proving that the practitioner was officially affiliated with a legitimate sect and was the disciple of an ordained head monk.

96. Ibid., pp. 838–39.

97. See *Shichū torishimari ruishū*, vol. 16, pp. 10–31, 61–69 for more details on how the shogunate tried to control itinerant religious practitioners working in the urban centers through regulatory measures, residential control, and institutional supervision via the *iemoto* system and head-branch relationship. In particular, for a discussion of the regulations directed toward the *gannin*, which peaked during the reform periods of Kyōhō, Kansei, and Tenpō, see Groemer, pp. 58–63 and Sakamto Tadahisa, pp. 60–68.

98. Ōkuwa, "Bakuhansei kokka no Bukkyō tōsei: shinji kinshirei o megutte," pp. 5–7. The Kan'ei head-branch registers, which lacked those for Jōdoshinshū and Enryakuji, were too porous to cover temples located in western Japan.

99. For more details, see ibid., pp. 7–11.

100. This strict policy was later eased, and some new temples holding funerary *danna* patrons were allowed the privilege of performing religious inspection. For more, see ibid., pp. 10–11.

101. *Meiji ishin shinbutsu bunri shiryō*, vol. 3, pp. 590–91 and Yoshida Toshizumi, p. 22.

102. *Meiji ishin shinbutsu bunri shiryō*, vol. 3, pp. 593–94. Some sources, including the *Meiji ishin shinbutsu bunri shiryō*, specify that the number of demolished temples was 997, but Tamamuro Fumio calculates that the number was actually 1,098. See Tamamuro Fumio (1987), pp. 116–21.

103. Yoshida Toshizumi, p. 22.

104. Ibid., pp. 22–23.

105. For more details on the edict of 1687, known as *Shōjiin jōmoku* (Regulations on all Buddhist temples), see *Tokugawa kinreikō*, vol. 5, pp. 34–36.

106. Here, it should be noted that, in return, Buddhist monks were required to be clean and precept-abiding. A series of laws enacted by the shogunate reiterated that Buddhist clergy were expected to study the sūtras and the teachings of their respective sects, preach the Buddhist truth, keep Buddhist precepts and regulations, provide religious service for the people regardless of their status and wealth, and maintain a simple and sumptuary life. They were also prohibited from having unnecessary contact with women, engaging in sexual indulgence, seeking entertainment, making excessive demands of patrons, pursuing worldly interests, engaging in acts of violence, and so on. The first article of the edict of 1722 — an edict that was addressed to monks of all sects — stated: "Those who have renounced the world are to be simple and honest, not to be seduced by flattery; to be soft and generous, not to fight for material gains; to stay away from external decorations, not to be swayed by the winds of the secular world; to attend to Buddhist studies, not to be self-indulgent; to pursue the Way of the Buddha day and night — this is the way and rule of renouncing the world." See Umeda, p. 296.

107. Okuno Hikoroku, p. 712. The *Kujigata osadamegaki*, a two-volume set, was compiled as the basic reference for all legal matters within the shogunal administration, and it was treated as a "secret" document. But its contents soon became known to officials in the local domains, particularly the list of ordinances in the second volume that provided the basis for dispensing punishments. For an English translation, see John C. Hall, *Japanese Feudal Law* (Washington, DC: University Publications of America, 1979), pp. 159–221. In order to keep abreast of new cases and documents, responsible *bakufu* officials routinely compiled their materials into reference works; these then passed from one office holder to another. By the mid-eighteenth century, records of punishments for temples and shrines were gathered into the *Jishakata oshioki reigaki* (Examples for punishing Buddhist and Shinto priests).

108. Ishii, vol. 4, p. 58.

109. Ibid., p. 367.

110. Ibid., pp. 49–50.

111. Kumazawa, p. 445.

112. Ibid., p. 446.

113. Ibid., p. 447. Kumazawa Banzan's radical opposition, expressed in his *Daigaku wakumon*, to the system of temple certification and to the daimyo's alternate attendance especially irritated *bakufu* leaders. He was sentenced to house arrest in Furukawa of Shimōsa, where he had been serving the Matsudaira Nobuyuki house. Banzan died in 1691 while serving his term of house arrest.

114. Quoted (with some modification) from Lidin, p. 266.

115. This proposal was in line with Ogyū Sorai's recurrent, albeit impractical and even anachronistic, call to return the samurai to the agricultural lands in order to restore an ideal social order. For more details, see Najita, pp. xli–xlvii.

116. Tsuji Zennosuke (1955), p. 97.

117. Ibid., p. 109. In his *Sōbō kigen*, Nakai Chikuzan mentions that when he was young, he often used to hear from his teachers that Shogun Yoshimune had well understood the evil practices of religious inspection and had tried to abolish it. Unfortunately, due to the opposition of his senior advisors, his efforts were to no avail. See Nakai Chikuzan, p. 504.

118. Tamamuro Fumio suggests that, in 1665, Buddhist temples had already arrived at a turning point in their relationship with the secular authorities, as was evidenced by two pieces of legislation: a nine-article edict promulgated by Shogun Tsunayoshi and a five-article directive issued by his senior councilors. Both of these were mainly designed to tame the behavior of Buddhist monks and to control their institutions. See Tamamuro Fumio (1987), pp. 84–85.

119. *Ofuregaki Kanpō shūsei*, p. 635. In fact, the issue of taking donations was not that simple, as the nature of donations was not uniform. Traditionally, donations were classified into three categories: donations of "gratitude," donations of "compassion," and donations of "reverence." The staunchest Fujufuse members took donations only when they were regarded as donations of "reverence."

120. *Ofuregaki Kanpō shūsei*, p. 633. For more details, see Takagi Yutaka, pp. 243–56.

121. For more details, see Kagawa, pp. 97–128.

122. For details, see ibid., pp. 137–68.

123. Okuno Hikoroku, pp. 709–11.

124. For details on how the Fujufuse was finally granted freedom of religion by the Meiji government, see Tsuji Zennosuke (1954), pp. 270–84.

125. Umeda, p. 101.

126. For more details on the guidelines of each sect, see Date, pp. 223–24.

127. Umeda, p. 101.

128. *Ofuregaki Kanpō shūsei*, p. 613.

129. Ibid., p. 613.

130. Umeda, pp. 298–99.

131. Ibid., p. 302.

132. For the meanings and origins of *kange* or *kanjin* campaigns in Japan, see Suzuki Yoshiaki, pp. 9–10.

133. According to a detailed study by Suzuki Yoshiaki, during the period of 144 years from 1722 to 1866 the shogunate issued 346 *gomen kange* permits. For its comprehensive list, see ibid., pp. 264–85.

134. For details, see ibid., pp. 85–100.

135. Tamamuro Fumio (1987), pp. 311–12. In 1774, the shogunate warned against this kind of practice: "Regarding the way in which items of donation are collected, the shogunate wants temples and shrines either to encourage people to bring their contributions to the collecting station by themselves or to arrange that ward or village officials collect and bring donations to the nearest collecting station. But the practice by which ward or village officials collect donations has gone out of control. This practice causes trouble to villages as well as to wards." See *Ofuregaki Tenmei shūsei*, p. 614.

136. *Ofuregaki Hōreki shūsei*, p. 314.

137. For more details on these anti-*kange* edicts, see ibid., pp. 325–26, 330, 332.

138. Ibid., p. 330.

139. For the origin and modus operandi of *kaichō* and *tomitsuki*, see Hur, pp. 80–82, 245, respectively.

140. *Ofuregaki Tenpō shūsei ge*, p. 15.

141. Quoted from Tamamuro Fumio (1987), pp. 338–39.

142. For an introduction to the origin and development of the *shidōkin* business, see Miura Toshiaki, pp. 17–65.

143. Based on who contributed to the fund or for what purposes the funds were raised, a *shidōkin* was operated under such titles as Mito *goyōkin* (a public fund donated by the Mito lord), Kishū *meimokukin* (a titular fund of the Kishū lord), Yakushidōkin (a fund for a Yakushi hall), or Kannondōkin (a fund for a Kannon hall). Debtors could hardly escape from the weight attached to such imposing titles, and the money owed to the temple was not something upon which they could easily default. In fact, moneylending was one of many traditional business ventures practiced by Buddhist monks. Originally, capital resources were collected from lay followers who sought religious merit for a better destiny in their future rebirth by contributing material goods to the monastic community, and the latter often managed such contributions as endowed funds and used income from them for clothing, food, and other communal needs. Because the funds generated interest and the principal deposits were not depleted, they were often called "inexhaustible storehouses" (*mujinzō*). And because these storehouses were "inexhaustible," it was often preached that the donor would therefore acquire inexhaustible merit.

144. Tamamuro Fumio (1987), p. 321.

145. In 1762, the shogunate warned against the unscrupulous expansion of cemetery space: "Small parcels of land are donated as cemetery space on the excuse that there is a shortage. This is how temple precincts come to be enclosed [by cemeteries]. This kind of practice should not occur." See *Ofuregaki Tenmei shūsei*, p. 548.

146. Ibid., p. 624.

147. *Ofuregaki Tenpō shūsei ge*, pp. 79–80.

148. Ibid., p. 29.

149. For more details, see Tamamuro Fumio (2002), pp. 512–17.

150. Nakai Riken, p. 630.

151. Ibid., pp. 621–22.

152. Fukaya (1995), p. 50 and Fujita Satoru (1999), pp. 73–74.

153. For a useful account of the Title Incident, see Ooms (1975), pp. 105–19.

154. Wakabayashi (1995), p. 36.

155. Fukaya (1995), p. 49.

156. Based on the quick and almost hysterical reaction the shogunate showed to those involved in these two incidents, Kinugasa Yasuki suggests that some political pundits began to pay attention to the issue of restoring the dormant imperial authority. See Kinugasa, pp. 97–99. On the other hand, Fujita Satoru notes that the increasing eruption of peasant rebellions

during this period demonstrated that the shogunal authority was, in fact, in decline, thereby giving rise to debates concerning the relationship between the court and the *bakufu*. For details, see Fujita Satoru (1999), pp. 111–24.

157. Fukaya (1995), p. 51 and Fujita Satoru (1999), pp. 74–75.

158. Umeda, p. 257. It should be noted that the shogunate's main intention was to keep the court from indiscriminately issuing purple robes in return for money. The court had previously granted the honor of wearing purple robes to the head monks of preeminent temples on its own initiative (or upon the recommendation of powerful daimyo). From 1613 onward, the shogunate, which was uneasy about this politico-religious nexus, wanted to keep the daimyo out of Buddhist politics while making the court and great temples more accountable to shogunal authority. The shogunate's high-handed intervention led to the purple robes incident in 1627–29.

159. Buyō Inshi, p. 686. The true identity of Buyō Inshi is not known. Based on his harsh tone and knowledge about government officials, merchants, peasants, Buddhist monks, and so on, he is often identified as a fallen samurai or a judicial clerk. His zeal for criticism was based on hearsay, gossip, or rumor, and it often drove him to exaggeration and despair. Certainly, the *Seji kenbunroku* has subtexts and silences of its own, and it should be read with caution. But this does not mean that Buyō Inshi's critique was entirely without ground. Much of it was also sober and down-to-earth.

160. Tamamuro Fumio, *Edo jidai no Sōtōshū no tenkai*, pp. 89–137. Dōshōan refers to a Buddhist brokerage house in Kyoto that offered lodgings as well as intermediary services for abbacy candidates affiliated with Sōtōshū. This brokerage house, which specialized in herbal medicine, made and sold drugs throughout the country via the networks of Sōtōshū temples. For more details on Dōshōan, see Williams (2005), pp. 96–97.

161. For more details, see Williams (2000), pp. 34–35.

162. Umeda, p. 63.

163. Buyō Inshi, p. 686.

164. In Sōtōshū, the monks in "black dress" were allowed to wear colored robes only when they were promoted to the rank of head monk through a "changing-clothes" ceremony conducted at Eiheiji or Sōjiji.

165. For a list of detailed itemized expenditures, see Hirose, pp. 628–32. Tamamuro Fumio, however, notes that it was no secret that this kind of title transaction required at least 30 or 40 gold pieces. See Tamamuro Fumio, *Edo jidai no Sōtōshū no tenkai*, pp. 84–87.

166. "Shūkyō kankei hōrei ichiran," p. 431.

167. Tamamuro Fumio, *Edo jidai no Sōtōshū no tenkai*, p. 138. Hirose Ryōkō provides yearly statistics on the number of successful applicants for head monk positions between 1615 and 1785. See Hirose, pp. 609–13.

168. Tokutomi, pp. 368–69.

169. Ibid., p. 379.

170. Kurimoto, vol. 1, pp. 229–30.

171. Katsu, vol. 2, pp. 2019–20.

172. Sakamoto Koremaru, pp. 419–20.

173. Ogyū, *Seidan*, p. 434.

174. Ibid., pp. 434–45.

175. Nakai Chikuzan, pp. 469–70.

176. Specifically, Nakai Chikuzan suggested that people living in rental houses should be scrutinized by their landlord; house owners should be scrutinized by their village or ward head; servants should be scrutinized by their master; and once this was done, then village or ward heads should compare a new register with the one drawn in the previous year and record any changes due to death, birth, marriage, or whatever. See ibid., pp. 470–71.

177. For more details on Nakai Chikuzan's criticism on "Buddhist degeneration," see ibid., pp. 477–80 (temples), 500–4 (annual memorial services), and 525–26 (monks).

178. Yamagata, p. 28.

179. For details on anti-Buddhist discussions in Mito, see *Meiji ishin shinbutsu bunri shiryō*, vol. 3, pp. 605–20. For a list of Buddhist temples affected by Tokugawa Nariaki's policy, see ibid., pp. 626–39.

180. Tsuji Zennosuke (1955), p. 246.

181. Ketelaar, p. 49.

182. For Buyō Inshi, fixed income from *danna* patrons, which he termed "temple salary" (*jiroku*), was unfair, particularly when compared to the samurai or merchants whose incomes moved up and down in accordance either with business cycles or with the success of crops. For him, the fixation on "temple salary" was a clear indication of Buddhist degeneration. Buyō Inshi, p. 679.

183. Ibid., p. 681.

184. Ibid., p. 681.

185. Shōji, vol. 34, p. 574.

186. Tsuji Zennosuke (1955), p. 334.

187. Shōji, vol. 34, p. 588.

188. Hirata, p. 193.

189. Tominaga Nakamoto, who was born into the merchant class in Osaka and educated in the Kaitokudō, wrote two works: a short essay entitled "Okina no fumi" ("The writings of an old man") and the much longer treatise *Shutsujō kōgo*. In the latter work, he suggested that the texts of Mahāyāna Buddhism were so different in language and content from the other sūtras that they could not be the direct teachings of the Buddha. This contention prompted numerous counterarguments and theories from Buddhists who felt their establishments threatened, but by the late nineteenth and early twentieth centuries most Japanese Buddhist scholars accepted Nakamoto's assertion and embraced the critical historical approach to the study of Buddhist texts.

190. For an English translation of this work, see Pye, pp. 71–183; for an introduction of the contents of the work, see Durt, pp. 12–21.

191. For a detailed discussion that contextualizes these two works within the discursive matrix of Buddhism, see Ketelaar, pp. 20–36.

192. This refers to Matsushita Gunkō, a military scholar who vilified Buddhist monks in the Kyōhō era. According to him: "[They] are the people of heavy crimes and numerous sins, who only look for the misfortune of their neighbors and are delighted when their acquaintances die." See Tsuji Zennosuke (1995), p. 266.

193. Hirata, p. 193.

194. Kanda, pp. 87–88. Nevertheless, ironically, National Learning ideologues were not able to liberate themselves from Buddhist death, sometimes due to their own choice and sometimes due to a lack of critical acumen, as was seen in the last wish of Motoori Norinaga. He asked his children to conduct his funeral at a Jōdoshū temple, the priest to recite the sūtras at the household altar in which his tablet and that of his wife would be placed, and the posthumous names for both of them to be carved on the gravestone in the temple cemetery. For Motoori Norinaga, Buddhist death was just a matter of "common sense" — too natural and too conventional to be questioned. For more details, see Kondō, p. 2 and Smith (1974), pp. 77–78.

195. Kashiwahara, "Kinsei no haibutsu shisō," pp. 522–23.

196. Ibid., p. 524. On the other hand, Kodama Shiki suggests that the real reason for such hostility toward Jōdoshinshū lay not in its corruption but in its massive centripetal force to pull the *monto* toward its leaders and head temples through pilgrimages, donations, and ritual events — an unsurpassable degree of solidarity with a potential to be able to destabilize the governing system of secular power. See Kodama Shiki, pp. 24–25.

197. Tsuji Zennosuke (1955), p. 494.

198. Ōkuwa, *Nihon Bukkyō no kinsei*, p. 7. A group of scholars (including Itō Yuishin, Kitanishi Hiromu, Sonoda Kōyū, Takeda Chōshū, Chiba Jōryū, and Fujii Manabu) formed the Kinsei Bukkyō kenkyūkai and began to publish the results of their collaborative research in the journal *Kinsei Bukkyō*. The journal dealt with three major issues of early modern Buddhism: transformation of sectarian institutions, social modes of Buddhist temples, and the religious teachings and their impact on Buddhist sects. However, Ōkuwa Hitoshi admits that in the end, a satisfactory perspective on how to overcome the theory of 'decadence' in early modern Buddhism was not found. On another front, scholars in the field of intellectual history have tried to locate elements of modernity in Tokugawa Buddhism to show how these elements empowered people to overcome the feudal society and to transform themselves into modern individuals. But this effort has also fallen by the wayside. See Ōkuwa, *Nihon Bukkyō no kinsei*, p. 8 and Ōkuwa (1989), p. 262. One positive impact of Tsuji Zennosuke's research has been to push scholars to uncover, collect, introduce, and examine a wide range of new materials pertaining to Tokugawa Buddhism. See Nishiwaki, "Kinsei Bukkyōshi kenkyū no dōkō," pp. 42, 48. For a useful account of research trends of Buddhism in early modern Japan, see Hōzawa (2004), pp. 1–14.

199. Cousins, p. 372. In a similar vein, James E. Ketelaar notes that the theory of "Buddhist decadence" is premised on "a preconception of Buddhism

as a philosophically complete system trapped within a hopelessly inept institutional framework, such that the historical object called 'Buddhism' could never be adequate to the standards set by those who desired to control its promulgation and sociality; 'Buddhism' could only ever be tending toward, or attempting to revive itself from, its 'destruction.'" Thus, Ketelaar concludes: "Analysis of mid-nineteenth-century Buddhism based upon this scheme has extended the predispositions of the analysis itself into the conclusions derived therefrom." See Ketelaar, p. 11.

200. For more details, see Nishiwaki, "Kinsei Bukkyōshi kenkyū no dōkō," p. 46; Ōkuwa (1989), pp. 261–66; and Takashima, p. 151.

201. For more details, see Kashiwahara, "Kinsei no haibutsu shisō," pp. 519–22. These claims were initially voiced by early Tokugawa ideologues such as Fujiwara Seika (1561–1619), Hayashi Razan (1583–1657), and Yamazaki Ansai (1618–82).

202. Theoretically, too, some Buddhists countered the claim that Buddhism was antithetical to filial piety and family values. For example, Ryūen (1759–1834), who became the seventeenth abbot of Sennenji in Kinki in 1796, divided filiality into two categories: filiality in the secular world, which nourishes the body, and filiality in the *sangha* world, which nourishes the mind. He then classified filial behaviors in each category according to three gradations. In secular filiality these were: being obedient to one's parents day and night, keeping oneself from behaving shamefully and disgracing one's parents, and practicing the five relationships in serving the parents. In *sangha* filiality these were: serving the Three Treasures of Buddhism and conducting Buddhist rituals, saving people from the world of transmigration and life and death, and regarding all sentient beings of the past and present as one's parents and helping them achieve the Buddhist Way. Ryūen elevated the action of filiality to the level of saving all sentient beings, and he criticized the self-indulgent narrowness of Confucian filiality. See Hasegawa, pp. 166–67.

203. LaFleur (1992), p. 82.

204. Fujii Manabu (1973), p. 586.

205. It did not mean, however, that there was no one who confronted or directly rebuked anti-Buddhist critics. For example, Daiga rebuffed Ogyū Sorai, Otsudō Kanchiku (?–1760, Sōtō) critiqued Dazai Shundai, and Nankei (1783–1873, Nishihonganji) negated the claims of Nakai Chikuzan. Some Jōdoshinshū monks, including Chūdō (1812–73, Nishihonganji), Hōren (1797–1884, Nishihonganji), Ryūon (1800–85, Higashihonganji), and Gidō (1805–81, Higashihonganji), tried to disqualify Hirata Atsutane's assertions. For more details, see Kashiwahara, "Kinsei no haibutsu shisō," pp. 533–37.

206. Kashiwahara, "Gohō shisō to shomin kyōka," p. 540.

207. Quote from Kashiwahara (1967), p. 117.

208. For more details, see Watt, pp. 200–212 and Takahashi, p. 158.

209. Yasumaru, "Sōron: Rekishi no naka de no kattō to mosaku," p. 43.

210. Kashiwahara (1967), pp. 120–23 and Kashiwahara, "Gohō shisō to shomin kyōka," pp. 544–47.

211. It should be noted that Gesshō's "loyal activities" were partly encouraged by Murata Seifū (1783–1855), the domain's senior councilor who tried to mobilize the exhortative influence of Jōdoshinshū monks upon the peasant *monto* in pushing forward a variety of reform measures. Murata thought that Jōdoshinshū might be useful as "teachings for governing the state" if effectively maneuvered. See Kodama Shiki, p. 29.

212. Ibid., p. 122. For a discussion of Gesshō's thought and activities, see ibid., pp. 279–86.

213. For a detailed discussion of Shōkai's thought on the unity of the essential and the secular, see Fukuma, pp. 8–12.

214. Ibid., pp. 1–2 and Yasumaru, "Sōron: rekishi no naka de no kattō to mosaku," pp. 50–51.

215. Contrary to the Nishihonganji subsect, the Higashihonganji subsect sided with the *bakufu* and called for volunteers to join the *bakufu* forces. However, after Tokugawa Yoshinobu surrendered his political authority to the emperor, the Higashihonganji quickly joined the Nishihonganji in support of the imperial court and its loyalists. See Ketelaar, p. 72.

Chapter 11

216. Shively (1991), p. 711.

217. Fujita Satoru (1989), pp. 10–12.

218. Fujita Satoru (1995), pp. 5–6.

219. Matsudaira Sadanobu (1789), p. 734.

220. This does not mean that sumptuary regulations (*ken'yakurei*) were directed only at the commoner class: they were issued in considerable numbers to all classes, including the samurai class, whose hierarchical gradations were complex and strictly kept. But by the time of Matsudaira Sadanobu, the conspicuous clothing worn by upper merchants had become so irritating to the regime that sumptuary regulations were increasingly focused on commoners. The main concern was to prevent the morale and discipline of the samurai class from being further eroded. For a useful discussion of the evolution and practice of sumptuary regulations and their effect on the samurai class, see Shively (1964–65), pp. 137–53.

221. Ibid., p. 133. Noting that breaches of customary practices with regard to clothing also tend to cause particular resentment in many other cultures, Shively discusses why this was especially so in Japan.

222. Naitō Chisō, p. 2870.

223. Matsudaira Sadanobu framed his view in the phrase "for the realm" (*tenka no ontame*), implying that all policies should be discreetly executed to the benefit of the realm. His rationale was extended to the point that luxury items, even those imported from China, should not be uniformly vilified because, whenever anyone bought them, the monies paid would eventually be circulated and so benefit the realm. See Fujita Satoru (1989), pp. 34–35.

224. See Hur, pp. 141–46 for a detailed discussion of the privation of shogunal retainers and vassals, and the shogunate's countermeasures, which

were devised to lessen their sufferings but which, in fact, often backfired and proved to be useless.

225. For early examples of sumptuary regulations, see Shively (1964–65), pp. 126–30.

226. Deuchler (1992), p. 110.

227. In the doctrinal tradition of Neo-Confucianism, the matter of nurturing *fūzoku* into becoming "good and rich" was the state's most important duty. The essence of *fūzoku* was represented by the three cardinal human relationships (between ruler and subject, father and son, and husband and wife) and the five moral imperatives (righteousness between sovereign and subject, proper rapport between father and son, separation of functions between husband and wife, proper recognition of sequence of birth between elder and younger brothers, and faithfulness between friends). In particular, these relationships were maintained by the concept of decorum (*rei* in Japanese, *li* in Chinese) — proper ritual behavior that could be fostered through the four rites of capping, wedding, mourning, and ancestor worship. Thus, proper ritual behavior was at the very core of the educative process aimed to make the people's minds firm and receptive to harmony and order. See Deuchler (1992), p. 110.

228. Quoted in Nakamura Shunsaku, p. 105.

229. Ogyū, *Taiheisaku*, p. 473.

230. Quoted in Nakamura Shunsaku, p. 111.

231. Hur, p. 160.

232. Fujita Satoru (1989), pp. 39–40, 42.

233. Quoted from ibid., pp. 42–43.

234. Ibid., p. 43.

235. Ibid., pp. 47–48.

236. Ibid., pp. 52–53.

237. Buyō Inshi, pp. 703, 725

238. Quoted in Nishiki (1999), p. 137.

239. Ibid., p. 138.

240. *Shichū torishimari ruishū*, vol. 1, p. 122.

241. *Edo machibure shūsei*, vol. 9, pp. 162–63.

242. *Shichū torishimari ruishū*, vol. 1, p. 123.

243. *Sen'yō eikyūroku ofuredome*, vol. 2, p. 744. The *Sen'yō eikyūroku ofuredome* is a collection of edicts and regulations imposed upon Edo and its townspeople from 1648 to 1862. It was compiled into 165 fascicles by the ward elder of Minami Denmachō, Takano Naotaka.

244. About this merchant family, see Nishiki (1999), p. 145.

245. Ibid., pp. 146–47.

246. Ibid., pp. 160–62.

247. Ibid., pp. 140–43.

248. Buyō Inshi, p. 714.

249. Ibid., p. 714.

250. *Shichū torishimari ruishū*, vol. 2, p. 41.

251. Ibid., p. 41.

252. Ibid., pp. 41–42.

253. It seemed that the lives of the have-nots were dependent upon the mercy of the haves to one degree or another, and the former showed subservience to the latter in the name of "gratitude." In return, the latter showcased the subservience of the former in their search for the social recognition of their wealth and influence.

254. *Shichū torishimari ruishū*, vol. 2, p. 42.

255. Ibid., p. 42.

256. *Shichū torishimari ruishū*, vol. 1, p. 50.

257. Why confraternity members made the occasion of their members' funerals eventful may also be seen in the genesis of *mokugyokō*. Originally, people agreed to save up monies that were to be used when their members' family had a funeral. At the funeral, when the coffin was carried, one member, who carried a big fish-shaped wooden block and beat it while chanting in a loud voice, led the remaining members (who formed a procession and chanted in response) to the burial site. This kind of group activity led to the formation of *mokugyokō*. This practice gradually spread to other confraternities, including *nenbutsukō* and *daimokukō*. See *Shichū torishimari ruishū*, vol. 2, pp. 12–13.

258. *Edo machibure shūsei*, vol. 7, p. 344.

259. Ibid., pp. 344–45.

260. For more details, see *Ofuregaki Tenpō shūsei ge*, pp. 436, 441 and Sawato, pp. 159–66.

261. Nishiki (1999), pp. 177–78.

262. *Sen'yō eikyūroku ofuredome*, vol. 3, pp. 450–53. The *bakufu* was prompted to issue this edict when Yahagi Tenmangū in Mikawa held a *degaichō* at Ekōin in Edo. When the portable shrine carrying the Tenmangū deity arrived at Shinbashi late in the fourth month of 1852, all the members of *mokugyokō* confraternities, along with some 50 groups of Fujikō and some 20 groups of labor associations, converged and followed the procession all the way to Ryōgoku. There was great havoc and noise, and this gravely irritated the public authorities. The *kaichō*, which was originally scheduled to last for two months, was soon stopped by the *bakufu*. For more details, see *Fujiokaya nikki*, vol. 5, p. 102.

263. Yoshida Nobuyuki (1998), p. 67.

264. *Fujiokaya nikki*, vol. 5, p. 74. The *Fujiokaya nikki* is a comprehensive collection of information on the events and happenings that occurred in Edo between 1804 and 1868, chronologically arranged and compiled by Yoshizō, who ran the Fujiokaya bookstore in Shitaya.

265. For more details, see Ikegami Akihiko (1978), pp. 112–37.

266. Yoshida Nobuyuki (1990), p. 220.

267. Matsumoto, pp. 315–16.

268. Yoshida Nobuyuki (1990), p. 216.

269. For details, see Sawato, pp. 164–66.

270. For a brief biography, the cause of his death, and his Osaka funeral, see *Fujiokaya nikki*, vol. 5, p. 46.

271. Ibid., p. 47.

272. Ibid., p. 47.

273. This honorific "cloister" rank alluded to the ideal path of a devoted lay follower who contributed to erecting temples and resolved to reside within them. By creating a fictive space of family pride, the survivors of the recipient were able to put themselves above their assigned status in society. See Vesey, pp. 374–76.

274. *Ofuregaki Tenpō shūsei ge*, p. 445.

Chapter 12

275. Ebrey, *Confucianism and Family Rituals in Imperial China*, p. 31.

276. It should be noted that, long before the *bakufu*'s compilation, several domain governments in Tsu, Aizu, Chikuzen, Tosa, Obama, and Higo had already published stories of filial sons and daughters (or other virtuous people found in their domains) for educational purposes. See Sugano (2003), p. 172.

277. *Kankoku kōgiroku*, vol. 1, p. 3. The channels through which the stories of filial piety and righteousness were disseminated, taught, or learned included: the processes of collection and compilation themselves; local editions published by domain governments for educational purposes; the publication and nationwide circulation of the *Kōgiroku* by the shogunate; lectures and lessons on these stories at Sekimon Shingaku schools and other educational institutions; novels and plays that featured these didactic stories; exhortations by officials, educators, Buddhist monks, and Shinto priests; and so forth.

278. Discussing the extent to which the *Kōgiroku* reached the populace, Sugano Noriko notes: "The *bakufu* intended to make the *Official Records* widely available for sale in local bookshops. Anecdotal evidence suggests that a variety of people ended up acquiring it, including women. Thus far I have not located any indication of the total number of copies produced. We know, however, that a complete string-bound edition from 1801 is housed in the National Diet Library in Tokyo today and that every prefectural and local library possesses at least the chapter pertaining to its region." See Sugano (2003), p. 172.

279. It is not known why cases in Hida were not included. For a list of examples, in terms of geography and category of virtues, see Sugano (1999), pp. 218–21.

280. For a detailed statistical data analysis of the entries in the *Official Records*, see Sugano (2003), pp. 174–77.

281. For comparison, see Sugano (1999), pp. 18–19 and (2003), pp. 180–81. In particular, Sugano offers examples from Yonezawa, Edo, Hiroshima, and Kumamoto that pertain to each of her categories, emphasizing the paramount importance of filiality in the *bakufu*'s cultural engineering. See Sugano (2003), pp. 181–85.

282. *Kankoku kōgiroku*, vol. 3, pp. 304–7.

283. Ibid., vol. 2, p. 300.

284. Ibid.

285. Ibid., vol. 1, pp. 103–4.

286. In the *Li-chi*, Confucius's disciple, Tseng Tzu, is quoted as saying, "Set up filial piety and it will fill the space from heaven to earth; spread it out and it will extend to the four seas; hand it down to future ages and from morning to night it will be observed." See Ebrey, *Confucianism and Family Rituals in Imperial China*, pp. 31–32.

287. For Chu Hsi, politics meant a process of education in which the ruler served as the teacher who exhorted and civilized the people. Through being taught, the people were to recover their original mind and realize it in their social life. In keeping with this line of thinking, when the social order was called into question in the early seventeenth century, Ogyū Sorai argued that the government should change its governing structure and proceed more actively to rectify people's customs and manners through the virtue of filial piety and other ethical values. See Tsujimoto, pp. 212–13.

288. For a detailed discussion, see ibid., pp. 216–17.

289. Quote from Rawski, p. 30. But even in China, the practice of filial piety was not uniformly Confucian. Patricia Ebrey notes: "Throughout the Sung, mourners regularly engaged Buddhist monks to perform funeral services for the recent dead, generally scheduled for each seventh day until the forty-ninth day after the death. Buddhist services were seen as a way to help the dead through these passages by transferring merit to them. The services could be held in the home of the deceased or in a temple; in either case the major activity was the chanting of sūtras. The monks who performed the services were fed vegetarian meals, and the relatives and guests who came to observe were also fed, making these services an expensive funeral activity for the bereaved family." See Ebrey, *Chu Hsi's Family Rituals*, pp. 79–80.

290. Sugano (2003), p. 171.

291. *Kankoku kōgiroku*, vol. 3, p. 436.

292. Ibid., vol. 1, pp. 151–52.

293. Ikegami (1973), pp. 145–46.

294. Ibid., pp. 147–48.

295. Ibid., pp. 148–50.

296. Ibid., p. 218.

297. See Bolitho (2003), p. 7 and Tamamuro Fumio (1987), p. 209.

298. For a typical example, see Ōhashi Shunnō, pp. 78–79.

299. For a representative compilation of these biographies, see Kasahara Kazuo, ed., *Kinsei ōjōden shūsei* (A collection of early modern biographies of rebirth in pure land), 3 vols. Tokyo: Yamakawa shuppansha, 1978–80.

300. Oguri (1979), pp. 604–5. For the whole text, see Kasahara, pp. 3–30.

301. For more details, see Oguri, "Shinshū kyōdan no risōteki nenbutsu-shazō," pp. 177–83.

302. Hasegawa, pp. 158–59 and Tamamuro Fumio (1987), pp. 231–32.

303. Oguri, "*Kuroshiro ōjōden* ni tsuite," p. 486.

304. Tamamuro Fumio (1987), pp. 232–33. For a similar analysis, see Hasegawa, pp. 144–45.

305. The six fascicles of the *Myōkōninden* were edited by Gōsei (the first fascicle, Jōsenji in Iwami), Sōjun (the second to fifth fascicles, Senshōji in Minō), and Shōō (the sixth fascicle, in Matsumae) and they introduced, all together, the life stories of 157 Jōdoshinshū adherents (64 peasants, 28 merchants, 10 Buddhist priests, 10 samurai, and others). For more details, see Kashiwahara (1992), pp. 74–85.

306. Oguri (1973), pp. 238–39.

307. On the issue of why the virtues of filiality, loyalty, and chastity were stressed more strongly upon Jōdoshinshū followers than upon other sectarians, Oguri Junko attributes it to the very teachings of Jōdoshinshū, which assure its followers of salvation in this world. The confidence of salvation in this life, suggests Oguri, made the followers highly receptive to what the secular power desired or demanded. Oguri, "Shinshū kyōdan no risōteki nenbutsushazō," pp. 236–37.

308. Arimoto (1997), pp. 64–65.

309. Yasumaru, "Sōron: rekishi no naka de no kattō to mosaku," p. 25.

310. In some regions, Jōdoshinshū followers refused to worship Shintō deities, to establish a household kami altar, and to place amulets and talismans on the post of the entrance door, while continuing to practice indoor household preaching against the shogunal ban. Some followers went so far as neither to make a grave for their deceased family members nor to install memorial tablets. This kind of ritual behavior invited criticism and social denial. For more details, see Yasumaru, "Sōron: rekishi no naka de no kattō to mosaku," pp. 25–26.

311. See *Kamioka chōshi*, pp. 382–91.

312. Arimoto Masao notes that the stronghold regions of Jōdoshinshū saw a steady increase in population in contrast to other regions and that this was attributable to the vigorous exhortatory activities of its monks, who preached against abortion, infanticide, and absconding while actively promoting the values of devotion to family business, frugality, and strict ethical life. In this sense, Arimoto suggests that the Jōdoshinshū was the most systematic educational institution and that its monks were the most influential popular educators in early modern Japan. For more details, see Arimoto (1997), pp. 37–54 and (2002), pp. 324–27.

313. There was a popular belief that anti-Kirishitan surveillance could last, in the case of males, for five or seven generations, and in the case of females, for three or five generations. For an example, see Tamamuro Fumio, *Edo jidai no Sōtōshū no tenkai*, p. 151.

314. Ibid., pp. 151–52.

315. As was seen in Shingaku teachings as well as in the movements led by such agricultural leaders as Ninomiya Sontoku (1787–1856) and Ōhara Yūgaku (1797–1858), from the late eighteenth century commoners were seriously engaged in the practice of what was known as popular morality (*tsūzoku dōtoku*), which featured diligence, industry, thrift, filial piety, and the like—ethical values practiced with the aim of restoring the strength of households and moral rectitude. For a detailed discussion, see Yasumaru (1974), pp. 29–37.

From a similar angle, Arimoto Masao examines the efforts of Miyaoi Sadao, a Hirata follower in Matsuzawa village, Shimōsa who promoted ethical values deemed essential for the good management of household properties, the collective well-being of the village community, and by extension, the safety of the country. Miyaoi Sadao, who recommended that the villagers read and practice the teachings found in such books as the *Honchō kōshiden* (Biographies of filial children of our country), authored by Fujii Raisai (1628–?) and *Fukeikun* (Admonitions of fathers and brothers), authored by Hayashi Shihei (1738–93), merged the ideals of Hirata nativist thought and the importance of family occupation and household institution into one, saying that the practice of filial piety, frugality, and hard work would invoke divine help and protection from deities and spirits. See Arimoto (2002), pp. 87–92.

316. Hur, pp. 182–83.

317. During the Tokugawa period there were some 3,000 peasant uprisings (on average, there were more than ten uprisings per year, but these were far more frequent in the late Tokugawa period) and another 3,000 intravillage conflicts. See Vlastos, pp. 10, 46, 75.

318. Buyō Inshi, p. 662.

319. *Shichū torishimari ruishū*, vol. 26, p. 16.

320. Scheiner, p. 51. For the original reference, see Fukaya (1986), p. 65.

321. For a detailed discussion, see Fukaya (1986), pp. 65–74.

322. Scheiner, p. 41. Irwin Scheiner notes that the "covenant paradigm" arose from the subsistence economy of agriculture, in which the survival of both benevolent lords and honorable peasants was interrelated. However, commenting that Scheiner's covenant paradigm falls short of explaining how reciprocal relationships became "socially dominant" in Tokugawa Japan, Stephen Vlastos suggests that "seigneurial benevolence was much more than a prescription for elite public morality, as in Chinese Confucianism. Rather, within the political economy of Tokugawa feudalism, seigneurial exploitation contained specific contradictions with respect to small cultivators that in the short run could only be resolved by regular administrative procedures to provide emergency aid and moderate tax extraction." See Vlastos, p. 16.

323. Kumazawa, p. 411. For the idea of "benevolent rule" as articulated in Confucian terms and played out in *bakuhan* politics, see Tahara, pp. 351–55.

324. Fujita Satoru (1989), pp. 129–30.

325. Ibid., pp. 133–34.

326. In contrast, those villagers who failed to fulfill their basic obligations were classified as "roguish peasants" (*itazura hyakushō*), and for the reason of "ethical decadence" could be excluded by the public authorities from the arena of benevolent rule. For villagers, plunging into the status of *itazura hyakushō* meant the loss of their legitimate social existence. See Fukaya (1986), pp. 68–69.

327. Hur, pp. 95–96.

328. For more details on Ekōin, see Saitō Gesshin, vol. 2, pp. 1852–61.

329. Tōkyōto kōbunshokan, vol. 7, p. 928.

330. Stupas erected in the precincts of Ekōin were for the victims of the Meireki fire of 1657, the Asama volcanic eruption of 1783, the tsunamis of 1827 and 1856, and the Ansei earthquake of 1855.

331. Tōkyōto kōbunshokan, vol. 37, pp. 187–89.

332. For example, see *Ofuregaki Tenpō shūsei ge*, pp. 6–7.

333. Hur, pp. 194–97.

334. Among the writers other than Tsuruya Nanboku who used the ghost story of Kasane to create their own versions of the "vengeful spirit" story were Takizawa Bakin (1767–1848) and San'yūtei Enchō (1839–1900). See Kawamura, pp. 378–40.

335. A full version of the story is found in the *Shirei gedatsu monogatari kikigaki* (A story of the salvation of dead spirits), which was published in two fascicles in 1690. For the full text, see Hattori, pp. 218–64.

336. Yūten Shōin, a renowned Jōdoshū monk, acted as an exorcist despite the criticism that temporarily disgraced him. The role of dealing with individual evil spirits existing outside the parameter of funerary Buddhism was considered to belong to petty exorcists rather than to the monks of institutional Buddhism, who were in charge of operating the *danka* system. For a detailed discussion on Yūten Shōnin, see Takada, pp. 106–30.

337. For a full text and an introduction, see Gunji Masakatsu (1981); for a summary, see Halford, pp. 373–74.

338. For more details, see Kawamura, pp. 381–84; for a chronology of the *Tōkaidō Yotsuya kaidan* staged at the kabuki theater, see Yokoyama, pp. 273–77.

339. Kawamura, p. 381.

340. Ibid., 384–85. Kawamura Minato suggests that Tsuruya Nanboku's reconstruction of a new image of female vengeful spirits represented an "early modern" mode of religious faith and social consciousness—one that embraced an element of rationality.

341. For how the Oiwa Inari shrine came into being, see Yokoyama, pp. 236–40.

Part IV

1. Ōta, p. 14.
2. Ibid., p. 17.
3. Ibid., p. 18.

Chapter 13

4. For details, see Ichimura, pp. 71–74.

5. By the late medieval period, Shinto families, including such prominent houses as the Urabe (Yoshida), Ōnakatomi, and Shirakawa, all followed funerary Buddhism. For example, Yoshida Kanehiro, great-great-grandfather of Kanetomo, who died in 1402, breathed his last while chanting the name of Amida Buddha. A week earlier, he had taken Buddhist vows, and his last wish was to be reborn in the Buddhist Paradise. His funeral, which his son

did not attend out of fear of death pollution, was performed by Buddhist monks. For details, see Okada Shōji, "Shintō sōsai no seiritsu to Yoshidake," pp. 33–35 and Kenney, pp. 242–43.

6. For a detailed account of Kanemigi's funeral based upon his son's diary, see Kenney, pp. 243–48 and Gilday, p. 282.

7. Based on the ideas of Chinese Daoists, who traditionally posited two possible fates for the human spirit after death — *kon* (*hun*), an ascent to heaven, and *haku* (*p'o*), a return to earth — Kanetomo suggested that the part of the human spirit that ascended to heaven would, if cared for through Shinto funerary rituals, eventually become a deity. For details, see Okada Shōji (1996), pp. 229–30 and Gilday, pp. 281–82. For a detailed discussion of Shinto funerals for the chieftains of the Yoshida house, see Okada Shōji, "Kinsei Shintō no jomaku," pp. 330–34.

8. For details, see Boot, pp. 150–56.

9. Endō Jun, p. 299 and Nishida, p. 14. For the manual of *Yuiitsu Shintō sōsai shidai*, see Kokugakuin daigaku Nihon bunka kenkyujo, ed., pp. 81–98. For a convenient summary of the ritual procedure for Yoshida funerals, see Okada Shōji (1989), p. 7.

10. The only exception to this rule involved funerals for the chief priests of the Yoshida house, the Shirakawa house, imperial shrines such as Ise, and other great shrines (such as Kamo and Izumo). These were not subject to Buddhist funerals. For details, see Nishida, pp. 24, 85–86 and Okada Shōji (1996), p. 238.

11. Date, p. 372. Conventionally, white vestments were worn by ordinary, unranked priests. For detailed discussions on this edict and its effects, see Hardacre (2002), pp. 48–54 and Maeda (2003), pp. 83–90.

12. On the Yoshida house's involvement in managing Shinto affairs for the imperial court and its practice of license issuance, see Hardacre (2002), pp. 46–47 and Maeda (2002), pp. 329–31 and (2003), pp. 68–74.

13. The major 22 shrines (commonly known as Nijūnisha) in the Ise, Kyoto, and Nara areas received special acknowledgment and patronage from the imperial court. They were ranked by three categories: the upper seven (Ise, Iwashimizu, Kamo, Matsuo, Hirano, Inari, and Kasuga), the middle seven (Ōharano, Ōmiwa, Isonokami, Ōyamato, Hirose, Tatsuta, and Sumiyoshi), and the lower eight (Hie, Umenomiya, Yoshida, Hirota, Gion, Kitano, Niukawakami, and Kibune).

14. For more details, see Maeda (2003), pp. 74–82.

15. Helen Hardacre has closely examined local gazetteers from Kōza county, Sagami and western Tama in Musashi and provides detailed statistical data on the sacerdotal lineage of the Yoshida house: "Shrine priests who were neither Buddhist priests (including the Shugen sects) nor customary ritualists of a community were rare in the survey area. There were 747 shrines in the survey area, but only seventy-seven of them (10 percent) were served by a professional shrine priest of any description. There were only forty-five shrine priests in the survey area, and only six of them were in the Yoshida line. None were in the Shirakawa line at the time of the compila-

tion of the gazetteers. Forty-three of the priests were located in western Tama and only two were in Kōza county." See Hardacre (2002), pp. 50–51.

16. Maeda (2002), pp. 332–34.

17. For a geographical distribution of rank and title certificates granted by the Yoshida house between 1535 and 1738, see ibid., pp. 336–37. The Shirakawa house, which was authorized to issue ordination writs to Shinto priests in the Kansei period, endeavored to expand its influence. Although the Shirakawa house could not match the Yoshida house with regard to the number of shrines under its control, which by the early nineteenth century was only some 290 shrines (mostly linked to the imperial house), the rivalry between the two Shinto houses intensified. The decision that allowed the Shirakawa house to issue ordination writs was made out of concern that the influence of the Yoshida house might be getting too great (even though this measure could not mend the situation). According to one estimate, the number of shrines affiliated with these Shinto houses showed a ratio of ten to one in favor of Yoshida. For more details, see Toki, p. 232 and Takano, pp. 94–102. For a useful discussion on the rise of Shirakawa's influence in Shinto-related affairs in general and its rivalry with the Yoshida house in the late Tokugawa period, see Maeda (2003), pp. 169–80.

18. Kikuchi Seiichi, pp. 545–46.

19. Tsuji Zennosuke (1997), p. 366.

20. *Meiji ishin shinbutsu bunri shiryō*, vol. 5, p. 1070.

21. Ibid., p. 1071.

22. Ibid., pp. 1077–78.

23. Ibid., pp. 1094–95.

24. It is hard to determine to what extent these documents are reliable, but the areas of Shinto funerals cited in them include the domains of Kaga, Aizu, Mito, Bizen, and Kii; the Matsusaka, Shirako, Kuwana, and Kameyama domains in Ise; the Muraoka and Toyooka domains in Tajima; Aida county and Shōboku and Ōniwa villages in Mimasaka; the domain of the Mizoguchi house in Echigo; Chichibu, Hanzawa, and Tama counties in Musashi; the Kameido area in Edo; Tsuru county in Kai; Nishinari county in Settsu; the Imabari domain in Iyo; the Matsushiro domain in Shinano; and various areas in Suō and Nagato. Ibid., pp. 1078–81; for a detailed discussion of the geographical distribution of Shinto funerals, see Nishida, pp. 77–82.

25. *Tokugawa kinreikō*, vol. 5, p. 192.

26. Ibid., p. 193. It cannot be verified, but the *Tokugawa kinreikō* cites a case in which a Shinto priest, Matsusaki Harima, and his entire family in Sashima county, Shimōsa were allowed Shinto funerals. On the other hand, Nishida Nagao indicates that in addition to the Harima case, the *Shintō sōsai kenbun-shū* (A collection of Shinto funeral rites seen and heard) introduces 37 cases in which permission for conducting Shinto funerals was granted to entire families of Shinto priests. See Nishida, pp. 32–41.

27. See Udaka (2002), pp. 566–67.

28. Ibid., pp. 572–73.

29. *Tokugawa kinreikō*, vol. 5, pp. 1079, 1083.

30. Ibid., p. 190.

31. For examples of severance fees, see Maeda (2003), p. 221 and Vesey, p. 333.

32. For more details, see Kikuchi Seiichi, pp. 549–50.

33. The two sources for this episode are *Meiji ishin shinbutsu bunri shiryō*, vol. 4, pp. 468–575 and Tsuji Zennosuke (1997), pp. 368–79. It should be noted that the main deity of Izumo Shrine, Ōkuninushi no Mikoto, was the *kami* that Hirata Atsutane believed to rule the world of spirits after he had turned this world over to the emperor (Sumeramikoto). Hirata's theology on Ōkuninushi no Mikoto, who was believed to facilitate and ensure communication between descendants and ancestral spirits, encouraged many Shinto activists to support the movement for Shinto funerals in the late Tokugawa period. See Kondō, pp. 26–27.

34. *Meiji ishin shinbutsu bunri shiryō*, vol. 4, p. 484.

35. Ibid., pp. 499–501.

36. For some details on how Shinto funerals were conducted, see ibid., pp. 509–10. Shōtatsuji secretly sent minor monks to observe what was going on and was shocked to find that the Masuno family buried its deceased with a Shinto funeral.

37. *Meiji ishin shinbutsu bunri shiryō*, vol. 4, p. 511.

38. Ibid., p. 468.

39. Ibid., pp. 482–83, 494. It is true that in the 1660s, Tokugawa Mitsukuni, the Mito lord, encouraged the families in his domain to adopt Confucian funerals. But the Kantō regulations, which the Shinto priest petitioners referred to as a legal foundation for Shinto funerals, were a fiction: there were no such regulations. Similarly, petitioners cited such areas as Suō, Nagato, Chikuzen, Bizen, Okayama, Kaga, Noto, Etchū, and so on as places where Shinto funerals were allegedly practiced. But this cannot be verified.

40. *Meiji ishin shinbutsu bunri shiryō*, vol. 4, p. 486.

41. Ibid., pp. 473, 487–88. Obviously, this Buddhist name was unprecedented, but the Enfukuji monk, upon being confronted, insisted that there were similar examples (even though he could not supply them).

42. For a specific example, the petitioners cited the misdeed of a head monk who "had an affair" with the widow of a Shinto priest named Kado Kazusa, claiming that when Kado died, the head monk of his *danna* temple conducted a funeral service for him; after that, he "approached Kado's wife," developed a relationship, and eventually impregnated her. In order to protect the widows and daughters of Shinto families (who had no option but to visit their *danna* temples to arrange memorial services for their fathers, husbands, and ancestors), the petitioners argued that, rather than having to go to *danna* temples, these women should have access "to the private funerals of Yuiitsu Shinto, as had been the case in ancient times." See *Meiji ishin shinbutsu bunri shiryō*, vol. 4, pp. 490–91.

43. Ibid., pp. 492–93.

44. For details, see ibid., pp. 571–74.

45. *Meiji ishin shinbutsu bunri shiryō*, vol. 3, pp. 609–10. It should be noted, however, that Nariaki called this type of funeral a "private funeral" (*jisō*), in which family members handled all matters.

46. Collcutt, pp. 147–48. For more details, see *Meiji ishin shinbutsu bunri shiryō*, vol. 3, pp. 612–20; in particular, for a discussion of the confiscation of temple bells and bone objects, see Tamamuro Fumio (1974), pp. 2–11.

47. See *Meiji ishin shinbutsu bunri shiryō*, vol. 3, pp. 622–23. Specifically, according to the suggestions of Mitogaku scholars and advisors, Nariaki got rid of all Ryōbu Shinto elements from Tōshōgū, over which Tōeizan Kichijōin had held power as an intendant temple (*bettōji*). In the fall of 1843, Nariaki converted the temple into a Yuiitsu Shinto shrine. Kichijōin, which had lost its power over Mito Tōshōgū, brought its grudge to the shogunal house, with which it maintained close connections. For more details, see *Meiji ishin shinbutsu bunri shiryō*, vol. 3, pp. 610–12. Similarly, attacks on Buddhism in the 1840s and 1860s in Chōshū and in the 1850s in Satsuma, all of which shared a rhetoric and severity similar to what had occurred in Mito, still fell far short of bringing sweeping changes in the mode of funeral rites.

48. Oka Kumaomi was the priest of Tomitakeyama Hachimangū and a teacher of National Learning at the domain school known as Yōrōkan. For more details concerning the role of Oka Kumaomi in the development of National Learning in the Tsuwano domain, see Katō, pp. 384–86.

49. For an account of the whole incident, see ibid., pp. 386–93.

50. For example, Shinto priests were granted the right to Shinto funerals over the course of several years. These included 28 priests in the Tsuchiura domain (1773), 63 priests in Ochi county of Iyo province (1832), all priests in the Hamada domain (1845), all priests in the Tsuwano domain (1847), 152 priests in the Owari domain (1848), and some priests in the Yoshida domain (in the *bakumatsu* period).

51. Asoya (1997), pp. 287–88 and Bernstein (1999), pp. 46–48.

52. Bolitho (2002), pp. 409–10; Kanda, pp. 90–91; and Kondō, p. 3. Hirata Atsutane distinguished the places in which spirits and descendants lived (*kakuriyo* and *utsushiyo*, respectively) and believed that the spirits staying in the former could watch the activities of descendants living in the latter, but not vice versa.

53. Asoya (1997), p. 288 and Kondō, p. 7.

54. Asoya (1997), pp. 292–93.

55. Nishida, pp. 92–99.

56. Sawa, p. 31.

57. For a detailed discussion on this first Urakami *kuzure*, see Ōhashi Yukihiro (2001), pp. 180–205 and Breen (1988), pp. 10–13. Breen notes that this whole incident, which was concluded with "the perfunctoriness of much of the investigation," marked "a great departure from the ruthless [anti-Christian] practices of the seventeenth century." Ibid., p. 16.

58. For details, see Ōhashi Yukihiro (2001), pp. 218–30.

59. For a detailed account, see Ebisawa (1968), pp. 14–61.

60. For a list of proscribed books and the procedure of inspecting imported books for Christian elements at Nagasaki, see Konta, pp. 7–13.

61. In this context, Yasumaru Yoshio determines that these preachers, who struggled to survive at the social margins, were executed as Kirishitan because their religious activities were defined as being "Kirishitan-ish" (Kirishitan *teki*). See Yasumaru, " 'Kindaika' no shisō to minzoku," pp. 437–38.

62. Regarding the kind of coexistence between the Kirishitan people and the state that features the "relationship of favor and reliance of paradox" (*gyakusetsu no onrai kankei*), see Ōhashi Yukihiro, "Ishū to Kirishitan," pp. 235–36.

63. "Urakami ishūto ikken," p. 852.

64. Ibid., p. 835.

65. Lu, p. 291.

66. The Roman Catholic Church (the Vatican), which tried to rebuild its missionary networks in Japan, had entrusted this task exclusively to the Society of Foreign Missions of Paris (Société des Missions Étrangères de Paris, or M.E.P.) long before the treaty was signed. From 1832 onward, the M.E.P. tried to send missionaries through the Korean peninsula, but it gave up the plan due to the Korean government's massive persecution of Roman Catholics in 1839. In 1844, after the Opium War, which enhanced the presence of France in East Asia, the M.E.P. was able to send missionaries to Okinawa and establish a foothold for future missions in mainland Japan. Once treaty ports were opened, it sent missionaries to Hakodate in 1859, to Nagasaki in 1863, and to the other treaty ports. In selecting missionaries to be sent to Japan, it excluded those who were not native speakers of French. Until the arrival of Spanish Dominicans in 1904, all the missionary groups were French in origin, although not all the missionaries were actually French nationals. For more details, see Gonoi, pp. 246–50 and Marnas, pp. 49–98, 128–242.

67. Marnas, p. 243. Santa Maria was at the epicenter of the religious lives of underground Kirishitan in Tokugawa Japan. Just as Buddhists enshrined images of the Buddha, so Kirishitan enshrined in secret places images (made of various materials) of the Santa Maria and prayed to them for food, rainfall, the prevention or healing of disease, and so on. For a summary of the encounter, see also Burkman, pp. 143–44.

68. It should be noted, however, that despite the underground Kirishitan having the "same heart," the French missionaries soon realized that Kirishitan faith and practice were polytheistic and deviated too far from the Roman Catholic faith. Over time, the missionaries showed less and less tolerance toward what they regarded as the "pagan traditions" of these underground "Christians"; many of the latter had long treasured "form over content, ritual over doctrine and continuity over meaning" while in hiding and so decided to stay separate from the Roman Catholic Church. For more details, see Turnbull, pp. 215–17 and Harrington, pp. 113–23.

69. Previously, at least on the surface, the Urakami Kirishitan received religious inspection from Shōtokuji and conducted Buddhist funerals offi-

ciated by Shōtokuji monks. However, they secretly undid those Buddhist funerals once the Shōtokuji priests had left the scene. They would open the casket, remove the Buddhist scrip attached to the dead, and replaced it with a piece of red cloth that was believed to be a relic of Christian martyrs. They then placed a natural stone in front of the grave instead of erecting a gravestone onto which a Buddhist name was to be inscribed. They also made offerings of chicken or fish, which were prohibited in Buddhism.

70. For more details, see "Urakami ishūto ikken," pp. 857–60.

71. Yasumaru and Miyachi, eds., p. 283.

72. Ibid., pp. 287–89.

Chapter 14

73. See *Hōrei zensho*, p. 336. For a useful discussion of the Meiji government's anti-Christian position, see Burkman, pp. 179–83.

74. "Shūkyō kankei hōrei ichiran," p. 425.

75. Yasumaru (1988), pp. 513–14.

76. For a list (albeit incomplete) of these Gotō Kirishitan prisoners and victims, including those who did not survive the harsh conditions of the prison, see Kataoka, ed., "Hijō nikki," pp. 893–900.

77. For an investigative report drawn by the Fukue domain based on the description of the murderer-samurai, see Yasumaru and Miyachi, eds., pp. 292–93.

78. Ibid., p. 303. How defiant and traitorous were they? In the second month of 1869, an imperial shrine was built in Urakami village. This was for integrating villagers into the system of State Shinto through daily worship of Amaterasu. However, the Urakami Kirishitan did not allow their children to enter the compound of the shrine, and when they had to pass the shrine, they took a detour to avoid it. Their Christian faith grew stronger day by day. On the decision-making process of the Urakami persecution, see Yoshiya Abe, pp. 121–23.

79. For statistics of the deportees and their destinations, see Iechika, pp. 91–93.

80. Yasumaru and Miyachi, eds., p. 291.

81. British Archival Material, F. O. 46–124. No. 6. Parkes to Clarendon. Jan. 22, 1870. Encl. 12, pp. 76–77 (microfilm page number).

82. Ibid., pp. 79–80.

83. Ibid., p. 37.

84. For these edicts and ordinances, see *Meiji ishin shinbutsu bunri shiryō*, vol. 1, pp. 81–85.

85. For an overview of the extent, severity, variety, and impact of the separation policy and its local enforcement, see Collcutt, pp. 150–65.

86. Ketelaar, p. 44. Up to this time, Sennyūji, a Shingonshū temple in Kyoto, served the imperial house as a funerary *danna* temple. But after the Restoration all members of the imperial house adopted Shinto funerals and memorial rites. Ancestral tablets in Buddhist style, which had been enshrined

in the palace, were removed, and Buddhist titles and posthumous names were no longer engraved on them.

87. "Shūkyō kankei hōrei ichiran," p. 427.

88. Tsuji Zennosuke (1984), p. 345.

89. Government bureaucracy dealing with state rituals and religious affairs went through drastic changes as state experimentation with Shinto kept running into problems. In the eighth month of 1871, the Department of Divinity (Jingikan) was demoted to the status of a ministry and renamed the Ministry of Divinity (Jingishō); in the third month of 1872, it was abolished and reconstituted as the Ministry of Doctrine (Kyōbushō). The demotion of Shinto-style government organs was due to the diminishing faith of secular leaders in Shinto administrators, who had failed to deliver the original vision of the Department of Divinity yet were hopelessly mired in factional infighting. For more details, see Hardacre (1989), pp. 29–31.

90. For details, see *Meiji ishin shinbutsu bunri shiryō*, vol. 5, pp. 809–20. The rationale for enforcing Shinto funerals was that funeral rites for the lord and the father could not be delegated to monks who had denounced the world.

91. Ketelaar, pp. 44–45.

92. From 1868 to 1871, the daimyo domains existed as local administrative units, and, as far as Shinto funerals were concerned, many of them promoted their own policies. See Endō Jun, pp. 296–97.

93. Murata (1999), p. 210.

94. "Shūkyō kankei hōrei ichiran," pp. 432–33, 437–38.

95. Ibid., pp. 422–23.

96. For example, the Satsuma domain legalized Shinto funerals in the sixth month of 1868. Even though it was not enforced at this stage, this legal measure soon brought about dramatic changes to funeral customs. Two episodes deserve attention. The first pertains to the establishment of shrines for dead spirits (*shōkonsha*). In the seventh month of 1868, the restored Department of Divinity built shrines for housing the spirits of those who had died in the battles to overthrow the *bakufu*. The second concerns the lord Shimazu Tadayoshi's young wife, who died in the third month of 1869. Her burial was carried out without any trace of Buddhist influence. After this, the domain issued a series of orders regulating Shinto funerals. All of this took place against the backdrop of (1) a policy aimed at decimating Buddhist institutions and (2) the domain's efforts to achieve unity under the tutelage of the Imperial household. For a more detailed account, see Ketelaar, pp. 54–60.

97. Jaffe, p. 60; see also Ishii, pp. 123–25.

98. See "Shūkyō kankei hōrei ichiran," p. 440.

99. It should be noted that the talisman each household was supposed to receive from its parish shrine was associated with the Ise Jingū. Each household was required to enshrine this talisman—the divided spirit of the Ise deities—in its *kamidana*. If this occurred, the state believed that each household would become a "branch shrine" of the Ise Jingū, which would then

link the entire populace to the cult center of State Shinto. See Hardacre (1989), pp. 29, 83.

100. Sakamoto Koremaru, pp. 421–22.

101. For a detailed discussion of clerical registration, see Jaffe, pp. 78–87.

102. Nevertheless, it should be noted that the Jinshin family register inherited two legacies from the system of temple certification: one was that, annually, in the eleventh month, Shinto shrines were required to report to the government the number of affiliates who died that year; the other was that each household was required to indicate its tutelary Shinto deity on the registration form. All these requirements were devised as a way of identifying the religious affiliation of each household.

103. British Archival Material, F. O. 46–143. No. 127. Adams to Granville. Dec. 12, 1871. Encl. 12.

104. Thelle, pp. 14–15; Yoshiya Abe, pp. 128–31; and Burkman, p. 204.

105. For details, see Iechika, pp. 178–82. In March of 1873, the Meiji government finally directed the local governments to release all of the Urakami Kirishitan held in their jurisdictions.

106. Protestantism was introduced by Anglican missionaries from England and the United States, and by American missionaries of various Protestant denominations rooted in New England Puritanism. John Liggins of the American Episcopal mission, who arrived in Nagasaki in May 1859, was the first Protestant missionary to arrive in Japan proper. For more details, see Ballhatchet, pp. 39–57.

107. "Shūkyō kankei hōrei ichiran," p. 448.

108. It is well known that since the 1868 founding of the Department of Divinity, government administrators were plagued with factional division — most notably the Hirata faction versus the Ōkuni faction — over the proper character of Shinto. The Hirata faction held that Shinto should principally be an agency for conducting the rites of state, and the Ōkuni faction argued that Shinto should be engaged in pastoral as well as in state rites. The 1872 edict urging Shinto priests to be more involved in funerals came from the line of Fukuba Bisei, who belonged to the Ōkuni faction. For the factional affiliations of Shinto government administrators, see Hardacre (1989), pp. 35–36.

109. "Shūkyō kankei hōrei ichiran," p. 452. For a discussion of the passage that led to the eventual removal of the anti-Christian clause, see Breen (1996), pp. 79–89.

110. Christian burials were nevertheless controlled until at least 1884 and the legal position of Christianity remained ambiguous until the Meiji Constitution of 1889, which, in theory, guaranteed religious freedom as long as it was not politically disruptive. See Miyazaki Kentarō, "Roman Catholic Mission in Pre-Modern Japan," pp. 4–5. With the lifting of the ban on the Kirishitan sect in 1873, a large number of underground Kirishitan contacted members of the M.E.P. Gradually they revealed their religious identity as members of the Roman Catholic Church. Miyazaki Kentarō suggests that

these people should be grouped as "resurrected Kirishitan" to distinguish them from those called Kakure Kirishitan (hidden Kirishitan) who, instead of rejoining the Roman Catholic Church, continued to follow the form of their faith as they knew it during their underground existence. These Kakure Kirishitan, who have survived to the present, were most numerous in such areas as Shimogotō, Sotome on the Nishisonogi peninsula, Hirado, and Ikitsuki. It should be noted that, due to significant changes during their underground period, the nature of their faith is very different from that of Christianity. As for why these people, even though they did not have to "hide," continued to remain Kakure Kirishitan, their common replies are that they cannot neglect a faith that their forebears risked their lives to defend, and that numerous marvelous experiences prove to them that the *kami* of their religion exist. The number of Kakure Kirishitan in the 1860s was estimated at some 40,000. See Miyazaki Kentarō, "Roman Catholic Mission in Pre-Modern Japan," p. 17.

111. For the whole text of this manual, see Katō, pp. 416–25 and Bernstein (1999), pp. 59–62.

112. For a detailed historical account of anti-cremation polemic as argued by Shinto funeral advocates, nativist scholars, and Confucian ideologues, see Bernstein (2000), pp. 304–9.

113. For example, Shimaji Mokurai (1838–1911), a prominent Jōdoshinshū monk, commented on the ban, but his words sounded rather conciliatory: "the matter of cremation or burial should be left to the desire of the people and to their convenience." He even suggested that Buddhist temples should entrust their cemetery spaces to their village or ward head so as to clear the way for those families who had switched to Shinto funerals. See Shimaji, pp. 69–73.

114. Before issuing the ban on cremation, the Meiji government asked the Tokyo, Kyoto, and Osaka municipal governments if they could deal with the expected demands of new burial spaces. The Tokyo and Kyoto governments were confident that they could secure new burial spaces, but the Osaka government was pessimistic, saying that the city really did not have idle spaces that could be converted into burial grounds. Sakamoto Koremaru, pp. 438–40.

115. For more details, see ibid., pp. 423, 432–35. In the local towns, too, finding new burial sites for Shinto funeral practitioners was a challenge. Some local governments tried to allocate new spaces for them. For the early 1871 example of the Matsumoto domain, see *Meiji ishin shinbutsu bunri shiryō*, vol. 5, p. 318.

116. Sakamoto Koremaru, pp. 441–42 and Bernstein (2000), pp. 318–21.

117. "Shūkyō kankei hōrei ichiran," p. 467. For a detailed discussion on the debates that led to the repeal of the ban on cremation, see Bernstein (2000), pp. 323–26.

118. In fact, the separation of the resting place of the deceased and the domain of Shinto remained an oddity within the Shinto funerary system.

119. For detailed information on this campaign and on the roles of the instructors of doctrine, see Hardacre (1989), pp. 42–48 and Ketelaar, pp. 96–122.

120. The Three Great Teachings were so vague that the government had to issue chapbooks on how to preach about them. These chapbooks, according to Helen Hardacre, "expounded the virtues of paying taxes, and of complying with conscription, compulsory education, and the solar calendar, as well as support for the military buildup and the importation of Western knowledge and culture." See Hardacre (1989), pp. 43–44.

121. See Kondō, pp. 19–20. In fact, these Shinto funeral manuals neither mentioned anything about death pollution nor included purification rites.

122. Sakamoto Koremaru, p. 436.

123. Hardacre (1989), p. 47.

124. Kanzaki Ichisaku, p. 253.

125. Ogawa Yoshiyasu (1831–1912), born the son of a farmer in Musashi, became a Japanese teacher with the help of David Thompson and later, in 1869, accepted Christianity after being inspired by Thompson's faith and personality. When the Itō Jōuemon incident occurred, Ogawa was an elder of the Tokyo Branch Church. He was anointed as pastor in 1877 and then traveled throughout the country to spread Christianity. Okuno Masatsuna (1823–1910), a former *hatamoto*, was introduced to James Curtis Hepburn, collaborated with Hepburn on an English-Japanese dictionary, and in 1872 accepted Christianity. Along with Ogawa, he was one of the first Japanese Christian pastors.

126. For their petition documents, see Yasumaru and Miyachi, eds., pp. 332–39.

127. Ibid., p. 342.

128. Ibid., p. 343.

129. Ibid., pp. 344–48.

130. The Pantheon Dispute refers to the rivalry between the Ise Jingū and the Izumo Taisha shrine. Izumo demanded that its main deity, Ōkuninushi no Mikoto, be added to the state pantheon as lord of the underworld. The pantheon consisted of Amaterasu and the Three Deities of Creation (Takamimusubi no kami, Amenominakanushi no kami, and Kamimusubi no kami) mentioned in the *Kojiki* and *Nihon shoki*. Ise refused this demand. This dispute lasted several years; it was brought to the imperial house for settlement but was never resolved. For details, see Hardacre (1989), pp. 43, 48–51 and Jaffe, pp. 87–88.

131. "Shūkyō kankei hōrei ichiran," p. 480.

132. The withdrawal of Shinto priests from the campaign resulted in boosting the development of Sect Shinto organizations whose instructors turned out to be the only clergy positioned to conduct Shinto funerals. Empowered with the monopoly of Shinto funerals, which could generate steady income, many Sect Shinto groups were able to expand their activities and consolidate their economic foundation. For more details, see Inoue Nobutaka, p. 376.

133. Date, p. 733.

134. Lay, p. 542.

135. Ibid., p. 535.

136. *Meiji ishin shinbutsu bunri shiryō*, vol. 4, p. 1047.

137. Ibid., p. 1052. Along with this Shinto funeral rite, the Shimazu family relinquished the custom of Bon memorial service, replacing it with the spring and autumn memorial services.

138. Ketelaar, pp. 54–55, 60–61 and *Meiji ishin shinbutsu bunri shiryō*, vol. 4, pp. 1053–55, 1103–9. Indeed, it was not unusual to chisel away the Buddhist name on the gravestone and replace it with a Shinto name (or to replace the gravestone bearing the Buddhist name with a new one bearing a new Shinto name). Families who could not afford to relocate their ancestral gravestones to a Shinto shrine often left them intact in their *danna* temple and carved new Shinto names on them. For the case of the Rikuchū area in Iwate, see *Meiji ishin shinbutsu bunri shiryō*, vol. 5, pp. 402–3.

139. For the example of Nohara village, see Sakurai Haruo, pp. 162–71.

140. Jinja honchō kyōgaku kenkyūjo, ed., pp. 206–7, 224–26.

141. Murata (1999), p. 215. Also see Kurokawa (1961), pp. 36–37 and (1988), pp. 365–67.

142. Quote from Murata (2000), p. 96.

143. Ibid., p. 96.

144. For the Meiji government's regulations on shrine-monks and *shugenja*, see Date, pp. 576–77, 579, 622.

145. Ibid., p. 246. In another example, the residents of the Ono village in the Atsugi area quickly moved, in protest, to abandon Buddhist funerals in 1871, when the village head had a big quarrel with the head monk of the village's dominant temple (Monshūji). See Nakamura Yasutaka, pp. 63–64.

146. Yasumaru and Miyachi, eds., pp. 119–20.

147. Ibid., pp. 121–24.

148. For more details, see *Meiji ishin shinbutsu bunri shiryō*, vol. 5, pp. 305–9.

149. Yasumaru and Miyachi, eds., pp. 124–35.

150. For details, see *Meiji ishin shinbutsu bunri shiryō*, vol. 2, pp. 290–301.

151. Yasumaru (1992), p. 215; for more details on this rebellion, see *Meiji ishin shinbutsu bunri shiryō*, vol. 3, pp. 763–74.

152. Bernstein (1999), pp. 80–82.

153. Murata (1999), pp. 240–43.

154. For details, see ibid., pp. 259–66.

155. For details, see *Meiji ishin shinbutsu bunri shiryō*, vol. 2, pp. 647–48, 701–3.

156. Ibid., vol. 2, p. 674.

157. Ōtō (1996), p. 102.

158. In 1890, the Meiji government promulgated a modern civil law, which it expected to put into effect in 1892. This civil law, known as the "Old Civil Law" (*kyūminpō*) and drafted under the influence of French civil law, did not provide the household head with absolute power over property rights, and it adopted an equal and divided inheritance system. But bureaucrats, legal scholars, and lawyers under the sway of the British legal system, who advo-

cated the absolute power of the household head (e.g., the right to designate a residence; arrange marriage or adoption; grant, re-grant, or cancel household membership; and so forth) and primogeniture, vigorously opposed the execution of the old civil law. Under mounting pressure spearheaded by Hozumi Yatsuka, the government gave up its original plan and began to re-draft a civil law, which was to be promulgated in June 1898 and put into effect the following month. Under this new civil law, a woman was not eligible for household headship.

159. Hozumi, p. 392.

160. Hardacre (1989), p. 122. Copies of the rescript, which were themselves treated as holy objects, were distributed to all public schools; beginning in the second grade, all schoolchildren were required to memorize it. Educators and government officials also held monthly assemblies at which this rescript was ceremonially read.

161. Tsunoda, p. 139.

162. Ōtō (1996), p. 104.

163. Irokawa, p. 16.

164. Quoted in Itō Mikiharu (1982), pp. 24–25.

165. Yanagita, "Jidai to nōsei," p. 38.

166. Itō Mikiharu (1982), p. 33.

Conclusion

1. In establishing the *bakuhan* order, Ieyasu had to control roaming Saikoku daimyo, masterless samurai, *ikki* organizations, bandits, gangs, and the like. He did this, fearing that Kirishitan might ally themselves with these anti-Tokugawa elements and pose grave danger to the foundation of his political authority.

2. Tsujimoto, pp. 219–10.

3. Asao, "The Sixteenth-Century Unification," p. 74.

4. This trend deepened in the Meiji period as the logic of the household institution combined with the ideal of the family-state and brought the individual faith of Buddhist followers under the political ambitions of Imperial Japan. According to Nagura Tetsuzō, within this context the task of modernizing Buddhism and creating a space for spiritual individuality depended on how Buddhists could "liquidate the *danka* system . . . as well as the household as a unit of religious life." But this liquidation never happened. See Nagura (November 1992), pp. 46–47.

5. Yasumaru (1979), pp. 28–30. As far as Confucian ideologues were concerned, this world could not escape the divine intervention of supernatural beings; therefore, it was essential that the state guide the populace through the world of "heaven, heavenly mandate, ghosts, and deities" by presiding over morally impeccable rites and ceremonies.

6. Accordingly, their concerns were directed to magicians, peripatetic religious practitioners, vagabond monks, *yamabushi*, healers, and diviners— all of whom were on the rise and seemed to coax the populace into a world

of fantasy that was detrimental to the social order. In this world of fantasy, the hearts and minds of people seemed to be shaken and confused, and in expectation of achieving their wishes, they threw their money and grain into the opulent halls of Buddhist institutions. Buddhism was not a threat to the Tokugawa system, to be sure; however, the framework within which it was couched came under question. See Yasumaru (1979), pp. 26–27.

7. Wakabayashi (1986), p. 211.

8. Ibid., pp. 271, 273.

9. See Kashiwahara (1990), pp. 20–25.

Works Cited

Abe Wakio 安部弁雄. "Kishū Tanabehan no shūmon aratame" 紀州田辺藩の宗門改め. *Chihōshi kenkyū* 地方史研究 21, no. 6 (December 1971): 23–34.

Abe, Yoshiya. "From Prohibition to Toleration: Japanese Government Views Regarding Christianity, 1854–73." *Japanese Journal of Religious Studies* 5, nos. 2–3 (June-September 1978): 107–38.

Akahori Seimei 赤堀正明 and Fujii Masao 藤井正雄. "Nichirenshū no sōgi" 日蓮宗の葬儀. Part 3 of "Shūkyō, shūhabetsu no sōgi no kenkyū" 宗教・宗派別の葬儀の研究. *Sogi* 3, no. 2 (March 1993): 21–29.

Akata Mitsuo 赤田光男. "Butsudō konryū katei no ichishiryō: Hiroshimaken Seragun Serachō Tsukuchi" 仏堂建立過程の一史料：広島県世羅郡世羅町津口. *Nihon minzokugaku* 日本民俗学, no. 73 (January 1971): 31–43.

——. "Sonraku shakai ni okeru butsudō no keitai to kinō ni tsuite (1)" 村落社会における仏堂の形態と機能について (1). *Bunka shigaku* 文化史学, no. 26 (March 1971): 58–76.

——. *Sorei shinkō to takaikan* 祖霊信仰と他界観. Tokyo: Jinbun shoin, 1986.

Amino Yoshihiko 網野善彦. *Muen, kugai, raku: Nihon chūsei no jiyū to heiwa* 無縁・公界・楽：日本中世の自由と平和. Tokyo: Heibonsha, 1978.

Andachi Itsuo 安達五男. "Buraku jiinsei ni tsuite" 部落寺院制について. *Buraku mondai kenkyū* 部落問題研究, no. 79 (1984): 49–65.

——. *Hisabetsu buraku no shiteki kenkyū* 被差別部落の史的研究. Tokyo: Akashi shoten, 1980.

Anesaki Masaharu 姉崎正治. *Kirishitan shūmon no hakugai to senpuku* 切支丹宗門の迫害と潜伏. Vol. 1 of *Anesaki Masaharu chosakushū* 姉崎正治著作集. Tokyo: Kokusho kankōkai, 1976.

Anno Masaki 安野真幸. *Geninron: chūsei no ijin to kyōkai* 下人論：中世の異人と境界. Tokyo: Nihon editāsukūru shuppanbu, 1987.

Aoki Kigen 青木紀元. *Nihon shinwa no kisoteki kenkyū* 日本神話の基礎的研究. Tokyo: Kazama shobō, 1970.

Arai Kōjirō 荒井貢次郎. "Sōbosei no hōminzokugakuteki kōsatsu" 葬墓制の法民俗学的考察. In *Bukkyō minzokugaku taikei: sosen saishi to sōbo* 仏教

民俗学大系：祖先祭祀と葬墓, ed. Fujii Masao 藤井正雄, pp. 341-57. Vol. 4 of *Bukkyō minzokugaku taikei*. Tokyo: Meicho shuppan, 1988.

Ariizumi Sadao 有泉貞夫. "Yanagita Kunio kō: sosen sūhai to sabetsu" 柳田国男考：祖先崇拝と差別. *Tenbō* 展望, no. 166 (June 1972): 204-24.

Arimoto Masao 有元正雄. *Kinsei Nihon no shūkyō shakaishi* 近世日本の宗教社会史. Tokyo: Yoshikawa kōbunkan, 2002.

——. *Shinshū no shūkyō shakaishi* 真宗の宗教社会史. Tokyo: Yoshikawa kōbunkan, 1995.

——. *Shūkyō shakaishi no kōsō: Shinshū monto no shinkō to seikatsu* 宗教社会史の構想：真宗門徒の信仰と生活. Tokyo: Yoshikawa kōbunkan, 1997.

Aruga Kizaemon 有賀喜左衞門. *Bunmei, bunka, bungaku* 文明・文化・文学. Tokyo: Ochanomizu shobō, 1980.

Asai Ryōi 浅井了意. "Tōkaidō meishoki" 東海道名所記. In *Tōkaidō meishoki, Tōkaidō bunken ezu* 東海道名所記・東海道分間絵図, ed. Fuji Akio 冨士昭雄, pp. 7-204. Tokyo: Kokusho kankōkai, 2002.

Asakura Haruhiko 朝倉治彦, ed. *Gofunai jisha bikō bessatsu* 御府内寺社備考別冊. Tokyo: Meicho shuppan, 1987.

Asano Hisae 浅野久枝. "Goryō to muenbotoke" 御霊と無縁仏. In *Bukkyō minzokugaku taikei: zokushin to Bukkyō* 仏教民俗大系：俗信と仏教, ed. Miyata Noboru 宮田登 and Sakamoto Kaname 坂本要, pp. 47-73. Vol. 8 of *Bukkyō minzokugaku taikei*. Tokyo: Meicho shuppan, 1992.

Asao Naohiro 朝尾直弘. "Higashi Ajia ni okeru bakuhan taisei" 東アジアにおける幕藩体制. In *Nihon no kinsei: sekaishi no naka no kinsei* 日本の近世：世界史のなかの近世, ed. Asao Naohiro, pp. 53-130. Vol. 1 of *Nihon no kinsei*. Tokyo: Chūō kōronsha, 1991.

——. "The Sixteenth-Century Unification." In *The Cambridge History of Japan: Early Modern Japan*, ed. John Whitney Hall, pp. 40-95. Vol. 4 of *The Cambridge History of Japan*. Cambridge, UK: Cambridge University Press, 1991.

Asoya Masahiko 安蘇谷正彦. *Shintō no seishikan: Shintō shisō to 'shi' no mondai* 神道の生死観：神道思想と「死」の問題. Tokyo: Perikansha, 1989.

——. "Shintō no seishikan: Shintō shisōka to 'shi' no mondai" 神道の生死観：神道思想家と「死」の問題. In *Shinsōsai daijiten* 神葬祭大事典, ed. Katō Takahisa 加藤隆久, pp. 282-95. Tokyo: Ebisu kōshō shuppan, 1997.

Atsugi shishi: kinsei shiryōhen 厚木市史：近世資料編, vol. 1. Ed. Atsugishi hishobu shishi hensanshitsu 厚木市秘書部市史編纂室. Atsugi, Kanagawa: Atsugishi, 1986.

Atsuta Kō 熱田公. *Nihon no rekishi: tenka ittō* 日本の歴史：天下一統. Vol. 11 of *Nihon no rekishi*. Tokyo: Shūeisha, 1992.

Ballhatchet, Helen J. "The Modern Missionary Movement in Japan: Roman Catholic, Protestant, Orthodox." In *Handbook of Christianity in Japan*, ed. Mark R. Mullins, pp. 35-68. Leiden and Boston: Brill, 2003.

Bernier, Bernard. "Yanagita's *About Our Ancestors*: Is It a Model for an Indigenous Social Science?" In *International Perspectives on Yanagita Kunio and Japanese Folklore Studies*, ed. J. Victor Koschmann, Ōiwa Keibō, and Yamashita Shinji, pp. 65-95. Ithaca, NY: Cornell University, East Asia Program, 1985.

Bernstein, Andrew. "Fire and Earth: The Forging of Modern Cremation in Meiji Japan." *Japanese Journal of Religious Studies* 27, nos. 3-4 (Fall 2000): 297-334.

——. "The Modernization of Death in Imperial Japan." Ph.D. diss., Columbia University, 1999.

Berry, Mary Elizabeth. *Hideyoshi*. Cambridge, MA: Council on East Asian Studies, Harvard University, 1982.

Bitō Masahide 尾藤正英. *Edo jidai to wa nanika* 江戸時代とはなにか. Tokyo: Iwanami shoten, 1992.

——. "Thought and Religion, 1550-1700." Trans. Kate Wildman Nakai. In *The Cambridge History of Japan: Early Modern Japan*, ed. John Whitney Hall, pp. 373-424. Vol. 4 of *The Cambridge History of Japan*. Cambridge, UK: Cambridge University Press, 1991.

Blum, Mark L. "Stand by Your Founder: Honganji's Struggle with Funeral Orthodoxy." *Japanese Journal of Religious Studies* 27, nos. 3-4 (Fall 2000): 179-212.

Bodiford, William. "Zen and the Art of Religious Prejudice: Efforts to Reform a Tradition of Social Discrimination." *Japanese Journal of Religious Studies* 23, nos. 1-2 (Spring 1996): 1-27.

——. *Sōtō Zen in Medieval Japan*. Honolulu: University of Hawai'i Press, 1993.

Bokhoven, Jeroen. "Butsudan no kigen ni tsuite no ichikōsatsu: bondana setsu to jibutsudōsetsu o megutte" 仏壇の起源についての一考察：盆棚説と持仏堂説を巡って. *Shūkyō kenkyū* 宗教研究 74, no. 4 (March 2001): 356-58.

Bolitho, Harold. *Bereavement and Consolation: Testimonies from Tokugawa Japan*. New Haven and London: Yale University Press, 2003.

——. "The Han." In *The Cambridge History of Japan: Early Modern Japan*, ed. John Whitney Hall, pp. 183-234. Vol. 4 of *The Cambridge History of Japan*. Cambridge, UK: Cambridge University Press, 1991.

——. "Metempsychosis Hijacked: The Curious Case of Katsugorō." *Harvard Journal of Asiatic Studies* 62, no. 2 (December 2002): 389-414.

Boot, W. J. "The Death of a Shogun: Deification in Early Modern Japan." In *Shinto in History: Ways of the Kami*, ed. John Breen and Mark Teeuwen, pp. 144-66. Honolulu: University of Hawai'i Press, 2000.

Boxer, C. R. *The Christian Century in Japan, 1549-1650*. Berkeley and Los Angeles: University of California Press, 1951.

Breen, John. "Beyond the Prohibition: Christianity in Restoration Japan." In *Japan and Christianity: Impacts and Responses*, ed. John Breen and Mark Williams, pp. 75-93. London: Macmillan Press, 1996.

——. "Heretics in Nagasaki: 1790-1796." In *Contemporary European Writing on Japan: Scholarly Views from Eastern and Western Europe*, ed. Ian Nish, pp. 10-16. Woodchurch, Ashford, Kent, UK: Paul Norbury Publications, 1988.

British Archival Material. F. O. 46-124. No. 6. Parkes to Clarendon. Jan. 22, 1870. Encl. 12.

British Archival Material, F. O. 46-143. No. 127. Adams to Granville. Dec. 12, 1871. Encl. 12.

Buke genseiroku 武家厳制録. In *Kinsei hōsei shiryō sōsho* 近世法制史料叢書, vol. 3, ed. Ishii Ryōsuke 石井良助, pp. 1–256. Tokyo: Sōbunsha, 1941.

Burkman, Thomas W. "The Urakami Incidents and the Struggle for Religious Toleration in Early Meiji Japan." *Japanese Journal of Religious Studies* 1, nos. 2–3 (June–September 1974): 143–216.

Butler, Lee A. "Tokugawa Ieyasu's Regulations for the Court: A Reappraisal." *Harvard Journal of Asiatic Studies* 54, no. 2 (December 1994): 509–51.

Buyō Inshi 武陽隠士. *Seji kenbunroku* 世事見聞録 (1816). In *Nihon shomin seikatsu shiryō shūsei: kenbunki* 日本庶民生活史料集成 : 見聞記, ed. Harada Tomohiko 原田伴彦 et al., pp. 641–766. Vol. 8 of *Nihon shomin seikatsu shiryō shūsei*. Tokyo: San'ichi shobō, 1969.

Chan, Wing-tsit. *A Source Book in Chinese Philosophy*. Princeton: Princeton University Press, 1963.

Chen, Ivan, trans. *The Book of Filial Piety*. London: J. Murray, 1908.

Chiba Jōryū 千葉乗隆. "Seiji to Bukkyō" 政治と仏教. In *Nihon Bukkyōshi: kinseihen kindaihen* 日本仏教史 : 近世編近代編, ed. Tamamuro Taijō 圭室諦成, pp. 19–72. Kyoto: Hōzōkan, 1967.

———. *Shinshū kyōdan no soshiki to seido* 真宗教団の組織と制度. Kyoto: Dōhō-sha, 1978.

Chijiwa Itaru 千々和 到. "Chūsei minshū no ishiki to shisō" 中世民衆の意識と思想. In *Ikki: seikatsu, bunka, shisō* 一揆 : 生活・文化・思想, ed. Aoki Michio 青木美智男 et al., pp. 1–42. Vol. 4 of *Ikki*. Tokyo: Tōkyō daigaku shuppankai, 1981.

Cho Kwang 趙珖. "Chosŏnjo hyo insik ŭi kinŭng kwa kŭ chŏngae" 朝鮮朝孝認識의 機能과그 展開. *Han'guk sasang sahak* 韓國思想史學 10 (1998): 257–90.

Cieslik, Hubert. "Edo no daijunkyō" 江戸の大殉教. In *Kirishitan kenkyū* キリシタン研究, vol. 4, ed. Kirishitan bunka kenkyūkai キリシタン文化研究会, pp. 55–112. Tokyo: Yōyōsha, 1957.

Cieslik, Hubert. *Sekai o aruita Kirishitan* 世界を歩いた切支丹. Tokyo: Shunjū-sha, 1971.

Cieslik, Hubert and Ōta Yoshiko 太田淑子, eds. *Nihonshi shōhyakka: Kirishitan* 日本史小百科 : キリシタン. Tokyo: Tōkyōdō shuppan, 1999.

Cocks, Richard. *Diary of Richard Cocks, Cape-Merchant in the English Factory in Japan, 1615–1622, with Correspondence*. 2 vols. Ed. Edward Maunde Thompson. London: The Hakluyt Society, 1883.

Collcutt, Martin. "Buddhism: The Threat of Eradication." In *Japan in Transition: From Tokugawa to Meiji*, ed. Marius B. Jansen and Gilbert Rozman, pp. 143–67. Princeton: Princeton University Press, 1986.

Cooper, Michael. *They Came to Japan: An Anthology of European Reports on Japan, 1543–1640*. Berkeley and Los Angeles: University of California Press, 1965.

———. *Rodrigues the Interpreter: An Early Jesuit in Japan and China*. New York: Weatherhill, 1974.

Cousins, L. S. "Buddhism." In *A New Handbook of Living Religions*, ed. John R. Hinnells, pp. 369–444. Oxford: Blackwell Publishers, 1997.

Date Mitsuyoshi 伊達光美. *Nihon shūkyō seido shiryō ruijūkō* 日本宗教制度史料類聚考. Kyoto: Rinsen shoten, 1974.

Deuchler, Martina. "Neo-Confucianism in Action: Agnation and Ancestor Worship in Early Yi Korea." In *Religion and Ritual in Korean Society*, ed. Laurel Kendall and Griffin Dix, pp. 26–55. Berkeley: Institute of East Asian Studies, University of California at Berkeley, 1987.

———. *The Confucian Transformation of Korea: A Study of Society and Ideology*. Cambridge, MA: Council on East Asian Studies, Harvard University, 1992.

"Doarute Korea no shuki" ドアルテ・コレアの手記. In *Nagasaki kenshi shiryōhen* 長崎県史資料編, vol. 3, ed. Nagasaki kenshi hensan iinkai 長崎県史編纂委員会. Tokyo: Yoshikawa kōbunkan, 1966.

Donner, Neal and Daniel B. Stevenson. *The Great Calming and Contemplation: A Study and Annotated Translation of the First Chapter of Chih-i's Mo-ho chih-kuan*. Honolulu: University of Hawai'i Press, 1993.

Dore, Philip R. *Education in Tokugawa Japan*. Berkeley and Los Angeles: University of California Press, 1965.

Douglas, Mary. *Purity and Danger: An Analysis of the Concepts of Pollution and Taboo*. London: Routledge and Kegan Paul, 1966.

Dumoulin, Heinrich. "The Consciousness of Sin and the Practice of Repentance in Japanese Buddhism." *The Japan Missionary Bulletin* 29, no. 2 (March 1985): 84–92.

Durt, Hubert. *Problems of Chronology and Eschatology: Four Lectures on the Essay on Buddhism by Tominaga Nakamoto (1715–1746)*. Kyoto: Istituto Italiano di Cultura Scuola di Studi sull'Asia Orientale, 1994.

Ebersole, Gary L. *Ritual Poetry and the Politics of Death in Early Japan*. Princeton: Princeton University Press, 1989.

Ebisawa Arimichi 海老沢有道. *Amakusa Shirō* 天草四郎. Tokyo: Jinbutsu ōraisha, 1967.

———. *Ishin henkakuki to Kirisutokyō* 維新変革期とキリスト教. Tokyo: Shinseisha, 1968.

———. *Takayama Ukon* 高山右近. Tokyo: Yoshikawa kōbunkan, 1958.

———. "Yamato Kōriyamahan ni okeru ko-Kirishitan to ruizoku shirabe" 大和郡山藩における古切支丹と類族調べ. *Seishin joshi daigaku ronsō* 聖心女子大学論叢, no. 26 (March 1966): 63–102.

———, comp. *Christianity in Japan: A Bibliography of Japanese and Chinese Sources, Part I (1543–1858)*. Tokyo: Committee on Asian Cultural Studies, International Christian University, 1960.

Ebisawa Arimichi et al. *Kirishitan sho, hai Yasho* キリシタン書・排耶書. Tokyo: Iwanami shoten, 1970.

Ebrey, Patricia Buckley. *Chu Hsi's Family Rituals: A Twelfth-Century Chinese Manual for the Performance of Cappings, Weddings, Funerals, and Ancestral Rites*. Princeton: Princeton University Press, 1991.

———. *Confucianism and Family Rituals in Imperial China: A Social History of Writing about Rites*. Princeton: Princeton University Press, 1991.

Edo machibure shūsei 江戸町触集成, 19 vols. Ed. Kinsei shiryō kenkyūkai 近世史料研究会. Tokyo: Hanawa shobō, 1994–2003.

Ekū 慧空. "Sōrinshū" 叢林集 (1698). In *Shinshū shiryō shūsei: jishi, iseki* 真宗 史料集成：寺誌・遺跡, ed. Hosokawa Gyōshin 細川行信, pp. 45–341. Vol. 8 of *Shinshū shiryō shūsei*. Kyoto: Dōhōsha, 1974.

Elisonas, Jurgis. "Christianity and the Daimyo." In *The Cambridge History of Japan: Early Modern Japan*, ed. John Whitney Hall, pp. 301–72. Vol. 4 of *The Cambridge History of Japan*. Cambridge, UK: Cambridge University Press, 1991.

Elison, George. *Deus Destroyed: The Image of Christianity in Early Modern Japan.* Cambridge, MA: Harvard University Press, 1973.

Endō Hiroaki 遠藤広昭. "Ōbakuha Edo hakkaan no koseki narabi gomen to sono kinō: Fukagawa no Ōbakuha jiin o jirei toshite" 黄檗派江戸八ヵ庵の 古跡並御免とその機能：深川の黄檗派寺院を事例として. *Kōtōku bunkazai kenkyū kiyō* 江東区文化財研究紀要, no. 1 (1990): 3–35.

Endō Jun 遠藤潤. "'The Shinto Funeral Movement' in Early Modern and Modern Japan." Trans. Norman Havens. *Kokugakuin daigaku Nihon bunka kenkyūjo kiyō* 國學院大學日本文化研究所紀要, no. 82 (September 1998): 282–312.

Endō Motoo 遠藤元男 and Yamanaka Yutaka 山中裕, eds. *Nenchū gyōji no rekishigaku* 年中行事の歴史学. Tokyo: Kōbundō, 1981.

Endō Shūsaku 遠藤周作. *Kirishitan jidai: junkyō to kikyō no rekishi* 切支丹 時代：殉教と棄教の歴史. Tokyo: Shōgakukan, 1992.

Faure, Bernard. *The Power of Denial: Buddhism, Purity, and Gender.* Princeton: Princeton University Press, 2003.

——. *The Rhetoric of Immediacy: A Cultural Critique of Chan/Zen Buddhism.* Princeton: Princeton University Press, 1991.

Fujii Jōji 藤井讓治. "Jūnana seiki no Nihon: buke no kokka no keisei" 十七 世紀の日本：武家の国家の形成. In *Iwanami kōza Nihon tsūshi: kinsei 2* 岩波 講座日本通史：近世 2, ed. Asao Naohiro 朝尾直弘 et al., pp. 1–64. Vol. 12 of *Iwanami kōza Nihon tsūshi*. Tokyo: Iwanami Shoten, 1994.

——. *Edo kaibaku* 江戸の開幕. Vol. 12 of *Nihon no rekishi* 日本の歴史. Tokyo: Shūeisha, 1992.

Fujii Manabu 藤井学. "Edo bakufu no shūkyō tōsei" 江戸幕府の宗教統制. In *Iwanami kōza Nihon rekishi: kinsei 3* 岩波講座 日本歴史：近世 3, ed. Ienaga Saburō 家永三郎 et al., pp. 133–70. Vol. 11 of *Iwanami kōza Nihon rekishi*. Tokyo: Iwanami shoten, 1963.

——. "Kinsei Bukkyō no tokushoku" 近世仏教の特色. In *Nihon shisō taikei: kinsei Bukkyō no shisō* 日本思想大系：近世仏教の思想, ed. Kashiwahara Yūsen 柏原祐泉 and Fujii Manabu, pp. 574–86. Vol. 57 of *Nihon shisō taikei*. Tokyo: Iwanami shoten, 1973.

Fujii Masao 藤井正雄. "Bukkyō no girei no kōzō hikaku: toku ni tsūjō hōyō to Bon segaki gyōji o megutte" 仏教の儀礼の構造比較：特に通常法要と盆 施餓鬼行事をめぐって. In *Nihon saishi kenkyū shūsei: matsuri no kigen to ten-kai* 日本祭祀研究集成：祭の起源と展開, ed. Kurahayashi Shōji 倉林正次, pp. 341–82. Vol. 1 of *Nihon saishi kenkyū shūsei*. Tokyo: Meicho shuppan, 1978.

——. *Bukkyō no girei* 仏教の儀礼. Tokyo: Tokyo shoseki, 1983.

——. "Jōdoshū no sōgi" Part 2 of "Shūkyō, shūhabetsu no sōgi no kenkyū" 浄土宗の葬儀：宗教・宗派別の葬儀の研究. *Sogi* 3, no. 1 (January 1993): 21–29.

——. "Muenbotoke kō" 無縁仏考. In *Nihon minzokugaku* 日本民俗学, no. 74 (March 1971): 55–61.

——. "Nihonjin no senzo kuyōkan no tenkai" 日本人の先祖供養観の展開. In *Bukkyō minzokugaku taikei: sosen saishi to sōbo* 仏教民俗学大系：祖先祭祀と葬墓, ed. Fujii Masao 藤井正雄, pp. 89–106. Vol. 4 of *Bukkyō minzokugaku taikei*. Tokyo: Meicho shuppan, 1988.

——, ed. *Bukkyō girei jiten* 仏教儀礼辞典. Tokyo: Tōkyōdō shuppan, 1977.

Fujii Masao et al. *Bukkyō sōsai daijiten* 仏教葬祭大事典. Tokyo: Yūzankaku shuppan, 1988.

Fujiki Hisashi 藤木久志. *Mura to ryōshu no sengoku sekai* 村と領主の戦国世界. Tokyo: Tōkyō daigaku shuppankai, 1997.

Fujiokaya nikki 藤岡屋日記, vol. 5. Ed. Suzuki Tōzō 鈴木棠三 and Koike Shōtarō 小池章太郎. Tokyo: San'ichi shobō, 1989.

Fujita, Neil S. *Japan's Encounter with Christianity: The Catholic Mission in Premodern Japan*. New York: Paulist Press, 1991.

Fujita Satoru 藤田覚. "Jūkyū seiki zenhan no Nihon: kokumin kokka keisei no zentei" 十九世紀前半の日本：国民国家形成の前提. In *Iwanami kōza Nihon tsūshi: kinsei 5* 岩波講座日本通史：近世5, ed. Asao Naohiro 朝尾直弘 et al., pp. 1–67. Vol. 15 of *Iwanami kōza Nihon tsūshi*. Tokyo: Iwanami shoten, 1995.

——. "Kan'ei kikin to bakusei (1)" 寛永飢饉と幕政（一）. *Rekishi* 歴史, no. 59 (1982): 38–54.

——. "Kan'ei kikin to bakusei (2)" 寛永飢饉と幕政（二）. *Rekishi* 歴史, no. 60 (1983): 39–59.

——. *Kinsei seijishi to tennō* 近世政治史と天皇. Tokyo: Yoshikawa kōbunkan, 1999.

——. *Tenpō no kaikaku* 天保の改革. Tokyo: Yoshikawa kōbunkan, 1989.

Fujiwara Arikazu 藤原有和. "Shiryō Sesshū Higashinarigun Tennōjimura korobi Kirishitan ruizoku shōshi aratemechō no kenkyū (1)" 史料摂州東成郡天王寺村転切支丹類族生死改帳の研究(1). *Kansai daigaku jinken mondai kenkyūshitsu kiyō* 関西大学人権問題研究室紀要 49 (August 2004): 49–94.

Fukaya Katsumi 深谷克己. *Hyakushō ikki no rekishiteki kōzō* 百姓一揆の歴史的構造. Tokyo: Azekura shobō, 1986.

——. "Jūhasseiki kōhan no Nihon: yokansareru kindai" 十八世紀後半の日本：予感される近代. In *Iwanami kōza Nihon tsūshi: kinsei 4* 岩波講座日本通史：近世4, ed. Asao Naohiro 朝尾直弘 et al., pp. 1–65. Vol. 14 of *Iwanami kōza Nihon tsūshi*. Tokyo: Iwanami shoten, 1995.

——. *Taikei Nihon no rekishi: shinōkōshō no yo* 大系日本の歴史：士農工商の世. Vol. 9 of *Taikei Nihon no rekishi*. Tokyo: Shōgakukan, 1988.

Fukuishi 福井市, ed. *Fukui shishi shiryōhen: kinsei 7* 福井市史 資料編：近世七. Vol. 9 of *Fukui shishi shiryōhen*. Fukui: Fukuishi, 1994.

Fukuma Kōchō 福間光超. "Bakumatsu Ishinki no kokka to Bukkyō: toku ni shinzoku nitai no seiritsu katei" 幕末維新期の国家と仏教：とくに真俗二諦の成立過程. *Kinsei Bukkyō* 近世仏教 4, no. 2 (September 1979): 1–19.

Fukuta Ajio 福田アジオ. "Kinsei jidan seido to fukudanka" 近世寺壇制度と複壇家. In *Bukkyō minzokugaku taikei: tera to chiiki shakai* 仏教民俗学大系：寺と地域社会, ed. Togawa Anshō 戸川安章, pp. 49–66. Vol. 7 of *Bukkyō minzokugaku taikei*. Tokyo: Meicho shuppan, 1992.

———. *Tera, haka, senzo no minzokugaku* 寺・墓・先祖の民俗学. Tokyo: Ōkawa shobō, 2004.

Gamaike Seishi 蒲池勢至. "Monto mono shirazu: Shinshū no sōsō girei to datsuraku shita shūzoku" 門徒もの知らず：真宗の葬送儀礼と脱落した習俗. In *Tōkai minzoku sōsho: sōsō girei to soreikan* 東海民俗叢書：葬送儀礼と祖霊観, ed. Kamiya Sachio 神谷幸夫 and Saitō Takushi 斉藤卓志, pp. 19–36. Vol. 1 of *Tōkai minzoku sōsho*. Matsusaka, Mie: Hikari shuppan insatsu, 1993.

———. "'Mubosei' to Shinshū no bosei" 「無墓制」と真宗の墓制. *Kokuritsu rekishi minzoku hakubutsukan kenkyū hōkoku* 国立歴史民俗博物館研究報告 49 (March 1993): 209–36.

———. "Ryōbosei to tanbosei" 両墓制と単墓制. In *Kōza Nihon no minzokugaku: kami to reikon no minzoku* 講座日本の民俗学：神と霊魂の民俗, ed. Akata Mitsuo 赤田光男 and Komatsu Kazuhiko 小松和彦, pp. 216–30. Vol. 7 of *Kōza Nihon no minzokugaku*. Tokyo: Yūzankaku shuppan, 1997.

———. *Shinshū to minzoku shinkō* 真宗と民俗信仰. Tokyo: Yoshikawa kōbunkan, 1993.

Genchi 玄智. "Kōshinroku" 孝信録 (1774). In *Shinshū shiryō shūsei: kyōdan no seidoka* 真宗史料集成：教団の制度化, ed. Chiba Jōryū 千葉乗隆, pp. 441–636. Vol. 9 of *Shinshū shiryō shūsei*. Kyoto: Dōhōsha, 1976.

Gilday, Edmund T. "Bodies of Evidence: Imperial Funeral Rites and the Meiji Restoration." *Japanese Journal of Religious Studies* 27, nos. 3–4 (Fall 2000): 273–96.

Gifuken 岐阜県, ed. *Gifu kenshi: shiryōhen kinsei 9* 岐阜県史：史料編近世 9. Gifu: Gifuken, 1973.

Gōda Hirofumi 郷田洋文. "Irori to hi" いろりと火. In *Nihon minzokugaku taikei: Seikatsu to minzoku* 日本民俗学大系：生活と民俗, ed. Ōmachi Tokuzō 大間知篤三, pp. 189–218. Vol. 6 of *Nihon minzokugaku taikei*. Tokyo: Heibonsha, 1958.

Gofunai jisha bikō 御府内寺社備考. Reprinted in 7 vols. Tokyo: Meicho shuppan, 1987.

Gombrich, Richard. "'Merit Transference' in Sinhalese Buddhism: A Case Study of the Interaction between Doctrine and Practice." *History of Religions* 11, no. 2 (November 1971): 203–19.

Gonoi Takashi 五野井隆史. *Nihon Kirisutokyōshi* 日本キリスト教史. Tokyo: Yoshikawa kōbunkan, 1990.

Gorai Shigeru 五来重. *Shūkyō saijiki* 宗教歳時記. Tokyo: Kadokawa, 1982.

———. *Sō to kuyō* 葬と供養. Osaka: Tōhō shuppan, 1992.

Gotō Haruyoshi 五島敏芳. "Shūmon ninbetsu okurijō no seiritsu: hikkoshi jirei no kentō o chūshin ni" 宗門人別送り状の成立：引越事例の検討を中心に. *Shiryōkan kenkyū kiyō* 史料館研究紀要 33 (March 2002): 1–77.

Gotōke reijō 御当家令条. Comp. Fujiwara Chikanaga 藤原親長. In *Kinsei hōsei shiryō sōsho* 近世法制史料叢書, vol. 2, ed. Ishii Ryōsuke 石井良助, pp. 1–300. Tokyo: Sōbunsha, 1940.

Gotō Shigemi 後藤重巳. "Edoki no ie ishiki: yuigonsho yon ten kara" 江戸期の家意識：遺言書四点から. *Beppu daigaku kiyō* 別府大学紀要, no. 32 (January 1991): 33–43.

Grapard, Allan G. "The Shinto of Yoshida Kanetomo." *Monumenta Nipponica* 47, no. 1 (Spring 1992): 27–58.

———, trans. "Yuiitsu Shintō Myōbō Yōshū." By Yoshida Kanetomo. *Monumenta Nipponica* 47, no. 2 (Summer 1992): 137–61.

Groemer, Gerald. "A Short History of the Gannin: Popular Religious Performers in Tokugawa Japan." *Japanese Journal of Religious Studies* 27, nos. 1–2 (Spring 2000): 41–72.

Gunji Masakatsu 郡司正勝, annot. and ed. *Tōkaidō Yotsuya kaidan* 東海道四谷怪談. Tokyo: Shinchōsha, 1981.

Haga Noboru 芳賀登. "'Murahachibu' no shinjitsu" 「村八分」の真実. In *Shiryō ga kataru Edoki no shakai jissō hyakuwa* 史料が語る江戸期の社会実相 100 話, ed. Nihon fūzokushi gakkai 日本風俗史学会, pp. 235–37. Tokyo: Tsukubanesha, 1998.

———. *Sōgi no rekishi* 葬儀の歴史. Tokyo: Yūzankaku shuppan, 1980.

"Hai Kirishitan bun" 排吉利支丹文. In *Nihon shisō taikei: Kirishitansho hai Yasho* 日本思想体系：キリシタン書排耶書, annot. and ed. Ebisawa Arimichi 海老沢有道, pp. 419–21. Vol. 25 of *Nihon shisō taikei*. Tokyo: Iwanami shoten, 1970.

Haketa, Yoshito S. *Kūkai: Major Works*. New York: Columbia University Press, 1972.

Halford, Aubrey S. and Giovanna M. Halford. *The Kabuki Handbook: A Guide to Understanding and Appreciation, with Summaries of Favourite Plays, Explanatory Notes, and Illustrations*. Rutland, Vermont and Tokyo: Charles E. Tuttle Company, 1956.

Hall, John Whitney. "The Bakuhan System." In *The Cambridge History of Japan: Early Modern Japan*, ed. John Whitney Hall, pp. 128–82. Vol. 4 of *The Cambridge History of Japan*. Cambridge, UK: Cambridge University Press, 1991.

Hamano Kiyoshi 浜野潔. "Kinsei Kyōto ni okeru jinkō idō to jidan kankei" 近世京都における人口移動と寺檀関係. *Kyōtogakuen daigaku keizaigakubu ronshū* 京都学園大学経済学部論集 12, no. 2 (December 2002): 53–70.

Hanzawa Toshirō 半澤敏郎. *Seikatsu bunka saijishi* 生活文化歳事史, vol. 3. Tokyo: Tōkyō shoseki, 1990.

Hardacre, Helen. "Creating State Shintō: The Great Promulgation Campaign and the New Religions." *Journal of Japanese Studies* 12, no. 1 (1986): 29–63.

———. *Religion and Society in Nineteenth-Century Japan: A Study of the Southern Kantō Region, Using Late Edo and Early Meiji Gazetteers*. Ann Arbor: Center for Japanese Studies, University of Michigan, 2002.

——. *Shintō and the State, 1868–1988.* Princeton: Princeton University Press, 1989.

Harrington, Ann M. *Japan's Hidden Christians.* Chicago: Loyola University Press, 1993.

Harufuji Hiroshi 服藤弘司. *Bakuhan taisei kokka no hō to kenryoku ı: Bakufuhō to hanpō* 幕藩体制国家の法と権力 1：幕府法と藩法. Tokyo: Sōbunsha, 1980.

Hasegawa Masatoshi 長谷川匡俊. "Jōdoshū nenbutsusha no risōteki ningenzō: kōki" 浄土宗念仏者の理想的人間像：後期. In *Kinsei ōjōden no sekai* 近世往生伝の世界, ed. Kasahara Kazuo 笠原一男, pp. 107–74. Tokyo: Kyōikusha, 1978.

Hattori Yukio 服部幸雄. *Hengeron: kabuki no seishinshi* 変化論：歌舞伎の精神史. Tokyo: Heibonsha, 1975.

Hayami Akira 速水融. *Rekishi jinkōgaku de mita Nihon* 歴史人口学で見た日本. Tokyo: Bungei shunjū, 2001.

——. *Rekishi jinkōgaku no sekai* 歴史人口学の世界. Tokyo: Iwanami shoten, 1997.

Hayashi Fukusai 林復斎. *Tsūkō ichiran* 通航一覧 (1853). Reprinted in 8 vols. Tokyo: Kokusho kankōkai, 1912–13.

Hayashi Masahiko 林雅彦. "Kumano bikuni to etoki" 熊野比丘尼と絵解き. In *Bukkyō minzokugaku taikei: hijiri to minshū* 仏教民俗学大系：聖と民衆, ed. Hagiwara Tatsuo 萩原龍夫 and Shinno Toshikazu 真野俊和, pp. 309–30. Vol. 2 of *Bukkyō minzokugaku taikei.* Tokyo: Meicho shuppan, 1986.

Hayashi Reiko 林玲子. *Edodana hankachō* 江戸店犯科帳. Tokyo: Yoshikawa kōbunkan, 1982.

——. *Nihon no kinsei: shōnin no katsudō* 日本の近世：商人の活動. Vol. 5 of *Nihon no kinsei.* Tokyo: Chūō kōronsha, 1992.

Hayashi Yukiko 林由紀子. "Edo bakufu bukkirei no igi to tokushitsu" 江戸幕府服忌令の意義と特質. In *Kazoku to shisha saishi* 家族と死者祭祀, ed. Kōmoto Mitsugi 孝本貢 and Yagi Tōru 八木透, pp. 69–128. Tokyo: Waseda daigaku shuppanbu, 1997.

——. *Kinsei bukkiryō no kenkyū: bakuhansei kokka no mo to kegare* 近世服忌令の研究：幕藩制国家の喪と穢. Osaka: Seibundō shuppan, 1998.

Higashibaba, Ikuo. *Christianity in Early Modern Japan: Kirishitan Belief and Practice.* Leiden: Brill, 2001.

Hiraide Kōjirō 平出鏗次郎. *Tōkyō fūzokushi* 東京風俗志 (1902). Reprinted in 3 vols. Tokyo: Nihon tosho sentā, 1983.

Hiramatsu Yoshirō 平松義郎. *Kinsei hōsei shiryōshū* 近世法制史料集, vol. 1. Tokyo: Sōbunsha, 1973.

Hirata Atsutane 平田篤胤. *Shutsujō shōgo* 出定笑語. In *Nihon shisō tōsō shiryō* 日本思想闘争史料, vol. 8, ed. Washio Junkyō 鷲尾順敬, pp. 1–299. Tokyo: Meicho kankōkai, 1969.

Hirayama Toshijirō 平山敏治朗. "Kamidana to butsudan" 神棚と仏壇. In *Sōsō bosei kenkyū shūsei: senzo kuyō* 葬送墓制研究集成：先祖供養, ed. Takeda Chōshū 竹田聴洲, pp. 204–32. Vol. 3 of *Sōsō bosei kenkyū shūsei.* Tokyo: Meicho shuppan, 1979.

———. *Saiji shūzokukō* 歳時習俗考. Tokyo: Hōsei daigaku shuppankyoku, 1984.

Hirose Ryōkō 広瀬良弘. "Bakufu no tōsei to Eiheiji" 幕府の統制と永平寺. In *Eiheijishi* 永平寺史, 2 vols, ed. Eiheijishi hensan iinkai 永平寺史編纂委員会. Eiheijichō, Fukui: Eiheiji, 1982.

Hitaken shoshū honmatsu jigō sonota meisaichō 日田県諸宗本末寺号其外明細帳 (1871, unprinted).

Hōjō Ujinaga 北条 氏長, ed. *Kirishitoki* (Kanbun era, 1652–62) 契利斯督記. In *Zokuzoku gunsho ruijū: shūkyōbu* 続々群書類従：宗教部, ed. Ichijima Kenkichi 市島謙吉, pp. 626–68. Vol. 12 of *Zokuzoku gunsho ruijū*. Tokyo: Kokusho kankōkai, 1907.

Honda Takashige 本多隆成. "Tenka tōitsu" 天下統一. In *Komonjo no kataru Nihonshi: Sengoku, Shokuhō* 古文書の語る日本史：戦国・織豊, ed. Minegishi Sumio 峰岸純夫, pp. 345–98. Vol. 5 of *Komonjo no kataru Nihonshi*. Tokyo: Chikuma shobō, 1989.

"Hōnen zeisho" 豊年税書 (1685). In *Nihon keizai taiten* 日本経済大典, vol. 3, pp. 687–749. Tokyo: Keimeisha, 1928.

Hōrei zensho 法令全書 (3/1867–12/1868). Compiled by Naikaku kanpōkyoku 内閣官報局. Tokyo: Hara shobō, 1974.

Hori Ichirō 堀一郎. *Hori Ichirō chosakushū: kodai bunka to Bukkyō* 堀一郎著作集：古代文化と仏教. Vol. 1 of *Hori Ichirō chosakushū*. Tokyo: Miraisha, 1977.

Hosotani Yoshiaki 細谷義秋. "Kirishitan denrai to sono seisaku ni tsuite: Toyotomi Hideyoshi no kinkyōrei happu made" キリシタン伝来とその政策について：豊臣秀吉の禁教令発布まで. *Nihon shigaku kyōiku kenkyūjo kiyō: kyōiku, keieihen* 日本私学教育研究所紀要：教育・経営編 19, no. 1 (1983): 257–87.

Hōzawa Naohide 朴澤直秀. "Bakuhan kenryoku to jidan kankei: ikka ichijisei o megutte" 幕藩権力と寺檀関係：一家一寺制をめぐって. *Shigaku zasshi* 史学雑誌 110, no. 4 (April 2001): 523–62.

———. *Bakuhan kenryoku to jidan seido* 幕藩権力と寺檀制度. Tokyo: Yoshikawa kōbunkan, 2004.

Hozumi Yatsuka 穂積八束. "Minpō idete chūkō horobu" 民法出でて忠孝亡ぶ. In *Nihon kindai shisō taikei: ie to mura* 日本近代思想体系：家と村, ed. Unno Fukuju 海野福寿 and Ōshima Mitsuko 大島美津子, pp. 391–94. Vol. 20 of *Nihon kindai shisō taikei*. Tokyo: Iwanami shoten, 1989.

Hugh-Jones, Stephen and James Laidlaw, eds. *The Essential Edmund Leach*. 2 vols. New Haven: Yale University Press, 2000.

Hur, Nam-lin. *Prayer and Play in Late Tokugawa Japan: Asakusa Sensōji and Edo Society*. Cambridge, MA: Harvard University Asia Center, 2000.

Hurvitz, Leon, trans. *Scripture of the Lotus Blossom of the Fine Dharma*. New York: Columbia University Press, 1976.

Ichikawa Hideyuki 市川秀之. "Senzo daidai no haka no seiritsu" 先祖代々之墓の成立. *Nihon minzokugaku* 日本民俗学, no. 230 (May 2002): 1–26.

Ichikawa shishi, dairokukan (jō) 市川市史第六巻(上). Ed. Ichikawashi shishi hensan iinkai 市川市史編纂委員会. Tokyo: Yoshikawa kōbunkan, 1972.

Ichimura Kisaburō 市村其三郎. "Shinsōsai mondai to sono hatten" 神葬祭問題とその発展. *Shigaku zasshi* 史学雑誌 41, no. 9 (September 1930): 70–85.

Ichioka Masakazu 市岡正一. *Tokugawa seiseiroku* 德川盛世録. Tokyo: Heibonsha, 1989.

Iechika Yoshiki 家近良樹. *Urakami Kirishitan ruhai jiken: Kirisutokyō kaikin e no michi* 浦上キリシタン流配事件：キリスト教解禁への道. Tokyo: Yoshikawa kōbunkan, 1998.

Ikedake rireki ryakki 池田家履歴略記 (Kansei era 1789–1800?). 2 vols., ed. Saitō Ikkō 斎藤一興. Okayama: Nihon bunkyō shuppan, 1963.

Ikeda Mitsumasa 池田光政. *Ikeda Mitsumasa nikki* 池田光政日記. Ed. Fujii Shun 藤井駿, Mizuno Kyōichirō 水野恭一郎, and Taniguchi Sumio 谷口澄夫. Tokyo: Kokusho kankōkai, 1983.

Ikegami Akihiko 池上彰彦. "Kōki Edo kasō chōnin no seikatsu" 後期江戸下層町人の生活. In *Edo chōnin no kenkyū* 江戸町人の研究, vol. 2, ed. Nishiyama Matsunosuke 西山松之助, pp. 139–226. Tokyo: Yoshikawa kōbunkan, 1973.

———. "Edo hikeshi seido no seiritsu to tenkai" 江戸火消制度の成立と展開. In *Edo chōnin no kenkyū* 江戸町人の研究, vol. 5, ed. Nishiyama Matsunosuke 西山松之助, pp. 91–169. Tokyo: Yoshikawa kōbunkan, 1978.

Inoguchi Shōji 井之口章次. *Bukkyō izen* 仏教以前. Tokyo: Kokon shoin, 1954.

Inoue Nobutaka 井上順孝. *Kyōha Shintō no keisei* 教派神道の形成. Tokyo: Kōbundō, 1991.

Inoue Tomokatsu 井上智勝. "Toshi no shōshi shōsha o meguru shomondai: shūkyō seisaku to no kakawari o chūshin ni" 都市の小祠小社をめぐる諸問題：宗教政策との関わりを中心に. *Nenpō toshishi kenkyū* 年報都市史研究 6 (1998): 19–28.

Irie Hiroshi 入江宏. *Kinsei shomin kakun no kenkyū: 'ie' no keiei to kyōiku* 近世庶民家訓の研究：「家」の経営と教育. Tokyo: Taga shuppan, 1996.

Irokawa Daikichi 色川大吉. "Tennōsei ideorogī to minshū ishiki" 天皇制イデオロギーと民衆意識. *Rekishigaku kenkyū* 歴史学研究, no. 341 (October 1968): 2–20.

Ise Sadatake 伊勢貞丈. "Sadatake kakun" 貞丈家訓 (1763). In *Nihon shisō taikei: kinsei buke shisō* 日本思想体系：近世武家思想, ed. Ishii Shirō 石井紫郎, pp. 85–103. Vol. 27 of *Nihon shisō taikei*. Tokyo: Iwanami shoten, 1974.

Ishida Mizumaro 石田瑞麿. *Bukkyō kyōtensen: minshū kyōten* 仏教経典選：民衆経典. Vol. 12 of *Bukkyō kyōtensen*. Tokyo: Chikuma shobō, 1986.

Ishige Tadashi 石毛忠. "Shisōshijō no Hideyoshi" 思想史上の秀吉. In *Toyotomi Hideyoshi no subete* 豊臣秀吉のすべて, ed. Kuwata Tadachika 桑田忠親, pp. 175–213. Tokyo: Shinjinbutsu ōraisha, 1981.

Ishii Ryōsuke 石井良助, ed. *Oshioki reiruishū koruishū* 御仕置例類集古類集, vols. 3–4. Tokyo: Meicho shuppan, 1971.

Isoda Michifumi 磯田道史. *Bushi no kakeibo: "Kagahan osan'yōmono" no bakumatsu ishin* 武士の家計簿：「加賀藩御算用者」の幕末維新. Tokyo: Shinchōsha, 2003.

Itō Mikiharu 伊藤幹治. *Kazoku kokkakan no jinruigaku* 家族国家観の人類学. Kyoto: Mineruva shobō, 1982.

———. "Sosen sūhai to ie" 祖先崇拝と家. In *Sorei shinkō* 祖霊信仰, ed. Akata Mitsuo 赤田光男, pp. 371-85. Tokyo: Yūzankaku shuppan, 1991.

Itō Takeshi 伊藤毅. "Edo jiin e no shikaku: kinsei no kyodai toshi to jiin" 江戸寺院への視角：近世の巨大都市と寺院. *Nenpō toshishi kenkyū* 年報都市史研究 3 (1995): 13-21.

Iwahashi Masaru 岩橋勝. *Kinsei Nihon bukkashi no kenkyū* 近世日本物価史の研究. Tokyo: Ōhara shinseisha, 1981.

Iwasaki Takeo 岩崎武夫. "Tennōji Nishimon kō: Shintokumaru denshō to ba no mondai o megutte" 天王寺西門考：しんとく丸伝承と場の問題をめぐって. In *Bukkyō minzokugaku taikei: seichi to takaikan* 仏教民俗大系：聖地と他界観, ed. Sakurai Tokutarō 桜井徳太郎, pp. 173-87. Vol. 3 of *Bukkyō minzokugaku taikei*. Tokyo: Meicho shuppan, 1987.

Izu no kuni honmatsu jigō sonota meisaichō 伊豆国本末寺号其外明細帳 (1871, unprinted).

Jaffe, Richard M. *Neither Monk Nor Layman: Clerical Marriage in Modern Japanese Buddhism*. Princeton: Princeton University Press, 2001.

"Jingi seishū" 神祇正宗. In *Zoku gunsho ruijū* 続群書類従, vol. 3, no. 1, pp. 58-69. Tokyo: Zoku gunsho ruijū kanseikai, 1932.

Jinja honchō kyōgaku kenkyūjo 神社本庁教学研究所, ed. "Kyōdō kenkyū 'shinsōsai no jittai chōsa' hōkoku" 共同研究「神葬祭の実態調査」報告. *Jinja honchō kyōgaku kenkyūjo kiyō* 神社本庁教学研究所紀要, no. 4 (February 1999): 193-238.

Jishōin iseki chōsadan 自証院遺跡調査団, ed. *Jishōin iseki: Shinjuku kuritsu Tomihisa Shōgakkō kaichiku ni tomonau kinkyū hakkutsu chōsa hōkokusho* 自証院遺跡：新宿区立富久小学校改築に伴う緊急発掘調査報告書. Tokyo: Tōkyōto Shinjukuku kyōiku inkai, 1987.

Johannes, Laures. "Hosokawake no Kirishitan" 細川家のキリシタン. In *Kirishitan kenkyū* キリシタン研究, vol. 4, ed. Kirishitan bunka kenkyūkai キリシタン文化研究会, pp. 19-54. Tokyo: Yōyōsha, 1957.

Jordan, Glenn and Chris Weedon. *Cultural Politics: Class, Gender, Race and the Postmodern World*. Oxford: Blackwell, 1995.

Kadomae Hiroyuki 門前博之. "Nihon kinsei ni okeru sōsei: Shimōsa no kuni Sashimagun Yama, Kutsukake ryōson ni miru" 日本近世における葬制：下総国猿島郡山・沓掛両村にみる. *Sundai shigaku* 駿台史学, no. 93 (January 1995): 150-82.

Kaempfer, Engelbert. *Kaempfer's Japan: Tokugawa Japan Observed*. Ed., trans., and annot. Beatrice M. Bodart-Bailey. Honolulu: University of Hawai'i Press, 1999.

Kagawa Haruyoshi 加川治良. *Bōsō kinsei shūmonshi* 房総禁制宗門史. Tokyo: Kokusho kankōkai, 1977.

Kajiyama Yūichi 梶山雄一. *'Satori' to 'ekō': daijō Bukkyō no seiritsu*「さとり」と「回向」：大乗仏教の成立. Tokyo: Kōdansha, 1983.

Kakudaken shoshū honmatsu jigō sonota meisaichō 角田県諸宗本末寺号其外明細帳 (1871, unprinted).

Works Cited

Kamiokachō 神岡町 ed. *Kamioka chōshi: shiryōhen bekkan* 神岡町史：資料編・別巻. Kamiokachō, Gifu: Kamiokachō, 1980.

Kamishima Jirō 神島二郎 and Itō Mikiharu 伊藤幹治, eds. *Yanagita Kunio: shinpojiumu* 柳田国男：シンポジウム. Tokyo: Nihon hōsō shuppan kyōkai, 1973.

Kanda Hideo 神田秀雄. "Kinsei kōki ni okeru kyūsai no ba" 近世後期における救済の場. *Edo no shisō* 江戸の思想, no. 1 (June 1995): 73-100.

Kan'ei nikki 寛永日記. (unprinted).

Kankoku kōgiroku 官刻孝義録, 3 vols. Annot. Sugano Noriko 菅野則子. Tokyo: Tōkyōdō shuppan, 1999.

Kanzaki Akitoshi 神崎彰利. "Tenpō gonen kokugun kokudakahyō" 天保五年国郡石高表. In *Nihonshi sōran: kinsei* 日本史総覧：近世, pp. 496-508. Vol. 4 of *Nihonshi sōran*. Tokyo: Shinjinbutsu ōraisha, 1984.

Kanzaki Issaku 神崎一作. "Kyōha Shintō" 教派神道. In *Shintō kōza: Shintōhen* 神道講座：神道篇, pp. 221-311. Vol. 2 of *Shintō kōza*. Tokyo: Hara shobō, 1981.

Kasahara Kazuo 笠原一男, ed. *Kinsei ōjōden shūsei* 近世往生伝集成, vol. 2. Tokyo: Yamakawa shuppansha, 1979.

Kasaya Kazuhiko 笠谷和比古. *Shukun 'oshikome' no kōzō: kinsei daimyō to kashindan* 主君「押込」の構造：近世大名と家臣団. Tokyo: Heibonsha, 1988.

Kashiwahara Yūsen 柏原祐泉. "Bukkyō shisō no tenkai" 仏教思想の展開. In *Nihon Bukkyōshi: kinsei, kindaihen* 日本仏教史：近世・近代篇, ed. Tamamuro Taijō 圭室諦成, pp. 73-168. Vol. 3 of *Nihon Bukkyōshi*. Kyoto: Hōzōkan, 1967.

———. "Gohō shisō to shomin kyōka" 護法思想と庶民教化. In *Nihon shisō taikei: kinsei Bukkyō no shisō* 日本思想大系：近世仏教の思想, ed. Kashiwahara Yūsen and Fujii Manabu 藤井学, pp. 533-58. Vol. 57 of *Nihon shisō taikei*. Tokyo: Iwanami shoten, 1973.

———. "Kinsei no haibutsu shisō" 近世の排仏思想. In *Nihon shisō taikei: kinsei Bukkyō no shisō* 日本思想大系：近世仏教の思想, ed. Kashiwahara Yūsen and Fujii Manabu 藤井学, pp. 517-32. Vol. 57 of *Nihon shisō taikei*. Tokyo: Iwanami shoten, 1973.

———. *Nihon Bukkyōshi: kindai* 日本仏教史：近代. Tokyo: Yoshikawa kōbunkan, 1990.

Kashiwahara Yūsen and Ōmine Akira 大峯顕. *Jōdo Bukkyō no shisō: Myōkōnin, Ryōkan, Issa* 浄土仏教の思想：妙好人、良寛、一茶. Vol. 13 of *Jōdo Bukkyō no shisō*. Tokyo: Kōdansha, 1992.

Kataoka Yakichi 片岡弥吉. *Nihon Kirishitan junkyōshi* 日本キリシタン殉教史. Tokyo: Jiji tsūshinsha, 1979.

———. "Ōmurahan kōri kuzure ikken kaidai" 大村藩郡崩れ一件解題. In *Nihon shomin seikatsu shiryō shūsei: minkan shūkyō* 日本庶民生活史料集成：民間宗教, ed. Tanigawa Ken'ichi 谷川健一, pp. 709-59. Vol. 18 of *Nihon shomin seikatsu shiryō shūsei*. Tokyo: San'ichi shobō, 1972.

———, ed. "Hijō nikki" 非常日記. In *Nihon shomin seikatsu shiryō shūsei: minkan shūkyō* 日本庶民生活史料集成：民間宗教, ed. Tanigawa Ken'ichi 谷川

健一, pp. 893–900. Vol. 18 of *Nihon shomin seikatsu shiryō shūsei*. Tokyo: San'ichi shobō, 1972.

Katō Takahisa 加藤隆久. "Tsuwanohan no shinsōsai fukkō undō to shinrei kenkyū" 津和野藩の神葬祭復興運動と心霊研究. In *Shinsōsai daijiten* 神葬祭大事典, ed. Katō Takahisa, pp. 381–99. Tokyo: Ebisu kōshō shuppan, 1997.

Katsuda Itaru 勝田至. "Chūsei minshū no sōsei to shie: toku ni shitai iki ni tsuite" 中世民衆の葬制と死穢：特に死体遺棄について. *Shirin* 史林 70, no. 3 (March 1987): 34–68.

————. *Shisha tachi no chūsei* 死者たちの中世. Tokyo: Yoshikawa kōbunkan, 2003.

Katsu Kaishū 勝海舟. *Kaikoku kigen* 開国起原. 3 vols. Tokyo: Kunaishō, 1893.

Kawamura Minato 川村湊. "Kasane to Oiwa" 累とお岩. In *Ōedo mandara* 大江戸曼陀羅, ed. Asahi jānaru 朝日ジャーナル, pp. 379–85. Tokyo: Asahi shinbunsha, 1995.

Kenney, Elizabeth. "Shinto Funerals in the Edo Period." *Japanese Journal of Religious Studies* 27, nos. 3–4 (Fall 2000): 239–71.

Ketelaar, James Edward. *Of Heretics and Martyrs in Meiji Japan: Buddhism and Its Persecution*. Princeton: Princeton University Press, 1990.

Keyes, Charles F. "Merit-Transference in the Kammic Theory of Popular Theravāda Buddhism." In *Karma: An Anthropological Inquiry*, ed. Charles F. Keyes and E. Valentine Daniel, pp. 261–86. Berkeley and Los Angeles: University of California Press, 1983.

Kibi gunshi (gekan) 吉備郡史(下巻). Ed. Nagayama Usaburō 永山卯三郎. Tokyo: Meicho shuppan, 1975.

Kikuchi Kiichirō 菊池貴一郎. *Ehon Edo fūzoku ōrai* 絵本江戸風俗往来. Tokyo: Heibonsha, 1965.

Kikuchi Seiichi 菊池誠一. "Akagi jinja shake no shinsōsai no jittai: Kanseiki o chūshin toshite" 赤城神社社家の神葬祭の実態：寛政期を中心として. In *Minshū shūkyō no kōzō to keifu* 民衆宗教の構造と系譜, ed. Tamamuro Fumio 圭室文雄, pp. 540–66. Tokyo: Yūzankaku shuppan, 1995.

Kikuchi Takeshi 菊池武. "Kumano bikuni saikō: toku ni shōbikuni o megutte" 熊野比丘尼再考：特に小比丘尼をめぐって. *Sangaku Shugen* 山岳修験, no. 13 (March 1994): 47–57.

Kinoshita Futoshi 木下太志. *Kindaika izen no Nihon no jinkō to kazoku: ushinawareta sekai kara no tegami* 近代化以前の日本の人口と家族：失われた世界からの手紙. Kyoto: Mineruva shobō, 2002.

Kinryū Shizuka 金龍静. "Shūkyō ikkiron" 宗教一揆論. In *Iwanami kōza Nihon tsūshi: chūsei 4* 岩波講座日本通史：中世 4, ed. Asao Naohiro 朝尾直弘 et al., pp. 59–88. Vol. 10 of *Iwanami kōza Nihon tsūshi*. Tokyo: Iwanami shoten, 1994.

Kinugasa Yasuki 衣笠安喜. "Bakuhanseika no tennō to bakufu" 幕藩制下の天皇と幕府. In *Tennōsei to minshū* 天皇制と民衆, ed. Gotō Yasushi 後藤靖, pp. 79–109. Tokyo: Tōkyō daigaku shuppankai, 1976.

Kirishitan bunka kenkyūkai キリシタン文化研究会, ed. *Kirishitan kenkyū* キリシタン研究, vol. 17 (1977), 19 (1979), 23 (1983), and 28 (1988). Tokyo: Yoshikawa kōbunkan.

Kitagawa Morisada 喜田川守貞. *Morisada mankō* 守貞漫稿 (1867). Reprinted in 2 vols. Tokyo: Kokugakuin daigaku shuppanbu, 1908.

Kitahara Itoko 北原糸子. "Edo Tokyo jiin shōshi: Hasshōji o chūshin toshite" 江戸・東京寺院小史：發昌寺を中心として. In *Hasshōji ato: shadan hōjin kin'yū zaisei jijō kenkyūkai shinkan kensetsu ni tomonau dainiji kinkyū hakkutsu chōsa hōkokusho* 發昌寺跡：社団法人金融財政事情研究会新館建設に伴う第二次緊急発掘調査報告書, ed. Shinjukuku Minamimotochō iseki chōsakai 新宿区南元町遺跡調査会, pp. 94-123. Tokyo: Shinjukuku Minamimotochō iseki chōsakai, 1991.

——. "Kinsei kōkogaku ni nozomu mono" 近世考古学に望むもの. In *Edo no kurashi: kinsei kōkogaku no sekai* 江戸のくらし：近世考古学の世界, ed. Shinjuku kuritsu Shinjuku rekishi hakubutsukan 新宿区立新宿歴史博物館, pp. 103-18. Tokyo: Shinjukuku kyōiku iinkai, 1990.

Kōanji monjo 講安寺文書. Ed. Bunkyōku kyōiku iinkai shakai kyōikuka 文京区教育委員会社会教育課. Tokyo: Bunkyōku kyōiku inkai, 1979.

Kobayakawa Kingo 小早川欣吾. *Zōho kinsei minji soshō seido no kenkyū* 増補近世民事訴訟制度の研究 (1957). Reprint. Tokyo: Meicho fukyūkai, 1988.

Kobayashi Daiji 小林大二. *Sabetsu kaimyō no rekishi* 差別戒名の歴史. Tokyo: Yūzankaku shuppan, 1987.

Kodama Kōta 児玉幸多 ed. *Nihonshi sōran: kinsei* 日本史総覧：近世. Vol. 4 of *Nihonshi sōran*. Tokyo: Shinjinbutsu ōraisha, 1984.

Kodama Shiki 児玉識. *Kinsei Shinshū no tenkai katei: nishi Nihon o chūshin toshite* 近世真宗の展開過程：西日本を中心として. Tokyo: Yoshikawa kōbunkan, 1976.

Koizumi Hiroshi 小泉弘. *Edo o horu: kinsei toshi kōkogaku e no shōtai* 江戸を掘る：近世都市考古学への招待. Tokyo: Kashiwa shobō, 1990.

——. "Maisō keishiki" 埋葬形式. In *Zusetsu Edo kōkogaku kenkyū jiten* 図説江戸考古学研究事典, ed. Edo iseki kenkyūkai 江戸遺跡研究会, pp. 142-45. Tokyo: Kashiwa shobō, 2001.

Kokan Shiren 虎関師錬. *Genkyō shakusho* 元亨釈書. Reprinted in *Shintei zōho kokushi taikei* 新訂増補 国史大系, vol. 31, ed. Kuroita Katsumi 黒板勝美 and Kokushi taikei henshūkai 国史大系編修会. Tokyo: Yoshikawa kōbunkan, 1965.

Kokugakuin daigaku Nihon bunka kenkyūjo 國學院大學日本文化研究所, ed. *Shinsōsai shiryō shūsei* 神葬祭資料集成. Tokyo: Perikansha, 1995.

Komori Ryūkichi 小森隆吉. "Edo ni okeru jiingai no keisei ni tsuite: Shitaya, Asakusa no baai" 江戸における寺院街の形成について：下谷・浅草の場合. *Nihon rekishi* 日本歴史, no. 496 (September 1989): 89-98.

Kōmoto Mitsugi 孝本貢. "Butsudan to ihai saishi" 仏壇と位牌祭祀. In *Kōza Nihon no minzokugaku: Kami to reikon no minzoku* 講座日本の民俗学：神と霊魂の民俗, ed. Akata Mitsuo 赤田光男 and Komatsu Kazuhiko 小松和彦, pp. 105-18. Vol. 7 of *Kōza Nihon no minzokugaku*. Tokyo: Yūzankaku shuppan, 1997.

——. "Jiin to danka no soshiki" 寺院と壇家の組織. In *Kōza Nihon no minzoku shūkyō: minzoku shūkyō to shakai* 講座日本の民俗宗教：民俗宗教と社会, ed.

Gorai Shigeru 五来重, pp. 100–23. Vol. 5 of *Kōza Nihon no minzoku shūkyō*. Tokyo: Kōbundō, 1980.

"Kōmyō shingonhō" 光明真言法. In *Dai Nihon Bukkyō zensho* 大日本仏教全書, vol. 53, ed. Suzuki gakujutsu zaidan 鈴木学術財団, pp. 117–27. Tokyo: Kōdansha, 1972.

Kondō Keigo 近藤啓吾. "Bakumatsu ishin ni okeru shinsōsetsu to sono jikkō" 幕末維新における神葬説とその実行. *Shintōgaku* 神道学, nos. 146–47 (November 1990): 1–28.

Kōnoike Shinroku 鴻池新六. "Yukimoto shison seishi jōmoku" 幸元子孫制詞条目. In *Nihon shisō taikei: kinsei chōnin shisō* 日本思想大系：近世町人思想, ed. Nakamura Yukihiko 中村幸彦, pp. 383–88. Vol. 59 of *Nihon shisō taikei*. Tokyo: Iwanami shoten, 1975.

Konta Yōzō 今田洋三. *Edo no kinsho* 江戸の禁書. Tokyo: Yoshikawa kōbunkan, 1981.

Kudamatsu Kazunori 久田松和則. "Nagasaki machishū ni okeru Ise shinkō: Kirishitan no machi kara no dappi" 長崎町衆に於ける伊勢信仰：キリシタンの町からの脱皮. In *Kinsei Nihon no seiji to gaikō* 近世日本の政治と外交, ed. Fujino Tamotsu sensei kanreki kinenkai 藤野保先生還暦記念会, pp. 285–310. Tokyo: Yūzankaku shuppan, 1993.

Kumazawa Banzan 熊沢蕃山. *Daigaku wakumon* 大学或問 (1686). Reprinted in *Nihon shisō taikei: Kumazawa Banzan* 日本思想大系：熊沢蕃山, ed. Gotō Yōichi 後藤陽一 and Tomoeda Ryūtarō 友枝隆太郎, pp. 405–63. Vol. 30 of *Nihon shisō taikei*. Tokyo: Iwanami shoten, 1971.

Kurahayashi Shōji 倉林正次. Naorai bunkaron: tatsu no hi sechie, mi no hi sechie ni tsuite 直会文化論：辰日節会・巳日節会について. *Kokugakuin zasshi* 國學院雑誌 91, no. 7 (July 1990): 22–48.

Kurashikiken honmatsu jigō sonota meisaichō 倉敷県本末寺号其外明細帳 (1871, unprinted).

Kurashiki shishi 倉敷市史, vol. 8. Ed. Nagayama Usaburō 永山卯三郎. Tokyo: Meicho shuppan, 1973.

Kurimoto Joun 栗本鋤雲. *Hōan ikō* 鉋庵遺稿 (1900). Reprint in 2 vols., ed. Nihon shoseki kyōkai 日本書籍協会. Tokyo: Tōkyō daigaku shuppankai, 1975.

Kuroda Hideo 黒田日出男. *Ō no shintai ō no shōzō* 王の身体王の肖像. Tokyo: Heibonsha, 1993.

Kuroda Toshio 黒田俊雄. *Nihon chūsei no kokka to shūkyō* 日本中世の国家と宗教. Tokyo: Iwanami shoten, 1975.

———. *Nihon chūsei no shakai to shūkyō* 日本中世の社会と宗教. Tokyo: Iwanami shoten, 1990.

Kurokawa Hirokata 黒川弘賢. "Haibutsu kishaku ni okeru shinsōsaika no katei to genjō: Gunma kenka no jittai" 廃仏毀釈における神葬祭化の過程と現状：群馬県下の実態. *Shūkyō kenkyū* 宗教研究 34-3, no. 166 (January 1961): 36–37.

———. "Shinbutsu bunri ikō ni okeru shinsōsai to Bukkyō minzoku" 神仏分離以降における神葬祭と仏教民俗. In *Bukkyō minzokugaku taikei: sosen saishi to sōbo* 仏教民俗学大系 : 祖先祭祀と葬墓, ed. Fujii Masao 藤井正雄, pp. 359–74. Vol. 4 of *Bukkyō minzokugaku taikei*. Tokyo: Meicho shuppan, 1988.

Kusatsu shishi 草津市史, vol. 2. Ed. Kusatsu shishi hensan iinkai 草津市史 編纂委員会. Kusatsu: Kusatsu shiyakusho, 1984.

"Kyōto oboegaki" 京都覚書. In *Nihon toshi seikatsu shiryō shūsei* 日本都市生活 史料集成. vol. 1, ed. Harada Tomohiko 原田伴彦, pp. 223–74. Tokyo: Gakushō kenkyūsha, 1977.

Kyūshū shiryō kankōkai 九州史料刊行会, ed. *Kyūshū shiryō sōsho: Nagasaki Hiradomachi ninbetsuchō* 九州史料叢書 : 長崎平戸町人別帳. Vol. 37 of *Kyūshū shiryō sōsho*. Fukuoka: Kyūshū shiryō kankōkai, 1965.

LaFleur, William R. *The Karma of Words: Buddhism and the Literary Arts in Medieval Japan*. Berkeley and Los Angeles: University of California Press, 1983.

——. *Liquid Life: Abortion and Buddhism in Japan*. Princeton: Princeton University Press, 1992.

Lay, Arthur Hyde. "Japanese Funeral Rites." *Transactions of the Asiatic Society of Japan*, vol. 19 (1891): 507–44.

Leach, Edmund. "Anthropological Aspects of Language: Animal Categories and Verbal Abuse." In *New Directions in the Study of Language*, ed. Eric H. Lenneberg, pp. 23–63. Cambridge, MA: The MIT Press, 1964.

Lidin, Olof G. *Ogyū Sorai's Discourse on Government (Seidan): An Annotated Translation*. Wiesbaden, Germany: Harrassowitz Verlag, 1999.

Lincoln, Bruce. *Discourse and the Construction of Society: Comparative Studies of Myth, Ritual, and Classification*. New York and Oxford: Oxford University Press, 1989.

Lu, David J. *Japan: A Documented History*. Armonk, NY: M. E. Sharpe, 1997.

Maeda, Hiromi. "Court Rank for Village Shrines: The Yoshida House's Interactions with Local Shrines during the Mid-Tokugawa Period." *Japanese Journal of Religious Studies* 29, nos. 3–4 (Fall 2002): 325–58.

——. "Imperial Authority and Local Shrines: The Yoshida House and the Creation of a Countrywide Shinto Institution in Early Modern Japan." Ph.D. diss., Harvard University, 2003.

Malalasekera, G. P. "'Transference of Merit' in Ceylonese Buddhism." *Philosophy East and West* 17, nos. 1–4 (January-October 1967): 85–90.

Marcure, Kenneth A. "The *Danka* System." *Monumenta Nipponica* 40, no. 1 (Spring 1985): 39–67.

Marnas, Francisque. *Nihon Kirisutokyō fukkatsushi* 日本キリスト教復活史. Trans. Kuno Keiichirō 久野桂一郎. Tokyo: Misuzu shobō, 1985.

Maruya Jinshichi 丸屋甚七. "Kagyōkō" 家業考. In *Nihon nōsho zenshū* 日本 農書全集, vol. 9, ed. Ozu Yūji 小都勇二, pp. 3–171. Tokyo: Nōsangyoson bunka kyōkai, 1978.

Massarella, Derek. *A World Elsewhere: Europe's Encounter with Japan in the Sixteenth and Seventeenth Centuries*. New Haven and London: Yale University Press, 1990.

Matsudaira Kanzan 松平冠山 ed. *Sensōjishi* 浅草寺志 (1813). Reprinted in 2 vols. Tokyo: Sensōji shuppankai, 1939, 1942.

Matsudaira Sadanobu 松平定信. *Uge no hitokoto* 宇下人言 (1793). Reprinted in *Uge no hitokoto, Shugyōroku* 宇下人言 • 修行録. Tokyo: Iwanami shoten, 1942.

———. "Matsudaira Etchū no kami kokoroegaki" 松平越中守心得書 (1789). In *Nihon shomin seikatsu shiryō shūsei: sesō 1* 日本庶民生活史料集成：世相一, ed. Harada Tomohiko 原田伴彦 and Asakura Haruhiko 朝倉治彦, pp. 733-35. Vol. 11 of *Nihon shomin seikatsu shiryō shūsei*. Tokyo: San'ichi shobō, 1970.

Matsudaira Tarō 松平太郎. *Edo jidai seido no kenkyū* 江戸時代制度の研究. Rev. ed. Shinji Yoshimoto 進士慶幹. Tokyo: Kashiwa shobō, 1971.

Matsuda Kiichi 松田毅一, ed. *Jūroku jūnana seiki Iezusukai Nihon hōkokushū: dainiki (1605-1625)* 十六・十七世紀イエズス会日本報告集：第二期, 3 vols. Kyoto: Dōbōsha shuppan, 1990-97.

Matsudo shishi: shiryōhen 松戸市史：史料編, vol. 1. Ed. Matsudoshi 松戸市. Matsudo, Chiba: Matsudoshi, 1971.

Matsumoto Ryōta 松本良太. "Hitoyado" 人宿. In *Iwanami kōza Nihon tsūshi: kinsei 5* 岩波講座日本通史：近世5, ed. Asao Naohiro 朝尾直弘 et al., pp. 313-32. Vol. 15 of *Iwanami kōza Nihon tsūshi*. Tokyo: Iwanami shoten, 1995.

Matsumurahan shoshū honmatsu jigō sonota meisaichō 松村藩諸宗本末寺号其外明細帳 (1871, unprinted).

Matsunaga, Alicia. *The Buddhist Philosophy of Assimilation: The Historical Development of the Honji-Suijaku Theory*. Tokyo: Sophia University, 1969.

Matsuura Shūkō 松浦秀光. *Zenke no sōhō to tsuizen kuyō no kenkyū* 禅家の葬法と追善供養の研究. Tokyo: Sankibō busshorin, 1969.

McMullin, Neil F. *Buddhism and the State in Sixteenth-Century Japan*. Princeton: Princeton University Press, 1984.

Meiji ishin shinbutsu bunri shiryō 明治維新神仏分離史料, 5 vols. Ed. Murakami Senjō 村上専精, Tsuji Zennosuke 辻善之助, and Washio Junkyō 鷲尾順敬. Tokyo: Meicho shuppan, 1970.

Michibata Ryōshū 道端良秀. *Bukkyō to Jukyō rinri: Chūgoku Bukkyō ni okeru kō no mondai* 仏教と儒教倫理：中国仏教における孝の問題. Kyoto: Heirakuji shoten, 1968.

Minkan jirei 民間時令 (1822). In *Minkan fūzoku nenchū gyōji (jō)* 民間風俗年中行事(上), ed. Mori Senzō 森銑三 and Kitagawa Hirokuni 北川博邦, pp. 69-211. Supplement vol. 11 of *Zoku Nihon zuihitsu taisei* 続日本随筆大成. Tokyo: Yoshikawa kōbunkan, 1983.

Mitamura Engyo 三田村鳶魚. *Edo nenchū gyōji* 江戸年中行事. Tokyo: Shunyōdō, 1927.

Miura Shumon 三浦朱門. "Haikyōsha" 背教者. In *Tanbō daikōkai jidai no Nihon: Kirishitan no higeki* 探訪大航海時代の日本：キリシタンの悲劇, ed. Endō Shūsaku 遠藤周作 et al., pp. 59-68. Vol. 3 of *Tanbō daikōkai jidai no Nihon*. Tokyo: Shōgakukan, 1978.

———. "Inoue Chikugo no Kami: dan'atsusha to iu na no korobi Kirishitan" 井上筑後守：弾圧社という名の転びキリシタン. In *Kirishitan jidai no chishikijin* キリシタン時代の知識人, ed. Endō Shūsaku 遠藤周作 and Miura Shumon 三浦朱門, pp. 10-47. Tokyo: Nihon keizai shinbunsha, 1967.

Miura Toshiaki 三浦俊明. *Kinsei jisha meimokukin no shiteki kenkyū: kinsei shomin kin'yū shijō no tenkai to yonaoshi sōdō* 近世寺社名目金の史的研究：近世庶民金融市場の展開と世直し騒動. Tokyo: Yoshikawa kōbunkan, 1983.

Miyachi Masato 宮地正人 ed. "Shūkyō kankei hōrei ichiran" 宗教関係法令一覧. In *Nihon kindai shisō taikei: shūkyō to kokka* 日本近代思想体系：宗教と国家, pp. 422–88. Vol. 5 of *Nihon kindai shisō taikei*. Tokyo: Iwanami shoten, 1988.

Miyaoi Sadao 宮負定雄. "Minka yōjutsu" 民家要術 (1831). In *Kinsei chihō keizai shiryō* 近世地方経済史料, vol. 5, ed. Ono Takeo 小野武夫, pp. 263–320. Tokyo: Yoshikawa kōbunkan, 1958.

Miyata Noboru 宮田登. *Edo saijiki: toshi minzokushi no kokoromi* 江戸歳時記：都市民族誌の試み. Tokyo: Yoshikawa kōbunkan, 1981.

——. "Nihonjin no seikatsukan: seikatsu no rizumu o tsukuru shin'i" 日本人の生活観：生活のリズムを作る心意. In *Nihon minzoku bunka taikei: koyomi to saiji – Nihonjin no kisetsu kankaku* 日本民俗文化大系：暦と祭事—日本人の季節感覚, ed. Miyata Noboru, pp. 7–66. Vol. 9 of *Nihon minzoku bunka taikei*. Tokyo: Shōgakukan, 1984.

——. "Yabuiri" 藪入り. In *Edo Asakusa o kataru* 江戸浅草を語る, ed. Sensōji hinamiki kenkyūkai 浅草寺日並記研究会, pp. 60–66. Tokyo: Tōkyō bijutsu, 1990.

Miyazaki Eishū 宮崎英修. "Fujufuseha no soshiki to sono tenkai: Miyakejima Zenshōan kakochō ni miru" 不受不施派の組織とその展開：三宅島善勝庵過去帳に見る. In *Nichirenshū Fujufuseha no kenkyū* 日蓮宗不受不施派の研究, ed. Kageyama Gyōo 影山堯雄, pp. 199–235. Kyoto: Heirakuji shoten, 1972.

Miyazaki Kentarō. "Roman Catholic Mission in Pre-Modern Japan." In *Handbook of Christianity in Japan*, ed. Mark R. Mullins, pp. 1–18. Leiden and Boston: Brill, 2003.

——. "The Kakure Kirishitan Tradition." In *Handbook of Christianity in Japan*, ed. Mark R. Mullins, pp. 19–34. Leiden and Boston: Brill, 2003.

Miyazaki Michio 宮崎道生, ed. *Shintei seiyō kibun* 新訂西洋紀聞. Tokyo: Heibonsha, 1968.

Mizubayashi Takeshi 水林彪. *Hōkensei no saihen to Nihonteki shakai no kakuritsu* 封建制の再編と日本的社会の確立. Tokyo: Yamakawa shuppansha, 1987.

Mogami Takayoshi 最上孝敬. "Handankasei ni tsuite" 半壇家制について. *Nihon minzoku gakkaihō* 日本民俗学会報, no. 50 (April 1967): 1–12.

Monbushō shūkyōkyoku 文部省宗教局, ed. "Daijusshū: Edo jidai ni okeru jiin seigen seisaku" 第十輯：江戸時代における寺院制限政策. In *Shūkyō seido chōsa shiryō* 宗教制度調査資料, vol. 4. Tokyo: Hara shobō, 1977.

——. "Dairokushū: jiin butsudō kyōkai no tōkei" 第六輯：寺院仏堂教会の統計. In *Shūkyō seido chōsa shiryō* 宗教制度調査資料, vol. 2. Tokyo: Hara shobō, 1977.

Monma Sachio 門馬幸夫. *Sabetsu to kegare no shūkyō kenkyū: kenryoku toshite no 'chi'* 差別と穢れの宗教研究：権力としての「知」. Tokyo: Iwata shoin, 1997.

Moran, J. F. *The Japanese and the Jesuits: Alessandro Valignano in Sixteenth-Century Japan.* London and New York: Routledge, 1993.

Morrell, Robert E. *Sand and Pebbles (Shasekishū): The Tales of Mujū Ichien, A Voice for Pluralism in Kamakura Buddhism.* Albany: State University of New York Press, 1985.

Mori Kenji 森謙二. *Haka to sōsō no shakaishi* 墓と葬送の社会史. Tokyo: Kōdansha, 1993.

———. "Sōbo no shokeitai to sosen saishi" 総墓の諸形態と祖先祭祀. *Kokuritsu rekishi minzoku hakubutsukan kenkyū hōkoku* 国立歴史民俗博物館研究報告 41 (March 1992): 255–315.

Morioka Kiyomi 森岡清美. "Kyōdan no kōzō" 教壇の構造. In *Nihon Bukkyō-shi: kinseihen kindaihen* 日本仏教史：近世篇近代篇, ed. Tamamuro Taijō 圭室諦成, pp. 169–250. Kyoto: Hōzōkan, 1967.

———. *Shinshū kyōdan to 'ie' seido* 真宗教団と「家」制度. Rev. ed. Tokyo: Sōbunsha, 1962.

Murai Sanae 村井早苗. "Bakufu wa naze Kanbunki ni shūmon aratamechō o seidoka shitaka" 幕府はなぜ寛文期に宗門改帳を制度化したか. In *Sōten Nihon no rekishi: kinseihen* 争点日本の歴史：近世編, ed. Aoki Michio 青木美智男 and Hosaka Satoru 保坂智, pp. 80–87. Vol. 5 of *Sōten Nihon no rekishi.* Tokyo: Shinjinbutsu ōraisha, 1991.

———. *Bakuhansei seiritsu to Kirishitan kinsei* 幕藩制成立とキリシタン禁制. Tokyo: Bunken shuppan, 1987.

———. *Kirishitan kinsei to minshū no shūkyō* キリシタン禁制と民衆の宗教. Tokyo: Yamakawa shuppansha, 2002.

———. "Sakoku taisei e" 鎖国体制へ. In *Komonjo no kataru Nihonshi: Edo zenki* 古文書の語る日本史：江戸前期, ed. Tokoro Rikio 所理喜夫, pp. 211–58. Vol. 6 of *Komonjo no kataru Nihonshi.* Tokyo: Chikuma shobō, 1989.

Murakami Kōkyō 村上興匡 and Fujii Masao 藤井正雄. "Tendaishū no sōgi" 天台宗の葬儀. Part 1 of "Shūkyō, shūhabetsu no sōgi no kenkyū" 宗教・宗派別の葬儀の研究. *Sogi* 2, no. 5 (September 1992): 43–49.

Murakami Naojirō 村上直次郎, ed. *Ikoku ōfuku shokanshū* 異国往復書翰集. Tokyo: Yushōdō shoten, 1966.

———, annot. and trans. *Zōtei ikoku nikkishō* 増訂異国日記抄. Tokyo: Yushōdō shoten, 1966.

Murakami Yasusuke 村上泰亮, et al. *Bunmei toshite no ie shakai* 文明としてのイエ社会. Tokyo: Chūō kōronsha, 1979.

Muramatsu Hyōzaemon 村松標左衛門. *Muramatsu kakun* 村松家訓 (1799–1841). Reprinted in *Nihon nōsho zenshū* 日本農書全集, vol. 27, ed. Shimizu Takahisa 清水隆久, pp. 3–389. Tokyo: Nōsangyoson bunka kyōkai, 1981.

Murata Yasuo 村田安穂. "Haibutsu kishaku to sōsai mondai" 廃仏毀釈と葬祭問題. In *Gendai Nihon to Bukkyō: kokka to Bukkyō—jiyū na shinkō o motomete* 現代日本と仏教：国家と仏教—自由な信仰を求めて, ed. Ikeda Eishun 池田英俊 et al., pp. 91–100. Vol. 2 of *Gendai Nihon to Bukkyō.* Tokyo: Heibonsha, 2000.

———. *Shinbutsu bunri no chihōteki tenkai* 神仏分離の地方的展開. Tokyo: Yoshikawa kōbunkan, 1999.

Naganuma Kenkai 長沼賢海. "Shūmon ninbetsu aratame no hattatsu" 宗門人別改めの発達. *Shigaku zasshi* 史学雑誌 40, no. 11 (November 1929): 13–62.

Nagasaki kenshi: taigai kōshōhen 長崎県史：対外交渉編. Ed. Nagasaki kenshi henshū iinkai 長崎県史編集委員会. Tokyo: Yoshikawa kōbunkan, 1985.

Nagazumi Yōko 永積洋子. "Orandajin no hogosha toshite no Inoue Chikugo no Kami Masashige" オランダ人の保護者としての井上筑後守政重. *Nihon rekishi* 日本歴史 321 (1975): 1–17.

——, trans. *Hirado Oranda shōkan, Igirisu shōkan nikki: hekigan no mita kinsei no Nihon to sakoku e no michi* 平戸オランダ商館・イギリス商館日記：碧眼のみた近世の日本と鎖国への道. Tokyo: Soshiete, 1981.

——, trans. *Hirado Oranda shōkan no nikki* 平戸オランダ商館の日記, vol. 4. Tokyo: Iwanami shoten, 1969.

Nagoyashi kyōiku iinkai 名古屋市教育委員会, ed. "Owari reijō" 尾張令条. In *Nagoya sōsho: hōseihen 1* 名古屋叢書：法制編 1, pp. 155–226. Vol. 2 of *Nagoya sōsho*. Nagoya: Nagoyashi kyōiku iinkai, 1960.

Nagura Tetsuzō 奈倉哲三. *Bakumatsu minshū bunka ibun: Shinshū monto no shiki* 幕末民衆文化異聞：真宗門徒の四季. Tokyo: Yoshikawa kōbunkan, 1999.

——. "Kinseijin to shūkyō" 近世人と宗教. In *Iwanami kōza Nihon tsūshi: kinsei 2* 岩波講座日本通史：近世2, ed. Asao Naohiro 朝尾直弘 et al., pp. 225–58. Vol. 12 of *Iwanami kōza Nihon tsūshi*. Tokyo: Iwanami shoten, 1994.

——. "Kinsei kōki Shinshū hōji no jittai to sono igi (ge): Echigo no kuni Kanbaragun Ganshōji to sono dōgyō" 近世後期真宗法事の実態とその意義(下)：越後国蒲原郡願正寺とその同行. *Bukkyō shigaku kenkyū* 仏教史学研究 35, no. 2 (November 1992): 36–60.

——. "Kinsei kōki Shinshū hōji no jittai to sono igi (jō): Echigo no kuni Kanbaragun Ganshōji to sono dōgyō" 近世後期真宗法事の実態とその意義(上)：越後国蒲原郡願正寺とその同行. *Bukkyō shigaku kenkyū* 仏教史学研究 35, no. 1 (July 1992): 1–19.

——. "Kinsei no Jōdoshinshū: kaimei e no soseki to kindai e no mitooshi" 近世の浄土真宗：解明への礎石と近代への見通し. *Nihon no Bukkyō* 日本の仏教, no. 4 (1995): 168–83.

——. *Shinshū shinkō no shisōshiteki kenkyū* 真宗信仰の思想史的研究. Tokyo: Azekura shobō, 1990.

——. "Shinshū jiin no eitaikyō shikkō ni tsuite" 真宗寺院の永代経執行について. *Bukkyō shigaku kenkyū* 仏教史学研究 36, no. 1 (July 1993): 104–8.

——. "Shōninteki 'ie' ideorogī no keisei to kōzō: Enomoto Yazaemon 'oboegaki' o chūshin ni" 商人的「家」イデオロギーの形成と構造：榎本弥左衛門「覚書」を中心に. *Nihonshi kenkyū* 日本史研究, no. 209 (January 1980): 30–68.

Naitō Chisō 内藤耻叟, ed. *Tokugawa jūgodaishi* 徳川十五代史, vol. 6. Tokyo: Hakubunkan, 1893.

Naitō Masatoshi 内藤正敏. "Toshi no sei kūkan to takai: Edo no juteki kosumoroji" 都市の聖空間と他界：江戸の呪的コスモロジー. In *Bukkyō minzokugaku taikei: seichi to takaikan* 仏教民俗学大系：聖地と他界観, ed.

Sakurai Tokutarō 桜井徳太郎, pp. 79-106. Vol. 3 of *Bukkyō minzokugaku taikei*. Tokyo: Meicho shuppan, 1987.

Najita, Tetsuo, ed. *Tokugawa Political Writings*. Cambridge, UK: Cambridge University Press, 1998.

Nakada Kaoru 中田薫. *Shinzokuhō, sōzokuhō* 親族法・相続法. Vol. 1 of *Hōseishi ronshū* 法制史論集. Tokyo: Iwanami shoten, 1926.

Nakagawa Manabu 中川学. "Edo bakufu narimono teishirei no tenkai to sono tokushitsu: kinsei zenchūki ni okeru Edo machibure o chūshin ni" 江戸幕府鳴物停止令の展開とその特質：近世前中期における江戸町触を中心に. *Rekishi* 歴史 79 (September 1992): 45-87.

Nakai Chikuzan 中井竹山. *Sōbō kigen* 草茅危言 (1791). In *Nihon keizai taiten* 日本経済大典, vol. 23, pp. 313-543. Tokyo: Keimeisha, 1929.

Nakai Riken 中井履軒. *Nenseiroku* 年成録 (duplicate 1844). In *Nihon keizai taiten* 日本経済大典, vol. 23, pp. 595-691. Tokyo: Keimeisha, 1929.

Nakajima Yōichirō 中島陽一郎. *Byōki Nihonshi* 病気日本史. Tokyo: Yūzankaku shuppan, 1982.

Nakamura Kōryū 中村康隆. "Higan'e to Hanamatsuri" 彼岸会と花祭り. In *Kōza Nihon no minzoku shūkyō* 講座日本の民俗宗教, vol. 2, ed. Gorai Shigeru 五来重, pp. 99-120. Tokyo: Kōbundō, 1980.

Nakamura Kōya 中村孝也. *Tokugawa Ieyasu monjo no kenkyū (gekan no ichi)* 徳川家康文書の研究(下巻の一). Tokyo: Nihon gakujutsu shinkōkai, 1960.

———. *Tokugawa Ieyasu monjo no kenkyū (gekan no ni)* 徳川家康文書の研究 (下巻の二). Tokyo: Nihon gakujutsu shinkōkai, 1961.

———. *Tokugawa Ieyasukō den* 徳川家康公伝. Nikkō: Nikkō Tōshōgū shamusho, 1965.

Nakamura Shunsaku 中村春作. "'Fūzoku' ron e no shikaku" 「風俗」論への視角. *Shisō* 思想, no. 766 (April 1988): 102-15.

Nakamura Tadashi 中村質. *Kinsei Nagasaki bōekishi no kenkyū* 近世長崎貿易史の研究. Tokyo: Yoshikawa kōbunkan, 1988.

———. "Shimabara no ran to sakoku" 島原の乱と鎖国. In *Iwanami kōza Nihon rekishi: kinsei 1* 岩波講座日本歴史：近世 1, ed. Asao Naohiro 朝尾直広, pp. 227-62. Vol. 9 of *Iwanami kōza Nihon rekishi*. Tokyo: Iwanami shoten, 1975.

Nakamura Yasutaka 中村康隆. "Haibutsu kishaku ni okeru shinsōsaika no katei to genjō: Kantō shoken no jittai (Kanagawaken)" 廃仏毀釈における神葬祭化の過程と現状：関東諸県の実態（神奈川県）. *Shūkyō kenkyū* 宗教研究 34-3, no. 166 (January 1961): 63-64.

Nakane, Chie. *Japanese Society*. Berkeley and Los Angeles: University of California Press, 1972.

Nakata Takaji 中田隆二. "Kagahan ni okeru Shinshū kyōdan no jidan kankei" 加賀藩における真宗教団の寺檀関係. *Ryūkoku shidan* 龍谷史談, nos. 81-82 (March 1983): 115-30.

Namihira Emiko 波平恵美子. "Ijō shisha no sōhō to shūzoku" 異常死者の葬法と習俗. In *Bukkyō minzokugaku taikei: sosen saishi to sōbo* 仏教民俗大系：祖先祭祀と葬墓, ed. Fujii Masao 藤井正雄, pp. 141-60. Vol. 4 of *Bukkyō minzokugaku taikei*. Tokyo: Meicho shuppan, 1988.

———. *Kegare* ケガレ. Tokyo: Tōkyōdō shuppan, 1985.

Nanzenji shūmu honjo 南禅寺宗務本所, ed. *Nanzenji monjo* 南禅寺文書. 2 vols, ed. Fujii Manabu 藤井学 and Sakurai Kageo 桜井景雄. Kyoto: Nanzenji shūmu honjo, 1972–78.

Narimatsu Saeko 成松佐恵子. *Shōya nikki ni miru Edo no sesō to kurashi* 庄屋日記にみる江戸の世相と暮らし. Kyoto: Mineruva shobō, 2000.

Narita Shunji 成田俊治. "Sonraku jidō no hyakumanben nenbutsu" 村落寺堂の百万遍念仏. In *Bukkyō minzokugaku taikei: Bukkyō nenchū gyōji* 仏教民俗大系：仏教年中行事, ed. Itō Yuishin 伊藤唯真, pp. 381–95. Vol. 6 of *Bukkyō minzokugaku taikei*. Tokyo: Meicho shuppan, 1986.

Negishi Yasumori 根岸鎮衛. *Mimibukuro* 耳袋 (1784–1814). 3 vols. Annot. Hasegawa Tsuyoshi 長谷川強. Tokyo: Iwanami shoten, 1991.

Nei Kiyoshi 根井浄. "Kumano bikuni to etoki" 熊野比丘尼と絵解き. *Kokubungaku kaishaku to kanshō* 国文学解釈と鑑賞 68, no. 6 (June 2003): 163–72.

Nichi-Ran gakkai 日蘭学会, ed. *Nagasaki Oranda shōkan nikki* 長崎オランダ商館日記, vol. 3. Tokyo: Yūshōdō shuppan, 1991.

Niigata kenshi shiryōhen: kinsei 2, Chūetsuhen 新潟県史資料編：近世 2 中越編, ed. Niigataken 新潟県. Vol. 7 of *Niigata kenshi shiryōhen*. Niigata: Niigataken, 1981.

Niikura Yoshiyuki 新倉善之, ed. *Edo Tōkyō hayari shinkō jiten* 江戸東京はやり信仰事典. Tokyo: Hokushindō, 1998.

Nishida Nagao 西田長男. *Nihon Shintōshi kenkyū: kinseihen (jō)* 日本神道史研究：近世編(上). Vol. 6. of *Nihon Shintōshi kenkyū*. Tokyo: Kōdansha, 1979.

Nishiki Kōichi 西木浩一. "Bohyō naki bochi no kōkei: toshi kasō minshū no shi to maisō o megutte" 墓標なき墓地の光景：都市下層民衆の死と埋葬をめぐって. In *Kinsei toshi Edo no kōzō* 近世都市江戸の構造, ed. Takeuchi Makoto 竹内誠, pp. 31–54. Tokyo: Sanseidō, 1997.

——. "Edo basue jiin ni kansuru ichikōsatsu: Yotsuya Samegabashi Ōbakushū Ennōji no boiki o megutte" 江戸場末寺院に関する一考察：四谷鮫河橋黄檗宗圓應寺の墓域をめぐって. In *Ennōji ato: Shinjuku kuritsu Wakaba kōreisha zaitaku sābisusentā kensetsu ni tomonau kinkyū hakkutsu chōsa hōkokusho* 圓應寺跡：新宿区立若葉高齢者在宅サービスセンター建設に伴う緊急発掘調査報告書, ed. Shinjukuku kōseibu iseki chōsakai 新宿区厚生部遺跡調査会, pp. 76–84. Tokyo: Shinjukuku kōseibu iseki chōsakai, 1993.

——. *Edo no sōsō bosei* 江戸の葬送墓制. Tokyo: Tōkyōto seisaku hōdōshitsu, 1999.

——. "Sōsō bosei kara mita toshi Edo no tokushitsu" 葬送墓制からみた都市江戸の特質. *Nenpō toshishi kenkyū* 年報都市史研究 6 (1998): 29–41.

Nishiwaki Osamu 西脇修. "Kinsei Bukkyōshi kenkyū no dōkō" 近世仏教史研究の動向. *Kinsei Bukkyō* 近世仏教 4, no. 2 (1979): 41–52.

——. "Kinsei jidan seido no seiritsu ni tsuite: bakufu hōrei o chūshin ni" 近世寺檀制度の成立について：幕府法令を中心に. In *Kinsei Bukkyō no shomondai* 近世仏教の諸問題, ed. Tamamuro Fumio 圭室文雄 and Ōkuwa Hitoshi 大桑斉, pp. 23–45. Tokyo: Yūzankaku shuppan, 1979.

Nittō Kazuhiko 日塔和彦. "Edo gofunai jiin no zentaiteki haaku: Gofunai jiin bikō kenkyū (1)" 江戸御府内寺院の全体的把握：『御府内寺社備考』研究 (1). In *Kenchikushi no kōmyaku* 建築史の鉱脈, ed. Ōkawa Naomi sensei tai-kan kinen ronbunshū kankōkai 大河直躬先生退官記念論文集刊行会, pp. 171-90. Tokyo: Chūō kōron bijutsu shuppan, 1995.

———. "*Gofunai jisha bikō* kara mita Edo no jiin" 『御府内寺社備考』からみた 江戸の寺院. *Nenpō toshishi kenkyū* 年報都市史研究 6 (1998): 3-18.

Noguchi Takenori 野口武徳. "Fukudankasei to fūfubetsu, oyakobetsu bosei: Nihon no shinzoku kenkyū e no ichishikaku" 複壇家制と夫婦別・親子別 墓制：日本の親族研究への一視角. *Seijō bungei* 成城文芸, no. 44 (1966): 34-53.

———. "Handankasei" 半壇家制. In *Kōza Nihon no minzoku shūkyō: minzoku shūkyō to shakai* 講座日本の民俗宗教：民俗宗教と社会, ed. Gorai Shigeru 五来重 et al., pp. 12-37. Vol. 5 of *Kōza Nihon no minzoku shūkyō*. Tokyo: Kōbundō, 1980.

Nōgyō yokoza annai 農業横座案内 (1777). Reprinted in *Nihon nōsho zenshū* 日本 農書全集, vol. 31, ed. Etō Akihiko 江藤彰彦, pp. 103-31. Tokyo: Nōsan-gyoson bunka kyōkai, 1981.

Nosco, Peter. "Keeping the Faith: *Bakuhan* Policy towards Religions in Seventeenth-Century Japan." In *Religion in Japan: Arrows to Heaven and Earth*, ed. P. F. Kornicki and I. J. McMullen, pp. 136-55. Cambridge, UK: Cambridge University Press, 1996.

———. "Secrecy and the Transmission of Tradition: Issues in the Study of the 'Underground' Christians." *Japanese Journal of Religious Studies* 20, no. 1 (March 1993): 3-29.

Nozawa Kenji 野沢謙治 and Yagi Yasuyuki 八木康幸. "Edo jidai no sosen sūhai" 江戸時代の祖先崇拝. In *Sosen saishi no rekishi to minzoku* 祖先祭祀 の歴史と民俗, ed. Tanaka Hisao 田中久夫, pp. 183-279. Tokyo: Kōbundō, 1986.

Ofuregaki Hōreki shūsei 御触書宝暦集成. Ed. Takayanagi Shinzō 高柳真三 and Ishii Ryōsuke 石井良助. Tokyo: Iwanami shoten, 1976.

Ofuregaki Kanpō shūsei 御触書寛保集成. Ed. Takayanagi Shinzō 高柳真三 and Ishii Ryōsuke 石井良助. Tokyo: Iwanami shoten, 1976.

Ofuregaki Tenmei shūsei 御触書天明集成. Ed. Takayanagi Shinzō 高柳真三 and Ishii Ryōsuke 石井良助. Tokyo: Iwanami shoten, 1976.

Ofuregaki Tenpō shūsei (ge) 御触書天保集成(下). Ed. Takayanagi Shinzō 高柳 真三 and Ishii Ryōsuke 石井良助. Tokyo: Iwanami shoten, 1976.

Ogawa Kyōichi 小川恭一. "Bakushin Fuseke monjo: moto ōban kumigashira no sōsō kiroku" 幕臣布施家文書：元大番組頭の葬送記録. *Fūzoku* 風俗 33, no. 2 (May 1995): 31-53.

Oguri Junko 小栗純子. "Edo jidai ni okeru seiji kenryoku to Bukkyō: *Myōkō-ninden* o chūshin toshite" 江戸時代における政治権力と仏教：『妙好 人伝』を中心として. In *Nihon ni okeru seiji to shūkyō* 日本における政治と 宗教, ed. Kasahara Kazuo 笠原一男, pp. 221-60. Tokyo: Yoshikawa kōbunkan, 1973.

———. "*Kinsei ōjōden* ni tsuite" 『近世往生伝』について. In *Kinsei ōjōden shūsei* 近世往生伝集成, vol. 2, ed. Kasahara Kazuo 笠原一男, pp. 601-5. Tokyo: Yamakawa shuppansha, 1979.

——. "*Kuroshiro ōjōden* ni tsuite" 『緇白往生伝』について. In *Kinsei ōjōden shūsei* 近世往生伝集成, vol. 1, ed. Kasahara Kazuo 笠原一男, pp. 481–86. Tokyo: Yamakawa shuppansha, 1978.

——. "Shinshū kyōdan no risōteki nenbutsushazō" 真宗教団の理想的念仏者像. In *Kinsei ōjōden no sekai* 近世往生伝の世界, ed. Kasahara Kazuo 笠原一男, pp. 175–252. Tokyo: Kyōikusha, 1978.

Ogyū Sorai 荻生徂徠. *Seidan* 政談 (1716–36). In *Ogyū Sorai* 荻生徂徠, annot. Tsuji Tatsuya 辻達也, pp. 259–445. Vol. 36 of *Nihon shisō taikei* 日本思想体系. Tokyo: Iwanami shoten, 1973.

——. *Taiheisaku* 太平策 (1719–22). In *Ogyū Sorai* 荻生徂徠, annot. Maruyama Masao 丸山真男, pp. 447–86. Vol. 36 of *Nihon shisō taikei* 日本思想体系. Tokyo: Iwanami shoten, 1973.

Ōhashi Shunnō 大橋俊雄. "Jōdoshū nenbutsusha no risōteki ningenzō: zenki" 浄土宗念仏者の理想的人間像：前期. In *Kinsei ōjōden no sekai* 近世往生伝の世界, ed. Kasahara Kazuo 笠原一男, pp. 45–106. Tokyo: Kyōikusha, 1978.

Ōhashi Yukihiro 大橋幸泰. "Ishū to Kirishitan" 異宗ときりしたん. In *Atarashii kinseishi: minshū sekai to seitō* 新しい近世史：民衆世界と正統, ed. Iwata Kōtarō 岩田浩太郎, pp. 204–44. Vol. 5 of *Atarashii kinseishi*. Tokyo: Shinjinbutsu ōraishia, 1996.

——. *Kirishitan minshūshi no kenkyū* キリシタン民衆史の研究. Tokyo: Tōkyōdō shuppan, 2001.

——. "New Perspectives on the Early Tokugawa Persecution." In *Japan and Christianity: Impacts and Responses*, ed. John Breen and Mark Williams, pp. 46–62. London: Macmillan Press, 1996.

——. "Shūmon aratame no seidoka to Kirishitan minshū: bakuhansei kokka to Kirishitan o megutte" 宗門改の制度化とキリシタン民衆：幕藩制国家とキリシタンをめぐって. *Rekishi hyōron* 歴史評論, no. 512 (December 1992): 50–66.

Ohnuki-Tierney, Emiko. *Illness and Culture in Contemporary Japan: An Anthropological View*. New York: Cambridge University Press, 1984.

Ōishi Kyūkei 大石久敬. *Jikata hanreiroku* 地方凡例録, ed. Ōishi Shinzaburō 大石慎三郎. 2 vols. Tokyo: Kondō shuppansha, 1969.

Ōishi Manabu 大石学. "Bakusei no shiren" 幕制の試練. In *Komonjo no kataru Nihonshi: Edo zenki* 古文書の語る日本史：江戸前期, ed. Tokoro Rikio 所理喜夫, pp. 417–42. Vol. 6 of *Komonjo no kataru Nihonshi*. Tokyo: Chikuma shobō, 1968.

Ōishi Shinzaburō 大石慎三郎. *Kinsei sonraku kōzō to ie seido* 近世村落構造と家制度. Tokyo: Ochanomizu shobō, 1968.

Okada Akio 岡田章雄. *Amakusa Tokisada* 天草時貞. Tokyo: Yoshikawa kōbunkan, 1960.

——. "Iwayuru 'nanban seishi' ni tsuite no ichikōsatsu" いわゆる「南蛮誓詞」についての一考察. In *Kirishitanshi ronsō* 切支丹史論叢, ed. Kirisutokyō shigakkai キリスト教史学会, pp. 156–68. Tokyo: Komiyayama shoten, 1953.

Okada Shigekiyo 岡田重精. *Imi no sekai: sono kikō to hen'yō* 斎忌の世界：その機構と変容. Tokyo: Kokusho kankōkai, 1989.

Okada Shōji 岡田莊司. "Kinsei no Shintō sōsai" 近世の神道葬祭. In *Kinsei no seishin seikatsu* 近世の精神生活, ed. Ōkura seishin bunka kenkyūjo 大倉精神文化研究所, pp. 215-51. Yokohama: Zoku gunsho ruijū kanseikai, 1996.

———. "Kinsei Shintō no jomaku: Yoshidake no sōrei o tsūro toshite" 近世神道の序幕：吉田家の葬礼を通路として. In *Shinsōsai daijiten* 神葬祭大事典, ed. Katō Takahisa 加藤隆久, pp. 323-43. Tokyo: Ebisu kōshō shuppan, 1997.

———. "Shintō sōsai no seiritsu to Yoshidake" 神道葬祭の成立と吉田家. In *Shinsōsai daijiten* 神葬祭大事典, ed. Katō Takahisa 加藤隆久, pp. 33-36. Tokyo: Ebisu kōshō shuppan, 1997.

———. "Yoshidaryū sōsai no hatten" 吉田流葬祭の発展. *Jinja shinpō* 神社新報 (15 May 1989): 7.

Okuno Hikoroku 奥野彦六. *Teihon osadamegaki no kenkyū* 定本御定書の研究. Tokyo: Sakai shoten, 1968.

Okuno Yoshio 奥野義雄. "Ishingo no shūzoku kinrei shiryō ni miru Meiji seifu no minshū tōsei ni tsuite" 維新後の習俗禁令史料にみる明治政府の民衆統制について. *Nara kenritsu minzoku hakubutsukan kenkyū kiyō* 奈良県立民俗博物館研究紀要, no. 12 (April 1990): 23-40.

Ōkuwa Hitoshi 大桑斉. "Handanka no rekishiteki tenkai" 半檀家の歴史的展開. *Kinsei Bukkyō* 近世仏教 6, nos. 3-4 (February 1986): 1-33.

———. *Jidan no shisō* 寺壇の思想. Tokyo: Kyōikusha, 1979.

———. "Jidan seido no seiritsu katei (jō)" 寺壇制度の成立過程(上). *Nihon rekishi* 日本歴史, no. 242 (July 1968): 23-36.

———. "Jidan seido no seiritsu katei (ge)" 寺壇制度の成立過程(下). *Nihon rekishi* 日本歴史, no. 243 (August 1968): 22-33.

———. "Bakuhansei kokka no Bukkyō tōsei: shinji kinshirei o megutte" 幕藩制国家の仏教統制：新寺禁止令をめぐって. In *Kinsei Bukkyō no shomondai* 近世仏教の諸問題, ed. Tamamuro Fumio 圭室文雄 and Ōkuwa Hitoshi 大桑斉, pp. 3-22. Tokyo: Yūzankaku shuppan, 1979.

———. "Kinsei ni okeru sosen sūhai: minshū shisō, ideorogī to Bukkyō" 近世における祖先崇拝：民衆思想・イデオロギーと仏教. In *Taikei Bukkyō to Nihonjin: kindaika to dentō—kinsei Bukkyō no henshitsu to tenkan* 大系仏教と日本人：近代化と伝統—近世仏教の変質と転換, ed. Yasumaru Yoshio, pp. 65-99. Vol. 11 of *Taikei Bukkyō to Nihonjin*. Tokyo: Shunjūsha, 1986.

———. "Kinsei sonraku no seikatsu bunka: haka, tera, senzo" 近世村落の生活文化：墓・寺・先祖. In *Nihon sonrakushi kōza: seikatsu 2, kinsei* 日本村落史講座：生活II、近世, ed. Fukuta Ajio 福田アジオ et al., pp. 189-204. Vol. 7 of *Nihon sonrakushi kōza*. Tokyo: Yūzankaku shuppan, 1990.

———. *Nihon Bukkyō no kinsei* 日本仏教の近世. Kyoto: Hōzōkan, 2003.

———. *Nihon kinsei no shisō to Bukkyō* 日本近世の思想と仏教. Kyoto: Hōzōkan, 1989.

"Ōmurahan Kōri kuzure ikken" 大村藩郡崩れ一件. In *Nihon shomin seikatsu shiryō shūsei: minkan shūkyō* 日本庶民生活史料集成：民間宗教, ed. Tanigawa Ken'ichi 谷川 健一, pp. 709-59. Vol. 18 of *Nihon shomin seikatsu shiryō shūsei*. Tokyo: San'ichi shobō, 1972.

Onuki Man'uemon 小貫萬右衛門. "Nōka shōkeishō" 農家捷径抄 (1808). Reprinted in *Nihon nōsho zenshū* 日本農書全集, vol. 22, ed. Sunaga Akira 須永昭, pp. 3-80. Tokyo: Nōsangyoson bunka kyōkai, 1980.

Ooms, Herman. *Charismatic Bureaucrat: A Political Biography of Matsudaira Sadanobu, 1758-1829*. Chicago: The University of Chicago Press, 1975.

———. *Sosen sūhai no sinborizumu* 祖先崇拝のシンボリズム. Tokyo: Kōbundō, 1987.

———. *Tokugawa Ideology: Early Constructs, 1570-1680*. Princeton: Princeton University Press, 1985.

———. *Tokugawa Village Practice: Class, Status, Power, Law*. Berkeley and Los Angeles: University of California Press, 1996.

Ōta Masahiro 太田正弘. "Atsuta daigūji Chiakike ridan no keika ni tsuite" 熱田大宮司千秋家離檀の経過について. *Kokugakuin zasshi* 國學院雑誌 75, no. 7 (July 1974): 13-19.

Ōtō Osamu 大藤修. "Kinsei nōminsō no sōsai, senzo saishi to ie, shinzoku, sonraku" 近世農民層の葬祭・先祖祭祀と家・親族・村落. *Kokuritsu rekishi minzoku hakubutsukan kenkyū hōkoku* 国立歴史民俗博物館研究報告 41 (March 1992): 67-131.

———. *Kinsei nōmin to ie, mura, kokka: seikatsushi, shakaishi no shiza kara* 近世農民と家・村・国家：生活史・社会史の視座から. Tokyo: Yoshikawa kōbunkan, 1996.

———. "Sonraku soshiki to nichijō seikatsu" 村落組織と日常生活. In *Nihon sonrakushi kōza: seikatsu 2, kinsei* 日本村落史講座：生活 II、近世, ed. Fukuta Ajio 福田アジオ et al., pp. 91-106. Vol. 7 of *Nihon sonrakushi kōza*. Tokyo: Yūzankaku shuppan, 1990.

"Owari reijō" 尾張令条. In *Nagoya sōsho* 名古屋叢書, vol. 2, ed. Nagoyashi kyōiku iinkai, pp. 155-226. Nagoya: Aichiken kyōdo shiryō kankōkai, 1982.

Ōyama Kyōhei 大山喬平. *Nihon chūsei nōsonshi no kenkyū* 日本中世農村史の研究. Tokyo: Iwanami shoten, 1978.

Ozawa Masahiro 小沢正弘. "Edo shoki Kantō ni okeru saidō kuji" 江戸初期関東における祭道公事. *Saitama kenshi kenkyū* 埼玉県史研究 9 (1982): 33-54.

Ōzuhan shoshū honmatsu jigō sonota meisaichō 大洲藩諸宗本末寺号其外明細帳 (1871, unprinted).

Pages, Leon. *Nihon Kirishitan shūmonshi* 日本切支丹宗門史, 3 vols. Trans. Yoshida Kogorō 吉田小五郎. Tokyo: Iwanami shoten, 1938.

Payne, Richard Karl. "Shingon Services for the Dead." In *Religions of Japan in Practice*, ed. George J. Tanabe, Jr., pp. 159-65. Princeton: Princeton University Press, 1999.

Poussin, Louis de La Vallée, trans. *Abhidharmakośa-bhāsya*, 4 vols. English trans. Leo M. Pruden. Berkeley: Asian Humanities Press, 1988.

Pye, Michael, trans. *Emerging from Meditation: Tominaga Nakamoto*. London: Duckworth, 1990.

Radcliffe-Brown, A. R. *The Andaman Islanders*. New York: The Free Press, 1964.

Ravina, Mark. *Land and Lordship in Early Modern Japan.* Stanford: Stanford University Press, 1999.

Rawski, Evelyn S. "A Historian's Approach to Chinese Death Ritual." In *Death Ritual in Late Imperial and Modern China,* ed. James L. Watson and Evelyn S. Rawski, pp. 20–34. Berkeley and Los Angeles: University of California Press, 1988.

Reis-Habito, Maria. "The Repentance Ritual of the Thousand-armed Guanyin." *Studies in Central & East Asia Religions* 4 (Autumn 1991): 42–51.

Ross, Andrew C. *A Vision Betrayed: The Jesuits in Japan and China 1542–1742.* Maryknoll, NY: Orbis Books, 1994.

Rowe, Mark. "Stickers for Nails: The Ongoing Transformation of Roles, Rites, and Symbols in Japanese Funerals." *Japanese Journal of Religious Studies* 27, nos. 3–4 (Fall 2000): 352–78.

Ruch, Barbara. "Woman to Woman: Kumano bikuni Proselytizers in Medieval and Early Modern Japan." In *Engendering Faith: Women and Buddhism in Premodern Japan,* ed. Barbara Ruch, pp. 537–80. Ann Arbor: Center for Japanese Studies, University of Michigan, 2002.

Ryori saijiki 閭里歳時記 (1780). In *Minkan fūzoku nenchū gyōji (jō)* 民間風俗年中行事(上), ed. Mori Senzō 森銑三 and Kitagawa Hirokuni 北川博邦, pp. 325–68. Supplement vol. 11 of *Zoku Nihon zuihitsu taisei* 続日本随筆大成. Tokyo: Yoshikawa kōbunkan, 1983.

Saitō Gesshin 斎藤月岑 et al. *Edo meisho zue* 江戸名所図絵 (1834–36). Reprinted in 2 vols. Tokyo: Jinbutsu ōraisha, 1967.

——. *Tōto saijiki* 東都歳時記 (1838). Reprinted in 3 vols., annot. Asakura Haruhiko 朝倉治彦. Tōyō bunko 東洋文庫 159. Tokyo: Heibonsha, 1970.

Saitō Natsuki 斎藤夏来. "Edo bakufu seiritsuki no seikyō kankei to shie jiken" 江戸幕府成立期の政教関係と紫衣事件. *Rekishigaku kenkyū* 歴史学研究, no. 715 (October 1998): 1–18.

Saitō Ryūzō 斎藤隆三. *Kinsei Nihon sesōshi* 近世日本世相史 (1925). Reprinted. Tokyo: Nihon tosho sentā, 1983.

Saitō Tadashi 斎藤忠. "Haka to Bukkyō" 墓と仏教. In *Bukkyō minzokugaku taikei: sosen saishi to sōbo* 仏教民俗大系：祖先祭祀と葬墓, ed. Fujii Masao 藤井正雄, pp. 213–32. Vol. 4 of *Bukkyō minzokugaku taikei.* Tokyo: Meicho shuppan, 1988.

Sakamoto Koremaru 阪本是丸. *Kokka Shintō keisei katei no kenkyū* 国家神道形成過程の研究. Tokyo: Iwanami shoten, 1994.

Sakamoto Tadahisa 坂本忠久. "Kinsei kōki no Edo ni okeru shūkyōsha tōsei to toshi mondai" 近世後期の江戸における宗教者統制と都市問題. *Hisutoria* ヒストリア, no. 137 (December 1992): 52–70.

Sakamoto Tarō. *The Six National Histories of Japan,* trans. John S. Brownlee. Vancouver: University of British Columbia Press, 1991.

Sakurai Haruo 桜井治男. "Chiiki shakai ni okeru shinsōsai no juyō to sono tenkai: Mie kenka no ichijirei" 地域社会における神葬祭の受容とその展開：三重県下の一事例. *Shūkyō kenkyū* 宗教研究 59, no. 1 (June 1985): 161–83.

Sakurai Tokutarō 桜井徳太郎. "Sanchū takaikan no seiritsu to tenkai: Ise Asamayama no take mairi" 山中他界観の成立と展開：伊勢朝熊山のタケ

参り. In *Bukkyō minzokugaku taikei: seichi to takaikan* 仏教民俗大系：聖地と他界観, ed. Sakurai Tokutarō, pp. 351-77. Vol. 3 of *Bukkyō minzokugaku taikei*. Tokyo: Meicho shuppan, 1987.

———. "Sōron: seichi to takaikan" 総論：聖地と他界観. In *Bukkyō minzokugaku taikei: seichi to takaikan* 仏教民俗大系：聖地と他界観, ed. Sakurai Tokutarō, pp. 1-24. Vol. 3 of *Bukkyō minzokugaku taikei*. Tokyo: Meicho shuppan, 1987.

Sano Kenji 佐野賢治. "Sanchū takai kannen no hyōshutsu to Kokūzō shinkō: jōdokan no rekishi minzokugakuteki ichikōsatsu" 山中他界観念の表出と虚空蔵信仰：浄土観の歴史民俗学的一考察." In *Kokūzō shinkō* 虚空蔵信仰, ed. Sano Kenji. Tokyo: Yūzankaku shuppan, 1991.

———. "Sanchū takai kannen to Kokūzō shinkō: Nihonteki sōsō, takai kannen no seiritsu to minzoku" 山中他界観念と虚空蔵信仰：日本的葬送・他界観念の成立と民俗. *Kokuritsu rekishi minzoku hakubutsukan kenkyū kiyō hōkoku* 国立歴史民俗博物館研究報告 68 (March 1996): 77-113.

Sasaki Kōshō 佐々木孝正. *Bukkyō minzokushi no kenkyū* 仏教民俗史の研究. Tokyo: Meicho shuppan, 1987.

Satō Hiroo. "Wrathful Deities and Saving Deities." In *Buddhas and Kami in Japan: Honji Suijaku as a Combinatory Paradigm*, ed. Mark Teeuwen and Fabio Rambelli, pp. 95-114. London and New York: RoutledgeCurzon, 2003.

Satō Yoneshi 佐藤米司. "Ano yo no iriguchi: seichi toshite no bosho" あの世の入口：聖地としての墓所. In *Bukkyō minzokugaku taikei: seichi to takaikan* 仏教民俗大系：聖地と他界観, ed. Sakurai Tokutarō 桜井徳太郎, pp. 131-46. Vol. 3 of *Bukkyō minzokugaku taikei*. Tokyo: Meicho shuppan, 1987.

Sauda Masayuki 左右田昌幸. "Kinsei 'buraku jiinsei' o megutte: Harima no kuni Kameyama Genshōji o chūshin ni" 近世「部落寺院制」をめぐって：播磨国亀山源正寺を中心に. *Ryūkoku shidan* 龍谷史壇, nos. 93-94 (March 1989): 108-32.

Sawa Hirokatsu 澤博勝. "Kinsei kōki no chiiki, Bukkyō, Shintō: Shinsōsai undō no igi" 近世後期の地域・仏教・神道：神葬祭運動の意義. *Shigaku zasshi* 史学雑誌 105, no. 6 (June 1996): 1-37.

Sawato Hirosato 澤登寛聡. "Fuji shinkō girei to Edo bakufu no Fujikō torishimarirei: juiteki shinkō girei toshite no Edo shichū e no kanjin o meguru mibunseiteki shakai chitsujo no dōyō o megutte" 富士信仰儀礼と江戸幕府の富士講取締令：呪医的信仰儀礼としての江戸市中への勧進をめぐる身分制的社会秩序の動揺をめぐって. *Hōsei daigaku bungakubu kiyō* 法政大学文学部紀要, no. 47 (2001): 147-79.

Scheiner, Irwin. "Benevolent Lords and Honorable Peasants: Rebellion and Peasant Consciousness in Tokugawa Japan." In *Japanese Thought in the Tokugawa Period 1600-1868: Methods and Metaphors*, ed. Tetsuo Najita and Irwin Scheiner, pp. 39-62. Chicago: The University of Chicago Press, 1978.

Schopen, Gregory. *Bones, Stones, and Buddhist Monks: Collected Papers on the Archaeology, Epigraphy, and Texts of Monastic Buddhism in India*. Honolulu: University of Hawai'i Press, 1997.

Sekiguchi Masayuki 関口正之. "Mikkyō no sekai" 密教の世界. In *Zusetsu Nihon no Bukkyō 2: Mikkyō* 図説日本の仏教 2 : 密教, ed. Sekiguchi Masayuki, pp. 18–46. Tokyo: Shinchōsha, 1988.

Sekiguchi Norihisa 関口慶久. "Kaimyō, hōmyōkō: Nara, Kyōto no bohyō shiryō kara" 戒名・法名考 : 奈良・京都の墓標資料から. *Kokuritsu rekishi minzoku hakubutsukan kenkyū hōkoku* 国立歴史民俗博物館研究報告 111 (February 2004): 125–46.

——. "Kinsei Tōhoku no ie to haka: Iwateken Maesawachō Ōmuro Suzukike no bohyō to kakochō" 近世東北の家と墓 : 岩手県前沢町大室鈴木家の墓標と過去帳. *Kokuritsu rekishi minzoku hakubutsukan kenkyū hōkoku* 国立歴史民俗博物館研究報告 112 (February 2004): 465–85.

Sensōji hinamiki kenkyūkai 浅草寺日並記研究会, ed. *Sensōji nikki* 浅草寺日記, vols. 2, 3, 4, and 14. Tokyo: Kinryūsan Sensōji, 1979–91.

Sen'yō eikyūroku ofuredome 撰要永久録御触留, 4 vols., ed. Hōmudaijin kanbō shihō hōsei chōsabu 法務大臣官房司法法制調査部. Tokyo: Shōji hōmu kenkyūkai, 1987.

Shibu Shōhei 志部昭平. "Genkai sankō gyōjitsuzu no denbon to sono keifu" 諺解三綱行実図の伝本とその系譜. *Tōyōgaku* 東洋学, no. 19 (October 1989): 65–91.

Shichū torishimari ruishū 市中取締類集. In *Dai-Nihon kinsei shiryō: shichū torishimari ruishū* 大日本近世史料 : 市中取締類集, vols. 1, 2, 4, 16, and 26, ed. Tōkyō daigaku shiryō hensanjo 東京大学史料編纂所. Tokyo: Tōkyō daigaku shuppankai, 1959–2004.

Shiiyahan honmatsu jigō sonota meisaichō 椎谷藩本末寺号其外明細帳 (1870, unprinted).

Shimada Katsuji 島田嘉津次. *Jinsuke banashi* 仁助噺. Vol. 9 of *Nihon nōmin shiryō shūsui* 日本農民史料聚粋, ed. Ono Takeo 小野武夫. Tokyo: Sakai shoten, 1970.

Shimaji Mokurai 島地黙雷. *Seikyō kankeihen* 政教関係編, ed. Futaba Kenkō 二葉憲香 and Fukushima Kanryū 福嶋寛隆. Vol. 1 of *Shimaji Mokurai zensho* 島地黙雷全書. Kyoto: Honganji shuppan kyōkai, 1974.

Shimizu, Akitoshi. "Ie and Dōzoku: Family and Descent in Japan." *Current Anthropology* 28, no. 4, Supplement: An Anthropological Profile of Japan (August-October 1987): S85–S90

Shimizu Hirokazu 清水紘一. "Kanbunki Owarihan no Kirishitan kinsei ni tsuite" 寛文期尾張藩のキリシタン禁制について. *Tokugawa rinseishi kenkyūjo kiyō* 徳川林政史研究所紀要 52, no. 10 (March 1978): 227–62.

——. "Kirishitan kankei hōsei shiryōshū" キリシタン関係法制史料集. *Kirishitan kenkyū* キリシタン研究 17 (1977): 251–438.

——. *Kirishitan kinseishi* キリシタン禁制史. Tokyo: Kyōikusha, 1981.

——. "Kirishitan sonin hōshōsei ni tsuite" キリシタン訴人褒賞制について. *Kirishitan kenkyū* キリシタン研究 19 (1979): 263–300.

——. "Kōri kuzurekō: Kanbunki shūmon aratamesei e no tenbō" 郡崩れ考 : 寛文期宗門改制への展望. *Nihon rekishi* 日本歴史, no. 554 (July 1994): 62–78.

——. "Shūmon aratameyaku nōto" 宗門改役ノート. *Kirisutokyō shigaku* キリスト教史学 30 (December 1976): 42–56.

Shimizu Masumi 清水真澄. *Dōkyō no sekai: nōdoku no tanjō* 読経の世界：能読
の誕生. Tokyo: Yoshikawa kōbunkan, 2001.

Shimura Kunihiro 志村有弘, annot. *Shimabara gassenki* 島原合戦記. Tokyo:
Kyōikusha, 1989.

Shingūhan shoshū honmatsu jigō sonota meisaichō 新宮藩諸宗本末寺号其外
明細帳 (1870, unprinted).

Shin Kumamoto shishi: shiryōhen, kinsei I 新熊本市史：史料編近世 I, vol. 3 of
Shin Kumamoto shishi. Ed. Shin Kumamoto shishi hensan iinkai 新熊本
市史編纂委員会. Kumamoto: Kumamotoshi, 1994.

Shinpen Chiyodaku tsūshi: shiryōhen 新編千代田区通史：資料編, ed. Sōmubu
sōmuka 総務部総務課. Tokyo: Tōkyōto Chiyodaku, 1998.

Shintani Takanori 新谷尚紀. "Ryōbosei ni tsuite no oboegaki" 両墓制につい
ての覚書. *Kokuritsu rekishi minzoku hakubutsukan kenkyū hōkoku* 国立歴史
民俗博物館研究報告 49 (March 1993): 273-321.

———. *Ryōbosei to takaikan* 両墓制と他界観. Tokyo: Yoshikawa kōbunkan, 1991.

Shiomi Sen'ichirō 塩見鮮一郎, ed. *Edo no kasō shakai* 江戸の下層社会. Tokyo:
Akashi shoten, 1993.

Shishiba Masako 紫芝昌子. "Kōdenchō ni tsuite no ichikōsatsu" 香奠帳につ
いての一考察. *Chihōshi kenkyū* 地方史研究 41, no. 6 (December 1991): 37-48.

Shisō zōshiki 祠曹雑識, vols. 7-9 of *Naikaku bunko shozō shiseki sōkan* 内閣文庫
所蔵史籍叢刊. Ed. Shiseki kankōkai 史籍刊行会. Tokyo: Kyūko shoin,
1981.

Shively, Donal H. "Popular Culture." In *The Cambridge History of Japan: Early
Modern Japan*, ed. John Whitney Hall, pp. 706-69. Vol. 4 of *The Cambridge
History of Japan.* Cambridge, UK: Cambridge University Press, 1991.

———. "Sumptuary Regulation and Status in Early Tokugawa Japan." *Harvard
Journal of Asiatic Studies* 25 (1964-65): 123-64.

Shizuoka kenshi: shiryōhen 静岡県史：資料編, vol. 12. Ed. Shizuokaken 静岡県.
Shizuoka: Shizuokaken, 1995.

Shōji Kōki 正司考祺. *Keizai mondō hiroku* 経済問答秘録 (1841). In *Nihon keizai
taiten* 日本経済大典, vols. 34 and 35, pp. 3-176. Tokyo: Keimeisha, 1929.

Shoke himonshū 諸家秘聞集 (1772-1802). In *Shinpen Meiji ishin shinbutsu bunri
shiryō* 新編明治維新神仏分離史料, vol. 1, ed. Tsuji Zennosuke 辻善之助,
Murakami Senjō 村上専精, and Washio Junkyō 鷲尾順敬, pp. 531-49. Tokyo: Meicho shuppan, 1984.

Shokoku fūzoku toijō kotae 諸国風俗問状答 (1814-18). "Awaji no kuni fūzoku
toijō kotae" 淡路国風俗問状答, pp. 776-90; "Awa no kuni fūzoku toijō kotae" 阿波国風俗問状答, pp. 794-820; "Bingo no kuni Fukatsugun Honjōmura fūzoku toijō kotae" 備後国深津郡本庄村風俗問状答, pp. 730-39;
"Bingo no kuni Fukuyamaryō fūzoku toijō kotae" 備後国福山領風俗問状
答, pp. 675-729; "Bingo no kuni Numakumagun Urasakimura fūzoku toijō
kotae" 備後国沼隈郡浦崎村風俗問状答, pp. 761-69; "Bingo no kuni Shinaharugun fūzoku toijō kotae" 備後国品治郡風俗問状答, pp. 740-60; "Dewa
no kuni Akitaryō fūzoku toijō kotae" 出羽国秋田領風俗問状答, pp. 492-
532; "Echigo no kuni Nagaokaryō fūzoku toijō kotae" 越後国長岡領風俗
問状答, pp. 540-57; "Higo no kuni Amakusagun fūzoku toijō kotae" 肥後

国天草郡風俗問状答, pp. 821-27; "Hitachi no kuni Mitoryō fūzoku toijō kotae" 常陸国水戸領風俗問状答, pp. 533-39; "Ise no kuni Shirakoryō fūzoku toijō kotae" 伊勢国白子領風俗問状答, pp. 619-26; "Kii no kuni Wakayama fūzoku toijō kotae" 紀伊国和歌山風俗問状答, pp. 770-75; "Mikawa no kuni Yoshidaryō fūzoku toijō kotae" 三河国吉田領風俗問状答, pp. 594-618; "Mutsu no kuni Shinobugun Dategun fūzoku toijō kotae" 陸奥国信夫郡伊達郡風俗問状答, pp. 472-77; "Mutsu no kuni Shira-kawaryō fūzoku toijō kotae" 陸奥国白川領風俗問状答, pp. 478-91; "Tango no kuni Mineyamaryō fūzoku toijō kotae" 丹後国峯山領風俗問状答, pp. 659-74; "Wakasa no kuni Obamaryō fūzoku toijō kotae" 若狭国小濱領風俗問状答, pp. 644-51. In *Nihon shomin seikatsu shiryō shūsei* 日本庶民生活史料集成, vol. 9, ed. Takeuchi Toshimi 竹内利美, Harada Tomohiko 原田伴彦, and Hirayama Toshijirō 平山敏治郎. Tokyo: San'ichi shobō, 1969.

"Shūkyō kankei hōrei ichiran" 宗教関係法令一覧. In *Nihon kindai shisō taikei: shūkyō to kokka* 日本近代思想体系 : 宗教と国家, ed. Miyachi Masato 宮地正人, pp. 422-88. Vol. 5 of *Nihon kindai shisō taikei*. Tokyo: Iwanami shoten, 1988.

Smith, Robert J. *Ancestor Worship in Contemporary Japan*. Stanford: Stanford University Press, 1974.

——. "Ihai: Mortuary Tablets, the Household and Kin in Japanese Ancestor Worship." *The Transactions of the Asiatic Society of Japan*, Third Series, vol. 9 (1966): 83–102.

——. "The Japanese Rural Community: Norms, Sanctions and Ostracism." *American Anthropologist* 63, no.3 (June 1961): 522–33.

Somada Yoshio 杣田善雄. "Kinsei no monzeki" 近世の門跡. In *Iwanami kōza Nihon tsūshi: Kinsei 1* 岩波講座日本通史 : 近世 1, ed. Asao Naohiro et al., pp. 301–22. Vol. 11 of *Iwanami kōza Nihon tsūshi*. Tokyo: Iwanami shoten, 1993.

Sone Hiromi 曽根ひろみ. "Kinsei no Kumano bikuni: kanjin to baishoku" 近世の熊野比丘尼 : 勧進と売色. *Josei shigaku* 女性史学, no. 5 (1995): 31–42.

Sōtōshū jinken yōgo suishin honbu 曹洞宗人権擁護推進本部, ed. *Sōtōshū jinken yōgo suishin honbu kiyō daisangō: 'kaimyō, kakochō, danka seido' ni kansuru chūkan hōkoku* 曹洞宗人権擁護推進本部紀要第三号 : 「戒名・過去帳・檀家制度」に関する中間報告. Tokyo: Sōtōshū jinken yōgo suishin honbu, 2002.

Stevenson, Daniel B. "The Four Kinds of Samādhi in Early T'ien-t'ai Buddhism." In *Traditions of Meditation in Chinese Buddhism*, ed. Peter N. Gregory, pp. 45–97. Honolulu: University of Hawai'i Press, 1986.

Sudō Hiroto 須藤寛人. "Butsudan, ihai shinkō no shiteki kōsatsu" 仏壇・位牌信仰の史的考察. *Komazawa daigaku Bukkyōgakubu ronshū* 駒澤大学仏教学部論集, no. 29 (October 1998): 329–45.

Sugano Noriko 菅野則子. *Edo jidai no kōkōsha: Kōgiroku no sekai* 江戸時代の孝行者 : 孝義録の世界. Tokyo: Yoshikawa kōbunkan, 1999.

——. "State Indoctrination of Filial Piety in Tokugawa Japan: Sons and Daughters in the Official Records of Filial Piety." In *Women and Confucian*

Cultures in Premodern China, Korea, and Japan, ed. Dorothy Ko, JaHyun Kim Haboush, and Joan R. Piggott, pp. 170–89. Berkeley and Los Angeles: University of California Press, 2003.

Sumitomo shiryōkan 住友史料館, ed. *Sumitomo shiryō sōsho: Asakusa kometen yorozu hikaechō (jō)* 住友史料叢書 : 浅草米店万控帳(上). Kyoto: Shibunkaku shuppan, 1997.

Sumitomo shūshishitsu 住友修史室, ed. *Sen'oku sōkō: fudasashigyō to Sumitomo–kinsei ni okeru Sumitomo no kin'yūgyō* (1) 泉屋叢考１６ : 札差業と住友－近世における住友の金融業 (1). Vol. 16 of *Sen'oku sōkō*. Kyoto: Sumitomo shūshishitsu, 1976.

Suzuki Kimio 鈴木公雄. "Chichū kara horidasareta kinseizō: rokudōsen no kōkogaku" 地中から掘り出された近世像 : 六道銭の考古学. In *Sōten Nihon no rekishi: kinseihen* 争点日本の歴史 : 近世編, ed. Aoki Michio 青木美智雄 and Hosaka Satoru 保坂智, pp. 373–81. Vol. 5 of *Sōten Nihon no rekishi*. Tokyo: Shinjinbutsu ōraisha, 1991.

Suzuki Masaharu 鈴木雅晴. "Segakiza sōdō to mura" 施餓鬼座騒動と村. *Komazawa shigaku* 駒沢史学, no. 55 (March 2000): 303–18.

Suzuki Yoshiaki 鈴木良明. *Kinsei Bukkyō to kange: boen katsudō to chiiki shakai no kenkyū* 近世仏教と勧化 : 募縁活動と地域社会の研究. Tokyo: Iwata shoin, 1996.

Tahara Tsuguo 田原嗣郎. "Jinsei no shisō to goke no shisō: bakuhansei seiji shisō no mujunteki kōzō" 仁政の思想と御家の思想 : 幕藩制政治思想の矛盾的構造. *Shisō* 思想, no. 633 (April 1977): 349–65.

Takada Mamoru 高田衛. *Edo no ekushoshisuto* 江戸の悪霊祓い師. Tokyo: Chikuma shobō, 1991.

Takagi Kazuo 高木一雄. *Edo Kirishitan no junkyō* 江戸キリシタンの殉教. Nagasaki: Seibo no kishisha, 1989.

Takagi Shōsaku 高木昭作. "Hideyoshi, Ieyasu no shinkokukan to sono keifu: Keichō jūhachi nen 'Bateren tsuihō no bun' o tegakari toshite" 秀吉・家康の神国観とその系譜 : 慶長十八年「伴天連追放之文」を手がかりとして. *Shigaku zasshi* 史学雑誌 101, no. 10 (October 1992): 1–26.

Takagi Yūshi 高木祐之 and Fujii Masao 藤井正雄. "Sōtōshū no sōgi" 曹洞宗の葬儀. Part 6 of "Shūkyō, shūhabetsu no sōgi no kenkyū" 宗教・宗派別の葬儀の研究. *Sogi* 3, no. 5 (September 1993): 37–45.

Takagi Yutaka 高木豊. "Kanbun hōnan zengo: Fujufuseshi kenkyū danshō" 寛文法難前後 : 不受不施史研究断章. In *Nichirenshū Fujufuseha no kenkyū* 日蓮宗不受不施派の研究, ed. Kageyama Gyōō 影山堯雄, pp. 236–67. Kyoto: Heirakuji shoten, 1972.

Takai Masatoshi 高井正俊 and Fujii Masao 藤井正雄. "Rinzaishū no sōgi" 臨済宗の葬儀. Part 11 of "Shūkyō, shūhabetsu no sōgi no kenkyū" 宗教・宗派別の葬儀の研究. *Sogi* 4, no. 4 (July 1994): 41–49.

Takahashi Fujitoshi 高橋藤俊. "Shuyō Tōshōgū ichiran" 主要東照宮一覧. In *Kokushi daijiten* 国史大辞典, vol. 10, pp. 112–13. Tokyo: Yoshikawa kōbunkan, 1989.

Takano Toshihiko 高埜利彦. *Kinsei Nihon no kokka kenryoku to shūkyō* 近世日本の国家権力と宗教. Tokyo: Tōkyō daigaku shuppankai, 1989.

Takashima Motohiro 高島元洋. "Kinsei Bukkyō no ichizuke to haibutsuron" 近世仏教の位置づけと排仏論. *Nihon no Bukkyō* 日本の仏教, no. 4 (1995): 151–67.

Takatori Masao 高取正男. *Shintō no seiritsu* 神道の成立. Tokyo: Heibonsha, 1978.

Takeda Akira 竹田旦. *Ie o meguru minzoku kenkyū* 家をめぐる民俗研究. Tokyo: Kōbundō, 1970.

Takeda Chōshū 竹田聴洲. "Kinsei shakai to Bukkyō" 近世社会と仏教. In *Iwanami kōza Nihon rekishi: kinsei 1* 岩波講座 日本歴史：近世1, ed. Asao Naohiro 朝尾直弘 et al., pp. 263–302. Vol. 9 of *Iwanami kōza Nihon rekishi*. Tokyo: Iwanami shoten, 1975.

———. *Minzoku Bukkyō to sosen shinkō* 民俗仏教と祖先信仰. Tokyo: Tōkyō daigaku shuppankai, 1971.

———. *Nihonjin no ie to shūkyō* 日本人の家と宗教. Vol. 6 of *Takeda Chōshū chosakushū* 竹田聴洲著作集. Tokyo: Kokusho kankōkai, 1996.

———. "Sōron: senzo kuyō no mondai shikaku" 総論：先祖供養の問題視角. In *Sōsō bosei kenkyū shūsei: senzo kuyō* 葬送墓制研究集成：先祖供養, ed. Takeda Chōshū, pp. 2–43. Vol. 3 of *Sōsō bosei kenkyū shūsei*. Tokyo: Meicho shuppan, 1979.

———. *Sosen sūhai: minzoku to rekishi* 祖先崇拝：民俗と歴史. Kyoto: Heirakuji shoten, 1957.

———. *Sōshi to shūshi* 葬史と宗史. Vol. 7 of *Takeda Chōshū chosakushū* 竹田聴洲著作集. Tokyo: Kokusho kankōkai, 1994.

Takemi Momoko, "Menstruation Sutra [Ketsubon kyo] Belief in Japan." *Japanese Journal of Religious Studies* 10, nos. 2–3 (June–September 1983): 229–46.

Taki Yoshinari 滝善成. "Shūhanken to handankasei: shūshi ninbetsu aratamechō no chōsa kara" 宗判権と半壇家制：宗旨人別改帳の調査から. *Saikō minzoku* 西郊民俗, no. 98 (1982): 3–8.

Tamamuro Fumio 圭室文雄. "Bakuhan taiseika no Bukkyō" 幕藩体制化の仏教. In *Ajia Bukkyōshi Nihonhen: Edo Bukkyō – taisei Bukkyō to chika shinkō* アジア仏教史日本編：江戸仏教—体制仏教と地下信仰, ed. Nakamura Hajime 中村元 and Kasahara Kazuo 笠原一男, pp. 7–70. Vol. 7 of *Ajia Bukkyōshi Nihonhen*. Tokyo: Kōsei shuppansha, 1972.

———. "Danka seido no seiritsu katei: Kumamoto hanryō o chūshin toshite" 檀家制度の成立過程：熊本藩領を中心として. In *Nihon Bukkyō no keisei to tenkai* 日本仏教の形成と展開, ed. Itō Yuishin 伊藤唯真, pp. 507–36. Kyoto: Hōzōkan, 2002.

———. "Danka seido no tenkai katei: Sagami no kuni Ashigarakamigun Senzushimamura shūmon ninbetsuchō no bunseki" 檀家制度の展開過程：相模国足柄上郡千津嶋村宗門人別帳の分析. *Meiji daigaku kyōyō ronshū* 明治大学教養論集 42 (1968): 20–38.

———. "Edo jidai no mura-chinju no jittai: Mito hanryō mura-chinju no sūryōteki kentō" 江戸時代の村鎮守の実態：水戸藩領村鎮守の数量的検討. *Meiji daigaku kyōyō ronshū* 明治大学教養論集, no. 368 (March 2003): 1–27.

———. *Edo jidai no Sōtōshū no tenkai* 江戸時代の曹洞宗の展開. Tokyo: Sōtōshū shūmuchō, 1999.

——. "Haibutsu kishaku to kindai jiin no jittai: Meiji shonen no jiin mei-saichō ni tsuite" 廃仏毀釈と近代寺院の実態：明治初年の寺院明細帳について. In *Gendai Nihon to Bukkyō II: kokka to Bukkyō – jiyū na shinkō o motomete* 現代日本と仏教 II：国家と仏教－自由な信仰を求めて, ed. Ikeda Eishun 池田英俊 et al., pp. 70–90. Tokyo: Heibonsha, 2000.

——. "Jiin honmatsuchō no seisaku to mondaiten" 寺院本末帳の政策と問題点. In *Edo bakufu jiin honmatsuchō shūsei (ge)* 江戸幕府寺院本末帳集成 (下), ed. Jiin honmatsuchō kenkyūkai 寺院本末帳研究会, pp. 5–26. Tokyo: Yūzankaku shuppan, 1981.

——. "Kaisetsu" 解説. In *Shinpen Meiji ishin shinbutsu bunri shiryō* 新編明治維新神仏分離史料, vol. 1, ed. Tsuji Zennosuke 辻善之助, Murakami Senjō 村上専精, and Washio Junkyō 鷲尾順敬, pp. 531–49. Tokyo: Meicho shuppan, 1984.

——. "Keichō jūkyūnen no terauke shōmon ni tsuite" 慶長十九年寺請証文について. *Fūzoku shigaku* 風俗史学 2 (Spring 1998): 2–27.

——. "Local Society and the Temple-Parishioner Relationship with the Bakufu's Governance Structure." *Japanese Journal of Religious Studies* 28, nos. 3–4 (Fall 2001): 261–92.

——. "Mitohan no dōshō chōshū seisaku" 水戸藩の撞鐘徴収政策. *Meiji daigaku kyōyō ronshū* 明治大学教養論集, no. 86 (February 1974): 1–12.

——. *Nihon Bukkyōshi: kinsei* 日本仏教史：近世. Tokyo: Yoshikawa kōbunkan, 1987.

——. *Sōshiki to danka* 葬式と檀家. Tokyo: Yoshikawa kōbunkan, 1999.

Tamamuro Fumio 圭室文雄 and Nemoto Seiji 根本誠二, eds. "Shaji torishirabe ruisan bunrui mokuji" 社寺取調類纂分類目次. In *Shinpen Meiji Ishin shinbutsu bunri shiryō* 新編明治維新神仏分離史料, vol. 1, ed. Tsuji Zennosuke 辻善之助, Murakami Senjō 村上専精, and Washio Junkyō 鷲尾順敬, pp. 531–49. Tokyo: Meicho shuppan, 1984.

Tamamuro Taijō 圭室諦成. "Chūsei kōki Bukkyō no kenkyū: toku ni Sengokuki o chūshin toshite" 中世後期仏教の研究：とくに戦国期を中心として. *Meiji daigaku jinbun kagaku kenkyūjo nenpō* 明治大学人文科学研究所年報, no. 3 (1961): 1–57.

——. *Sōshiki Bukkyō* 葬式仏教. Tokyo: Daihōrinkaku, 1963.

——. "Sōshiki hōyō no hassei to sono shakai keizaishiteki kōsatsu" 葬式法要の発生とその社会経済史的考察. In *Nihon shūkyōshi kenkyū* 日本宗教史研究, ed. Nihon shūkyōshi kenkyūkai 日本宗教史研究会, pp. 171–213. Tokyo: Ryūshōkaku, 1933.

Tanabe, George J. *Myōe the Dreamkeeper: Fantasy and Knowledge in Early Kamakura Buddhism.* Cambridge, MA: Harvard University Press, 1992.

Tanabe Tadafumi 田辺忠史. "Sōryo oyobi jiin no shakaiteki yakuwari: danshinto no ishiki o megutte" 僧侶および寺院の社会的役割：檀信徒の意識をめぐって. *Bukkyō keizai kenkyū*, no. 22 (May 1993): 21–35.

Tanaka Hisao 田中久夫. "Heian jidai no kizoku no sōsei ni tsuite: toku ni jūisseiki o chūshin toshite" 平安時代の貴族の葬制について：特に十一世紀を中心として. In *Sōsō bosei kenkyū shūsei: haka no rekishi* 葬送墓制研究

集成：墓の歴史, ed. Uwai Hisayoshi 上井久義, pp. 186–204. Vol. 5 of *Sōsō bosei kenkyū shūsei*. Tokyo: Meicho shuppan, 1979.

Tanaka Kyōshō 田中教照 and Fujii Masao 藤井正雄. "Jōdoshinshū no sōgi" 浄土真宗の葬儀. Part 8 of "Shūkyō, shūhabetsu no sōgi no kenkyū" 宗教・宗派別の葬儀の研究. *Sogi* 4, no. 1 (January 1994): 31–39.

Tanaka Sen'ichi 田中宣一. "Nenchū gyōji no kōzō" 年中行事の構造. In *Nihon minzoku bunka taikei: koyomi to saiji – Nihonjin no kisetsu kankaku* 日本民俗文化大系：暦と祭事—日本人の季節感覚, ed. Miyata Noboru, pp. 67–126. Vol. 9 of *Nihon minzoku bunka taikei*. Tokyo: Shōgakukan, 1984.

Tanaka Takaji 田中隆二. "Kagahan ni okeru Shinshū kyōdan no jidan kankei" 加賀藩における真宗教団の寺檀関係. *Ryūkoku shidan* 龍谷史壇, nos. 81–82 (March 1983): 115–30.

Tanaka Yasuo 田中康雄. "Mitsuiten hōkōnin no sōbo" 三井店奉公人の総墓. *Mitsui bunko ronsō* 三井文庫論叢, no. 11 (1977): 391–420.

Tanigawa Akio 谷川章雄. "Edo no bochi no hakkutsu: mibun, kaisō no hyōchō toshite no haka" 江戸の墓地の発掘：身分・階層の表徴としての墓. In *Yomigaeru Edo* 甦る江戸, ed. Edo iseki kenkyūkai 江戸遺跡研究会, pp. 79–111. Tokyo: Shinjinbutsu ōraisha, 1991.

———. "Ennōji ato ni okeru maisō shisetsu to fukusōhin" 圓應寺跡における埋葬施設と副葬品. In *Ennōji ato: Shinjuku kuritsu Wakaba kōreisha zaitaku sābisusentā kensetsu ni tomonau kinkyū hakkutsu chōsa hōkokusho* 圓應寺跡：新宿区立若葉高齢者在宅サービスセンター建設に伴う緊急発掘調査報告書, ed. Shinjukuku kōseibu iseki chōsakai 新宿区厚生部遺跡調査会, pp. 106–12. Tokyo: Shinjukuku kōseibu iseki chōsakai, 1993.

———. "Jishōin iseki ni okeru bohyō to maisō shisetsu" 自証院遺跡における墓標と埋葬施設. In *Jishōin iseki: Shinjukuku Tomihisa shōgakkō kaichiku ni tomonau kinkyū hakkutsu chōsa hōkokusho* 自証院遺跡：新宿区立富久小学校改築に伴う緊急発掘調査報告書, ed. Jishōin iseki chōsadan 自証院遺跡調査団, pp. 188–94. Tokyo: Tōkyōto Shinjukuku kyōiku iinkai, 1987.

———. "Kinsei bohyō no hensen to ie ishiki: Chibaken Ichiharashi Takataki, Yōrō chiku no kinsei bohyō no saikentō" 近世墓標の変遷と家意識：千葉県市原市高滝・養老地区の近世墓標の再検討. *Shikan* 史観 121 (September 1989): 2–16.

Taniguchi Keitarō 谷口恵太郎. "Shimabara Amakusa no ran ni kansuru kōsatsu" 島原天草の乱に関する考察. *Ryūkoku shidan* 龍谷史壇, no. 92 (October 1988): 50–67.

Teiser, Stephen F. *The Ghost Festival in Medieval China*. Princeton: Princeton University Press, 1988.

———. *The Scripture on the Ten Kings and the Making of Purgatory in Medieval Chinese Buddhism*. Honolulu: University of Hawai'i Press, 1994.

Tejima Toan 手島堵庵. "Zenkun" 前訓. In *Nihon shisō taikei: Sekimon Shingaku* 日本思想史大系：石門心学, ed. Shibata Minoru 柴田実, pp. 159–83. Vol. 42 of *Nihon shisō taikei*. Tokyo: Iwanami shoten, 1971.

Terakado Seiken 寺門静軒. *Edo hanjōki* 江戸繁昌記 (1832–36). Reprint. Tokyo: Misaki shobō, 1972.

Tezuka Hiroshi 手塚浩司. "Kinsei Shinano ni okeru kyūri, kandō, chōgai ni tsuite: 'Kubota monjo' o jirei ni shite" 近世信濃における旧離・勘当・帳外について：「久保田文書」を事例にして. *Shinano* 信濃 54, no. 10 (October 2002): 715-34.

Thelle, Notto R. *Buddhism and Christianity in Japan: From Conflict to Dialogue, 1854-1899.* Honolulu: University of Hawai'i Press, 1987.

Titsingh, Isaac. *Illustrations of Japan.* Translated from the French by Frederic Shoberl. London: Ackermann, 1822.

Toki Masanori 土岐昌訓. "Kinsei no shinshoku soshiki: Musashi no kuni no jirei" 近世の神職組織：武蔵国の事例. *Kokugakuin daigaku Nihon bunka kenkyūjo kiyō* 國學院大學日本文化研究所紀要 12 (March 1963): 191-254.

Tokugawa jikki 徳川実紀, vols. 1-6. Ed. Kuroita Katsumi 黒板勝美 and Kokushi taikei henshūkai 国史大系編集会. Tokyo: Yoshikawa kōbunkan, 1964-65.

Tokugawa kinreikō 徳川禁令考, vols. 3 and 5. Comp. Shihōshō shomuka 司法省庶務課. Tokyo: Shihōshō shomuka, 1895.

Tokutomi Sohō 徳富蘇峰. *Kinsei Nihon kokuminshi: Tenpō kaikakuhen* 近世日本国民史：天保改革篇. Vol. 28 of *Kinsei Nihon kokuminshi.* Tokyo: Kinsei Nihon kokuminshi kankōkai, 1964.

Tōkyōto Bunkyōku kyōiku iinkai 東京都文京区教育委員会, ed. *Bunkyō kushi* 文京区史, vol. 2. Tokyo: Tōkyōto Bunkyōkyu, 1968.

Tōkyōto kōbunshokan 東京都公文書館, ed. *Tōkyō shishikō: sangyōhen* 東京市史稿：産業編, vols. 6, 7, and 37. Tokyo: Tōkyōto kōbunshokan, 1958, 1960.

Tōkyōto Edo-Tōkyō hakubutsukan toshi rekishi kenkyūshitsu 東京都江戸東京博物館都市歴史研究室, ed. *Yotsuya Shiochō itchōme ninbetsu kakiage* 四谷塩町一丁目人別書上. 2 vols. In *Edo-Tokyo hakubutsukan shiryō sōsho* 江戸東京博物館史料叢書. Tokyo: Tōkyōto Edo-Tōkyō hakubutsukan, 1998-99.

Toyoda Takeshi 豊田武. *Myōji no rekishi* 苗字の歴史. Tokyo: Chūō kōronsha, 1971.

——. *Shūkyō seidoshi* 宗教制度史. Tokyo: Yoshikawa kōbunkan, 1982.

Tsuji Mayumi 辻まゆみ. "Kinsei sonraku to chōgai" 近世村落と帳外. *Shien* 史苑 49, no. 1 (April 1989): 6-23.

Tsujimoto Masashi 辻本雅史. "Kinsei kōki ni okeru minshūkan: kyōkaron o chūshin ni" 近世後期における民衆観：教化論を中心に. In *Tenbō Nihon rekishi: kinsei no shisō to bunka* 展望日本歴史：近世の思想と文化, ed. Aoki Michio 青木美智男 and Wakao Masaki 若尾政希, pp. 212-25. Vol. 16 of *Tenbō Nihon rekishi.* Tokyo: Iwanami shoten, 2002.

Tsuji Tatsuya 辻達也. "Tokugawa seiken kakuritsu katei no kōbu kankei" 徳川政権確立課程の公武関係. In *Nihon no kinsei: tennō to shōgun* 日本の近世：天皇と将軍, ed. Tsuji Tatsuya, pp. 57-94. Vol. 2 of *Nihon no kinsei.* Tokyo: Chūō kōronsha, 1991.

Tsuji Zennosuke 辻善之助. *Nihon Bukkyōshi: kinseihen no ni* 日本仏教史：近世編の二. Tokyo: Iwanami shoten, 1953.

——. *Nihon Bukkyōshi: kinseihen no san* 日本仏教史：近世編の三. Tokyo: Iwanami shoten, 1954.

——. *Nihon Bukkyōshi: kinseihen no yon* 日本仏教史：近世編の四. Tokyo: Iwanami shoten, 1955.

———. "Shinshoku ridan mondai ni tsuite" 神職離檀問題について. In *Shinsōsai daijiten* 神葬祭大事典, ed. Katō Takahisa 加藤隆久, pp. 364–80. Tokyo: Ebisu kōshō shuppan, 1997.

Tsūkō ichiran 通航一覧, vol. 5, ed. Hayakawa Junzaburō 早川純三郎. Tokyo: Kokusho kankōkai, 1913.

Tsunoda, Ryusaku, et. al. *Sources of Japanese Tradition*, vol. 2. New York: Columbia University, 1958.

Turnbull, Stephen. *The Kakure Kirishitan of Japan: A Study of Their Development, Beliefs and Rituals to the Present Day*. Richmond, Surrey, UK: Japan Library, 1998.

Udaka Yoshiaki 宇高良哲. *Edo bakufu no Bukkyō kyōdan tōsei* 江戸幕府の仏教教団統制. Tokyo: Tōyō bunka shuppan, 1987.

———. *Kinsei Kantō Bukkyō kyōdanshi no kenkyū: Jōdoshū, Shingonshū, Tendaishū o chūshin ni* 近世関東仏教教団史の研究：浄土宗・真言宗・天台宗を中心に. Tokyo: Bunka shoin, 1999.

———. "Kinsei ni okeru Shugensō no jishin indō mondai ni tsuite: toku ni Musashi no jirei o chūshin ni" 近世における修験僧の自身引導問題について：とくに武蔵の事例を中心に. In *Nihon Bukkyō no keisei to tenkai* 日本仏教の形成と展開, ed. Itō Yuishin 伊藤唯真, pp. 558–74. Kyoto: Hōzōkan, 2002.

———. *Tokugawa Ieyasu to Kantō Bukkyō kyōdan* 徳川家康と関東仏教教団. Tokyo: Tōyō bunka shuppan, 1987.

Umeda Yoshihiko 梅田義彦. *Nihon shūkyō seidoshi: kinseihen* 日本宗教制度史：近世編. Rev. ed. Tokyo: Tōsen shuppan, 1972.

Unno, Mark T. "*Recommending Faith in the Sand of the Mantra of Light*: Myōe Kōben's *Kōmyō Shingon Dosha Kanjinki*." In *Re-Visioning "Kamakura" Buddhism*, ed. Richard K. Payne, pp. 167-218. Honolulu: Unversity of Hawai'i Press, 1998.

"Urakami ishūto ikken" 浦上異宗徒一件. In *Nihon shomin seikatsu shiryō shūsei: minkan shūkyō* 日本庶民生活史料集成：民間宗教, ed. Tanigawa Ken'ichi 谷川健一, pp. 761–888. Vol. 18 of *Nihon shomin seikatsu shiryō shūsei*. Tokyo: San'ichi shobō, 1972.

Uranishi Tsutomu 浦西勉. "Higan'e: minkan ni okeru Higan no fūshū" 彼岸会：民間における彼岸の風習. In *Bukkyō minzokugaku taikei: Bukkyō nenchū gyōji* 仏教民俗大系：仏教年中行事, ed. Itō Yuishin 伊藤唯真, pp. 65-96. Vol. 6 of *Bukkyō minzokugaku taikei*. Tokyo: Meicho shuppan, 1986.

Ury, Marian. *Tales of Times Now Past: Sixty-two Stories from a Medieval Japanese Collection*. Ann Arbor, MI.: Center for Japanese Studies, University of Michigan, 1979.

Ushiki Yukio 丑木幸男. *Kōzuke no kuni jiin meisaichō* 上野国寺院明細帳, 8 vols. Maebashi, Gunma: Gunmaken bunka jigyō shinkōkai, 1993-98.

Varley, H. Paul, trans. *A Chronicle of Gods and Sovereigns: Jinnō Shōtōki of Kitabatake Chikafusa*. New York: Columbia University Press, 1980.

Vesey, Alexander Marshall. "The Buddhist Clergy and Village Society in Early Modern Japan." Ph.D. diss., Princeton University, 2003.

Vlastos, Stephen. *Peasant Protests and Uprisings in Tokugawa Japan*. Berkeley and Los Angeles: University of California Press, 1986.

Wakabayashi, Bob Tadashi. *Anti-Foreignism and Western Learning in Early Modern Japan: The New Theses of 1825*. Cambridge, MA: Council on East Asian Studies, Harvard University, 1986.

———. *Japanese Loyalism Reconstrued: Yamagata Daini's Ryūshi Shinron of 1759*. Honolulu: University of Hawai'i Press, 1995.

Wakao Masaki 若尾政希. *'Taiheiki yomi' no jidai: kinsei seiji shisōshi no kōsō* 「太平記読み」の時代 : 近世政治思想史の構想. Tokyo: Heibonsha, 1999.

Wakisaka Akio 脇坂昭夫. "Kan'eiki no Onomichimachi shūmon ninbetsuchō ni tsuite" 寛永期の尾道町宗門人別長について. *Hiroshima daigaku bungakubu kiyō* 広島大学文学部紀要, no. 15 (March 1959): 72–90.

Watanabe Hiroshi 渡辺浩. *Kinsei Nihon shakai to Sōgaku* 近世日本社会と宋学. Tokyo: Tōkyō daigaku shuppankai, 1985.

Watanabe Kenji 渡辺憲司. *Edo yūri seisuiki* 江戸遊里盛衰記. Tokyo: Kōdansha, 1994.

Watanabe Shōgo 渡辺章悟. *Tsuizen kuyō no hotokesama: jūsanbutsu shinkō* 追善供養の仏様 : 十三仏信仰. Tokyo: Keisuisha, 1989.

Watanabe Toshio 渡辺敏夫. *Nihon no koyomi* 日本の暦. Tokyo: Yūzankaku shuppan, 1976.

Watt, Paul B. "Jiun Sonja, 1718–1804: A Response to Confucianism within the Context of Buddhist Reform." In *Confucianism and Tokugawa Culture*, ed. Peter Nosco, pp. 188–214. Princeton: Princeton University Press, 1984.

White, James W. *The Demography of Sociopolitical Conflict in Japan, 1721–1846*. Berkeley: The Institute of East Asian Studies, University of California at Berkeley, 1992.

Whitlock, Greg. "Concealing the Misconduct of One's Own Father: Confucius and Plato on a Question of Filial Piety." *Journal of Chinese Philosophy* 21 (1994): 113–37.

Williams, Duncan Ryūken. "Representations of Zen: An Institutional and Social History of Sōtō Zen Buddhism in Edo Japan." Ph.D. diss., Harvard University, 2000.

———. *The Other Side of Zen: A Social History of Sōtō Zen Buddhism in Tokugawa Japan*. Princeton and Oxford: Princeton University Press, 2005.

Yamada Kazuma 山田一真 and Fujii Masao 藤井正雄. "Shingonshū no sōgi" 真言宗の葬儀. Part 7 of "Shūkyō, shūhabetsu no sōgi no kenkyū" 宗教・宗派別の葬儀の研究. *Sogi* 3, no. 6 (November 1993): 21–29.

Yamagata Bantō 山片蟠桃, *Yume no shiro* 夢の代 (1820). In *Nihon shisō tōsō shiryō* 日本思想闘争史料, vol. 6, ed. Washio Junkyō 鷲尾順敬, pp. 193–384. Tokyo: Meicho kankōkai, 1969.

Yamamoto Hirofumi 山本博文. *Kan'ei jidai* 寛永時代. Tokyo: Yoshikawa kōbunkan, 1989.

Yamamoto Naotomo 山本尚友. "Kinsei buraku jiin no seiritsu ni tsuite (jō)" 近世部落寺院の成立について(上). *Kyōto burakushi kenkyūsho kiyō* 京都部落史研究所紀要, no. 1 (1981): 80–126.

———. "Kinsei buraku jiin no seiritsu ni tsuite (ge)" 近世部落寺院の成立に ついて(下). *Kyōto burakushi kenkyūsho kiyō* 京都部落史研究所紀要, no. 2 (1982): 34–62.

Yamamoto Shūsei 山本秀惺. *Edo Kirishitan yashiki no shiseki* 江戸キリシタン 屋敷の史跡. Tokyo: Ideā shoin, 1924.

Yamamoto Shigeo 山本殖生. "Kumano bikuni no haisatsu" 熊野比丘尼の 配札. *Sangaku Shugen* 山岳修験, no. 23 (March 1999): 47–58.

Yamamoto Shinkō 山本真功, ed. *Kakunshū* 家訓集. Tōyō bunko 東洋文庫 687. Tokyo: Heibonsha, 2001.

Yamanaka Hisao 山中寿夫. "Bakuhan taiseika ni okeru Shinshū jiin to Aki monto" 幕藩体制下における真宗寺院と安芸門徒. In *Chiiki shakai to shūkyō no shiteki kenkyū* 地域社会と宗教の史的研究, ed. Ogura Toyofumi 小倉 豊文, pp. 127–55. Tokyo: Yanagihara shoten, 1963.

Yamanoshirimura no nanushi nikki: Gotenba shishi shiryō sōsho 山の尻村の名主 日記：御殿場市史史料叢書, vol. 2. Gotenbashi, Shizuoka: Gotenba shishi hensan iinkai, 1977.

Yamaori Tetsuo 山折哲雄. "Reikon no jōka: ikotsu sūhai no genryū" 霊魂の 浄化：遺骨崇拝の源流. In *Nihon minzoku bunka taikei: gendai to minzoku – dentō no henyō to saisei* 日本民俗文化大系：現代と民俗—伝統の変容と 再生, ed. Tanigawa Ken'ichi, pp. 309–72. Vol. 12 of *Nihon minzoku bunka taikei*. Tokyo: Shōgakukan, 1986.

———. *Wandering Spirits and Temporary Corpses: Studies in the History of Japanese Religious Tradition*. Ed. and trans. Dennis Hirota. Kyoto: International Research Center for Japanese Studies, 2004.

Yanagita Kunio 柳田国男. "Jidai to nōsei" 時代ト農政. In *Teihon Yanagita Kunio shū* 定本柳田国男集, vol. 16, pp. 1–160. Tokyo: Chikuma shobō, 1969.

———. "Nihon nōminshi 日本農民史. In *Teihon Yanagita Kunio shū* 定本柳田 国男集, vol. 16, pp. 161–236. Tokyo: Chikuma shobō, 1969.

———. "Nihon no matsuri" 日本の祭. In *Teihon Yanagita Kunio shū* 定本柳田 国男集, vol. 10, pp. 153–314. Tokyo: Chikuma shobō, 1969.

———. "Senzo no hanashi" 先祖の話. In *Teihon Yanagita Kunio shū* 定本柳田 国男集, vol. 10, pp. 1–157. Tokyo: Chikuma shobō, 1969.

Yasumaru Yoshio 安丸良夫. *Kamigami no Meiji ishin: shinbutsu bunri to haibutsu kishaku* 神々の明治維新：神仏分離と廃仏毀釈. Tokyo: Iwanami shoten, 1979.

———. "'Kindaika' no shisō to minzoku" 「近代化」の思想と民俗. In *Nihon minzoku bunka taikei: fūdo to bunka – Nihon rettō no isō* 日本民俗文化大系： 風土と文化—日本列島の位相, ed. Tanigawa Ken'ichi 谷川健一, pp. 407– 66. Vol. 1 of *Nihon minzoku bunka taikei*. Tokyo: Shōgakukan, 1986.

———. "Kindai tenkanki ni okeru shūkyō to kokka" 近代転換期における宗教 と国家. In *Nihon kindai shisō taikei: shūkyō to kokka* 日本近代思想体系： 宗教と国家, ed. Yasumaru Yoshio and Miyachi Masato 宮地正人, pp. 490–564. Vol. 5 of *Nihon kindai shisō taikei*. Tokyo: Iwanami shoten, 1988.

———. *Kindai tennōzō no keisei* 近代天皇像の形成. Tokyo: Iwanami shoten, 1992.

———. *Nihon no kindaika to minshū shisō* 日本の近代化と民衆思想. Tokyo: Aoki shoten, 1974.

———. "Sōron: rekishi no naka de no kattō to mosaku" 総論：歴史のなかでの 葛藤と模索. In *Taikei Bukkyō to Nihonjin: kindaika to dentō – kinsei Bukkyō no henshitsu to tenkan* 大系仏教と日本人：近代化と伝統ー近世仏教の変質と 転換, ed. Yasumaru Yoshio, pp. 3-64. Vol. 11 of *Taikei Bukkyō to Nihonjin* 大系仏教と日本人. Tokyo: Shunjūsha, 1986.

Yasumaru Yoshio 安丸良夫 and Miyachi Masato 宮地正人, eds. *Nihon kindai shisō taikei: shūkyō to kokka* 日本近代思想体系：宗教と国家. Vol. 5 of *Nihon kindai shisō taikei*. Tokyo: Iwanami shoten, 1988.

Yoda Sōzō 依田惣蔵. *Kakun zensho* 家訓全書 (1760). Reprinted in *Nihon nōsho zenshū* 日本農書全集, vol. 24, ed. Ōi Takao 大井隆男, pp. 257-361. Tokyo: Nōsangyoson bunka kyōkai, 1981.

Yokoōji Katsuoki 横大路勝興. *Nenchū kokoroegaki* 年中心得書. Reprinted in *Nihon nōsho zenshū* 日本農書全集, vol. 31, ed. Hidemura Senzō 秀村選三, pp. 63-88. Tokyo: Nōsangyoson bunka kyōkai, 1981.

Yokota Akira 横田明 and Kobayashi Yoshitaka 小林義孝. "Kōmyō shingon to sōsō girei" 光明真言と葬送儀礼. *Rekishi minzokugaku* 歴史民俗学 8 (October 1997): 214-47.

Yokoyama Yasuko 横山泰子. *Yotsuya kaidan wa omoshiroi* 四谷怪談は面白い. Tokyo: Heibonsha, 1997.

Yoshida Eijirō 吉田栄治郎. "Kinsei Yamato no sanmai hijiri: ikkoku nakama soshiki o megutte" 近世大和の三昧聖：一国仲間組織をめぐって. In *Sanmai hijiri no kenkyū* 三昧聖の研究, ed. Hosokawa Ryōichi 細川涼一, pp. 135-72. Tokyo: Sekibunsha, 2001.

Yoshida Kanetomo 吉田兼倶. "Yuiitsu Shintō myōhō yōshū" 唯一神道名法 要集. In *Zoku gunsho ruijū* 続群書類従, vol. 3, no. 2, pp. 636-61. Tokyo: Zoku gunsho ruijū kanseikai, 1932.

Yoshida Nobuyuki 吉田伸之. "Hitoyado" 人宿 and "Tobi" 鳶. In *Nihon toshishi nyūmon: hito* 日本都市史入門：人, ed. Takahashi Yasuo 高橋康夫 and Yoshida Nobuyuki, pp. 216-17, 220. Vol. 3 of *Nihon toshishi nyūmon*. Tokyo: Tōkyō daigaku shuppankai, 1990.

———. "Kōjū to minshū sekai" 講中と民衆世界. *Nenpō toshishi kenkyū* 年報 都市史研究 6 (1998): 60-72.

———. *Nihon no rekishi: seijuku suru Edo* 日本の歴史：成熟する江戸. Vol. 17 of *Nihon no rekishi*. Tokyo: Kōdansha, 2002.

Yoshida Tokkō 吉田徳晃. "Tsuizen butsuji ni kansuru kōsatsu: chūin ni kanshite" 追善仏事に関する考察：中陰に関して. *Bukkyōgaku kaihō* 仏教学 会報, no. 7 (December 1981): 36-40.

Yoshida Toshizumi 吉田俊純. "Tokugawa Mitsukuni no jisha seiri to sonraku" 徳川光圀の寺社整理と村落. *Chihōshi kenkyū* 地方史研究, no. 253 (February 1995): 20-39.

Yoshie Akio 義江彰夫. *Shinbutsu shūgō* 神仏習合. Tokyo: Iwanami shoten, 1996.

Yoshihara Mutsumu 吉原睦. "Kinsei danka seido no minzokugakuteki kōsatsu: 'ikka ichiji gensoku' no umu ni tsuite" 近世檀家制度の民俗学的 考察：「一家一寺原則」の有無について. *Minzokugaku ronsō* 民俗学論叢, no. 15 (April 2000): 19-31.

——. "Nijū no danka kankō ni kansuru ichikōsatsu: Saitamaken Miyashiro-machi no jirei kara" 二重の檀家慣行に関する一考察：埼玉県宮代町の事例から. *Nihon minzokugaku* 日本民俗学, no. 221 (February 2000): 65–95.

Yoshii Toshiyuki 吉井敏幸. "Sanmai hijiri to bosei no hensen" 三昧聖と墓制の変遷. *Kokuritsu rekishi minzoku hakubutsukan kenkyū hōhoku* 国立歴史民俗博物館研究報告 68 (March 1996): 109–33.

Yoshizawa Satoru 吉澤悟. "Nara bonchi to sono shūhenchi ni okeru kinsei sekitō no zōritsu keikō ni tsuite" 奈良盆地とその周辺地における近世石塔の造立傾向について. *Kokuritsu rekishi minzoku hakubutsukan kenkyū hōkoku* 国立歴史民俗博物館研究報告 112 (February 2004): 161–79.

Zenkoku minji kanrei ruishū 全国民事慣例類集 (1880). Ed. Shihōshō 司法省. Reprint. Tokyo: Seishisha, 1976.

Zuikei Shūhō 瑞渓周鳳. *Zenrin kokuhōki* 善隣国宝記. Ed. and annot. Tanaka Takeo 田中健夫. Tokyo: Shūeisha, 1995.

ꝏ

List of Characters

Abe Masahiro　阿部正弘
Abe Tadaaki　阿部忠秋
aisatsu　挨拶
Aizawa Seishisai　会澤正志斎
Akagi Jinja　赤城神社
Akechi Mitsuhide　明智光秀
akedango　明け団子
Akiyama Keizan　秋山景山
akutai shibai　悪態芝居
Amakusa kuzure　天草崩れ
Amakusa-Shimabara　天草島原
Amakusa Shirō　天草四郎
Amida　阿弥陀
Amida darani　阿弥陀陀羅尼
Amidadō　阿弥陀堂
Amidakyō　阿弥陀経
an　庵
anatsurushi　穴吊るし
Andō Shigenobu　安藤重信
angō　庵号
anshitsu　庵室
anshu　庵主
An'yōin　安養院
An'yōji　安養寺
Aoyama Naomichi　青山直道
Arai Hakuseki　新井白石
aramitama　荒魂、新霊
Arima Harunobu　有馬晴信
Asai Ryōi　浅井了意

Asakusa komemise yorozu hikaechō
　浅草米店万控帳
Asamayama　朝熊山
Ashikaga Yoshiaki　足利義昭
ashura　阿修羅
asobi　遊び
Atsuta Jingū　熱田神宮

Baba Toshishige　馬場利重
bakuhan　幕藩
bateren　伴天連
bateren monto　伴天連門徒
bateren shūshi　伴天連宗旨
Bateren tsuihō no bun
　伴天連追放之文
bettōji　別当寺
Birushanabussetsu kongōchōgyō
　kōmyōshingon giki
　毘盧遮那仏説金剛頂経
　光明真言儀軌
Bishamonten　毘沙門天
bodai　菩提
bodaiji　菩提寺
Bon　盆
Bonku　盆供
Bon matsuri　盆祭り
Bonmōkyō　梵網経
Bonshun　梵舜
botamochi　牡丹餅

bu 武
bui 武威
Buke shohatto 武家諸法度
bukki 服忌
bukkiryō 服忌令
Bukkyō 仏教
bumin 撫民
bun 文
Bungo kuzure 豊後崩れ
Buppō gokokuron 仏法護国論
burakumin 部落民
butsudan 仏壇
butsudan aratame 仏壇改め
butsudō 仏堂
butsuji 仏事
butsuma 仏間
Butsujō 仏定
Buyō Inshi 武陽隠士

Ch'an-yüan ch'ing-kuei 禅苑清規
chasen 茶筅
chazuke 茶漬け
chesa 祭祀
Chiaki Kijō 千秋季条
Chiba Jōryū 千葉乗隆
Chih-i 智顗
chikushō 畜生
chingo kokka 鎮護国家
chinju 鎮守
Chinjuchō 鎮守帳
chinjugami 鎮守神
chinjusha 鎮守社
chinkon 鎮魂
Chinmoku 沈黙
Chion'in 知恩院
Chōemon 長右衛門
Chōenji 長遠寺
chōgai 帳外
chōhazure 帳外
Chokugo engi 勅語衍義
Chōnen 超然
chōnin 町人
Chōrakuji 長楽寺
Chōsenji 長泉寺
Chōsenji 超専寺
Chūdō 中道

chūin 中陰
chūindan 中陰壇
Chūkōshi 忠孝誌
Chung-yüan 中元
chūu 中有

Daiga 大我
Daigoji 醍醐寺
daigongen 大権現
daihishin darani 大悲心陀羅尼
daijōdaijin 太政大臣
Daijōin 大乗院
Daijuji 大樹寺
daimoku 題目
daimokukō 題目講
Daimonji 大文字
daimyōjin 大明神
Dainichi 大日
Dainichi Nyorai 大日如来
daishi 大姉
Daishi 大師
daishigō 大姉号
Daishōji 大聖寺
Daitokuji 大徳寺
Daiyūin-dono 大猷院殿
dajōtennō 太上天皇
danchū 檀中
danka 檀家
dankadera 檀家寺
danka seido 檀家制度
dankata 檀方
danna 檀那
dannadera 檀那寺
dan'otsu 檀越
danto 檀徒
dan'yaku 檀役
daraku Bukkyō 堕落仏教
darani 陀羅尼
Date 伊達
degaichō 出開帳
Denkō Fuchū 田孝不忠
Denkō Fuchū Shinnyo
　　田孝不忠信女
Denzūin 伝通院
dōhōgyō 同朋行
Doi Toshikatsu 土井利勝

dōji　童子
dōjo　童女
dōjō　道場
dōjuku　同宿
Domingo Matsugorō
　　ドミンゴ松五郎
dōmyō　同苗
doshakaji　土砂加持
Dōshōan　道正庵
dōshuku　同宿
dōzoku　同族
dōzokudan　同族団

ebumi　絵踏み
Echū　恵中
Edo meisho zue
　　江戸名所図絵
ehōdana　恵方棚
Eiheiji　永平寺
Eishōji　永照寺
Eitaiji　永代寺
eitaikyō　永代経
eji　穢寺
ekō　回向
ekōchō　回向帳
Ekū　慧空
ema　絵馬
Endō Shūsaku　遠藤周作
Enfukuji　圓福寺
enkadera　エンカ寺
enkaridera　縁借寺
Enma　閻魔
Enmaō　閻魔王
Enma mairi　閻魔参り
Enmanji　圓満寺
Ennin　円仁
en no tsuna　縁の綱
Ennōji　円応寺
Enryakuji　延暦寺
Enryūji　円龍寺
Enshōji　圓正寺
Entokuji　圓徳寺
En'ya　塩治
eta　穢多
etoki　絵解き
etoki bikuni　絵解比丘尼

Fa-hua san-mei ch'an-i
　　法華三昧懺儀
fudai　譜代
fudasashi　札差
Fudō　不動
Fudōin　不動院
Fudōmyōō　不動明王
Fugen　普賢
fuhō deiri　不法出入
Fujii Raisai　藤井懶斎
Fujii Umon　藤井右門
Fujikō　富士講
Fujimori Kōan　藤森弘庵
Fujiokaya nikki　藤岡屋日記
Fujita Kenzō　藤田顕蔵
Fujita Tōko　藤田東湖
Fujiwara Seika　藤原惺窩
Fujufuseha　不受不施派
Fukagawa Fudōdō　深川不動堂
Fukahori Yasuzaemon
　　深堀安左衛門
Fukansai Habian
　　不干斎巴鼻庵
Fukeikun　父兄訓
Fukuba Bisei　福羽美静
fukudanka　複檀家
*Fukūkenjaku Birushanabutsu
　　daikanjō kōshingonkyō*
　　不空羂索毘盧遮那仏大灌頂
　　光真言経
Fukūkenjaku jinben shingonkyō
　　不空羂索神変真言経
Fukusenji　福専寺
Fukushima Masanori
　　福島正則
Fukushōji　福昌寺
Fukuzenji　福善寺
fumie　踏絵
fumiechō　踏絵帳
Fu-mu en-chung ching
　　父母恩重経
Funahashi Hidekata　船橋秀賢
funanushi　船主
Furansudera　フランス寺
furegashira　触頭
fushin　普請

gaki 餓鬼
gakki 月忌
gannin 願人
Ganshōji 願正寺
gappei 合併
gekokujō 下剋上
Genchi 玄智
Genkakuji 源覚寺
Genki 元亀
Genna 元和
Genroku 元禄
Genroku gōchō 元禄郷帳
Gensanji 玄珊寺
Genshin 源信
Genshōji 源正寺
Gen'yūin 厳有院
genze annon 現世安穏
genzoku 還俗
Gesshō 月性
Gidō 義導
Gionji 祇園寺
gōchō 郷帳
Gofunai bikō 御府内備考
Gofunai fūdoki 御府内風土記
Gojiin 護持院
Gojōmoku shūmon danna ukeai no okite
　御条目宗門檀那請合之掟
goke 御家
gokoku 護国
Gokokuji 護国寺
Gokurakuin 極楽院
Gokurakuji 極楽寺
Gomizunoo 後水尾
Gomontoshū 御門徒宗
gondainagon 権大納言
gongen 権現
Gongen-sama 権現様
goningumi 五人組
goningumichō 五人組帳
gorin (Five Relationships) 五倫
gorin 五輪
gorintō 五輪塔
goryō 御霊
goryōsho kaikaku 御料所改革
Gōsei 仰誓

goshō zensho 後生善処
goshuinchi 御朱印地
Gōtokuji 豪徳寺
Goyōzei 後陽成
Gozan Jissatsu shozan
　五山十刹諸山
Guzeiji 弘誓寺
gyakusetsu no onrai kankei
　逆説の恩頼関係
gyakushu 逆修
Gyokusen'in 玉泉院
Gyokutan 玉潭
gyōnin 行人
Gyōzenji 行善寺

hachibu 八分
Hachiman gudōkin 八幡愚童訓
Ha Daiusu 破提宇子
hafuru ハフル、波不流
Ha Kirishitan 破吉利支丹
haibutsu kishaku 廃仏毀釈
hairidango 入団子
hairyōchi 拝領地
Hai Yaso 排耶蘇
hakaishi 墓石
haku (p'o) 魄
Hakusan 白山
Hakuun'an 白雲庵
hakyaku 破却
han 藩
handanka 半檀家
Hanju zanmaikyō 般舟三昧経
hannya haramitsu 般若波羅蜜
Hannya haramitta shingyō
　般若波羅蜜多心経
Hanshichi 半七
Harada Toshiaki 原田敏明
harae 祓 (祓え)
haramitsu 波羅蜜
Hara Mondo 原主水
Harimaya Nakaike 播磨屋中井家
Haru はる
Hasegawa Fujihiro 長谷川藤広
Hassenju hannya 八千頌般若
Hasshōji 発昌寺
Hasugesan 八菅山

hatamoto 旗本
hatsuho 初穂
hatsumiyamairi 初宮参り
hayamonoya 早物屋
hayaokeya 早桶屋
Hayashi Gonzaemon 林権左衛門
Hayashi Razan 林羅山
Hayashi Shihei 林子平
hei 幣
Heiroku 平六
hiaburi 火焙り
Hidenshū 悲田宗
Hieizan 比叡山
Higan 彼岸
Higaneyama 日金山
Higashichōshōji 東超勝寺
Higashihonganji 東本願寺
hijiri 聖
Hijō nikki 非常日記
hikan 被官
hiki 疋
Hikimigumi 疋見組
Himon'ya Hokkeji 碑文谷法華寺
hinagata 雛形
hinin 非人
hi no gan 日の願
Hiradomachi Yokoseuramachi
    ninzū aratame no chō
    平戸町横瀬浦町人数改之帳
Hirata Atsutane 平田篤胤
Hirayama Jōchin 平山常陣
Hirose Tansō 広瀬淡窓
hito-nanuka 一七日
hitoyado 人宿
hizamoto 膝元
hōbi 褒美
Hōdōji 宝幢寺
hōgō 法号
hōji 法事
Hōjiji 法持寺
Hōjō Ujinaga 北条氏長
Hokekyōji 法華経寺
hokke senbō 法華懺法
hokke zanmai 法華三昧
Hokkeji 法華寺
Hōkōji 方広寺

hōkyōintō 宝篋印塔
hōmuru 葬る
hōmyō 法名
honbyakushō 本百姓
Honchō 本朝
Honchō kōshiden 本朝孝子伝
Honda Masazumi 本田正純
Hōnen zeisho 豊年税書
Honganji 本願寺
Hongan jiin 本願寺院
hongoku 本国
Hongū 本宮
Honjakuji 本迹寺
honji suijaku 本地垂迹
honke 本家
honmatsu 本末
honmatsuchō 本末帳
Honmyōji 本妙寺
honnin dōzen 本人同前
Honshōji 本照寺
honzan 本山
Hōonkō 報恩講
Hōren 法蓮
Hōrenji 法蓮寺
Horie Buzen 堀江豊前
Horie Hitachi 堀江常陸
Horie Inaba 堀江因幡
Hōseiji 法誓寺
Hoshina Masayuki 保科正之
Hōshōin 宝生院
Hosokawa Garashiya
    細川ガラシヤ
Hosokawa Tadaoki 細川忠興
hossu 払子
hossu 法主
hotoke 仏
Hōzōji 宝蔵寺
Hsiao-ching 孝経
hyakumanben nenbutsu
    百万遍念仏
hyakushō 百姓
hyakushōkabu 百姓株
hyakushō no naritachi
    百姓の成り立ち
hyakushō shōgatsu 百姓正月
Hyōjōsho 評定所

ibutsu 異仏
Ichigorō 市五郎
ichinomiya 一ノ宮
Ichizō 市蔵
ie 家
iegoroshi 家殺し
ieishiki 家意識
iemochi 家持
iemoto 家元
ie no kami 家の神
ie shakai イエ社会
igaku no kin 異学の禁
Igi Tanomo 伊木頼母
ihai 位牌
Ihei 伊兵衛
ihō 異法
Ikeda Mitsumasa 池田光政
ikidokoro no kami 生所神
ikimitama 生御魂、生見玉
ikitsuki take 息つき竹
ikka-ichijisei 一家一寺制
ikki 一揆
Ikkō ikki 一向一揆
Ikkōshū 一向宗
Ikkyū 一休
Ikoku nikki 異国日記
imiake 忌明け
imoi 斎
Inaba Kagemichi 稲葉景道
Inaba Nobumichi 稲葉信道
Inaba Norimichi 稲葉典道
Ina Hanzaemon
  伊奈半左衛門
inaka danrin 田舎檀林
indengō 院殿号
indō 引導
ine 稲
ingō 院号
inke 院家
Inoue Masashige 井上政重
Inoue Tetsujirō 井上哲次郎
Inoyama Nobuyuki 猪山信之
inshi 淫祀
Iōin 医王院
Ise Jingū 伊勢神宮
Ishigai Sadakiyo 石谷貞清

Ishihara Seizaemon
  石原清左衛門
Ishiyama Honganji 石山本願寺
ishū 異宗
Itakura Katsushige 板倉勝重
Itakura Shigemasa 板倉重昌
Itakura Shigemune 板倉重宗
itazura hyakushō 徒百姓
Itō Jōuemon 伊藤定右衛聞
Itō Kihee 伊藤喜兵衛
ito wappu 糸割符
Itō Yuishin 伊藤唯真
itsu-nanuka 五七日
Iwakura Tomomi 岩倉具視
Izumiya Jinzaemon
  泉屋甚左衛門
Izumo Taisha 出雲大社

ji 持
jibutsu 持仏
jibutsudō 持仏堂
jichū 寺中
jidan seido 寺檀制度
jigari 地借
Jigenji 慈眼寺
jigoku 地獄
jigoku zōshi 地獄草紙
jiin 寺院
jiin hatto 寺院法度
jiin honmatsuchō 寺院本末帳
Jiin kaikichō 寺院開基帳
jiin meisaichō 寺院明細帳
jiin seiri 寺院整理
Jikata hanreiroku 地方凡例録
Jikōji 慈広寺
jinchiku aratamechō
  人畜改帳
Jingikan 神祇官
Jingi seishū 神祇正宗
Jingishō 神祇省
jingūji 神宮寺
Jingūkyō 神宮教
jinnin 神人
Jinnō shōtōki 神皇正統記
jinsei 仁政
Jinshin koseki 壬申戸籍

Jinsuke banashi　仁助噺
jiriki　自力
jiroku　寺祿
jisha bugyō　寺社奉行
Jishakata oshioki reigaki
　　寺社方御仕置例書
jishin indō　自身引導
Jishōin　自証院
Jishū　時宗
jisō　自葬
Jitsunyo　実如
Jiun　慈雲
Jizō　地蔵
Jizōdō　地蔵堂
Jizō Bosatsu hosshin innen jūōkyō
　　地蔵菩薩発心因縁十王経
Jizō hongankyō　地蔵本願経
Jizōkyō　地蔵経
jō　定
jōbutsu　成仏
jochi　除地
jōdo　浄土
Jōdoji　浄土寺
Jōdoshinshū　浄土真宗
Jōdoshū　浄土宗
Jōdoshū hōyōshū　浄土宗法要集
Jōdoshū shoji no chō　浄土宗諸寺之帳
Jōenji　浄円寺
Jōenji　常圓寺
Jōgyōan　常行庵
jōgyō zanmai　常行三昧
Jōkagumi　城下組
Jōkanji　浄閑寺
Jōkenji　浄見寺
Jōkōin　充行院
Jōkōji　乗光寺
Jōkyō　貞享
Jōkyūji　常久寺
Jōrenji　常蓮寺
Jōrinji　常林寺
Jōsenji　浄泉寺
Jōshinji　浄心寺
Jōshinji　常真寺
Jōshin Koji　浄心居士
Jūgōen raijugiki　充洽園礼誦儀記
Jūjōin　十乗院

jukai　授戒
Jumyōin　寿命院
Jun'yo　遵誉
Jūōkyō　十王経
Jūō sandanshō　十王讃歎抄
Jurakutei　聚楽第
jūsanbukyō　十三部経
jūsan butsuji　十三仏事
jūsanbutsu mandara　十三仏曼荼羅
jūsanbutsu nenbutsu　十三仏念仏
jūsan sotoba　十三卒塔婆
Jutokuji　寿徳寺

ka　加
ka　家
kabu　株
kabunakama　株仲間
Kado Kazusa　門上総
kadomatsu　門松
kafuken　家父権
kagami　鏡
kagamimochi　鏡餅
kago　駕籠
kagura　神楽
kagyō　家業
Kagyōkō　家業考
kaichō　開帳
kaichō kanjin　開帳勧進
Kaifukuji　海福寺
kaigō　改号
Kaijō monogatari　海上物語
kaiki danna　開基檀那
kaimyō　戒名
Kaizōji　海蔵寺
kaji　加持
Kajūji　勧修寺
kakaebyakushō　抱百姓
kakaku　家格
kakochō　過去帳
kakun　家訓
Kakun zensho　家訓全書
Kakure Kirishitan　隠れキリシタン
kakuriyo　幽界、幽世
kamei　家名
Kamei Koremi　亀井茲監
kami　神

kamidana 神棚
kamishimo 裃
kanbō 看坊
Kanbun 寛文
Kan'ei honmatsuchō 寛永本末帳
Kan'eiji 寛永寺
Kan'eiji Gokokuin 寛永寺護国院
Kan'ei tsūhō 寛永通宝
kaneuchi 鉦打ち
Kan Fugen Bosatsu gyōbōkyō
　　観普賢菩薩行法経
kange 勧化
kanjin 勧進
kanjin hijiri 勧進聖
Kanjin jikkai mandara
　　観心十界曼荼羅
kanjō 灌頂
kanjō bugyō 勘定奉行
Kankoku kōgiroku 官刻孝義録
Kan muryōjukyō 観無量寿経
Kannondō 観音堂
Kannondōkin 観音堂金
Kannongyō 観音経
kannushi 神主
Kannōji 感応寺
kanpaku 関白
kanpei 官幣
Kanpu gosata ryakki
　　官府御沙汰略記
Kansei 寛政
Kantei hisetsu 函底秘説
Kanzeon 観世音
karahafu 唐破風
Kareutafune tokai kinshirei
　　かれうた船渡海禁止令
karoku 家禄
kasan 家産
kasanaru 累なる
Kasane 累
kashin 家臣
Kasshi yawa 甲子夜話
katoku 家督
Katsu かつ
Katsugorō 勝五郎
Katsu Kaishū 勝海舟

Katsuzō 勝蔵
kawa-segaki 川施餓鬼
Kawasumi Yukitaka 川澄幸隆
kazoku kokka 家族国家
kechimyaku 血脈
kegare 穢れ
keidaichi 境内地
Keizan 瑩山
Keizan shingi 瑩山清規
kenchichō 検地帳
Kengiroku 顕偽録
kengō 軒号
ken'yakurei 倹約令
keshōdera ケショウ寺
Ketsubonkyō 血盆経
Kibe Pedoro 岐部ペドロ
Kichizō 吉蔵
Kichijirō 吉次郎
kichū 忌中
kichū harai 忌中祓い
Kihachi 亀八
Kiheitai 奇兵隊
Kijin jippen 畸人十篇
Kikkawa 吉川
Kiku 菊
Kinchū narabi ni kuge shohatto
　　禁中並公家諸法度
kinichi 忌日
kinnōsō 勤王僧
kinō 帰農
Kinsei awaumi nenbutsu ōjōden
　　近世淡海念仏往生伝
Kinsei Bukkyō 近世仏教
Kinsei ōjōden 近世往生伝
Kinsei ōjōden shūsei 近世往生伝集成
Kinshirō 金四郎
Kinu きぬ
kirikami 切紙
Kirishitan キリシタン、切支丹
Kirishitan aratame 吉利支丹改
Kirishitan bugyō 吉利支丹奉行
Kirishitan gojōmoku 切支丹御條目
Kirishitan ruizoku キリシタン類族
Kirishitan ruizoku aratame
　　切支丹類族改
Kirishitan shihai 吉利支丹支配

Kirishitan teki　キリシタン的
Kirishitan yashiki　切支丹屋敷
kishinchi　寄進地
kishōmon　起請文
Kishū meimokukin　紀州名目金
Kitabatake Chikafusa　北畠親房
Kitagawa Morisada　喜田川守貞
Kitanishi Hiromu　北西弘
kitōji　祈祷寺
kō　講
Kōanji　講安寺
koban　小判
Kōbōdaishi　弘法大師
Kobotoke Kohei　小仏小平
kōden　香奠
Kōgakuji　光岳寺
kōgi　公儀
kōgimei　公儀名
Kōgiroku　孝義録
Kogi Shingonshū　古義真言宗
Kōgyō　興教
Kōjakuji　広寂寺
koji　居士
kojigō　居士号
Kōkaku　光格
Kokawadera　粉河寺
Kōken　好堅
kokka ankō　国家安康
kokka Shintō　国家神道
koku　石
Kokubu Naoichi　国分直一
kokudaka　石高
Kokugaku　国学
kokuhei　国幣
kokumin dōtoku　国民道徳
kokuze　国是
Kokūzō　虚空蔵
Kokūzō Bosatsu　虚空蔵菩薩
Kominato Tanjōji　小湊誕生寺
komusō　虚無僧
kōmyōku　光明供
kōmyō shingon　光明真言
kon (hun)　魂
Konchiin　金地院
Konchiin Sūden　金地院崇伝
konfurariya　コンフラリヤ

Konishi Yukinaga　小西行長
Konjaku monogatarishū　今昔物語集
Konnyaku Enma　こんにゃく閻魔
Konpukuji　金福寺
Konsenji　金泉寺
Kōnoike Shinroku (Shin'emon)
　　鴻池新六（新右衛門）
Koori kuzure　郡崩れ
korobi Kirishitan　転びキリシタン
korobu　転ぶ
korosareta haka　殺された墓
kōsatsu　高札
koseki jiin　古跡寺院
Kōshinroku　孝信録
kōshō　高勝
koshōgatsu　小正月
koshuken　戸主権
kōsori　頭剃
kotodama　言霊
Kōtokuji　弘徳寺
kowameshi　強飯
Kōya hijiri　高野聖
Kōyasan　高野山
Kōyasan Myōōin　高野山明王院
koyorikō　小寄講
Kuan wu-liang-shou-ching shu
　　観無量寿経疏
Kujigata osadamegaki　公事方御定書
Kūkai　空海
Kumano bikuni　熊野比丘尼
Kumano no e　熊野の絵
Kumazawa Banzan　熊沢蕃山
Kume Jirō　久米次郎
Kuno　くの
Kurasaki Kauemon　鞍崎加右衛門
Kurokawa Masanao　黒川正直
Kuruma Zenshichi　車善七
Kusakabe Takeemon
　　日下部武右衛門
Kūya　空也
Kuze Hirotami　久世広民
kuzure　崩れ
Kyōbushō　教部省
Kyōbushō shiryō　教部省資料
kyōdōshoku　教導職
kyōgen　狂言

Kyōgyōshinshō 教行信証
Kyōhō 享保
kyōka 教化
kyōkai 教会
kyōkatabira 経帷子
Kyōtokuji 教徳寺
Kyōto oboegaki 京都覚書
Kyoto shoshidai 京都所司代
Kyōzenji 教善寺
Kyūgorō 久五郎
kyūminpō 旧民法
kyūri 久離
Kyūshōji 久昌寺

li 禮

machi 町
machihikeshi 町火消
Maeda Toshinaga 前田利長
maegaki 前書き
magireyasuki
　　まぎれ（紛れ）やすき
mai 枚
mairibaka 詣墓
maitsuki meinichi 毎月命日
Makashikan 摩訶止観
makuradango 枕団子
makuragyō 枕経
Manabe Akikatsu 間部詮勝
Mansenji 万宣寺
Manshōji 万祥寺
marudanka 丸檀家
Maruya 丸屋
Maruya Jinshichi 丸屋甚七
masu 枡
Masudagumi 益田組
Masuda Tokisada 益田時貞
Masumida Jinja 真清田神社
Masuno Sahee 増野佐兵衛
matsuage マツアゲ
Matsudaira Nobutsuna 松平信綱
Matsudaira Norinaga 松平乗寿
Matsudaira Sadamasa 松平定政
Matsudaira Sadanobu 松平定信
Matsudaira Yasuyoshi 松平康福
Matsuemon 松右衛門

matsugo no mizu 末期の水
matsuji okite 末寺掟
Matsukura Katsuie 松倉勝家
Matsuoka Yukiyoshi 松岡行義
Matsura Seizan 松浦静山
Matsusaki Harima 松崎播磨
Matsushita Gunkō 松下郡高
Matsuya Tōkichi 松屋藤吉
Meguro Fudō 目黒不動
meinichi 命日
Meireki 明暦
Meishō 明正
metsuzai 滅罪
mibun 身分
miko 神子
miko 巫女
Mimibukuro 耳袋
minagoroshi 皆殺し
Minamoto no Yorimasa 源頼政
mi-nanuka 三七日
Minkan seiyō 民間省要
Minka yōjutsu 民家要術
minpō 民法
Minpō idete chūkō horobu
　　民法出でて忠孝亡ぶ
minshū kyōka 民衆教化
Miroku 弥勒
misogi 禊
Misumigumi 三隅組
Mito goyōkin 水戸御用金
Mito kaikichō 水戸開基帳
Miura Anjin 三浦按針
Miura Baien 三浦梅園
Miyagi Kazumi 宮城和澄
Miyaoi Sadao 宮負定雄
Mizuno Gunki 水野軍記
mizunomi byakushō 水呑百姓
Mizuno Morinobu 水野守信
mogari 殯
Mo-ho chih-kuan 摩訶止観
Mokichi 茂吉
mokubazeme 木馬責
mokugyōkō 木魚講
Mokurin 黙霖
monjin 門人
Monju 文殊

Monshūji　聞修寺
monto　門徒
monzeki　門跡
monzen　門前
monzenmachi　門前町
Morioka Tashichi　森岡多七
Motochi　元地
motsugo sasō　没後作僧
moya　喪屋
mubosei　無墓制
muen　無縁
muenbotoke　無縁仏
Muenji　無縁寺
Mujū Ichien　無住一円
mukaebi　迎火
mukaetaimatsu　迎松明
mura　村
murahachibu　村八分
murakata sōdō　村方騒動
Muramatsu Hyōzaemon
　　村松標左衛門
Murata Seifū　村田清風
murauke　村請
Muro Kyūsō　室鳩巣
Muryōjukyō　無量寿経
mushiokuri　虫送り
Myōe　明恵
Myōgiji　妙義寺
Myōgyōji　妙行寺
Myōhen　明遍
myōji　苗字
myōjin　明神
Myōki　妙喜
Myōkōji　妙光寺
Myōkōninden　妙好人伝
Myōōji　明応寺
Myōsenji　妙泉寺
Myōshinji　妙心寺
Myōshun　明春

Nabeshima Naotaka　鍋島直孝
Nachi　那智
nagarekanjō　流灌頂
Nagase Tokie　長瀬時衛
nago　名子
naidaijin　内大臣

naisai　内済
Naitō Joan　内藤如庵
naiyū gaikan　内憂外患
Nakai Chikuzan　中井竹山
Nakai Riken　中井履軒
Nakamura Utaemon　中村歌右衛門
Nakamuraza　中村座
nakayado　中宿
nakayashiki　中屋敷
Namu Myōhōrengekyō
　　南無妙法蓮華経
nanban seishi　南蛮誓詞
Nankei　南渓
Naojirō　直次郎
naorai　直会
narimono　鳴物
nayosechō　名寄帳
negi　禰宜
Negoroji　根来寺
nenbutsu　念仏
Nenbutsuji　念仏寺
nenbutsukō　念仏講
nenchū gyōji　年中行事
nenguchi　年貢地
nenki　年忌
nenkiage　年忌アゲ
Nichiki　日輝
Nichirenshū　日蓮宗
Nihon nijūroku junkyōsha kyōkai
　　日本二十六殉教者教会
Nihon nijūroku junkyōsha
　　tenshudō
　　日本二十六殉教者天主堂
Nihon ryōiki　日本霊異記
Nihon sandai jitsuroku
　　日本三代実録
Nihon shoki　日本書紀
nijūgo zanmai　二十五三昧
Nijūnisha　二十二社
Nikka nenbutsu tōshukuhen
　　日課念仏投宿編
ninbetsu aratamechō　人別改帳
ninbetsuchō　人別帳
ninbetsu okurijō　人別送り状
ningen　人間
ninjuchō　人数帳

Ninnaji　仁和寺
Ninomiya Sontoku　二宮尊徳
Ninsei　任誓
Nintoku　仁徳
Nishihonganji　西本願寺
Nishikawa Tokuzō　西川徳蔵
nobe okuri　野辺おくり
Nōbi kuzure　濃尾崩れ
Nōka shōkeishō　農家捷径抄
Nōmin kagami　農民鑑
noren　暖簾
nue　鵺
nyobon　女犯

Ōbakushū　黄檗宗
Oda Nobunaga　織田信長
odori nenbutsu　踊念仏
Ogawa Yoshiyasu　小川義綏
Ōgimachi　正親町
Ogyū Sorai　荻生徂徠
Ōhara Yūgaku　大原幽学
Oiwa　お岩
Oiwa Inari　お岩稲荷
ōjō　往生
ōjōden　往生伝
ojōdo mairi　お浄土詣り
Oka Kumaomi　岡熊臣
Okamoto Daihachi　岡本大八
Okamoto San'emon　岡本三右衛門
Ōkubo Tadachika　大久保忠隣
Ōkuninushi no kami　大国主神
Ōkuni Takamasa　大国隆正
Okuno Masatsuna　奥野昌綱
okuri　送り
okuribi　送り火
okuri issatsu　送り一札
okuri tegata　送手形
Ōkuwa Hitoshi　大桑斉
ōmetsuke　大目付
omononari　御物成
Ōmura Sumitada　大村純忠
Ōnakatomi　大中臣
onbyakushō　御百姓
Ono Naokata　小野直方
Ono Sōemon　小野摠右衛門
onryō　怨霊

onshi　御師
Onuki Man'uemon　小貫萬右衛門
Ōoka Tadasuke　大岡忠相
oshi　御師
oshikome inkyo　押込隠居
Ōshio Heihachirō　大塩平八郎
ōshōgatsu　大正月
Osorezan　恐山
osukui　御救い
Ōtani honbyō　大谷本廟
Ōtani sobyō　大谷祖廟
Ōta Sukemune　太田資宗
otoki　御斎
Otsudō Kanchiku　乙堂喚丑
Ōyama　大山
Oume　お梅
Ōura tenshudō　大浦天主堂

p'en　盆

Raigōji　来迎寺
Rai Mikisaburō　頼三樹三郎
Rai San'yō　頼山陽
rei　礼
Reiganji　霊岸寺
reigō　霊号
reigenki　霊験記
reijingō　霊神号
reisha　霊社
reizan　霊山
Renchōji　蓮長寺
Rengein　蓮花院
Renkyōji　蓮教寺
Rennyo　蓮如
ri　里
ridan　離檀
Riemon　利右衛門
Rihee　利兵衛
Rinnōji　輪王寺
Rinshōan　隣松庵
Rinzaishū　臨済宗
Rishukyō　理趣経
Risshakuji　立石寺
risshun　立春
rokudō　六道
rokudōsen　六道銭

ruizoku　類族
ruizoku keizu　類族系図
ryō　両
Ryōbu Shintō　両部神道
Ryōkan　良寛
Ryōnyo　良如
Ryori saijiki　閭里歳時記
ryūmin　流民
Ryūen　隆円
Ryūon　竜温
Ryūseiji　龍性寺
Ryūsenji　龍泉寺
Ryūshōin　龍松院
Ryūtakuji　柳澤寺

Sahimeyama Jinja　佐毘売山神社
Saifukuji　西福寺
Saigenji　最玄寺
Saihōji　西方寺
saijin ronsō　祭神論争
Saijōji　最乗寺
Saikōin　西光院
Saikokuji　西国寺
Saimyōin　西明院
saisei itchi　祭政一致
Saitō Gesshin　斎藤月岑
Saitō Ryūzō　斉藤隆三
Sajirō　佐治郎
Sakai Tadakatsu　酒井忠勝
Sakai Tadakiyo　酒井忠清
sakayaki　月代
sakuji bugyō　作事奉行
Samgang haegsildo　三綱行實圖
Sandai jitsuroku　三代実録
San'emon　三右衛門
sangai　三界
sangi　参議
sankei　参詣
sanki　三季
sankyō edaha hanami setsu
　三教枝葉花実説
sanmai　三昧
sanmai hijiri　三昧聖
Sannō ichijitsu Shintō
　山王一実神道
Sannō Shintō　山王神道

Sano　さの
Sanpachi　三八
Sanpōin　三宝院
Santō Kyōden　山東京伝
San'yūtei Enchō　三遊亭円朝
Sanzen'in　三千院
Sanzu no kawa　三途の川
Saruwakaza　猿若座
Sawano Chūan　沢野忠庵
se　畝
segaki　施餓鬼
segakiza　施餓鬼座
Seidan　政談
Seigen'in　清源院
Seikichi　清吉
Seikōin　清光院
Seikōji　清光寺
Seishi　勢至
Seiunji　盛雲寺
Seiyō kibun　西洋紀聞
Seji kenbunroku　世事見聞録
Sendara　旃陀羅
sendatsu　先達
Sengan'en　仙巌園
sengoku　戦国
senju darani　千手陀羅尼
senkyōshi　宣教師
Senmyō　宣明
Sennenji　専念寺
Sen no Rikyū　千利休
Sennyūji　泉涌寺
Sen'oku Jinzaemon　泉屋甚左衛門
sensaku　穿鑿
Senshōji　専精寺
Sensōji　浅草寺
senzo daidai no haka
　先祖代々之墓
senzo matsuri　先祖まつり
seppuku　切腹
Sessō Sōsai　雪窓宗崔
setai　世帯
Shajikyoku　社寺局
Shaji torishirabe ruisan
　社寺取調類纂
Shaka　釈迦
shaku　尺

shanin　社人
Shan-tao　善導
Shasekishū　沙石集
shasō　社僧
Shibahashi　柴橋
Shibano Ritsuzan　柴野栗山
shibochi　新発意
Shibukawa Harumi　渋川春海
Shichiemon　七右衛門
shichi-go-san　七五三
shidōkin　祠堂金
shie　紫衣
shigoto hajime　仕事始め
Shimada Katsuji　島田嘉津次
Shimaji Mokurai　島地黙雷
Shimazu Nariakira　島津斉彬
Shimazu Takahisa　島津貴久
shimojimo no kutabire　下々の草臥
shimoyashiki　下屋敷
shinbutsu bunri　神仏分離
shinbutsu reikenki　神仏霊験記
shinchi jiin　新地寺院
Shingi Shingonshū　新義真言宗
Shingon Risshū　真言律宗
Shingū　新宮
Shingū myōjin　新宮明神
shinji　信士
shinjigō　信士号
Shinjikankyō　心地観経
shinkoku　神国
Shinkunsama gojōmoku jūgokajō
　神君様御條目十五ケ條
shinnyo　信女
Shinnyodō　真如堂
shinnyogō　信女号
Shinpen Musashi fūdoki
　新編武蔵風土記
Shinran　親鸞
Shinron　新論
Shinseiji　真盛寺
shinshokuuke　神職請
shinshū　神州
Shinshū　真宗
shinsō　神葬
shinsōsai　神葬祭
shintai　神体

Shintan　震旦
Shintō sōsai　神道葬祭
Shintō sōsai kenbunshū
　神道葬祭見聞集
Shintō sōsai ryakushidai
　神道葬祭略次第
Shintō shūmon shokoku ruireisho
　神道宗門諸国類例書
Shintōuke　神道請
shinzoku-nitai　真俗二諦
Shirakawa　白川
shirei　死霊
Shirei gedatsu monogatari kikigaki
　死霊解脱物語聞書
Shirokiya　白木屋
shiryō　死霊
Shisō zōshiki　祠曹雑識
shissōke　執奏家
Shitennōji　四天王寺
shō　升
shōbō　正法
shobun　処分
Shōdenji　正伝寺
Shōgenji　正眼寺
Shōgoin　聖護院
Shōgyōji　唱行寺
Shojiin jōmoku　諸寺院条目
Shōji Kōki　正司考祺
Shōkai　性海
Shōkakuji　勝覚寺
shōkoku　生国
shokoku junkenshi　諸国巡見使
Shokoku fūzoku toijō　諸国風俗問状
Shōkoku-sama　相国様
shōkon　招魂
shōkonsha　招魂社
Shoku Nihon kōki　続日本後記
shōmono　抄物
sho-nanoka　初七日
shōnin　上人
shōnō keiei　小農経営
Shōō　象王
Shōrenji　青蓮寺
Shōrin'in　少林院
shōryō　精霊
shōryōdana　精霊棚

shōryō-sama　精霊様
shōsha　小社
Shosha negi kannushi hatto
　諸社禰宜神主法度
shōshi　小祠
shōshinge　正信偈
shōshin nenbutsuge　正信念仏偈
Shoshū jiin hatto　諸宗寺院法度
Shoshū sōryo hatto　諸宗僧侶法度
shōsoku　消息
Shōsuke　庄助
shotai　所帯
Shōtatsuji　勝達寺
Shōtokuji　聖徳寺
shōtsuki meinichi　祥月命日
Shōzaburō　庄三郎
Shugen　修験
Shugendō　修験道
shugenja　修験者
Shūgi gaisho　集義外書
shūhanken　宗判権
shuinsen　朱印船
shukkan　出棺
shukke　出家
shukkesha　出家者
shūmei　襲名
shūmon aratame　宗門改め
shūmon aratamechō　宗門改帳
shūmon aratame goninchō
　宗門改五人帳
shūmon aratameyaku　宗門改役
shūmon bugyō　宗門奉行
Shūmon danna ukeai no okite
　宗門檀那請合之掟
shūmon ikki　宗門一揆
Shūmon jūgokajō gojōmoku utsushi
　宗門十五箇條御條目寫
shūmon ninbetsuchō　宗門人別帳
shūmon ninbetsu aratamechō
　宗門人別改帳
shūmon ninbetsu okurijō
　宗門人別送り状
shūmon okuri tegata　宗門送手形
shūmon ukejō　宗門請状
Shunhyakuan　春百庵
shūshi　宗旨

shūshi aratamechō　宗旨改帳
shūshi okuri tegata　宗旨送手形
shusseken　出世間
Shutsujō kōgo　出定後語
Shutsujō shōgo　出定笑語
sōbo　総墓
Sōbō kigen　草茅危言
sōdō　惣堂
Soeda Ichirōji　添田一郎次
Soga Hisasuke　曽我古祐
sōgen senji　宗源宣旨
sōjaban　奏者番
sōji　惣寺
Sōjiji　総持寺
Sōji ryakki　葬事略記
Sōjun　僧純
sōkon　送魂
sokushin jōbutsu　即身成仏
sondō　村堂
Sonoda Kōyū　薗田香融
sorei　祖霊
Sōrinji　雙林寺
Sōrinshū　叢林集
Sōsai ryakushiki　葬祭略式
sosei　蘇生
sosen saishi　祖先祭祀
sosen sūhai　祖先崇拝
sōshiki Bukkyō　葬式仏教
sotoba　卒塔婆
Sōtōshū　曹洞宗
Ssu-ma Kuang　司馬光
Suijinroku　吹塵録
sujiai　筋合
Suke　助
Sukehito　典仁
Sumeramikoto　天皇命
Sumitomo　住友
sutebaka　捨墓
Suzuki Shigenari　鈴木重成
Suzuki Shōsan　鈴木正三

tachikaeri Kirishitan
　立帰りキリシタン
Tachino Kyūen　館野久円
Tadasuke　忠助
Tadayoshi　忠義

taihō 大法
Taikyō senpu undō 大教宣布運動
taima 大麻
taiya 逮夜
taka 高
Takaaki 敬明
Takahashi Ichiemon 高橋市右衛門
Takano Naotaka 高野直孝
Takaya Eizaemon 高谷永左衛門
Takayama Ukon 高山右近
Takebee 武兵衛
Takeda Chōshū 竹田聴洲
Takeda Shingen 武田信玄
Takenaka Shigeyoshi 竹中重義
Takenouchi Shikibu 竹内式部
Takizawa Bakin 滝沢馬琴
Tamamuro Fumio 圭室文雄
Tamamuro Taijō 圭室諦成
tamashii 魂
tamashiro 霊代
tama yobai 魂呼ばい
tamayobi 魂呼び
Tamiya Iemon 民谷伊右衛門
Tamura Yoshishige 田村吉茂
tanagari 店借
tanagyō 棚経
Tanaka Daizen 田中大膳
Tanaka Kyūgu 田中丘愚
Tanaka Sahei 田中左兵衛
Tanjōji 誕生寺
Tankeiji 擔景寺
ta no kami 田の神
tankon shōkazoku 単婚小家族
Tashichi 太七
tatari 祟り
tatchū 塔頭
tawara 俵
tedai 手代
Tejima Toan 手島堵庵
Tendaishū 天台宗
tendō 天道
Tenjiku 天竺
tenka 天下
tenka fubu 天下布武
Tenkai 天海
tenka no ontame 天下の御為

Tenna 天和
tennin 天人
tennōsei 天皇制
Tenpō gōchō 天保郷帳
Tenshō 天正
Tenshōkō Daijin 天照皇大神
Tenshu jitsugi 天主実義
Tenshukyō kōsatsu 天主教考察
teppō aratame 鉄砲改
Terakado Seiken 寺門静軒
terakoya 寺子屋
Tera-machi-kan himonshū
　寺町勘秘聞集
Teranishi Zōtai 寺西蔵太
tera okurijō 寺送り状
tera okuri shōmon 寺送り証文
terauke 寺請
teraukejō 寺請状
terauke shōmon 寺請証文
Terazawa Katataka 寺沢堅高
tetsugitera 手次寺
to 斗
tobi 鳶
toburaiage とぶらひ上げ
Toda Mitsunori 戸田光則
Toda Tadamasa 戸田忠昌
Tōdaiji 東大寺
Tōdenji 東伝寺
Tōeizan 東叡山
Tōemon 藤右衛門
Tōhokuji 東北寺
toiage トイアゲ
toikiri トイキリ
toikiri 問ひきり
tojaku 戸籍
Tōjiemon 藤次右衛門
Tōkaidō meishoki 東海道名所記
Tōkaidō Yotsuya kaidan
　東海道四谷怪談
Tōkaiji 東海寺
Tōkōji 東光寺
Tokuganji 徳願寺
Tokugawa Hidetada 徳川秀忠
Tokugawa Ienari 徳川家斉
Tokugawa Ieyasu 徳川家康
Tokugawa jikki 徳川実紀

Tokugawa kinreikō 徳川禁令考
Tokugawa Mitsukuni 徳川光圀
Tokugawa Nariaki 徳川斉昭
Tokugawa Tsunaeda 徳川綱條
Tokujuan 徳寿庵
Tominaga Nakamoto 富永仲基
Tomitakeyama Hachimangū
　富長山八幡宮
tomitsuki 富突
tomoraishimai トモライシマイ
tomuraiage 弔上 (弔い上げ)
Tongguk sinsok samgang haengsildo
　東國新續三綱行實圖
torii 鳥居
Tōrinji 東林寺
toshidana 年棚
toshigami 年神、歳神
toshigomori 年籠
toshikoshi 年越
toshiotoko 年男
toshitokudana 年徳棚
toshitokujin 歳 (年) 徳神
Tōshō Daigongen 東照大権現
Tōshō Gongen 東照権現
Tōshōgū 東照宮
Tōshōgū jūgokajō 東照宮一五ヵ条
Tōshō shinkun shūmon hikae
　東照神君宗門控
Tosotsuten 兜率天
Tōto saijiki 東都歳時記
Tōyama Kagemoto 遠山景元
Toyoda Mitsugi 豊田貢
Toyokuni Daimyōjin 豊国大明神
Toyotomi Hideyori 豊臣秀頼
Toyotomi Hideyoshi 豊臣秀吉
tozama daimyō 外様大名
Tōzan 当山
tsubo 坪
Tsuchiya Atsunao 土屋篤直
Tsuchiya Morinao 土屋守直
tsuizen 追善
tsuizen kuyō 追善供養
Tsuji Zennosuke 辻善之助
tsuketodoke 付届け
tsūmei 通名
Tsuruya Nanboku 鶴屋南北

tsuya 通夜
tsūzoku dōtoku 通俗道徳

ubugami 産神
ubusunagami 産土神
Ueda Engoemon 上田演五右衛門
Uesugi Kagekatsu 上杉景勝
Uge no hitokoto 宇下人言
ujidera 氏寺
ujigami 氏神
ujiko 氏子
ujiko aratame 氏子改
ujiko shirabe 氏子調
umarekawari 生まれかわり
umebaka 埋墓
Unryūji 雲龍寺
Urabe 卜部
uradana 裏店
Uramachi 裏町
utsushiyo 現界、顕世

wasan 和讃
wabijō 詫状
Waemon 和右衛門

yabu 薮
yabuiri 薮入り
yadonushi 宿主
Yahagi Tenmangū 矢作天満宮
yakkai 厄介
yaku 役
Yakushi 薬師
Yakushidō 薬師堂
Yakushidōkin 薬師堂金
yamabushi 山伏
Yamada Emosaku 山田右衛門作
Yamagata Bantō 山片蟠桃
Yamagata Daini 山片大弐
Yamamoto Shinkō 山本真功
yama no kami 山の神
yamayashiki 山屋敷
Yamazaki Ansai 山崎闇斎
yamori 家守
Yanagita Kunio 柳田国男
Yanaka Kannōji 谷中感応寺
yashikigami 屋敷神

Yashiro Hirokata　屋代弘賢
Yaso　耶蘇
yasu　康
Yasuda Muneyuki　保田宗雪
Yen-lo-wang shou-chi ssu-chung
　ni-hsiu shen-ch'i wang-shen
　ching-t'u ching
　閻羅王授記四衆逆修生七往生
　浄土経
Yoda Sōzō　依田惣蔵
Yodo　淀
Yoemon　与右衛門
Yokoōji Katsuoki　横大路勝興
yomi no kuni　黄泉の国
yorishiro　依代
Yōrōkan　養老館
Yoshida　吉田
Yoshida Kanehiro　吉田兼煕
Yoshida Kanemi　吉田兼見
Yoshida Kanemigi　吉田兼右
Yoshida Kanetomo　吉田兼倶
Yoshida Shintō　吉田神道
Yoshida Shōin　吉田松陰
Yōtokuji　養徳寺
Yugashijiron　瑜伽師地論
Yuigyō　唯行
Yuiitsu Shintō　唯一神道
Yuiitsu Shintō myōbō yōshū
　唯一神道名法要集

Yui Shōsetsu　由井正雪
yukan　湯灌
yukidaore　行倒れ
yü-lan　盂蘭
Yü-lan-p'en　盂蘭盆
Yume no shiro　夢の代
Yūtenji　祐天寺
Yūten Shōnin　祐天上人

zatō　座頭
Zenjōji　禅定寺
zenjōmon　禅定門
zenjōni　禅定尼
Zenkōji　善光寺
zenmon　禅門
Zennen shingi　禅苑清規
zenni　禅尼
Zenrin kokuhōki　善隣国宝記
Zenroku　善六
Zenshōji　善正寺
Zenshōji　善勝寺
zetsuen　絶縁
zhenyen　真言
Zōjōji　増上寺
zokuuke　俗請
zōni　雑煮
Zōryū　増隆
Zuikei Shūhō　瑞渓周鳳

Index

Harvard East Asian Monographs
(*out-of-print)

203. Robert S. Ross and Jiang Changbin, eds., *Re-examining the Cold War: U.S.-China Diplomacy, 1954–1973*

204. Guanhua Wang, *In Search of Justice: The 1905–1906 Chinese Anti-American Boycott*

205. David Schaberg, *A Patterned Past: Form and Thought in Early Chinese Historiography*

206. Christine Yano, *Tears of Longing: Nostalgia and the Nation in Japanese Popular Song*

207. Milena Doleželová-Velingerová and Oldřich Král, with Graham Sanders, eds., *The Appropriation of Cultural Capital: China's May Fourth Project*

208. Robert N. Huey, *The Making of 'Shinkokinshū'*

209. Lee Butler, *Emperor and Aristocracy in Japan, 1467–1680: Resilience and Renewal*

210. Suzanne Ogden, *Inklings of Democracy in China*

211. Kenneth J. Ruoff, *The People's Emperor: Democracy and the Japanese Monarchy, 1945–1995*

212. Haun Saussy, *Great Walls of Discourse and Other Adventures in Cultural China*

213. Aviad E. Raz, *Emotions at Work: Normative Control, Organizations, and Culture in Japan and America*

214. Rebecca E. Karl and Peter Zarrow, eds., *Rethinking the 1898 Reform Period: Political and Cultural Change in Late Qing China*

215. Kevin O'Rourke, *The Book of Korean Shijo*

216. Ezra F. Vogel, ed., *The Golden Age of the U.S.-China-Japan Triangle, 1972–1989*

217. Thomas A. Wilson, ed., *On Sacred Grounds: Culture, Society, Politics, and the Formation of the Cult of Confucius*

218. Donald S. Sutton, *Steps of Perfection: Exorcistic Performers and Chinese Religion in Twentieth-Century Taiwan*

219. Daqing Yang, *Technology of Empire: Telecommunications and Japanese Expansionism, 1895–1945*

220. Qianshen Bai, *Fu Shan's World: The Transformation of Chinese Calligraphy in the Seventeenth Century*

221. Paul Jakov Smith and Richard von Glahn, eds., *The Song-Yuan-Ming Transition in Chinese History*

222. Rania Huntington, *Alien Kind: Foxes and Late Imperial Chinese Narrative*

223. Jordan Sand, *House and Home in Modern Japan: Architecture, Domestic Space, and Bourgeois Culture, 1880–1930*

224. Karl Gerth, *China Made: Consumer Culture and the Creation of the Nation*

225. Xiaoshan Yang, *Metamorphosis of the Private Sphere: Gardens and Objects in Tang-Song Poetry*

226. Barbara Mittler, *A Newspaper for China? Power, Identity, and Change in Shanghai's News Media, 1872–1912*

227. Joyce A. Madancy, *The Troublesome Legacy of Commissioner Lin: The Opium Trade and Opium Suppression in Fujian Province, 1820s to 1920s*

252. Hiroshi Aoyagi, *Islands of Eight Million Smiles: Idol Performance and Symbolic Production in Contemporary Japan*

253. Wai-yee Li, *The Readability of the Past in Early Chinese Historiography*

254. William C. Kirby, Robert S. Ross, and Gong Li, eds., *Normalization of U.S.-China Relations: An International History*

255. Ellen Gardner Nakamura, *Practical Pursuits: Takano Chōei, Takahashi Keisaku, and Western Medicine in Nineteenth-Century Japan*

256. Jonathan W. Best, *A History of the Early Korean Kingdom of Paekche, together with an annotated translation of* The Paekche Annals *of the* Samguk sagi

257. Liang Pan, *The United Nations in Japan's Foreign and Security Policymaking, 1945–1992: National Security, Party Politics, and International Status*

258. Richard Belsky, *Localities at the Center: Native Place, Space, and Power in Late Imperial Beijing*

259. Zwia Lipkin, *"Useless to the State": "Social Problems" and Social Engineering in Nationalist Nanjing, 1927–1937*

260. William O. Gardner, *Advertising Tower: Japanese Modernism and Modernity in the 1920s*

261. Stephen Owen, *The Making of Early Chinese Classical Poetry*

262. Martin J. Powers, *Pattern and Person: Ornament, Society, and Self in Classical China*

263. Anna M. Shields, *Crafting a Collection: The Cultural Contexts and Poetic Practice of the Huajian ji* 花間集 *(Collection from Among the Flowers)*

264. Stephen Owen, *The Late Tang: Chinese Poetry of the Mid-Ninth Century (827–860)*

265. Sara L. Friedman, *Intimate Politics: Marriage, the Market, and State Power in Southeastern China*

266. Patricia Buckley Ebrey and Maggie Bickford, *Emperor Huizong and Late Northern Song China: The Politics of Culture and the Culture of Politics*

267. Sophie Volpp, *Worldly Stage: Theatricality in Seventeenth-Century China*

268. Ellen Widmer, *The Beauty and the Book: Women and Fiction in Nineteenth-Century China*

269. Steven B. Miles, *The Sea of Learning: Mobility and Identity in Nineteenth-Century Guangzhou*

270. Lin Man-houng, *China Upside Down: Currency, Society, and Ideologies, 1808–1856*

271. Ronald Egan, *The Problem of Beauty: Aesthetic Thought and Pursuits in Northern Song Dynasty China*

272. Mark Halperin, *Out of the Cloister: Literati Perspectives on Buddhism in Sung China, 960–1279*

273. Helen Dunstan, *State or Merchant? Political Economy and Political Process in 1740s China*

274. Sabina Knight, *The Heart of Time: Moral Agency in Twentieth-Century Chinese Fiction*